Sensation and Perception

Sensation and Perception

STANLEY COREN
UNIVERSITY OF BRITISH COLUMBIA

CLARE PORAC
UNIVERSITY OF VICTORIA

LAWRENCE M. WARD
UNIVERSITY OF BRITISH COLUMBIA

ACADEMIC PRESS
NEW YORK
SAN FRANCISCO
LONDON
A SUBSIDIARY OF HARCOURT BRACE JOVANOVICH, PUBLISHERS

Cover photo © Carroll H. Weiss, RBP, 1978

Text illustrations prepared by Rino Dussi

Academic Press, Inc.
111 Fifth Avenue, New York, New York 10003

United Kingdom Edition published by
Academic Press, Inc. (London) Ltd.
24/28 Oval Road, London NW1

ISBN: 0-12-188550-X
Library of Congress Catalog Card Number: 78-54526

PRINTED IN THE UNITED STATES OF AMERICA

Preface

THE JAY.   THE BAY.

The Blue Jay, as we clearly see,
Is so much like the green Bay tree
That one might say the only clue.
Lies in their dif-fer-ence of hue,
And if you have a color sense,
You'll see at once this difference.*

—R. W. Wood 1917

The wood-cut above is an amusing example of how one form of sensory information can tell us about the ways in which objects in our world are similar or different. Without our senses, our experiences would be incredibly limited. Consider the impossible problem of explaining the difference between the color blue and the color green to a person who has been blind since birth. Or how would you explain to a person who has no taste buds how the taste of chocolate and vanilla differ from each other? Such aspects of the world will never exist for these individuals. For the blind person, salt and pepper differ only in taste. For the person with no ability to taste, salt and pepper differ only in color. For those of us who have senses of sight, hearing, taste, touch, and smell, our world is a continuous flow of changing percepts. Each new sensation carries with it information about our world.

This book provides an introduction to the

* From *How To Tell the Birds from the Flowers and Other Wood-Cuts* by Robert William Wood, reprint of the original edition, Dodd, Mead and Company, New York, 1917.

study of Sensation and Perception. We have incorporated several features into this volume in order to create a more useful teaching tool. For instance, concrete examples are used throughout the text in order to make the subject matter "come alive" for students. Whenever possible, common or natural instances of perceptual phenomena are described during the discussion of the concepts underlying them.

Each chapter is preceded by an outline, which serves as a preview to its contents. These outlines also provide a structure that can guide students as they review the chapters.

Although terms are defined at the time of their introduction in the text, a glossary has been provided as well. Any item printed in SMALL CAPITAL LETTERS in the chapters is also listed in the glossary at the back of the book. Students will find the glossary particularly helpful when looking up a term if it is referred to at a later point in the text.

One special feature of our text is the inclusion of *80 Demonstration Boxes*. Each box describes a simple demonstration that students can conduct for themselves, using stimuli provided with the box or materials found in most homes and dormitory rooms. These demonstrations allow the students to actually experience many of the perceptual phenomena described in the text. Although most demonstrations require only a few moments of preparation, we feel this is time well spent in improving understanding of the concepts under discussion and in maintaining student interest. Of course, the demonstrations can be performed in class if the instructor desires. In this case the demonstrations may also serve as the focal point for a lecture or for classroom discussion.

Another feature is the inclusion of *Special Topics,* which are appended to five of the chapters. These sections give a more detailed discussion of some of the material introduced

in the chapter. These special topics are optional and can be omitted without breaking the flow of the text. Instructors may wish to cover some of these topics in class or to assign them in conjunction with individual student projects.

The text is designed to survey the broad range of topics generally included under the heading of Sensation and Perception. Since a single author can only know a limited portion of the literature in so vast a field, we decided to form a team in order to present a more complete and balanced picture. Nevertheless, this volume has been a truly collaborative effort of all members of the team. While each of us had primary responsibility for specific chapters, all three authors made comments, suggestions, and contributions to every one of them. In addition, each chapter of the final draft has been reviewed by all of us and rewritten in order to provide a uniform tone and flow throughout the book.

The reader will notice that no single theory of perception is championed. This is partly because we often hold divergent opinions about how any particular perceptual problem should be approached. In general, we have attempted to be as eclectic as we could, since we felt that nearly every alternative viewpoint of a problem contained some kernel of truth.

The topics in this book were selected on the basis of our experience in teaching our own courses; therefore, much of the material has already been class tested. We have included two chapters, *Attention and Search* and *Individual Differences,* that are not often seen in Sensation and Perception textbooks. These areas have attracted a good deal of experimental work in recent years, and they are sufficiently relevant to many issues in perception that we felt that students should be aware of their existence.

In order to keep the book a manageable size, we have occasionally been selective in our coverage. It was our first priority to cover the central concepts of each topic in enough detail to make the material clear and coherent. To have included all of the topics ever classified as part of the field of Sensation and Perception, we would have had to present a "grocery list" of concepts and terms, each treated superficially. Such an alternative was unacceptable to us.

In our attempts to collect and interpret the information for this text, we have been assisted at various stages by some of our colleagues, including R. Corteen, R. Lakowski, R. Hare, and R. Tees, all of the University of British Columbia, and J. Kess of the University of Victoria. In addition, L. Elfner of Florida State University and J. Hoffman of the University of Delaware read the entire manuscript and provided useful comments and criticism. We have also been assisted by a number of very capable typists, including S. Dixon, P. Waldron, E. Turner, J. Brazier, R. Lee, and H. Baudreau. Our research assis-

tants, C. Behman, L. McRae, C. Ensworth, and J. Foster, provided support in terms of duplicating, library work, and all of the small but necessary chores that eat up innumerable hours of a textbook writer's time. We would also like to thank our editor and the production team at Academic Press for their careful work and enthusiastic support.

Finally, the reader might notice that there is no dedication page. This is not to say that we do not wish to dedicate the book to anyone. It reflects the fact that there are too many people who have been important in our personal and professional lives to list on any single page (no matter how small the print). Perhaps it is best to simply dedicate this book to all of those researchers who have provided the knowledge that we have attempted to organize and review between these covers, and to all of those researchers who will provide further insights into Sensation and Perception for future authors to collate, review, digest, wonder at, and learn from.

S.C.
C.P.
L.M.W.

Contents

Demonstration Boxes

1
Sensation and Perception

SENSATION, PERCEPTION, COGNITION,
AND INFORMATION PROCESSING

THE PLAN OF THE BOOK

Can you answer the following questions? What color is the sky? Which is warmer—fire or ice? Which tastes sweeter—sugar or vinegar? Which has a stronger smell—burning wood or burning rubber? Which sounds louder—a chirping bird or the crack of a rifle? Such questions probably seem quite trivial, and the answers obvious. Well, perhaps we should phrase the questions differently. How do you know what color the sky is? How do you know how hot fire is relative to ice? How do you know that sugar is sweet? Again, you might feel that the answer is obvious, you *saw* the color of the sky, you *felt* the temperature of the flame and an ice cube, and you *tasted* the sweetness of sugar—in other words, the answers come through your senses.

Now, let us push our questioning one step further. How do you know *anything* about your world? You might say that you learn from books, television, radio, films, lectures, or the actual exploration of places. And how do you obtain the information from these sources? Again, the answer is through your senses. In fact, without your senses of vision, hearing, touch, taste, and smell, your brain, the organ that is responsible for your conscious experience, would be an eternal prisoner in the solitary confinement of your skull. You would live in total silence and darkness. All would be a tasteless, colorless, feelingless, floating void. Without your senses, the world would simply not exist for you. The philosopher Thomas Hobbes recognized this fact in 1651 when he wrote: "There is no conception in man's mind which hath not at first, totally or by parts, been begotten upon the organs of sense." The Greek philosopher, Protagoras, was actually stating the same position around 450 B.C. when he said "Man is nothing but a bundle of sensations."

You may protest what seems to be a rather extreme viewpoint. Certainly, much of what we know about the world does not arrive through our eyes, ears, nose, and other sense organs. We have complex scientific instruments, such as telescopes that tell us about the size and the shape of the universe by analyzing images too faint for the human eye to see. We have sonar to trace out the shape of the sea bottom, which may be hidden from our eyes by hundreds of feet of water. We have spectrographs to tell us about the exact chemical composition of many substances, as compared to the crude chemical sensitivity of our noses and tongues. While such pieces of apparatus exist, and measure phenomena not directly available to our senses, this does not alter the fact that it is the perception of the scientist that constitutes the subject matter of every science. It is the eye of the scientist that presses against the telescope or examines the photograph of the distant star. It is the ear of the scientist that listens to the sound of sonar tracing out the size and distance of objects. While the tongue of the scientist does not taste the chemical composition of some unknown substance, his eye, aided by the spectrograph, provides the data for the analysis. In reality, the only data that reach the mind of the scientist come, not from his instruments, but from his senses. The instrument can be perfectly accurate, yet if the scientist misreads a dial, or does not see a critical shift in a measurement device, the obtained information is wrong and the resulting picture of the world is in error. The minds of the scientist, the nonscientist, our pet dog sniffing about the world, or a fish swimming about in a bowl, in fact, the minds of all living, thinking organisms, are prisoners that must rely upon information smuggled in to them by the senses. Your world is what your senses tell you. The limitations of your senses set the boundaries of your conscious existence.

Since our knowledge of the world is dependent upon our senses, it is important to know how our senses function. It is also important to know how well the world that is created by our senses corresponds to the external reality. At this point, you are probably smiling to yourself and thinking, "Here comes another academic discourse which will attempt to make something that is quite obvious appear to be complex." You are probably saying to yourself "I see my desk in front of me because it is there. I feel my chair pressing against my back because it is there. I hear my phone ringing because it contains a bell which makes sounds. What could be more obvious?" Such faith in your senses is a vital part of existence. It causes you to jump out of the way of an apparently oncoming car, thus preserving your life. It provides the basic data that cause you to step back from a deep hole, thus avoiding a fall and serious bodily harm. Such faith in our senses is built into the very fabric of our lives. As the old saying goes, "Seeing is believing." Long before the birth of Christ, Lucretius stated this article of faith when he asked, "What can give us surer knowledge than our senses? With what else can we distinguish the true form from the false?" Perhaps the most striking example of this faith is found in our courts of law where people's lives and fortunes rest solely upon the testimony of the eyes and ears of witnesses. While a lawyer might argue that a witness is corrupt or lying, or even that his memory has failed, no lawyer would have the audacity to suggest that his client should be set free because the only evidence that was available was based upon what the witnesses saw or heard. Certainly no sane person would charge the eye or ear with perjury!

The philosophical position that perception is an immediate, almost godlike knowledge of external reality has been championed, not only by popular sentiment, but also by philosophers of the stature of Immanual Kant (1724–1804). Unfortunately, it is wrong. Look at the drawings shown in Figure 1-1.

Clearly, they are all composed of outlined forms on various backgrounds. Despite what your senses tell you, A, B, and C are all perfect squares. Despite the evidence of your senses, D is a perfect circle, and despite the evidence of your senses, the lines in E are both straight and the lines marked X and Y in F are both the same length.

The ease with which we use our senses, seeing apparently through the simple act of opening our eyes or touching apparently by merely pressing our skin against an object, masks the fact that perception is an extremely sophisticated activity of the brain. Perception calls upon stores of memory data. It requires subtle classifications, comparisons, and myriad decisions before any of the data in our senses becomes our conscious awareness of what is "out there." Contrary to what you may think, the eyes do not see. There are many individuals who have perfectly functioning eyes yet have no sensory impressions. They cannot perceive because they have injuries in those parts of the brain that receive and interpret messages from the eyes. As Epicharmus said 450 years before the birth of Christ, "The mind sees and the mind hears. The rest is blind and deaf."

"So what?" you mutter to yourself. "So, sometimes we make errors in our perceptions, the real point is that the senses simply carry a picture of the outside world to the brain. The picture in the brain represents our percept. Of course if we mess up the brain we will distort or destroy perception." Again, this answer is too simple. If we look outside and see a car, are we to believe that there is a picture of a car somewhere in our brains? If we notice that a traffic light is green, are we to believe that some part of the brain has turned green? And suppose that there were such images in the brain, carried without distortion from the senses, would this help us to see? Certainly, images in the brain would only be of value if there were some other eyes in the

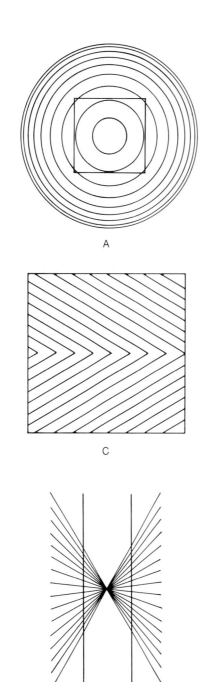

A

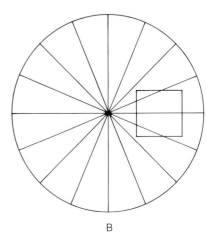

B

C

D

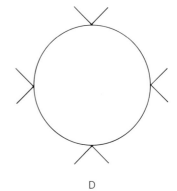

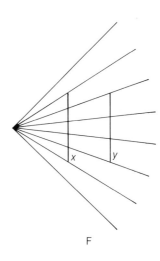

E

F

Figure 1-1.
Some instances where the senses tell lies.

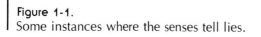

head, which would look at these pictures and interpret them. If this were the case, we would be left with the question of how these internal eyes see. Thus, we would eventually be forced to set up an endless chain of *pictures* and *eyes* and *pictures* and *eyes,* because the question of who is perceiving the percept and how still remains.

If we are to understand perception we must consider it in its natural context. Sensation and perception are the first of many complex processes that occur when an individual initiates a behavior. There is no clear line between perception and many other behavioral activities. No perception gives direct knowledge of the outside world, rather such knowledge is the end product of many processes. The wet-looking black spot on the edge of a desk could be the place where ink was spilled. Of course, this could be wrong. The ink may be dry, or the spot might not be there at all. The desk that is seen and touched, might not really exist. We might be dreaming, drugged, or hallucinating. Too extreme, you say? Consider the following example that actually happened to one of the authors. One night he walked across the floor of his darkened home. In the dim gloominess of the night, he saw his dog resting on the floor, clearly asleep. When he bent to touch the dog, he found that it was a footstool. He stepped· back, somewhat startled at his stupidity, only to bump against the cold corner of a marble-topped coffee table. When he reached back to steady himself, he found that the corner of the table was, in fact, his dog's cold nose. Each of these perceptions, dog, stool, table, and dog again, seemed to represent reality. Yet, sensory data are not always reliable. Sometimes they can be degraded or not completely available. There seems to be no sudden break between perceiving or sensing an object and guessing the identity of an object. In some respects, one can say that all perception of objects re-

quires some guessing. Sensory stimulation provides the data for our hypotheses about the nature of the external world, and it is these hypotheses that form our perceptions of the world.

Many human behaviors have been affected by the fallible and often erroneous nature of our percepts. For example, the most elegant of the classic Greek buildings, the Parthenon, is bent. The straight clean lines, which bring a sense of simple elegant grandeur, are actually an illusion. If we schematically represent the east wall of the building as it appears, it is square (as shown in Figure 1-2A). Actually, the Parthenon was built in a totally distorted fashion in order to offset a series of optical illusions. There is a common visual distortion in which placing angles above a line (much like the roof is placed over the architrave) causes the line to appear bowed. One form of this illusion is shown as Figure 1-2B. If the Parthenon were built physically square, it would appear to sag as a result of this visual distortion. This is shown in an exaggerated manner in Figure 1-2C. The sagging does not appear because the building has been altered to compensate for the distortion. Figure 1-2D illustrates what an undistorted view of the Parthenon would look like. The upward curvature is more than 6 cm on the east and west walls and almost 11 cm on the longer north and south sides. The vertical features of the Parthenon (such as the columns) were inclined inwards in order to correct for a second optical illusion in which the features of rising objects appear to fall outward at the top. Thus, if we projected all of the columns of the Parthenon upward, they would meet at a point about a mile above the building. Furthermore, the corner columns were increased in thickness since it was found that when these columns were seen against the sky, they appeared to be thinner than those seen against the darker background formed by the interior wall.

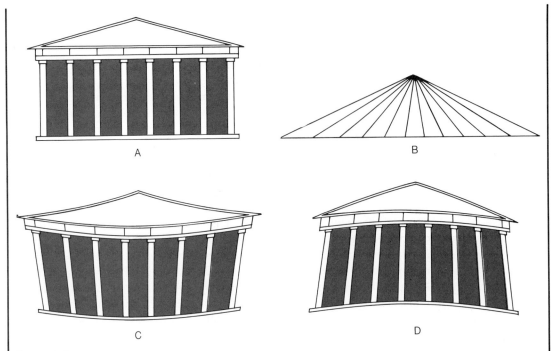

Figure 1-2.
(A) The Parthenon as it appears, (B) an illusion that should cause the Parthenon to appear as (C), and (D) the way the Parthenon is built to offset the illusion.

These were conscious corrections made by the Greek architects. To quote one of them, Vitruvius, writing around 30 B.C.: "For the sight follows gracious contours, and unless we flatter its pleasure by proportionate alterations of these parts (so that by adjustment we offset the amount to which it suffers illusions) an uncouth and ungracious aspect will be presented to the spectators." In other words, the Parthenon appears to be square, with elegant straight lines, because it has been consciously distorted to offset perceptual distortions. If it were geometrically square, it would not be perceptually square.

Many perceptual errors are merely amusing. For instance, Figure 1-3A shows a picture frame. Unfortunately, the grain of the wood is too prominent. Despite the fact that the picture is perfectly rectangular, it appears to be distorted. Such distortions, disagreements between percept and reality, are quite common. We call them illusions, and they occur in predictable circumstances for normal observers. The term illusion is drawn from the Latin root *illudere,* meaning "to mock." In a sense, they do mock us for our blind reliance upon the validity of our sensory impressions. Unfortunately, some perceptual errors or illusions are quite serious. In Figure 1-3B, we have shown a surgeon probing for a bullet. She is using a fluoroscope, which presents the outline of her patient's ribs. We have positioned her probe so that it is exactly on line with the bullet lodged below the rib. As you can see, it appears that she will miss and pass too far below the bullet despite the fact that the probe is perfectly angled and aimed. Figure 1-3C shows an even more disastrous oc-

7
SENSATION,
PERCEPTION,
COGNITION,
AND
INFORMATION
PROCESSING

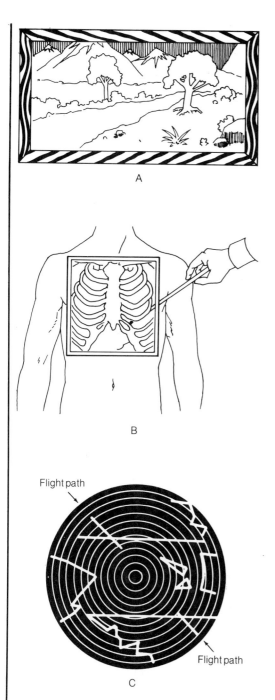

A

B

Flight path

Flight path

C

Figure 1-3.
Some perceptual distortions in common situations.

currence of an illusion. It represents a radar screen with various flight regions marked across its face. The two oblique luminous streaks represent jet aircraft approaching the control region, both flying at about 950 kph. The information displayed is the same as that which an air traffic controller might use. From it he might conclude that if these two aircraft continue in the same direction they will pass each other with a safe distance between them. At the moment represented here, however, these aircraft are traveling on a direct line. If they are both flying at the same altitude it is very likely that they will collide. This example illustrates how important discrepancies between perception and reality can be. Therefore it becomes important for us to know how our perceptions arise, how much we can rely upon them, under what circumstances they are most fallible, and under what conditions our perceptions most accurately present a picture of the world. An exploration of these questions is the purpose of this book.

SENSATION, PERCEPTION, COGNITION, AND INFORMATION PROCESSING

There is a tremendous amount of diversity in the study of perception. Part of this comes from the length of time that perceptual problems have been studied. The Greek philosophers, the pre-Renaissance thinkers, the Arabic scholars, the Latin scholastics, the early British empiricists, the German physicists and the German physicians who founded both physiology and psychology considered issues in sensation and perception as basic questions. When Alexander Bain wrote the first English textbook on Psychology in 1855 it was entitled *The Senses and the Intellect,* with the most extensive coverage reserved for sensory and perceptual functions. The major portion of both the theorizing and the empirical work produced by Wilhelm Wundt, who is generally credited with the founding of experimental psychology, was oriented toward sensation and perception. In addition to the diversity caused by a long and varied history, perception has been affected by many "schools" of thought. Each has its own major theoretical viewpoint and its own particular set of methodological techniques. Thus we encounter psychophysicists, gestaltists, functionalists, analytic introspectionists, transactionalists, sensory physiologists, sensory–tonic theorists, "new look" psychologists, and efferent theorists, to name but a few. There are even theorists (such as some behaviorists) who deny the existence of, or at least deny our ability to study, the conscious event we call perception. Despite this chorus of diverse voices and viewpoints, there seems to be a consensus about the important aspects of perceptual study.

Before we look at the major areas of emphasis in the study of the perceptual process let us first offer a disclaimer. We recognize that it is difficult, perhaps impossible, and most certainly unwise to attempt to draw sharp lines separating one field of inquiry from another. However, there are certain problem areas, or orientations, that have been designated by groups of investigators, and these seem to be definable. The study of SENSATION, or *sensory processes,* is concerned with the first contact between the organism and the environment. Thus, someone studying sensation might look at the way in which electromagnetic radiation (light) is registered by the eye. This investigator would look at the physical structure of the sense organ and would attempt to establish how sensory experiences are related to physical stimulation and physiological functioning.

These types of studies tend to focus upon less complex (although not less complicated) aspects of our conscious experience. For instance, these investigators might study how we perceive brightness, loudness, or color; however, the nature of the object having a given brightness, sound, or color would not make much difference to them.

Someone who is interested in the study of PERCEPTION is interested in our conscious experience of objects and object relationships. For instance, the sensory question might be "How bright does the target appear to be?", while the perceptual questions would be "Do you recognize what that object is?", "Where is it?", "How far away is it?", or "How large is it?" In a more global sense, those who study perception are interested in how we form a conscious representation of the outside environment, and the accuracy of that representation. For those of you who have difficulty in drawing a hard and fast line between the concepts of perception and sensation, rest easy. Since Thomas Reid introduced the distinction in 1785, some investigators have championed its use, while others have totally ignored the difference, choosing to treat sensation and perception as a unitary problem.

COGNITION is a term used to define a very active field of inquiry in contemporary psychology. The word itself is quite old, probably first introduced by St. Thomas Aquinas (1225–1274). He divided the study of behavior into two broad divisions. One he labeled *cognition,* meaning how we know the world, and the other he labeled *affect,* which was meant to encompass feelings and emotions. Today's definition of cognition is equally as broad as that of Aquinas. While many investigators use the term to refer to memory, association, concept formation, language, and problem solving (all of which simply take the act of perception for granted), other investigators include the processes of attention and the conscious representation and interpretation of stimuli as part of the cognitive process. In other words, cognition tends to be somewhere between the areas that were traditionally called *perception* and *learning;* and it incorporates elements of both. The similarity between many of the problems studied by cognitive psychologists and those studied by perceptual psychologists is best seen by the fact that both often publish in the same journals and on similar topics.

INFORMATION PROCESSING is a relatively new term. It is a recent attempt to avoid making distinctions between sensation, perception, and cognition. Information processing describes behavior by assuming that the way in which observers process information includes a *registration* or sensory phase, an *interpretation* or perceptual phase, and a *memoric* or cognitive phase. When one looks at the entire scheme the global term information processing seems to be appropriate. Actually, information processing should be viewed as an approach rather than as a separate subdiscipline. It relies upon a LEVELS-OF-PROCESSING analysis in which each stage of sensory processing, from the first registration of the stimulus on the receptor to the final conscious representation entered into memory, is systematically analyzed.

None of these labels should be taken as representing inflexible, or completely separate, areas of study. At a recent professional meeting one well-known psychologist lamented, "When I first started doing research, people said I studied perception. After a while, they said I studied cognition. Now they say that I am studying human information processing. I don't know what is going on—I've been studying the same set of problems for the last ten years!"

This book will address the problem of how people build a conscious picture of their environment through the use of information

reaching their senses. What we call this endeavor is of considerably less importance than the answer itself.

THE PLAN OF THE BOOK

The orientation of this book is implicit rather than explicit. While theories are introduced and discussed in the various chapters, no all-encompassing theoretical orientation has been adopted. We have chosen to be "militantly eclectic" in our orientation. Thus, this text is mostly concerned with perceptual and sensory processes. In general, the presentation of the material follows a levels-of-processing approach that is somewhat similar to that found in the information-processing literature. The way in which levels of processing can be used to gain a fuller understanding of perception is demonstrated in the last chapter.

Each individual chapter is relatively self-contained. We begin by explaining how sensations and perceptions are measured (Chapters 2 and 3). These chapters present the basic psychophysical techniques of measurement, and try to orient you toward some of the issues and approaches that will appear later in the text. Chapters 4–6 describe the physiological functioning of the receptors themselves. Without knowledge of how the eye, ear, or any of the other senses work at the physiological level, we can never fully build a picture of how perception is achieved. Chapters 7–10 deal with the basic sensory responses. These include, among others, the sensory qualities of brightness, color, loudness, touch, and taste. Chapters 11–14 deal with those problems that have traditionally been treated as part of classical perception. They discuss our conscious representation of space, time, motion, form, and size. Chapters 15–17 deal more with the cognitive aspects of perception. They focus upon attentional processes and how learning and development can alter our percepts or cause the perception of one individual to disagree with that of another. The last chapter (18) attempts to illustrate how all of these levels of processing can be combined to demonstrate how perception operates. It also sets a series of puzzles or problems for you to consider. Some of these have agreed-upon solutions, while others are still on the frontiers of current research, begging for answers.

You will notice that each chapter includes a series of Demonstration Boxes. These are experimental demonstrations that you can perform for yourself using materials that are easily found. They illustrate many aspects of the perceptual process. Quite often they illustrate concepts that are very difficult to put into words, but which, when experienced, are immediately understandable. You are encouraged to try these demonstrations as they are an integral part of the book. In the same way that perception involves interaction with the world, these demonstrations allow you to interact with your senses in a controlled manner and to gain some insight into yourself.

We hope that this book will provide you with some understanding of the limits and the abilities of your senses. This knowledge should expand your comprehension of many behavioral phenomena that depend upon perception as a first step. For humans perception seems to be the final judge of the truth or the falsity of everything we encounter. How often have you heard the phrase, "Seeing is believing" or "I didn't believe it until I saw it with my own two eyes"? Yet you have already seen in this chapter that such faith in the truthfulness of our conscious percepts is often misplaced. In 500 B.C. Parmenides considered the way in which perception can deceive us. He summarized his feelings when he said "The eyes and ears are bad witnesses when they are at the service of minds that do not understand their language." In this book we will try to teach you their language.

2
Detection, Recognition, and Discrimination

The ocean liner glides slowly through the thick stormy night. Somewhere in the distance is New York harbor. With the visibility near zero the Captain is forced to rely solely upon the ship's radar system for information about the position of obstacles impeding the passage of his ship. The ship is in a heavily traveled trade route, and the crew must continually be alert for possible collisions with other ships. The radar operator is watching his screen intently. He is searching for a radar "echo" caused by the presence of another ship nearby. Actually, he is also wrestling with a basic sensory–perceptual problem, that of DETECTION. He is trying to answer the question "Is there anything there?"

He is sure that he sees an echo. Now the question becomes "what is it?" Is this an echo from another ship or just a "ghost," a false echo often encountered in stormy weather? The radar operator is faced with a second basic problem: RECOGNITION. These are two problems that we normally solve quickly and automatically, since we generally encounter stimuli which are so strong, and provide so much information, that they pose little problem for us. The complex nature of detection and recognition only emerges in the context of a difficult or degraded stimulus situation.

The echo turns out to be just a "ghost" and the order is given to maintain the previous heading (compass direction). The Helmsman has been given the bearing and now holds the ship's direction so that the compass needle always points to the correct place on the dial. At this moment, he is asking himself "Has the needle drifted slightly toward the north?" If so, he must compensate by turning the wheel so that the needle moves back to the desired compass point. He is continuously concerned with the problem of whether the compass needle is centered on the desired heading. This task also evokes an important perceptual process called DIS-

CRIMINATION. "Is this stimulus different from that one?" is the general discrimination question.

Finally, through the clearing weather the entrance to New York harbor appears. The ship is taken in tow by a tugboat and maneuvered toward its berth at the dock. The Captain of the tugboat peers from the bridge, carefully judging the distance between the ship and the concrete wall of the pier. He must continually ask himself, "How far does the ship appear to be from the pier?" Such questions are part of another sensory problem, "How much of X is there?" This is the problem of SCALING.

These four problems, *detection, recognition, discrimination,* and *scaling* are the central concerns of the area of perceptual psychology called *psychophysics.* Psychophysics owes its name and origin to Gustav Theodor Fechner (1801–1887), a physicist and philosopher who set out to determine the relationship between the magnitude of a sensation registered in the mind and the magnitude of the physical stimulus that gave rise to it. Hence, the name psychophysics (from the Greek roots *psyche* or mind, and *physike,* which refers to naturally occurring phenomena). Fechner not only established the philosophical rationale for studying the relationship between sensations and physical stimuli, but he also developed and utilized many of the experimental methods still in use today. These methods, and ways of treating data produced by them, are employed in every aspect of the study of perception.

DETECTION

The basic problem for any sensory system is to detect the presence of energy changes in the environment. Those energy changes may take the form of light, sound, chemical, or mechanical stimulation. The problem of detection is centered around the problem of how much of such a stimulus (relative to a zero energy level) is necessary for an individual to say that the stimulus is heard, tasted, smelled, or felt. Classically, this minimal amount of energy has been called the ABSO-LUTE THRESHOLD. The notion of threshold was first introduced into psychology by Johann Herbart in 1824, when he defined the "threshold of consciousness." Gustav Fechner used this notion when he defined a threshold stimulus as one that "lifted the sensation or sensory difference over the threshold of consciousness." The idea is that below some critical value of the stimulus, a person would not be expected to detect a stimulus. However, as soon as this threshold value is exceeded one would expect the observer to always detect its presence.

We can represent this relationship by a graph, which plots the percentage of time that an observer would be expected to detect the presence of a stimulus (values along the ordinate or vertical axis) against stimulus magnitude (plotted in arbitrary values along the abscissa or horizontal axis). This has been done in Figure 2-1. Notice that the percentage of time that the stimulus is detected takes a sudden step up from 0% to 100% when the stimulus reaches a value of 3.5. Three point five, then, is the absolute threshold.

Method of Limits. How do we measure absolute thresholds? Let us conduct a relatively simple but typical experiment to measure the threshold of hearing. We will use a situation in which an observer sits in a soundproof room wearing headphones. The experimenter sits outside the test area and, starting with a very faint undetectable tone, gradually increases the intensity of the stimulus until the observer reports "I hear it." On alternate trials the experimenter starts with a clearly perceptible stimulus level and decreases the intensity until the observer reports "I no

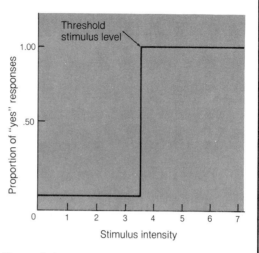

Figure 2-1.
Absolute threshold.

longer hear it." This method of determining the threshold is called the METHOD OF LIMITS. Kraepelin named this procedure the method of limits in 1891, because a stimulus series always ends when the observer reaches a limit or a point of change in his judgments. Some authors, such as J. P. Guilford (1954), prefer to call it the *method of minimal changes,* which more accurately describes the way the stimulus sequence is varied.

The two modes of presenting (increasing or decreasing) the stimulus are usually called ascending or descending stimulus series. A sample of the kind of data such an experiment might generate is shown in Table 2-1.

The first thing we notice is that our "absolute threshold" for hearing is not a fixed value as we first proposed, but appears to vary from trial to trial. For instance, on trial 6 the observer could no longer detect the stimulus when we presented a sound with an intensity of 8; on trial 4, a stimulus intensity of only 5 was detected. Such data indicate that the "absolute threshold" is anything but absolute. It seems that the threshold varies from measurement to measurement, or moment to moment. As early as 1888, Joseph Jastrow

Table 2-1 *Determination of the Absolute Threshold of Hearing by the Method of Limits*

Sound Intensity (Scale Units)	Trials					
	↑ 1	↓ 2	↑ 3	↓ 4	↑ 5	↓ 6
16						+
15						+
14		+				+
13		+				+
12		+		+		+
11		+		+		+
10		+		+		+
9		+		+		+
8		+	+	+	+	−
7		−	−	+	+	
6	$+^a$	−	−	+	−	
5	$-^b$		−	+	−	
4	−		−	−	−	
3	−		−	−	−	
2	−		−	−		
1				−		
Threshold for series	5.5	7.5	7.5	4.5	6.5	8.5

Computations

$$\text{Mean descending threshold} = \frac{7.5 + 4.5 + 8.5}{3} = 6.8$$

$$\text{Mean ascending threshold} = \frac{5.5 + 7.5 + 6.5}{3} = 6.5$$

$$\text{Mean absolute threshold} = 6.65 \text{ sound units}$$

[a] "I hear it."
[b] "I don't hear it."

speculated on the variability in the threshold over time. He theorized that lapses of attention, slight fatigue, and other psychological fluctuations could cause the obtained fluctuations of the threshold. Demonstration Box 2-1 shows how you can experience this threshold variability for yourself.

We can compute an estimate of the average absolute threshold from the tabled data by simply taking the average stimulus intensity at which a response shifted either from an "I hear it" to an "I don't hear it," or from an "I don't hear it" to an "I hear it." This gives us a threshold value of 6.65 sound units. These computations are shown at the bottom of the table. Table 2-1 also shows that there is a slight difference in the threshold value depending upon whether it was computed from an ascending or a descending series of stimuli. Such differences may arise from ob-

Demonstration Box 2-1:
*The Variability of the
Threshold*

For this demonstration you will need a wrist watch or an alarm clock that ticks. Place the clock on a table and move across the room, so that you can no longer hear the ticking. If the tick is faint, you may accomplish this by merely moving your head away some distance. Now gradually move toward the clock. Note that by doing this, you are actually performing a method of limits experiment since the sound level steadily increases as you approach the sound. At some distance from the watch you will just begin to hear the source of the sound. This is your momentary threshold. Now hold this position for a few moments and you will notice that occasionally the sound will fade out and you may have to step forward to reach threshold, while at other times it may get noticeably louder and you may be able to step back further and still hear it. These changes are due to your changing threshold sensitivity.

servers continuing to report "yes" in a descending series and "no" in an ascending series, a tendency called the ERROR OF PERSEVERATION. It is also possible to have an ERROR OF ANTICIPATION. Here an observer feels that he has said "yes" too often and decides that it is time to say "no" even though he still faintly hears the tone. It is to balance out such possible constant errors that we use alternating ascending and descending stimulus series, and begin the series of the same kind at different stimulus intensities.

Part of the theoretical difficulties associated with the fluctuations in the threshold disappear when we recognize that we have been assuming throughout this discussion that the only stimulus present is the stimulus we are asking our observer to detect. This is of course quite false. There is a constantly present and ever changing background of stimulation for any signal that we present to the observer. Place both of your hands over your ears in order to block out the room noises, and you will hear a sound that one observer poetically called "the sound of waves from a distant sea" and another, somewhat less poetically, "the faint hissing of radio static."

Similarly, if you sit in a completely light-proof room in absolute darkness, you do not see complete blackness. Your visual field appears to be filled with a grayish mist (which has been termed "cortical gray") and occasionally you can even see momentary bright pinpoint flashes here and there. Any stimulus that we ask an observer to detect must force itself through this spontaneously generated fluctuating background. It is as if every stimulus that must be detected is superimposed on a background of noise generated within the observer.

As the noise level changes so does our measured threshold, in the same way that a person standing in the midst of a noisy crowd must talk louder in order to be heard. Some experimenters have resorted to the introduction of experimentally controlled background noise level in order to achieve more constant conditions than would be possible if we simply relied on the constancy of internally generated noise. Under these circumstances, the experimenter has a crude idea of the noise level with which the stimulus is competing. In fact many of the experiments we will discuss have employed a controlled background noise level. We are using *noise* to define any background stimulus other than the one to be detected. Defined in this way we may have visual, chemical, mechanical, and thermal, as well as auditory, noise.

Method of Constant Stimuli. Let us discuss another method that will allow us to see the nature of the threshold more clearly. Suppose we take a set of stimuli ranging from clearly imperceptible to clearly perceptible and present them, one at a time, to our observer. We present each stimulus many times in a prearranged mixed order. The observer is simply required to respond "yes" when she detects the stimulus and "no" when she does not. This procedure is called the METHOD OF CONSTANT STIMULI, a name derived from the fact that a fixed or constant set of stimuli is chosen beforehand and presented a fixed or constant number of times to each observer. Some typical data obtained through the use of this method are presented graphically in Figure 2-2.

In the figure we see that as the stimulus energy increases, the relative number of times that the observer says "yes" (meaning that the stimulus was perceived) gradually

increases. It is not the single jump that we might have originally predicted from the definition of absolute threshold illustrated in Figure 2-1. These S-shaped curves are commonly obtained in all sensory systems when using the method of constant stimuli. Let us take a look at what the "proportion of yes responses" might indicate in such experiments. One basic assumption made by psychophysicists is that any type of behavior, such as saying "Yes, I see it," has some *strength*. The strengths of various behaviors can be represented by numbers, which indicate their relative magnitude. The measure that has found most favor among contemporary workers in the field is a numerical estimate of the likelihood that the particular response in question will occur. We will call this likelihood the *response probability*. We can estimate the response probability for detecting the stimulus, or more exactly for saying "Yes, I see it," by using the formula

$$p(\text{Yes}) = \frac{\text{Number of ``Yes'' Responses}}{\text{Number ``Yes'' + Number ``No''}}$$

The data of Figure 2-2 make it clear that the probability that an observer will detect a stimulus is not an "all or none" affair (as in Figure 2-1), but rather it changes gradually as the stimulus intensity increases. Then where is the absolute threshold? Here we must make a somewhat arbitrary decision.

The point usually taken as the absolute threshold is that value where the probability of saying "Yes" is the same as the probability of saying "No," in other words where $p(\text{Yes}) = p(\text{No}) = 0.50$. Conceptually, this is simply the stimulus value that is detected 50% of the time when it is present. In Figure 2-2 we have indicated this threshold value by dotted lines. We would say that the threshold value for detecting light is about 3.5 energy units for this observer.

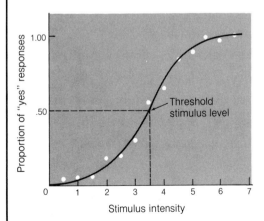

Figure 2-2.
Typical data from method of constant stimuli in detection; average absolute threshold.

It might be interesting to mention some examples of approximate threshold values as measured by these methods. The visual system is so sensitive that a candle flame can be seen from a distance of more than 48 km on a dark clear night. In the auditory system, we can detect the ticking of a wristwatch in a quiet room at a distance of 6 m. With more sensitivity in this system we would hear the sound of air molecules colliding. As for our other senses, we can taste one teaspoon of sugar dissolved in $7\frac{1}{2}$ liters of water and smell one drop of perfume diffused through the volume of an average three-room apartment (Galanter, 1962).

Signal Detection Theory. Some of you may have been bothered by one aspect of the psychophysical measurement techniques that we have been discussing. We are supposedly studying an observer's sensory capacities, yet we have not been talking about the probability that an observer detects a stimulus, but rather the probability that a "Yes, I hear a stimulus" response is made. One can imagine that if an observer feels that this is a "test" of some sort, where it would be good for him to look as if he were quite sensitive, he might end up saying "yes" on almost every trial. What is to prevent this from happening? We might argue that people are basically honest, and would not lie about whether or not they heard a stimulus. Yet this is not the sort of guarantee upon which scientists would like to rest their conclusions. We are not criticizing the reliability of observers in psychophysical experiments, for most are quite sincere and honest. Rather, we are pointing out that at the very low stimulus energies used in most detection experiments, the observer may be unsure about whether the sensation has been experienced. This may result in his being unsure as to whether or not he should respond "yes" on any particular trial. Thus, on some trials a "guess" response

is made. Therefore, in order to accurately assess sensory capacities, we must take into account an observer's decision-making behavior.

Experimenters became aware of this problem early in the history of psychophysics. They first attempted to cope with it by inserting CATCH TRIALS, which were trials in which no stimulus was presented. They reasoned that if the observers were honest in reporting what was detected, they would respond "no" on these catch trials. If the "yes" response came too frequently, the observer was warned by the experimenter. Alternatively, an attempt was made to adjust the calculated threshold to account for the guesses, or the data were simply discarded. However, over many experiments it became clear that the observers were not trying to fool anyone. Somehow their behavior was reasonable, although it was not clear what it was they were doing.

If we now change our classical absolute threshold experiment so that we can study not only the observer's ability to detect a stimulus when it is there, but also his guessing behavior as reflected in a "yes" response when no signal is present, we have entered the domain of SIGNAL DETECTION THEORY. Signal detection theory has aroused a good deal of contemporary interest and research (see Egan, 1975; Green & Swets, 1966). It is a mathematical, theoretical system, which recognizes that the observer is not merely a passive receiver of stimuli, but is also engaged in the process of deciding whether or not he is confident enough that the stimulus was present to say "Yes, I detected it."

For the purposes of the following discussion we will list all of the possible behaviors in our new type of detection experiment and give them names. Table 2-2 is a schematic representation of the standard signal detection experiment. There are two types of

Table 2-2 *Outcomes of a Signal Detection Experiment*

Signal	Response	
	Yes	No
Present	Hit	Miss
Absent	False alarm	Correct negative

"stimulus" presentations (at the left of the table). A *signal absent* presentation is like a classical catch trial—no stimulus is presented and the observer sees or hears only the noise generated by the sensory system. *Signal present* is when the signal is actually presented. It is, of course, superimposed on the noise in the sensory system. There are also two possible responses in the experiment (at the top of the table). These are "yes" to indicate that the observer thinks a stimulus was indeed presented on a particular trial (i.e., signal present), and "no" to indicate that the observer thinks that the signal was absent. The combination of the two possible stimulus presentations with the two possible responses leads to four possible outcomes on a given trial (the four cells of the table). When the signal was present and the response was "yes" the observer has made a HIT. But if the observer responds "yes" when the signal was absent, then he has made a FALSE ALARM. The other cells are called MISSES and CORRECT NEGATIVES. The relationships between these responses will depend not only upon the nature of the signal, but also upon the decision processes occurring within the observer.

Let us consider an experiment in which an observer is presented with a stimulus that can be heard above the noise level most of the time, although not always. Tanner, Swets, and Green (1956) performed an auditory detection experiment in which the signal was a tone that was presented for 0.1 sec in the presence of a controlled noise background.

Following a ready signal, the observer was required to respond by pushing a button to signify "yes" when the signal (the tone) was detected and a different button to signify "no" when it was not. For the case of interest to us, there were 300 judgments and the signal was presented on 50% (or 150) of the trials. The extrapolated data (proportions) for one observer are shown in Table 2-3.

Notice that on 40% of the trials when no signal was present, our observer responds "Yes, the signal was present." Why should the observer report that a signal was heard when no signal was presented? One variable that might influence the occurrence of such false alarms is the observer's expectations. For instance, if the observer knows that the signal is very likely to occur on any given trial, he might decide that even if he experiences only the faintest of sensations he will say "yes," since by doing this he will very often be correct. However, if he knows that the signal rarely occurs, he would be tempted to wait until he experienced a very strong sensation before saying "yes." If this is the case, then we should be able to alter the observer's response pattern by altering his expectations. Thus, if we present a signal on almost every trial with only infrequent catch trials, the observer would soon come to expect a signal and would say "yes" frequently. Under these conditions we might expect that the false alarm rate (saying "yes" when no signal is present) would be higher than if the signal were presented only occasionally. On the other hand, if we rarely present the

Table 2-3 *Stimulus Present 50% of the Time (Based upon Tanner, Swets & Green, 1956)*

Signal	Response	
	Yes	No
Present	.72	.28
Absent	.40	.60

to be present and, hence, would be more likely to respond "no" on the infrequent trials when the signal occurs. Actual results from our same observer are presented in Table 2-4. In one case the signal was present on 90% of the trials and in the other on only 10% of the trials.

If we systematically explore this relationship by holding constant the strength of the signal and varying the relative frequency with which the signal occurs, we may plot a curve that indicates the relationship between the proportion of hits and false alarms across various situations. Figure 2-3 presents such a curve. Along the ordinate we have plotted the probability that a person will say "yes" when a signal is present (hit) and along the abscissa the probability that he will say "yes" when no signal is present (false alarm). This function is called a RECEIVER OPERATING CHARACTERISTIC CURVE (frequently abbreviated ROC CURVE). The terminology was inherited from the communications engineers who first developed signal detection theory. A more descriptive term for those interested in perception would be to call it an *isosensitivity curve*. The figure shows that when the signal is rare, the observer frequently says

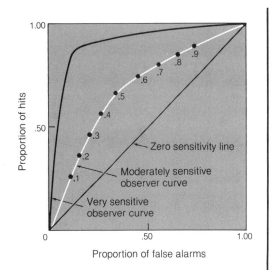

Figure 2-3.
ROC curves. Notice how the shape of the curves changes for different levels of sensitivity. Black dots on white curve represent results of experiments with indicated probability of signal presentation.

"no" even when the signal is presented. At the high end of the curve, where the signal occurs frequently, our observer says "yes" quite often even when the signal is not there.

An ROC curve reflects an observer's response pattern for one signal strength. If we increase the strength of the signal, we find that the curve has a more pronounced bow, as shown by the dotted line in Figure 2-3. If we lower the signal strength, the curve becomes flatter and approaches the 45° line, which represents chance responding. Thus, the amount of bow in the curve can serve as a measure of the perceived signal strength, or alternatively of the sensitivity of the observer to a particular signal. The measure of the observer's sensitivity, which is reflected by the curvature of the ROC curve, is called d'. A high d' indicates greater sensitivity and a small d' lower sensitivity.

We may also vary our observer's response pattern, while holding the signal intensity constant, by varying the importance or the payoff for a given response. For instance, if

Table 2-4 *Stimulus Present 90% of the Time (Based upon Tanner, Swets & Green, 1956)*

Signal	Response	
	Yes	No
Present	.96	.04
Absent	.80	.20

Stimulus Present 10% of the Time

Signal	Response	
	Yes	No
Present	.39	.61
Absent	.05	.95

we pay 10 cents for every correct detection of the stimulus and do not penalize the observer for false alarms, the optimal strategy is to guess "yes" on every trial. This will maximize the amount of money that can be earned in the test situation. Contrast this to a situation where we deduct 10 cents for each false alarm and do not reward for correct detections. Here a reasonable observer would maximize the gains by saying "no" on every trial. Actually most situations are somewhere between these two extremes. For instance, we might pay our observer 10 cents for every correct response and deduct 5 cents for every wrong response. This situation may be represented in a matrix of numbers as shown in Table 2-5. Such a set of rewards and penalties is called the PAYOFF MATRIX. Changing the payoff matrix causes changes in an observer's response pattern in much the same way as varying our observer's expectations concerning stimulus frequency. Thus our observer's *motives* as well as *expectations* affect responses during the detection experiment.

By systematically varying the payoff matrix of an experiment, we can vary an observer's numbers of hits and false alarms and produce an ROC curve similar to that generated by varying the relative frequency of signals. Such an experiment has been done by Swets, Tanner, and Birdsall (1961) among others. It is important to note that it is the observer's response pattern (the number of "yes" responses) that varies as the ROC curve is produced, and not the d' value that is a measure of sensitivity to the stimulus. Since

the manipulation of motivation in this case is done by varying the payoff matrix, and thus the amount of money paid to an observer, this type of experiment has been snidely termed "sweatshop psychophysics."

Perhaps the theoretical and methodological position of signal detection theorists will become clearer if we look at the detection problem from a different conceptual angle, one more similar to that used by signal detection theorists themselves. We have said that even when no stimulus is present, an observer's sensory systems are still active, generating sensory noise. The amount of noise probably varies from moment to moment, and thus will almost certainly be different at various moments when a signal absent presentation is initiated. This fluctuation in noise level is probably caused by the operation of physiological, attentional, and other variables upon the sensory and perceptual systems of the observer. Signal detection theorists represent these fluctuations in the form of a PROBABILITY DISTRIBUTION. This distribution is graphed in Figure 2-4 as the *signal absent curve*. The abscissa is the amount of sensory activity (or sensation level) and the ordinate can be thought of as the likelihood of occurrence of any particular level of sensation over a great many trials. This means that even in the absence of any external signal, the observer experiences some level of sensation that is represented by a particular location along the abscissa. This level is experienced with a frequency proportional to the height of the curve at that point.

Now when a signal is actually presented it is presented against this background of sensory noise. We may assume that the signal elicits some sensation of its own, which then adds to whatever amount is already present. The effect of this would be the creation of a new distribution of sensory activity. Generally, the new level of activity elicited by the signal is more intense. This is shown by its

Table 2-5 *A Typical Payoff Matrix for a Psychophysical Experiment*

	Response	
Signal	Yes	No
Present	10¢	−5¢
Absent	−5¢	10¢

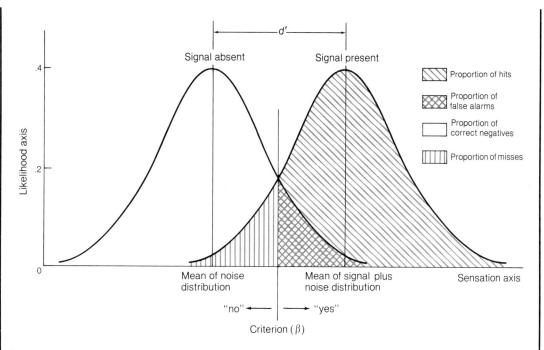

Figure 2-4.
Illustration of how overlapping noise and signal plus noise
distributions result in hits, misses, false alarms, and correct
negatives for a particular criterion setting.

higher position on the sensation level scale in Figure 2-4. Usually, the signal does not add enough sensory activity to make the two distributions (signal absent vs. signal present) completely distinct. Thus, we have drawn two overlapping distributions in Figure 2-4 to indicate that some levels of sensation could either result from applications of the signal or simply be a product of noise alone.

Imagine you are an observer sitting inside the head trying to decide if a signal has been presented. The only information you have is the intensity of the sensation, but sometimes the noise produces a sensation that is just as intense as that produced by the signal (remember the overlapping distributions in Figure 2-4). In order to solve this problem you might set a CRITERION or cutoff point for sensation level. This value is usually

symbolized with the Greek letter β (which is pronounced "beta"). If a sensation level is below the criterion (to the left in Figure 2-4), you respond "no"; if it is above the criterion, you respond "yes." This simplifies the problem greatly, since you must only decide, based on your motives and expectations, where to put the criterion. From that point onward, the experienced level of sensation more or less automatically determines the response. Theoretically, this is the optimal policy for an observer to follow. An observer who does follow this policy, and who has no other perceptual or mental limitations, is called the IDEAL OBSERVER.

When the problem is presented in this way it is easy to specify the proportions of hits and false alarms that one might expect. According to signal detection theory, the proportions of the various outcomes observed in an experiment (see Table 2-2) may be represented as that proportion of the *area* under the appropriate probability distribution curve to the right or left of the criterion location. Thus, if Figure 2-4 represents the real situation, the proportion of signal present trials on which a "yes" response would be given (the proportion of hits) is represented by the area under the signal present curve to the right of the criterion, since the observer would say "yes" whenever the sensation level was above, or to the right of, the criterion. Similarly, the proportion of false alarms is represented by the area under the signal absent curve to the right of the criterion, since that is the proportion of the trials on which the sensation level generated by the sensory system in the absence of a signal exceeded the criterion level set up for the "yes" response. The other two possible outcomes have similar representations within the two distributions of Figure 2-4.

The motivation and expectation effects on an observer's response pattern in a detection experiment now become interpretable. Essentially, these variables affect the placement of the criterion and, hence, the proportion of hits and false alarms. For instance, suppose that the observer is a radiologist looking for a light spot in a set of chest X rays, which might be evidence of cancer. If she thinks she has found such a spot, she calls the patient back for additional tests. Now the penalty for a false alarm (additional tests when no cancer is present) only involves some added time and money on the part of the patient, whereas the penalty for a miss (not catching an instance of real cancer) might be the patient's death. Thus, the radiologist may set a criterion that is quite low. This means she will have many hits and few misses, but also many false alarms. This situation is shown in Figure 2-5A. If, on the other hand, the observer is a radar operator looking for blips on

a screen signifying enemy missiles, he might be much more conservative. Here the penalty for a false alarm could be a war, while the penalty for a miss might only be a few seconds lost in sounding the alarm. He would set a much higher criterion to avoid false alarms, but at the penalty of reducing the number of hits. This would be equivalent to the situation shown in Figure 2-5B. In this same manner, each point on any given ROC curve simply represents a different criterion setting.

Although we indicated that the location of the criterion alters the pattern of responses, we never mentioned the effect of criterion lo-

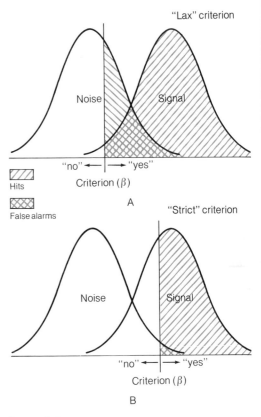

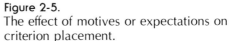

Figure 2-5.
The effect of motives or expectations on criterion placement.

cation on the sensitivity of the observer. That is because there is no such effect. In signal detection theory, sensitivity refers to the average amount of sensation generated by a given signal as compared with the average amount of noise generated alone. This is similar to the everyday use of the word sensitivity. Thus, a radio receiver that produces a large electrical response that lets a small signal be heard is more sensitive than one that produces only a small electrical response to the small signal. In the second case, the response may be obscured by static and noise.

Within our present framework, the perceptual analog is the distance between the centers (means) of the signal absent and the signal present distributions. This is merely a measure of the difference in average sensation levels as a function of the presence or absence of a signal. This distance is the measure of sensitivity that we called d'. When the distributions are close together, and overlap to a great extent, the d' is relatively small as in Figure 2-6A. The corresponding ROC curve is close to the diagonal, which represents zero sensitivity. When the distributions are far apart, and overlap very little, as in Figure 2-6B, d' is large and the ROC curve is far from the diagonal and sharply curved. Signal detection theory attempts to measure an observer's sensitivity to a signal independently of his decision strategy, while acknowledging that both might affect the actual responses made in the experimental setting. Actual computation of d' and criterion values from hit and false alarm proportions is demonstrated in a Special Topic at the end of this chapter.

Is this an unusually elaborate procedure for investigating a seemingly simple problem, namely, the determination of the minimal amount of energy necessary for stimulus detection? No, since this type of analysis is quite necessary. An observer is a living organism whose expectations and motives affect be-

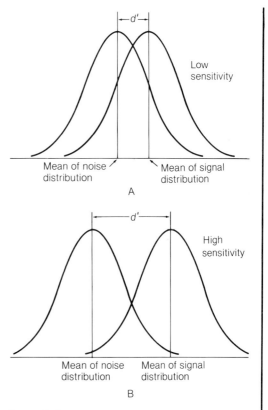

Figure 2-6.
The effect of sensitivity on d'.

haviors and judgments as well as stimulus reception. These nonperceptual effects must be removed if we are to look at the pure sensory responses. Our original notion of an absolute threshold has proved to be far too primitive. The detection threshold is simply a convenient statistically defined point. As an alternative we may use the d' measure, which provides an index of the observer's sensitivity to stimuli, instead of the traditional but less stable threshold measures.

RECOGNITION

The doctor listened very carefully, paused for a moment to adjust the stethoscope to a more comfortable position and listened again to the sounds emanating from the patient's chest. The sounds were quite clear and distinct. The problem was simply to decide whether they indicated a normal or a pathological heartbeat. This doctor is wrestling with a problem that does not involve stimulus detection, for the sounds are clearly above the detection threshold. However, it does involve the *recognition* of the occurrence of one of a number of possible alternative stimuli. To recognize or identify a stimulus is one of the major tasks that the perceptual system is asked to perform.

The difficulty of any recognition task depends, in part, upon the number of possible stimulus alternatives an observer is asked to distinguish. Consider an observer who claims he can discriminate his brand of cola from all others. Suppose we gave him two unmarked glasses of cola and asked him to sample them and to try to recognize his own favorite brand. If he did select the correct brand we would not be very surprised, since he would be expected to select his own brand 50% of the time, by chance alone; even if his taste buds were nonfunctional. If our expert selected his own brand out of 25 brands presented to him we would be much more likely to take his claim seriously, since the probability that he would by chance alone find his brand out of 25 alternatives is only 1/25. Measures of the difficulty of the recognition task must therefore take into account the number of stimulus alternatives.

Information Theory. To solve the problem of specifying the difficulty of a recognition task psychologists in the early 1950s turned to work arising from the efforts of engineers to assess the performance of radio and telephone communications systems. With the publication of books by Shannon and Weaver (1949) and by Wiener (1948), it became clear that the problems faced by the psychophysicist and by the communication engineer were

quite similar. The engineer deals with a message that is transmitted through a communication channel and decoded by someone or something at the receiver end. The degree to which the final decoded message reflects the original message depends, in part, upon the ability of the system to transmit information without distortion (this is what is meant by the fidelity of a system), and upon the complexity of the input. The psychophysicist has an analogous problem. Stimulus information is transmitted to an observer through a sensory system, and is then decoded in the central nervous system. The degree to which the observer's identification of the stimulus corresponds to the actual stimulus input will be affected by both the ability of the sensory system to handle the stimulus input without distortion and upon the complexity of the input.

The quantitative system for specifying the characteristics of the input message is known as INFORMATION THEORY. Information theory is *not* really a theory at all, but rather it is simply a system of measurement. The amount of information in a given stimulus display is defined so that the nature of the object being measured is irrelevant. What, then, do we mean by information? We mean what the everyday use of the word would imply. If you tell us that this week will contain a Sunday morning, you have conveyed very little information, since we know that every week contains a Sunday morning. If you tell us that this Sunday morning there will be a parade in honor of Jiffy the Kangaroo, you have conveyed a great deal of information because you have specified which one of the total number of possible alternative events was about to occur.

One way to quantify information is to define it in terms of the number of questions a person must ask to discover which member of a stimulus set had occurred. Suppose we had only two possible alternatives, A or B, and you were to search for the target among them. You need only to ask "Is it A?" to determine unambiguously which alternative had been selected as the target. If you receive an answer of "no" you know immediately that B is correct. Similarly, if you had to determine which of four stimuli, A, B, C, or D, had been chosen as the target, you could determine it in two questions. The answer to the question "Is it A or B?" reduces your number of possible alternatives to two, since a "no" answer reveals that it is either C or D, while a "yes" indicates that it is A or B. We already know that only one more question is necessary in order to identify the correct item. Each necessary question, structured to eliminate exactly *half* of the alternatives, defines a BIT of information. Bit is a contraction of the words *binary digit* (which can be either a "0" or a "1," i.e., there are *two* possible digits).

The number of bits of information needed to determine exactly one stimulus alternative is given by a number that is the logarithm to the base 2 of the total number of possible stimulus alternatives. The logarithm of a number n to the base 2, which is written $\log_2 n$, is merely the power to which the number 2 must be raised to equal n. Thus, if we have four alternatives we must raise 2 to the second power (i.e., $2^2 = 2 \times 2 = 4$) and $\log_2 4 = 2$. Similarly, Table 2-6 gives the corresponding number of bits for n alternatives (a more detailed table can be found in Garner, 1962). Each time the number of stimulus alternatives is doubled the amount of information rises by one bit. Of course, for intermediate values the number of bits will not be a whole number (for example, 7 alternatives gives 2.81 bits).

Channel capacity. How many bits of stimulus information can an observer process and still have perfect recognition? Let us first look at a group of stimuli selected from a one-dimensional physical continuum, such as sound or light intensity. The number of

Table 2-6 *$\log_2 n$ for Selected Numbers*

Number of Stimulus Alternatives (n)	Number of Bits ($\log_2 n$)
2	1
4	2
8	3
16	4
32	5
64	6
128	7
256	8

stimuli from one continuum that a subject can differentiate has been found to be surprisingly small. For the judgment of the pitch of a tone, Pollack (1952) found it to be about 2.3 bits, which is equivalent to about 5 stimulus alternatives. Garner (1953) found much the same result for loudness, around 2.1 bits. Eriksen and Hake (1955) measured several visual continua and found information transmission to be limited to 2.34 bits for brightness, 2.84 bits for size, and 3.08 bits for hue. Overall, the number of stimuli that may be perfectly recognized on any single continuum turns out to be approximately 7 ± 2, depending on the particular stimulus continuum being tested (see Miller, 1956).

It is important at this point to define the concept of INFORMATION TRANSMISSION. To do this, let us consider an observer as a channel, in the way that communication engineers do. Our observer can be represented as in Figure 2-7. A stimulus is presented to the observer and he is asked to try to recognize it. By recognition we mean giving a response that is the correct, agreed-upon label for the particular stimulus presented. We can say that information is transmitted by the observer to the extent that the responses given match the actual labels of the stimuli presented. That is, if the observer correctly recognizes a stimulus, and gives the correct

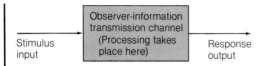

Figure 2-7.
A human information channel.

label as a response, information (the correct label) has been transmitted from one end to the other of the channel represented by the observer. If the response matches the stimulus perfectly for all stimuli, then the observer is a perfect information transmitter.

Consider an example where we are calling out alphabetic letters from a set containing 8 items: A B C D F G H X. If the observer correctly identifies the letter (response) that we have called out (stimulus) then she has reduced her uncertainty from 3 bits of information (8 alternatives) to zero, hence, she has transmitted 3 bits of information. Suppose that recognition is not perfect. This means that only some of the information is being transmitted. Thus, if the observer hears a faint "eee" sound, with the first part of the letter cut off, she does not know exactly which letter was called out. However, she can eliminate A, F, H, and X which have no "eee" sound; hence, she has reduced the number of stimulus alternatives by half, and we would say that 1 bit of information has been transmitted. In general, the greater the probability that the observer will recognize the stimulus, that is the more she "picks up" from the presentations, the more information she is capable of transmitting.

Consider a hypothetical experiment in which each of 4 stimuli are presented 12 times and observers are asked to identify which stimulus was presented. In Table 2-7 observer A shows perfect information transmission because every time stimulus 1 is presented our observer correctly recognizes it, and every time 2 is presented it is named correctly. In Table 2-7 observer B shows

Table 2-7 *Stimulus–Response Matrices for Three Observers*

Observer A: Perfect information transmission

Stimulus	Response			
	1	*2*	*3*	*4*
1	12			
2		12		
3			12	
4				12

Observer B: Some information transmission

Stimulus	Response			
	1	*2*	*3*	*4*
1	8	2		
2	4	8	2	
3		2	8	4
4			2	8

Observer C: No information transmission

Stimulus	Response			
	1	*2*	*3*	*4*
1	3	3	3	3
2	3	3	3	3
3	3	3	3	3
4	3	3	3	3

poorer information transmission. Notice here that when stimulus 2 is presented, the observer calls it stimulus 2 most of the time; but, sometimes, he calls it stimulus 1 and sometimes he calls it stimulus 3. However, when he does say that it is stimulus 2, there is a fair likelihood that it is stimulus 2. He is much better than observer C who seems to be responding without reference to the stimulus presented. Observer C is transmitting none of the available stimulus information. Formulas for computing the amount of information transmitted in such experiments may be found in Garner and Hake (1951).

If we now consider the information transmission measured in a number of experimental studies, we find that when the number of stimuli are few observers are capable of perfect recognition. However, when the number of stimuli begins to exceed 7 or so, that is 2.5–3.0 bits of information, errors are made. We have reached the limit of the observer's ability to differentiate among the stimuli. This limit is called (again using communication theory terminology) our observer's CHANNEL CAPACITY. A typical channel capacity is shown in Figure 2-8. Notice that even though we increase the amount of information available in the display, our subject has reached his limit of recognition (about 2.5 bits) and can transmit no more information.

Seven seems to be a very small number of stimuli to be able to recognize. Each of us knows that singers, for example, seem able to recognize (indeed sing) hundreds of different songs. Every one of us can certainly recognize and differentiate dozens of faces and thousands of words. How can this be, in light of our inability to transmit more than about 3 bits of information per stimulus dimension? In other words, how could we go about increasing our channel capacity, or our ability to recognize stimuli?

One technique that was tried was to space the stimuli farther apart in an attempt to increase their discriminability. However, this was not very effective (Pollack, 1952). Practice does help, and this explains the phenomenal abilities of wine tasters to discriminate varieties of wines. It also explains how some individuals in the cosmetics industry can not only recognize but name hundreds of distinct colors in the range from orange to red. Some recognition behavior is quite accurate yet involves very little practice and stimuli that are

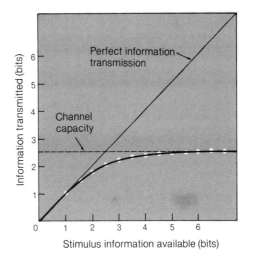

Figure 2-8.
Channel capacity. The straight diagonal represents perfect information transmission. The curve represents typical performance. The dotted horizontal line is channel capacity.

not very discriminable. For instance, you hear a new word today and now you can recognize that word with ease, even though you have seen it only once. You can recognize that the new word is different from any other word in your vocabulary. We are not at all surprised at such a performance, yet this type of recognition may involve the reduction of uncertainty by some 16 bits (or more accurately, the quantity associated with the selection of one word out of the total number of English words in your vocabulary). Given that our channel capacity is so limited for any single stimulus dimension, how can this occur? The answer seems to depend upon the *number of dimensions* along which the stimulus varies.

As an example, Pollack (1953) found that if he varied only pitch the amount of transmitted information was 1.8 bits, and if he varied only loudness the information transmitted was 1.7 bits. If he varied both simultaneously, the total transmitted information was 3.1 bits (this is somewhat less than a simple sum of the information transmitted by both channels independently, which would be equal to 3.5 bits). The greater the number of stimulus dimensions, the better the recognition. Thus, one can now play a sort of a recognition game. By using highly over-learned stimulus dimensions (for we have already seen that extended practice can lead to increased performance along a unidimensional continuum) and a large number of stimulus dimensions we can continue to increase the amount of transmitted information. Anderson and Fitts (1958) varied stimuli using numbers, colors, and varying spatial position. They obtained an information transmission of 17 bits for single brief exposures. This means that their subjects could perfectly discriminate one stimulus out of a set of more than 131,000 alternative stimuli (cf. Garner, 1962).

The importance of stimulus dimensions has led modern investigators to place less emphasis upon the *quantity* of information available and more emphasis upon the *quality* or kind of information and the characteristics of the information processor (see Garner, 1974; Neisser, 1967). The basic ideas of information theory, especially those associated with the number of stimulus alternatives, have been important in calling attention to critical issues in recognition. They have taken their place as foundational concepts, almost assumptions, and modern researchers build on them rather than study them for their own sake. Chapter 13 considers some of these modern extensions of and alternatives to information theory in the study of pattern recognition.

The Detection–Recognition Hierarchy. In the previous section we were dealing with stimuli that were presented at levels well above some average detection threshold. Al-

though an observer might have been unable to recognize any given stimulus, he was at least certain that a stimulus was present. Suppose we work at levels around the average detection threshold, where an observer is unsure about whether or not a stimulus is present, and suppose we simultaneously conduct a detection and a recognition experiment. Can the observer recognize the stimulus at greater than chance levels of performance, given the fact that he is unsure of whether it is there at all? In other words, is some information about very weak stimuli still available to the subject?

Some interesting data on this issue have been provided by Shipley (1961). She presented observers with a series of auditory stimuli in the presence of noise. The observer was presented with either a high or low pitched tone, or noise alone. The observer was required to say whether or not a tone was present (this is a simple detection experiment) and then, regardless of whether the response was "yes" or "no," the observer was asked to guess which of the 2 tones was present. The results indicated that on those trials when the observer answered "no" when the tone was indeed present (a miss), recognition of which of the 2 tones was present was not above chance levels. This experiment seems to indicate that a hierarchical relationship exists between detection and recognition. Before a stimulus can be recognized it must cause sufficient sensation to elicit a fairly confident "yes" response. This hierarchical relationship was suggested as early as 1905 by Davies, who briefly presented geometrical shapes to observers. His observers always reported that they were able to detect the presence of light before they were able to perceive or recognize the geometrical form of the stimulus. Recognition, then, seems to require that more of the stimulus information be available than does simple detection.

DISCRIMINATION

The artist glances at his model's hair and then back down at the paint on his palette. He mutters to himself, "Still not the same." He daubs a bit more black, mixes the color through, and glances up again. "That is a perfect match," he grunts. This artist is engaging in a special form of recognition task. He is determining whether two colors are the same or different. He does not care what the color actually is, it can be "burnt sienna" or just plain "brown." He cares only whether or not it matches his model's hair color. The artist is engaged in an act of *discrimination*. Discrimination problems ask the question "Is this stimulus different from that?"

The study of discrimination has focused upon the question "By how much must two stimuli differ in order to be discriminated as not the same?" It must be clear at once, that this question needs some additional specification. Suppose the melody "Oh Susanna" were to be played on a piano once in the key of C and once in the key of G. Are these two musical stimuli the same or different? Clearly, the answer to this question depends upon the stimulus dimension being judged. If we are judging whether the melodies are the same or different, we would answer differently than if we were judging the key in which the melodies are played.

To avoid such confusions the standard discrimination experiment involves variation of stimuli along only one dimension. Thus, in a study of the sense of touch, we might hold the size and the shape of our stimuli constant and vary only the weight. In the earlier studies, observers were presented with pairs of stimuli and asked to make the appropriate response, "heavier," "lighter," or "same," or some similar set of judgments appropriate to the stimulus dimension being judged. One of these stimuli is designated as the STANDARD.

This is a stimulus that appears on every trial. It is compared to a graded set of similar stimuli differing along the dimension being studied. These comprise the set of COMPARISON STIMULI. This is simply a variant of the method of constant stimuli, which is used to determine the absolute threshold, with the addition of a standard. We are also measuring a threshold here, only this is a threshold for the perception of a difference between the standard and the other stimuli. It is called a DIFFERENCE THRESHOLD.

As psychophysicists worked with the measurement of difference thresholds for various stimulus dimensions, it became clear that the "same" response category was very unstable. It tended to fluctuate a great deal and to obscure an observer's ability to judge stimulus differences. Suppose we present an observer with only 2 response alternatives instead of 3. Thus, in this weight judgment experiment, the observer will only be permitted to respond that the comparison stimulus is either "heavier" or "lighter." If he feels that the comparison and the standard are the same, he is still forced to indicate (by guessing) in which direction they appear to differ. This is an example of a FORCED-CHOICE procedure. Its advantage is demonstrated by the painstaking work of Brown (1910), who was able to show that in a weight judgment experiment stimulus differences as small as 0.2 g (which is about 0.008 ounces) produced more right than wrong judgments. Thus, when we force the observer to respond to small stimulus differences, we find that the "same" response has been used as a kind of a "doubtful" category. It is used when the observer feels that the stimuli may indeed be different but he is not sure enough to make a commitment. There may even be a tendency to make the number of same and different responses equal, which would result in apparently poorer discrimination performance.

The results from a forced-choice experiment are easy to display. In the weight judging paradigm, for instance, we have presented the standard with each comparison stimulus many times. We can plot the proportion of the presentations on which any given stimulus was judged heavier than the standard. Such a plot is illustrated in Figure 2-9. The data are typical of those from an experiment on weight judgment such as that of Brown (1910). Brown used a 100-g standard and a set of comparison weights ranging from 82 to 118 g in one gram steps. Each comparison stimulus was judged 700 times against the standard stimulus. We find that the shift from reports of "lighter" to reports of "heavier" is not very abrupt, as it would be if the threshold were always a single, unique value. Rather we find a gradual, continuous change in the probability of a "heavier" response as the stimulus changes from much lighter than the standard to much heavier. Given the fact that the change is gradual we

again must make some decision as to how we will define the difference threshold. Clearly the point where p(heavier) $= 0.5$, that is the stimulus called "lighter" 50% of the time and "heavier" 50% of the time, is not appropriate. This 50% point probably represents the stimulus that appears most like the standard, since the choices appear to be evenly divided on either side of it. Therefore, this point has been defined as the POINT OF SUBJECTIVE EQUALITY. Since we know that the stimuli for which p(heavier) $= 1.0$ represents perfect discrimination (because here a physically heavier stimulus is judged heavier 100% of the time), and we have already noted that the stimulus where p(heavier) $= 0.5$ represents no perception of difference, then we can easily see that the p(heavier) $= 0.75$ point represents a value where the *difference* is noted 50% of the time. Following similar reasoning, p(heavier) $= 0.25$ is the point at which a lighter stimulus difference is recognized 50% of the time. By convention we take the interval from the 0.25 point to the 0.75 point, called the INTERVAL OF UNCERTAINTY, and divide it by 2 to give us a value that we call the JUST NOTICEABLE DIFFERENCE or *jnd*. The *jnd* is computed for the data in Figure 2-9, and it is about 4 g. This means that given a pair of stimuli that are separated by 4 g, the subject will be able to notice or detect the difference between them about half of the time. You can probably see that the *jnd* is nothing more than the average of the threshold for greater and the threshold for less than. In other words it represents the threshold for "different" regardless of the direction of differences.

If discrimination is good we would expect very small differences between stimuli to be noticed. This corresponds to a small *jnd*. In Figure 2-10 the solid line shows a good discriminator with a *jnd* of 0.5 units, while the dashed line shows a poor discriminator with a *jnd* of 2 units. As the *jnd* increases in size

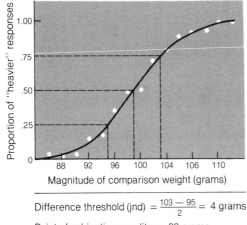

Difference threshold (jnd) $= \dfrac{103 - 95}{2} = 4$ grams

Point of subjective equality $= 99$ grams

Figure 2-9.
Typical data from the method of constant stimuli in discrimination with calculations of difference threshold (*jnd*) and point of subjective equality.

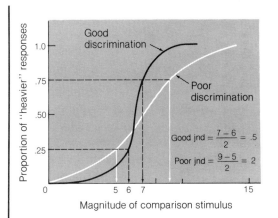

Figure 2-10.
Difference thresholds (*jnd*s) for observers of different sensitivity.

and discrimination ability decreases, the curve begins to flatten. The extreme of no discrimination at all would be represented by a horizontal line parallel to the abscissa at p(heavier) = 0.5.

There is an interesting aspect of the data pictured in Figure 2-9 that you may have noticed. The point of subjective equality is not equal to the standard in these data. The stimulus that *appears* to be equal to the standard of 100 g is actually 1 g lighter. This is a typical result in many psychophysical experiments involving the presentation of stimuli that are separated in time. The stimulus presented first (generally the standard) is judged to be less intense than the later stimulus. This effect has been named the NEGATIVE TIME ERROR. It is negative because the standard is now judged as less intense than it should be. Gustav Fechner (1860) and Wolfgang Kohler (1923) thought that this error was caused by the fading of the image or the trace of the sensation of the standard with the passage of time. However, work done with auditory stimuli has shown that with proper selection of a time interval the error can be positive rather than negative (Köhler, 1923), and practice effects can re-

verse the direction of the error (Needham, 1934). A fading trace cannot handle these peculiarities in any obvious way. Suffice it to say that time errors exist in most psychophysical data although they are not readily explainable.

Weber's Law. Is the *jnd* a fixed value for any given sense modality, or does it vary as a function of the nature of the stimulus input or the state of the observer? Following the lead of Ernst Heinrich Weber (1834), Gustav Fechner (1860) conducted an experiment in which he measured the *jnd*s for lifted weights using standard weights of different magnitudes. We may plot the size of the *jnd,* that is, the amount by which we must increase the stimulus so that it is discriminable as different from the standard 50% of the time, against the magnitude of the standard. This has been done for illustrative data in Figure 2-11. First, we notice that the *jnd* is not a constant value. It appears to increase in a linear fashion with the size of the standard. In other words, as the stimulus magnitude increases so does the size of the change needed for discrimination to occur. The intuitive force of this relationship is well illustrated in an example proposed by Galanter (1962), ". . . if in a room with ten candles you had to add one more in order to detect an increase in illumination, then if the room contained one hundred candles it would be necessary to add ten candles in order to detect the same apparent increase in illumination . . ." (p. 133). This relation between the size of the *jnd* and the size of the standard intensity is called WEBER'S LAW after its discoverer.

Weber's Law is simply written as

$$\Delta I = KI$$

where ΔI is the size of the *jnd,* I is the intensity of the standard stimulus, and K is a constant. The constant K is always a fraction and is equal to $\Delta I/I$. It indicates the proportion by which the standard stimulus must be increased in order to detect a change. This fractional value is called the WEBER FRACTION. Thus, if the Weber fraction is .5, it means that we must increase the intensity of one stimulus by one half for a difference between it and another stimulus to be detected. This proportion (the Weber fraction) is the same regardless of the strength of the standard stimulus. In a weight judgment, for example, to discriminate a stimulus as different from a 2-gm standard, the weight must be increased by only 1 gram. To discriminate a stimulus as different from a 200-gm standard, it must be increased by 100 gm. A simple demonstration of

Weber's Law is given in Demonstration Box 2-2.

You may consider the Weber fraction to be a measure of the overall sensitivity of a sensory system to differences along a stimulus continuum. On the average, the larger the Weber fraction, the larger will be the *jnd*s for any stimulus dimension. Note that K has no units (like grams), so that it does not depend on the physical units used to measure I and ΔI. Thus, we can compare Weber fractions across different stimulus dimensions without having to worry about how the stimulus values were measured. The Weber fraction

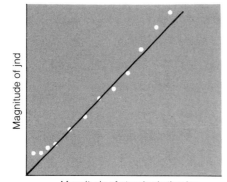

Figure 2-11.
Effect of intensity of standard on difference threshold (*jnd*).

Table 2-8 *Typical Weber Fractions $\Delta I/I$ (Based upon Teghtsoonian, 1971)*

Continuum	Weber Fraction
Brightness	.079
Loudness	.048
Finger span	.022
Heaviness	.020
Line length	.029
Taste (salt)	.083
Electric shock	.013
Vibration (fingertip)	
60 Hz	.036
125 Hz	.046
250 Hz	.046

It is quite easy to demonstrate Weber's Law for the perception of heaviness. For this you will need 3 quarters, 2 envelopes, and your shoes. Take one quarter and put it in an envelope and put the remaining two quarters in the other. If you now gently lift each envelope and put it down (use the same hand) it is quite easy to distinguish the heavier envelope. Now insert one envelope into one of your shoes, and the other envelope into your second shoe and lift them one at a time. The weight difference should be almost imperceptible. Notice that in the first instance, the targets differed by the weight of the quarter and the difference was easily discriminated. In the second instance, although the weight differential was the same (one quarter), the overall stimulus intensity was greater since shoes weigh much more than the envelopes and the quarters alone.

Demonstration Box 2-2:
Weber's Law

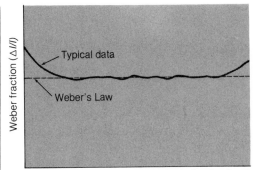

Logarithm of magnitude of standard stimulus (log *I*)

Figure 2-12.
Typical data for test of Weber's Law. The dotted line is predicted by Weber's Law:
$\Delta I/I = K$.

simply represents the average ratio of *jnd* size to the size of the standard level at which the *jnd* was measured, over an entire range of standard values. Table 2-8 presents typical Weber fractions for a variety of continua. As you can see, some of the Ks are relatively large (e.g., those for brightness and loudness), while some are quite small (e.g., electric shock).

How well does Weber's Law fit the data? For many years there was considerable argument about this issue. Measurements were taken in many sense modalities to check the relation. The clearest picture of the results is given by plotting the value of the Weber fraction $\Delta I/I$ against the standard stimulus intensity. If this fraction is actually constant we should see a horizontal line, parallel to the abscissa. Figure 2-12 shows a composite of data from a series of loudness discrimination experiments by Miller (1947) and Riesz (1928). It is quite clear that there is considerable deviation from the expected constancy at both extremes. Although these deviations look very large when compared to the area over which the curve appears to be flat, it is important to note that this is only because we have plotted the stimuli in logarithmic units. The flat part of the curve actually exceeds

99.9% of the total range of intensities used. Thus Weber's Law is a useful summary in spite of the deviation of the data from a perfect fit.

There is a difficulty that has occupied much time and effort in psychophysics, namely the interaction of measurement technique with the results obtained. We have just seen that with a *constant stimulus method,* where the standard is presented first and then the comparison stimulus, we find that Weber's Law holds over almost all of the stimulus range except for the extremes. Ono (1967), however, has found that the Weber fraction may change, depending upon the way in which stimuli are presented; hence, we must be careful about assuming that a Weber fraction measured in one circumstance will be the same as in all others.

Signal Detection Theory in Discrimination. Although signal detection theory was presented (and first developed) in the context of the detection problem, it can be extended to the discrimination situation since there are certainly decisional components that influence whether or not an observer responds that a difference between two stimuli exists. In order to use the signal detection procedure to assess discrimination, we must redesign our method of constant stimuli experiment so that the observer is asked to say which of two very similar stimuli was actually presented on a given trial. This is rather like a recognition experiment with only two stimuli.

The signal detection analysis of this experiment is quite similar to that used for detection. Instead of trying to ascertain whether the sensation experienced on a given trial came from the signal or the noise distribution, the observer must decide whether it came from the signal 1 or signal 2 distribution. If the stimuli were very similar the curves would overlap, and an observer would be faced with a situation very similar to that faced by the observer in the absolute detection situation. Thus, you might look back at Figure 2-4 and mentally relabel the two distributions "signal 1" and "signal 2." Each stimulus can give rise to a variety of different sensation levels, with different probabilities. Since the curves overlap, there is no way to be certain which stimulus elicited a given sensation level on any one trial. The best the ideal observer can do is to place a criterion somewhere on the sensation axis, and simply determine whether the sensation level experienced is above or below that criterion. If above, the appropriate response would be that the presented stimulus was a 2; if below, a 1. Just as in the absolute detection situation, where the observer places the criterion will greatly affect the proportions of different responses he gives. In turn, criterion placement will be affected by the observer's expectations as to the relative frequency of presentation of the two stimuli, and the observer's present motivational biases.

As in the detection experiment, different criterion placements will define an isosensitivity curve as we plot the proportion of hits against the proportion of false alarms. The measure of sensitivity to the difference between the two stimuli is still called d' and is still unaffected by changes in the criterion. Actually, d' is determined by the physical difference between the two stimuli and the sensitivity of the observer's sensory system; both are factors that determine the difference between the levels of sensation evoked by the stimuli. Thus d' represents a measure of just how discriminable two very similar stimuli are. As such, it is closely related to the difference threshold and to the Weber fraction (Treisman, 1976; Treisman & Watts, 1966).

Reaction Time. We have been looking at stimuli that are difficult to discriminate correctly. Even when we are working with stimuli well above the difference threshold, we intuitively sense that some discriminations are easier to make than others. Red is more easily differentiated from green than from orange. When we are working with sets of stimuli that exceed the difference threshold, the frequency methods we have used up to this point are too crude to measure interstimulus differences in detectability or discriminability. To provide a more sensitive measure we must turn to one of the oldest techniques in sensory psychology— REACTION TIME. Reaction time is defined as the time between the onset of a stimulus and the beginning of an overt response. It was first introduced by one of the early giants in perception and physiology, Hermann von Helmholtz, in 1850, who used it as a crude measure of the speed of neural conduction in a limb. When Wundt established his pioneer psychological laboratory in 1879 most of the experiments he conducted utilized reaction time as a measure of the speed of various mental operations.

There are two varieties of reaction time. SIMPLE REACTION TIME involves pressing or releasing a telegraph key (or making some other simple stereotyped response) immediately upon detecting a stimulus. CHOICE REACTION TIME involves making one of several responses depending upon the stimulus presented (i.e., press the right-hand key for a red stimulus and the left for a green). Simple reaction times are generally used in detection paradigms. We have known for a long time that the stronger a stimulus the faster the reaction time. Figure 2-13 shows typical median reaction times to the onset of a tone plotted against the stimulus intensity (Chocolle, 1945). Notice that as the stimulus intensity decreases and approaches the detection threshold (although it is still quite detectable) the reaction times begin to lengthen. Thus as the stimulus becomes more difficult to ap-

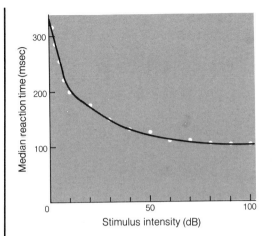

Figure 2-13.
Effect on simple reaction time of stimulus intensity (based upon Chocolle, 1945).

prehend, the reaction time grows longer. Similar results have been obtained for visual stimuli (Berger, 1896; Cattell, 1886).

Simple reaction time has also been used to measure discrimination. Here, however, the subject must detect a change in stimulus intensity. Steinman (1944) had observers sit 60 cm in front of a 2.5-cm diameter ground-glass screen. This target was centered on a brightly lit background. Observers were instructed to react as soon as they detected any change in brightness of the target. Changes could be either increases or decreases in intensity. Steinman found that as the magnitude of the change increased, the reaction time decreased. Chocholle (1943) found similar results for changes in auditory intensity.

Choice reaction time has been used in studies of discrimination and recognition. These reaction times tend to be somewhat longer than simple reaction times. The classic discrimination experiment utilizing reaction time comes from Henmon (1906). In this experiment the observer had two response keys: one for each hand. In one experiment, the observer was presented with pairs of lines differing only in length. She was to depress the key corresponding to the side on which the line was longer. Henmon found that as the difference between the line lengths increased the reaction time decreased. He also reported similar results for colors and tones.

A striking example of the relationship between choice reaction time and the discriminability of stimuli utilized a slightly different technique. In an experiment by Shallice and Vickers (1964), observers were required to sort decks of cards into piles according to which of two lines on the cards appeared longer. The time it took for them to sort the cards was the measure of their reaction time. This measure is, of course, the sum of a number of reaction times, where we consider the sorting of each card as a single response. The standard stimulus in this experiment was a 4.5-cm line. In the data shown in Table 2-9, we see that as the discrimination becomes more difficult the sorting time increases. A simple demonstration of this effect is given in Demonstration Box 2-3. Crossman (1953) has shown that these reaction time differences are related both to the discriminability of the stimuli and the amount of infor-

Table 2-9 *Differences in Reaction Time as a Function of Differences in Line Lengths Measured via Card Sorts (Based upon Shallice & Vickers, 1964)*

Difference in Length (cm)	Sorting Time (sec)
1.1	39.4
0.9	40.0
0.7	40.1
0.5	41.0
0.4	42.0
0.3	42.9
0.2	46.5
0.1	52.4

Table 2-10 *Reaction Time as a Function of Number of Stimulus Alternatives (Based upon Merkel, 1885)*

Number of Alternatives	Reaction Time (msec)
1	187
2	316
3	364
4	434
5	487
6	534
7	570
8	603
9	619
10	632

mation they contain. We are referring to information in the technical sense that was discussed in the section on recognition. If this is the case, then we would expect choice reaction times to increase as we increase the number of response alternatives, and indeed, this result has been known for many years. Merkel (1885) showed, using numbers as stimuli, that as the number of response alternatives increased so did the reaction time.

This is clearly seen in the data in Table 2-10.

Hick (1952) attempted to explain these results by postulating that the observer extracts information from the stimulus display at a constant rate. The more information, that must be obtained from the display, the longer the reaction time. In an experimental situation, where a display of lights served as stimuli and finger pressings of telegraph keys served as responses, he found that the reaction time was a linear function of the logarithm of the number of stimulus alternatives. This relation has been called HICK'S LAW and states that choice reaction time is a linear function of the amount of information in the stimulus. This result has been confirmed by a number of investigators. You may demonstrate these effects of the number of stimulus alternatives on reaction time by consulting Demonstration Box 2-4.

The techniques introduced in this chapter will appear in many disguises throughout the rest of this book. We will not generally stop and identify these techniques, or the means of analyzing and speaking about data that they involve. Do not ignore their importance, however, for the way in which data are collected is important. As demonstrated for

---

Take a deck of common playing cards and select out of it 10 of the picture cards (Kings, Queens, and Jacks) and 10 numbered cards from the red suits (hearts and diamonds) to make up a new deck of 20 cards. Compose another deck of 20 by using the numbered cards (include the aces) of the black suits (clubs and spades). Shuffle each deck separately and place it in front of you, face down. Next you need a clock or a watch with a sweep second hand. Wait till the second hand reaches the 12, pick up one of the decks and begin to sort it into two piles. The first deck gets sorted into number and picture cards, while the second gets sorted into spades and clubs. Note the time it takes to sort each deck. You may want to repeat the task a couple of times so that you are sorting smoothly. Notice that the sorting time for the spades and clubs (a more difficult task since it involves making small form discriminations on similarly colored cards) is longer than the easier discrimination task of sorting picture and number cards.

Demonstration Box 2-3:
Reaction time and Stimulus Discriminability

Again take a deck of playing cards and separate 16 cards using only the low numbers, A, 2, 3, and 4. Next, make up another deck of 16 cards using two each of the 5, 6, 7, 8, 9, 10, J, Q. Now shuffle each deck. Measure the time it takes to sort each deck into piles by number (4 for the first and 8 piles for the second deck) using a watch or clock with a sweep second hand as you did in Demonstration Box 2-3. Notice that the reaction time is longer (measured by sorting time) as the number of alternative stimuli that must be recognized and responded to is greater. Thus, sorting the 4 stimulus deck is more rapid than sorting the 8 stimulus deck.

Demonstration Box 2-4:
Number of Stimulus Alternatives and Reaction Time

Weber's Law, the measurement technique will frequently interact with the phenomena to be measured. We find, when we look at raw recognition scores, that red and green are both easily discriminated 100% of the time from orange, yet when we measure reaction times it takes longer to discriminate red from orange than green from orange. Is this a contradiction of fact? The answer is "not really." The reason is, as we will find later, that such differences as a function of measurement technique frequently indicate that the two methods of measurement are not measuring the same processes. With this warning in mind, we will move on to the problem of scaling.

SPECIAL TOPIC: HOW TO CALCULATE d' AND THE CRITERION VALUE β

To calculate d' and β you must have at hand the matrix of outcomes of the detection or discrimination experiments (for example, Table 2-3). You need to use only the *proportion of hits* [p(HIT)] and the *proportion of false alarms* [p(FA)]. When you have these values, consult Table ST2-1. This table defines several situations according to the values of p(HIT) and p(FA). Find the situation appropriate to your data ("defining conditions" in Table ST2-1) and then carry out the operations specified in the order given for calculating d' and the criterion β. These operations are listed by number in Table ST2-3. Consult the indicated part of Figure ST2-1 for an example of a graphical representation of your own data within the signal detection theoretical model.

Example.

$$p\,(\text{HIT}) = .7 \qquad p\,(\text{FA}) = .2$$

The indicated values for p(HIT) and p(FA) indicate situation A in Table ST2-1 [p(FA) < .5 and p(HIT) > .5]. Figure ST2-1A shows a typical example of this situation. Following steps 1–5–4–6–7 to obtain d' yields:

1. $A(\text{HIT}) = .7 - .5 = .2$
5. $Z(\text{HIT}) = .52$
4. $A(\text{FA}) = .5 - .2 = .3$
6. $Z(\text{FA}) = .84$
7. $d' = .52 + .84 = 1.36$

Following steps 1–11–4–12–13 to obtain β yields:

1. $A(\text{HIT}) = .7 - .5 = .2$
11. $O(\text{HIT}) = .348$
4. $A(\text{FA}) = .5 - .2 = .3$
12. $O(\text{FA}) = .280$
13. $\beta = .348/.280 = 1.24$

Table ST2-1 *Situations*

	A	B	C	D	E	F
Defining conditions	p(FA) < .5 and p(HIT) > .5	p(FA) ≥ .5 and p(HIT) > .5	p(FA) < .5 and p(HIT) ≤ .5	p(FA) > .5 and p(HIT) < .5	p(FA) = p(HIT)	p(FA) = 0,1 and/or p(HIT) = 0,1
Look at figure	ST2-1A	ST2-1B	ST2-1C	ST2-1D	ST2-1E	No figure
d' calculation operations	1–5–4–6–7	1–5–3–6–8	2–5–4–6–9	2–5–3–6–10	$d' = 0$	d' and β cannot be calculated under these conditions
β calculation operations	1–11–4–12–13	1–11–3–12–13	2–11–4–12–13	2–11–3–12–13	$\beta = 1$	
β value range	$0 < \beta < \infty$	$0 < \beta < 1$	$1 < \beta < \infty$	$0 < \beta < \infty$		

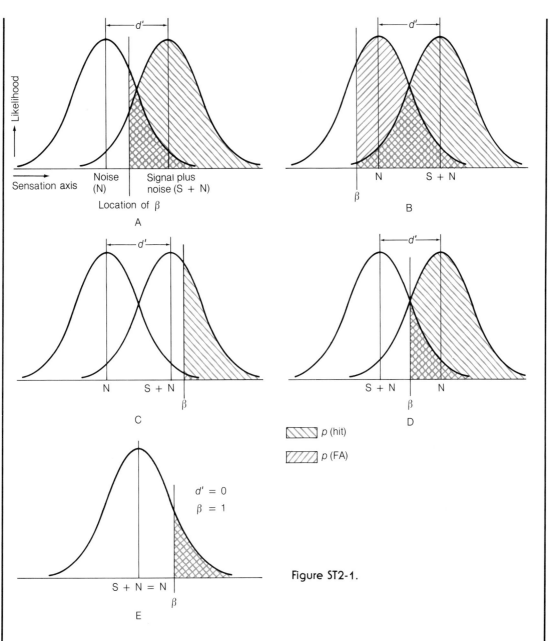

Figure ST2-1.

Table ST2-2 *Z and Ordinate Values for Areas under the Normal Curve*

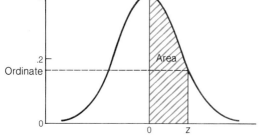

Area	Z	Ordinate
.00	0.00	.399
.05	0.13	.396
.10	0.25	.387
.15	0.39	.370
.20	0.52	.348
.25	0.67	.319
.30	0.84	.280
.35	1.04	.232
.40	1.28	.176
.45	1.65	.102
.46	1.75	.086
.47	1.88	.068
.48	2.05	.049
.49	2.33	.026
.492	2.41	.022
.494	2.51	.017
.496	2.65	.012
.498	2.88	.006

Table ST2-3 *Operations*

1. Calculate $A(\text{HIT}) = p(\text{HIT}) - .5$
2. Calculate $A(\text{HIT}) = .5 - p(\text{HIT})$
3. Calculate $A(\text{FA}) = p(\text{FA}) - .5$
4. Calculate $A(\text{FA}) = .5 - p(\text{FA})$
5. Find the value of $A(\text{HIT})$ in the area column of Table ST2-2. Read across to the corresponding value in the Z column. This is $Z(\text{HIT})$.
6. Find the value of $A(\text{FA})$ in the area column of Table ST2-2. Read across to the corresponding value in the Z column. This is $Z(\text{FA})$.
7. Calculate: $d' = Z(\text{HIT}) + Z(\text{FA})$
8. Calculate: $d' = Z(\text{HIT}) - Z(\text{FA})$
9. Calculate: $d' = Z(\text{FA}) - Z(\text{HIT})$
10. Calculate: $d' = -[Z(\text{HIT}) + Z(\text{FA})]$
11. Find the value of $A(\text{HIT})$ in the area column of Table ST2-2. Read across to the corresponding value in the ordinate column. This is $O(\text{HIT})$.
12. Find the value of $A(\text{FA})$ in the area column of Table ST2-2. Read across to the corresponding value in the ordinate column. This is $O(\text{FA})$.
13. Calculate: $\beta = O(\text{HIT})/O(\text{FA})$.

3
Measurement, Scaling, and Adaptation Level

The dog trainer glanced at her new St. Bernard pupil and estimated his shoulder height to be 75 cm and his weight to be 80 kg. The boy scout leader considered his aching feet and glanced up the trail to where smoke was rising from the permanent campsite. Wistfully, he appraised the distance to be about two kilometers. Both of these individuals were engaged in the perceptual act that we call *scaling*. Scaling attempts to answer the question, "How much of X is there?" X can be a stimulus magnitude, a sensation magnitude, or the magnitude of such other complex psychological variables as similarity or even pleasantness.

THE NATURE OF SCALES

Basically, a scale is a rule by which we assign numbers to objects or events. The scale attempts to represent numerically some property of objects or events. There are a variety of different types of representations that can be established, and each has its own characteristics (see Stevens, 1946). Perhaps the most primitive and unrestricted type of scale is a NOMINAL SCALE. Its etymology specifies its nature, since "nomin" is derived from the Latin word for "name." When numbers are assigned in a nominal scale, they serve only as identity codes or surrogate names. The numbers imply nothing more about the quantity of some property than does the number on a football jersey. An example of a nominal scale of this type is the labeling of dogs at a dog show. All Collies might be labeled with a number "1," German sheperds with a "2," and Pomeranians with a "3." In this case, the only property of numbers that can be used in a valid way is the property that the various numerals are different. Thus, someone at the

dog show could announce "All number 4s to the judging area please," and the announcement would have the effect of gathering all of the Doberman Pincers but none of the Collies. If a number 2 answered the call, it would not be included in the round of judging simply because the number was different, thus designating a different type of object (breed). As has been pointed out by Snodgrass (1975), in order to perform a recognition experiment there must first be a nominal scale that can be used to signal the observer's perception of the identity of the stimuli that are to be judged. This type of scale has also been called an "identification function" (see Bush, Galanter, & Luce, 1963).

Whenever we are dealing with something for which it is possible to say that an object or event contains more or less of the property than some other object or event, it is possible to create an ORDINAL SCALE of that property. An ordinal scale simply ranks items on the basis of some quantity. An example might be the "Best Seller" or "Top Fifty" lists that order books or records on the basis of how many have been sold. Similarly, we rank order horses in a race according to the sequence in which they crossed the finish line. Now the sequential properties of the number system become important. We can be sure that the horse that is labeled "2" was slower than the horse labeled "1" and faster than the horse labeled "3." Of course, if we only know these labels, we cannot tell by *how much* 2 was slower than 1. The second place horse could have lost the race by 20 lengths or by a nose, and he would still have received the number "2" on our ordinal scale of horse speed. It is clear that although this scale may prove to be more useful for measurement than a nominal scale, we are still very restricted in what we can do with the numbers on such a scale. We may also find the scale too insensitive for many purposes. However, since it is often very difficult to do much more than determine the rank order of a group of objects or events, an ordinal scale may be the best we can create for some problems.

The third type of scale is the INTERVAL SCALE. It not only answers the questions implied by the labels "more" or "less" but also tells "by how much." It employs not only the sequential properties of numbers but also their spacing, or the *intervals* between them. A good example of an interval scale is the scale of temperature represented by the common household thermometer. Here we can say that the size of the difference between 10 and 20°C is exactly equal to the size of the difference between 40 and 50°C. Such scales are very useful, as they allow for the application of most statistical techniques. However, these scales suffer from one major drawback. They do not have a *true* 0 point; rather, convenience or convention usually dictates where the 0 will be. Thus, in the Centigrade scale of temperature, the 0 point is located at the freezing point of pure water; 0 for the Farenheit scale is at the freezing point of a specified salt water brine, which is much colder. This lack of a true 0 point means that we can't really ask "how many times more" of a quality something has, relative to something else. For example, although 100 is numerically twice as large as 50 ($2 \times 50 = 100$), it makes no sense to say that 100° is twice as warm as 50°C. What is twice as warm as −2°C? Certainly not −4°C [even though $2 \times (-2) = -4$].

The most numerically powerful scale is the RATIO SCALE. The creation of this type of scale is possible only when all four relations, equality, rank order, equality of intervals, and equality of ratios, can be experimentally determined. These scales do possess a true 0 point. Unfortunately, ratio scales are most often found in the physical rather than in the behavioral sciences. Such things as weight, density, and length can be measured on ratio scales since the 0 points are not arbitrary. For example, 0 g represents the complete absence of weight, and we can now meaningfully say that 10 g is twice as heavy as 5 g. Minus values of weight only exist in the fantasies of dieters. Psychologists would love to have ratio scales for all of the variables that they manipulate and measure. However, few are available, so they usually have to be content with measuring their behavioral variables on interval or ordinal scales.

All sensory qualities cannot be scaled in the same way. Some perceptual experiences have an underlying aspect of intensity (for instance, brightness) while others do not (such as color). When we are dealing with a stimulus or an experience in which it makes sense to ask "How much?" or "How intense?" we have a PROTHETIC CONTINUUM. Changes from one level of sensation to another come about by adding or subtracting from what is present. Thus, when we increase the weight of a stimulus, the corresponding psychological sensation of "heaviness" increases. Such prothetic continua can be meaningfully scaled using any of the scale types we have discussed. Unfortunately, in the other type of sensory continuum changes in the physical stimulus result in a change in the apparent quality rather than the apparent quantity of a stimulus. When we have a stimulus or experience in which the only question that it makes sense to ask is "What kind?" we are dealing with a METATHETIC CONTINUUM. Thus, systematic changes in the wavelength of light may cause the appearance of light to change from red to green. Psychologically, there is no quantitative difference between these two hues, they just appear to be different. Occasionally both types of continua will be present in the same sense impressions. For instance, in touch, the amount of pressure applied is a prothetic continuum, while the location of the touch is a metathetic continuum. Metathetic continua can be dealt with using nominal scales, but any scales that imply order have generally not been successfully applied to such sensory qualities.

INDIRECT SCALING: FECHNER'S LAW

When the perceptual investigator attempts to establish a sensory scale in which he will assign numbers to the intensity of sensations, he can take two alternative approaches. The first is a DIRECT procedure in which individuals are asked to assess directly some aspect of the strength of the sensation. Although this might seem to be the easiest procedure, it is often difficult for the untrained observer. In addition, many early psychologists distrusted the accuracy of such direct reports because there seemed to be no easy way to convert them to numerical values. For this reason IN-DIRECT methods, based upon discrimination ability, formed the basis for the first psychological scales. It must not be thought that using an indirect procedure is necessarily bad. After all, we measure temperature indirectly, using the height of a column of mercury as our indicator.

The first person to attempt to describe the relationship between stimulus intensity and sensation intensity was Gustav Theodor Fechner. To do this, he had to invent some sort of measurement unit that could be used to describe the quantity of the sensory experience. As his starting point, he assumed that Weber's Law was correct. As we have seen, it does hold over a large part of the range of those stimuli that are likely to be encountered. His next assumption engendered a good deal of controversy and hundreds of pages of theory and experimental work.

Fechner assumed that the subjective impression of the difference between 2 stimuli separated by one *just noticeable difference* (or *jnd*) was the same regardless of the absolute magnitude of the 2 stimuli. Thus, if we take 2 dim lights that are separated by one *jnd* and we take 2 lights which are 30 or 40 times brighter, but again separated from each other by one *jnd,* we should perceive the 2 pairs of stimuli as differing by equal sensory steps. Finally, Fechner assumed that sensation differences could be represented by adding or subtracting *jnd*s.

If we accept Fechner's postulate that Weber's law is true and that the subjective sizes of all *jnd*s are equal, then only a small *physical* change is necessary to achieve a one *jnd* change for a weak stimulus, while a *large* change is needed for a one *jnd* change when the physical stimulus is intense. Perceptually, this means that the intensity of the sensation grows rapidly for weak physical stimuli and more slowly as the physical stimulus is made more intense. The relationship between the intensity of the sensation and the intensity of the physical stimulus is shown in Figure 3-1. Mathematically, this curve is described by the equation,

$$S = K \log I$$

where S is the magnitude of sensation that a stimulus elicits, I is the physical magnitude of the stimulus (units above the absolute threshold stimulus magnitude), and K is a constant that depends upon the value of the Weber fraction ($\Delta I/I$). This equation is called FECHNER'S LAW. The actual mathematical procedures by which Fechner derived this relationship are discussed in Guilford (1954) and Falmagne (1974). It is important to remember that we are using the number of *jnd*s above the absolute threshold as a measure of the strength of the sensation generated by a given stimulus, and we are saying that this number

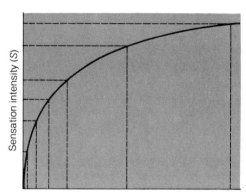

Figure 3-1.
Fechner's Law. Notice that it takes larger and larger differences between stimuli (*I*s) as stimulus intensity increases in order to give rise to the same size differences between sensations (*S*s).

is simply related to the physical intensity of the stimulus by the above equation. The constant *K* is different for differing sensory and psychological continua.

Our discussion clearly shows that Fechner was indirectly measuring sensation with his *jnd* scale. The resultant scale seems to be an interval scale. To create this scale the only thing that must be measured is the size of the *jnd*. Once that has been determined, the rest is easy, and requires only counting *jnd*s. Fechner believed that this was the best one could do, and spent much of his later life refining his measurements of *jnd*s for various sensory continua. The essence of Fechner's technique was to use some aspect of the discriminability of stimuli as an index of the intensity of an observer's sensory impression. A number of contemporary attempts have extended this notion. They employ more modern statistical procedures that take into account the fact that the same stimulus may not always produce an identical sensory re-

sponse (using the same rationale that we discussed as part of signal detection theory). These modifications were originally instituted by Thurstone (1927) and essentially comprise an extension of Fechner's original approach.

DIRECT SCALING

Since Fechner's time, there have been many psychophysicists who have insisted that indirect scaling is neither necessary nor preferable. Since we are interested in the *apparent* intensity of a stimulus to an observer, why not simply require judgments based upon how intense a stimulus seems to be? The observer's responses could then be used directly to establish a scale of measurement for the psychological attribute. The first attempt to do this was undertaken in 1872 by one of Fechner's contemporaries, a French investigator named Plateau. To test Fechner's Law he had eight artists mix a gray that was halfway between a particular black and a white. Notice that this requires direct relative judgments of three stimuli, the black, white, and gray. Fechner's Law predicts that this psychological midpoint should correspond to the average of the logarithm of the intensity of the black stimulus and that of the white stimulus. Unfortunately, the results, although somewhat similar to the prediction, did not fully support Fechner's Law. Rather, the grays mixed by Plateau's artists seemed to fall halfway between the cube roots ($\frac{1}{3}$ power) of the intensities of the black and the white stimuli. This numerical discrepancy suggests that Fechner's law may only be a coarse approximation to the relationship between physical and sensory intensity. Some other early investigations, using somewhat different techniques, did seem to support Fechner more closely.

Category Judgment. Sanford was among the investigators who attempted to measure sensation directly (see Titchner, 1905). As early as 1898, he had worked out a technique that involved having observers judge a number of envelopes, each of which contained different weights. The subjects were instructed to sort the weights into 5 categories. Category 1 was to be used for the lightest weights, and category 5 for the heaviest, with the remaining weights distributed in the other categories in such a way that the *intervals between the category boundaries would be subjectively equal*. Thus, the difference in sensation between the upper and the lower boundaries of category 1 should be the same as that of category 2. In other words all categories should be the same size. This method has been called CATEGORY SCALING or EQUAL INTERVAL SCALING. There is a similarity between this method and a recognition task, except that in category scaling we usually have fewer categories than stimuli. Here, of course, there is no such thing as a correct or an incorrect answer, since the very nature of the experiment implies that we cannot know in advance what a correct category assignment might be.

If our observer has spaced the category boundaries equally in terms of the magnitude of the sensory differences between them, we can, without making any other assumptions, mark off equal category intervals (to represent the midpoints of the categories) along our ordinate and label them with the category names. We can plot the average category label assigned to each stimulus intensity over several trials. The obtained curve for typical data shown in Figure 3-2 is concave downward, and closely approximates the curve that would be predicted by Fechner's Law (Figure 3-1). You can demonstrate this result for a similar set of stimuli in Demonstration Box 3-1. The fact that we can predict the shape of this category scale from simple discrimina-

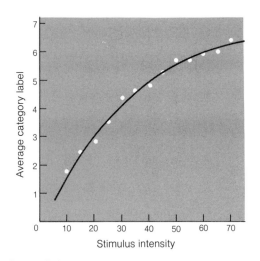

Figure 3-2.
Some typical data from a category judgment experiment. The dots represent average category judgments of the various stimulus intensities.

tion data is quite an impressive feat. To Sanford it seemed to provide support for the contention that a logarithmic relationship exists between physical stimulus intensity and perceived magnitude.

Since Sanford, category scaling has been studied in great detail. One important series of studies was reported by Stevens and Galanter (1957). They explored the stability of the category scaling function over a variety of situations. In one series, observers were required to judge the loudness of white noise. White noise is simply a random mixture of tones of all frequencies, which sounds very much like radio static or the hissing of air through your teeth. Observers were either asked to sort the stimuli into 7 categories labeled 1–7, or to sort them into 7 categories, each designated with a verbal label, such as *very very loud; very loud; loud; medium; soft; very soft; very very soft*. The shape of the obtained scaling function did not change as a result of the different category labels. In addi-

The demonstrations in this chapter involve more work than those in any other chapter in this book. This is because we can only make sense of a psychophysical scale if we take a number of measures and actually draw the results on a graph so that we can see them. Despite the extra effort involved, this demonstration should help you to understand what types of perceptual judgments the observer must make and what types of analyses the psychophysicist attempts.

For this demonstration (and for the others in this chapter) you will need a series of weight stimuli. These are easily provided by getting 2 rolls of nickels (or 80 nickels). If you are feeling wealthy 2 rolls of quarters will give you a greater weight range (remember that your stimuli are available for spending after the demonstrations have been tried). You will also need 12 envelopes of the same size.

Put 1 nickel in the first envelope, 2 in the second, and so forth until you have 12 nickels in the last envelope. Write the number of nickels contained in each of the envelopes lightly on the back. These are your weight stimuli. Label a sheet of paper with 12 lines marked 1–12. Now find the envelope with one nickel and the one with 12. Alternately lift each one. Remember 1 represents your lightest and 12 your heaviest stimulus. Next shuffle the set of envelopes (be sure the number side is turned away from you).

Your task is to categorize each envelope on the basis of its heaviness into one of 4 categories. Category 1 will represent the lightest stimuli and category 4 the heaviest. Now lift the first envelope from the shuffled pile and judge the weight category to which it belongs. Write the category number on the line marked 1 and carefully set it aside. Judge each envelope in turn, carefully placing them down in order, and writing your numbers on the paper. When you have finished, turn the envelopes over and write the actual number of nickels in each next to the judged category. Now simply compute the average number of nickels that you placed into each category. For instance, if you called the envelopes with 1, 2, and 3 nickels category 1, the average stimulus intensity for this category would be 2 nickels. Make a graph with categories 1–4 indicated on the vertical axis and number of nickels shown on the horizontal axis. Plot the 4 points (average number of nickels in each category). Draw a smooth curve through the points. Notice that they do not follow a straight line but, rather, approximate the curve shown in Figure 3-1. This shows that, when you categorize your sensations of heaviness, the intensity of sensations caused by adding weight to weaker stimuli grows more rapidly than the sensations caused by adding weight to more intense stimuli. This is predicted by Fechner's logarithmic relationship.

Save this set of stimuli for further use in this chapter. Also save the curve you have just drawn until you have completed Demonstration Box 3-2.

Demonstration Box 3-1:
Category Scaling of Weight

tion to varying the labels on categories we can vary the number of categories. Stevens and Galanter (1957) presented subjects with white noise varying in intensity and gave them either 3 categories or 100 categories into which to sort the stimuli. We find, again, that the variation does not affect the overall shape of the curve. There is one class of experimental manipulations that does seem to have a large effect on the shape of the obtained curve. These manipulations involve the spacing or distribution of stimuli along the physical dimension, a variable that should be irrelevant if we are actually measuring the underlying psychological process.

Suppose we present a large number of relatively strong stimuli and only a few weak stimuli, such as in a logarithmic spacing, and compare this to the situation where we present a group of equally spaced stimuli. Carter and Hirsch (1955) did this with lifted weights. They found that the shape of the obtained curve of category judgments versus stimulus magnitudes varied significantly with the distribution of stimuli. These results have been confirmed by Pollack (1965). Parducci (1965) held the spacing of the stimuli constant and varied the frequency with which any one stimulus was presented. He found similar distortions in the shape of the curve. The nature of these distortions indicates that differences in sensory magnitude are more salient for the intensity region where the stimuli are most heavily concentrated; hence, the curve is steeper. Such changes could also result if, in addition to responding to the magnitude of the stimuli, observers were trying to make their responses in a way that would use each category name about equally often. Thus, we find that category judgment results can be affected by observers' expectations (just as are the detection and the discrimination responses discussed in Chapter 2). Category judgments are also affected by a variety of other biases. The range of the stimuli is important, and repetitively occuring stimuli affect the resulting judgments (Parducci, 1965). A variety of studies have demonstrated that category judgments are altered by the memories of previous stimuli and responses (see Ward, 1972). These biases indicate that we should use caution in the interpretation of scales of measurement formed from category judgments.

Magnitude Estimation and Stevens' Power Law. In category judgments observers are directly responding to variations in stimulus magnitude; however, there is still some "indirectness" involved. Thus, stimuli that are similar but still discriminably different from one another may be grouped into the same category. Also, responses are limited to a few category labels. S. S. Stevens has popularized a procedure called MAGNITUDE ESTIMATION that avoids these problems. The method is so simple and direct that one wonders why it had to be "invented" at all. In this procedure, observers are simply asked to assign numbers to a stimulus on the basis of how intense it appears to be. Stimuli are usually judged one at a time and the only restriction on responses is that numbers of 0 and lower cannot be used.

In a typical magnitude estimation experiment, in which we wish to scale the apparent length of lines, we would start by showing a *standard stimulus* that serves as the starting point for the observer's judgments. We might then instruct her by saying "This stimulus has a value of 10. You will be presented with a variety of stimuli that differ in length. Your task is to assign numbers to these other stimuli in relation to the one with a value of 10. Thus, if you see a line that appears to be twice as long as this one, you should assign to it the number 20. If you see a line $\frac{1}{5}$ as long, you should assign to it the number 2. You may use any numbers you choose as long as they are larger than zero." In this task the number assigned to the standard stimulus is called the MODULUS. It serves to keep the numerical estimates of different subjects within the same general range of values. As you can see this is a very direct way to attempt to measure sensation. The very nature of the task (where a stimulus judged to be *n* times larger than the standard is given a number *n* times as large) implies that the resultant scale might be a ratio scale. There is, however, continuing debate on this point.

Stevens fully expected the results of such experiments to confirm Fechner's Law. However, when he plotted the data from an experiment in the magnitude estimation of loudness (Stevens, 1956), he found that the graph differed from what a logarithmic relationship would lead us to expect. When he ascertained the equation that best described the relationship of the median magnitude estimates to the stimulus intensities, it was

$$L = aI^{0.6}$$

where *L* is the subjective loudness obtained through the observer's magnitude estimates, *a* is a constant, *I* is the physical intensity of the sound, and 0.6 is a power to which *I* is raised. In the years that followed, Stevens and a host of others produced magnitude estimation scales for a multitude of sensory continua. All of these scales seemed to be related to the physical stimulus intensities by the general relationship

$$S = aI^n$$

where *S* is the sensory intensity and *n* is a characteristic exponent which differs for different sensory continua. Since this relation states that the magnitude of the sensation is simply the intensity of the physical stimulus raised to some power, this relationship is often called the POWER LAW or, after its popularizer, STEVENS' LAW.

The actual rate of sensation change with changes in stimulus intensity depends upon the size of the exponent. Thus, it would be disturbing if the exponents varied at random. However, the exponent for any one continuum is quite stable. As long as the experimental situation is kept reasonably standard, the average exponents produced by different groups of observers for the same continuum are quite close together. Some of them are small fractions, like 0.3 for brightness, some are near 1, as for line length, while others are quite large, as 3.5 for electric shock. Some typical exponents for a number of continua are given in Table 3-1.

If we plot some of the relationships between sensory intensity and stimulus intensity, we find that the curves for power functions with different exponents (*n*) have dramatically different shapes. This can be seen in Figure 3-3. With exponents of less than 1 (i.e., brightness) the curves are concave downward, meaning that as the stimulus becomes more intense, greater stimulus changes are needed to produce the same degree of perceptual change. When exponents are greater than 1 (i.e., shock) the curves are concave upward, meaning that as stimuli become more intense, the same physical stimulus change produces an even larger perceptual change than at lower stimulus intensities. With so many differently shaped curves describing the relationship between sensory and physical intensity, it is fortunate that there is a simple procedure that allows us to assess rapidly all of the values in any power function. If we plot the logarithm of the average magnitude estimates (the average numbers observers assign to their sensations) against the logarithms of the stimulus intensities, any curves of the general form $S = aI^n$ will appear as straight lines. In Figure 3-4 the curves in Figure 3-3 have been replotted in this way. We can now estimate *n* from the curve by measuring the distances marked Δy

Table 3-1 *Representative Exponents of the Power Functions Relating Psychological Magnitude to Stimulus Magnitude (Based upon Stevens, 1961)*

Continuum	Exponent	Stimulus Conditions
Loudness	0.6	Both ears
Brightness	0.33	5° target—dark
Brightness	0.5	Point source—dark
Lightness	1.2	Gray papers
Smell	0.55	Coffee odor
Taste	0.8	Saccharine
Taste	1.3	Sucrose
Taste	1.3	Salt
Temperature	1.0	Cold—on arm
Temperature	1.6	Warmth—on arm
Vibration	0.95	60 Hz—on finger
Duration	1.1	White noise stimulus
Finger span	1.3	Thickness of wood blocks
Pressure on palm	1.1	Static force on skin
Heaviness	1.45	Lifted weights
Force of handgrip	1.7	Precision hand dynamometer
Electric shock	3.5	60 Hz—through fingers

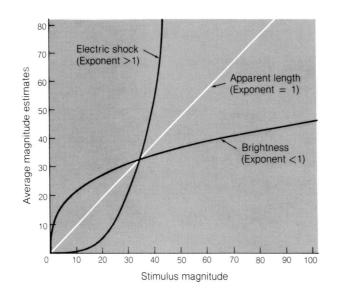

Figure 3-3.
Power functions for brightness, length, and shock. Notice how the shape of the curve changes as the exponent changes.

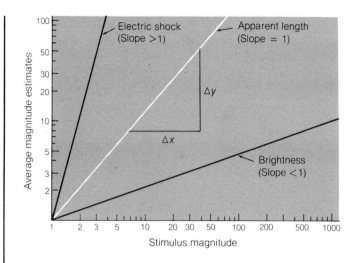

Figure 3-4.
The same power functions as in Figure 3-3 plotted on logarithmic axes. In such "log–log" plots all power functions become straight lines, with the slope of the straight line determined by the exponent (n) of the power function.

and Δx in the figures and computing $\Delta y/\Delta x$. The constant a is the point at which the line crosses the ordinate. Demonstration Box 3-2 allows you to perform a magnitude estimation experiment for yourself.

You might wonder why it is the case that category judgments seem to give a logarithmic relationship that supports Fechner's law, while magnitude estimates seem to give a power law to describe the growth of the sensation. Actually, Stevens and Galanter (1957) found that category judgments only approximately fit a logarithmic scale. Since then many investigators (Marks, 1974, 1968; Gibson & Tomko, 1972; Ward, 1971, 1972, 1974) have shown that category judgments also fit the power law, but with exponents (n) that are about half the size of those produced by magnitude estimation. Marks (1974) and Torgerson (1961) have suggested that these different results reflect the fact that the two types of procedures require different but equally valid types of judgments reflecting sensory experiences. Each may have quite different relationships to the size of the physical stimulus. For example, if my 10-kg dog and my 100-kg brother both gain one kilogram in weight we may ask, "Have they both gained the same amount?" If we are making

an equal interval judgment (analogous to that required for category scaling) the answer is "yes," since both have increased by one kilogram. If we are making an equal ratio judgment (magnitude estimate), my dog has increased his body weight by 10% and my brother by only 1%. Thus, the weight gain is far from the same. Both judgments require estimates of stimulus magnitude, and both are useful, but the scales (and resultant stimulus–sensation curves) are different.

An alternate interpretation of the difference between the two types of scales emerges from the fact that the ranges of responses are different (Ward, 1971, 1973, 1975). With a restricted response range, magnitude estimates produce smaller exponents. Category scales almost always have a restricted number of responses, as opposed to magnitude estimates, which are usually relatively unrestricted. When the response ranges for category judgments and magnitude estimations are equated they produce highly similar sensory scales (Gibson & Tomko, 1972).

Cross-modality matching. If the size of the exponent varies with the nature of the response, one might wonder whether these scales tell us more about how humans use numbers than they do about how sensation

You will need the weight stimuli you have already prepared, and another sheet of paper with 12 lines labeled 1–12. Select the envelope that has 4 nickels and lift it so that you can assess its heaviness. Call this stimulus 10 units of heaviness. If you feel that a stimulus is twice as heavy as this one, call it 20; if half as heavy, call it 5. You may use any numbers that you feel are appropriate (as long as they are larger than zero). Shuffle the envelopes and judge each stimulus one at a time, writing your first judgment on line 1, your second on line 2 and so forth. Now carefully turn the pile of envelopes over, as you did in the experiment in Demonstration Box 3-1, and write the actual number of nickels next to each judgment. Make a graph with your numerical magnitude estimates on the vertical axis and the number of nickels on the horizontal axis. Plot your estimates (number of nickels and judged magnitude) and draw a smooth line through it. Notice that the shape of this curve is quite different from that obtained from your category judgments.

You can determine whether these estimates follow the power law by plotting them on log–log coordinates. These are provided on the accompanying graph. The vertical axis is the logarithm of the magnitude estimate while the horizontal axis is the logarithm of the number of nickels. You can simply trace these axes onto a piece of paper and plot your data points again. Now you can see that the points fall along a straight line. Actually, you can directly compute the exponent (n in the power law $S = aI^n$) by computing the slope. Simply pick two points on the line and measure Δx and Δy for these points as pictured in Figure 3-4, with a ruler. Now divide Δy by Δx and you should get a value between 1.0 and 1.5. This exponent means that the feeling of heaviness increases more rapidly than the actual physical weight.

Demonstration Box 3-2:
Magnitude Estimation of Weight

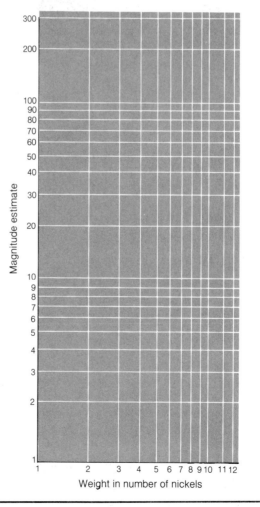

varies with stimulus intensity. In order to counter this criticism, Stevens invented a scaling procedure that does not use numbers at all. In this technique, an observer adjusts the intensity of a stimulus until it appears to be as intense as another stimulus from a different sensory continuum. Thus you might be asked to squeeze a handgrip until the pressure felt as strong as a particular light was bright. This procedure is called CROSS-MODALITY MATCHING, since the observer is asked to match sensory magnitudes *across* sensory modalities. Actually, magnitude estimation can also be viewed as a form of cross-modality matching in which the number continuum is matched to a stimulus

continuum (see Oyama, 1968; Stevens, 1975).

When we plot the data from cross-modality matching experiments on log–log axes (as we did for magnitude estimation experiments), we find that the average matches fall onto a straight line. Despite the fact that we no longer use numerical estimates from the observers, the data still obey the power law for sensory intensities. Figure 3-5 shows this for a number of modalities matched against handgrip pressure. Demonstration Box 3-3 will allow you to try a cross-modality matching task for yourself.

The theoretical importance of cross-modality matching rests in the exponents

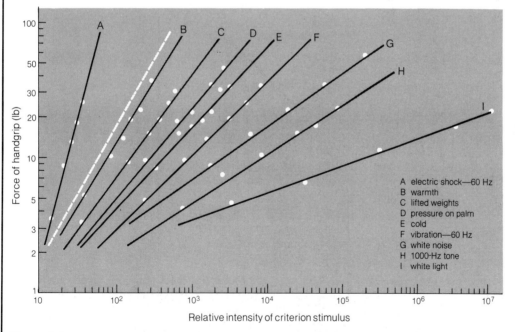

Figure 3-5.
Cross-modality matching data for 9 different psychological stimulus continua with force of handgrip as the response continuum. Since the values on both axes are logarithmically spaced, all of the straight lines indicate a power function relationship between stimulus and response magnitude. The dotted line has an exponent of 1.0 (from Stevens, S. S. In W. A. Rosenblith (ed.), *Sensory Communication*. New York: Wiley, 1961. © 1961 by the MIT Press).

Again you will need your weight stimuli, only now you will need 13 sheets of plain paper. Your task is to estimate the heaviness of each envelope by drawing a line of an appropriate length. Pull out the envelope with 4 nickels in it. Draw a line about 5 cm long. This line represents the heaviness of the envelope. If you feel an envelope is twice as heavy, the line you draw should be twice as long (about 10 cm). If an envelope is one-half as heavy, the line you draw should be one-half as long. Now shuffle the envelopes and judge the heaviness of each by drawing an approximate line length on separate pieces of paper. When you are done, turn the stack of envelopes over and write the actual number of nickels judged on the appropriate pages. Now measure each line with a ruler, so that you will have a measured line length associated with each number of nickels. Tracing the scales marked on the accompanying graph (which represent the logarithm of the line length on the vertical axis and the logarithm of the weight in nickels on the horizontal) onto another sheet of paper, plot your data points. Notice that they again fall onto a straight line.

Actually, if you compute the exponent (n) by measuring the slope as you did in Demonstration Box 3-2, you should again get a value of about 1.5. In other words, the magnitude estimations made with numbers and with cross-modality matches using line lengths reach the same conclusions.

Demonstration Box 3-3:
Cross-Modality Matching of Line Length to Heaviness

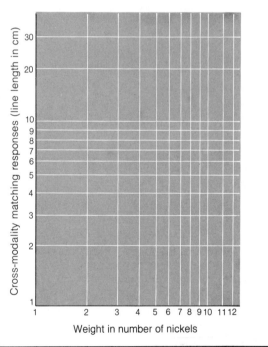

computed from such experiments. These exponents indicate how the perceived intensities of stimuli change as we change the physical intensities. Remarkably, these exponents usually agree regardless of the modalities used to estimate them. In addition, they agree with the values obtained from traditional magnitude estimation techniques (Stevens, 1975; Teghtsoonian, 1975). Thus, it seems likely that the power law is a reasonable description of how perceived intensity is related to stimulus intensity.

Interpretation of the power law. Sensory scaling data provide much information that is of everyday importance. For instance, most radio and stereo dials are calibrated in a roughly logarithmic manner so that equal turns of the dial produce approximately equal changes in sound intensity. Similarly, photographic filters, in order to appear to alter lightness in equal steps, must be spaced at intervals that keep the cube root of the physical stimulus about equal. Why is it the case that perceived intensity increases do not directly follow physical intensity differences? Why is it the case that equal changes in physical intensity do not produce equal changes in sensation (which in terms of the power law would be an exponent of 1)?

Stevens (1961, 1970) suggested that the power functions describe the operating characteristics of the sensory transducers. That is, each sensory organ has the function of changing or transducing energy from one form to another (e.g., light or sound energy to electrical energy in the nervous system). The power function, then, is a mathematical description of the relationship between the incoming energy (i.e., light or sound) and the neural electrical energy sent to the brain. The differences in exponents for different modalities may reflect the fact that different sensory transducers operate on different forms of energy in different ways, and hence with different operating characteristics. Such a theory predicts that if and when such operating characteristics can be measured more directly, for example, by recording the electrical activity in the optic nerve, these direct measurements will reveal power functions with exponents similar to those obtained by psychophysical techniques. Stevens (1970) has provided convincing evidence that this is the case for at least some sensory continua.

The above theory is in direct conflict with the classical view of the logarithmic nature of the operating characteristics of sensory transducers, as is found in Fechner's Law. In fact, early investigators were very excited when they found logarithmic functions at the transducer level, for they tended to confirm Fechner's Law. Lipetz (1969) presented a review of the evidence for logarithmic transducer functions and concluded that although power functions are sometimes

found, logarithmic functions characterize the majority of sensory transducers. In addition, there are many who argue (e.g., Galanter, 1966) that whether or not sensory transducers operate according to power functions, there can always be later transformations that could cause the electrical activity representing the intensity of the sensation to follow one or the other of the proposed psychophysical laws. In this view, the physiological data can only be supplementary to the psychological understanding. This viewpoint is also supported by the fact that the direct methods of scaling work quite nicely on sensory continua that certainly have no simple transducer; for example, pain, electric shock, numerosity, line length, duration, and so on. In addition, even nonsensory continua can be successfully scaled by direct methods. For example, Stevens (1966) summarized several studies that scaled such things as heinousness of crimes. All of these scales follow the power law just as well as do those constructed for simple sensory transducers, such as the intensity transducer in the ear or the eye.

Recently, a different explanation of the power law has been offered. It is based upon the assumption that the shape of the psychophysical scaling function is caused by the inability of the observer to discriminate constant physical differences equally well over the range of stimuli. This has been supported by the fact that the Weber fraction (which we noted in Chapter 2 was a measure of discrimination ability) is related to the exponent of the power function. This can be seen in Table 3-2, where it is apparent that small Weber fractions (high discrimination ability) are associated with larger exponents (rapid changes in sensory intensity as the stimulus varies), as for heaviness or shock. Large Weber fractions, on the other hand, are associated with small exponents, as for brightness and taste. Using some sophisticated analyses, it is possible to show that the

Table 3-2 *Relationship between Weber Fractions ($\Delta I/I$) and Power Law Exponents (n) (Based upon Teghtsoonian, 1971)*

Continuum	Weber Fraction ($\Delta I/I$)	Power Exponent (n)
Brightness	.079	.33
Loudness	.048	.60
Finger span	.022	1.30
Heaviness	.020	1.45
Length	.029	1.04
Taste, NaCl	.083	.41
Electric shock	.013	2.50

power law can emerge from such discrimination considerations (Poulton, 1968; Teghtsoonian, 1971).

ADAPTATION LEVEL THEORY

Part of the circus strongman's job was to carry various members of the animal cast onto the circus train. One visitor watched in amazement as one after another he lifted the dancing ponies and placed them in their railroad car. "Aren't they heavy?" asked the visitor. "Not if you've just carried three elephants," came the reply. The essence of this apocryphal tale is that no stimulus can be appreciated in isolation. Stimuli are always seen in the context of the stimuli that precede them. Thus, a sportscaster of average height looks like a midget when interviewing a group of professional basketball players, but like a giant when interviewing professional jockies. He has, of course, not changed his height, but his apparent size has changed as a result of the frame of reference provided by the heights of those around him.

Contextual effects have long been known to influence judgments of sensory magnitude in many psychophysical tasks. Let us look at an experiment by Engen and Tulunary (1956) in which subjects were required to determine which weight of an ascending or a descending series was exactly half the weight of a standard. They found that the mean weight judged to be one-half as heavy as the standard was consistently lighter for an ascending series of comparison weights (starting with the light weights and moving gradually to heavier) than for a descending series. This is clearly seen in Table 3-3. Similar series effects have been found for the judgment of pitch by Cohen, Hansel, and Sylvester (1954) and Pedley and Harper (1959), of time by Weinstein, Goldstone, and Boardman (1958), and even of pain by Swartz (1953).

A systematic attempt to explain such effects has been offered by Helson (1964). This theory has both quantitative and qualitative aspects. In Helson's theory, the organism is thought to accommodate itself to the changing environment around it. This accommodation involves the establishment of a *reference level* against which all other stimuli are judged. Stimuli below this reference or ADAPTATION LEVEL are judged in one way (to be weak) and stimuli above it in another way (to be intense). Stimuli at or near the adaptation level are judged to be medium or neutral. This implies that all judgments are rela-

Table 3-3 *Effects of Preceding Stimuli on Weight Judgments (Based upon Engen & Tulunary, 1956)*

Standard (g)	Average Weight Judged to Be $\frac{1}{2}$ Standard: Ascending Series (g)	Average Weight Judged to Be $\frac{1}{2}$ Standard: Descending Series (g)
150	22.7	104.3
300	140.0	178.8
550	306.5	344.2
700	501.7	581.2

tive. A stimulus is not simply weak or intense, it is weak or intense when judged against the subjective adaptation level.

For Helson, adaptation levels are established by pooling the effects of three classes of stimuli. The first of these classes of stimuli is that of the so-called FOCAL STIMULI. These are the stimuli that are the center of an observer's attention and are usually the stimuli that she is asked to judge. It is clear that the magnitude of these stimuli will in some way determine the observer's judgments. This is the basic assumption of all scaling procedures. The second class of stimuli is the so-called BACKGROUND STIMULI. These are stimuli in which the focal stimulus is embedded. They provide the immediate background against which a focal stimulus is judged. The final set of stimuli is the so-called RESIDUAL STIMULI. These are stimuli that are not current for the observer. They are the residue of stimuli the observer has experienced in the past. If you like, they are the sum of the observer's past experiences. To be more concrete, consider the example where we judged the height of a sportscaster surrounded by basketball players or jockies. The physical height of the sportscaster comprises the focal stimulus. The contextual stimuli are provided by the heights of the surrounding athletes. The residual stimuli come from having seen athletes of different heights in the past. All of these stimuli pool together to form the adaptation level.

Let us look at each of these classes of stimuli, and their separate contributions to the adaptation level. The general methodology used in studies of adaptation level employs the method of category judgment in which the categories have verbal labels. For instance, if we are judging weights the labels might be: *very, very heavy; very heavy; heavy; medium heavy; medium; medium light; light; very light; very, very light.* When we look for the adaptation level, we are looking for a stimulus that is judged neither heavy nor light, in other words, that stimulus judged to be medium. Helson and Nash (1960) presented subjects with 7 successive series of weights, each containing 5 stimuli. The weights were to be judged using the 9-point scale that we have just described. As the mean weight of the series increased the weight of the stimulus judged *medium* also increased. Thus, for a set of stimuli ranging from 100 to 300 g the stimulus judged to be medium was 165 g, while for a stimulus series ranging from 200 to 400 g this value had moved up to 227 g. For a series ranging from 300 to 500 g, it had risen to 301 g. It should be clear that at some point we will reach a situation where the stimulus that we perceive to be medium (neither heavy nor light) will no longer be found in the stimulus array. Thus, if we ask a person to judge the apparent weight of a series of stimuli ranging from 300 to 500 kg, in absolute terms, we would not be particularly surprised if heavy was the best description for all of these stimuli. Helson and Nash found that for a series of stimuli ranging from 400 to 600 g no stimulus in the series was judged medium. All were perceived to be heavy. Results such as this point out that the absolute value of the focal stimulus is clearly a major determinant of the judgment of stimulus magnitude when all other factors remain constant.

The effect of context upon judgments of magnitude was basically the consideration that originally brought us into a discussion of the problem of adaptation level. Several well-controlled studies have explored this issue. Helson (1964) reports a number of weight estimation studies that have provided consistent backgrounds against which the focal weights are to be judged. Helson (1947) and Helson and Nash (1960) are typical in both their methodology and findings. To provide a background for weight judgment, we need some weight that is always present, but never actually judged. To do this we provide an additional weight, not one of the set of focal stimuli, which is lifted before each weight judgment. This stimulus, which provides the background against which the judgments will be made, is generally called an ANCHOR STIMULUS. Let us look at some typical results. Using a series of 5 stimuli, ranging from 200 to 400 g, Helson (1947) had observers judge the apparent heaviness of weights using a 9-point scale. Without any anchor, the medium stimulus was 250 g. With a 900-g stimulus lifted before each judgment, the stimulus judged to be medium rose to 338 g. With a 90-g anchor or background stimulus, the stimulus perceived to be medium in weight sank to 185 g. It seems as if observers are not judging stimuli in isolation, but comparing them to the overall context of stimuli in which they appear. Thus a 250-g stimulus seems quite light in the context of an ever-present 900-g background, but quite heavy when one's adaptation level

is dominated by an ever-present 90-g stimulus. Context can affect our judgments of stimulus intensity even when the context is not in the same stimulus modality. You can demonstrate this for yourself using Demonstration Box 3-4.

As soon as we begin to separate the background or the context from the focal stimuli to be judged, we are forced to consider the nature of the way in which the observer attends to the stimulus array as well as the stimulus array itself. Clearly, if the observer pays careful attention to the background, it has shifted its identity from background to focal stimulus. Can such simple attentional shifts vary the perceived magnitude of a stimulus? If stimuli are differentially weighted in their contribution to the establishment of the reference or adaptation level, then such attentional shifts should certainly make a difference in the judgment of the magnitude of stimuli. This should happen simply on the basis of the fact that by shifting the observer's attention, we are subtly (or grossly) altering the context itself. Bevan, Maier, and Helson (1963) directly investigated this issue. They devised a situation in which observers were asked to judge the number of beans in jars. The number of beans could vary from 60 to 410, while the jar could be either large or small. Two types of instructions were used. In one, the observers were instructed to consider the beans and the jar as one organic unit, set off from their surroundings; in the other, they were instructed to treat the jar as a container and to view it as part of the surroundings. Bevan, Maier, and Helson argued that the first instruction set would make the jar part of the focal stimulus array, hence, allowing jar size to exert more influence on the judgment of the number of beans. The second set of instructions, on the other hand, would minimize this effect by relegating the jar to the background. Their results were in accord with their expectations. Making the large jar part of the focal array increased the estimate of the number of beans, while making the small jar focal made the estimate smaller. Restle (1971) has shown similar effects in a length judging task.

This leaves us with the class of residual stimuli to consider. We have reasons for expecting the residual stimulus effects to appear. When we see a toy poodle in the street, we are apt to remark "Isn't that a small dog?" If there are no other dogs in the street at the moment when we assess the size of this one, it means that at some time in our past experience we have internalized an adaptation level corresponding to medium dog size. A clear demonstration of the effects of past experience on the judgment of sensory magnitude comes from an experiment by DiLollo (1964). Using lifted weights, one group of subjects judged the apparent heaviness of a heavy series of weights (ranging from 400 to 600 g), while another group judged the heaviness of a light series of weights (ranging from 100 to 300 g). After 2 practice trials, and 10 training trials in which the weights were judged, one-half of the group that had judged the heavy series was shifted to judging the light series, while one-half of the group that had judged the light series was switched to the heavy series. The results (which are shown in Figure 3-6) were quite striking. The group that had originally judged the light series of weights now judged the heavy series of weights to be much heavier than did the group that had been judging the heavy series continually. The group shifted from the heavy series to the light series judged the light series to be much lighter than did the group that had been judging the light series throughout. This result demonstrates that stimuli that occurred in the past, although no longer physically present in the judgment situation, can still affect the perception of sensory magnitude. Similar results are reported for the visual modality by Helson and Bevan (1964) and for loudness by Ward and Lockhead (1970).

We have dealt with the formulation of adaptation level theory in a general and qualitative manner. It is important to point out, however, that Helson's formulation (Helson, 1964) is not merely qualitative, but is quantitative enough to allow for some specific tests. Helson defines the adaptation level as a weighted product of all three classes of stimuli, the focal, which we will designate F, the background, B, and the residual, R. Thus, the formula for adaptation level becomes,

$$\text{Adaptation level} = F^{W_1} B^{W_2} R^{W_3}$$

where W_1, W_2, and W_3 are simply weighting coefficients that reflect the importance of any one class of stimuli in the determination of the overall adaptation level. Helson (1959) generally rewrites this formula as,

$$\text{Log AL} = W_1 \log F + W_2 \log B + W_3 \log R$$

which shows clearly that we are dealing with a weighted logarithmic mean. This formula-

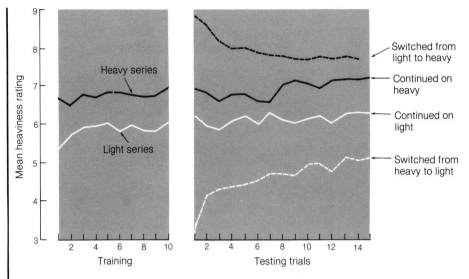

Figure 3-6.
The effect of past experience on weight judgments. Notice that weights seem particularly light after judging the heavy series and heavy after judging the light series (based upon DiLollo, 1964).

tion is not totally arbitrary. It is based upon data similar to those used to verify the logarithmic scaling function, and it provides a surprisingly good approximation to a large class of judgmental data. While there have been some interesting recent extensions of adaptation level (Restle, 1971, 1977), there are also a number of other quantitative formulations that make some slightly different assumptions about how stimulus magnitudes affect each other. These result in some different mathematical expressions (Anderson, 1970, 1975). However, all of these alternatives still acknowledge the fact that surrounding stimuli, stimuli experienced in the past, and patterns of attention, as well as the actual stimulus judged, can affect our judgments of stimulus intensity.

There may be no simple relationship be-tween stimulus magnitude and perceived magnitude. One is forced by the data to take into consideration a large class of variables and influences, which includes attentional factors and the observer's past history of stimulation. Thus, what we perceive is not simply a photographic reproduction of the stimuli in the environment, but is affected by all of the myriad of forces that have impinged upon us in the past and provide the context for the perceptual situation in which we presently find ourselves. We will find that these conditions hold for all of the sensory modalities that we will study in the following chapters. Perception is an active process, and processes within the observer can be more important in determining what the sensory experience will be than factors in the external environment.

4
The Visual System

Although perception occurs within the brain, our only contact with the external environment is through our sense organs. Thus, one is reminded of the old homily that says "The eyes are the windows to the world." The physical properties of this "window" should affect the nature of our perception in the same manner as the physical properties of a glass window affects the view. If the window is colored, our perception of the world will be tinted. If the window is dark, or dirty, our ability to discern objects will be reduced. If the window is curved, so as to magnify the images, our perception of the size of objects viewed through the glass may also be distorted. Thus, it is important for us to know the nature of the "window" through which we look at the world, or, more simply, to understand the physiological makeup of the eye.

LIGHT

Each of the sensory systems is responsive to a different form of physical stimulation. Thus, we find that taste and smell respond to chemical stimuli, touch to mechanical pressure, and hearing to the vibration of air molecules. The physical stimulus for sight is electromagnetic radiation. If the electromagnetic radiation produces a visual response we call it light. Later, when we discuss the perception of brightness and color, we will deal with the physical properties of light in more detail. For the moment, let us deal only with some basic concepts.

In 1704, Sir Isaac Newton advanced the theory that light, or for that matter any form of electromagnetic radiation, acts as if it were a stream of particles travelling in a straight line. Each particle is called a QUANTUM. When these are particles of radiation that we register as light they are called PHOTONS. The intensity of light is then given by the number of photons. Although this conception of light is extremely useful in physics, it is only important to the understanding of vision when we deal with stimuli that are relatively dim. At low levels of light one often describes intensities as the number of photons reaching the visual receptors. Clearly, the smallest amount of light possible is a single photon.

While light often acts as if it were a stream of particles, at other times it acts as if it were made up of waves. James Clerk Maxwell (1873) showed that light does not travel in a straight line but rather as an oscillating wave. He suggested that if we consider the change in the electromagnetic field surrounding the train of photons, we can treat light as if it were purely a wave phenomenon, with the wavelength defined as the physical distance between the peaks of the photon waves.

Electromagnetic energy can have wavelengths over a broad range, varying from trillionths of a centimeter to many kilometers in length. Very short wavelengths are not registered as light, nor are very long wavelengths. As can be seen in Figure 4-1 very short wavelengths include gamma rays, X rays, and ultraviolet rays. Longer wavelengths vary from those that we call electricity through the broadcasting wavelengths associated with T.V. and radio (which may be over 100 meters in length). The section of the electromagnetic spectrum that we see as visible light is really quite small, extending from 380 to about 760 nanometers. A NANOMETER is a billionth of a meter and is usually abbreviated *nm*. The older method of specifying wavelength was MILLIMICRONS which was abbreviated *mμ*. The abbreviation for this unit (mμ) contains a Greek letter and it is difficult to type on an English typewriter; hence, the change was made to *nm*. Perceptually, variations in wavelengths correspond roughly to the hue

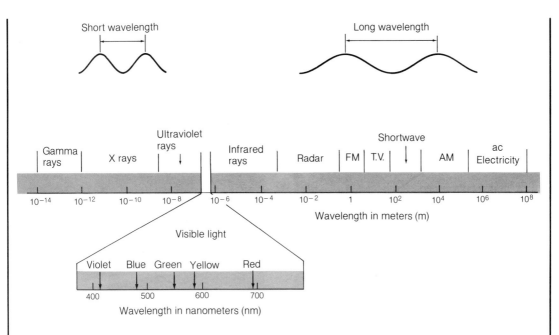

Figure 4-1.
The electromagnetic energy spectrum. We have enlarged the region containing visible light.

or color of light. Wavelengths of about 400 nm are seen as violet, 500 nm are seen as blue-green, 600 nm are seen as yellow-orange, and 700 nm are seen as red. Unfortunately, the perception of color depends upon much more than simply wavelength, as you will find out in Chapter 9.

The sensitivity of animals to wavelengths differs somewhat. Many nocturnal (night active) vertebrates are not sensitive to light of long wavelengths, which humans see as red. Some insects are sensitive to wavelengths too short to be seen by human beings (usually called *ultraviolet light*). Actually the photosensitive receptors of vertebrates will respond when exposed to ultraviolet light. However, these short wavelengths are normally filtered out by the fluid in the eyeball and never reach the photoreceptors.

THE STRUCTURE OF THE EYE

The photoreceptive portion of an animal is not always anything like what one typically calls an eye. Some simple animals, such as worms, have light sensitive receptors distributed over their entire body. Although such animals may be able to discriminate light intensity and may be able to localize its source roughly, they do not have vision in the sense of being able to recognize objects in their environment. In order to accomplish that task it is necessary to have a set of individual receptors, each of which responds to light coming from only a specific direction or region of the environment. The simplest optical system for achieving this result is shown in Figure 4-2A. This is the diagram of the eye of a mollusk called the *nautilus,* which is related to the squid. Basically, this eye is simply a hollow sphere lined with light sensitive cells. The light enters through a small hole in the top. Simple geometry demonstrates that this arrangement would limit the reception of each light sensitive unit to a narrow angular region in line with the hole. This is the principle of the pinhole camera.

Arthropods, such as crabs or locusts, have more complex eyes. Each so-called "compound eye" consists of a bundle of thin translucent cylinders called OMMATIDIA. Each of these is essentially a simple eye, which picks up light from a small angle and uses it to excite its own set of receptor cells. Each ommatidium points in a slightly different direction, hence, each is receptive to a different part of the environment. Figure 4-2B shows how this works. By integrating the activity of several receptors, the central nervous system is able to discriminate patterns (Walls, 1963).

When we turn to the vertebrate eye we find that a single basic plan is common from the level of the fish all the way up through the higher mammals. The vertebrate eye improves on the basic pinhole camera idea by placing a lens at the opening to the eye. In terms of image formation the lens serves the same function as the hole. It gathers light hitting it and concentrates it to a single point of focus. Since the lens has a larger surface than a pinhole, it gathers more of the light without increasing the angle seen by each receptor. This may be seen in Figure 4-2C, which presents a diagram of the structure of a typical human eye. It is important to note that the presence of the lens complicates matters somewhat. Only objects at a certain distance can be brought into sharp focus at the level of the receptors. Thus, the lens must have some ability to adjust its point of focus, or the amount by which the light rays are bent. Before we consider how this is done let us first follow the pathway light must travel through the eye, in order to understand the structures it encounters, and their general function.

The eyes of most vertebrates may be found lying in protective bony sockets within the skull. They are spherical structures about 20–25 mm in diameter. The outer covering, which is seen as the "white" of the eye, is a strong elastic membrane called the SCLERA. Since the eye is not made of rigid materials, it maintains its shape by means of fluid pressure from within. In the front of the eye there is a place where the sclera bulges forward to form a domelike window called the CORNEA. The cornea is the first optically active element in the eye. It serves as a simple fixed lens that begins to gather light and concentrate it. Because the cornea is extended forward, it actually allows reception of light from a region behind the observer as is shown in Demonstration Box 4-1. Behind the cornea is a small chamber filled with a watery fluid called the AQUEOUS HUMOR. This fluid is similar in nature to the cerebral spinal fluid which bathes the inner cavities of the brain. This is not surprising since embryological evidence has shown that the neural components of the eye actually develop from the same structures that eventually form the brain.

When you look at a human eye your attention is usually captured by a ring of color that has what appears to be a black hole through its center. The colored membrane is called the IRIS; its color determines whether you have blue or brown eyes. The actual color, which may vary from blue through black, appears to be genetically determined. The function of the iris seems to be to control the amount of light entering the eye. It may be of some interest to note that although blue eyes

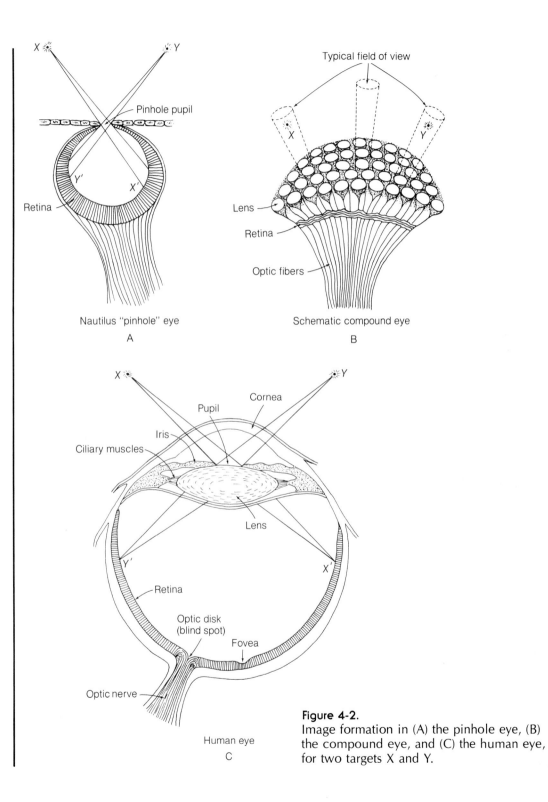

Nautilus "pinhole" eye
A

Schematic compound eye
B

Human eye
C

Figure 4-2.
Image formation in (A) the pinhole eye, (B) the compound eye, and (C) the human eye, for two targets X and Y.

It is easy to demonstrate that the visual field actually extends to a region somewhat behind the eye. In order to do this, simply choose a point that is some distance in front of your head and stare at it. Now raise your hand to the side of your head as is shown in the figure, with your index finger extended upward. Your hand should be out of view when you stare at the distant point. Now, wiggle your finger slightly, and bring your hand slowly forward until the wiggling finger is just barely visible in your peripheral vision. At this point stop and, with your head as still as possible, move your finger directly in toward your head. You will notice that your hand will touch a point on your temple somewhat behind the location of the eye, indicating that you were actually seeing somewhat "behind yourself."

Demonstration Box 4-1:
Vision "behind" the Eye

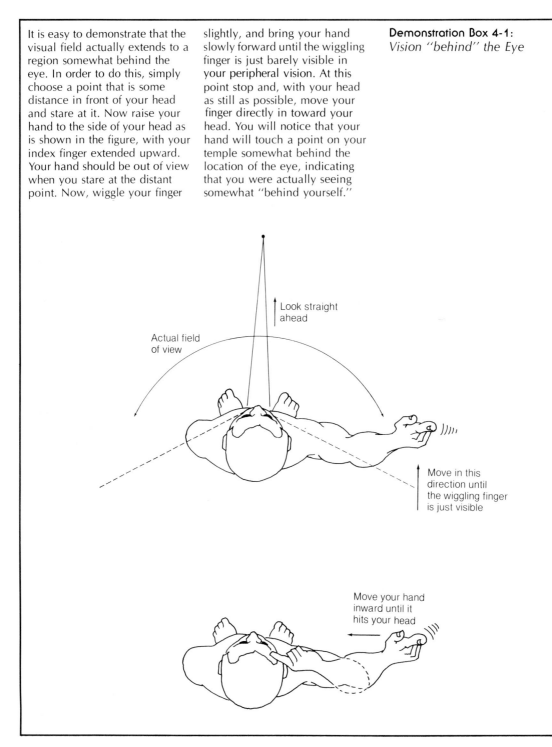

Look straight ahead

Actual field of view

Move in this direction until the wiggling finger is just visible

Move your hand inward until it hits your head

may be more appealing to the poet or the romantic, dark irises, such as brown or black, more effectively shield the eye from light. The light enters through the dark hole which is called the PUPIL. The size of the pupil appears to be controlled by a light reflex. When the light is bright the pupil may contract to as little as 2 mm in diameter, while in dim light it may dilate to more than 8 mm. This is about a sixteenfold change in the area of the aperture. Demonstration Box 4-2 shows how you may observe the effect of light on pupil size.

The construction of the pupil serves an important function. Despite the fact that the eye needs light to function there are some advantages to viewing the world with a small pupil. Although the amount of light entering the eye is reduced, imperfections in the lens produce fewer distortions with a small pupil, and the depth of focus (which is the range of distances over which objects are simultaneously in focus) is vastly increased. We might say that the eye takes advantage of better light by improving its optical response. In dim light, the ability of the eye to resolve or discriminate details (called ACUITY) becomes less valuable than the increased sensitivity obtained by increasing the amount of light entering the eye; thus the pupil increases in size to let in more light (Duke-Elder, 1963). The pupil size also changes as a function of emotional and attentional variables. Under conditions of high interest the pupil tends to be large, a cue often used by smart traders as an index of a customer's interest in an item (Hess, 1965). Clever customers often negate the usefulness of this cue in bargaining situations by wearing dark glasses. Similarly, candlelight with all of its dimness dilates the pupils and makes lovers appear to be more attentive and interested.

The Lens: Focusing the Eye. Most vertebrate eyes contain a LENS. The lens is located directly behind the pupillary aperture. Since the curvature of the lens determines the amount by which the light is bent, it is critical in bringing an image into focus at the rear of the eye. The process by which the lens varies its focus is called ACCOMMODATION. The lens changes focus by changing its shape. The natural shape of the human lens tends to be spherical, but when the ciliary muscles that control it relax, the pressure of the fluid in the eyeball causes it to flatten. Under these conditions, distant objects should be in focus. Contraction of the ciliary muscles, from which the lens is suspended, takes some of the tension from the lens and it regresses to a more spherical shape. When it is rounder, near objects are in focus. The effect of lens shape on point of focus is shown in Figure 4-3.

An individual's age is important in determining the focusing ability of the lens. It is

For this demonstration you need a friend. Dim the light in the room, but leave enough light so that you can still see the size of the pupil. Notice how large your friend's pupil appears to be under these conditions. Now turn on an overhead light, or shine the beam of a flashlight into your friend's eye and note how the pupil constricts. Removal of the light will cause the pupil to dilate again. The light reflex of the pupil was the first reflex ever studied by Whytt (1751), who is credited with the discovery of reflex action. It is still sometimes called Whytt's reflex.

Demonstration Box 4-2:
The Pupillary Light Reflex

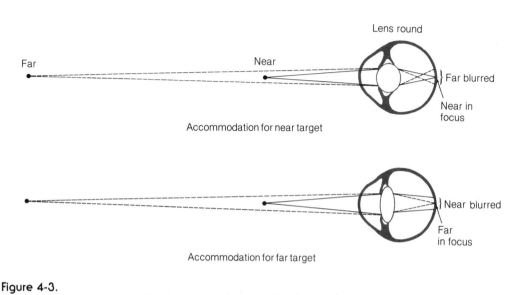

Figure 4-3.
Accomodation (focusing) of an image by changing the shape of
the crystalline lens of the eye.

interesting to note that the ability to accommodate is not present at birth. A newborn
infant, until about the age of one month, can
only focus upon objects that are approximately 19 cm away. Images of targets closer
or farther away than 19 cm are proportionally
blurred. However, during the second month
of infancy, the accommodative system begins to respond more adaptively (see Chapter
16). The ability of the lens to change focus
decreases with age after about age 16. This is
because the inner layers of the lens die, and
lose some of their elasticity (Duke-Elder,
1963). Thus, it becomes more difficult for the
ciliary muscles to change the lenses' curvature to accommodate to the near object. This
results in a form of REFRACTIVE ERROR (light
bending or focusing error) called PRESBYOPIA,
which simply translates to "old sighted."
Functionally, this condition increases the NEAR
POINT distance. The near point simply refers
to the nearest point to which an object may

be brought to the eye before it can no longer
be held in focus and becomes blurry. Thus,
older persons without corrective lenses often
may be seen holding reading material ab-
normally far from their face in order to focus
upon it adequately.

Another feature of the lens, which war-
rants mention, is the fact that it is not perfectly
transparent. The lens is tinted somewhat yellow, and the density of this yellow tint increases with age (Coren & Girgus, 1972a).
The yellow pigment serves to screen out some
of the blue light and ultraviolet light entering
the eye. It also alters our perception of color
somewhat because it selectively absorbs
some wavelengths of light and not others.
Thus, one may frequently find a mother and
daughter vehemently arguing about whether
the color of a particular garment is blue or
green, totally oblivious to the fact that each
views the world through a different yellow
filter because of their difference in age. Their

eyes may be receiving totally different wavelengths of light.

An eye having normal accommodative ability is called EMMETROPIC. Sometimes there is too much or too little curvature in the cornea or, alternatively, the shape of the eye is too short or too long, so that the accommodative capacity of the lens is not sufficient to bring targets into focus. If the eye is too short, distant objects are seen quite clearly, but it is difficult to bring near objects into focus. The common term for this is farsightedness, while the technical term is HYPERMETROPIA. The opposite occurs if the eye is too long. Now far objects are difficult to bring into focus. This condition is called nearsightedness or MYOPIA. The optical situations that result from these difficulties are shown in Figure 4-4.

The Retina. The large chamber of the eye is filled with a jellylike substance called the VITREOUS HUMOR. This substance is generally clear, although shreds of debris can often be seen floating in it. Try steadily viewing a clear blue sky and note the shadows that move across it; these shadows are from floating debris in the vitreous humor.

The actual image formed by the optical system of the eye is focused upon a screen of neural elements at the back of the eye called the RETINA. The term retina derives from the Greek word meaning *net,* because when one surgically opens up an eye (or views its interior with an optical device such as an ophthalmoscope) the most salient feature is the network of blood vessels lining the inner cavity of the eye. Demonstration Box 4-3 shows how you can observe these blood vessels in your own eyes.

The neural sheet of elements that makes up the retina extends over most of the interior of the eye. In diurnal or daylight-active animals, the retina is backed by a light absorbing dark layer called the PIGMENT EPITHELIUM.

This dark pigment layer serves the same purpose as the black inner coating in a photographic camera. It reduces the amount of reflected and scattered light that could blur or fog the image. In nocturnal or night-active animals, where the detection of light is more important than image clarity, the light that penetrates the retina is reflected back through the retina by a shiny surface known as the REFLECTING TAPETUM. This permits the light to

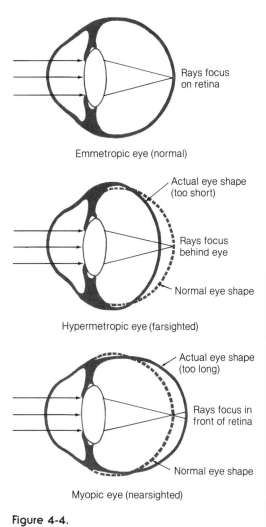

Emmetropic eye (normal)

Hypermetropic eye (farsighted)

Myopic eye (nearsighted)

Figure 4-4.
Three common refractive states of the eye.

Demonstration Box 4-3:
Mapping the Retinal Blood Vessels

For this demonstration you will need a pocket penlight, and a white paper or light-colored wall. Hold the penlight near the outside canthus (corner) of your eye. Now, shaking the bulb up and down you will see a netlike pattern on the light surface. This pattern is generated by the movements of the shadows of your retinal blood vessels across your retina. By steadily shaking the bulb with one hand and tracing the shadows with the other, you can produce a map of your own retinal blood vessels.

pass through the retina twice (once as it enters and once as it is reflected out), effectively doubling its intensity. Although this results in a considerable increase in sensitivity, it is obtained at the expense of a considerable degrading of the image through fogging and blur. This is especially true at higher illumination levels. The existence of this reflecting surface explains why cats have eyes that seem to glow in the dark when a flashlight is pointed toward them.

The retina of the eye is a predominantly neural layer of tissue, about the thickness of a sheet of paper. It is in the retina that the light is changed or *transduced* into a neural response. Structurally, the retina consists of three main neural layers, which are diagrammed in Figure 4-5. The first is that of the PHOTORECEPTORS. There are two types of photoreceptors that are distinguishable on the basis of their shapes. There are long, thin, cylindrical cells, called RODS, and shorter, thicker, somewhat more tapered cells, called

CONES. The outer segments of these cells contain pigments that actually absorb the light and start the visual process. The next layer consists of BIPOLAR CELLS, which are neurons with two long extended processes. One end synapses, or receives information from, the photoreceptor; and the other end synapses, or sends information to, the third layer of the retina, which consists of large retinal GANGLION CELLS. In addition to these three basic layers, there are two types of cells that have lateral connections. Closest to the receptor layer are the HORIZONTAL CELLS. These cells typically have short dendrites and a long horizontal process that extends some distance across the retina. The second set of cells that are lateral interconnections are called AMACRINE CELLS. These are large cells, which are found at the layer between the ganglion and bipolar cells and seem to interact with spatially adjacent units (Dowling, 1970).

As we noted, the actual photoreception occurs within the rod and cone cells. Con-

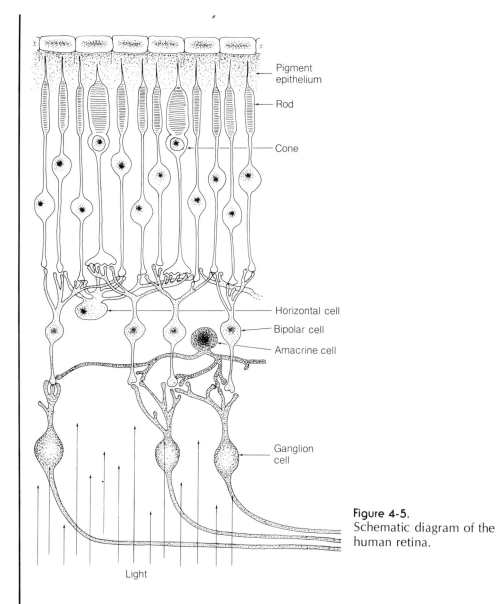

Pigment epithelium

Rod

Cone

Horizontal cell

Bipolar cell

Amacrine cell

Ganglion cell

Light

Figure 4-5.
Schematic diagram of the human retina.

trary to what one might expect, the orientation of rods and cones is inverted, with the pigment-bearing end pointing toward the rear of the eye rather than toward the lens. Thus, the retina may be viewed as if it were a transparent carpet lying upside down on the floor of the room, with the pile of the carpet corresponding to the rods and cones. The incoming light must therefore transverse its way through the carpet (the retina) before reaching the photoreceptors. The photoreceptors need a rich oxygen supply. To meet this need, many blood vessels lie in the epithelial layer. If the retina were "right-side up," so many blood vessels would be needed that the light input would be partially blocked. Therefore, the "upside-down" organization is more functional.

The Fovea. Not all parts of the retina are of equal importance in the perceptual process. The most important section of the human retina is located in the region around the OPTIC AXIS. The optic axis is an imaginary line that passes through the center of the pupil. If one views a human retina through an ophthalmoscope one notes a yellow patch of pigment located in the region of the optic axis. This area is called the MACULA LUTEA (or just macula), which simply translates to the "yellow spot." Demonstration Box 4-4 describes a procedure in which you can actually see your own macula. In the center of the macula is a small depression that looks much like the imprint of a pinpoint about $\frac{1}{3}$ mm in diameter. This small circular depression is called the FOVEA CENTRALIS, or translated, the "central pit." The fovea is critical in visual perception. Whenever one "looks" at a target, it means that the eyes are rotated so that the image of the target falls upon the foveal region.

The fovea is quite unique in its structure, and is schematically depicted in Figure 4-6.

In the center of the foveal depression, the upper layers of cells are apparently pushed away so that the light passes through a much thinner cellular layer before reaching the photoreceptors. The photoreceptors themselves are very densely packed in this region. This section of the retina contains only cones. There are no rods at all here. Foveal cones have a different shape from the cones of the periphery that we saw in Figure 4-5. They are much longer and thinner, so that they somewhat resemble rods. While cones normally vary between 0.002 and 0.008 mm in diameter elsewhere on the retina, in the fovea they are as thin as 0.001 mm.

In an incredibly laborious study Osterberg (1935) examined the retina of a human eye that had been removed as the result of an accident. By fixing the fresh retina in a suitable fluid it is possible to preserve it indefinitely. Thus the topography, or distribution, of the rods and cones can be studied at leisure in such a preparation. Osterberg actually counted the number of rods and cones in this human retina. He found that there were no rods in the center of the fovea at all, as we have already indicated. Outside of the fovea

---

Under appropriate conditions it is possible to see the macular spot in your own eye. In order to do this you will need a dark blue or purple piece of cellophane. Brightly illuminate a piece of white paper with a desk lamp. Now, while looking at the paper with one eye, quickly bring the piece of cellophane between your eye and the paper. Now as you look at the paper you will see what appears to be a faint circular shadow in the center of it. The sight of the shadow may only last for a couple of seconds. Sometimes its visibility can be improved by moving the cellophane in front of and away from your eye, so that you have a flickering colored field. Some individuals can see the spot when staring at a uniform blue field, such as a clear summer sky. This percept is caused by the fact that the yellow pigment in the macula absorbs the blue light and does not let it pass. This causes a circular shadow which can be briefly seen. It is often called Maxwell's spot, after James Clerk Maxwell, who noticed its presence during some color-matching experiments.

Demonstration Box 4-4:
The Macular Spot

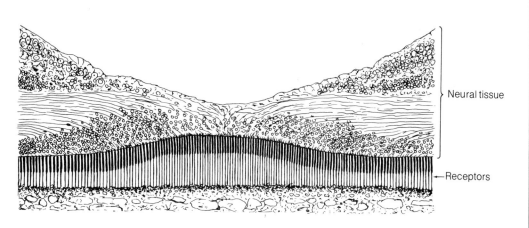

Figure 4-6.
Sketch of a cross section through the fovea. Light comes from
the top.

the number of cones rapidly decreases. The number of rods, on the other hand, rapidly increases as one leaves the foveal region and reaches a peak concentration at about 20° in the periphery; they then decrease in frequency again. The general distribution (which has been verified several times) is shown in Figure 4-7.

Rods and Cones. The presence of two types of retinal photoreceptors suggests the existence of two types of visual function. In

Figure 4-7.
The distribution of rods and cones in the human retina. The left figure gives the locations on the retina of the "angle" axis on the right figure (from Lindsay & Norman, 1977).

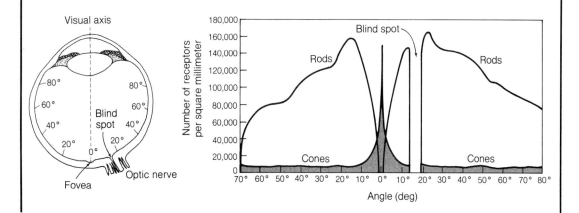

the early 1860s, the famous retinal anatomist Max Schultz found that animals that are predominantly nocturnal, such as owls, have retinas that contain only rods. Animals that are diurnal, or only active during the day, such as the chipmunk or pigeon, have retinas that are all cones. Animals that are active in the twilight, or during both day and night, such as rats, monkeys, or man, have retinas comprised of both rods and cones. On the basis of this observation Schultz offered what has been called the DUPLICITY or DUPLEXITY THEORY of vision. He maintained that there are two separate visual systems. The first is for dim vision and is dependent upon the rods, and the other is for vision under daylight or bright conditions and is dependent upon the cones. Vision under bright light is called PHOTOPIC (which translates to "light vision"), while vision under dim light is called SCOTOPIC ("dark vision"). Since that time, much evidence has been offered to support this theory. Perhaps the most spectacular evidence comes from clinical studies in which humans who were born with retinas lacking in rods or cones were studied. In individuals whose retinas contain no rods, or only nonfunctioning rods, an interesting visual anomaly occurs. Although these individuals seem to have normal vision under daylight conditions, as soon as the light dims beyond a certain point (into what we would call a twilight level of intensity) they lose all sense of sight and become functionally blind. These individuals are called NIGHT-BLIND. The implication is that in the absence of rods, scotopic vision is lost. A quite different pattern is found for individuals lacking in functioning cones. For these unfortunates, normal levels of daylight are quite painful. These individuals are totally lacking in the ability to discriminate colors, and have very poor visual acuity. Under dim levels of illumination, however, they function normally. Such individuals, called DAY-BLIND, show that a functioning

cone system is necessary for normal photopic vision and also for the perception of color. The specifics of the perception of brightness and color will be discussed in Chapters 8 and 9.

Before a rod or a cone can signal the presence of light, it must first interact with the light in some way. Chemically, such interaction involves absorbing, or capturing, one or more photons. Any substance that absorbs light is called a pigment. A substance that absorbs a lot of light would appear to be darkly pigmented, since most of the photons hitting it would be absorbed and very few would be left to bounce back to the eye of the viewer. As we noted earlier, the outer segments of both the rods and the cones contain a visual pigment. Figure 4-8 shows a more detailed sketch of these cells, in which the pigment may be seen as horizontal dark layers in the outer segment.

Rods and cones do not contain the same pigment. The visual pigment contained in the rods of vertebrates has been experimentally isolated. The first successful isolation of this pigment was in 1876 when Franz Boll isolated a brilliant red pigment from the frog retina (which contains predominantly rods). He noted that this pigment bleached, or lost its apparent coloration, when exposed to light. This reaction indicated that the substance was photosensitive. He further noted that the pigment regenerated itself in the dark. Thus, it fulfilled the elementary requirements of the visual pigment in that it responded by changing chemically in the presence of light, yet it still remained capable of resynthesizing itself. Kuhne took up the study of this pigment in 1877, and, in one extraordinary year, laid the groundwork for our understanding of its action. This pigment has been named rhodopsin (which means "visual red" rather than "visual purple" as it is sometimes called). In the century since the work by Boll and Kuhne, we have been able

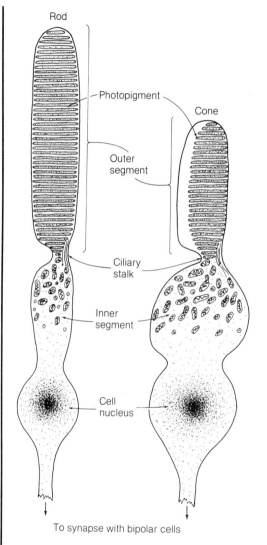

Rod

Cone

Photopigment

Outer
segment

Ciliary
stalk

Inner
segment

Cell
nucleus

To synapse with bipolar cells

Figure 4-8.
Schematic diagram of a typical human rod
and cone.

to work out much of the photochemical reaction in rhodopsin.

Basically rhodopsin is a compound that is made up of two parts, a RETINENE part and an OPSIN part. The retinene part is structurally very similar to vitamin A, which is in fact necessary for its synthesis. The retinene portion of the rhodopsin molecule is quite complex. As is the case for many organic compounds, the molecule can exist in several different shapes called *isomers*. When a molecule of rhodopsin absorbs light it isomerizes, or changes shape. That is the only effect light has on rhodopsin. The resultant substance is unstable and rapidly goes through several chemical changes (all resulting in unstable intermediate substances) until the molecule splits into retinene and opsin. The energy for this chain reaction is provided by light. The isomerization triggers a neural response through some mechanism not yet fully understood. Some theories suggest that the process punches a hole in the rod membrane which allows ions to flow in and out; others suggest that tiny vibrations are set up by the process. Rhodopsin regenerates in the dark from the retinene and opsin with the help of vitamin A and a set of enzymes. There is some evidence that indicates that light actually provides the energy to resynthesize rhodopsin, although this process is somewhat too complex to discuss here. The chemical chain of events involved in the bleaching and resynthesis of rhodopsin is shown in Figure 4-9 (see Rodieck, 1973, for a more complete review). Notice that vitamin A is vital to the resynthesis and in the absence of vitamin A, rhodopsin cannot be formed. In isolated communities where fish products or appropriate vegetables are not available, the absence of vitamin A in the diet shows up in "epidemics" of night blindness, as the rods become nonfunctional (Wald, 1968).

The identification and analysis of cone pigments has proved to be more difficult and elusive than that of rhodopsin. However, we have learned that a purple colored pigment IODOPSIN ("visual purple") is present in the cone cells of some birds. Iodopsin breaks down upon exposure to light into retinene and another form of opsin. Opsins are large complex protein molecules. The opsin found

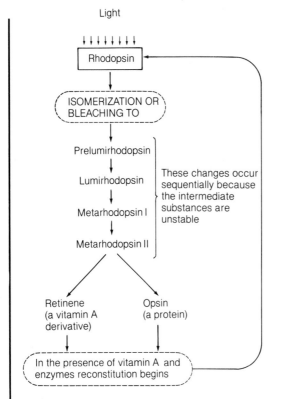

Figure 4-9.
The rhodopsin cycle.

in cones is often called PHOTOPSIN to distinguish it from that in rods which is called SCOTOPSIN. It is a slightly different protein from the opsin found in the rods. The retinene, however, appears to be the same in rods and cones. Research indicates that all photopigments, regardless of the animal species studied, are composed of the same retinene and a specific protein or opsin that is characteristic of each pigment (Dartnall, 1957; Wald, Brown, & Gibbons, 1963). In some manner, these photochemical reactions result in electrochemical neural responses that pass on to the bipolar cells. From the bipolar cells, the neural information is passed on to the retinal ganglion cells, and from the retinal ganglion cells the information passes out of the eye.

NEURAL RESPONSES TO LIGHT

In order to get the information out of the eye and up to the brain, the axons of the retinal ganglion cells move transversely across the retina and gather together to exit from the eye. This is done by punching a hole through the retina and the scleral wall. The resulting bundle of axons (the long fibers of nerve cells) forms the OPTIC NERVE. Through the center of the optic nerve come the blood vessels that sustain the metabolic needs of the eye. Since the bundle of axons must push its way through the retina, there are no photoreceptors in this region. Because of this there can be no visual response to light striking this portion of the retina and it is appropriately called the BLIND SPOT. The circular pattern of neural axons as they form the nerve to exit the eye has led anatomists to refer to this as the OPTIC DISK. One may easily demonstrate the absence of vision in this region of the retina by referring to Demonstration Box 4-5.

The output of the retina is transmitted to the brain via the optic nerves. The nerve impulses transmitted via the ganglion cell axons that make up the optic nerve are not "raw" sense data, but are the result of a large amount of neural processing that has already taken place in the retina itself. In order to understand how much processing has occurred, one might consider that there are some 120,000,000 rods and another 5,000,000 cones in each human eye. There are only about 1,000,000 axons in each optic nerve. Clearly, then, each receptor cell does not have its own private pipeline to the brain, but

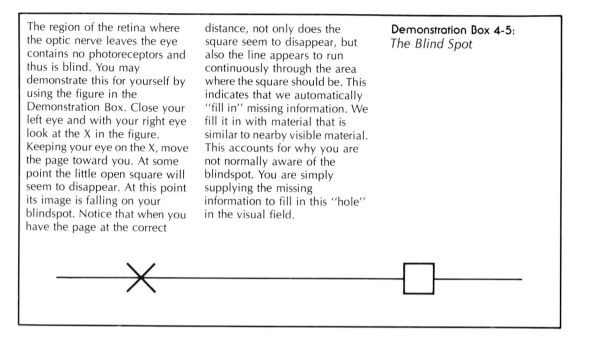

Demonstration Box 4-5:
The Blind Spot

The region of the retina where the optic nerve leaves the eye contains no photoreceptors and thus is blind. You may demonstrate this for yourself by using the figure in the Demonstration Box. Close your left eye and with your right eye look at the X in the figure. Keeping your eye on the X, move the page toward you. At some point the little open square will seem to disappear. At this point its image is falling on your blindspot. Notice that when you have the page at the correct distance, not only does the square seem to disappear, but also the line appears to run continuously through the area where the square should be. This indicates that we automatically "fill in" missing information. We fill it in with material that is similar to nearby visible material. This accounts for why you are not normally aware of the blindspot. You are simply supplying the missing information to fill in this "hole" in the visual field.

rather the responses of over 125 photoreceptors may be represented in one optic nerve fiber. This comes about when the combined activity of the 125,000,000 rods and cones, plus the output of several million more intervening bipolar, horizontal, and amacrine cells, converge upon the much smaller number of ganglion cells. It seems reasonable to assume that the information is modified and distilled as it is collected. Since the information carried to the brain by a single ganglion cell represents the combined activity of a large number of rods and cones, a single ganglion cell may respond to light from a sizable region of the retina. Such a region, or area of the retina, in which light alters the firing rate of a cell, is called that cell's RECEPTIVE FIELD. Thus, a single ganglion cell serves as a clearing house for information coming from a substantial zone of receptor cells in the retina.

In order to understand how visual information is processed, we would want to know how specific ganglion cells respond to various forms of light stimuli. To begin with, the response of all neurons is electrical in nature. For those of you who do not know how neurons work, it would be useful to stop at this point and read the Special Topic at the end of this chapter entitled "What is the neural response?" Basically, each time a nerve cell fires, there is a momentary change in electrical activity that can be recorded by means of an electrode inserted into the cell. The use of microelectrodes to record the activity of single neurons has produced some of the most exciting data in the field of sensory physiology. The general procedure involves use of an anesthetic or a paralyzing agent such as *curare* combined with local anesthetics to reduce the discomfort of the restraining device used to hold the animal. Such devices are called STEREOTAXIC INSTRUMENTS. A stereotaxic instrument is a device that permits accurate placement of electrodes in the brain, and the advancement of the electrode forward in very small steps. Figure 4-10 shows a cat in a stereotaxic instrument.

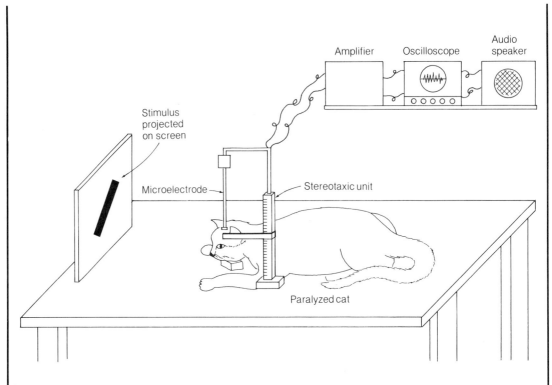

Figure 4-10.
Recording of neural responses from the visual system of a cat.

Note that the cat is viewing a screen upon which stimuli may be presented. The electrode is attached through a set of amplifiers to an oscilloscope and it is also attached to a speaker. As the special topic on the neural response indicates, we can display the responses of a neuron as a series of rapid, brief, electrical changes, which produce the characteristic nerve "spike" on an oscilloscope screen. For an experimenter attempting to record from a neuron, a much more useful procedure is to feed the neural responses into an audio-amplifying system and from there into a loudspeaker. This transforms the neural response into a series of pops or clicks, each click being caused by a single neural impulse. One can then listen to the neural response, thus keeping the eyes free to tend to

other matters. An increase in the rate of clicking means an increase in the frequency of cell firing, and a decrease means a reduction. Whether there is an increase or a decrease in the rate of response is easily recognized by the observer.

Following the lead of Hartline (1940), Kuffler (1953) recorded the neural impulses occurring in retinal ganglion cells. This was done by inserting the electrode through the eye of an anesthetized cat and recording from single ganglion cells in the retina. Kuffler found that when he displayed a single spot of light on the screen he could elicit three different types of responses from a cell, depending upon the location of the stimulus in the field. The first type of response is the one most typically expected when a neuron is excited. This type of response is a burst of neural impulses immediately following the onset of the stimulus. This response has been dubbed an ON RESPONSE. Alternatively, the cell can give a burst of impulses coincident with the termination of the stimulus. Such a response is termed an OFF RESPONSE. There are some responses that appear to be hybrids because either the presentation of, *or* the removal of, the stimulus causes a burst of neural impulses. These are designated as ON–OFF RESPONSES. Typical examples of these responses are shown in Figure 4-11.

Kuffler found that when he used very small stimulus lights (about 0.2 mm in diameter) the nature of the retinal ganglion cell response varied from on, through on–off, to off, depending upon the location of the stimulus. When he mapped the shape of the overall receptive field of the retinal ganglion cell (the region of retinal stimulation to which the cell responds), he found that it tended to be circular. There were three distinct zones within each receptive field. Typically, the receptive field had a relatively circular center that gave on responses when stimulated. That is, it responded with an on response to the onset of a light stimulus. The outer portion of the receptive field gave the opposite result. That is, the onset of a light did not produce a response, but its offset did. Between these two regions was a boundary area where on–off responses occurred. A typical receptive field is shown as Figure 4-12, where on response regions are marked by +, off by −, and on–off by ±. Some receptive fields have the opposite organization, with the central region giving off responses when stimulated and the surrounding region showing on responses. There are approximately equal numbers of off-center cells and on-center cells. (Rodieck & Stone, 1965; Rodieck, 1973).

A very small percentage of the receptors in the primate retina is particularly important. These receptors have their own direct lines to the higher centers, rather than a broad, extended receptive field. Thus, a single receptor can lead to a single bipolar cell that in turn synapses directly with a single ganglion cell. This produces a ganglion cell with a receptive field containing an exquisitely small center, reflecting the output from one photoreceptor, although the annular surround may reflect the output from others. Such receptors are most likely all cones clustered together in the fovea. Some evidence indicates that there are fewer than 50,000 of these important receptors in each eye. This amounts to less than one-tenth of one percent of all the receptors present. Strangely, it is this small percentage of cells upon which we rely for precise photopic vision. Outside of the fovea, the degree of convergence from the receptors to the retinal ganglion cells is much greater. Consequently, the size of the receptive fields grows proportionately.

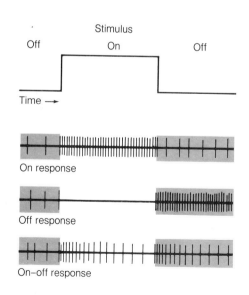

Figure 4-11.
On, off, and on–off neural responses in the optic nerve.

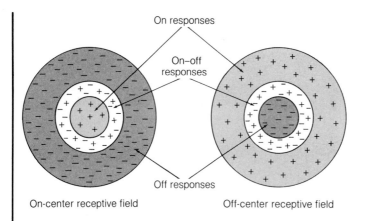

On responses

On–off
responses

Off responses

On-center receptive field   Off-center receptive field

Figure 4-12.
Circular center–surround
retinal receptive fields of two
types.

Recently, attention has turned toward an analysis of the speed with which neural information is conducted out of the retina as well as the form of the response. On the basis of these observations it seems as though there are actually three types of cells in the retina. Each has different characteristics, and they have been given the rather unexciting names of W, X, and Y cells. W cells are very tiny, conduct very slowly (10 meters per second) and do not seem to have a center–surround organization in their receptive fields (Stone & Hoffman, 1972; Rodieck, 1967). The X retinal cells are physically small and have small center–surround receptive fields. They are usually found near the center of the retina. They send relatively slow signals into the visual pathways, the speed of which is about 20 meters per second (Fukada & Saito, 1971; Cleland, Dubkin, & Levick, 1971). The Y cells are physically larger, with large receptive fields. They are located in the peripheral retina and have much faster responses than X cells (about 40 meters per second).

Although we are just learning about these units, it seems that they serve different functions. X cells seem to be sensitive to continued stimulation and, perhaps, provide information about the general state of illumination. Their small receptive field size seems to allow good localization information. On the other hand, Y cells respond to any change, and seem particularly sensitive to movement, although their large receptive fields do not permit very accurate localization (Schmitt & Worden, 1974). As we shall see in Chapter 12, X and Y cells may play an important role in the perception of movement. Such a variety of cells at the retinal level may indicate that much processing of visual information has already taken place before the sensory data have even left the eye.

THE VISUAL PATHWAYS

The axons of the retinal ganglion cells gather together and push their way out of the eye at the blindspot. This bundle of axons, which forms the optic nerve, is the beginning of the pipeline of information that eventually ends in the brain. A basic map of the pathways of the visual system is given in Figure 4-13A and B. Notice that the two optic nerves come together at a point that looks like an X. This point is called the OPTIC CHIASM (from the Greek letter χ, which is called chi). In lower animals, the optic nerve from the right eye crosses completely to the left side of the head and vice versa. In many mammalian species, particularly those who seem to use combined input from the two eyes to obtain better depth perception (this will be discussed more fully in Chapter 11), some of the fibers do not cross. In primates, such as man, approximately one-half of the optic nerve fibers cross to the opposite side of the head. These are the

Figure 4-13.
The visual pathway from the eye to the visual cortex (from Lindsay & Norman, 1977).

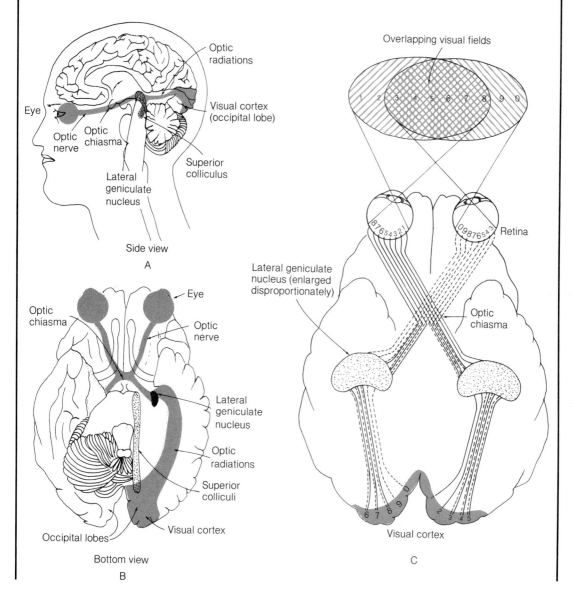

fibers that represent the two inside or *nasal* retinas. Those from the outside or *temporal* halves of each retina do not cross but continue on the same side. Such an arrangement implies that each half of the visual field will be projected to the opposite side of the brain. At the risk of being confusing, since the crystalline lens in the eye reverses the image up–down and right–left, this means that the *right visual field* is projected onto the nasal half of the retina of the right eye and the temporal half of the retina of the left eye. The axons from both of these half-retinas (or hemiretinas) end up on the left side of the brain. Thus information from the right side of your field of view ends up on the left side of your brain, and vice versa as shown in Figure 4-13C.

The Superior Colliculus. Beyond the optic chiasm the pathway is no longer called the optic nerve, but rather the OPTIC TRACT. There are two major branches in the optic tract. The first ends in a region of the brain stem where there are four small bumps or nodules. The optic fibers terminate on the upper pair of bumps called the SUPERIOR COLLICULI. In lower vertebrates this area is the primary end point for optic fibers. It may be regarded, in an evolutionary sense, as an older, more primitive, visual center. In lower animals, it is frequently referred to as the *optic tectum.* Although much remains to be learned about the superior colliculus, recent work has shown that the collicular centers are important in the localization of targets and the guidance of eye movements. Surgical removal of the colliculi in cats results in eye movement inaccuracies, and the animals seem to have difficulty locating targets in order to bring them into view. This latter ability seems to recover after a few months (Sprague & Meikle, 1965). In general, the superior colliculus seems to have cells that are specially adapted to monitor the position

of a target (Gordon, 1976), and also to indicate eye position when looking at targets (Wurtz, 1976). The importance of the superior colliculus in locating objects in space was dramatically shown by Schneider (1969). He removed the colliculus from golden hampsters and found that, although the animals could still recognize objects or patterns when they encountered them, they acted as if they could not localize targets well enough to walk over to them. It is almost as if localization and recognition were handled by separate visual mechanisms.

The Lateral Geniculate Nucleus. For most primates the major termination for the optic tracts is reached after the fibers pass around the hypothalamus and synapse in the LATERAL GENICULATE NUCLEUS of the thalamus. There seem to be about 1,000,000 cells in the primate lateral geniculate nucleus. This is about the same as the number of ganglion cells in the optic nerve. The lateral geniculate is arranged in layers. There are six such layers, each of which seems to receive input from only one eye, with little binocular interaction.

Electrophysiological studies of the lateral geniculate have shown that these neurons are spontaneously active. This means that they produce a steady train of nerve impulses even in the dark. Although this may seem somewhat surprising, spontaneity is a characteristic of brain cells. We do not fully understand why this activity maintains itself. It may simply be due to the fact that the neurons are alive and announce this by occasional random responses. This continuing train of responses does augment the information coding capacity of the cells, as we shall see.

As is the case with the retinal ganglion cells, lateral geniculate cells do not respond to visual stimuli unless the stimulation occurs within their receptive fields. Thus, a particular lateral geniculate neuron provides information about the location of an object in space because it responds only to those objects projected onto the patch of retinal receptors that define its receptive field. These receptors, in turn, respond only to objects in a particular region of the visual field. Generally speaking, there is much similarity between the lateral geniculate cell receptive fields and those of the retina. If we map a lateral geniculate cell by projecting points of light onto a screen in the visual field in front of an animal, we find that the cell response appears somewhat similar to that of a retinal ganglion cell. For instance, most such cells have an on-center and an off-surround, or the reverse.

There is, however, one quirk that makes these responses somewhat different. Experiments by DeValois (1971) and by Wiesel and Hubel (1966) have shown that these cells respond differentially not only to the location of a light, but also to its color. DeValois discovered that there are cells in the lateral geniculate of monkeys that respond with an increase in their base firing rate when the center of their receptive field is stimulated by a red spot of light, whereas they show an off response (or a decrease in their activity levels over the spontaneous firing rate) when the center is stimulated by a green light. This finding suggests the possibility of recording both color and location information from the same cells. Out of 203 cells recorded by Wiesel and Hubel 77% were color coded. For instance, the red might produce an on response in the center of these cells and an off response in the periphery. The green would then produce an off response in the center and an on response in the periphery. Some cells show a pairing of blue and green, and although other subtypes are theoretically possible, they were not observed in this experiment. It is of course possible that further testing will show other color pairings. There are some cells in the lateral geniculate that do not appear to be color sensitive, but they merely show the same circular distribution of on- and off-responses that has been observed in retinal ganglion cells. On the other hand, there are some cells that respond only to color changes, increasing their firing rate for some colors and decreasing it for others. This is the case regardless of where in the receptive field of these cells the target is imaged. Cells of this type are found only infrequently (see DeValois & DeValois, 1975).

Very little is known about the actual function of the lateral geniculate. Although we find specifically tuned cells that seem to extract properties of the visual input, the geniculate is only a "way station." The experience of vision does not arise here any more than it does in the retina. A human or a monkey with retina and lateral geniculate intact, but deprived of the cortical portion of the visual system is, as far as can be determined, blind. If the connections to the superior colliculis are still intact, some rudimentary perception of the brightness and crude localization of targets still may be possible; however, the perception of form, pattern or any of the aspects of the visual experience we associate with "seeing" would be absent. We would say that the organism is functionally blind, with some residual light sense. Thus, if we are to understand vision, we must consider the operations of other portions of the brain, most particularly the cerebral cortex.

THE VISUAL CORTEX

When the axons of the lateral geniculate neurons leave the geniculate, they spray out and form a large fan of fibers called the OPTIC RADIATIONS. These fibers eventually synapse with cells in the cortex in the rear portion of the brain. This portion of the brain is known as the OCCIPITAL LOBE. Several alternate labels have been used to refer to this region of the brain. Since, when viewed under a light microscope the cells are arranged regularly, giving a banded appearance to the cortex, this region is also called the STRIATE (striped) CORTEX. Alternatively, the region may be designated using the numbering system devised by Brodmann (1914) based upon the appearance of cells. In Brodmann's numbering system this major area of visual function is demarcated as AREA 17. To simplify these complexities of labeling, we will simply say that the axons of the lateral geniculate cells branch out and synapse with the neurons in the VISUAL CORTEX.

There are over 100,000,000 neurons in the visual cortex. Only the smallest fraction of these have been thoroughly studied in attempts to discover their response characteristics. What we do know of these cells is based largely on research done with microelectrodes. These studies have employed techniques similar to those used in the mapping of the receptive fields for the retinal ganglion and lateral geniculate cells. Much of the pioneer work was done by Hubel and Wiesel using the cat as their primary subject (although similar results have been obtained in the monkey and the rabbit).

In the early 1930s, Lashley (1931) established the importance of the visual cortex for the perception of patterns and forms. He removed the visual cortex of rats, while Klüver and Bucy (1937) did the same for monkeys. They were able to establish that with this section of the cortex missing, the animals were unable to discriminate patterns, although brightness perception was still intact. Thus, decorticate animals could be trained to discriminate light from dark, but could not respond to the shape of the targets.

Within the striate cortex there is a rather direct topological (point for point) mapping of the external visual world, with specific points in the environment corresponding to specific points in the cortex. Most information about this mapping has been obtained with the aid of various military organizations, since one consequence of war is the prevalence of penetrating missile wounds that injure specific parts of the cortex. When a piece of the occipital cortex is so damaged, the patient is blind in part of the visual field. Such a damaged area is technically called a *lesion*. This blind patch is called a SCOTOMA (meaning dark spot). It is interesting to note that if the scotoma is small, and not too close to the region represented by the fovea, the patient may not even be aware of its presence. Such scotomas must be plotted laboriously by means of an instrument known as a PERIMETER. In this device, the observer looks at the center of a hemisphere, and a small light or other target is placed at some known point on the surface. The observer has to report whether he sees it or not. Target presentations are repeated until an extensive map of the field, including the blindspots, has been derived. One interesting fact that emerges from such measurements on observers with lesions is that the fovea is represented by an inordinately large quantity of cortex, relative to its actual size on the retina. This is in accord with its disproportionate importance relative to other retinal regions.

It is important to note that the point-for-point representation of the visual field on the cortex is not perfect. If you view a picture of a house in the environment, that does not mean that there is a house-shaped pattern of electrical excitation in the cortex. Rather, much of the analysis of features of visual input occurs within individual cortical neurons. Hubel and Wiesel (1962) mapped the receptive fields in cats by implanting electrodes in cortical cells in Area 17, and flashing stimuli on a screen in front of an animal. When cortical cells are mapped in this way, the familiar circular on and off regions found for ganglion and geniculate cells are not present. Instead the typical receptive fields have elongated central regions. A map of some such cells is shown in Figure 4-14. This type of cell, which Hubel and Wiesel labeled a SIMPLE CELL, generally has no spontaneous activity at all and never seems to respond to diffuse illumination of the whole screen. Sometimes such cells respond, albeit grudgingly, to small spots of light. However, because of the elongation of the central region of the receptive field, the best stimulus for such a cell is a white or black bar or line, or a white or black border, flashed in the appropriate location in the receptive field. Figure 4-14 shows the receptive fields that might be mapped from several simple cells. Beneath each of them you will see the stimulus that produces the maximal

response for each of these receptive fields. Notice that in every case the edge between the light and the dark areas must be at a particular orientation in a particular location. If the edge of the line is flashed on the receptive field at a different angle, a greatly reduced response may be obtained, or perhaps no response at all. For this reason such cortical cells have been called ORIENTATION or LINE DETECTORS.

There are other kinds of neurons in the visual cortex that seem to be tuned to even more complicated pattern properties of the stimulus. Such cells are usually not located in Area 17, but in some regions very close to Area 17 and slightly forward in the brain. These visual areas in the primate brain are numbered in Brodmann's mapping system as Areas 18 and 19. These more elaborate

Figure 4-14.
Receptive fields of "simple" cortical cells:
+ means the cell gives an on response;
− means the cell gives an off response.

Receptive field shape

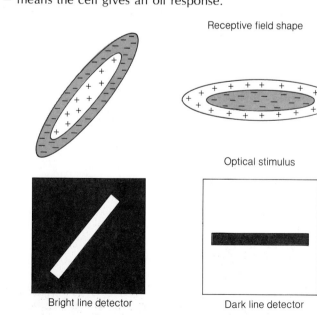
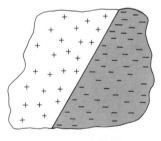

Optical stimulus

Bright line detector   Dark line detector   Edge detector

feature-analyzing neurons have been labeled COMPLEX CELLS. Generally speaking, they have larger receptive fields than do simple cells, although their size may vary tremendously. Like simple cells they are most responsive to visual stimuli in the shape of lines or bars. Also, like simple cells, complex cells respond maximally to such stimuli when they are in a particular orientation. However, they rarely respond to any flashing patterns. What they prefer is a bar or edge moving somewhere within the receptive field. The location within the receptive field does not appear to be particularly important. In other words, the complex cells seem to generalize their response over a wider area of the visual field. Figure 4-15 shows the response of a complex

cell to two different moving light slits, one in the optimal, and the other in a nonoptimal orientation.

Unfortunately, complex cells do not exhaust the types of cells recorded in the cortex. At a slightly more sophisticated level are HYPERCOMPLEX CELLS, which respond not only to the orientation and to the direction of movement of the stimulus, but also to the length, to the width, or even to the selective features of shape. Figure 4-16 shows an example of some hypercomplex cell responses as described by Hubel and Wiesel (1968).

This catalog does not exhaust the complexity of cortical cell responsiveness. There are also cells that are apparently tuned to SPATIAL FREQUENCIES. This term refers to the rapidity of luminance changes in adjacent areas in the field of view. For instance, a sharp, crisp contour (such as the contours of the print on this page) will have many high spatial frequencies or frequently occurring luminance changes. However, a blurred image will not have the high spatial frequencies but only low frequencies, since the luminance changes are neither that dramatic nor frequent. The existence of these frequency-tuned cells has been shown using patterns that contain bars with different widths and spacings. Broad stripes represent low spatial frequencies while narrow stripes provide high spatial frequencies. Some cells respond to one grid pattern but not to others (Robson, 1975); however, the implications of the existence of these cells for visual processing is still being investigated (Campbell & Maffei, 1974). You may demonstrate a spatial frequency effect for yourself using Demonstration Box 4-6.

We could ask what possible anatomical connections could result in the response specificity observed in cortical cells. Although we do not know the detailed neuroanatomy very well, it seems clear that

Preferred orientation and direction

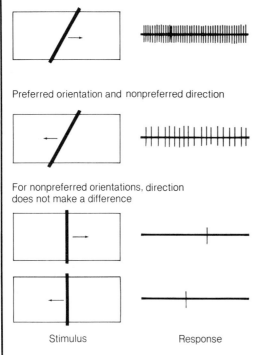

Preferred orientation and nonpreferred direction

For nonpreferred orientations, direction does not make a difference

Stimulus   Response

Figure 4-15.
Some typical "complex" cortical cell responses.

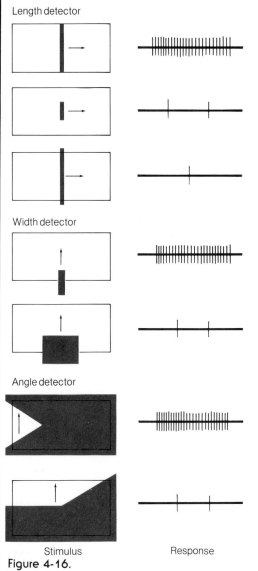

Length detector

Width detector

Angle detector

Stimulus   Response

Figure 4-16.
Some typical "hypercomplex" cortical cell responses.

feature-specific cortical cell. Notice that if the lateral geniculate cells are connected as shown, we have changed the responsiveness from fields that prefer spots or dot-shaped stimuli to ones that prefer lines at given orientations. It is possible to hypothesize a series of interconnections between simple cells that might produce complex cells, and even hypercomplex cells, although such speculation is essentially guesswork in the absence of hard anatomical data. Recent data seem to suggest that this viewpoint may be too simple. It seems that complex cells often respond more quickly to stimuli than do simple cells. This seems like an impossible state of affairs if complex cells are made up of hierarchical connections of simple cells (Barlow, 1972; Blakemore, 1975). Perhaps all cells are directly connected to the lateral geniculate, which serves a switching and traffic control function.

The existence of orientation-specific or feature-specific cells in the cortex suggests that pattern perception may take place by decomposing visual stimuli into component features or contours. These are then resynthesized at a later point according to some plan or template. Certainly, many pattern-recognition machines have been built using this principle. For instance, the machine that reads the numbers on your bank check is tuned to respond to certain, highly stylized, numerical stimuli by matching the patterns on paper to internally represented codes. Unfortunately, in mammalian species the significance of such feature extraction cells for the perceptual process has not yet been determined. It is known that if we alter an animal's visual experience from birth, we can alter the distribution of orientations to which simple cells are responsive. This has been elegantly shown by Hirsch and Spinelli (1970), who reared cats with special goggles that only allowed them to see horizontal or vertical stripes. The effect of such a restriction

simple cells can be synthesized by assuming that a series of concentric receptive fields, such as those observed in the lateral geniculate, all converge on a single cortical neuron. The pattern of such convergence, as diagrammed in Figure 4-17, could result in a

If you look at the pattern below, you will see that one of those on the left has broad bars (low spatial frequency) and the other has narrow bars (high spatial frequency). The pattern on the right contains two gratings, both of which have the same spatial frequencies, which are neither as high nor as low as the ones on the left. Hold the illustration about 80 cm away from you. Now look at the horizontal bar between the upper and lower patterns on the left for about 20 or 30 sec. Move your gaze from one portion of the bar to another, but keep your eyes on the bar. As you steadily look at the bar, the receptive fields attuned to low spatial frequencies from the upper part of your visual field and those attuned to the high spatial frequencies from the lower part of your visual field are fatiguing. Now if you quickly transfer your gaze to the dot between the identical gratings on the right, you will notice that they no longer seem to be the same. The top part of the grating now appears to be more finely spaced than the bottom. This implies that the visual system has special detectors for recognizing bars or gratings of specific spacing. Looking at a particular spatial frequency for a length of time, until it is fatigued, results in an aftereffect in which the apparent spacing of the new stimuli are shifted away from the frequencies of the fatigued detectors.

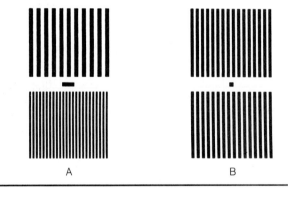

A   B

of visual experience was an alteration in the distribution of cortical cells. Thus an eye exposed to only vertical stripes since birth seems capable of only driving cells in the cortex that respond to vertical orientations.

We might now suppose that a cat has been created that is blind to horizontal contours. However, such is not the case. Early reports indicated that there were large visual losses when orientation deprivation had been imposed (Blakemore & Cooper, 1970). In reviewing the effects of this type of selective rearing, Hirsch and Jacobson (1975) noted that despite the drastic alterations in the responses and cortical distributions of orientation-specific cells, cats reared in this fashion seem to be otherwise normal in their visual behaviors. Given the complexity of the feature extraction cells in the cortex, it is puzzling that such massive disruptions do

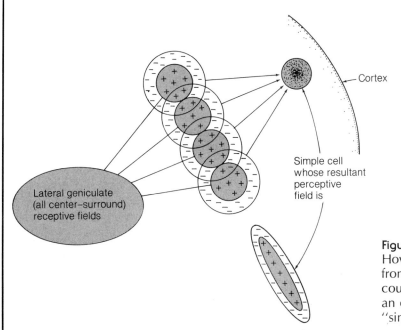

Cortex

Simple cell
whose resultant
perceptive
field is

Lateral geniculate
(all center–surround)
receptive fields

Figure 4-17.
How center–surround cells
from the lateral geniculate
could be connected to form
an orientation-specific
"simple" cortical cell.

not seem to affect the perceptual process more significantly.

The Inferotemporal Cortex. Recently, evidence has accumulated indicating that a region of the cortex that formerly had not been identified with the visual system is, nonetheless, involved in the visual process. This is the INFEROTEMPORAL CORTEX, located in the temporal lobes of the brain. This area roughly corresponds to the region of your skull called the temples. This portion of the brain receives input from several other regions, including Areas 18 and 19, which we already know have important visual functions. The visual significance of this area was accidentally discovered by Klüver and Bucy in 1937 while observing monkeys who had undergone surgery that removed most of both temporal lobes. They called the syndrome that they observed PSYCHIC BLINDNESS. The animals could reach for, and accurately pick up, small objects; hence, they were clearly not blind. However, they did appear to have lost

the ability to identify objects by sight. An example of this is shown in what was named the CONCENTRATION TEST. Here, a piece of food or a metal object is presented to the monkey approximately every 30 sec. Generally, a normal monkey will eat the food, and discard the nail or steel nut after examination by mouth. Within a few trials, a normal monkey will let the metal objects pass by and select only the food. For animals with inferotemporal lobe loss, however, both the food and the inedible object were picked up on virtually every trial. The animal seemed to show no evidence of learning to discriminate visually between the targets. Wilson (1957) found that such monkeys could discriminate between an inverted and an upright L by touch, yet with inferotemporal lesions, they could not make the same discrimination visually. This syndrome is similar to a human defect called VISUAL AGNOSIA. Such patients can see all parts of the visual field, but the things they see mean nothing to them. Milner (1954, 1958) showed that patients with lesions of the right temporal lobe also show deficits on a variety of visual tests. For instance, they have difficulty in placing pictures in a sequence that relates a meaningful story or pattern. They also have difficulty in learning to recognize new faces. Kimura (1963) showed that such patients make poor visual estimates of the number of dots in an array, and have difficulty recognizing overlapping figures, have poor memory for nonsense forms, and generally have poor picture memory.

Needless to say, some investigators have begun to map single neurons in the inferotemporal cortex. Some microelectrode measurements in the monkey brain have produced startling results, suggesting that neurons found in this part of the brain have amazing response specificities. Although this research area is quite new, neurons sensitive to size, shape, color, orientation, and direction of movement have already been discovered in this region of the brain. There is even a report that one neuron produced its best response when the stimulus was the outline of a monkey's paw. Gross, Rocha-Miranda, and Bender (1972) report that one day they discovered a cell that seemed unrespon-

sive to any light stimulus. When they waved their hand in front of the stimulus screen, however, they elicited a very vigorous response from the previously unresponsive neuron. They then spent the next twelve hours testing various paper cutouts in an attempt to find out what feature triggered this specific unit. When the entire set of stimuli were ranked according to the strength of the response they produced, they could not find any simple *physical* dimension that correlated with this rank order. However, the rank order of stimuli, in terms of their ability to drive the cell, did correlate with their apparent similarity (at least for the experimenters) to the shadow of a monkey's hand. The relative adequacy of a few of these stimuli is shown in Figure 4-18. Interestingly enough, fingers pointing downward elicited very little response when compared to fingers pointing upward or to the sides. An animal looking at his own hand would most likely see a hand with fingers pointing upward. Thus, it seems possible that in your inferotemporal cortex there might be a template for the perception of your grandmother, your car, or many other familiar stimulus shapes.

Most vigorously responded to stimuli

Stimuli producing moderate response

Stimuli producing weak response

Figure 4-18.
The stimuli in the figure were used to excite a neuron in the inferotemporal cortex of a monkey. Notice that the more handlike a stimulus is, the more vigorous is the response.

SPECIAL TOPIC: WHAT IS THE NEURAL RESPONSE?

In several sections of this book, we discuss research that has focused upon the activity of cells within various portions of sensory systems. This *Special Topic* will help you to understand the nature of the neural response, and it will also give you a brief overview of how cellular recording is done.

The human nervous system contains approximately 10–14 billion neurons. Each of these neurons is a separate unit composed of three parts. These three parts are a CELL BODY, an AXON, and DENDRITES. The axon and dendrites are extensions of the cell body. Figure ST4-1 shows a typical cell. Although each neuron or cell is discrete, it communicates with other cells by means of its AXON TERMINALS (the ends of the axon). The place where the axons of one cell come into proximity with the cell body or dendrites of another cell is called a SYNAPSE.

Basically, all neural activity is electrical. The inside of a cell is charged relative to the outside. This electrical difference, or POTENTIAL, is about 70 millivolts (mV). Under these conditions, we say that the cell is at rest or POLARIZED, which is the technical term for this resting state. When an external stimulus causes a reaction in a cell, electrical or potential changes are seen. Either the resting potential of the cell becomes less negative by moving toward 0 mV, or it increases its degree of negativity by moving away from 0 mV. The word DEPOLARIZATION describes the movement of the potential toward zero, while the movement toward increasing negativity is called HYPERPOLARIZATION. When a stimulus evokes a response in a neuron, this response is elec-

Figure ST4-1.
A typical neuron and a few connections to other neurons.

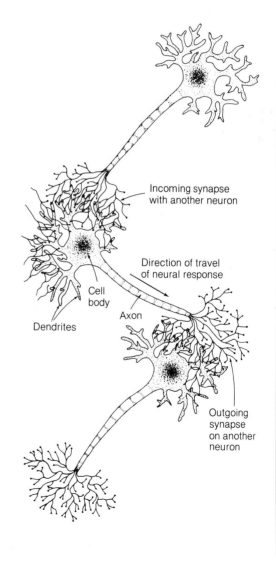

Incoming synapse with another neuron

Direction of travel of neural response

Cell body

Axon

Dendrites

Outgoing synapse on another neuron

trical, and it either involves depolarization or hyperpolarization.

For most cells the neural response is not a graded change in potential. Instead there is a complex and rapid change in electrical state. First, there is a small depolarization (movement from −70 mV toward 0 mV), which is suddenly followed by a large and rapid shift from a negative to a positive potential. This shift occurs within about 1 msec and it is diagrammed in Figure ST4-2. This rapid depolarization is followed by a period of hyperpolarization where the potential returns to the resting level of −70 mV. These changes in electrical potentials in the axon constitute the ACTION POTENTIAL or SPIKE POTENTIAL that is recorded by various cellular recording devices. Increased stimulation does not change the size of the spike potential, but rather it increases the number of responses per unit time. You might imagine that each neural response is a gun shot and the excitement of the gunman is measured by the speed at which he is firing his weapon. Thus the number or frequency of responses shows level of stimulation.

Neural responses are measured using microelectrodes (the tip of which might be .01 mm in size, or smaller). The electrical activity of the cell is detected by the electrode, amplified, and usually displayed on an OS-CILLOSCOPE, which is nothing more than a sensitive voltmeter that displays voltage changes over a period of time. Typical cell responses are shown in Figure ST4-3, which shows an excited cell and a relatively unexcited neural cell.

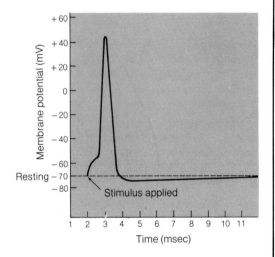

Figure ST4-2.
Electrical response of neuron ("spike potential") to a stimulus.

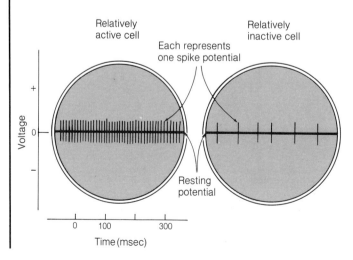

Figure ST4-3.
Oscilloscope records of electrical responses of a neuron.

5
The Auditory System

It is one of those strange historical occurrences that while studying the physiology of the ear in order to help the deaf learn to deal with a world of sound, Alexander Graham Bell developed the telephone. Perhaps the leap was not too great however, for if the eye is our window to the world, then the ear must be our microphone. Just as an understanding of the physical nature of light and of the anatomy and physiology of the eye is important to understanding the psychology of vision, an understanding of the physical nature of sound and of the anatomy and physiology of the auditory system is crucial to our understanding of hearing. The ear is a remarkable physical instrument. An engineer trying to duplicate the function of the ear would have to compress a sound system of immense complexity into a space of approximately two cubic centimeters. It would have to contain many sophisticated components including an impedence matcher, a wide-range mechanical analyzer, a mobile relay-and-amplification unit, a multichannel transducer to convert mechanical energy to electrical energy, a system to maintain a delicate hydraulic balance, and an internal two-way communications system (Stevens & Warshovsky, 1965). So much complicated apparatus suggests that the path of sound waves, from their origin in the external environment to the final stage where we "hear a sound," will involve several different mechanisms and stages of information processing.

SOUND

Sound is quite similar to mechanical pressure. If you have ever attended a very loud rock concert, you probably have felt the actual mechanical pulsations, especially those from the bass instruments that may cause the floor, seat, or the air about you to seem to vibrate. You are feeling the results of the movements of air molecules being pushed forward in waves by the cone of the speaker. Perhaps it is easier to understand this process if we consider what happens when we pluck a guitar string, causing a sound. You can see the string vibrate. It is this vibration that causes the sound as the strand of steel or nylon collides with the air molecules around it. These molecules, in turn, collide with others causing air compression as the string moves forward and rarefaction as it moves back. This movement results in a WAVE of mechanical energy, as is shown in Figure 5-1. Such collisions are of course not perfectly efficient in transferring the original collision energy, so that the wave tends to become less intense as it moves further away from the original source. Consequently, its ability to move or vibrate other objects decreases. Sound waves are in fact alternations of rarefaction and compression of any elastic medium (for example, water, air, and walls) in which they are traveling. For instance, in air the original vibrating surface first compresses the nearby air molecules into a smaller space by bumping into them and moving them closer together. Then when it moves away from the air molecules, during the second part of its vibration, it causes a rarefied region where there are relatively few air molecules. This cycle is repeated in the vibration, and the alternations of compression and rarefaction are transmitted for great distances through the medium, while the individual air molecules simply move back and forth over very small distances. Since sound involves actual vibration of parts of the medium through which it travels, it cannot pass through a vacuum. The necessity of a medium for the existence of sound waves was demonstrated by Robert Boyle in 1660, when he pumped the air out of a jar and then failed to hear the ringing of a watch suspended by a thread in the jar.

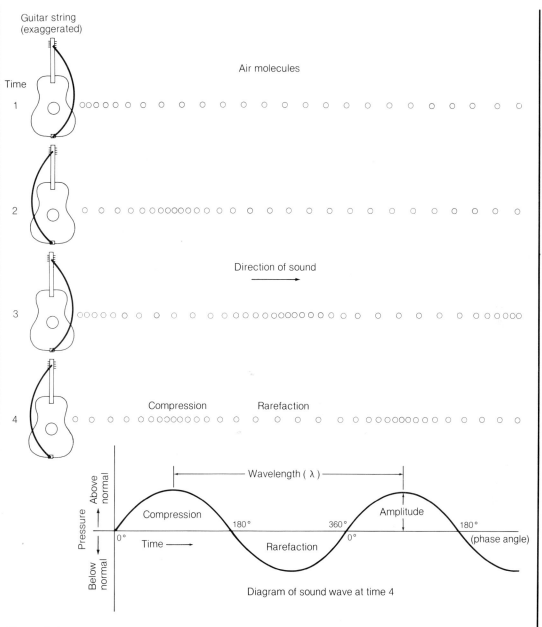

Figure 5-1.
Nature of a sound wave in air.

The speed of sound varies according to the medium in which it travels. The elasticity and density of the medium are important, with sound traveling faster in a denser and/or more elastic medium. The speed of sound is rather slow compared to that of electromagnetic waves. Sound travels at approximately 340 m/sec in air, while it travels in water at about 1360 m/sec.

Describing a Simple Sound Wave. Any sound waves can be described by specifying certain values. The simplest wave is sinusoidal (so-called because the trigonometric sine function describes it mathematically). In Figure 5-1, we presented a representation of the alternate compressions and rarefactions over time from the vibrating string of a guitar. When we plot the air pressure as it varies over time we get the wave shown in the figure. Its WAVELENGTH (λ) is the distance from one peak to the next peak. The wavelength represents a single CYCLE of the wave. The FREQUENCY (f) of the wave is, by convention, the number of cycles the wave is able to complete in one second. The unit used to measure frequency is CYCLES PER SECOND or HERTZ (Hz), named after the German physicist Heinrich R. Hertz. The frequency of a sound wave is important to our later discussion, since it is related to (although not the same as) the perceived pitch of the sound. The range of frequencies important to human hearing is from about 20 to 20,000 Hz, although other animals such as bats or dolphins can hear frequencies several times as high as the upper limit for humans.

The measure of the intensity of a sound wave is directly related to the mechanical pressure it exerts. The unit used to measure this intensity is called the BEL (after Alexander Graham Bell). This unit is rather large, hence most intensities are measured in tenths of a bel, which are simply designated DECIBELS (dB). This value is logarithmically related to

the pressure exerted by the sound waves (sound pressure level or SPL). The most commonly used starting point (0 dB) is close to the absolute threshold of hearing, and all values are then decibels above threshold. Table 5-1 indicates representative values of SPL for some representative sounds. The table shows that as the measured intensity of a sound increases, subjective loudness also increases. Intensity is related to (but not identical to) loudness. The actual procedures used to compute decibels are given in the Special Topic at the end of this chapter entitled Sound Pressure and Decibels.

A final important parameter of sound waves is PHASE, which becomes important when two or more simple waves are to be compared. Phase refers to the particular part of the compression–rarefaction cycle a wave has reached at a given instant of time. If two waves are at exactly the same part of their respective cycles at the same instant (so that their peaks and valleys will always coincide), they are said to be IN PHASE. If their peaks and valleys do not coincide exactly over time, the two waves are OUT OF PHASE. How much they are out of phase can be measured by means of PHASE ANGLE. A single cycle is assigned 360° (as in circular motion); thus a portion of a cycle can be specified by number of degrees from 0 to 360 (see Figure 5-1). If one wave is at its 90° point (its peak) when another wave is at its 180° point (crossing the zero pressure difference line), then the two waves are 90° out of phase. If we remember that these waves simply describe increases and decreases in mechanical pressure at various moments in time, it should be obvious that different sound waves (patterns of pressure) that occur at the same time can interact with each other. Thus if two waves are perfectly in phase (0° out of phase) their peak and minimum pressures coincide; hence they strongly add to each other's intensity. If the two waves are 180° out of phase,

Table 5-1   *Sound Pressure Levels (Intensity Levels) of Various Sound Sources*

Source	Sound Level (dB)
	200
Manned spacecraft launch (from 45 m)	180
Loudest rock band on record	160
Pain threshold (approximate)	140
Large jet motor (at 22 m)	120
Loudest human shout on record	111
Heavy auto traffic	100
Conversation (at about 1 m)	60
Quiet office	40
Soft whisper	20
Threshold of hearing	0

then when one reaches its minimum the other is reaching its maximum and they will serve to cancel out each other's effects.

Most of the everyday sounds to which we are exposed are more complex than the simple sine waves we have been discussing. Only a few sound sources, such as tuning forks or electronic instruments, produce "pure" sounds, which are composed of a simple sine wave variation of compression and rarefaction. Sounds produced by musical instruments, the human voice apparatus, cars, waterfalls, and so on have enormously complex cycles of compression and rarefaction. These complexities are due to the interaction of many different waves of different frequencies and phases. Such complex wave forms produce the TIMBRE of the sounds. Thus we can tell the difference between a trumpet, a clarinet, a piano, and a violin quite easily, because the wave forms they produce, even when playing the same musical "note," are very different. You can see this in Figure 5-2. Clearly, these are very complicated wave forms. The secret in describing them is to break each one up into a set of simpler sine waves, which then add together to produce

these more complicated wave forms. This method was invented by the French scientist Jean B. J. Fourier in the course of his studies

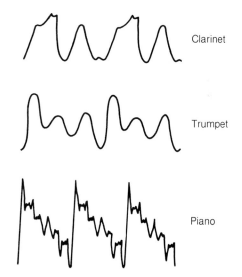

Clarinet

Trumpet

Piano

Figure 5-2.
Complex sound waves produced by three musical instruments.

of heat conduction. Fourier proved a mathematical theorem that states, in essence, that *any* wave form that is continuous and periodic can be represented as the sum of a series of simple sine waves with appropriate wavelengths, phases, and amplitudes. As it turns out, these simple waves have frequencies related to each other by simple mathematical ratios. Figure 5-3 shows an example of the decomposition of a complex wave form into its FOURIER COMPONENTS. Speech sounds may also be analyzed into their Fourier components, with results that are very useful for the understanding of speech perception (see Chapter 13). The ear itself seems to act in some ways as a sound analyzer, breaking down complex sounds into their individual components. This fact is known as OHM'S ACOUSTICAL LAW after the physicist George Ohm. You may demonstrate this effect for yourself using Demonstration Box 5-1.

Figure 5-3.
Fourier components (simple sine waves) of a complex sound wave.

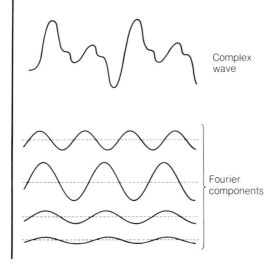

Complex wave

Fourier components

THE STRUCTURE OF THE EAR

Evolution and Anatomy of the Ear. The human ear is a complex piece of biological engineering. Yet biologists have traced its origins to simple organs in quite primitive animals. All ears seem to have evolved out of the sense of touch (see Figure 5-4). Whether primitive or advanced, they seem to be specializations of groups of cells with protruding hairs, much like those found on the skin of your arm. In fact we can use the skin to demonstrate a number of the phenomena that comprise human hearing. One of the first steps in the evolution of the modern mammalian ear is the "lateral line." This is a linear array of nerve endings in the skin of fish and some amphibians from which protrude jellylike masses in which are embedded sensory hairs. Often they are pigmented and form a horizontal line that runs the length of the animal's body. As the water moves or vibrates due to sound or other stimuli these sensory hairs bend. In a sense the fish does not so much "hear" sound as "feel" it.

Some types of fish have, in addition to the lateral line system, primitive internal ears that work on much the same principles as do human ears. It is believed that these internal ears evolved from a specialized, deeply sunken part of the lateral line system. In such fish, vibrations in the water cause similar vibrations in an air bladder in the fish's body cavity. From there the vibrations are passed on to a series of small bones, derived from some of the vertebrae and ribs, and then to a complex organ called the labyrinth, whose looping passages are filled with fluid. In this fluid are found (you guessed it) hairs that are sensitive to the movements of the liquid in

Demonstration Box 5-1:
Ohm's Acoustical Law

This demonstration is best done with a piano or a guitar. If neither are available take two glasses and fill one with water so that it makes a fairly high note when struck with a butter knife. The other should be relatively empty so that it produces a low note. Using piano, guitar, or glasses, sound a high note and then a low note. Now sound both simultaneously. Although the resultant chord is a complex sound, you can still pick out both the high and the low notes that have been combined. They do not lose their individual identities. A few moments practice will help you to resolve the sound. With enough practice a person can learn to separate as many as six or seven different harmonics (Fourier components) of a complex "clang." This separation of sound components in the ear is known as Ohm's Acoustical Law.

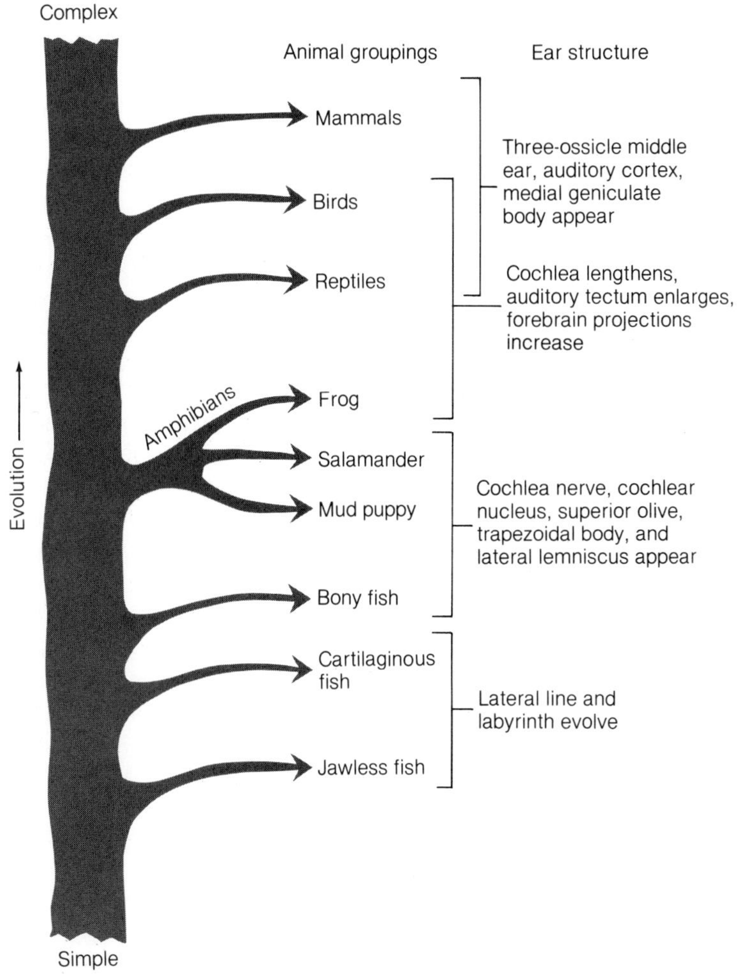
Complex
Animal groupings
Ear structure
Mammals
Birds
Reptiles
Amphibians
Frog
Salamander
Mud puppy
Bony fish
Cartilaginous fish
Jawless fish
Three-ossicle middle ear, auditory cortex, medial geniculate body appear
Cochlea lengthens, auditory tectum enlarges, forebrain projections increase
Cochlea nerve, cochlear nucleus, superior olive, trapezoidal body, and lateral lemniscus appear
Lateral line and labyrinth evolve
Evolution
Simple

Figure 5-4.
Major developments in the evolution of the ear.

the labyrinth caused by the vibrations picked up by the air bladder. These hairs send the auditory information to the fish's brain via sensory nerves. In all of its elements this system is quite similar to that found in man, even to the composition of the fluid in the labyrinth. A variety of other animals have ears that are considered to be outgrowths of these primitive versions. An interesting transition form is that of the frog. When it is a tadpole, it has a hearing apparatus similar to those of fishes. Sound waves are picked up by the lung and transmitted to the inner ear (the labyrinth) and from there to the brain. During metamorphosis into a frog, however, the ear changes. It develops an external membrane (the eardrum) that takes the place of the lung in the tadpole hearing system.

Another major component, which is common to all mammals and birds, is the COCHLEA. It also appears in the "crocodilian" reptiles. The cochlea is a specialized extension of the labyrinth that contains a long membrane covered with sensory cells from which (of course) hairs protrude. Its name (which means "shell") is derived from its coiled appearance in mammals.

All mammalian ears have the same basic parts, although they differ somewhat in proportions (with the elephant of course having one of the largest). There are also differences in sensitivity. Bats, dolphins, and dogs have extraordinarily keen hearing over a very wide range of frequencies. The ears of mammals differ from those of birds, reptiles, and fish in that mammalian ears typically have three small bones to transmit vibrations to the labyrinth, rather than the single bone found in these other species. Von Békésy (1960), in a series of detailed studies, established that all of these various types of ears function in a similar manner. He was able to link many of the performance differences with differences in the physical properties of the ears (such as in the length of the cochlea). Thus the human

ear, with which we will be concerned in the remainder of this chapter, is a part of a large family of roughly equivalent organs. This fact makes it possible to extend the results of studies of other mammalian ears to the human auditory system as well.

Let us now tackle the task of following a sound wave through the structures of the human ear, and trace the information pathways to the brain. The ear can be divided into three major parts, the OUTER, MIDDLE, and INNER ears. Figure 5-5 is a schematic representation of the human ear. The outer ear consists of the PINNA, which is the fleshy part of the ear visible from the outside. Only mammals have pinnae, and they are thought to function mainly to channel the sound waves into the AUDITORY CANAL. The pinna may also be involved in the localization of sound. Some mammals, such as bats and dogs, have highly mobile pinnae that allow them partially to select the direction from which sounds are received. At any rate, the sound waves that enter the auditory canal are channeled along it until they encounter the EARDRUM (or TYMPANUM). The eardrum vibrates in resonance with incoming sound waves, moving back and forth at a high rate for high-frequency sounds, and more slowly for low-frequency sounds. These vibratory movements are small. The shape of the auditory canal actually helps to concentrate the sound and to increase its force against the eardrum.

The middle ear consists of a set of three tiny bones (ossicles): the MALLEUS (hammer), the INCUS (anvil), and the STAPES (stirrup). These bones transmit the vibrations of the eardrum to the transducer mechanism located in the inner ear. There are some interesting and important subtleties of operation of this part of the ear that may explain why the complex system of ossicles evolved. First there is a problem associated with the fact that air is highly compressible and elas-

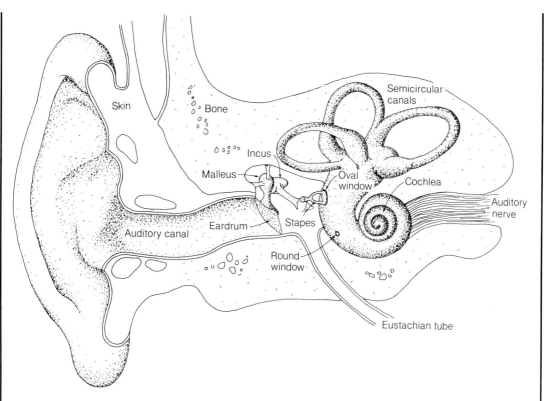

Figure 5-5.
The human ear (based upon Lindsay & Norman, 1977).

tic, while the fluid filling the inner ear is less compressible and elastic. As we mentioned above, the properties of sound depend greatly on the characteristics of the medium in which it occurs. The outer and middle ears together form an intricate system that amplifies the sound energy received from the air so that equivalent vibrations can be set up in the fluid medium of the inner ear. This process is called IMPEDENCE MATCHING. It is accomplished by three separate mechanisms in the ear. First, the auditory canal provides an approximate doubling of the energy in the sound wave. Second, the ossicles form a system of levers which again double the force of the vibrations at the eardrum. Finally, the difference between the size of the eardrum and that of the oval window upon which the stapes rests provides additional amplification. This is the result of the simple physical principle that an identical physical force applied to two surfaces of different areas yields a larger force per unit area on the smaller surface. The oval window is about $\frac{1}{30}$ of the area of the eardrum. In sum, sound waves are amplified by a factor of about 120 in their short journey through the ear.

A second important aspect of the operation of the middle ear is the ability of the ossicle system to vary the amplification it provides by means of a partial decoupling of the eardrum from the oval window. When sounds are in the normal range of intensity they cause the stapes to press directly on the fluid in the vestibular canal. For very intense sounds, however, the axis of rotation changes and the effect of the stapes on the fluid of the vestibular canal is greatly reduced (see von Békésy, 1960). In addition, a muscle attached to the stapes contracts via a neuromuscular reflex when intense low-frequency sounds strike the ear. This makes the ossicle system a less effective amplifier. Also, another muscle attached to the eardrum contracts to stiffen the eardrum and it thereby becomes less able to vibrate in sympathy with sounds in the canal. These mechanisms tend to protect the ear from long-lasting excessive stimulation.

The bones of the middle ear are surrounded by air. The pressure of this air is kept approximately the same as that of the atmosphere surrounding the observer by means of the EUSTACHIAN TUBES, which open into the back of the throat. The equalization of pressure on either side of the eardrum is important since a pressure differential would cause the membrane to bulge and stiffen, resulting in less responsiveness of the eardrum to the sound striking it. If the eustachian tubes were not present, the pressure on the inner side would gradually drop due to absorption of the air by the surrounding tissue. However, the eustachian tubes open briefly every time we swallow, which is quite often, allowing air to flow into the middle ear cavity from the mouth and lungs. This equalizes the air pressure on both sides of the eardrum.

The footplate of the stapes rests on a membrane called the OVAL WINDOW, which is the only part of the inner ear directly receiving sound vibrations. The oval window is at one end of one of the three canals that make up the COCHLEA. In man and other mammals the semicircular canals containing the organs of balance (see Chapter 6) make up the rest of the labyrinth. As can be seen from Figure 5-6, the cochlea consists of three canals that run down its length. Two of these, the VESTIBULAR and the TYMPANIC CANALS, are connected at the apex of the cochlea by an opening called the HELICOTREMA. They are filled with a fluid resembling saltwater. Since this fluid is relatively noncompressible, one needs a point where the pressure from the vibration of the stapes at the oval window is released. This release point is provided by the ROUND WINDOW, which is a membrane at the base of the cochlea that opens onto the middle ear. When a movement of the stapes causes the fluid to move away from the oval window, the round window can be seen to bulge. This indicates that some fluid has been displaced, and the resulting pressure change has been transmitted through the helicotrema into the tympanic canal and to the round window at its base. Of course this system allows any vibration of the stapes to set up similar vibrations in the internal fluid in the cochlea.

The third canal of the cochlea, the COCHLEAR DUCT, is relatively self-contained. It neither opens to the middle ear nor joins the vestibular or tympanic canals. It is formed by two membranes that run the length of the cochlea: REISSNER'S MEMBRANE and the BASILAR MEMBRANE. Together they form a rough triangle with the wall of the cochlea (Figure 5-6B). The cochlear duct is also filled with a different kind of fluid. Reissner's membrane is very thin (only two cells thick) and has no function other than to form one wall of the cochlear duct. The basilar membrane is the functionally important one. In man it is about 3 cm long and varies in width from about .08 mm near the base (where the windows are) to about .5 mm at the apex (where the helicotrema is). It is also about 100 times stiffer at the base than at the apex. A third membrane within the cochlear duct is also of importance. The TECTORIAL MEMBRANE extends into the cochlear duct from Reissner's membrane, and embedded in it are the hairs

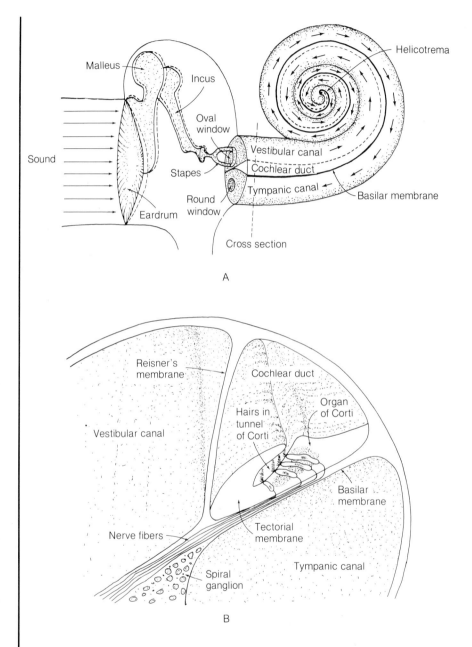

Figure 5-6.
Detailed structure of the inner ear (A), the ossicles connect the
eardrum to the coiled cochlea and (B) a cross section through
the cochlea reveals its three canals and the organ of Corti, the
actual auditory receptor (based upon Lindsay & Norman,
1977).

of the ORGAN OF CORTI. This is the part of the cochlear duct that accomplishes the final transduction of the mechanical energy of a sound wave into electrochemical energy interpretable by the nervous system. The organ of Corti rests on the basilar membrane along its entire length. It is composed of about 23,500 cells, which resemble the cells of the skin in that hairs protrude from them to embed themselves in the tectorial membrane. Each hair cell may have as many as 100 hairs portruding from it. Nerve fibers come from neurons of the SPIRAL GANGLION to the base of the hair cells. The axons of these spiral ganglion cells make up the auditory nerve, which is the neural pathway to the brain.

Wave Motion on the Basilar Membrane.
Sound waves cause the bones of the middle ear to vibrate, and the last of these bones (the stapes) transmits the vibration to the fluid in the cochlea. The pressure changes are transmitted virtually instantaneously (in one twenty-millionth of a second) to all parts of the cochlea, including the cochlear duct suspended inside the cochlea. Such pressure changes cause movement in the cochlear duct, and this stimulates the sensory cells of

the organ of Corti. There are two important aspects to the transduction of mechanical energy into electrochemical energy accomplished here. The first is the movements of the basilar membrane that result in the bending of the hair cells, and the second is the actual transduction mechanism itself. We will discuss each of these in turn.

The pressure changes of the cochlear fluid cause mechanical waves to travel down the basilar membrane from the base (near the oval window) to the apex. This wave is really a traveling bend or kink that moves down its length, much like what happens when you crack a whip. Figure 5-7 shows a schematic drawing of such a wave. The existence of these traveling waves was demonstrated by Georg von Békésy, who received the Nobel Prize for his work on the mechanics of the ear. The waves themselves travel very quickly, going from the base to the apex in about 2.5 msec. The wave is initiated first in the stiffer, narrower part of the basilar membrane, and travels toward the looser, broader part. The stiffer parts react first, and the reaction is progressively slower as the membrane becomes broader and looser.

The variations in elasticity and width of the basilar membrane are responsible for the

Figure 5-7.
A traveling wave on the basilar membrane.

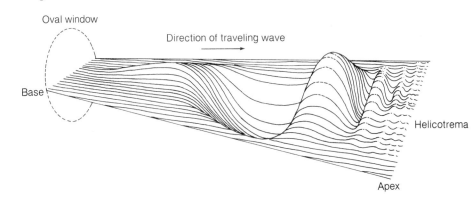

direction and the speed of the traveling wave. They are also responsible for differences in the size or amplitude of the wave. Von Békésy was able to demonstrate that the basilar membrane reacts differently to sound stimuli of different frequencies. Although the entire basilar membrane vibrates for any given stimulus, each different frequency of a sound wave has a different place along the basilar membrane at which the traveling wave reaches its maximum. Traveling waves caused by low-frequency sounds grow steadily in size as they travel toward the end of the membrane, and do not reach a maximum until they reach a place near the apex. High-frequency sounds, on the other hand, cause traveling waves that reach their maximum near the base of the basilar membrane, and then quickly dissipate, causing little deformation of the membrane near the apex. This is shown in Figure 5-8, which demonstrates the amplitude of the traveling wave at different places along the basilar membrane for pure tones of several different frequencies. This property of the basilar membrane provides a basis for the frequency analysis of complex tones, as well as for the more basic ability of distinguishing between pure tone stimuli of different frequencies. You can demonstrate the differences in the ability of low and high frequencies to travel down a membrane in Demonstration Box 5-2.

Mechanisms of Transduction. Thus far we have been discussing the ear as if it were a purely mechanical device. The organ of Corti, which rests on the basilar membrane, is the site of the transduction of sound energy from its mechanical form to the electrochemical energy that is the language of the nervous system (see the Special Topic in Chapter 4, entitled: What is the neural response?). As was mentioned above, the entire cochlear duct moves with the pressure changes in the fluid caused by the vibrations of the stapes. We have already pointed out the movements of the basilar membrane. However, it must also be noted that the tectorial membrane, in which the outer hair cells are embedded, moves as well but in a different manner. The

Figure 5-8.
A graph of the relative size of traveling waves on the basilar membrane for three different frequencies of tone. Notice that as the frequency increases the waves reach their maximum nearer the oval window and stapes.

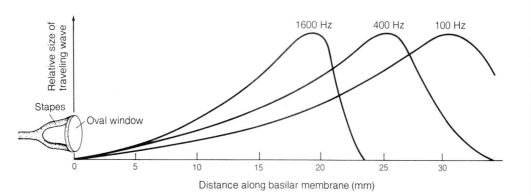

Demonstration Box 5-2:
The Skin as a Model for the Basilar Membrane

As we noted in the text, the basilar membrane is set into vibration by incoming sound stimuli. The points along the membrane that actually vibrate, however, depend upon the frequency of the sound input. Low frequencies tend to cause vibrations that travel the entire length of the membrane, while high frequencies are much more localized. You can easily demonstrate the frequency-specific nature of membrane vibration by using your forearm as a model of the basilar membrane; forearm skin has about the same resiliancy and elasticity as the basilar membrane. First, lightly rest your forearm against a surface that is vibrating at a high frequency (such as an electric shaver with nonrotating heads). Notice that the vibratory feeling (transmitted from the vibrations of the skin) covers only a small, localized region. Next rest your forearm lightly against a surface vibrating at a lower frequency (a washing machine is an excellent source of such vibrations). Notice that the lower frequency pulsations seem to travel the entire length of the arm, up to the elbow. In a similar fashion, lower sound frequencies induce waves that extend over the length of the basilar membrane, while higher frequency waves are more spatially restricted in their effects.

two membranes move laterally with respect to one another (see Figure 5-9). Since the outer hair cells are attached at their base to structures connected to the basilar membrane, and their hairs are embedded in the tectorial membrane, a shearing force is applied to the hairs. This causes the hair cells to bend, and it is thought that this bending of the hairs is the final mechanical step in the transduction process. The bending is thought somehow to produce electrical and/or chemical changes in hair cells that in turn trigger electrical activity (spike potentials) in the neurons of the spiral ganglion.

The actual process by which the neural message is generated from this mechanical action is not fully understood. In the most recent theories (see Gulick, 1971; Brown, 1975) it is thought that the forces acting on the hairs lead (via chemical action around the top of the hair cells) to a hypopolarization or hyperpolarization (difference in electrical charge on the two sides of the cell membrane). This in turn causes an electrical current to flow, releasing transmitter substances that trigger the spike potentials. An interesting alternative theory has been offered by Spoendlin (1968). He proposes that the sensory hairs themselves have piezoelectric properties (the ability to directly generate electricity from mechanical deformations).

Figure 5-9.
Bending of the outer hair cells as a result of movement of the basilar and tectorial membranes.

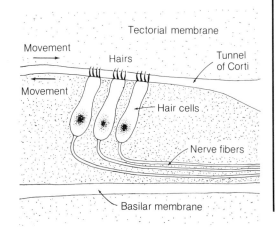

Thus the bending may produce electrical activity directly, rather than through chemical processes. However, for the time being it is sufficient to say that the bending of the hair cells stimulates neural activity in the auditory nerve.

ELECTRICAL ACTIVITY OF THE AUDITORY NERVE

We have followed sound energy to the point at which it is converted into patterns of spike potentials in the auditory nerve. From this point onward we can use the same techniques of electrophysiological recording that we used to investigate the visual system, in order to study the neural processing of auditory information. When electrodes are inserted into single axons in the auditory nerve, we can record the electrical activity of individual neurons in response to a variety of sounds.

As a first guess, one might suppose that the auditory system would be mainly responsive only to simple physical aspects of the sound, namely frequency and intensity. Actually some cells seem to mimic visual processing in that they are quite selective and respond to complex aspects of the stimulus. Thus when we record the responses of single axons in the auditory nerve, we find that some respond only to complex noises and are completely unresponsive to pure tones. Others respond only to brief transient sounds such as clicks. Still others respond to a wide variety of different frequencies of pure tones. Apparently, auditory encoding is very complex even at this peripheral level. Thus in much the same way that we found selective analysis taking place early in the visual system, similar selec-

tivity seems to be characteristic of audition.

Although neurons possessing a great many different types of response characteristics seem to be present in the auditory nerve, there is one type of neuron that is extremely common. Figure 5-10 shows the response (recorded from a microelectrode) of a typical neuron of this type. The neuron responds to pure tones of reasonably long durations (1 sec or so) with an increased rate of firing. While it responds to pure tones over a wide range of frequencies, the vigor of its response differs for different frequencies. The curve displayed in Figure 5-10 is called a TUNING CURVE because it exhibits a single maximum rate of firing to a particular frequency of sound wave (about 400 Hz in the example of Figure 5-10). This neuron is said to be "tuned" to that frequency. Other neurons are tuned to other frequencies, and the range of frequencies to which neurons are tuned corresponds roughly to the range of frequencies that an animal can hear.

A simple explanation for this type of tuning curve is to assume that the hair cells from which a given tuned neuron collect information are all in the same area of the basilar membrane, and that the rate of firing induced in the neuron is proportional to the amplitude of movement of the basilar membrane at that

Figure 5-10.
Tuning curve of a typical neuron in the auditory nerve (from Lindsay & Norman, 1977).

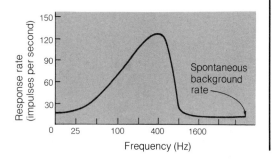

point. The obtained tuning curve is what would then be predicted from the fact that a given part of the basilar membrane moves with different amplitudes depending upon the frequency of the sound stimulus. If you will look back to Figure 5-8, you will see that this follows from the fact that the traveling waves on the basilar membrane have maximum amplitudes at different places depending upon sound frequency. Pick a particular location on the basilar membrane (say at about 20 mm from the stapes) and observe how the amplitude of the traveling wave varies as frequency varies. The tuning curves, then, seem to reflect both the spatial distribution of the hair cells along the basilar membrane (and the corresponding spatial distribution of the dendritic endings of the auditory neurons) and the relative amounts of membrane activity caused by sounds of different frequencies.

The thresholds (minimum intensity that stimulates a neuron to fire above its back-ground rate) of different tuned neurons that are most sensitive to the same frequency may vary over a range of about 20 dB (see Evans, 1975). Also, there is a wide range of thresholds over all of the fibers in the auditory nerve for a stimulus of any particular frequency because of the fact that they are tuned to different frequencies. Thus for a sound of any given intensity and frequency, there might be a fairly large number of neurons responding with a wide range of firing rates. This situation is represented hypothetically in Figure 5-11. Stimuli of different frequencies tend to cause different populations of neurons to fire above their background rates. As the intensity of the stimulus is increased, neurons already firing increase their firing rate, while still others begin to fire for the first time. These patterns of neural activity in the auditory nerve provide a basis for the transmission of information regarding the frequency and intensity of the stimulus to higher areas of the brain.

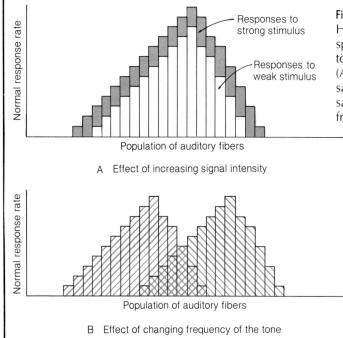

A   Effect of increasing signal intensity

B   Effect of changing frequency of the tone

Figure 5-11.
Hypothetical distributions of response rates for populations of auditory nerve fibers firing in response to (A) weak versus strong stimuli of the same frequency and (B) stimuli of same strength but different frequencies.

Frequency seems to be indicated by *which* neurons are firing, while intensity seems to be roughly indicated by *how many* are firing, and *how fast* they are firing.

At low frequencies of sound the responses seem to be directly related to the physical stimulus. Thus if the frequency of the stimulus is 100 Hz, the firing in the auditory nerve will tend to be at approximately this frequency. Any given individual neuron does not necessarily fire at exactly 100 Hz. Individual neurons seem to fire at fixed points in the cycle of the sound wave. For example, one neuron may fire at every second peak of the wave (and thus at 50 Hz) while another may fire at every fifth peak (and thus at 20 Hz). For a great many neurons firing out of phase with one another there will tend to be a spike (or several) occurring at every peak of the wave (and thus at 100 Hz). This ability of the auditory nerve to follow the frequency of the stimulating sound wave (up to about 4000 Hz) has been a central component of several theories of pitch perception (e.g., Wever, 1970) that will be discussed in Chapter 9.

THE AUDITORY PATHWAYS

Figure 5-12 diagrams the more important pathways taken by auditory information in the brain. The auditory pathways are somewhat more complex than the visual pathways. First, as can be seen in this figure, the bipolar cells of the spiral ganglion, which send dendritic processes to the organ of Corti, send their axons (which make up the auditory nerve) to both the DORSAL and VENTRAL parts of the COCHLEAR NUCLEUS. This is located in the lower back part of the brain. The cells of the dorsal cochlear nucleus (where the majority of the auditory nerve fibers termi-

nate) send their axons to the SUPERIOR OLIVE on the opposite side of the brain, while those of the ventral cochlear nucleus (the minority) send their axons to the superior olive on the same side of the brain. Thus most of the information from the right ear is processed first by the left side of the brain, and vice–versa. The cells of the superior olives send most of their fibers to the INFERIOR COLLICULI (located just below the superior colliculi, which we discussed under visual processing in Chapter 4). At the level of the inferior colliculus there is considerable fiber crossing from one side of the brain to the other, so that both inferior colliculi have full information about what is going on in the other inferior colliculus.

Most cells in the inferior colliculi go on through the MEDIAL GENICULATE and up to the cortex, although a few go to the superior colliculus as well. Since the superior colliculus has been implicated in visual localization, this seems to be an understandable projection. Sound information must have an opportunity to be related to visual data to yield a more complete "picture" of space. From the medial geniculate the fibers project to the TEMPORAL CORTEX, which is often called the PRIMARY AUDITORY PROJECTION AREA or Brodman's area 41.

Electrical Activity of the Lower Auditory Centers. We already discussed the response patterns found in the fibers of the auditory nerve. Although some of them respond only to clicks or other non-pure-tone stimuli, the majority of the fibers are axons from "tuned" neurons. These neurons respond to a range of frequencies of pure-tone sounds, but each has a "preferred" band of frequencies that produces a maximum response. We find similar "tuned" neurons in the cochlear nucleus, superior olive, inferior colliculus, and medial geniculate. However, as we get higher into the auditory system the tuning becomes more

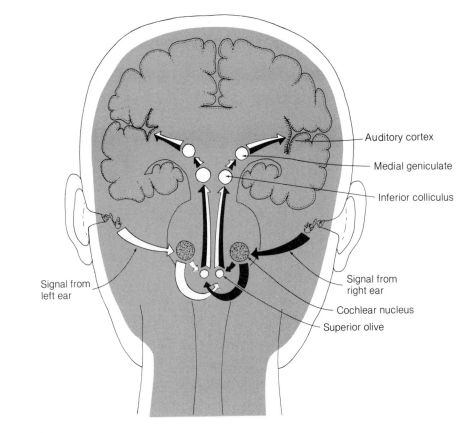

Figure 5-12.
Major auditory pathways in the brain (from Lindsay & Norman, 1977).

precise, and the band of frequencies to which the neurons respond becomes smaller.

In addition to the finer tuning in higher cells, a number of complex neural response patterns appear. When Pfeiffer (1966) recorded from single neurons of adult cats at the cochlear nucleus, he found a variety of different types of neural responses to a simple tone. ON NEURONS gave a burst of responses immediately after the onset of the tone burst and then responded no further to the tone, whether it was of long or short duration. PAUSER NEURONS exhibited a similar burst of firing at the onset of a tone; this was followed

by a pause and then a weaker sustained response until the tone was turned off. CHOPPERS gave repeated bursts of firing followed by short pauses, with the vigor of successive bursts decreasing. PRIMARYLIKE NEURONS gave an initial vigorous burst of firing when the tone was turned on, then the firing rate decayed to a lower level that was sustained for the duration of the tone. Both choppers and pausers showed somewhat different responses to longer duration stimuli, but these were related to their typical patterns.

In addition to these response patterns, there seems to be a response analogous to the

OFF RESPONSES observed in the visual system. These cells actually reduce their response rate below their spontaneous activity level at the onset of the tone, and then give a burst of activity at its offset. An interesting variation of this is the presence of "tuned" cells that reduce their activity level when a stimulus that is not the optimally tuned one is present. A more complex example of this response pattern is demonstrated in the work of Whitfield and Purser and Aitkin and Prain (see Webster & Aitkin, 1975). They have described cells in the medial geniculate with "W-shaped" receptive patterns. That is, these neurons respond above their background rate of firing to a particular "best" frequency, and below the background rate for frequencies close to that frequency on either side. The firing rate gradually returns to background level for frequencies progressively more removed from the "best" frequency and its surrounding "worst" frequencies. These cells resemble on-center, off-surround cells found in the visual system (see Chapter 4). This type of correspondence between properties of neurons in different sensory systems is very common, although each sensory system also displays coding principles idiosyncratic to its own stimulus modality. We are dealing with basically the same kinds of neural units whatever the input, and it is not surprising to find considerable similarity among the different sensory systems at the electrophysiological level.

Because different points along the basilar membrane vibrate most strongly for various different frequencies of sounds, we can refer to the response of the basilar membrane as TONOTOPIC (from the Greek *tono* for tone and *topus* for place). This means that we are actually representing sound frequencies with a sort of spatial code. This spatial encoding seems to be preserved to some extent at other points in the auditory system. In the cochlear nucleus of the cat, Rose, Galambos, and

Hughes (1960) recorded the responses of single cells to pure tones as a microelectrode was moved through the tissue. As the electrode was pushed along, the frequency of stimulus that gave the best response (highest rate of firing) changed systematically, going from high near one edge of the nucleus to low near the other. This indicated that the cells were arranged in an orderly spatial layout, with cells tuned to similar frequencies lying closer together in the nucleus than those tuned to different frequencies. Similar tonotopic arrangements of cells have been reported for other noncortical nuclei, although evidence has been difficult to obtain because of the extreme complexity of the anatomy of the system (see Gulick, 1971; Webster & Aitkin, 1975). In general, however, we can conclude that the tonotopic organization of the basilar membrane is preserved in the electrical responses of the neurons of the auditory system from the lowest to the highest levels. Thus even in the cortex we find cells that respond to high frequencies clustered in some areas, and cells that respond to low frequencies clustered in other areas. You can see this clustering in Figure 5-13 (where H marks high-frequency response areas and L marks low-frequency response areas). This fact is very important for the plausibility of the idea that the frequency of sound waves is coded mainly by *place*, both on the basilar membrane and in the central auditory system.

THE AUDITORY CORTEX

Studies of nonhuman animals have provided us with the bulk of the information we now have on the physiology of sensory systems. For the lower levels of analysis we can be

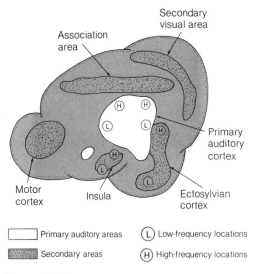

Primary auditory areas
Secondary areas
(L) Low-frequency locations
(H) High-frequency locations

Figure 5-13.
Auditory areas of the cat cortex.

fairly confident that the generalizability of the concepts to the human is straightforward and generally valid. However, when we begin to discuss the cortex it must be realized that we are on shakier ground. The human cortex is more complex than those of most of the common experimental animals (such as the cat, which seems to be the preferred subject of such studies), so that generalization of findings to humans is more tenuous. Nonetheless, animal studies have yielded a significant amount of useful information on the activity of the auditory cortex. Figure 5-13 shows the wide variety of areas on the cat cortex that have been shown to be responsive to sound stimuli. In this chapter we will be mainly concerned with the primary auditory areas, but a large number of nonauditory areas respond to sound stimuli, especially association and visual areas. Presumably, similar responses occur in the human cortex, especially in the speech centers and general association areas.

Cells in the auditory cortex exhibit a variety of complex responses to sound stimuli. In the approximately 60% of the cells that respond to pure tones, there occur *on* responses, *off* responses, *on–off* responses, and more general *ex*citatory and *inhibitory* responses (see Figure 5-14). These, of course, resemble the response patterns of cells in the visual system. The other 40% of the cells seem to respond selectively to more complex sounds, including noise bursts, clangs, or clicks.

Another complex type of neuron found in the auditory cortex of the cat is the FREQUENCY SWEEP DETECTOR (Whitfield, 1967). These cells respond only to sounds that change frequency in a specific direction and range. Some cells respond only to increases but not to decreases in frequency in the same range. Others respond to decreases in frequency but not to increases. A third type responds only to increases in frequency for low-frequency tones, and only to decreases for high-frequency tones. Since these types of stimuli are often encountered in everyday speech and music, such detectors, if present in humans, could have an important role in speech and music perception. Certainly they have obvious utility for the cat, whose "war cries" and "love calls" consist of just these types of sounds. These cortical neurons respond to sound patterns in much the same way that visual cortical neurons respond selectively to light patterns. There are even auditory analogs to the "grandmother detectors" we talked about in Chapter 4. Swarbrick and Whitfield (1972) found cells in the auditory cortex of the squirrel monkey that are sensitive only to the vocalizations of other squirrel monkeys, while Funkenstein *et al.* (1971) demonstrated that some of these cells are unresponsive to the presentation of simple tones, although they respond vigorously to the presentation of extremely complex vocalizations.

Such response specificity opens up some interesting experimental possibilities. For in-

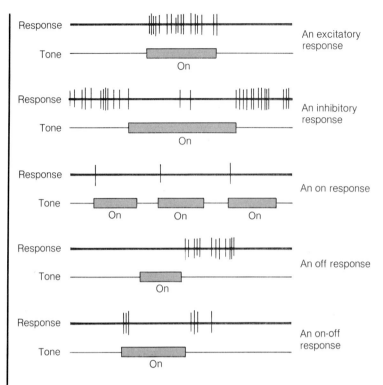

Response — An excitatory
Tone — response
On

Response — An inhibitory
Tone — response
On

Response — An on response
Tone
On   On   On

Response — An off response
Tone
On

Response — An on-off
Tone — response
On

Figure 5-14.
Different types of responses to
pure tones recorded from
neurons in the auditory cortex
of the cat (from Whitfield, I. C.
The Auditory Pathways. London: Arnold, 1967).

stance, if we could fatigue the cells that respond to a given sound quality we might expect individuals to become less sensitive to
this particular aspect of the stimulus. Eimas
and Corbit (1973) did exactly this. They presented observers with the speech sound "ta"
several hundred times in very quick succes-
sion. They reasoned that this would fatigue
neurons that selectively respond to this
speech sound, and if so, the observer should
become less sensitive to "ta" sounds. To verify this, observers were presented with a
sound that was ambiguous in that it could be
interpreted as either "ta" or "da." This ambiguity implied that the population of
neurons selectively tuned to "ta" and that
tuned to the sound "da" were being activated. For observers in whom the "ta" population had been fatigued or adapted, rela-

tively more of the neurons that respond to
"da" should have been active when this ambiguous stimulus was presented (simply because the "ta" neurons were too tired to respond). Thus these individuals should have
been more likely to hear the sound as "da."
This was the result that was actually obtained. The importance of such psychophysical findings lies in the fact that they begin to
translate some of the neurophysiological responses into predictable patterns of perceptual behavior. We are spending the time to
understand the physiology of the auditory
system so that we can better understand how
individuals hear. Thus the ultimate test of any
hypotheses about the significance of neural
encoding or analysis patterns must rest upon
data based upon an individual's actual auditory percepts.

SPECIAL TOPIC: SOUND PRESSURE AND DECIBELS

The intensity of a sound wave is related to its PRESSURE AMPLITUDE. This is a measure of the degree of compression or rarefaction in the air, or other medium, at the peaks or valleys of the sound wave. For a sine wave in air, the pressure amplitude is the maximum amount by which the wave causes the pressure (force per unit area) to differ from the normal atmospheric pressure (which is about 1,000,000 dynes/cm²). The maximum pressure *variation* the ear can tolerate is about 280 dynes/cm² above atmospheric pressure, whereas the minimum pressure variation detectable is of the order of .0002 dynes/cm² (above atmospheric). For these threshold-level sound waves, the air molecules are displaced (on average) about .0000000001 cm, which is about $\frac{1}{10}$ the diameter of an average air molecule. Obviously the ear is an extremely sensitive organ with a broad response range.

In order to conveniently express this wide range of sounds to which the ear is sensitive, we express *sound pressure level* (*SPL*) in terms of how many powers of 10 (which is simply the logarithm) one *SPL* is greater than another one. If one *SPL* is one million times greater than another (10^6 times greater), we say that it is 12 (2×6) bels greater. Since a bel is a rather large unit relative to normal hearing levels, the most common unit used is the decibel. The actual formula for a decibel is

$$\text{Number of dB} = 20 \log (P/P_0)$$

where P is the *SPL* we wish to measure, and P_0 is the standard reference level, which is the average value of the threshold for sound at 1000 Hz (.0002 dynes/cm²). Decibels are particularly suited to measure *SPL*, since they compress the large range of possible pressures into more manageable units. In addition, since the scale is logarithmic, it more closely follows the human sensation scale (as we noted in Chapter 3).

6
The Chemical
and Mechanical Senses

". . . I guessed vaguely from my mother's signs and from the hurrying to and fro in the house that something unusual was about to happen, so I went to the door and waited on the steps. The afternoon sun penetrated the mass of honeysuckle that covered the porch, and fell on my upturned face. My fingers lingered almost unconsciously on the familiar leaves and blossoms which had just come forth to greet the sweet southern spring. I did not know what the future held of marvel or surprise for me. . . We walked down the path to the well-house, attracted by the fragrance of the honeysuckle with which it was covered. Someone was drawing water and my teacher placed my hand under the spout. As the cold stream gushed over one hand . . ." (Keller, 1931, pp. 21–22).

In reading the passage above, what can you say of the person who wrote it? Did it occur to you that all of those vivid sensory impressions came from someone who was completely blind and deaf? It takes someone like a Helen Keller to point out that the so-called "minor senses" (touch, taste, and smell) can provide us with a rich and accurate picture of the world. Humans, primates, and birds are somewhat unique in their reliance on the visual and auditory sensory systems. Most other animals are equipped with less effective visual and auditory organs, or none at all. However, they perform amazing feats through the use of a variety of other sensory systems, which are often much more sensitive and discriminative than ours. In this chapter, we will explore the physiology of some of these "other" sensory systems, including *smell, taste,* the *skin senses,* the *kinesthetic* senses, the *vestibular* senses, and the sensation of *pain*.

THE GUSTATORY (TASTE) SENSE

Life presumably began in a bowl of chemical soup (the sea). Various substances suspended or dissolved in water were important to the survival of primitive living things. Some substances provided food, some gave warning, some caused destruction. The most primitive, one-celled organisms clearly could not use anything like visual or auditory sensory systems, which require large numbers of specialized cells. They must have relied, and still do, on chemical or mechanical interactions with their environment. For such simple organisms, the only contact with the outside world came from chemical and mechanical events that affected the cell's outer membrane. This was the first, primitive, "sensory system" to be used by living things. As life evolved, multicelled animals could afford a "division of labor" among the many cells composing an animal's body. Specialized cells were grouped together to pick up chemical information from the surroundings. For example, fish have pits on the surfaces of their bodies lined with cells responsive to a variety of chemical and mechanical stimuli. Some insects and other invertebrates have these cells located on their antennae.

At first, in the sea, there was little differentiation between taste and smell. All substances were dissolved or suspended in the same substance, water. When life moved on to land, however, it became necessary to have different cells to respond to substances suspended in air. The "taste" system that had been already developed would only suffice for substances dissolved in water (such as food dissolved in saliva, which is mostly water). Thus taste became a "close-up" sense, which provided the last check on the acceptability of food. Smell in turn evolved as a distance sense, and as we shall see later, may be based on an entirely different principle of animal–environment interaction.

Taste Stimuli and Receptors. The physical stimuli for the taste system are substances that can be dissolved in water. As is usual for physical stimuli, the amount of a substance present is related to the intensity of the taste that we experience. However, what property (or collection of properties) gives rise to the various different taste qualities is still unknown. There are a variety of possibilities, such as the size of the individual molecules of the substance, how a molecule breaks apart when it is dissolved in water, or how the molecule interacts with cell membranes. Unfortunately, just what aspects of the stimulating substance cause its characteristic taste will be known only when we agree on the basic dimensions of taste. This is still a controversial topic, as we will see in Chapter 10.

There is, however, general agreement that there are at least four primary taste qualities: *sweet, salty, sour,* and *bitter.* These taste qualities have been connected to some general types of molecules. A sweet taste is associated mainly with so-called "organic" molecules, which are made up mostly of carbon, hydrogen, and oxygen in different combinations. These are commonly called sugars, alcohols, and so forth. Other sweet substances like saccharine are also organic chemicals, but they are quite different from "natural" sweeteners, such as sugars, in their molecular structure. Bitter taste is closely related to sweet taste. Many substances that

taste sweet when present in small amounts taste bitter when present in large amounts (e.g., saccharine). Also, a number of chemicals containing nitrogen (such as strychnine, caffeine, quinine, and nicotine) taste bitter. A salty taste is elicited by molecules that, when dissolved in water, break into two electrically charged parts called *ions.* For example, common table salt is composed of two atoms, one sodium and one chlorine. When dissolved in water, the atoms break apart and go their separate ways. The sodium atom is now a positively charged ion, and the chlorine atom is a negatively charged ion. The ratio of the weights of these positively and negatively charged ions may be related to how salty a substance tastes. When the ratio is relatively low, substances taste salty. A high ratio is associated with substances that taste bitter (see Wyburn, Pickford, & Hirst, 1964). In very low concentrations, salts tend to taste sweet. Finally, we have the sour taste. Sour substances also break up into two parts when in solution, but they are usually acids (such as hydrochloric, sulphuric, acetic, and nitric acid) rather than salts. These substances all have hydrogen as the positively charged ion. The behavior of the hydrogen seems to be directly related to the sourness of such acids, but other properties must also be important since most acids taste sweet or bitter instead of sour. Thus while we can relate some aspects of chemical stimuli to the tastes they produce, this relationship is not simple. Any given taste is probably the result of the interaction of several different properties of the physical stimulus with the properties of the receptor cells.

The major receptors for taste are groups of cells called TASTE BUDS. These are located in little bumps on the tongue called PAPILLAE.

Although there are three different types of papillae, there is no simple relationship between their locations and the sensitivity to different taste sensations. There are also some taste receptors scattered over parts of the mouth other than the tongue, but they do not appear to play a major role (except perhaps in wine tasting and other gourmet activities). Figure 6-1A shows how the taste buds are distributed within one kind of papilla. Each taste bud consists of several receptor cells (perhaps up to 30) arranged like the closed petals of a flower (Figure 6-1B). There are about 10,000 taste buds in your mouth when you are young, but their number decreases with age.

Within each taste bud, the individual cells are continually developing. Each cell has a life span of only a few days so that the composition of the taste bud is continually changing, with some immature cells (around the outside), some mature cells (near the inside), and some dying cells always present (Beidler & Smallman, 1965). No one knows why these cells have such a short life span; perhaps it is because they are somehow damaged when they respond to substances in the mouth. Each taste cell in the taste bud is a leaflike cell that resembles a skin cell, from which it probably evolved. From the top end of each cell there is a slender projection that lies near an opening onto the surface of the tongue called a TASTE PORE. It is thought that the actual reception mechanism for taste is located in these slender processes, but it is at present unknown exactly how the mechanism operates. Presumably, some aspect of the stimulating substance causes a change in the cell wall of the taste cell, which in turn causes the cell to generate electrical energy and stimulate the nerve cell(s) connected to it. Since there are several different taste qualities, there may well be several specialized receptor processes that encode the taste information.

Neural Responses in Taste. Neural fibers from the taste buds run from the tongue to a

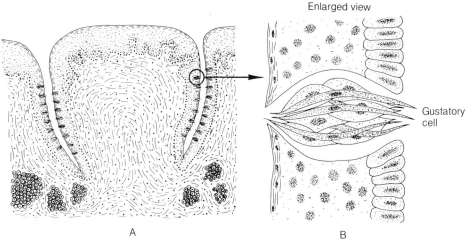

Enlarged view

Gustatory
cell

A   B

Figure 6-1.
(A) A typical papilla with taste buds (one is circled). (B) Enlarged picture of a single taste bud (from Wyburn *et al.,* 1964).

nucleus in the brainstem (the lower back part of the brain) via three different large nerves. From the nucleus in the brainstem, taste information is carried to the thalamus, and from there to the area of the sensory cortex that receives information from the face region.

As in vision and audition, most of our knowledge of the electrical activity of the taste system has come from many studies on nonhuman animals. It seems clear from a variety of studies that taste fibers respond to increasing intensity (concentration) of the stimulus by increasing their overall rate of firing. One study actually used 17 human subjects for direct recording (Diamant, Funakoshi, Strom, & Zotterman, 1963). One of the taste pathways from the front of the tongue had to be cut during a certain kind of ear operation. The recording of electrical activity in response to taste stimuli was made from this nerve. The data from these patients show that the amount of neural response grows as the logarithm of the intensity of the stimulus (in this case, table salt). Thus in taste, as in vision and audition, the code for intensity seems to be the overall amount of firing of all of the sensory fibers.

How is taste *quality* encoded? At first it was thought that there would prove to be "sweet receptors" and "salt receptors." However, every receptor cell seems to respond to all of the four basic kinds of taste stimuli (Kimura & Beidler, 1961). In addition, many studies have found that every taste fiber in the nerves leading away from the tongue responds to any sort of taste stimulus, although different rates of response may appear for different stimuli. The same sort of general responsiveness has been found in the brainstem nucleus mentioned above and in the thalamus as well (Doetsch, Ganchrow, Nelson, & Erickson, 1969; Scott & Erickson, 1971).

Actually, there is no theoretical need for specialized taste receptors as long as the various neural units have different stimulus-specific response rates. If this condition is met then the code for taste quality could be an ACROSS-FIBER PATTERN of neural activity (Erickson & Schiffman, 1975). Figure 6-2 shows how this might work. Notice that although all of the fibers respond to all taste inputs to some extent, the pattern of firing of the population of fibers changes for each quality. Erickson (1963) was actually able to show such across-fiber pattern differences. These patterns become somewhat less distinct in the thalamus (Doetsch et al., 1969; Scott & Erickson, 1971). It is likely that some recoding of the taste information may take place in the cortex. There is some evidence that there may actually be specific cortical cells that give an "on" response to some taste stimuli and an "off" response to others, in much the same way that there are feature-specific cells in the visual cortex (Funakoshi, Kasahara, Yamamoto, & Kawamura, 1972).

THE OLFACTORY (SMELL) SENSE

When we have a bad head-cold food seems tasteless, and yet it is our nasal passages that are most affected by the cold, not our mouths where the taste receptors are located. It seems that a major part of the experienced "taste" of food and drink is related to the *odor* of the substance. When our nasal passages are clogged with mucus our olfactory (smell) receptors cannot function properly. This affects both our ability to smell and to

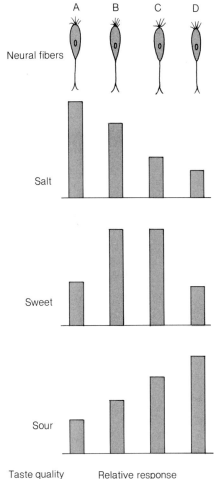

Neural fibers

Salt

Sweet

Sour

Taste quality   Relative response

Figure 6-2.
A schematic representation of across-fiber patterns encoding taste quality. Notice that all of the neural fibers respond to each of the three stimuli, but not each to the same extent. You could easily tell what stimulus had been presented by simply recognizing the across-fiber pattern.

"taste," since much of the richness and subtlety of our experiences with food and drink come from their odor.

As we mentioned in the previous section, organisms that live in water presumably do not need a special odor sense, since all substances with which they interact would have to be dissolved in water. But life on land can exploit the fact that molecules of various types are continually floating about in the air. These molecules carry information about the organisms or objects from which they have been detached. For instance, we leave molecules of ourselves on the ground and in the air near the ground whenever we take a walk. Insects and some higher animals secrete volatile chemicals (pheromones) whose molecules waft through the air to other members of the species. The specific molecules secreted can carry messages about fear and sexual availability, among other things. Species that possess sensory systems that respond to these low concentrations of molecules in the air can take advantage of this information, hence improving their ability to survive.

Smell Stimuli and Receptors. What aspects of a molecule give it the quality of evoking the sensation of smell? First, it must come from a volatile substance (one that has a gaseous state at ordinary temperatures—in other words something that can evaporate) since air currents carry the molecules to the smell receptors in the nose. However, the most volatile substances do not necessarily smell the strongest. Water, which has a high volatility, has no smell at all, while musk, which has a low volatility, is a very powerful odorant. Musk is used in making some of our most expensive perfumes.

In general, any molecules may be described as having a specific size, weight, shape, or *vibration frequency.* This last property has to do with the fact that atoms in a given molecule are often not held firmly in place, but move around in a characteristic pattern, at predictable speeds that are different for different substances. Wright (1977) has suggested that the vibration frequency may be the critical property that determines the quality of a smell. We can measure the vibration frequency of a molecule by determining how infrared light (wavelength longer than 700 nm) is absorbed by the substance. Such measurements have turned out to be quite useful in predicting smell responses to various substances. Substances that have similar infrared absorption characteristics (vibrate at the same frequencies) seem to have similar smells (Wright & Burgess, 1975).

Another possible critical property of smell molecules is the shape of the molecule (Amoore, Johnston & Rubin, 1964). This is an old suggestion, but in its most modern form it is supposed that there are holes of different shapes on the receptor surface, and only molecules of a certain "shape" can fit into these holes (as a key fits into a lock). This changes the state of the cell membrane and produces a neural response. It seems likely that several different properties of odorous molecules play a part in determining the quality of our sensory response to them.

The receptor cells that interact with the smell stimuli are located in a relatively small area in the upper nasal passages (see Figure 6-3). This area is called the OLFACTORY EPITHELIUM or "smell skin." The actual receptor cells are oval in shape. Each sends a long extension (called the OLFACTORY ROD) toward the surface of the olfactory epithelium. In addition, the receptors send their axons toward the brain. The olfactory rod of the receptor cell reaches up toward the surface of the epithelium, where it expands to form a knob. From this knob protrude a number of OLFACTORY CILIA, which are embedded in mucus secreted by a set of special glands found nowhere else in the nasal passages.

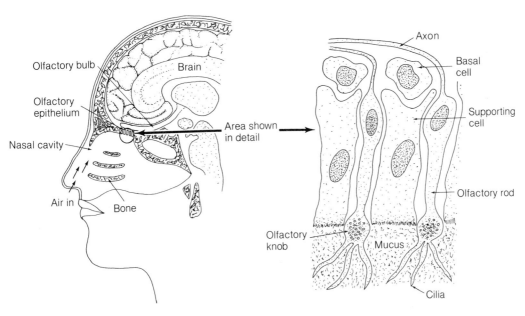

Figure 6-3.
Anatomy of the olfactory system and a detail of the structure of the olfactory epithelium.

These cilia are probably the receptor elements that actually make contact with the smell stimulus. Both the number of cilia per receptor and the total number of receptors seem to be correlated with olfactory sensitivity. Animals that have more receptors and more cilia per receptor have much keener senses of smell than do humans. Humans are at the lower end of the scale of smell sensitivity. For example, a dog has about 100 million receptors as opposed to 5 million in the human. Similarly a dog will have 100–150 cilia per receptor as opposed to our paltry 6–8 cilia (Brown, 1975).

As is the case with the other senses, the mechanism by which the stimulus molecules cause an electrical response in the receptors of the olfactory epithelium is still a mystery. There are two major theories. The LOCK-AND-KEY THEORY maintains that variously shaped molecules fit into holes on the receptor membrane (probably on the cilia or the knobs from which they protrude) like a key into a lock. When a molecule fits into a hole, a change in the structure of the cell membrane results, perhaps allowing electrically charged substances into or out of the cell and generating an electrical current (Amoore et al., 1964).

The VIBRATION THEORY maintains that the stimulus molecule ruptures certain chemical bonds in the cell membrane, causing the release of stored-up energy, which in turn generates an electrical current. Which bonds are ruptured in which cells depends on the unique vibrational frequency of each stimulus molecule. Again, the interaction should take place in the cilia (Wright, 1977).

One difference between these views is that in the lock-and-key theory, once a stimulus molecule served as a key for a particular lock it would be stuck there. In the vibration theory a single stimulus molecule could bounce along over the olfactory epithelium like a rubber ball, having broken chemical bonds in cell after cell (and thus causing them to give a neural response) without being detained by any of them. This mechanism is consistent with the high sensitivity of the olfactory sense, which can respond to the presence of only a few molecules of a volatile substance. For example, a dog can detect butyric acid (contained in sweat) at a concentration of 1 g spread throughout the entire volume of air above a city of the size of Boston, up to a height of 100 m (Dröscher, 1971). A difficulty of the vibration theory, however, is that the stimulus molecule may have to penetrate the mucous covering in order to contact the receptor cell. This would make it unlikely that a single molecule could move very far over the receptor surface. This is no problem at all for the lock-and-key theory.

Neural Responses in Smell. The axons of the receptor cells form the OLFACTORY NERVE, which passes through a bone at the top of the nasal cavity. It goes straight to the OLFACTORY BULB, which is located in front of and below the main mass of the brain (see Figure 6-3). In the olfactory bulb, the axons of the receptors and the dendrites of other cells form complex clusters of connections. One type of cell seems to send axons directly to the primary sensory cortex for smell, which is located on the temporal lobe of the cortex. Another type of cell sends axons to a variety of lower brain centers, as well as to the smell cortex. The number of fibers leaving the olfactory bulb is *much* smaller than the number entering it, so presumably many receptor cells contribute to the activity of each of the cells in the olfactory bulb and later centers (Allison, 1953). The major route of information from the olfactory bulb to the smell cortex is called the LATERAL OLFACTORY TRACT. It contains axons from the olfactory bulb cells. After the primary smell cortex, as with the other senses, the neural pathways become extremely complex and are not well understood.

Although the electrophysiology of the smell system has not been studied very thoroughly, we know enough to suggest that the sense of smell is very similar to the other sensory systems. A number of studies have found that the intensity of the neural response varies directly with the intensity of the stimulus. However, most investigators have focused on the problem of how different smell qualities are signaled to the brain. They have tried to find evidence of specific types of receptors for different types of stimuli. One major study was that of Ottoson (1956), who measured the electrical response of the entire olfactory epithelium to various stimuli. He discovered that the passing of a puff of odor-laden air across the epithelium resulted in a unique type of electrical response. This is a slow change in the electrical charge of the receptor cells. It is this change that is thought to generate spike potentials in their axons.

With improved experimental techniques, Gesteland, Lettvin, Pitts, and Rojas (1963) were able to record the responses of single receptors in the olfactory epithelium. They recorded both the slow potential response to stimuli and the spike potentials generated in the axons of the receptors by the same stimuli. These two types of electrical responses are shown one on top of the other in Figure 6-4. As you can see in the figure, this particular receptor seems to respond vigorously to a musky odor, less well to nitrobenzene, hardly at all to benzonitrite, and not at all to pyridine. Gesteland et al. (1963) thought these responses indicated the existence of the various receptor types that they had been looking for, although they were cautious in making this interpretation. Such caution seems to have been well founded, since later recordings from single cells in the

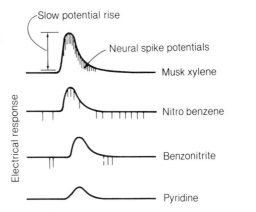

Figure 6-4.
Slow potential and spike potential responses of olfactory receptor cells to four different smell stimuli (based upon Gesteland et al., 1963).

epithelium, olfactory bulb, and in cortical and lower brain centers that receive olfactory information, have tended to indicate that each neural unit responds to a broad range of stimuli (Giachetti & MacLeod, 1975; Cain & Bindra, 1972; MacLeod, 1971; O'Connell & Mozell, 1969). The same sort of across-fiber patterns that we found in taste reception seem to be present, and it seems likely that the "code" for smell qualities will be found in these patterns (Erickson & Schiffman, 1975).

THE CUTANEOUS (SKIN) SENSES

All living things can be said to have a "skin." Probably the most important function of the skin is to *define* the organism, that is, to set boundaries in space, inside of which we can talk about the organism and outside of which we can talk about the environment. The skin is an *interface* (a place where two systems meet) between the organism and the environment. It is surrounded by the environment, and it is in intimate contact with it. In the most primitive one-celled organisms the skin is the cell membrane, and it is responsible for all of the organism's contacts with its environment. Taking in food, excreting waste, isolating the inside of the cell from damaging outside substances, and responding to external stimuli of all sorts, are all functions of this primitive skin. Although evolutionarily more advanced organisms, such as mammals (including humans), have more specialized organs to handle these tasks, their skins are also complex and important organs. The skin plays a role in respiration, temperature regulation, and protection. It also has a wide variety of sensory functions. It produces the sensations that we call touch, heat or cold, and pain. Unfortunately, although we can easily distinguish these sensations, so far we have not been able to discover any distinct physiological response differences corresponding to these different sensory qualities. However, we do know which physical stimuli tend to provoke different sensory qualities, so we can at least start at that level.

Skin Stimuli and Receptors. The skin responds to a variety of physical stimuli. When we press an object against the skin, it deforms the surface and we experience the sensation of touch or pressure. When an object makes contact with a hair, causing it to bend, we also experience touch. The temperature of the object with which we touch the skin also elicits a sensation. Whether it is warmth or cold depends upon both the temperature of the stimulus and upon the temperature to which the skin has been previously exposed (see Chapter 10). Finally, the skin responds to electrical stimulation. For mild stimulation a type of touch sensation is usually felt, although temperature can also be experienced.

When the stimulation becomes more intense, the sensation usually becomes painful.

In humans the skin has a very complex structure. Figure 6-5 is a diagram of the most important structures in HAIRY SKIN, which covers most of the human body. A different kind of skin, found on the palms of the hands, soles of the feet, fingers and toes, and other places, has no hairs protruding from it. The outer layer of dead skin cells is thicker, and there are more nerve endings embedded in the skin, making such skin effective protection and also extremely sensitive to stimulation. This is called GLABROUS SKIN. All skin consists of two basic layers. The outer layer, called the EPIDERMIS, consists of several layers of tough dead cells on top of a single inner layer of cells, which divide constantly to generate the protective layers above. The inner layer, called the DERMIS, contains most of the nerve endings in the skin. Under these two layers is usually a layer of fat cells. In addition to these layers, there are a variety of hairs, muscles, glands, arteries, veins and capillaries, and nerve endings in the skin. Some of these are also shown in Figure 6-5.

The skin also contains a variety of different types of nerve endings. Some of the most common forms are shown in Figure 6-6. Although it is certain that at least some of these nerve endings must be the receptors for the skin sensations, it has been difficult to specify exactly which ending is responsible for which sensation. In fact, all of the endings seem to respond somewhat to all of the different types of stimulation. Some argue that it is only the free nerve endings that have developed properly, and that the other types are "rejects" that have been left to adapt themselves to their local surroundings; they have done so by forming the observed configurations (see Geldard, 1972). The striking thing about all of these nerve endings in the skin is that they seem to respond directly to physical stimulation. These fibers don't seem to be

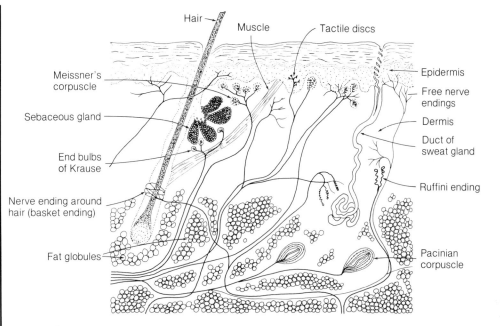

Figure 6-5.
A piece of hairy skin in cross section (based upon Woolard
Weddell, & Harpman, 1940).

modified in any special way to respond to
mechanical or temperature stimuli.

As an example of how a skin receptor responds to stimulation, let us consider the
PACINIAN CORPUSCLE (see Figure 6-6). It has
been well studied because it is large, easily
accessible, and occurs in nearly all animals
that have complex nervous systems. The
elegant work of Loewenstein and his colleagues (see Loewenstein, 1960) on the Pacinian corpuscle has indicated that a mechanical stimulus operates directly on the
axon of the nerve. To show this they peeled
away the surrounding cell layers as we
would peel an onion, until they were touching the axon itself. The basic idea is that the
deformation of the axon membrane causes
numerous tiny holes in the membrane to
open, allowing electrically charged particles

to flow from one side of the membrane to the
other. This causes an electrical current to
flow between the point of stimulation and
another point on the axon. This electrical current then generates a spike potential that
jumps along the axon and carries the message of stimulation to the brain. The surrounding layers of material in the Pacinian
corpuscle seem to be present simply to make
the effect of the stimulus less intense. Temperature could act in a similar way, perhaps
by controlling chemical reactions that would
affect the ability of electrically charged particles to cross the cell's membrane. Electrical
stimuli probably trigger spike potentials directly. We do not know whether this is the
case for all of the cutaneous nerve endings,
but it is reasonable to suppose that they all
operate in a similar way.

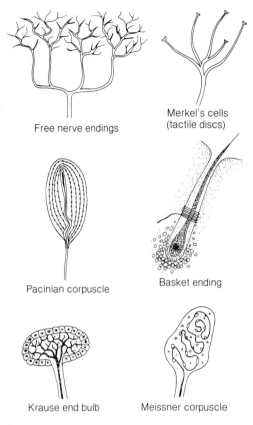

Free nerve endings

Merkel's cells
(tactile discs)

Pacinian corpuscle

Basket ending

Krause end bulb

Meissner corpuscle

Figure 6-6.
Some representative types of nerve endings.

Neural Responses in the Skin Senses. Because there are so many different types of nerve endings in the skin, you might be thinking that the nerve pathways to the brain would be hopelessly complex. Yet there is a fairly simple organizational plan at work here. The major principle seems to be that *where* on the skin a particular nerve ends determines where its information goes in the brain, regardless of the type of cell it represents. All of the sensory information is passed from the skin on to the spinal cord through 30 pairs of nerves (one member of each pair for each side of the body). There are also four cranial nerves that collect cutaneous information from the head region. These inputs are gathered into two main pathways to the brain, each of which seems to carry different types of information.

The first system is called the LEMNISCAL SYSTEM. The nerve fibers that comprise this path are large and conduct information quickly. The inputs are passed through the MEDULLA, then the THALAMUS, and finally arrive at the sensory cortex, which is located in the PARIETAL region of the brain (the upper central region). An interesting aspect of the lemniscal system is that the inputs from the right side of the body end up on the left side of the brain, and vice versa. This system has fibers that respond mostly to touch and movement, although temperature fibers have also been found (Hensel, 1968).

The second major pathway is called the SPINOTHALAMIC SYSTEM. This pathway is rather slow, and is made up of many short fibers instead of a few long axons. It also passes through the thalamus (but through a different area), but then moves on through the RETICULAR FORMATION to the sensory cortex. It seems to have relatively equal inputs to both sides of the brain. This pathway seems to carry information about temperature as well as touch. Some recent evidence suggests that one of its prime functions is to convey the sensation of pain (discussed in the last section of this chapter).

An important property of the skin is the fact that sensory activity in one region can interfere with sensory activity in nearby regions. If the distance between two stimuli is appropriate, one may even get a reduction in the perceived magnitude of the sensation. This seems to indicate that the receptive fields in the skin have the same sort of excitatory-center, inhibitory-surround organization that we observed in the visual system (von Békésy, 1967). Demonstration Box 6-1 shows how you can demonstrate this for yourself with touch stimuli.

In this demonstration you will see how skin sensations interact. You will need two fairly sharply pointed objects such as two toothpicks or two bristles from a hairbrush. The demonstration will work better if you get a friend to control the stimuli. Do not use anything like a knife, for you will be pushing the point quite strongly against your skin. First, try pressing one point against the skin of your palm. Notice the spread of sensation around the stimulated point. Now put the two points as close together as you possibly can. Push them together on the same place on your palm. Notice that you feel only one point, although two are present. Now move the two stimulating points slightly apart. You should *still* feel only one point. Repeat this procedure several times, moving the points apart by a little more each time, and paying careful attention to whether the sensation feels like two points or one on your skin. If you are pushing hard enough, and paying close attention to your sensations, at just about the separation where the two points begin to feel like two distinct points on the skin, you should have a surprising experience. The magnitude of the sensation from the two points should diminish greatly, perhaps vanish altogether for a short time. The sensation should be very faint, even though two toothpicks (or brush bristles) are pushing with some force against the skin. As you then move the points even further apart, you will perceive two distinct, full strength sensations, appropriately separate on the skin. This phenomenon is explained by the overlapping of regions of excitation and inhibition in adjacent receptive fields of the skin, as shown in the accompanying figure.

Demonstration Box 6-1:
Inhibitory Interactions on the Skin

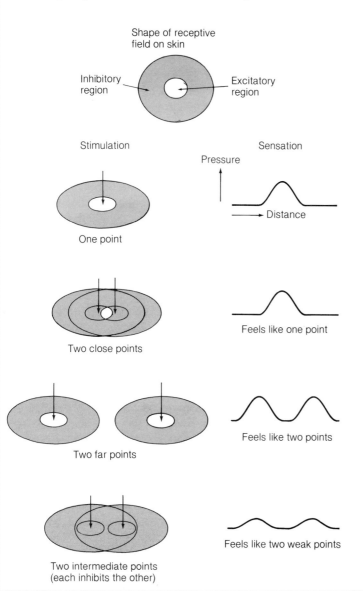

Shape of receptive field on skin

Inhibitory region — Excitatory region

Stimulation — Sensation

Pressure / Distance

One point

Two close points — Feels like one point

Two far points — Feels like two points

Two intermediate points (each inhibits the other) — Feels like two weak points

Specific brain regions respond to stimuli at particular parts of the body. Just as in vision, neurons in the cutaneous system have RECEPTIVE FIELDS. That is to say, each neuron in the brain that responds to cutaneous stimulation does so for only a limited area of the skin. Poggio and Mountcastle (1960) reported that certain cells in the thalamus of the cat respond to specific regions of the cat's skin (e.g., a specific paw). The receptive fields for neurons in the part of the thalamus that receives nerves from the lemniscal system are quite small, while large fields are found for neurons in that part of the thalamus receiving projections from the spinothalamic system. The finding of distinct receptive fields for most neurons in these systems seems to indicate that *which* neurons are firing is an indication of *where* the stimulus is touching the skin.

At the level of the cortex the relationship between regions of the body that are stimulated and regions of the brain that respond is quite regular. One "map" of these relationships was created by Penfield and Rasmussen (1950). These investigators electrically stimulated the sensory cortex of patients during brain operations. As various points on the cortex were stimulated, the patients reported what they felt (such as a tingling of their leg). The resulting sensory map of the body is shown in Figure 6-7. Thus the spatial location of stimulation on the skin is preserved in the spatial location of activity in the cortex.

The skin responds not only to touch, but also to temperature. There seem to be two types of nerve fibers that respond when the skin is cooled or warmed. COLD FIBERS respond to cooling of the skin with an increase in firing relative to their resting rate, and to warming with a decrease. WARM FIBERS respond to warming with an increase in firing rate and to cooling with a decrease (see Hensel, 1966, 1968). Also, after an initial change in firing rate in the direction appropriate to

the type of stimulus and the type of receptor, both types of fibers gradually go to a steady rate of firing. This "resting" rate is related to the *absolute* temperature of the skin (and thus of the receptor).

Cold and warm fibers have different patterns of response over a broad range of skin temperatures. This is shown in Figure 6-8, which is from the work of Zotterman (1959). As you can see in the figure, the cold fibers respond in the range from about 13–35°C and again from about 45–50°C. Above this limit the receptors become damaged and the response falls off. Warm receptors respond from about 23°C to about 47°C with a peak at about 38°C (just above body temperature). The cold fibers have peaks at about 25°C and again at about 50°C. These *steady-state* responses provide us with information about the absolute temperature of the skin. This information is quite important since *internal body temperature* must be maintained within a narrow range of values (around 37°C) if the body is to survive.

THE KINESTHETIC SENSES

Thus far we have been talking about receptors of information generated by the world around us. Now we will consider some of the vast array of sensory information generated within our own bodies. In this section we will discuss some of the more general systems that signal that we are moving, inform us of the position of bodily parts, and also tell us something of the body's chemical state.

One of the things that distinguishes animal from plant life is the ability to move about in the world. In order to inform the brain about the position of the limbs or the orientation of the body, higher organisms have developed specialized receptor systems. The bodies of

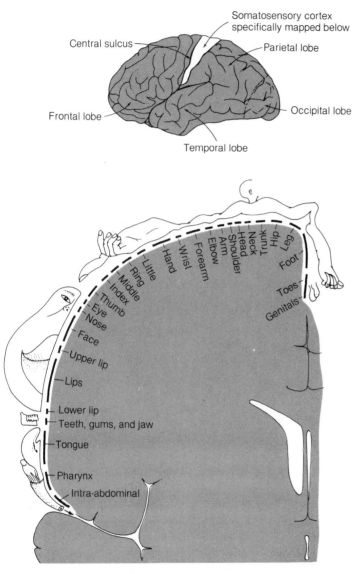

Central sulcus

Somatosensory cortex
specifically mapped below

Parietal lobe

Frontal lobe

Occipital lobe

Temporal lobe

Little
Ring
Middle
Index
Thumb
Eye
Nose
Face
Upper lip

Hand
Wrist
Forearm
Elbow
Arm
Shoulder
Head
Neck
Trunk
Hip
Leg

Foot

Toes

Genitals

Lips

Lower lip
Teeth, gums, and jaw

Tongue

Pharynx

Intra-abdominal

Sensory homunculus

Figure 6-7.
Penfield and Rasmussen's
(1950) topographic map of
projections of "touch" nerve
fibers on the sensory cortex.
The length of the line next to
each body part is proportional
to the area of sensory cortex
receiving information from
that body part (From Penfield,
W., & Rasmussen, T. *The
Cerebral Cortex of Man*. ©
1950 by MacMillan Publishing Co., Inc., renewed 1978
by Theodore Rasmussen).

such organisms (including humans) are liter-
ally enmeshed in a web of sensory receptors,
which accurately monitor the positions of
various parts so that appropriate action can
be initiated. In many cases the signals of
these sensory systems are not consciously
perceived, but rather they are used in controlling reflex actions that maintain an upright
posture.

Kinesthetic Stimuli and Receptors. The
overt physical stimulus to which the kinesthe-

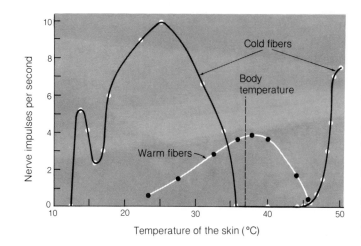

Figure 6-8
Steady discharge of cold and warm nerve fibers in the cat as it varies with skin temperature. Notice that the cold fibers (O–O) have two major response ranges, from about 13–35°C and from 45–50°C. The warm fibers (●–●) respond only in the range of 23–47°C (based upon Zotterman, 1959).

tic system responds is movement (the root *kine* is from the Greek word for movement). However, there is also some information about position available even when no movement is taking place. This information comes from our continual battle against the force of gravity. Both movement and these postural responses involve tension, compression, or twisting forces on the muscles, tendons, or joints of limbs. These physical forces should be considered as the stimuli for kinethesis. Any position of the body, even prone and fully relaxed, results in a complex pattern of muscular tensions and compressions, and the consequent mechanical forces acting on tendons and joints. The intensity of the various forces, or changes in intensity over time, signal body movement and posture.

Just as in the surface layers of the skin, there are a great many sensory receptors scattered throughout the remainder of the body. First, there are at least two types of nerve endings in the deeper layers of tissue beneath the skin: FREE NERVE ENDINGS and PACINIAN CORPUSCLES (both of which we encountered in the last section). The free nerve endings are thought to be responsible for pain sensations. The Pacinian corpuscles provide our sense of deep pressure (which can be felt even when the overlying skin has been anesthetized). There are also a variety of receptors (such as the carbon dioxide sensor) that are located on or in many of our vital organs. Although the visceral organs themselves are rather insensitive to touch, temperature, or pain stimuli (with the obvious exception of stretching or twisting forces that cause, for example, gas pains), these organs are surrounded by muscle. This muscle is freely supplied with a variety of nerve endings that are responsive to the movements of the viscera. Finally, there are a number of types of nerve endings located in the muscles that move our limbs in and around the joints.

Matthews (1933) divided these receptors in the muscles into three major types, two of which are shown in Figure 6-9. His first type is called the A endings. There are two subtypes of A endings. The A_1 endings are often

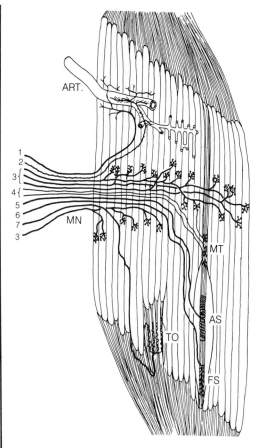

Figure 6-9.
Nerve endings in muscle. (1) Free nerve
endings around an artery; (2) efferent nerves
that regulate the size of the artery; (3) motor
nerves that cause the muscle to contract; (4)
more motor nerves; (5) Matthews type A_2 (or
annulospiral) nerve endings on a muscle
spindle; (6) Matthews type A_1 (or
flower-spray) nerve endings on the same
muscle spindle; (7) Matthews type B (Golgi
tendon organs) nerve endings on a muscle
tendon. Matthews type C (Pacinian
corpuscles) endings are not shown (from
Creed, Denny-Brown, Eccles, Liddell, &
Sherrington, 1932).

called "flower-spray" endings because they
look just like a bunch of flowers against the
muscles to which they have synapses. The A_2
type are wound around strands of muscle
fibers, which are called muscle spindles.
Both types respond to stretching of the muscle and therefore have been called STRETCH
RECEPTORS or SPINDLE ORGANS, since they
both attach to muscle spindles. This type of
nerve ending is found also in great numbers
in the joints between limbs. Matthews' second type, the B endings, look much like the
flower-spray endings but are attached to the
tendons that connect the muscles to the
bones. B endings are also called GOLGI TEN-
DON ORGANS. They seem to respond to both
stretching and contraction of the muscle,
while the spindle organs respond only to
stretching. Matthews' third type of receptor,
which he labeled C, is thought to be the
Pacinian corpuscle (Geldard, 1972). Although it is important in the cutaneous
senses, it probably plays little role in kinesthesis. There seem to be few such Pacinian
corpuscles in muscles or near joints. In addition to all of the above, muscles and joints
are well supplied with the free nerve endings
that may be responsible for pain sensations in
these areas.

Neural Responses in Kinesthesis. The variety of receptors we have described send their
messages to the brain via the two major
neural pathways described previously, the
lemniscal system and the spinothalamic system. Most of the fibers follow the lemniscal
pathway, except for the free nerve endings,
many of which follow the spinothalamic
pathway. There are also a great many branch-
ings and interactions of these two pathways
with others of lesser importance. The nerves
that terminate on muscles or tendons and in

joints project to the same region of the cortex we described for the skin senses (Wyburn et al., 1964). Thus information about stimuli touching the skin of the arm and about the position and the movement of the arm are both projected onto the same general area of the cortex. However, the cutaneous and the kinesthetic systems activate separate cortical units, which are not shared between systems. This means that the cutaneous information is kept separate from the position and movement information even at the cortical level.

Let us look at the signals generated by these kinesthetic receptors. Figure 6-10 shows an electrophysiological recording

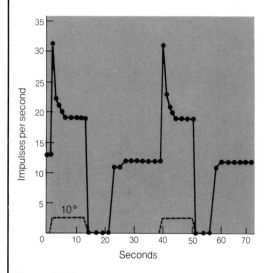

Figure 6-10.
Response of a single nerve fiber that terminates in the knee joint of a cat. The dotted lines represent bending of the knee joint by 10°. This "slow-adapting" fiber gives a large initial burst of impulses to the bending, which gradually declines to a stable rate of firing above background (no bending). When the limb is "unbent" there is an inhibition of responses, so that nerve firing is below background rate, and then the firing rate climbs back to the background rate (from Boyd & Roberts, 1953).

from a nerve fiber that terminates in the knee joint of a cat. The limb is being bent and returned to its original position. The movement of the limb is signaled by a sudden change in neural response rate. The size of the change indicates the speed of movement. The static position of the limb is signaled by the resting level of neural response. Fibers that act in this manner are often called SLOW-ADAPTING FIBERS, because it takes several seconds for them to find a new resting rate of firing corresponding to a new limb position. Cells with similar response characteristics are also found higher up in the kinesthetic system at sites in the thalamus and cortex (Mountcastle, Poggio & Werner, 1963; Mountcastle & Powell, 1959). The consensus is that virtually all positional and movement information comes from the receptors located in the joints (Adams, 1977). All of the other receptors may serve to give us the sensation of strain when lifting something, or of pain. Their major role seems to be to provide information to control our postural reflexes, automatically adjusting our muscle tension to the requirements of whatever load we are carrying.

THE VESTIBULAR SENSE

In the last section, we mentioned that much sensory input does not give rise to conscious sensations. In these cases the information that is gathered is used to regulate various physiological states such as muscular tension. This is also true of the vestibular system. This system's major functions are to assist in the maintenance of an upright posture and to control eye position as we move our heads while viewing various stimuli. Both of these operations take place outside of consciousness.

Some of the most primitive organisms

have organs that are sensitive to changes in motion of the body. In primitive invertebrates such as the crayfish these are called STATO-CYSTS. They consist simply of a fluid-filled cavity that is lined with hair cells. In the cavity is a tiny stone, called a STATOLITH or "still stone," that rests on the hairs. When the animal accelerates, the stone tends to stay behind because of its inertia, thus bending the hairs on which it rests. This action generates an electrical response to the movement. If the animal is tilted, the stone rolls along over a number of different hairs, bending them and generating a different response indicating tilt. The function of such organs is to signal the animal's orientation with respect to gravity.

Primitive vertebrates have organs that have a similar function; they are called OTO-CYSTS and the bones they contain are called OTOLITHS. Notice that these terms each contain the root *oto* meaning ear. These organs are usually closely associated with the ears, since both the auditory receptors and the vestibular organs probably evolved from pits on the surface of hairy skin. In mammals these organs are protected by the skull from damaging outside forces. In man the BONY LABYRINTH in the head is the area that contains the cochlea (which is the auditory organ) and the SEMICIRCULAR CANALS, the UTRI-CLE, and the SACCULE, which comprise the vestibular organs (see Figures 6-11 and 5-5).

Vestibular Stimuli and Receptors. The effective physical stimulus for the vestibular organ is *change* of rate of motion, or ACCELERATION, like that which occurs when we jump up and

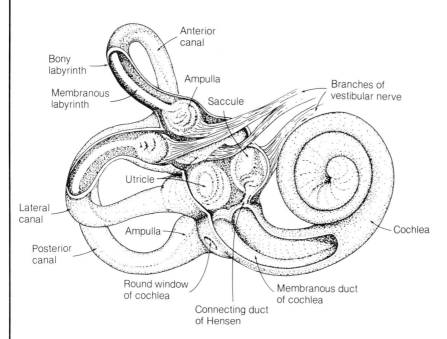

Figure 6-11.
A diagram of the right inner ear showing the cochlea (the auditory receptor), the semicircular canals, and the utricle and saccule (from Geldard, F. A. *The Human Senses,* 2nd ed. New York: Wiley, 1972).

down, spin in a barber chair, take off in a jet plane or rocket, or simply stand up and walk. The semicircular canals and their associated receptor organs seem particularly well suited for monitoring rotary motion (as when turning around). The other two organs, the utricle and the saccule, seem mainly to respond to linear acceleration (as when taking off in a plane).

The movement-receptive portion of the semicircular canals is called the CRISTA, which is found in swellings (called AMPULLAE) at the bases of the semicircular canals (see Figure 6-11). The crista consists of an array of sensory cells from which tiny hairs protrude. This is shown in Figure 6-12A. These hairs are embedded in a jellylike material called the CUPOLA. When the head accelerates, the fluid in the canals causes the cupola to move. This in turn causes the hairs to bend, generating neural responses. As the head continues to move at a particular rate of speed, the

cupola gradually comes back to its resting position, no longer bending the hairs, and no longer causing a response in the sensory cells. This is why the effective stimulus is acceleration rather than steady movement.

The receptor organ found in the utricle and the saccule is called the MACULA, shown in Figure 6-12B. It functions much like the statocyst we discussed before. As in the crista, tiny hairs protrude from the sensory cells in the macula. These hairs are embedded in a jellylike substance. In the macula, however, a layer of otoliths ("ear stones") covers the jellylike substance. These lag behind when the head is accelerated, bending the hair cells and generating an electrical response to the acceleration. When the otoliths catch up to the rest of the head, which would happen if the acceleration ceased and motion became steady, the hairs are no longer bent. This means no response would be generated, even though the head may be traveling at

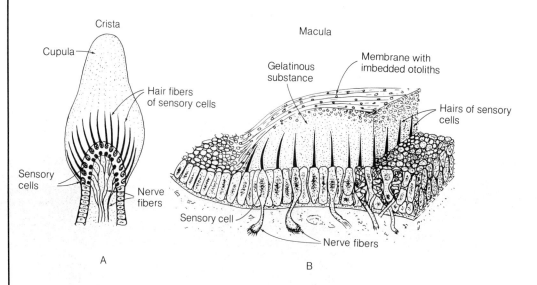

Figure 6-12.
(A) Diagram of the crista, the receptor found in the ampulla of the semicircular canals. (B) Diagram of the macula, the receptor found in the utricle and the saccule (from Geldard, F. A. *The Human Senses,* 2nd ed. New York: Wiley, 1972).

thousands of kilometers per hour relative to the earth.

Neural Responses in the Vestibular Sense. The hair cells from both the crista and the macula send their information to the brainstem via the eighth cranial nerve. From there most of the nerve fibers go to the VESTIBULAR NUCLEI (still in the brainstem). After this the sensory pathways are complicated and little is known about them. There seem to be projections to the cerebellum and perhaps to the cortex. It is important to note that most of the fibers leaving the vestibular nuclei are motor (or EFFERENT) fibers. One major group of these fibers forms a pathway to the muscles that move the eyes. Szentágothai (1950) discovered that each pair of eye muscles receives fibers from a different semicircular canal. The arrangement indicates that muscles that move the eye in a particular plane are controlled by nerve fibers that originate in the semicircular canal that responds to acceleration in that plane. Acceleration in a particular direction causes compensatory eye movements in the opposite direction. This allows the eyes to remain fixed on an object even though the head is turning in various directions. The relationship between eye movements and vestibular stimulation is shown in Demonstration Box 6-2.

Löwenstein and Sand (1940) performed a classic study that illustrates the elec-trophysiology of the vestibular system. They recorded the electrical activity of single nerve fibers from the crista of a ray (a kind of fish) while the entire labyrinth was rotated on a turntable. They found that as long as the head was accelerating, the fibers responded. They increased their response rate for acceleration in one direction and, when the acceleration was in the *opposite* direction, these fibers responded by giving *fewer* impulses per second than the resting rate. Thus, as in other sensory systems, both excitatory and inhibitory responses to physical stimuli occur. Löwenstein and Sand (1940) also showed that the magnitude of the response (impulses per second in single fibers) varies directly with the magnitude of the stimulating acceleration. Thus stimulus intensity seems to be encoded in a manner similar to that in other sensory systems. There are at least two other types of nerve fibers, one of which always responds to acceleration (regardless of direction) with an increase in firing rate. The other only responds with decreases in its firing rate.

The fibers connected to the hair cells of the macula seem to respond to their stimuli somewhat more simply. Two types of responses have been described. The first is an increase in the rate of neural firing when the head is tilted; the second is a rate increase when the head is returned to its original position (Wyburn *et al.,* 1964). Although there have been some studies that have found cor-

---

For this demonstration you will need a friend and a little space. Have your friend hold his or her arms out and spin around (like a whirling ice skater) until they become dizzy. This continuous rotation sets up currents in the semicircular canals that trigger the compensatory eye movement system. Now stop your friend from turning and look into his or her eyes. You will notice that the eyes drift steadily in one direction, and then snap back and start to drift again. This type of repetitive eye movement is called NYSTAGMUS. It is a reflex movement that is evoked automatically by the vestibular stimulation caused by fluid currents in the semicircular canals.

Demonstration Box 6-2:
Vestibular Stimulation and Eye Movements

tical responses to acceleration of the head, little is known about higher level vestibular responses (Andersson & Gernandt, 1954).

PAIN

The shrill squeal of the siren seemed to pierce his head like a knife. The pain was exquisite. Then came a brilliant flash of light; he blinked, trying to somehow relieve the savage pain flooding in through his eyes. He stumbled, barking his shin on a log, and another bright, fierce pain penetrated his consciousness. On top of all this, the old World War II shrapnel wound in his hip began to throb with a dull, sickening ache. Finally, he found the water, diving into a dark, cool world that promised to soothe his battered body. But something was wrong with the water; instead of cooling it was burning. His head seemed to explode as the caustic liquid burned its way along his nasal passages and forced its way between his lips. Finally, and almost gratefully, he lost consciousness, his body succumbing to an assault it was never meant to experience.

Pain is a complex perceptual experience. It is usually associated with damage to the body of an animal, and, in humans, it is also accompanied by a myriad of other emotions and thoughts. Some sensory psychologists consider it to be a sensation in its own right. Other psychologists argue that pain is not a sensation at all, but rather an emotion. Perhaps the best view is a compromise. There seem to be identifiable sensory characteristics to the experience of pain; therefore we will treat it as a separate sensory modality. We must be aware, however, that interactions with other sensations and with more complex cognitive processes are important for a complete understanding of pain phenomena.

Pain Stimuli and Receptors. The evolutionary significance of pain is obvious. It is absolutely essential that an animal be able to respond appropriately to environmental situations that could destroy it. It must respond by avoiding these situations in the future or terminating the ongoing, dangerous stimulus. Light, sound, touch, and temperature, when they occur at very high intensities or for prolonged durations, can destroy the receptors that are specialized to receive these energies. Such potentially damaging intensities must be signaled quickly to the brain, or the organism will be damaged beyond repair. This is often the unfortunate fate of those humans who are born without a well-functioning pain sense (see Sternbach, 1963). Still, all pain does not come from overstimulation. Certain kinds of painful experiences arise from only moderately intense stimulation, such as a pin prick or salt touching an open wound. On the other hand, overstimulation can sometimes occur without eliciting pain. For instance, pain is not experienced as one increases the concentration of sugar stimulating the tongue. At present it is difficult to say exactly what stimulus properties are responsible for the experience of pain. The best statement would probably be that there are several different stimulus qualities that can arouse pain. What they share in common is, perhaps, the potential for causing damage to the integrity of the organism.

The best candidates for pain receptors are the free nerve endings with which the skin and the rest of the body are particularly well supplied. It has been suggested that we could isolate the pain receptors if we could find some area of the body that only experiences pain. For a while it was thought that the cornea of the eye was such a place. This area is exquisitely sensitive and almost any stimulus will cause pain there, as anyone who has had to endure the process of adapting to hard contact lenses knows well. Also, it is known to contain only free nerve endings (Tower, 1943). However, very careful work by Nafe and Wagoner (1937), and by several others, has established that the cornea is capable of a variety of sensory experiences, including touch and perhaps temperature. So free nerve endings must be capable of responding with signals that are interpreted as sensations other than pain.

Another view puts less emphasis on the receptors than on the nerve fibers that carry information away from the stimulated site on the body. As we mentioned above, some of the fibers are fast conductors and some conduct nerve impulses more slowly. Many authors, stimulated by the early work of Henry Head (1920), have proposed that the fast system (lemniscal) is specialized for highly discriminative, complicated processing of information. The slower system (spinothalamic), which is also the more primitive one, is said to carry less complicated information such as pain, temperature, and rudimentary touch. Since all types of nerve endings can send information through both types of systems, it is uncertain just how such a division of labor comes about. This view, however, is appealing on some physiological grounds, and is consistent with some interesting psychological phenomena. Consider for example the phenomenon called DOUBLE PAIN. This is the experience of two distinct peaks of pain, differing in quality and separated in time, arising from a single pain stimulus. One explanation has the first pain arising from the fast fibers, while the second arises from the slow ones. You may be able to experience this for yourself if you try Demonstration Box 6-3.

Neural Responses to Pain Stimuli. The electrophysiology of the pain system(s) has been studied by applying noxious stimuli (such as electric shock, pinching, or pricking) to animals and recording the responses of neurons at various levels of the nervous system. It is assumed that these stimuli cause pain for the animals, as they usually do for humans, but this may not always be the case. Injured humans, particularly those engaged in some demanding activity such as war or athletics, often do not feel pain although horribly wounded. At any rate, certain nerve fibers appear to fire only when their receptive fields are stimulated by noxious stimuli. For example, the study of Poggio and Mountcastle (1960) found such neurons in the cat's thalamus. Another group of investigators stimulated various areas of animals' brains while looking for responses indicating discomfort. Several candidates for a pain center in the brain have been found, but it is probable that no one region of the brain can claim to be exclusively responsible for pain (see Milner, 1970).

Perhaps the most interesting electrophysiological fact about pain is that the two types of fibers that are involved in pain, and in the other cutaneous and kinesthetic sensations, seem to act in opposition to each other. Melzack and Wall (1965) and Melzack (1973a) devised an ingenious theory of pain, called the GATE-CONTROL THEORY, based upon the interaction of these two systems. This theory provides the foundation for most modern accounts of a variety of pain phenomena (see Craig, Best & Ward, 1975). Figure 6-13 is a diagrammatic presentation of this theory. Let us go through the theory step by step, since there are several aspects to keep in mind.

First, notice that both fast and slow fibers have connections with the SUBSTANTIA GELATINOSA (a part of the spinal cord) and with the first TRANSMISSION CELLS (T cells) that send the information up the spinal cord to the brain. The fast fibers also have a direct connection to the brain ("central control" in the figure), which can in turn send information back down the spinal cord to the GATE-CONTROL SYSTEM. Notice in the figure that the connections of both the fast and the slow

In this demonstration we will use the method of Sinclair and Stokes (1964) to generate two pains for the price of one. Double pain is experienced only under certain conditions. When these are met, people report a first, sharp stinging sensation, followed about a second later by a more intense burning pain that may spread to a wider area and fades more gradually. Although most people, under the appropriate conditions, experience this sequence without being told what to expect, we are telling you now so that everybody will have a good chance to experience it. For this demonstration you will need to find a source of hot water, something to measure it with, and two medium-size bowls to hold it in. We want to produce two water baths: one at 35°C (95°F) and one at 57°C (135°F). If you have access to a thermometer (a meat thermometer is fine for this demonstration), this would obviously be the best way to measure the temperatures of the baths. If you don't have a thermometer, simply mix $3\frac{1}{2}$ cups of very hot tap water with $3\frac{1}{2}$ cups of cold tap water for the 35° bath. To keep it at about this temperature, add a little hot water every minute or so. To create the 57° bath, combine $6\frac{2}{3}$ cups of hot tap water with $\frac{1}{3}$ cup of cold tap water. You are going to immerse your entire hand in the 35° bath for about 10 minutes. When this time has elapsed, mix the 57° bath and carefully insert your finger into it until the water comes up past the second joint of the finger, count "one-thousand-one" to yourself, and then withdraw your finger. Pay careful attention to the sensations you experience. Notice that first you feel a sharp stinging and then about a second later a burning feeling. You may try the experiment again and again, without fear of any damage, if you immerse your hand in the 35°C bath between trials, and always limit your immersion in the 57°C bath to one second. If you wish, you can try varying the temperatures of the two baths to find the limits of the conditions under which the phenomenon will occur. Also, in calculating the formulas for the two baths we assumed that the cold tap water in your area had a temperature of about 10°C, and the hot tap water a temperature of about 60°C. If your water temperatures vary significantly from these, you will have to adjust the proportions of each to make up the baths.

fibers to the T cells are marked + (meaning that they increase neural activity). The fast fibers, however, excite the substantia gelatinosa (+), while the slow fibers inhibit its action (−). When the T cells are stimulated beyond some value, we experience pain. A normal stimulus, say a touch, would mostly stimulate the fast fibers, which have lower thresholds. This would excite the substantia gelatinosa, thus causing it to inhibit the T cells, keeping them well below the value that is sensed as pain. A noxious stimulus, however, would stimulate slow as well as fast fibers. Since the slow fibers inhibit the substantia gelatinosa, this allows the T cells to fire more vigorously, and pain is experienced. The substantia gelatinosa then is the "gate" for the T cells. The fast fibers close this gate, while the slow fibers open it. Melzack and Wall (1965) suggest that pain is the result of

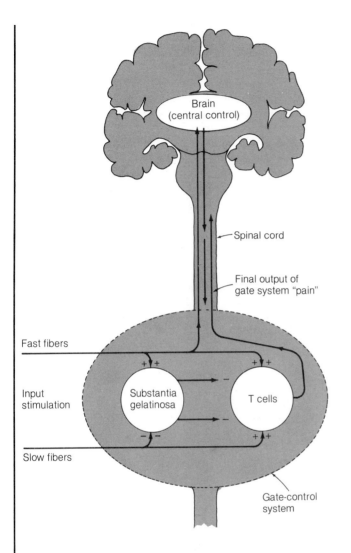

Figure 6-13.
The "gate-control theory" of pain. The fibers labeled "fast" are fast, large-diameter fibers; those labeled "slow" are slower, small-diameter fibers.

an open gate, in other words, a high rate of firing in the T cells. Melzack and Casey (1968) have suggested that the central pathway to the gate can also be responsible for closing it, so that other perceptions, cognitions, and emotions could be responsible for changing the nature of a potentially painful experience.

A fascinating extension of gate-control theory deals with the traditional Chinese technique for alleviating pain called *acupuncture* (from the Latin *acus* meaning needle and *pungere* meaning to sting). In this technique, long thin needles are inserted at various sites on the body (see Figure 6-14). These needles may be occasionally twirled, heated, or may have electrical current passed through them. Although Western doctors have been cautious about accepting acupuncture as a valid means of reducing

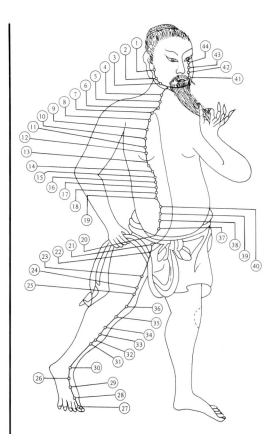

Figure 6-14.
A typical acupuncture chart. The numbers
indicate the sites at which needles can be
inserted, and then either twisted, electrified, or
heated. An impressive analgesia results in
many cases.

pain, most (though not all) studies support its
effectiveness (see P. E. Brown, 1972; Cheng,
1973; Clark & Yang, 1974; Taub, 1972).
Generally speaking, chemical anesthetics act
to inhibit the slow fibers, but do not affect the
fast fibers. This allows the substantia
gelatinosa to inhibit the T cells and close the
pain gate. Perhaps acupuncture works by increasing the activity in the fast fibers. This
would have the effect of stimulating the substantia gelatinosa more strongly, and thus
again reducing the pain-producing activity of
the T cells. In order to explain how a needle
in the arm can ease a toothache, or a needle
in the foot can ease sinus pain, we would
have to postulate higher level gates, perhaps
in the thalamus, that work in a similar fashion. Perhaps the anesthetic of the future will
not be a needle filled with novacaine, but
merely a needle.

7
Brightness

It is hard to know how many times the following scene has been played on cinema screens in Grade B movies.

It is night, and in the darkness two old, ragged beachcombers can be barely seen moving along the water's edge. Suddenly, one stops.

"Hey, Charlie, I think there's something out there."

"W-what is it?"

"I can't make it out. It's some sort of glow. It's too dim to make out what it is."

This scene illustrates a basic property of the visual system. Vision depends upon the presence of light, and the most primitive visual percepts are simply reactions to the intensity of the incoming energy. These responses are represented in consciousness as a brightness or glow. We may sense the presence of light before there is sufficient energy for us to apprehend shape or form. Thus, the next line in the above scenario usually goes, "It's getting brighter," and then as the energy becomes sufficient to apprehend the object itself "Oh my God! It's some sort of creature!" As we shall soon see, the perception of brightness is much more complex and surprising than the script of the above film.

PHOTOMETRIC UNITS

As you may recall from Chapter 4, electromagnetic energy, which we call light, varies along two dimensions: intensity and wavelength. Both are important in the perception of brightness, although brightness varies most directly with the intensity. Of course, to make sense of the perceptual effects, we must first be able to specify the physical intensity of the stimulus. This is not as simple as it seems.

The process of light measurement is based upon the visual effects produced by the radiation being studied and is known as PHOTOM-

ETRY. Photometric units are used to describe the stimulus, and these are, by convention, expressed in terms of energy. Unfortunately, over the years a confusing array of photometric units has sprung up. Most of these were designed for some specific purpose or by some technical or academic subdiscipline that needed to specify the amount of light present. The result is chaos. Even among the most scholarly, there are few who can tell you how many *nits* there are in an *apostilb* or a *blondel*, or how any of these units are related to a *candle* or a *lambert*. In 1960, an International Conference on Weights and Measures established the *Système International d'Unites*, which is a uniform system of measurement. Throughout this book we use these "standard" (SI) units. Should your reading bring you into contact with some of the older forms of photometric measurement, we can only refer you to some more advanced texts such as Wyszecki and Stiles (1967) to try to make sense of the quantities involved. Basically, there are two ways in which light can reach the eye: (1) Directly from a radiating source such as a light bulb, fluorescent tube, or the sun, or (2) by reflection from surfaces that have radiant energy falling about them, such as walls and paper. Different types of measures are used for these different types of light input. However, all photometric units are ultimately based upon the light from a single candle. The nature of this *standard candle*, its photic energy, and the specific measures derived from it have been fixed (albeit somewhat arbitrarily) by an international body called the *Commission Internationale de l'Eclairage*, usually known as the CIE.

Separate terms designate the different aspects of light. Each has its own name and requires a different measurement unit. Thus, the amount of energy coming from a light source is called its RADIANCE. Its unit is defined in terms of the standard candle, which produces an energy of slightly more than one

one-thousandth of a watt at a wavelength of 555 nm. This quantity of luminous energy is called a LUMEN. The amount of light falling upon a surface is another photometric quantity called ILLUMINANCE. The amount of light reflected from a surface is called its LUMINANCE while the proportion of light falling on a surface that is reflected is called its REFLECTANCE. The amount of light reaching the retina is called the RETINAL ILLUMINANCE. Finally, the phenomenal impression of the light intensity of a stimulus is called its BRIGHTNESS. Thus, if we have a slide projector shining upon a screen, the amount of energy leaving the bulb determines its *radiance,* the amount of light falling upon the screen is its *illuminance,* the amount of light reflected from the screen is its *luminance,* and your phenomenal impression is the *brightness* of the screen. Table 7-1 summarizes the most common photometric quantities, how they are measured, the units used, and some of their specific properties.

Before we become too involved with measurement, however, it is important to remember that perceptually, brightness is not explained simply by the amount of light reaching the eye. As we noted in Chapter 3, when we plot the brightness sensation against the physical stimulus intensity we get a nonlinear relationship. The intensity of this sensation grows in a nearly logarithmic manner as we increase the physical intensity of the stimulus (to be precise the phenomenal sensation grows as a function of the intensity raised to the .33 power). This relationship is shown in Figure 7-1. Because of this approximately logarithmic relationship, various photometric values are frequently presented in logarithmic units when reporting visual

Table 7-1 *Photometric Units*

Photometric Term	What is Measured?	Unit	How Measured?	Comments
Radiance or luminous flux	Radiant energy from a light source	Lumen	A candela is the light of a 1 lumen source at a distance of 1 m shone on a square meter	Defined in terms of a standard candle
Illuminance	Light falling on a surface	Lux	Actually 1 lumen/m²	As the source moves father away illuminance decreases
Luminance	Light reflected from a surface	Candela per meter	Lumens reflected from a surface	Independent of distance of eye from surface
Reflectance (albedo)	Proportion of light reflected from surface	% reflectance	$\dfrac{\text{Luminance}}{\text{Illuminance}} \times 100$	Really ratio of reflected to incident light
Retinal illuminance	Amount of light incident on the retina	Trolands	1 candela/m² seen through pupil of 1 mm² area	Roughly 0.0036 lumens/m² through a 1-mm² pupil
Brightness	Phenomenal impression of light intensity	Not yet agreed upon but bril is best contender	Relative matching and scaling techniques	Psychological rather than physical quantity

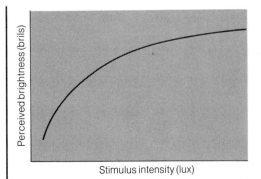

Figure 7-1.
The nonlinear relationship between stimulus intensity and brightness.

data. This serves to equalize more closely the sizes of the sensory changes as a function of changes in physical intensity. The unit of brightness in the graph in Figure 7-1 is the BRIL, which was suggested by S. S. Stevens. Each bril represents about one-tenth of a log unit above threshold, in much the same way that a decibel represents one-tenth of a log unit above threshold in audition.

FACTORS IN BRIGHTNESS PERCEPTION

Adaptation. The perception of brightness depends upon the state and the sensitivity of the eye in much the same way that the brightness of the final photographic image depends upon the sensitivity of the film. An amount of light that will produce a faint image on insensitive film will produce an overly bright image on very sensitive film. You may have been aware of the effects of changing sensitivity when you walked from a darkened room into the bright sunlight, only to find that everything appeared to be so bright and "washed out" that a few moments

had to pass before objects began to be clearly visible. The opposite occurs when you walk from a bright exterior into a darkened room. Now everything appears to be very dark, and objects are difficult to resolve in the gloom. After a while you can discern objects, although the accommodation to the darkness takes somewhat longer than the adaptation to the brighter environment. We call this first process DARK ADAPTATION and the second LIGHT ADAPTATION. Although we cannot slip off our daylight retina and put on the twilight one in the way that we change film in a camera to accommodate changes in lighting conditions, the sensitivity of our eyes still changes. This general process is called ADAPTATION.

We can track these changes in sensitivity experimentally. First, we adapt an observer to bright light by putting him in a brightly lit room for a few minutes; then we turn off the lights. Now we test to find the observer's absolute threshold for the detection of light. This is done at fixed time intervals following the onset of darkness, using one of the standard psychophysical methods outlined in Chapter 2. Such an experiment usually reveals that at first the observer needs relatively strong stimuli to reach threshold; however, the eye rapidly becomes more sensitive over the first minute or two. At this point, it begins to stabilize at a level that is about 100 times more sensitive (2 log units) than when we initially turned off the light. After about 10 min of darkness, the sensitivity begins to rapidly increase again. During this second period, the threshold drops quickly for 5 or 10 min, then begins to stabilize, reaching a relatively constant level after about one-half hour. When we graph the change in threshold for a typical observer, as we have done in Figure 7-2A, we can see a break, or *kink,* in the sensitivity curve, which indicates a change in the rate of dark adaptation. Whenever a sudden transition or break is

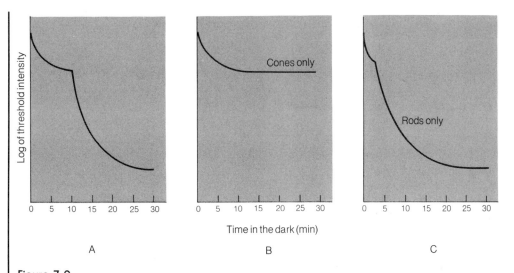

Figure 7-2.
(A) Normal time course of dark adaptation, (B) dark adaptation in
the cones (or central fovea), and (C) dark adaptation in the rods
(periphery).

found in a curve, it suggests that a second mechanism or process has come into operation. This is confirmed by the fact that there are phenomenal changes that occur at about the same time. For instance, if we used a greenish light (or nearly any color, for that matter) to measure the threshold, the observer would be able to identify the color throughout the first 10 min or so of the test session. At about the point where the sensitivity suddenly begins to increase again, the test stimulus would seem to lose its color and become greyish. There is an old proverb that is based upon this loss of color vision under dim levels of illumination; it says "At night, all cats are gray." The technology associated with photography employs an analog to this perceptual change. It is fruitless to attempt to take a snapshot with color film when the illumination is poor. Color film requires a lot of light. The only way to get a picture under these conditions is to use a very sensitive black and white film. Thus, for both the eye

and the camera, if the light signal is only sufficient to resolve vague outlines, it cannot provide the additional information necessary for the discrimination of color.

In Chapter 4 we talked about the differences between rods and cones. At that time, we reviewed some evidence that indicated that rods were found predominantly in animals that are active during the twilight hours (or in conditions of dim illumination), while cones are found predominantly in the retinas of animals that are active during daylight. It was suggested that cones function to provide photopic or daylight vision (including the perception of color), while rods provide scotopic or twilight vision. In humans, we find both rods and cones; hence, it seems possible that the two segments of the dark adaptation curve represent separate rod and cone contributions. The cones seem rapidly to reach their level of maximal sensitivity. The rods take longer to adapt. When they do, the threshold begins to drop, but at the expense of a loss in color vision. The point at which the adaptation of the rods catches up to that of the cones is the break in the dark-adaptation curve shown in Figure 7-2A. We can verify this experimentally.

Suppose we return to the experimental situation that we used to track the course of dark adaptation. Now we change the stimulus so that we are focusing a tiny pencil of light only on the fovea when we take threshold measurements. Since the fovea contains only cones (Chapter 4), this method will allow us to track dark adaptation in cones. Such an experiment gives us the data shown in Figure 7-2B. Notice that this looks just like the first segment of the curve in Figure 7-2A. No second increase in sensitivity occurs, no matter how long we continue in darkness. There is an even more spectacular means of making the same point. We could deprive a person of vitamin A for a period of time. Since this vitamin is critical for the synthesis of rhodopsin, the pigment in rods, vitamin A deprivation will "knock out" the action of these receptors. Hecht and Mandelbaum (1938) placed a normal observer on a vitamin A deficient diet, and after 57 days he had a dark adaptation curve quite similar to that in Figure 7-2B. Not only was the rod portion of the curve almost totally absent, but the individual was almost completely "night-blind" and unable to see dimly illuminated targets. By the way, the observer recovered his night vision when he went back to a normal diet.

We can now demonstrate the lower or rod portion of the curve in a normal observer by repeating our original experiment. This time, however, we focus our pencil of light about 20° from the center of the fovea, where the retina contains predominantly rods. When we do this, we get the curve shown in Figure 7-2C, in which the first rapid change (attributable to cone action) is almost completely absent. It is because the rods and cones are unequally distributed across the retina, with the fovea completely consisting of cones (which are less sensitive to weak stimuli), that looking directly at a dim object, such as a star, may actually cause it to disappear from view. A trick used by early astronomers was to look at some point off to the side of a star in order to let its image fall upon the more sensitive peripheral retina (which contains mostly rods). This technique allowed it to be perceived more clearly. Overall, these lines of evidence indicate that two separate physiological mechanisms are involved in the perception of brightness: the cone system for bright illumination and the rod system for dim illumination.

Glancing back at the time course of our sensitivity increase in darkness (as shown in Figure 7-2A), it is clear that it takes some 15–30 min to achieve full twilight vision. It would seem that the long period of time to achieve full adaptation to the dark of night would be maladaptive. Such a visually deficient animal could easily fall prey to other animals under these conditions. Fortunately, however, rapid changes from light to dark tend to occur only in technologically advanced societies such as ours. In nature, the natural transition from light to dark, which occurs at twilight, takes about 20 min, or about the amount of time it takes the eye to dark adapt. On the other hand, light adaptation is considerably faster. This is also in accord with natural conditions. An animal awakening in the morning must go from a fully dark-adapted state (from having his eyes closed throughout the night), to a light-adapted state suitable for the morning light. For optimal survival this change must occur within a few seconds, and it does.

Wavelength. The wavelength of the light hitting the eye will also affect our perception of its brightness. For instance, yellows (medium wavelengths) are almost always brighter than blues (short wavelengths); hence, color, or rather its physical analog, wavelength, partially determines our perception of brightness. The usual procedure for assessing the relative brightness of lights of different colors is to use a *bipartite target*. This is simply a circular target that has been divided in half. One half contains the standard color that is to be matched in brightness, and the other half is the comparison color that is adjustable. The energy level of the two halves of the target is adjusted until all parts of the spectrum have been examined. This provides a set of measures of the relative amounts of energy needed to produce equal sensations of brightness for various wavelengths of light. For convenience, the wavelength requiring the least energy to equal the brightness of the standard is set at a value of 1.0. All other wavelengths, being less effective, are assigned values less than 1, depending upon their relative brightnesses. Once this conversion has been made, a curve can be plotted as in Figure 7-3. Such a curve is called a LUMINOSITY CURVE. Notice that we actually have two curves in this figure. The first is labeled *photopic* and represents the results we would obtain from the matching experiment if we were working at daylight levels of light intensity. It has a peak sensitivity for wavelengths around 555 *nm* and the apparent

brightness falls off rapidly as the wavelengths grow shorter (toward the blue) or get longer (toward the red). If we repeat this matching experiment under conditions of dim illumination, where we are operating only on rod vision, no color differences will be present, and both halves of the field will appear gray regardless of their wavelength. Nonetheless, some wavelengths still look brighter than others. Thus, we can map out the luminosity curve that is marked *scotopic* in Figure 7-3. Under these conditions the curve is somewhat different, with a peak around 505 *nm*. Thus the curve is shifted toward the short wavelengths, suggesting that we may be more sensitive to blue light under dim viewing conditions.

The change in the apparent brightness of different wavelengths as we alter the intensity of the light was first noted by the Czechoslovak phenomenologist Johannes E. Purkinje, and in his honor this phenomenon is referred to as the PURKINJE SHIFT. He took note of this while looking at his garden as twilight was falling. He found that as the light dimmed certain colors began to change their apparent brightness. Thus, reds that had been bright relative to blues and greens began to look darker, while the bluer tones appeared to brighten. Recalling that scotopic vision actually lacks the sensation of color, this means

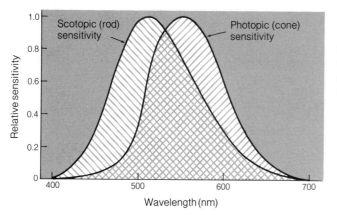

Figure 7-3.
Differences in relative sensitivity to various wavelengths under photopic and scotoptic illumination conditions.

that daylight greens or blues change to moonlight grays, while daylight reds change to moonlight blacks. Demonstration Box 7-1 allows you to experience this shift in sensitivity for yourself.

There is an interesting application of the Purkinje shift. In war movies, the briefing rooms next to air strips or the control rooms of ships are often depicted as illuminated by red light. This is not done solely for dramatic effect. It actually occurs in such settings. Rods are relatively insensitive to the red end of the spectrum but the cones still function at these longer wavelengths if there is sufficient stimulus intensity. Thus, the cones may be used while the rods are beginning to dark adapt. The dotted line in Figure 7-3 shows a wavelength where this is true. Thus, pilots about to fly night missions, or sailors about to stand the night watch, can be briefed or can check their instruments, then go directly into the dark without waiting the many minutes necessary to completely dark adapt.

Time and Area. In addition to the intensity, wavelength, and retinal location of the stimulus, our ability to detect a spot of light depends upon other stimulus properties. For

---

Demonstration Box 7-1:
The Purkinje Shift

For this demonstration, you will need a dark room and some way of providing a light whose intensity you can vary without altering its color. A good method is to use a television set as a light source. This may be done by turning the set to an unused channel and by turning the contrast control to a minimum. This reduces the visibility of the random dots that normally appear on the screen. Now, if you darken the room so that the television is the only source of illumination, the brightness control of the set will be a means of controlling the room light. An alternate procedure in the absence of a television is to turn on a light in a room and enter a closet, shutting the door after you. The amount of light entering the closet can be controlled by opening the door by differing amounts. Turning your back to the door allows for a diffusion of the light to any target that you wish to be illuminated. Unfortunately, if the outside room is well lit, opening the door by a few centimeters will provide a good deal of light; hence, control of illumination may be improved by dimming the light in the outside room.

Now, look at Color Plate 1 in Chapter 8. Here we have two colored spots, one blue and one red. When viewed in moderate or bright light (the brightness control on the television is set to high, or the closet door is more widely ajar) the blue and the red spot appear to be approximately equal in brightness. Now, make the light very dim (close the door almost completely, or turn down the brightness control of the television). In the bright light, you were viewing the spots with cone vision. Now, if you dim the lights sufficiently only rod vision will be activated. After 5–10 min, as your eye dark adapts, the blue spot will appear to be significantly brighter than the red spot. In fact, the red spot may actually disappear. The effect may be accentuated by staring at the white spot. This shifts the images away from the fovea to an area of the retina containing a greater number of rods.

instance, a photographer knows that when she is taking a picture under dim illumination she may have to lengthen the exposure time in order to collect enough light to adequately register the image on the film. In bright sunlight a short exposure will usually do. Actually the same amount of physical energy is necessary to expose the film properly in each case; it just takes longer to collect the requisite amount under dim illumination. In physics this relationship is known as the BUNSON–ROSCO LAW. It describes the photochemical reaction of any light-sensitive substance, whether it be film or visual pigment. We find that there is a similar trade-off between stimulus duration and stimulus intensity in vision, at least for periods of $\frac{1}{10}$ sec or less. We can express this relationship using simple algebra. If we define C as the critical value necessary to reach threshold (i.e., the minimum perceptable brightness), I as the stimulus intensity, and T as the stimulus duration, the relationship becomes $T \times I = C$. When applied to vision, this is known as BLOCH'S LAW. Thus, for a given stimulus, we may increase the likelihood of detection by either increasing the intensity of the stimulus or increasing its duration of presentation. If, however, the duration is greater than about $\frac{1}{10}$ sec, the probability that you will detect a stimulus is not affected by stimulus duration, but depends only on stimulus intensity.

The size of the stimulus is also important in determining its detectability. In Chapter 4, we noted that there is a good deal of convergence in the visual system. A number of rods or cones may converge upon the same bipolar cell. Similarly, several bipolar cells may converge upon the same retinal ganglion cell. Let us consider a hypothetical example. Suppose that it takes four neural responses per unit of time to activate a given bipolar cell. If we provide a tiny spot of light, which is only strong enough to elicit one response per unit of time for the retinal receptor, and

the light is only large enough to cover two receptors, clearly the bipolar cell will not respond. However, if we double the size of the stimulus so that four receptors are illuminated, we have enough neural activity to trigger the bipolar cell. Thus as the area of a stimulus increases, even if its intensity does not change, the likelihood increases that we will recruit enough photoreceptors to begin a chain of neural activity. For relatively small areas, covering visual angles of 10 minutes of arc (') or less (about 1 mm viewed at arm's length), there is a direct relationship between area and intensity. If A signifies the area stimulated, and I and C are the same as before, we can describe the relationship as $A \times I = C$. This is known as RICCO'S LAW. Perceptually, this means that we can increase the likelihood of stimulus detection by either increasing its intensity or increasing its area. For stimulus sizes greater than 10', increasing the area has a somewhat reduced effect. The effect of area on detection for larger stimuli is described by $\sqrt{A} \times I = C$. In other words, for larger stimuli a greater increase in area is needed to achieve the same reduction in threshold as before. This second area–intensity relationship is known as PIPER'S LAW. Beyond 24° of visual angle no further benefit is gained by increasing the size of the stimulus, and the likelihood of detection depends solely upon the intensity.

After this discussion, you may be wondering just what the ultimate limit of sensitivity might be if the stimulus were adjusted to the optimal wavelength, size, and retinal position, and the observer were fully dark adapted. The classic experiment to answer this question was conducted by Hecht, Schlaer, and Pirenne (1942). They found that the threshold for the perception of a brightness sensation occurred when only 10 quanta of light were reaching the retina. Further computations and experiments have shown that one gets a visual response when only one quantum of light stimulates one rod, which actually is the greatest sensitivity that would be theoretically possible (Cornsweet, 1970).

BRIGHTNESS CONTRAST

Strange as it may seem, our perception of the brightness of targets often depends more upon the luminance of adjacent objects than upon the actual luminance of the target itself. Figure 7-4 demonstrates this. Here we have four small squares, each of which is surrounded by a larger square. The central squares are printed in the same gray; thus, the amount of light that reaches your eye from each is the same. Notice, however, that the apparent brightnesses of these small squares are not equal. Their brightnesses vary depending upon their background, with the grays printed on dark backgrounds appearing lighter than the grays printed on light backgrounds. This perceptual effect is called SIMULTANEOUS BRIGHTNESS CONTRAST.

Common sense tells us that our conscious experience of brightness will increase as the amount of light that reaches our eye increases. Unfortunately, our perceptual experiences often defy common sense. Increasing the amount of light reaching our eye from a target may actually *decrease* its apparent brightness, depending upon the brightness of the background upon which it rests. This surprising result is shown in Demonstration Box 7-2.

The fact that the targets are varying in brightness as a function of the intensity of their background suggests that there is some form of spatial interaction present, perhaps between adjacent retinal regions that are illuminated by the target. Notice that targets on a light background, such as target 4 in Figure 7-4, appear to be darkened. The brightness response from target 4 has been reduced. This seems to suggest some sort of inhibition of the brightness response as a function of activity in surrounding retinal areas.

Actually, there is physiological evidence that indicates that such inhibitory spatial interaction does take place in the eye. Most of this evidence has been collected from *Limulus* (the horseshoe crab), which is an animal commonly found on the Eastern shores of the United States. *Limulus* has several sets of eyes, but the ones that are most important for research purposes are the lateral eyes, which are faceted (as in the eye of a

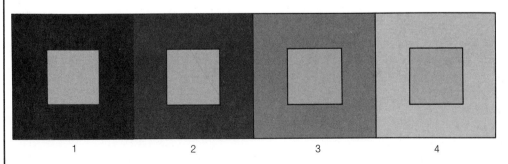

Figure 7-4.
Simultaneous brightness contrast, showing how the background can alter the perception of the central gray regions.

Demonstration Box 7-2:
The Interaction of Luminance and Background

For this experiment you will need your variable light source again (either the closet or the television). Hold up Figure 7-4 and look at the central squares, with your light source providing a low (but not dim) level of illumination. As you increase the level of illumination from its lowest value, the center target in square 1 should grow brighter. Now repeat the procedure while looking at the center target in square 4. Notice that as the luminance level increases, this target square actually gets darker. Since all of the center squares are identical in reflectance, the differences in their apparent brightnesses depend solely upon their backgrounds. This may seem strange because we tend to associate black with the absence of light. Since you are already in a room or a place that potentially can be darkened, turn off all of the light sources and close your eyes (to eliminate any stray illumination). Notice that what you are seeing is not black, but rather a misty gray (often called "cortical gray"). Thus, the absence of light is gray, not black. Only in fields that contain some areas of bright illumination can real black be seen.

fly). In such a compound eye, there is a separate optical system for each facet, and each has its own primitive retina. Since each eyelet has its own optic nerve, this arrangement spreads out the neural fibers somewhat.

With skill (and a dissecting microscope) it is possible to separate a single nerve fiber and drape it over an electrode. Much of the work on the visual system of *Limulus* has been carried out in the laboratories of H. K. Hartline and Floyd Ratliff. They were able to demonstrate the inhibitory neural interactions between nearby receptors via a very simple, but elegant, experiment (Hartline & Ratliff, 1957). First, they monitored the responses from a ganglion cell while the receptor attached to it was stimulated. The fact that the onset of the light increased the activity of the ganglion cell, of course, indicated that its activity was controlled by stimulation of the particular receptor they had illuminated. Let us call this ganglion cell and its receptor A. Next Hartline and Ratliff illuminated a receptor located a short distance away (call this one B). Since there was no change in the activity of A, it indicated that there were no excitatory connections between A and B. Next they went back and again stimulated A and, while that light was still on, they turned on the light at B. Stimulation of B actually *decreased* the response of the A ganglion cell. This experiment is shown diagramatically in Figure 7-5. These results demonstrate that the activity in one cell may be modified by the activity of its neighbors, and specifically, that adjacent visual units may inhibit one another. This process is called LATERAL INHIBITION because the inhibition acts laterally (sideways) on adjacent cells. The amount of inhibition any given cell imparts to its neighbors depends upon how strongly it is responding. The more a cell is stimulated, the more intensely it responds and the more it inhibits its neighbors.

Glancing back at Figure 7-4, it is now easy to understand why the target in square 1 is seen to be brighter than the target in square 4. In the bright surround (square 4) many cells are active and, as a consequence of this activity, they are actively inhibiting their neighbors. This inhibition from the bright surround should reduce the neural response rate in the

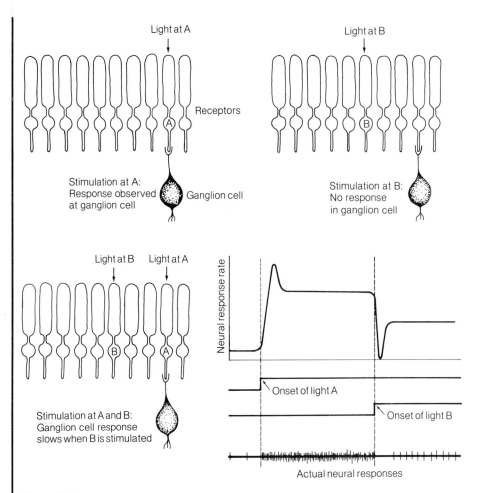

Figure 7-5.
Lateral inhibition: Stimulation at A produces a response in the ganglion cell, while stimulation at B does not. Stimulating B while A is active depresses its response due to lateral inhibition (from Lindsay & Norman, 1977).

central square, making it appear dimmer. The target on the dark background does not receive as much inhibition from its less strongly stimulated neighbors. Since the amount of stimulation from the target is the same, but square 1 is undergoing a lesser amount of inhibition, it appears to be brighter. Thus, lateral inhibition provides a basis for predicting brightness contrast effects.

Complex effects can also be predicted for other stimulus configurations. In the 1860s, Ernst Mach (see Ratliff, 1965) studied patterns with an intensity distribution like that shown in Figure 7-6B. In this figure, we have a uniform dark and a uniform light area, with an intermediate zone that gradually changes from dark to light. However, when we look at the actual stimulus depicted in Figure 7-6A,

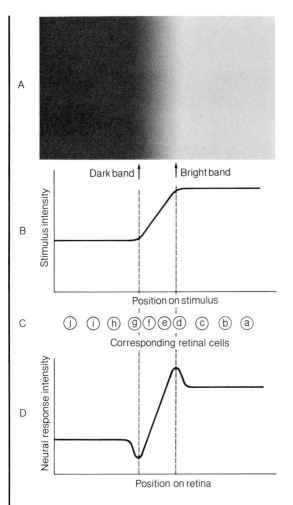

Figure 7-6.
(A) A Mach band pattern, (B) the actual stimulus distribution of intensity, (C) corresponding retinal cells (see text), and (D) neural response intensity distribution. (A and B based upon Cornsweet, 1970).

we do not see a uniform change in brightness flanked by two uniform areas. Instead two bands or blurry lines are visible at the points marked by the arrows in the figure. One is darker than any other part of the figure and the other is brighter. They are called MACH BANDS, in honor of their discoverer, and their

presence can be predicted from a consideration of the process of lateral inhibition.

We have indicated the location of some retinal cells illuminated by the Mach-band-producing pattern in Figure 7-6C. Cell b is stimulated by bright incoming light, but it is also strongly inhibited by the activity of the adjacent cells a and c. Cell d is stimulated to the same extent as cell b. But on one side it is strongly inhibited by c while on the other side it is somewhat more weakly inhibited by e, which is not receiving as much light. The important thing to derive from this discussion is the fact that cells b and d have the same degree of stimulation, but d is less strongly inhibited. In this case, we might expect that its corresponding response will be more vigorous than that in cells like b. This should cause a relatively bright region to appear in the region of d. Next consider cell i, which is not stimulated very much, but neither are the nearby cells h and j. This means that i is not being strongly inhibited by surrounding units. On the other hand, g is receiving the same small amount of stimulation as i. But while g is weakly inhibited on one side by h, it is more strongly inhibited on the other side by f which is responding more vigorously because of the higher intensity of light falling upon it. Thus although g and i receive the same amount of stimulation, g is more strongly inhibited than i. This means that its response will be lowered, causing a darker band to appear in this region. The relationship between the input and the neural (and perceptual) response is diagrammed in Figure 7-6D. It is actually quite easy to produce a Mach band pattern for yourself. Demonstration Box 7-3 shows how this can be done.

Lateral inhibition explains not only the brightness phenomena associated with Mach bands and brightness contrast, but also the percept associated with Figure 7-7B. Here we have a series of gray stripes, each of which is uniform in brightness although different from

Mach band patterns do not show up well in printed representations. This is probably due to the fact that the range of luminances possible from ink on paper is not very large. It is actually quite easy to produce your own Mach band pattern using a distribution of light. All you need is a card or a book that is opaque and has a straight edge, and a large light source. If you are in a room that has fluorescent or large frosted light fixtures in the ceiling, these produce a fine uniform source of illumination. When you hold the card near a surface, you cast a shadow. As is shown in the accompanying diagram, there is a full shadow under the surface and full light on the other side. In between there is a graded shadow, the *penumbra,* which gradually moves from light to dark. Hold the card still and look at the brightness pattern and you will easily see the dark and light Mach bands. You may increase the visibility of the bands by moving the card closer to the surface. This reduces the size of the penumbra and makes the area of gradual change in intensity steeper, as shown in the diagram. Since this puts the bright and dim areas nearer one another it enhances the effect of the inhibitory process.

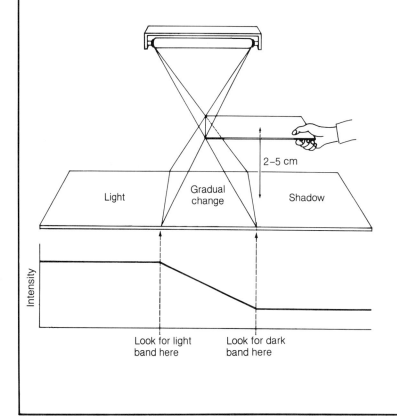

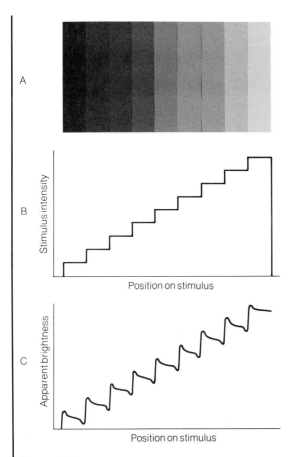

Figure 7-7.
(A) Staircase brightness pattern, (B) actual stimulus intensity distribution, and (C) resultant brightness perception (A and B based upon Cornsweet, 1970).

its neighbors. Notice, however, that the stripes do not appear to be uniformly bright (Figure 7-7A). Rather they are somewhat scalloped in appearance. The left edge, toward the darker neighbor, appears to be somewhat lightened, while the right edge, next to the lighter neighbor, appears to be somewhat darkened. The resultant percept is diagrammed in Figure 7-7C. Again, it is quite easy to predict this result from the lateral in-

hibitory response, with brighter regions inhibiting adjacent areas more strongly than darker regions.

COGNITIVE FACTORS IN BRIGHTNESS PERCEPTION

The relatively simple manner in which changes in brightness can be predicted from spatial interactions between retinal cells appears to be quite exciting, especially given the apparent precision suggested by some relatively sophisticated mathematical descriptions of these interactions (Ratliff, 1965). Unfortunately, brightness perception is much more complex, and there are many instances where predictions made from lateral inhibitory considerations can be wrong. As an example, consider Figure 7-8. The gray under the white stripes is identical to that under the black stripes. Notice, however, that the gray under the white stripes appears to be lighter than the gray under the black stripes. This is opposite to the prediction one would make based upon the action of lateral inhibition. The white should darken the gray rather than lighten it. The phenomenal impression, then, is the reverse of brightness contrast, and it is called BRIGHTNESS ASSIMILATION. The appearance of this effect seems to depend upon a cognitive factor. The term cognition is used to cover all mental processes by which we come to know the world. Thus processes such as learning, reasoning, intuition, or attention are all cognitive factors, as we noted in Chapter 1.

Attention seems to be a relevant variable for the appearance of brightness assimilation. Coren (1969a) demonstrated that the part of

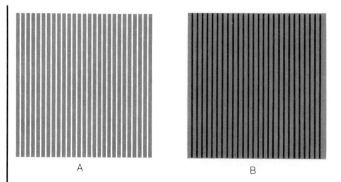

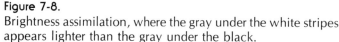

Figure 7-8.
Brightness assimilation, where the gray under the white stripes appears lighter than the gray under the black.

the visual field to which you pay attention seems to show greater brightness contrast. Festinger, Coren, and Rivers (1970) extended this observation to explain brightness assimilation. They showed that regions of a field to which you pay attention show the usually expected brightness contrast against their surround, while regions of the field to which you are not attending show brightness assimilation. Observers usually describe the pattern shown in Figure 7-8A as a gray field with white lines *on* it and Figure 7-8B as a set of black lines *on* a gray background. Festinger *et al.* (1970) reasoned that the lines have a "figurelike" quality that captures the attention (this aspect of perception will be discussed more fully in Chapter 13). Since the gray is then a nonfigural background, to which we pay little attention, it shows assimilation. If this is the case then voluntary shifts in attention, so that concentration is focused on the gray regions, should alter the brightness effect from one of assimilation to one of contrast. The gray under the white stripes should now appear to be the darker member of the pair, and this is exactly what happens (Festinger *et al.*, 1970).

Some brightness effects depend upon other cognitive factors, namely the assump-

tions that the observer makes about the nature of the world. Consider the gray tube shown as Figure 7-9. Notice that the gray of the interior of the tube appears to be lighter than the gray of the exterior. In actuality they are the same gray. Coren and Komoda (1973) suggest that this apparent brightness difference involves a cognitive adjustment based upon presumptions that we make about the environment. The interior of a real tube is apt to receive less light than the exterior of the tube; however, in Figure 7-9 the same amount of light reaches the eye from both the interior and the exterior surfaces. In reality, this could only happen if the interior surface reflects a greater proportion of the light that reaches it. In other words, if we had a bit of the external surface and a bit of the internal surface together under the same illumination, the internal surface material would appear brighter since its reflectance is greater. Apparently the visual system makes similar presumptions about the amount of light reaching surfaces, and adjusts the percept so that the apparent brightness corresponds to the presumed relative reflectances rather than to the actual distribution of light reaching the eye. This is actually an example of BRIGHTNESS CONSTANCY, a

Figure 7-9.
A reversible tube in which the inner gray always appears lighter (from Coren, S., & Komoda, M. *Am. J. Psych.*, 1973, **86,** 346. Copyright © University of Illinois Press).

process that adjusts brightness percepts in order to take into account varying environmental conditions. Thus a pair of black shoes in bright sunlight still appears black, while a white shirt in a dim room still looks white. This is the case despite the fact that the shoes may actually be delivering more light to the eye than the shirt (this topic is discussed in greater detail in Chapter 14). These demonstrations indicate that brightness depends not only upon the amount of light reaching the eye, or upon retinal interactions, but also upon higher level, more "cognitive," processes.

VISUAL ACUITY

VISUAL ACUITY refers to the ability of the eye to resolve details. There are different types of visual acuity, each dependent upon the specific task or specific detail to be resolved. These details almost always involve brightness differences between a target, or part of a target, and its background. The type of visual acuity most commonly measured is RECOGNITION ACUITY, which was introduced by Herman Snellen (1862). This task uses the familiar *eye chart* found in most ophthal-

mologists' or optometrists' offices. It is composed of rows of letters of progressively smaller size. The observer is simply asked to recognize the letters on the chart. The smallest recognizable letters determine the acuity. Acuity is usually measured relative to the performance of a normal observer. Thus, an acuity of 6/6 indicates that an observer is able to recognize and identify letters, at a distance of 6 m, that a normal observer can also read at that distance (you may be more familiar with the designation 20/20, since 6 m is equivalent to 20 ft). In other words, the measured acuity is normal. An acuity of 6/9 would mean that an observer is able to read letters at 6 m that are large enough for a normal observer to read at a distance of 9 m. Here, the visual acuity is less than normal. A more general means of specifying the limits of acuity is to use the minimum VISUAL ANGLE of a detail that can be resolved. The visual angle is simply a measure of the size of the retinal image. Figure 7-10 shows what the visual angle is and demonstrates a simple computation based upon the size and the distance of the object. Generally speaking, a normal observer can resolve details of one minute of arc (about the size of a quarter seen at a distance of 81 m).

The recognition of letters on a Snellen chart is not the best way to measure acuity since letters differ in their degree of recognizability. For instance O and Q or P and F are easily confused, whereas L and W or O and I are quite easy to discriminate. Because these differences might affect acuity measurements, Hans Landolt (1889) introduced a different recognition task that used circles with a gap in them as targets (see Figure 7-11). The gap can be oriented either up, down, to the right, or to the left, and the observer's task is to indicate the position of the gap. The circles differ in size and the smallest detectable gap is the measure of acuity.

There are a variety of other tasks used to

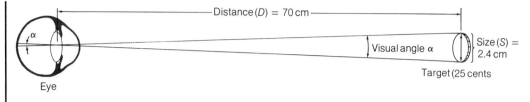

Figure 7-10.
Computation of the size of the visual angle in the image of a quarter viewed at a distance of 70 cm (approximately arm's length). Tangent of visual angle = size/distance, therefore tan $\alpha = S/D = 2.4/70 = 0.034$. Thus α is approximately 2°.

measure visual acuity. RESOLUTION or GRATING ACUITY is measured by an observer's ability to detect a gap between two bars, or the orientation of a grid of lines. VERNIER or DIRECTIONAL ACUITY requires an observer to distinguish a broken line from an unbroken line. The most primitive measure of acuity is simply the specification of the smallest target of any type that can be detected. The relationship between brightness perception and the acuity task is most apparent for this task, where the target is a light line or spot against a dark background, or a dark line or spot against a light background. Figure 7-11 shows examples of the above-mentioned acuity targets with arrows pointing to the detail to be recognized. Each detail is merely a region of the field where there is a change in luminance.

Since acuity tasks are really forms of brightness discrimination, it is not surprising to find that acuity varies as a function of the many factors that were shown to be important in the perception of brightness. For instance, the adaptive state of the eye determines the minimum details that can be discriminated under particular viewing conditions. If you step out of the bright sunlight into a dim room, you may find it impossible to read even the large type of the headlines of a newspaper for a few moments. As your eyes adapt to the dim surroundings, however, you can soon easily read even fine print. Miller (1965) demonstrated that even a brief flash of light, bright enough to alter an observer's state of adaptation, could markedly reduce an observer's ability to detect and recognize acuity targets.

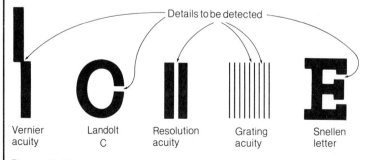

Figure 7-11.
Some typical acuity targets and the details to be discriminated.

Retinal position is also as important for acuity as it is for brightness perception. Demonstration Box 7-4 provides a figure that allows you to experience the drastic reductions in visual acuity for targets that are imaged some distance away from the fovea. When we measure relative acuity for various locations on the retina, we find that it varies as shown in Figure 7-12. Notice that acuity is best in the central fovea and drops off rapidly as we move out into the periphery. Look at the shape of this curve and then turn back and look at Figure 4-7 in Chapter 4, which shows the distribution of rods and cones. It is easy to see that relative acuity almost perfectly follows the distribution of cones. Where cones are plentiful acuity is good; where cones are sparse acuity is poor. Hershenson (1969) showed that letter detection drastically decreased when the letters were positioned only 3°–4° away from the fovea.

To the extent that the presence of cones seems to determine the limits of acuity, and cones are only operative at higher levels of illumination, we would expect acuity to be quite dependent upon levels of illumination. When we measure this relationship directly we obtain results such as those shown in Figure 7-13. Notice that when the illumination is low, in the scotopic (rod) range, acuity is

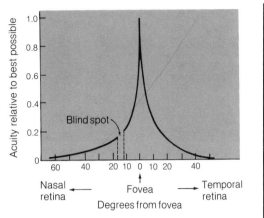

Figure 7-12.
The distribution of visual acuity across the retina.

poor, and it improves only slightly as the light intensity is increased. However, as we begin to shift into the photopic (cone) range acuity improves rapidly. Demonstration Box 7-5 provides a stimulus figure and instructions for demonstrating the relationship between acuity and illumination.

Let us reconsider the experiment we performed in Demonstration Box 7-2. In that demonstration, we saw that increasing the light falling upon a light target on a dark background made the target appear lighter

---

Visual acuity is best in the fovea. The range of clear vision extends less than 10° away from the foveal center. Lay this book flat on the table and view the accompanying diagram from a distance of approximately 12 cm. Cover your left eye with your left hand and look directly at the point marked 0°. Without moving your right eye, you will note that the letter over the 0° mark is relatively clear, and that the letter at 5° is also legible. However, the letters at 10° and beyond begin to appear fuzzy, and the letters at 40° or 50° are virtually unreadable.

Demonstration Box 7-4:
Visual Acuity as a Function of Retinal Location

K	B	X	M	P	A	S
+	+	+	+	+	+	+
50°	40°	30°	20°	10°	5°	0°

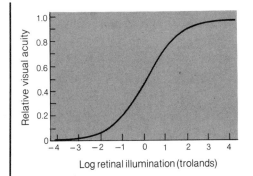

Log retinal illumination (trolands)

Figure 7-13.
The effect of illumination on visual acuity.

and the background darker. Exactly the opposite occurred for a dark target on a light background, with the target apparently darkening and the surround lightening. Clearly, this means that under higher illumination there is a larger apparent difference between background and target. In other words, this change in relative brightness should make it easier to discriminate details marked by areas of different intensities. Thus the brightness paradox in Demonstration Box 7-2 may actually form the basis of the acuity increase with increasing illumination. Recently, a new and more powerful linkage between the perception of brightness and visual acuity has been suggested. This analysis is discussed in the Special Topic that follows.

You will need your variable intensity light source again (either television or closet). Under very dim illumination, view the bundle of converging lines shown in the diagram. Notice that at some point, where the lines are relatively close together, you can no longer resolve individual lines and the bundle appears to be gray. This is the limit of your grating acuity under these conditions. Place your finger or the point of a pencil at the point where the individual lines are no longer resolvable. Now gradually increase the intensity of the light source and notice that you can now begin to resolve lines at a higher point in the bundle. In fact, under normal room illumination, the lines in the area where acuity began to fail under lower illumination may now be discriminable. Notice also that the apparent blackness of the lines and whiteness of the paper (in other words the psychological contrast) also improves under higher light conditions.

Demonstration Box 7-5:
Acuity and Intensity

SPECIAL TOPIC: THE MODULATION TRANSFER FUNCTION

In Chapter 7 we have seen that perceived brightness greatly depends upon the relationship between the luminous intensities of various parts of the stimulus. We might wish to know just how changes in the pattern of stimulus intensities in the visual field alter our perception of brightness. One rather inefficient experimental procedure would be to present visual displays consisting of every shape, intensity, or size we can think of, and carefully form a catalog of brightness judgments made by observers for each part of each display. Of course, since the potential number of displays is infinite, our catalog will never be finished. For this reason, researchers found it necessary to try to find some reasonably small set of relationships, among the variables that affect brightness perception, that could adequately explain all of the data, and perhaps shed some light on the relationship between brightness and acuity. The most successful attempt has been to use a mathematical technique based upon FOURIER'S THEOREM, which says that it is possible to take any light pattern and analyze it into a set of sine waves (see Chapter 5). Thus we can generate any light distribution by summing the appropriate sine waves. This means that any visual pattern can be completely described mathematically by breaking it up into the set of sine waves that produce it when added together.

You might recall from trigonometry (and Chapter 5) that a sine wave is simply a regular smooth periodic function that has precisely specified mathematical properties. Figure ST7-1A shows a graph of a sine wave,

and beside it is a distribution of light that follows this mathematical description, growing more intense where the function rises and less intense where it falls. Such a pattern is properly called a SINE WAVE GRATING, because its intensity varies sinusoidally as we move across the figure. Fourier's theorem says that by adding together (synthesizing) a number of such waves we can produce any specified brightness distribution. For instance, we can even produce a brightness distribution (such as that in Figure ST7-1B) that will contain sharp corners. This pattern is commonly called a SQUARE WAVE GRATING. You can see graphically how this is done in Figure ST7-2. Here we have a series of sine waves (or rather the light intensities that they represent) that we add together progressively until we begin to get good approximations to a square wave.

Fourier analysis and synthesis are more than mathematical curiosities. They provide the basis for a powerful tool that may be used to analyze how some sensory systems respond to stimuli. Consider for a moment how one might test the fidelity of a photographic system. One might take a series of gratings, such as those shown in Figure ST7-1, some of which have very broad bars and spaces (these are low spatial frequencies as we defined them in Chapter 4) and some of which have very narrow bars and spaces (high spatial frequencies). One may now photograph each grating to see how well it can be reproduced. At some point, when the grating becomes quite fine, the system will reach its limit. The lens will no longer be able to resolve the individual lines, and all of the fine

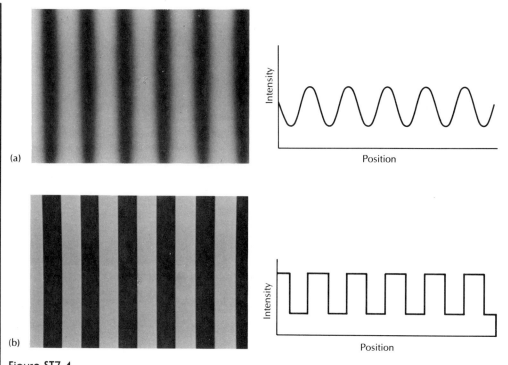

Figure ST7-1.
(A) A sine wave spatial distribution of light and (B) a square wave spatial distribution of light (based upon Cornsweet, 1970).

lines will merge into a gray blur. This is exactly the same type of task that we used when we were discussing the resolution acuity of observers, except that here we are looking at the resolution acuity of an optical system. When photographic engineers do this type of analysis for an optical system, they measure its resolution in terms of the maximum number of lines per inch that can be resolved. Since very finely packed arrays of lines, corresponding to high spatial frequencies, cannot be resolved and are simply blurred, this system is *attenuating* the high-frequency components of the pattern. A description of the way in which certain frequencies are lost, while others are not, is called the SPATIAL MODULATION TRANSFER FUNCTION. It measures the system's ability to "transfer" to the final image a spatial modulation (or intensity change) present in the target stimulus.

In order to assess the visual system's limitations in resolving spatial changes in brightness, *contrast matching* is used to measure the modulation transfer function in humans. Consider the two targets shown in Figure ST7-3. Both are square wave gratings; however, the one on the left is of a lower spatial frequency than the one on the right. Despite the fact that the physical contrast is the same in the two figures, the psychological contrast (the apparent difference between light and dark regions) is much less for the high frequency (you can probably increase this difference by propping the book up and stepping back a foot or two). In a contrast match-

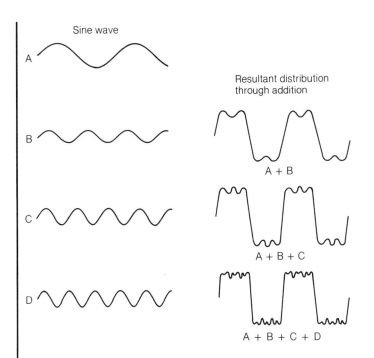

Figure ST7-2.
Gradually adding higher
frequency sine waves to the
distribution leads to better
approximations of a square
wave through the process of
Fourier synthesis.

ing task, observers would be asked to match the apparent contrast of such targets (or more usually sine wave gratings) by adjusting the intensities of the light and the dark regions. In this way, we could map the differences in visibility for various spatial frequencies. An alternative method involves measuring the threshold for detecting sine wave gratings as being different from uniform stimuli. Subjects are presented with a sine wave grating at a particular spatial frequency. Using one of the psychophysical procedures we discussed in

Chapter 2, the size of the intensity variation between the bright and the dark regions of the grating is adjusted until the observer can just barely distinguish the grating pattern from a uniform gray.

When we measure a typical modulation transfer function for a human observer, it might look like the one shown in Figure ST7-4. As can be seen from the graph, it indicates that human observers are quite sensitive to spatial frequencies around six cycles per degree. As spatial frequencies become

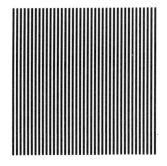

Figure ST7-3.
The effect of spatial frequency
on the apparent brightness
and contrast of patterns.
Notice that the higher
frequency pattern has less
apparent contrast.

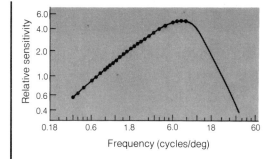

Figure ST7-4.
The modulation transfer function, which shows the relative visibility of targets of various spatial frequencies (from Cornsweet, 1970).

higher, we tend to lose our ability to resolve spatial intensity differences. This loss at high-frequency is probably due to the fact that the eye is an optical system, containing a lens, and any such system tends to have a high-frequency cutoff. Notice also that there is some loss of resolution in the lower spatial frequencies (less than six cycles per degree). This loss is due to the fact that as the variation in image intensity widens, the lateral inhibitory interactions, which tend to sharpen the contours and increase apparent brightness differences between adjacent regions, be-

come less effective. In much the same way, Demonstration Box 7-3 showed that the Mach bands were accentuated when the brightness changes were near one another.

Fourier analysis and knowledge of the modulation transfer function provide us with important information. With this information, we can summarize much of our knowledge about the perception of brightness and the determinants of visual acuity. Intensity changes are most effective in producing the phenomenal impression of a brightness difference when these changes occur in patterns containing, or predominated by, intermediate spatial frequencies (as determined by the Fourier analysis). When intensity changes occur too frequently within the visual image, the brightness differences become difficult to resolve. Similarly, when the physical changes are too infrequent, there is no perception of brightness differences. Thus, the modulation transfer function provides a convenient summary as to what we can expect in terms of the apparent brightness of many types of stimulus configurations. However, as we have seen before, higher level cognitive factors may still play a role in the brightness percept. Therefore, Fourier analysis only provides us with an introduction, and not the whole story.

8
Color

They sat watching the new color television set. When a commercial appeared on the screen, she commented, "I often wonder why humans developed color vision. After all, if we never saw anything but shades of gray, history would have run its course, science would have emerged, and, except for the effect it would have had on art, we would have survived well enough as a species."

"I'm not so sure," he replied. "My dad was color-blind, but didn't find out until he was nearly fifty. He was always doing strange things. He couldn't be trusted to pick tomatoes from the garden because he was always mixing up the ripe and the green ones. We finally suspected that something was wrong when he commented that he really admired cherry pickers for their ability to recognize shapes. 'After all,' he said, 'the only thing that tells 'em it's a cherry is the fact that it's round and the leaves aren't. I just don't see how they find 'em in those trees!'"

It is surprising to many of us to find out how important a factor color is in determining our ability to discern aspects of our world. For instance, consider Figure 8-1. Although the figure appears to be a random collection of gray shapes, there is a word hidden in it. Each letter is spelled out by a series of similar shapes. If you study the figure for a moment, you will begin to see how difficult it is to pick out the word (if you can do it at all). Now flip to Color Plate 2, where we have added the dimension of color to the figure. Notice that in this color plate the word actually "leaps out." Thus, color provides an important stimulus dimension that aids in the localization and identification of targets. For some species, color vision is a matter of life and death. If bees lacked color vision, their task of locating the nectar-bearing flowers hidden among shrubs, grasses or leaves would be almost impossible. The survival of this species depends upon the ability to spot the glints of color that indicate the presence of blossoms.

THE COLOR STIMULUS

The human eye registers as light wavelengths between 400 and 700 nm. Sir Isaac Newton was able to show that stimuli of different

Figure 8-1.
Can you find the hidden word? If not, turn to Color Plate 2.

wavelengths within this range produce different color sensations. Newton's experiment was quite simple. He took a glass prism and allowed some sunlight to pass through it from a slit in a window shade. When he held a sheet of white paper on the other side of the prism, the light no longer appeared to be white; rather, it took the form of a colored spectrum, looking much like the arrangement of lights in a rainbow (see Figure 8-2A). Newton knew that light bends when passing through a prism, and that the amount of bending (technically called refraction) depends upon wavelength. There is less refraction of the longer wavelengths. Thus a prism takes various wavelengths of light, which make up sunlight, and separates them according to wavelength. The fact that we see this spread of light as varying in hue seems to show that color perception depends upon the wavelength of the light. Table 8-1 shows

some typical color names associated with some selected wavelengths of light. Newton inserted another prism (in opposite orientation) that recombined all of these wavelengths; when he placed a piece of paper into this beam it again appeared to be white. This indicates that the sensation of white results from a mixture of many different wavelengths (see Figure 8-2B).

Figure 8-2 does not describe how white light is broken up into colored light. Colored light does not exist; rather, what does exist is visible radiation of different wavelengths. If there were no observer, there would be no color. Newton pointed this out when he said, "For the rays, to speak properly, are not coloured. In them is nothing else than a certain Power and Disposition to stir up a sensation of this or that Colour." Thus when we talk about the color stimulus, we should speak of radiation of different wavelengths, since the sensations of red, green, blue, or any other color reside in the observer. Having made this protest, we must admit that it is extremely convenient to talk about red light or green light, and for the sake of brevity we will not hesitate to do so in some of our later

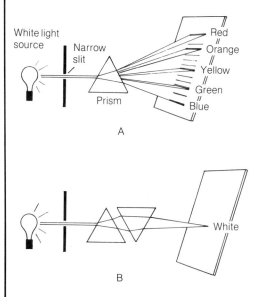

Figure 8-2.
Newton's experiments: (A) separation of white light into its various wavelengths gives the color spectrum; (B) recombination of the colors gives white light.

Table 8-1 *Wavelengths of Light and Associated Color Sensations*

Color Name	Wavelength (nm)
Violet	450
Blue	470
Cyan	495
Green	510
Yellow-Green	560
Yellow	575
Orange	600
Red	660
Purple	Not a spectral color but a mixture of "red" and "blue"

descriptions. Remember, however, that when we refer to a blue light, we are referring to those wavelengths of light *that elicit the sensation of blue,* namely, the shorter wavelengths.

Objects appear to be colored because they reflect to our eyes only selected wavelengths of light. Consider a common object, such as an apple with white light falling upon it. It appears to be red. We have already seen that white light, such as sunlight, is a combination of all wavelengths. Since the light stimulus that reaches your eyes produces the sensation of red, all of the wavelengths except the longer (red-appearing) ones must have been absorbed by the surface of the apple. Objects, surfaces, or pigments selectively absorb wavelengths of light, and it is the unabsorbed wavelengths reflected from the surface that give an object its color. If a surface appears white, then it reflects all wavelengths uniformly. Since it does not absorb or alter the wavelengths reaching the eye, it does not appear to have a color. Color filters work in much the same way. For instance, if a white light is projected through a green filter, the resulting beam is green. This means that the filter has absorbed most of the long and short wavelengths, leaving only the medium range or green-appearing wavelengths to reflect to the eye. Unfortunately, simply specifying the wavelength, or wavelengths, in a stimulus does not seem to fully describe the way the color appears to an observer. For instance, a stimulus with a dominant wavelength of 570 nm may appear yellow, while another with the same wavelength composition might appear brown. For this reason, additional factors other than wavelength are used to classify colors.

Color Appearance Systems. Suppose that you were marooned on a desert island that had a beach covered with many colored pebbles. Lacking anything else to do, you set about the task of classifying the colors of all of the pebbles in some meaningful way. The first classification scheme that might come to mind would involve grouping stones together on the basis of their hues. Thus you would end up with a pile of red stones and another of green stones. Once you have your piles of stones, you would next have to look for some meaningful arrangement for the piles. For instance, you might notice that orange seems to fall, in terms of appearance, somewhere between red and yellow. The yellow-greens, of course, seem to fall between yellow and green. Once you reach the blue end of your line of stones, however, you might find yourself running into a bit of a problem. The purple stones seem to fall somewhere between the blues and the reds. This means that a straight line arrangement is not adequate. Instead, you might arrange the pebbles as shown in Figure 8-3.

This crude color arrangement scheme is circular in form. You have probably seen it before in books on art, decorating, or design. It is usually called the COLOR CIRCLE or COLOR WHEEL in such sources. In this arrangement, you have separated the colors according to HUE, which is the psychological dimension that most clearly corresponds to variations in wavelength. Let us consider the effect of wavelength on sensation by looking at the effects produced by pure or MONOCHROMATIC stimuli. A monochromatic stimulus contains only one wavelength (from the Greek *mono* meaning one and *chroma* meaning color). These stimuli are similar to those found in the spectrum generated by Newton's prismatic separation of light and therefore are often called SPECTRAL COLORS. Such monochromatic stimuli do not produce all of the hues found in the color wheel. For instance, we find that there is no single wavelength that produces the sensation of purple. This sensation requires a mixture of

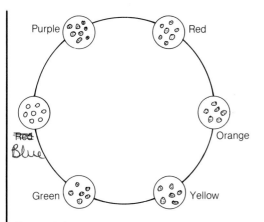

Figure 8-3.
A primitive color circle for encoding the colors of pebbles.

blue and red wavelengths. Similarly, there is no place in the spectrum where we can find a red that doesn't have a tinge of yellow. In order to achieve such a hue, we must add a bit of blue (short wavelength) light.

Meanwhile, back on the beach, it has become clear that our color wheel classification scheme based only upon the psychological attribute of hue seems incomplete. A close look at the piles of pebbles reveals marked color differences. For instance, among the red pebbles, you might find that some are a deep red color, while others are more pink. Another group may be almost pure white with only a hint of red coloration. Physically, this observation corresponds to the dimension of PURITY. Clearly the purest color one could get would correspond to a monochromatic or spectral hue. As we add other wavelengths, or white light, the color appears to become more "washed out." This attribute of color appearance is called SATURATION. It is actually quite easy to integrate saturation into the color circle by simply placing white in the center. Now imagine that the various degrees of saturation correspond to positions along the spokes or radii

from the center of the wheel. The center represents white and the perimeter represents the purest or most saturated color possible. Figure 8-4 shows the color wheel now modified to include saturation. Notice that the point corresponding to pink (a moderately desaturated red) would be plotted near the center along the line connecting red and white, while a crimson would be plotted further away from the center along the same line.

Unfortunately, hue and saturation do not completely describe all nuances of color. It is quite possible to have two colors match in both of these attributes but still appear to be different. For instance, a blue spot of light projected onto a screen would not appear to be the same as another spot identical in all regards except that it has been dimmed by putting a light-reducing filter in front of it. Thus the sensory quality of BRIGHTNESS (which we discussed in Chapter 7) must be worked into our system of describing colors.

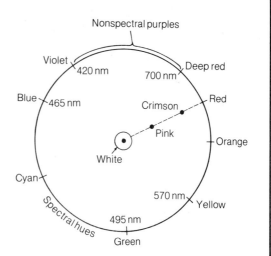

Figure 8-4.
The color circle modified to allow the encoding of both hue and saturation. Spectral colors are on the outer rim, white is in the center.

Since we have already used the two dimensions capable of being reproduced on a flat piece of paper, it is clear that the addition of a third color dimension (brightness) must force us to use a solid instead of a flat representation. The shape of this three-dimensional surface becomes clear if we recognize that at high brightness levels or at very low brightness levels colors seem "weak" or "washed out," meaning that they are of low saturation. Thus, one can imagine the hue circle shrinking, as saturation judgments become less spread out. If we combine the three attributes of hue, saturation, and brightness, we get something that looks like Figure 8-5. We have what seem to be a pair of cones placed base to base. This is usually called the COLOR SPINDLE, or the COLOR SOLID. The central core

as we move up or down represents brightness. We can imagine that at each brightness level, if we sliced through the color solid in the direction shown in the diagram, we would get a color circle in which the hue would be represented along the perimeter. Totally desaturated colors (those ranging from white through gray and black) represent the central core; hence, saturation is represented by moving from the center outward. This is the basic representation used in many color appearance systems. Probably the most popular among psychologists is the one developed by Munsell (1915) and modified by Newhall, Nickerson, and Judd (1943) to agree with the way in which typical observers arrange color stimuli. To actually classify colors, you can use a COLOR ATLAS in which each page represents a horizontal or a vertical slice through the color solid. Color samples that illustrate colors found in varying locations in the color solid are given in such atlases. This allows the observer to identify and to label any given test color.

Color Mixture. Pure colors of a single wavelength are usually produced under precise laboratory conditions. Most of the light reaching your eye is composed of a mixture of many different wavelengths. Generally, the DOMINANT WAVELENGTH will determine what hue you see, although this is not always the case. When we combine two or more wavelengths of light a new color, with a different psychological hue and saturation, is seen. Once the colors are mixed, the eye can no longer determine the individual wavelengths that make up the mixture. Thus, you can have a pure yellow made up of 570 nm light and another that matches it, composed of a mixture of a 500 nm green and a 650 nm red. Colors that appear to be the same but are made up of different wavelengths of light are called METAMERIC

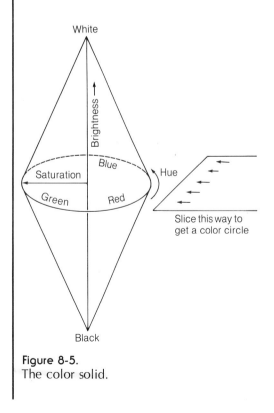

Figure 8-5.
The color solid.

COLORS. You will not be able to distinguish between these hues, nor will you be able to isolate the red and the green that went into the mixture.

There are two types of color mixtures. The first, and the simplest to describe, is called ADDITIVE COLOR MIXTURE. Additive mixtures occur when we mix light. For instance, if we project a red circle on a screen, the light reaching our eye from the projected point is red. If we project a blue circle on the screen so that it partially overlaps with the red circle, the light reaching our eye from the region where the circles overlap contains both blue and red light. Thus, each new wavelength projected onto the screen adds to the mixture of wavelengths reaching the eye. Figure 8-6A shows a situation that might occur if we used three projectors with the first projecting a red beam, the second a green beam, and the third a deep blue beam. If the circles of light were arranged so that they partially over-lapped with one another, we would get a series of additive mixtures. For instance, where red and the deep blue overlap we get a reddish-purple generally called magenta. Where the deep blue and the green overlap we get a lighter hue tending toward a green, usually called cyan. Something quite surprising happens where the red and green overlap. In this region we get the sensation of yellow. Where all three beams overlap we get the sensation of white. Demonstration Box 8-1 shows another way to get additive color mixtures.

These results cannot be duplicated using paints. If you tried mixing all of your paints together to get white, you would get a shade of gray instead. This is because pigments do not work in the same way that lights do. Something that appears red, such as a to-mato, will have a surface pigment that ab-sorbs most of the short and medium wavelengths, reflecting to your eyes only wavelengths in the vicinity of about 620 nm.

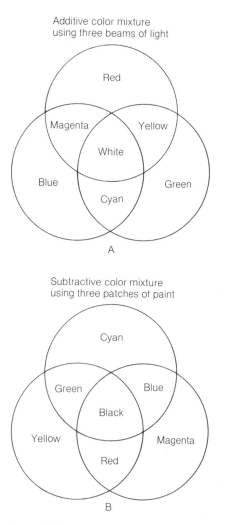

Figure 8-6.
Color mixture systems: (A) additive, (B) subtractive.

On the other hand, a pigment that gives you a color similar to grass green might absorb most of the long wavelengths and the short wavelengths, reflecting to your eye mainly wavelengths around 500 nm. Thus when you mix the red and the green paints together, you effectively *subtract all* the wavelengths, leaving you with a muddy gray.

Since pigments work by subtracting or absorbing wavelengths of light, mixtures of pigments are called SUBTRACTIVE COLOR MIXTURES. Such pigment mixtures produce colors that are considerably less predictable than mixtures of lights, because the wavelength-absorbing property of pigments is complex and often varies. For example, Figure 8-7 shows the wavelengths reflected by some typical pigments. If we painted circles of a yellow pigment, a cyan pigment, and a magenta pigment so that they overlapped, we would get a crude representation of what would generally be expected in subtractive color mixtures. Since yellow pigments work by absorbing all of the short wavelengths, and the cyan pigment absorbs all the long wavelengths, their mixture absorbs both the short and the long wavelengths, leaving us only with the middle or green-appearing portion of the spectrum. When we combine yellow with magenta, we find that the yellow subtracts the short wavelengths and the magenta subtracts the middle wavelengths; hence only the long, or red-appearing, wavelengths remain. In a similar fashion, overlapping cyan and magenta leaves us

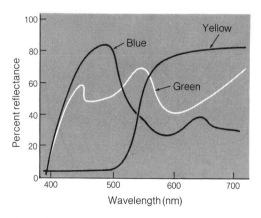

Figure 8-7.
The relative wavelength composition of a blue, yellow, and a green pigment.

with only the blue wavelengths, because all others are subtracted; hence, the mixture produces blue. Clearly, when all three pigments overlap, everything is absorbed and we get black, as shown in Figure 8-6B. In general, it is more convenient to deal with additive color mixtures since they are easier to conceptualize.

The color wheel, which we have already discussed, provides a convenient means of predicting the appearance of additive color mixtures. It is important to note that the color wheel describes, rather than explains, how colors interact. To use the color wheel to predict a color mixture is actually quite simple. Suppose we mix a spectral red (about 650 nm) with a spectral yellow (about 570 nm). We can depict this as in Figure 8-8, where the two colors to be mixed are represented by the line connecting these two colors. For instance, if we combine the yellow and the red in equal proportions we will get a color that corresponds to the dot in the center of the line. We can determine what this color will look like by simply drawing a line from the center of the color circle through the dot to the perimeter. When this is done, we find that we would get an orange corresponding to about a 600-nm spectral stimulus. Increasing the amount of yellow would shift the point along the line in the direction indicated, making it closer to the yellow hue. Adding more red would shift the point in the other direction along the line. You will notice that we started out with two spectral, or pure hues (marked on the perimeter). However, the resultant mixed color is a hue that is no longer on the perimeter. It is closer to the center of the color wheel. The purest colors possible are placed on the perimeter of the color wheel, since colors become more desaturated as they move toward the center (toward white). Thus, the color mixture is less saturated than either of the two component colors that compose it. *It is the case that no mix-*

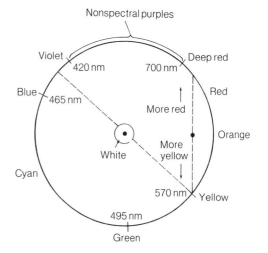

Figure 8-8.
Using the color circle to predict color mixtures.

ture of colors can ever be quite as saturated as a monochromatic or spectral color.

Mixing more than two hues (or hues containing more than a single wavelength) is a little more complex. If we were mixing three colors, the resultant color sensation would be given by the center of a triangle produced by connecting the three colors. If the amount of each hue differs, the center point of the triangle would shift toward the dominant hue. An interesting effect occurs when we mix two colors that are opposite to each other on the color circle. For instance, mixing a violet with a yellow along the lines shown in Figure 8-8 results in a colorless gray or white. This is because, when the proportions are correct, this mixture lies in the center of the circle. Colors whose mixture produces such an achromatic gray or white are known as COMPLEMENTARY COLORS.

One of the most important facts about color mixtures emerged in the 1850s. The German physicist and physiologist Hermann von Helmholtz (1821–1894) and the Scottish physicist James Clerk Maxwell (1831–1879) carried out a set of color matching experiments. They reported that by combining an appropriate set of three monochromatic light sources in appropriate amounts, they could match any other hue. These three wavelengths were to be known as PRIMARIES. Actually the choice of primaries is rather arbitrary. One must select colors that are reasonably far apart, with the requirement that the mixture of any two of them alone will not match the third one. In 1929, Wright made a set of measurements in which observers matched the hue of the various spectral sensations. He selected as his primary colors a red of 650 nm, a green of 530 nm, and a blue of 460 nm. The observers matched the color of two patches of light, where the first was the test color, and the second could contain any combination of the three primaries. His results are shown in Figure 8-9, which indicates the relative amount of each of the three primaries needed to match any given wavelength. You might notice that some of the values are negative. This indicates that some of the particular primary had to be added to the test sample in order to reduce its saturation to the point where it could be matched by a mixture of the two remaining primaries. The fact that any given color can be matched by an appropriate combination of the three

others has important theoretical implications, which we will discuss later. In addition, it has led to another means of specifying colors that has been agreed upon by the Commission Internationale de l'Eclairage (CIE). This international commission adopted a set of standard primary wavelengths, and by adopting a certain shape of color diagram, they created the CIE COLOR SPACE, which can more accurately describe color mixtures. How one arrives at this color description is described in the Special Topic at the end of this chapter entitled The Color Space.

THE PHYSIOLOGY OF COLOR VISION

To this point, we have dealt with the physical stimulus, some methods of specifying the appearance of a color, and some aspects of combining various wavelengths of light. None of the foregoing descriptions specify *how* a particular color sensation arises. In order to understand this, we must deal with both physiological and psychological factors. Let us consider these in light of the two major theoretical positions that have emerged during the last 150 years.

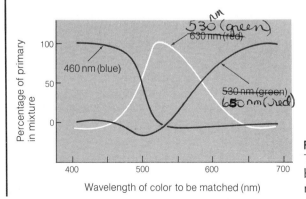

Figure 8-9.
The proportion of each primary (a 460-nm blue, a 530-nm green, and a 650-nm red) needed to match any pure spectral color.

Trichromatic Color Theory. Much research has gone into the search for the physiological basis of color vision. One of the earliest findings was discussed in Chapter 7, where it was reported that under scotopic levels of illumination, when only the rods are active, no color vision is found. On the basis of these observations, it was concluded that cones are the retinal receptors that provide the first stage of the color response. Thus how the cones provide information about the wavelength of the incoming light becomes the first question to be answered.

The average human observer can discriminate approximately 200 different hues. Conceptually, the simplest procedure to build an eye with color vision would be to have a separate cone that responded to each of the discriminable hues. Unfortunately, such a scheme is not particularly practical. For any given colored stimulus, we would only have 1/200 of the cones active. This means that our visual acuity would be much poorer than research has shown it to be. In addition, such a system would mean that our acuity measured under white illumination would be 200 times better than our acuity measured under monochromatic stimulation. This is experimentally false.

An alternate scheme would be to have only one type of retinal cone with 200 different signal codes, by which it could indicate the discriminable hues. This could be done via a sort of neural Morse code. Although it may be the case that such a neural Morse code can play a part in color vision (as we shall see later), it does not seem to work well. Research evidence seems to indicate that each cone contains only one pigment. If this is the case, how would the cone itself recognize the wavelength of the light? The only thing that the cone "knows" is the amount of pigment that has been bleached. Although different wavelengths of light may bleach more or less pigment, simply increasing or decreas-

ing the intensity of the stimulus could also bring about such a state of affairs. It seems unlikely that a single cone would be able to discriminate 200 hues.

An answer was suggested almost 200 years ago by Thomas Young (1773–1829). Young suggested that only a few different retinal receptors, operating with different wavelength sensitivities, would be necessary to allow humans to perceive the number of colors they do. He further suggested that perhaps as few as three would do. His theoretical notion was revived in the 1850s by Helmholtz. As we have already noted, Helmholtz and Maxwell were able to show that normal observers need only three primaries to match any color stimulus. These data were taken as evidence for the presence of three different receptors in the retina. Since the usual color matching primaries consisted of a red, a green, and a blue, it was presumed that there were three types of receptors, one responsive to red, one to green, and one to blue. Since these receptors are cones, and cones operate by the bleaching of pigment, we may suggest three hypothetical pigments. The first we would call ERYTHROLABE (translated from the Greek this means red-catching), another called CHLOROLABE (meaning green-catching) and the third pigment would be called CYANOLABE (meaning blue-catching). This TRICHROMATIC THEORY (from the Greek *tri* meaning three and *chroma* meaning color) finds some very convincing support in the realm of defective color vision.

Color vision defects. Virtually all individuals differ from what is usually called "normal" color vision in some ways. However, some individuals show drastic deficiencies in their ability to discriminate colored stimuli. In popular speech, such individuals tend to be called COLOR-BLIND. This term is much too strong, since only a very small percentage of individuals are totally incapable of discriminating colors. According to a trichromatic theory of color vision, we should be able to predict that there would be five different varieties of color abnormality. The first, and most drastic, would be found in individuals who have no functioning cones. Since these individuals would be required to do all of their seeing with the rod system, they would be expected to have no color discrimination ability. In addition, these individuals should find photopic, or daylight, levels of illumination to be quite uncomfortable. A slightly less drastic malady is one in which only one variety of cone is functioning in addition to the rods. With this problem, you should be able to see under both photopic and scotopic conditions but you would still lack any color discrimination ability. Any wavelength of light hitting one of the functioning rods (or the single cone system) would produce some bleaching of the pigment. Even though different wavelengths might bleach different amounts, this is not enough to allow color discrimination since the response produced by any one wavelength of light can be matched by merely adjusting the intensity of any other. In other words, the individual with no functioning cones, or the one with only one functioning cone type, responds to light in much the way that a sheet of black and white film does. All colors are recorded simply as gradations in intensity of the response. Such individuals are called MONOCHROMATS.

One might also suppose that some individuals, rather than lacking two or three sets of cones as does the monochromat, might only have one malfunctioning cone system. Given two functioning cone systems, individuals should have some color perception. Of course their color perception would differ from that of a normal observer. In effect they should be able to match all other colors with a mixture of two primaries. Such individuals are usually called DICHROMATS (from the Greek di meaning two and chroma meaning

color). The existence of such individuals has been known since the 1700s. The famous English chemist, Dalton, was such a dichromat, a fact he learned rather late in his life. Supposedly, it first came to his attention when he wore a scarlet robe to receive his Ph.D. degree. Since he was a Quaker, a sect that shuns bright colors, this caused quite a stir, until it became clear that woolen yarn dyed crimson or dark blue-green appeared to be the same to him.

There are three predictable forms of dichromacy, depending upon whether it is the red, green, or blue responding cones that are inoperative. The specific confusions one would get are predictable from the color matching curves of normal observers shown in Figure 8–9. Dalton's type of color defect is usually referred to as PROTANOPIA (the Greek prefix protos means first, and red light is generally designated as the first primary). A protanope would be insensitive to long wavelengths of red light. If a red light were made very much brighter than a green light, a protanope could easily confuse them. A color normal observer would perceive that the red light was brighter than the green and also that they differ in hue. Dalton described his subjective experiences when viewing a spectrum such as that produced by Newton's prism. Most individuals perceive six different colors, blending one into another. Dalton reported that "To me it is quite otherwise. I see only two, or at most three distinctions. These I should call yellow and blue, or yellow, blue, and purple. My yellow comprehends the red, orange, yellow, and green of others and my blue and purple coincide with theirs."

The most common form of dichromacy is called DEUTERANOPIA (the Greek prefix deuteros means second, and green light is by convention the second primary). Individuals with deuteranopia presumably have a malfunction in the green cone system. With deuteranopia, you are still able to respond to green light, however, you cannot distinguish green from certain combinations of red and blue.

Trichromatic theory would also predict that there would be a third form of dichromacy based upon the absence or malfunction of the blue cone system. Although a name existed for this phenomenon, TRITANOPIA (from the Greek *tritan,* for the third primary), there was no report of this difficulty for many years. However, some years ago a magazine article began an intensive search throughout England and managed to find 17 such individuals. These individuals, instead of seeing the spectrum as composed of blue and of yellow as do other dichromats, see the longer wavelengths as red and the shorter ones as bluish-green. The discovery of this last class of individuals seems to provide strong support for a trichromatic theory of color vision.

Color defects are a fairly common problem. Some instances of it are relatively mild and result in what we call ANOMALOUS TRICHROMATISM. Such individuals do not act exactly as a dichromat would, however their matches require more red (PROTOANOMALY) or more green (DEUTERANOMALY) than the color matches of nondefective individuals. They look more like a dichromat than like a color-normal individual. If we count all of the individuals with any form of color deficiency, we find that just over 8% of all males show such color weaknesses, while slightly less than .05% of all females are afflicted.

What colors does a dichromat actually see? It is really not possible to know how the colors of a dichromat compare with those seen by a color-normal observer. However, a glimpse into the visual world of the color defective has been provided by a rare person who was deuteranope in her left eye, but color-normal in her right eye. Graham and Hsia (1958) had this observer adjust the color seen by her normal eye so that it appeared to be the same hue as the color seen by her defective eye. The results of her matches are shown in Figure 8-10. As can be seen from this figure, the colors over the entire range of red to green (from about 700 to 502 nm) all appear to have the same yellow hue (about 570 nm), while all of the colors from green to violet appeared to be blue (matching a 470-nm stimulus). The region that appears to be blue-green to the normal observer (around 502 nm) was perceived as being a neutral gray in the defective eye.

Physiological evidence. Although the data from color mixing and color defects seem to support a trichromatic theory of color vision, direct physiological evidence for three cone pigments did not appear until the 1960s. The most elegant measurements were done by Marks, Dobelle, and MacNichol (1964) and Brown and Wald (1964). Their procedure was conceptually simple, but technically quite difficult. It involved a device called a MICROSPECTROPHOTOMETER. With this device a tiny spot of monochromatic light is focused upon the pigment-bearing outer segment of a cone. Now tiny amounts of light of various wavelengths are passed through the cone, and the amount of light absorbed at each wavelength is measured. The more light of a given wavelength that is absorbed by the cone pigment, the more sensitive is the cone to light of that particular wavelength. Such measurements were taken using cones from the retina of goldfish, monkeys, and finally on cones from the retinas of humans. The results were unambiguous. There were three major groups of cones. One had a maximum absorption in the range 445–450 nm, another in the range 525–535 nm and the third in the range 555–570 nm. Figure 8-11 shows the relative absorption of these three pigments (where 1.0 is the maximum amount absorbed by the pigment). Clearly, on the basis of their sensitivity peaks we should call the short-wavelength-absorbing pigment "blue violet," the middle

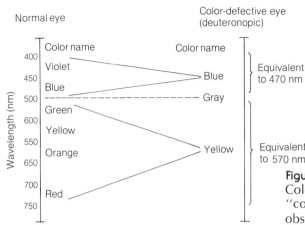

Figure 8-10.
Color matches of a normal eye to a "color-blind" eye (deuteranopic) in the same observer (based upon Graham & Hsia, 1958).

"green," and the long wavelength "yellow-red" if we wished to be more precise than the red, green, and blue labels we have been using.

At about the same time, Rushton (1962, 1965) measured the absorption of cone pigments in living human observers. He used a technique in which a beam of light is sent into the eye, with measurements taken on the amount of light reflected back out of the eye. By taking the difference between the amount of light sent into the eye and the amount re-

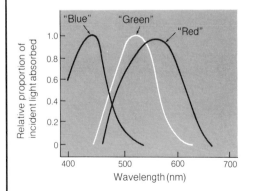

Figure 8-11.
Relative spectral absorption of pigments in cones taken from a human eye.

flected (corrections are also applied for various interfering factors, such as absorption by blood vessels and light scattering in the eye), an estimate is obtained of the amount of light at each wavelength absorbed by the photo-pigments in the living human eye. Rushton concentrated his beam on the fovea, since cones alone populate this region. He was able to obtain absorption curves similar to those shown in Figure 8-11 for pigments marked "red" and "green." He reasoned further that protanopes and deuteranopes, according to trichromatic theory, should be missing one or the other of the two longer wavelength pigments. When he used his procedure with color-defective observers, he found that they were missing the appropriate pigments.

Rushton could not find evidence for cones containing blue-matching pigment in the fovea. This fact suggests that all observers are dichromats for targets seen in central vision. Actually, we have known for a long time that the color response varies over regions of the retina. The central foveal region is relatively blue-blind. The distribution of sensitivity to red and green is limited to an area of about 20°–30° around the fixation point. Yellow and blue can be discriminated at up to 40°–

60°. If we go into the far periphery of the retina, we find that individuals are totally color-blind in this region. Figure 8-12 shows a map of the color sensitivity of the retina. You may trace this sensitivity for yourself, to see how your own color discrimination varies across the retina, by using Demonstration Box 8-2. Although the evidence for trichromatic theory is quite strong at the retinal level, there are a number of perceptual phenomena that cannot be explained by the existence of three pigments alone. Such data suggest that the actual neural coding of color information is not simply the addition of responses from three separate color channels, as we shall see in the next section.

Opponent-Process Theory. The German physiologist Ewald Hering (1878) was not completely satisfied with a trichromatic theory of color vision. It seemed to him that human observers acted as if there were four,

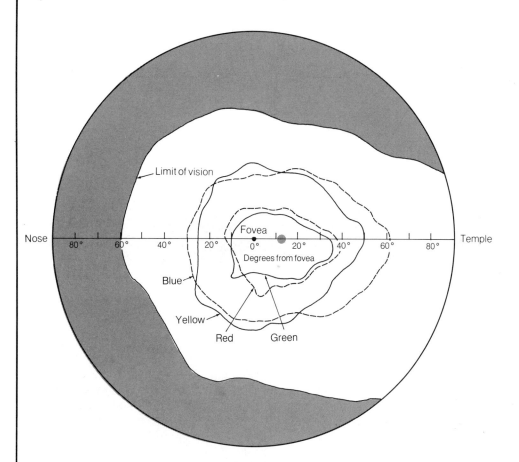

Figure 8-12.
Map of the zones of color sensitivity of one observer's right eye. Each line represents the limit of the area (from the center out) in which the marked colors can be seen.

Demonstration Box 8-2:
Color Sensitive Zones on the Retina

Color perception is best in the central region of the retina. You can observe the changes in color discrimination for different parts of the retina by using Color Plate 5. Lay this book flat on a table and view the color plate from a distance of approximately 12 cm. Cover your left eye with your left hand and look directly at the point marked 0°. Without moving your right eye, you will notice that the four colored dots (red, green, blue, and yellow) have clearly discriminable hues at the point marked 5°. At 10°, you may find some difficulty discriminating between the red and the green. At 20°, only the blue and the yellow should have clearly discriminable hues, while at 50° or 60°, the four dots should be virtually indistinguishable as far as hue is concerned, with each taking on a shade of gray.

rather than three, primary colors. For instance, when observers are presented with a large number of color samples, and asked to pick out those which appear to be *pure* (defined as not showing any trace of being a mixture of colors) they tend to pick out four, rather than three, colors. These unique colors almost always include a red, a green, and a blue, as trichromatic theory would predict; however, they also include a yellow (Bornstein, 1973). Boynton and Gordon (1965) showed that with the color names red, yellow, green, and blue, English-speaking observers can categorize the entire range of visible hues (some stimuli seem to require a combination term containing two primaries, such as yellow-green). The way in which adult observers distribute their hue names is shown in Figure 8-13. One can see that there are four overlapping hue name categories corresponding to red, green, blue, and yellow. One cannot simply attribute the results to learning or language use. For example, Bornstein, Kessen, and Weiskopf (1976) showed that four-month-old infants tend to see the spectrum as if it were divided into four hue categories. They did this by repeatedly presenting a given wavelength of light until the infant became visually bored (a process called HABITUATION). They next monitored how much time an infant spent looking at a second wavelength of light. They

found that when the second wavelength was selected from another hue name category (based upon the adult data) the infants spent more time looking at it than they did at a wavelength selected from the same hue category. This suggests that infants think that stimuli within a given hue category are somehow familiar; hence it seems they are categorizing hues into the same four groups that the adults do.

Hering looked at another aspect of the subjective experience of hue. He noted that certain color combinations were never reported by observers. For instance, one cannot have a yellowish-blue, nor can one have a greenish-red. This led Hering to suggest that

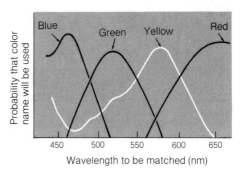

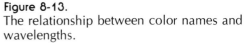

Figure 8-13.
The relationship between color names and wavelengths.

Color Plate 1

Color Plate 2

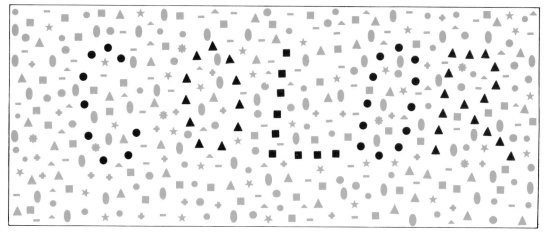

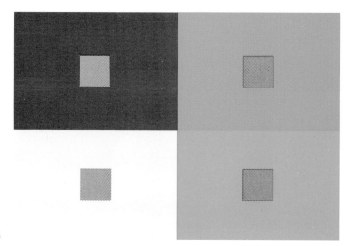

Color Plate 3

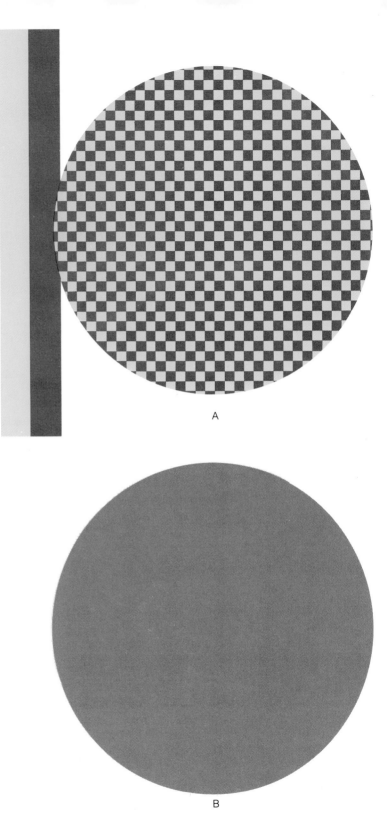

Color Plate 4

A

B

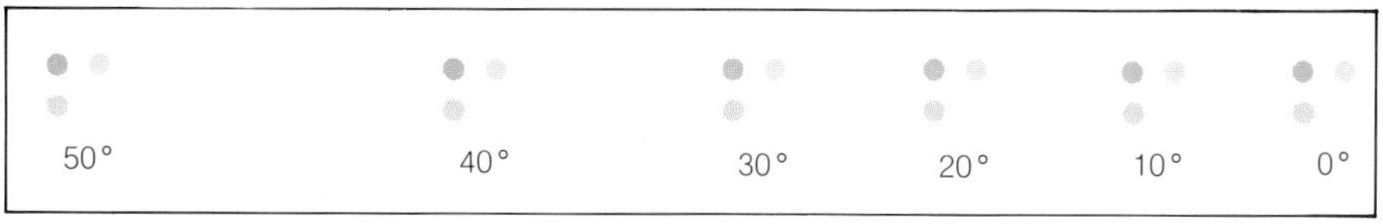

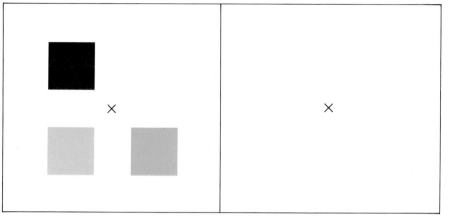

50°   40°   30°   20°   10°   0°

Color Plate 5

Color Plate 6

A Read through this list of color names as quickly as possible.
   Read from right to left across each line.

RED	YELLOW	BLUE	GREEN
RED	GREEN	YELLOW	BLUE
YELLOW	GREEN	BLUE	RED
BLUE	RED	GREEN	YELLOW
RED	GREEN	BLUE	YELLOW

B Name each of these color patches as quickly as possible.
   Name from left to right across each line.

C Name the color of ink in which each word is printed as quickly as possible.
   Name from left to right across each line.

RED	BLUE	GREEN	YELLOW
YELLOW	BLUE	RED	GREEN
BLUE	YELLOW	GREEN	RED
GREEN	BLUE	YELLOW	RED
BLUE	YELLOW	RED	GREEN

Color Plate 7

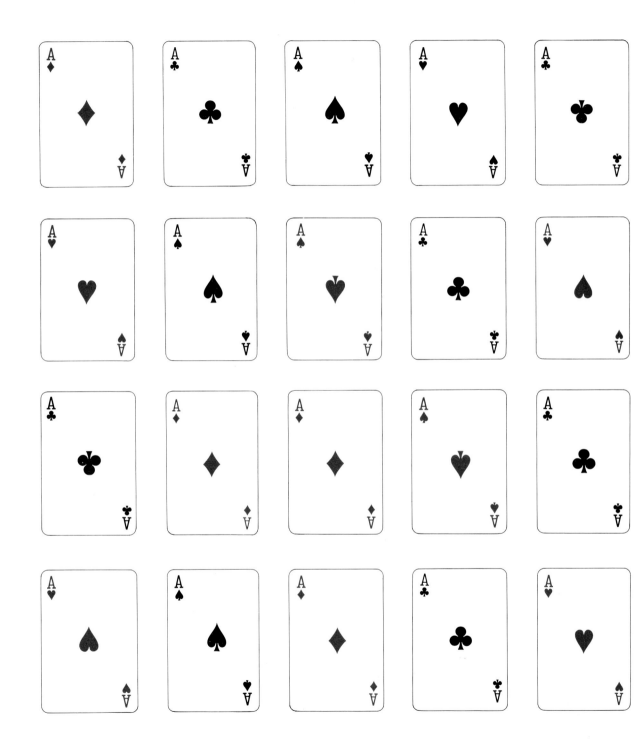

Color Plate 8

the four primaries were arranged in opposing pairs. One pair would signal the presence of red or green, while a separate pair would signal blue or yellow. This might be accomplished by having a single neuron whose activity rate increased with the presence of one color (red) and decreased in the presence of its opponent color (green). Since the cell's activity cannot increase and decrease simultaneously, one could never have a reddish-green. A different opponent process cell might respond to blue and yellow. A third unit was suggested to account for brightness perception. This unit might be called a black–white opponent-process cell. One need not limit the discussion to speculation, however, since there exists physiological evidence that bears directly on the issue of opponent-process coding of color information.

Physiological evidence. At the time when Hering first suggested an opponent-process mechanism for the neural encoding of hue information, there was no physiological evidence to support such a speculation. Perhaps the single most important finding of 20th century sensory physiology was that neural responses are subject to both excitatory and inhibitory influences caused by interaction between neighboring units. We introduced such systems in Chapters 4 and 7. In fact, in Chapter 7 we saw that many brightness phenomena can be explained by the presence of a *spatially* opponent mechanism on the retina, where excitation in one region might cause inhibition in another. If we could also find *spectrally* opponent organization, where stimulation by one wavelength of light causes excitation in a cell, and stimulation by a wavelength in another region of the spectrum causes inhibition of that cell's neural response, then we would have the mechanism postulated by Hering.

The first evidence that different wavelengths of light could cause opponent effects in neural response was offered by Svaetichin (1956), who inserted an electrode into the cell layers of the retina of the goldfish. When he recorded the responses to light, he found that they varied depending upon its wavelength. He found that not only did the strength of response vary as one changed the wavelength, but more importantly the electrical sign of the response was different for long and short wavelengths. Figure 8-14 shows the pattern of responses recorded by Svaetichin and MacNicol (1958). Notice that the spectral sensitivity of the units marked R–G and B–Y are exactly what we would need for a red–green cell and

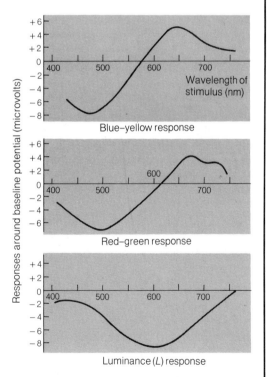

Figure 8-14.
Graded electrical response of retinal cells to various wavelengths of light (based upon Svaetichin & MacNichol, 1958).

a blue–yellow cell. For instance, the cell marked R–G would respond with a large negative signal if the unit is stimulated with a long-wavelength light (around 650 nm). This negative response could signal red. If the unit is stimulated with a greenish hue (around 500 nm), it would give its peak positive response, thus signaling the presence of green. If we simultaneously stimulated this unit with both a red and a green stimulus, the positive and negative responses would cancel each other and no signal would result. Thus indeed, red and green oppose each other, and one can never have the same unit simultaneously signaling both red and green. Such graded potentials are usually called S POTENTIALS after their discoverer, Svaetichin. Notice the cell marked *L* in the figure. It simply responds to the intensity of the light regardless of wavelength. This could be the black–white cell hypothesized by Hering.

As we move further back into the nervous system to the lateral geniculate nucleus we find more signs of the action of a spectrally opponent-process. In Chapter 4, we discussed some of the work of DeValois and his co-workers (DeValois & DeValois, 1975). They found that cells in the lateral geniculate of monkeys were also color coded. These units showed a resting level of activity (in terms of neural responses per unit time) even in the absence of any light stimulation. When the eye was stimulated by light, the response pattern changed. Some cells responded more vigorously when the eye was stimulated with short wavelengths of light, and decreased their response rate below their spontaneous (dark) activity level for long wavelengths of light. Other cells acted in exactly an opposite manner. As with the S potentials, two different classes of cells were reported. Each had different patterns of response as a function of wavelength, similar to what is needed for a red–green cell and a blue–yellow cell. Another group of cells responded to increases

or decreases in illumination but showed little spectral sensitivity. These responses from lateral geniculate cells can be seen in Figure 8-15. DeValois further reports that whether a given wavelength will produce an increase or a decrease in neural response may also vary as one varies the spatial position of the stimulus spot within the receptive field of the cell (an issue we discussed in Chapter 4).

Unfortunately, there have only been about a dozen studies on the color response of cortical cells in higher animals. It seems clear at this moment that some cortical cells respond quite similarly to those of the lateral geniculate, although often with a narrower range of response (Boles, 1971; Poggio, 1972; Dow &

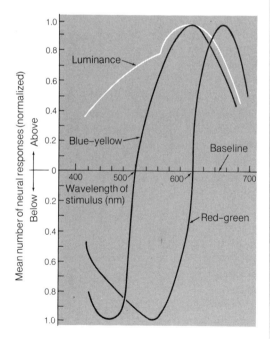

Figure 8-15.
The neural response rate for cells in the lateral geniculate relative to their resting response rate, for stimulation by monochromatic lights (based upon DeValois & DeValois, 1975).

Gouras, 1973). There are some reports of cells in the cortex that respond to monochromatic light but not to white light (Boles, 1971; Dow & Gouras, 1973). This could indicate that the color response becomes more specific in the cortex. Much more research must be done before we will have the full picture, however.

How can a four-primary, opponent-process (or "push–pull") system exist when we already provided physiological and psychophysical evidence indicating that the retina operates with a three-color pigment system? Actually, Hurvich and Jameson (1974) have suggested a NEURAL WIRING DIAGRAM that indicates the way in which cones, each containing only one of three pigments, could produce opponent responses at the postretinal level. An example of how such a wiring diagram might work is shown in Figure 8-16. Notice that we only have to require that certain cones excite cells further along in the system, while other cones inhibit or decrease the response rates of other cells. Engineers hit upon a similar system when they designed color television. The color in the original scene is first analyzed into its red, green, and blue components by the camera, and then transformed into two color-difference (or opponent-process) signals (plus an intensity signal). After reception at its distant location, the signals are reconverted into red, green, and blue signals by your television set. This technique was selected because it required considerably less information to be transmitted through each channel. Thus one could have good fidelity and increased economy. Perhaps similar considerations of economy and fidelity underlie the organization of our visual systems.

There is an alternative neural coding theory for color. It was first suggested by Troland (1921) and recently revived by Festinger, Allyn, and White (1971). It suggests that separate neural channels may not be

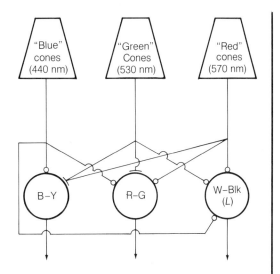

Figure 8-16.
Schematic diagram indicating how a three-pigment system might be connected to produce an opponent-process neural response. The lines represent the connections. The round and the flat connections differ in that one is excitatory and the other is inhibitory (which is which is arbitrary). Numbers indicate the wavelength of maximum sensitivity.

needed for the various primary hues. Instead, information may be sent through common channels, with the color information carried via a sort of neural Morse code. Here, specific patterns of neural responses with specified time intervals could signal various colors. If this is the case, then it should be possible to create the subjective impression of color by flickering white light on and off in a pattern that mimics the usual neural code. Festinger et al. (1971) have been able to do exactly this. Until there is neurophysiological verification of such a neural Morse code, however, this notion must remain an intriguing speculation, and the phenomenon of SUBJECTIVE COLORS must remain an interesting puzzle. A procedure for creating subjective colors for yourself is shown in Demonstration Box 8-3.

An interesting array that produces the subjective experience of colors from flickering black and white patterns began as a toy invented by Benham in 1894. It was painted on a top and meant to be spun; hence the pattern is often referred to as BENHAM'S TOP. The pattern is shown in the figure below. Cut out this pattern (or carefully reproduce it) and mount it on a piece of thin cardboard. Punch a hole in the marked center region and insert a nail or a round pencil. Now spin the pattern as shown. At a moderate speed, colors should appear. If you are spinning clockwise the inner bands should be slightly red, the next yellow, then green, and the last blue or violet. The order of the colors should reverse if you spin the pattern counterclockwise. The color effects arise because of the specific patterns of flickering white and black set up by each band. These mimic the flashing on-and-off light patterns used to study subjective colors in a laboratory setting.

THE PERCEPTION OF COLOR

The wavelength or combination of wavelengths of light are not the only factors that determine our perception of hue. Stimulus intensity and duration, as well as the characteristics of surrounding stimuli, can also alter the perceived color.

Intensity and Duration. Earlier in this chapter, we noted one way in which the perception of hue and the intensity of the stimulus interact. If intensity levels are low, only rods will be active and no color will be seen. Beyond the cone threshold however, the perceived hue of a stimulus varies as we change stimulus intensity. When we increase the intensity of red or yellow-green stimuli, they begin to take on a more yellow hue. Similarly, blue-greens and violets begin to appear

bluer when the intensity is increased. This phenomenon is called the BEZOLD–BRUCKE EFFECT after its two discoverers. It is quite easy to demonstrate, as is shown in Demonstration Box 8-4. Although the basis of the Bezold–Brucke effect is not yet fully understood, it is clear that it is neural in its origin (Coren & Keith, 1970). This effect may come about because the red–green cells are slightly more sensitive than the blue–yellow cells. Thus we can discriminate between red and green at lower intensity levels. Because the blue–yellow units become more active at higher intensity levels, hues tend to be dominated by these colors when stimuli are bright (Hurvich & Jameson, 1974).

Prolonged exposure to colored stimuli also produces a shift in the perception of hue. For instance, should you view the world through a deep red filter for a sufficient period of time, you would find that when the filter was removed the world would take on a blue-green tint. The fatiguing of a specific

For this demonstration you will need three pieces of colored cellophane, glass, or celluloid to serve as color filters. One should be a red, the other a green, and the last a yellow. Take a white sheet of paper that is brightly illuminated with room lighting and cast a shadow over one-half of it. Looking through the red filter, you will notice that the hue of the red seen on the bright half of the paper is noticeably yellower than the hue seen on the shadowed portion. When you peer through the green filter, you should experience the same effect. On the other hand, looking through a yellow filter should not cause an apparent change in hue. Thus the brighter one makes a red or a green, the more yellow it will appear. This is a demonstration of the hue shift, associated with increasing stimulus intensity, called the Bezold–Brucke effect. Another way to see this effect is to simply look at an incandescent light bulb (60–100 W) through the red or the green filter. You will notice that the light bulb appears to be yellow, despite the presence of the filter. Since the red filter only allows the long (red) wavelengths of light to pass, and the green only allows the middle (green) wavelengths through, no yellow light is reaching your eye. Thus the yellow appearance of the bulb is caused by the Bezold–Brucke hue shift that occurs when the intensity of the stimulus is high.

Demonstration Box 8-4: *The Bezold–Brucke Effect*

color response is called CHROMATIC ADAPTA-TION. It is believed that these adaptation effects are due either to selective bleaching of one particular photopigment, or to fatigue of one aspect of an opponent-process color response system. Suppose you looked through the red filter for a long period of time. The red-catching pigment becomes bleached, or the red response in the R–G unit becomes fatigued. Now, when you view a white surface, the absence of red pigment (or the weakness of the red response) causes the blue and green systems to account for a greater proportion of the total activity. This gives the white a cyan (blue-green) tint. When such fatigue effects, due to prolonged stimulation, are localized (that is confined to one region of the retina), they are called AFTERIMAGES. Demonstration Box 8-5 provides a stimulus for the production of color afterimages. You will notice when performing this demonstration that the hue of the afterimage tends to be a *complementary* hue of the stimulus producing the afterimage.

Spatial Interactions. In Chapter 7 we found that the brightness of a stimulus could be affected by the intensity of adjacent stimuli. The general nature of the interaction was in-

hibitory with the effect that a bright surround made a target appear dim. Inhibitory interactions between adjacent color systems can also occur. This results in hue shifts. The phenomenon is called SIMULTANEOUS COLOR CONTRAST. Consider Color Plate 3. Notice that this figure has four brightly colored patches, each of which surrounds a small central target. The target on the red patch appears to be slightly green, while that on green appears to be slightly red. The target on the blue patch appears to be slightly yellow, while that on the yellow patch appears slightly blue. However, each target is exactly the same gray. The apparent tinge of hue that appears in the target results from spatial interactions. You might be able to increase the strength of this effect by viewing Color Plate 3 through a sheet of tracing paper or thin tissue.

Jameson and Hurvich (1964) have suggested that color contrast arises from mechanisms similar to those that cause brightness contrast (discussed in Chapter 7); namely, an active retinal neuron tends to inhibit the responding of adjacent units. If we consider the target on the red background, we have a situation where the red response system is highly activated. In turn, these active neurons will

---

You can easily demonstrate negative or complementary color afterimages using Color Plate 6. Here you will see four square patches of color: a red, green, blue, and yellow. Notice that there is a black x in the middle of this pattern. Stare at the black x for about two minutes while keeping the plate under reasonably bright illumination. At the end of this period, transfer your gaze to the black x to the right of the figure. You should see a pattern of colored squares that is the exact complement of the pattern originally viewed. Where the red patch was, you will see green; where the green patch was, you will see red; where the blue patch was, you will see yellow; and where the yellow patch was, you will see blue. These are the complementary color afterimages caused by the fatiguing of the color response during the time you were staring at the color patches.

Demonstration Box 8-5:
Color Afterimages

inhibit the red response in the gray patch. Inhibition of the red response results in the emergence of the complementary, or opponent, green response in this region. A tinge of hue is then seen in the gray. The mechanism is similar to that in chromatic adaptation except that there is an instantaneous neural response, rather than a prolonged fatigue effect.

Age and Physical Condition. An individual may have normal color vision when tested at any one stage in life. However, color discrimination ability may change over a lifetime. For instance, the process of aging seems to alter color vision. This may be due to the fact that the crystalline lens of the eye grows more yellow as an individual ages; hence we look at the world through a gradually darkening yellow filter (Coren & Girgus, 1972a). Other effects may also account for age changes in color vision. For instance, aging seems to bring about a gradual deterioration in blue–yellow vision (Lakowski, 1962; Verriest, 1974). Most individuals are unaware of such changes because the onset is quite slow; however, the effect gradually accumulates. Since the perception of hue is subjective, you seldom have opportunities to assess whether your hue perception agrees with that of others. Does your red appear the same as that of your friends? Clearly, this is an unanswerable question.

Physical conditions can also result in losses in the ability to discriminate colors. Such acquired color vision losses are called DYS-CHROMATOPSIAS. There are several diseases or physical conditions that lead to such dys-chromatopsias. For instance, diabetics tend to suffer losses of color discrimination in the blue–yellow system, although the red–green system appears to be relatively unaffected (Lakowski, Aspinall, & Kinnear, 1972). These color losses can be aggravated by a number of factors. For instance, diabetic women who take oral contraceptives show significantly greater discrimination losses in the blue–yellow range (Lakowski & Morton, 1977). Thus changes in the perception of color are possible throughout an individual's lifetime.

Cognitive Factors in Color Perception.

Memory color. Although color is a basic sensory experience, there are also nonsensory factors that affect the perceived color of an object. In addition, color may interact with other nonperceptual behaviors. For example, the remembered color of familiar objects often differs from the object's actual color. When observers are shown color samples and later asked to match them from an array of colored chips, systematic errors are made. Observers tend to pick chips of greater brightness when asked to remember bright colors and greater darkness when asked to remember dark colors. (Bartleson, 1960; Newhall, Burnham, & Clark, 1957). When asked to remember and match colors of familiar objects with characteristic hues, we remember apples or tomatoes as being more red than the actual objects, bananas are more yellow in memory than in the bunch, and grass is greener than it is on the lawn. Because of this memory, film manufacturers have been forced to modify the spectral reproduction ability of colored film so that the reproduced colors are richer than they are in nature. Since television engineers have not made a similar correction, color memory distortions may account for our feeling that the picture reproduced on a color television set is an unfaithful reproduction of real color.

Memory color effects tend to creep into certain other matching tasks. For instance, if you are asked to match the color of a Valentine's Day heart or an apple, both of which have been cut out of orange paper, you will match them with a truer red than you would match an oval or a triangle cut out of the same material. A banana-shaped figure, or one labeled "lemon," is matched with a truer yellow. It seems as if the remembered color blends with the observed stimulus, altering the percept toward the ideal, or prototypical, color of an object (Bruner, Postman, & Rodrigues, 1951; Delk & Fillenbaum, 1965; Duncker, 1939; Harper, 1953). The color you remember is probably "better" than the color that was actually there; on the other hand, the color you see now may be tinged by your memory's hue.

Culture and color. As we noted earlier, an English speaker is content to describe hue differences using four basic categories: red, yellow, green, and blue. This is not the case for many other languages. Many languages have no separate names for green and blue, while others have the same name for yellow and green, or red and yellow. There are some languages that only distinguish red as a separate color and have no names for the other hues. It is often argued that there is an interaction between language and perception, and that when one has separate names for separate sensory experiences these labels make discriminations easier. In other words, the Iakuti tribe, who only have a single term for blue and green, may see the two colors as being more similar to each other than English speakers, who have separate words for these stimuli (Whorf, 1956).

The suggestion that different language terms for colors indicate different perceptual abilities has been presented in many different forms. For instance, Robertson (1967) suggested that there has been an evolutionary development in both the color-perceiving ability of humans and in the color terms encoded in the language. He suggested that the first discriminations were between red and green, then the discrimination ability for yellow evolved, and finally, that for blue. He analyzed a number of ancient languages and found such evolutionary trends. One could

conclude from such evidence that the ancient Greeks were relatively weak in their ability to perceive colors because their language has only a limited set of color names. Actually, when one directly measures the ability of individuals to match, discriminate, or reproduce colors (rather than just to name colors) the picture changes. It seems as if the number of color names in a language does not affect one's ability to make such discriminations (Berlin & Kay, 1969; Bornstein, 1973; Bornstein, 1975). Such findings indicate the danger in assuming that cognitive effects are occurring in the absence of direct perceptual measurements. Culture and color perception do not seem to interact.

Color impressions. Color does more than provide us with additional information about stimuli. It has emotional consequences. It delights and depresses. It makes humans feel warm or cold, tense or relaxed. For instance, a manufacturer of detergent found that the color of the detergent box made a difference in how the user evaluated the strength of the detergent. Women were given the same detergent in three boxes, which differed only in color. When the detergents were rated after use, the women felt that the detergent in a yellow-orange box was too strong, and supposedly had ruined some of the clothes. The detergent in a blue box was too weak, while the one with both blue and yellow-orange flashes seemed to be most effective (Kupchella, 1976).

Color can even produce sensory impressions that are characteristic of other senses. It is almost universal to call the short-wavelength (blue) colors "cool," while the longer wavelengths (yellow) tend to be called "warm." Perhaps these labels arise because the cool of the night is first broken by the red of the dawn, with midday characterized by the yellow of sunlight and warmth. As the yellow begins to disappear and the blue of twilight begins to predominate, temperatures again grow cool. Many years and many generations of such an association might stamp in this warm–cool relationship. In an era when the conservation of energy is important, it is interesting to note that people will turn a heat control to a higher setting in a blue room than they will in a yellow one. It is as if they are trying to compensate thermally for the coolness that has been visually induced (Boynton, 1971).

Color adds an aesthetic quality to our lives. We refer to an interesting person as a "colorful" character. We refer to the announcer who adds extra detail and insight to a sports broadcast as the "color man." We refer to exciting events as being "colorful." Certainly, in the absence of our ability to distinguish chromatic stimulation, our life would be "colorless" in all senses of that word.

SPECIAL TOPIC: THE COLOR SPACE

As we noted in Chapter 8, any color can be matched by a mixture of three appropriately chosen primary colors. This fact suggests an alternate way of specifying the hue of a stimulus. We can specify the stimulus in terms of the proportion of the three primaries needed to mix it. We could represent such a space as a triangle with a primary color at each corner. Color mixtures are represented in the same way as they are on the color circle. Thus yellow, which is a mixture of red and green, is represented by a point on the line between red and green. If we add more red the point moves toward the red primary, and if we add more green it moves toward the green. As in the color circle, white is represented by a point in the middle, representing an equal proportion of the three

primaries. Thus a red of lower saturation (the whitish red or pink) would be represented by a point moved inward toward the center. Such a diagram is shown in Figure ST8-1.

In 1931 a special commission of the CIE standardized the procedure for specifying the color of a stimulus. They decided to use a color space created by the mixing of three primaries as we did above. Unfortunately, if we select any three real primary colors, a number of perceptual and mathematical problems result. The major perceptual problem is the fact that there are some colors that cannot be accurately represented within the triangle. Thus a pure spectral yellow cannot be represented, since as we noted in Chapter 8 any color mixture can never be as saturated as the pure spectral color itself. To solve this perceptual problem, the CIE selected three *imaginary* primary colors. They arranged the primaries at the corners of the triangle shown in Figure ST8-2. These imaginary primary colors are more saturated than it is possible to get with any real colors. (Remember, this is simply done so that all real colors can be

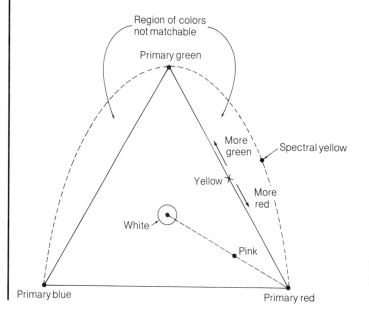

Figure ST8-1.
Specifying colors using a color triangle.

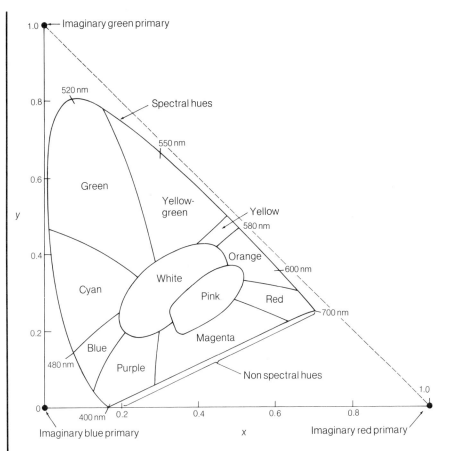

Figure ST8-2.
The CIE chromaticity space, which is a variant of the color
triangle system, using three imaginary "super" primaries.

represented within the space.) Notice that we have labeled the horizontal and vertical axes of the triangle with the labels X and Y.

We can now represent any color as a point in the color space. The reason that we can plot a mixture of three colors by using a point that has only two spatial coordinates is because the CIE CHROMATICITY SPACE has been arranged so that Y represents the proportion of green in the mixture, and X represents the proportion of red in the mixture. Clearly the proportions of red and green and blue in any mixture must sum to a proportion of 1.0 (you

can think of these as representing percentages where all of the items must sum to 100% of the light). If we know the total proportion of green and red in the mixture, we need only subtract this value from 1.0 to find the proportion of blue. Arranging the color space as shown automatically gives us these totals when we plot the X and Y coordinates of any color. The actual colors that can be perceived do not fill the full triangle (remember the primaries we are using are imaginary super colors). Instead they fill a horseshoe-shaped area with the spectral colors forming the outside boundary. We have labeled this area on the figure so that you can see the regions filled by various colors. Thus if we had a color $.2X$ and $.6Y$, we would know that it is comprised of 20% red and 60% green, and subtracting from a total of 100% we would know that it contained 20% blue. Looking at the figure you can trace out the X and Y coordinates and see that this color would look green.

Notice that brightness is not represented any place on this diagram. As for the color spaces we discussed in Chapter 8, brightness requires a third dimension. Thus the color space in the figure can be pictured as a single slice through a three-dimensional color space just as we demonstrated in Figure 8-5. This third dimension would be called Z. Using the CIE color system we can specify any color stimulus by using its TRISTIMULUS VALUES, which are simply the X and Y coordinates for the hue of the stimulus, and a Z coordinate for the brightness of the stimulus.

9
Loudness and Sound Qualities

DETECTION OF SOUNDS
TEMPORAL, FREQUENCY, AND BINAURAL INTERACTIONS
AUDITORY MASKING
SOUND DISCRIMINATION

SUBJECTIVE DIMENSIONS OF SOUND
LOUDNESS
PITCH
THEORIES OF PITCH PERCEPTION

VOLUME, DENSITY, AND SUBJECTIVE IMPRESSIONS

The young dancers moved in unison. Two lines of lithe bodies in black leotards swayed, seemingly pulled about like marionettes by the throbbing beat of the loud music. The choreographer watched a moment, then turned to her visitor and said, "It's really hard to believe that they are all deaf, isn't it? I never understand how they keep in time to the music. They claim that they just 'feel' the rhythm and the sound."

There are in fact many striking similarities between the sense of touch and the sense of hearing. The sense of touch is generally evoked by mechanical pressure against some part of the body, and the sense of hearing is similarly evoked by mechanical pressure. For auditory sensation, the pressure is caused by the collision of vibrating air molecules with parts of the ear, as we discussed in Chapter 5. We can often actually "feel" some sounds. For instance, at a loud rock concert, we might feel the pulsating throb of the bass guitar, or the drum, physically assailing the whole surface of our body. This aspect of sound recently led some movie theaters to install large speakers that emit intense low-frequency sound, thus giving audiences an opportunity not only to hear but to feel the presence of an earthquake or an explosion. The close relationship between touch and hearing is also apparent in the evolutionary history of hearing organs. Modern ears seem to have evolved from a vibration-sensitive line that extends the length of the body of certain species of fish. Scientists have not yet agreed as to whether this primitive "lateral line" represents an organ of touch or one of hearing.

At the subjective level, however, the senses of hearing and touch have many qualitative differences. Although we may feel the air vibration associated with the sound stimulus, we also "hear" it, which is quite a different sensory experience. Psychologically, a sound has many attributes of its own. While the sensation of touch shares with sound the psychological attributes of location and duration, sound also has the qualities of *loudness, pitch, timbre, volume,* and *density.* Some of these sensory qualities seem to be associated with particular aspects of the physical stimulus. However, sometimes the sensation is not directly predictable from a knowledge of the physical stimulus, and it seldom varies directly (in a simple manner) as we vary any one physical dimension.

DETECTION OF SOUNDS

Clearly, the minimum auditory experience is the detection of the presence of a sound. What determines the minimum loudness we can hear? The physical dimension that most closely predicts our perception of loudness is the amount of pressure exerted by the vibrating air molecules against the eardrum. You may recall that in Figure 5-1 we showed a simple auditory stimulus (pure tone) as a sine wave. In that representation the amplitude of the sine wave represented the intensity of the stimulus, or the pressure exerted by the vibrating air molecules. In determining an observer's absolute threshold for sound presented through earphones, we measure the sound pressure level associated with the threshold stimulus near the eardrum. This value is called the MINIMUM AUDIBLE PRESSURE. One might argue that this is a rather artificial situation since the sound wave at the eardrum has already been somewhat amplified and distorted. Another, perhaps more natural, procedure would be to determine the absolute auditory threshold for an observer sitting in an open space that is free of echoes and other distortions. In this situation sounds are presented by a speaker placed at various angles to the observer's ear and the intensity of the threshold stimulus is measured at the location of the observer's head. This measurement of threshold is called the MINIMUM AUDIBLE FIELD (indicating that the intensity of the threshold stimulus was measured in a free field, rather than directly at the eardrum).

In a classic study at Bell Telephone Laboratories, Sivian and White (1933) systematically varied the frequency of the pure tone stimulus as they took a series of threshold measures under carefully controlled conditions. (As you may recall from Chapter 5, frequency represents the number of sound vibrations, or cycles of the sine wave, that reach the ear per second. Its unit is the hertz, abbreviated Hz, which is simply cycles per second.) Sivian and White's results are shown in Figure 9-1. Notice that the threshold for hearing varies as we vary the frequency of the stimulus. The ear appears to be most sensitive to sounds with frequencies between 2000 and 5000 Hz. We are about 100 times less sensitive to a sound at 100 Hz than we are to a sound at 3000 Hz. Notice that the minimum audible field measurements are considerably lower than the minimum audible pressures. The reasons for

this are rather complex, the most important of which is probably that the free field situation allows resonances and amplifications from the shape of the pinna (the outer cup of the ear) and the ear canal to come into play. This is supported by the fact that we are most sensitive to a sound of 3000 Hz in free field presentation. This value corresponds to the natural resonance frequency of the external ear canal. From an adaptive point of view, the benefit that humans derive from increased sensitivity in this particular range of frequencies may at first be obscure, since most of the frequencies associated with language are around 1000 Hz or lower. A somewhat macabre answer seems to be that screams of pain or agony sometimes reach the 3000 Hz range. Thus Milne and Milne (1967) speculate that we leave a ". . . channel open—as though reserved for emergencies—for any high pitched scream." It is actually possible to demonstrate for yourself the effect of frequency on your ability to detect sounds using the procedure outlined in Demonstration Box 9-1.

The lower limit of sensitivity for the ear seems to be determined by the sound of blood rushing through the tiny vessels in the middle and inner ear, while the upper limit is determined by those stimuli that are so intense that they produce the sensation of pain. The difference between the absolute threshold and the pain threshold for a particular frequency of sound waves defines what is called the DYNAMIC RANGE of the ear for that frequency. In the range of about 1000–5000 Hz the ear has a dynamic range of up to 150 dB, which is equivalent to a 7.5 millionfold increase in sound pressure from the weakest sound detectable to the most intense sound tolerable. Few stereo systems can approach the dynamic range with which you were born. Young people can hear sounds between about 20 and 20,000 Hz. Unfortunately, with age, there is a loss in hearing

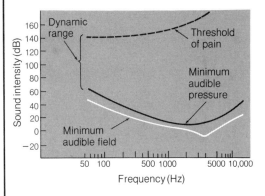

Figure 9-1.
The dynamic range of hearing from minimum audible intensities to the threshold of pain (based upon Sivian & White, 1933).

Many people are aware of the problems associated with replaying recorded music so that it sounds as it did when it was recorded. Recording techniques reproduce the frequency produced by musical instruments, but the replay is usually at a lower intensity. Most of the sounds of musical instruments lie in frequency ranges where the absolute threshold is most affected by changes in frequency. Thus unless you listen to recordings of an orchestra at reasonable intensity levels, you will not hear many of the frequencies produced by the instruments. Many high-quality audio amplifiers have been modified to include circuits that compensate for such psychological mechanisms. These circuits are set to emphasize very low and very high frequency sounds. For this demonstration you will need a radio or another sound source that produces orchestral music. A cheaper unit, such as a portable radio or your car radio,

both of which lack loudness compensation circuits, would be perfect. Find a station (or a record) where there is a full orchestra playing. Turn down the sound and listen to the instruments you can hear. Now gradually turn up the sound. As you do this you will find that you become more aware of the bass violin and cello, the larger brass pieces, such as the tuba, and some of the lower notes of the harp or bassoon, as well as some of the higher tones from the violins, flutes, and piccolos. When the volume has been considerably increased so that you can now hear the entire orchestra and many of the pieces (placing your ear close to the speaker helps), gradually turn down the volume again. Now many of the lower and higher frequency instruments seem to disappear as certain frequencies they produce drop below threshold. However, the middle frequencies of the orchestra are still quite audible.

Demonstration Box 9-1:
Sound Frequency and Threshold

capacity, particularly for higher frequencies, so that this range gradually shrinks as we grow older. Demonstration Box 9-2 provides a simple test for the upper limits of your own hearing.

Temporal, Frequency, and Binaural Interactions. There are a number of factors other than frequency and intensity that determine our ability to detect sounds. One of these factors is the duration of the stimulus. When a stimulus is brief, say 10 msec or so, the intensity of the stimulus necessary to give us the threshold sensation of sound is greater than for a sound of the same frequency but of longer duration. The auditory system seems to act as if a certain amount of sound energy

is necessary to stimulate the ear sufficiently so that we hear a sound, and it doesn't matter if this energy comes at a high intensity over a short interval or at a lower intensity over a longer time interval. We can describe this relationship algebraically as:

$$T = I \times D$$

where I is the intensity of the sound, D is its duration, and T is a constant value necessary to reach threshold. This relationship holds approximately for threshold sounds up to a duration of about 200 msec. Beyond 200 msec, increasing stimulus duration does not seem to improve our ability to detect sound. You may recall that in Chapter 7 we observed

Demonstration Box 9-2:
*High-Frequency Hearing
Limits*

A simple test of your own high-frequency hearing can be made using your television set. Turn it on and then lower the sound completely. Now lean over the back of your set and listen for a soft, high-pitched whine. If you can hear it, this means that you can detect frequencies on the order of 16,000 Hz. Now try this test on someone who is considerably older than you are and then with someone who is much younger.

You should find that the older individual cannot hear this sound, while the younger one can. You might also try moving away from the set (if possible) until you can just hear the sound. This is your "threshold distance." Now have your other observers do the same and determine their threshold distances. The greater your threshold distance, the more sensitive is your ear to these high-frequency sounds.

a similar relationship between time and intensity in the visual system.

We have been talking about increasing the likelihood that a sound will be heard by increasing its duration. We may also increase the likelihood that a sound will be heard by increasing the number of different tones, or frequencies, that are presented together. It has been shown that adding another tone of a different frequency to a stimulus improves our ability to detect the presence of sound. Thus we may add together two tones, neither of which would reach threshold by itself, and achieve an audible stimulus. Each could actually be about half the intensity needed for threshold. It seems that the nervous system adds the neural responses of different tones, producing a composite response based upon the sum of the intensities of the various single stimuli.

However, the tones cannot differ in frequency by too much. If they are very different in frequency their energies will not sum, and the threshold intensities will be the same as if we presented each tone alone. Just as there was a critical duration beyond which the temporal summation did not occur, there is a critical band of frequencies beyond which adding tones does not facilitate detection (Scharf, 1975). This critical band is not the same width for all frequencies. It is much narrower for low frequencies than it is for high frequencies. Thus if we start with a 400-Hz tone, adding a tone between 350 and 450 Hz will improve our detection ability, while tones beyond these limits will not. If we started with a 5000 Hz tone, however, any added tone between about 4500 and 5500 Hz would improve our detection ability. Figure 9-2 demonstrates how the critical bandwidth varies with frequency.

There is an additional factor that affects our ability to detect the presence of sound stimuli. When sounds are presented to both ears, as opposed to only one, the thresholds are lowered. Presentations to one ear are called MONAURAL (from the roots *mon* for one and *aural* for ear); presentations to two ears are called BINAURAL (from the root *bi* for two). At first it was believed that this was only because one of the ears was more sensitive than the other, and the most sensitive ear determined the absolute threshold (Sivian & White, 1933). However, more recent work (Chocolle, 1962) has shown that the threshold for two-ear stimulation is about one-half of that for one-ear stimulation. An interesting aspect of the interaction between the ears was shown by Schenkel (1967), who found that the two stimuli did not have to occur simultaneously in the two ears. If the tones are presented to the ears one at a time,

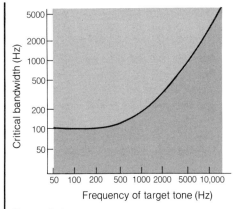

Figure 9-2.
Relation between critical bandwidth in which added tones will facilitate detection and frequency of stimulus tone.

and the total stimulus duration of the combined input is less than 200 msec, the pair of tones will be detected even if each individual tone is only about one-half of the intensity needed to reach threshold when presented monaurally.

As well as lowering the absolute threshold, presentation of the same stimulus to the two ears causes the subjective impressions of loudness from each ear to add together. Thus a binaural presentation will sound about twice as loud as a monaural presentation of the same tone. If you have a sound source nearby such as a radio or a T.V., you can demonstrate this for yourself by assessing the loudness when you hear the source with two ears, then covering one ear, and noting how the apparent loudness diminishes. It is likely that the summation of input from the two ears occurs at fairly central regions of the brain, since information from the two ears does not meet until fairly late in the neural pathways.

Auditory Masking. All of us have been in a noisy meeting, convention, or theater and

have found that we could not hear or understand a speaker very well. When the crowd quiets down, however, we find that the speaker's voice is immediately audible. This observation illustrates that whether a particular sound can be heard or not depends not only upon its own intensity, but also upon the presence of other sounds in the environment. In the last section we saw one way in which sounds can interact with one another to facilitate hearing. In this situation the effects are reversed. Now we present an observer with a sound, which is audible by itself, and then add another sound only to find that the target tone can no longer be heard. We usually say that the second tone has MASKED the first.

A masking sound does not simply make all other tones more difficult to hear. Masking sounds act rather selectively. A set of measurements demonstrating this was taken by Zwicker (1958), who masked target tones using a narrow band of noise whose middle frequency was 1200 Hz. He measured the threshold intensity for a listener to detect a target tone with and without the masking stimulus. When he measured the effects of various frequencies of target tone he obtained the results shown in Figure 9-3. As you can see from the figure, as we increase the intensity of the masking stimulus we must increase the intensity of the test tone for it to be audible.

Another striking aspect of these data is the asymmetry of the masking effect. The most strongly masked tones have frequencies that are very similar to that of the masker itself. The effect of the masker seems to spread upward, affecting tones higher in frequency than the masking sound, although the effect becomes less and less as the frequency increases. Tones of a lower frequency are relatively unaffected. In Zwicker's experiment, tones more than 500 Hz lower in frequency than the masker were hardly affected by the masking noise at all.

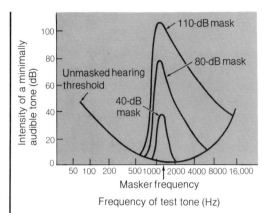

Figure 9-3.
Thresholds for a pure tone target in the presence of a narrow band of masking noise centered at 1200 Hz. The higher the curve, the higher the threshold, hence the more effective the masking. Tones with a lower frequency than the mask are affected much less than are tones of frequency higher than the mask (based upon Zwicker, 1958).

Why does the added noise only mask tones higher in frequency than itself? The answer may lie in the physiology of the ear. Turn back to Figure 5-8, which shows how the pattern of vibration of the basilar membrane varies with the frequency of a pure tone. Notice that tones of low frequencies produce a very broad vibration pattern, extending over much of the membrane, while tones of higher frequencies produce vibration patterns nearer to the oval window, and do not extend as far along the membrane. Now look at Figure 9-4. Notice that when we have a weak test tone, and the noise is of a higher frequency than the target, the pattern of vibrations set up in the basilar membrane by the masking noise only extends part way up the membrane. Since the lower frequency target tone vibrates more of the membrane, the target's pattern can peek out from around the flank of the vibration pattern produced by the masker. Thus the target is

detectable. However, the vibration pattern produced by the target tone when the noise is of a lower frequency than the target is completely covered by the masker's vibration pattern, and it is thus not detectable as a separate tone. The intensity of the higher frequency test tone in the presence of low-frequency noise must be increased before its own vibration pattern at last emerges from behind that of the masker and can be detected as a separate tone.

An interesting prediction emerges from this analysis. When the intensities of target and masker are increased even further, as in the bottom picture in Figure 9-4, you can see that the lower frequency target begins to produce a vibration pattern that actually hides that of the masker. Thus the target is masking the mask! You can experience some aspects of the frequency-specific effect of a masker by performing Demonstration Box 9-3 for yourself.

Although sound masking effects seem to be largely explained by the interaction of the patterns of vibration on the basilar membrane, this explanation is clearly not adequate for all masking phenomena. For example, it is possible to mask a target sound presented to one ear by presenting a masking sound to the other. In this situation the masker must be much more intense (about 50 dB) than when a masking sound is presented to the same ear as the target tone. Under these conditions it can be shown that the effect of the mask is much more symmetrical as we vary the frequency of the test tone (Zwislocki, Damianopoulos, Buining, & Glantz, 1967).

When one looks at the interaction between the two ears, one occasionally encounters some strange and interesting phenomena. For example, Hirsh (1948) presented a pure tone plus a broad band noise (that is, one containing many frequencies) to the same ear. He adjusted the target tone so that it

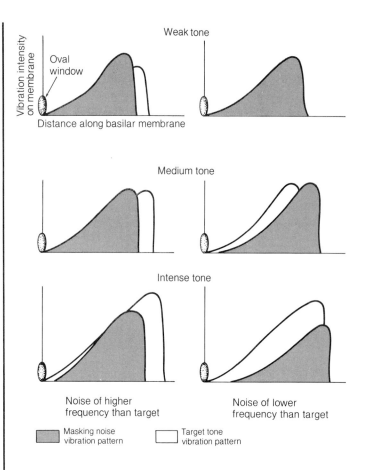

Figure 9-4.
The interactions of patterns of vibration of the basilar membrane resulting from a target and a noise stimulus. (based upon Scharf, 1964)

could just be heard above the background of noise. Next he presented some additional noise to the other ear, so that the two noises were in phase (meaning that the peaks and valleys of sound pressure coincide, as we discussed in Chapter 5). Under these circumstances the target tone, instead of being more difficult or perhaps impossible to hear, becomes more clearly audible. To reach the threshold value again, it is necessary to *lower* the target's intensity. What seems to be happening is that the two masking tones are masking each other. Again, since the two noise masks are coming into different ears and do not share the same basilar membrane,

the interaction must be occurring more centrally, that is, in the brain. These central interactions become very important when we consider the processing of meaningful sounds, such as occur when we are listening to speech (see Chapter 13).

Sound Discrimination. In some respects the problem of masking is really a discrimination problem, of much the same sort as that discussed in Chapter 2. Basically, the observer's task is to discriminate the target tones from the mask, which serves as a noise stimulus. We may simplify this problem somewhat by asking the basic discrimination question for

To experience several different masking phenomena, you need two major sources of sound, one for a masking sound, and one for the target sound which will be masked. Good sources are the noise of a car engine for a masking sound and the car radio for a source of target sounds. If you have a car with a radio, get into it and turn on the radio without starting the engine. Find some music with a good range of frequencies. Classical music is best, but any music will do. Modern music with a lot of steel guitar (country) or electrically amplified guitar (rock) is also good. Take particular note of the high and the low frequencies. Turn the volume knob on the radio to an intensity where you can just barely hear these frequencies. Now start the car motor. Press on the accelerator (with the car out of gear!) to make the engine turn over at high rpm. This creates a source of intense broad-band masking noise. Now listen for the high and the low frequencies that were clearly audible in the music before you started the car engine. Turn up the volume until the high and low frequencies (which should now be masked) are just barely audible again and take notice of the difference between the volume settings before and after the noise was introduced. You could map out a masking curve for particular frequencies in a piece of music by varying the rpm of the motor to vary the intensity of the noise, and by varying the frequency of the sounds whose audibility you are using as a criterion for radio volume adjustment. Note that even with intense masking noise, you can still hear the middle frequencies, where most of the singing is, while the higher and lower frequencies are masked. This is a reflection of the superior sensitivity of the ear to these frequencies. You also experience *speech masking* in your car. When the masking noise is of sufficient intensity (be careful not to damage your engine), even the middle frequencies (where most speech sounds occur) are masked, and you cannot understand the singer or the radio announcer.

the perception of sound, "How different must two sounds be in order for the difference to be reliably detected?" To answer this question precisely, we must separate the two physical dimensions upon which a sound stimulus may differ, namely, intensity and frequency.

Let us begin by considering our sensitivity to intensity changes. A good deal of care must be taken when studying such abilities, since turning a tone on or off, or changing its frequency or intensity abruptly, can cause the perception of a "click." In a threshold situation an observer might respond to this click rather than to the actual intensity or fre-quency change in which we are interested. Because of this, Riesz (1928), at the Bell Telephone Laboratories, resorted to a rather elaborate technique based upon a phenomenon known as BEATS. When you simultaneously listen to two tones that are similar in intensity but slightly different in frequency, you may perceive the occurrence of beats. These may be described as the perception of a single tone that seems to throb, much like the vibrato of a singer. In short, the perception is of an alternate rising and falling in loudness. The frequency with which the loudness fluctuates is precisely the frequency difference between the two sounds that are combined. The air compressions in the sound waves will add to each other when the maximum of one wave is occurring at the same time as the maximum of the other, and subtract from each other when a maximum of one wave coincides with the minimum of another. For example, when two tones differ by 3 Hz, the maxima of the two sound waves will coincide (add) three times each second and subtract three times each second. The sound will thus seem to wax and wane at 3 Hz (three times per second). As you increase the size of the frequency difference, the beats will soon no longer be discriminable. At a large enough difference between the two tones, the sound begins to take on a harsh or rough and grating quality. Figure 9-5 shows how two sound signals can combine to form a separate beat frequency.

Riesz (1928) used the perception of beats to determine the limits of intensity discrimination in an observer. He presented a tone that was clearly audible by itself (say, at a frequency of 1000 Hz). He next presented another tone that was close enough in frequency (say, 1003 Hz) so that it would cause the perception of beats if it were intense enough. He gradually increased the intensity of the added sound until the listener first detected the fluctuation in loudness caused by the beating. On the basis of this he could compute the difference threshold, without contaminating the sound with the harsh clicking of sudden changes in intensity or onset and offset of the stimulus.

You probably recall from Chapter 2 that one measure of our ability to discriminate between two stimuli is given by Weber's fraction. We defined the Weber fraction as $\Delta I / I$ where ΔI equals the intensity change necessary to be just noticed, and I is the standard stimulus from which the change is taken. This fraction represents the proportion by which a stimulus must be changed in order for us to detect that change. Thus a Weber fraction of 0.5 means that we must increase (or decrease) a stimulus by 50% in order for a subject to discriminate the change.

We can use this Weber fraction as a measure of our ability to discriminate sounds from one another. In general, studies of the difference threshold for intensity have shown that a Weber fraction of about 0.33 describes auditory performance. Figure 9-6 shows how the Weber fraction varies as we vary the in-

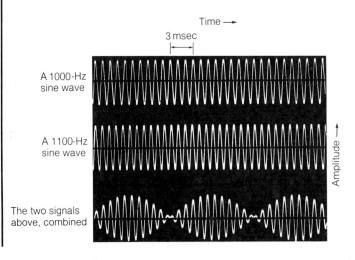

Figure 9-5.
A 1000-Hz sine wave is added to a 1100-Hz sine wave to give a beat frequency of 100 Hz. This means that the beat pattern repeats every 10 msec as the overall envelope of sound pressures varies (from Lindsay & Norman, 1977).

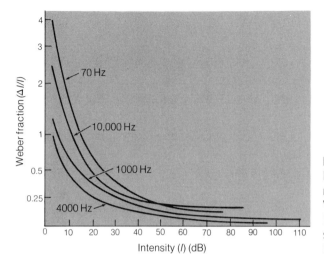

Figure 9-6.
Intensity discrimination
measured in terms of the
Weber fraction for various
intensities and frequencies of
standard stimuli (based upon
Riesz, 1928).

tensity of the standard (*I*) stimulus. Notice
that we have plotted four different curves for
four different frequencies. As you can see, the
size of the Weber fraction is smallest (hence
discrimination is best) for stimuli in the middle range of frequencies. Increasing or decreasing the frequency results in a decrease
in our ability to discriminate intensity
changes. For moderate stimulus intensities,
the Weber fraction is rather constant. (It
would, of course, be perfectly constant if
Weber's law were completely true, as we
discussed in Chapter 2.) This graph shows
that the auditory system is sensitive enough to
reliably detect a 20% change in stimulus intensity across a rather broad range of frequencies and a broad range of intensities,
covering those frequencies and intensities
where most of our everyday hearing takes
place.

Thus far we have dealt with the question
of discrimination of differences in intensity of
sound stimuli. We may also ask, "By how
much must two tones differ in frequency for
this difference to be noticed?" Again, the
classic study was done at the Bell Telephone
Laboratories (you might guess that the telephone company would have an interest in
discovering the limits of our ability to discriminate sounds), this time by Shower and
Biddulph (1931). The basic experiment involves presenting an observer with a tone of a
given frequency and intensity and then varying the frequency of the tone until the observer is just able to detect a change in pitch.
Again, we may measure the limits of discrimination using the Weber fraction. How-
ever, in this case the fraction consists of $\Delta f/f$,
where *f* represents the frequency of the standard tone and Δf represents the change in
frequency necessary to be just noticed as different from the standard. Figure 9-7 shows
the Weber fraction for frequency discrimination for a number of different intensity levels
and a broad range of frequencies. Notice that
above 1000 Hz the Weber fraction is constant and quite small (around 0.005). This
means that if we presented a listener with a
tone with a frequency of 1000 Hz, and
another tone of 1005 Hz, this small difference
in frequency (only half of one percent) would
be detectable. It is important to note that at

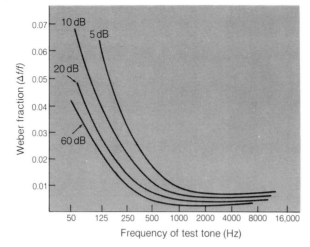

Figure 9-7.
Frequency discrimination measured in terms of the Weber fraction for various intensities and frequencies of standard stimuli (based upon Shower & Biddulph, 1931).

lower intensity levels our discrimination of frequency differences is not quite this accurate.

SUBJECTIVE DIMENSIONS OF SOUND

So far we have concentrated on an observer's ability to detect the presence of a sound, or to discriminate one sound from another. However, such analyses do not deal directly with the subjective quality of a sound as experienced by an observer. Early in the history of the psychological investigation of audition, experimenters were inclined to believe that there would be a direct correspondence between the experienced qualities of the sensation and the physical stimulus. For a long period of time it was taken for granted that every *qualitative psychological variable* would almost perfectly reflect some corresponding *quantifiable physical variable*. For example, it was firmly believed that the subjective dimension of loudness was a direct consequence of the physical dimension of *amplitude* of the sound wave stimulus. In

similar fashion it was believed that the subjective dimension of *pitch* (whether a sound is high or low) depended directly upon the *frequency* of the sound wave. Even today one occasionally finds careless references to frequency and intensity when one really should be speaking of perceived pitch and loudness. This sort of mechanistic viewpoint has been vehemently opposed by many investigators, who have pointed out that we should separate concepts and expressions that describe our conscious or phenomenal experience from those that describe the physical stimulus. The subjective qualities of loudness and pitch are complex perceptions that depend upon the interaction of several physical characteristics of the stimulus, as well as the physical and psychological state of the observer. Thus we must distinguish between the physical dimensions that refer to the characteristics of the vibrations we call sound stimuli and the phenomenal qualities or subjective experiences, which should probably be called *sound attributes*. These attributes are of special concern to the perceptual psychologist.

The deeply rooted older view maintained that at best the observer could be expected to distinguish only two phenomenal dimensions (loudness and pitch), because there are two predominant physical dimensions (intensity and frequency). Actually, we can differentiate many qualitative differences in sound stimuli. These include not only *pitch* and *loudness,* but also the LOCATION of a sound (where it seems to come from), its DURATION (how extended in time it appears), its TIMBRE (that complex quality that allows us to distinguish a note played on a clarinet from the same note played on a violin), its VOLUME (the sense in which it fills space and seems large or small), its DENSITY (a complex feeling of the compactness or hardness of the sound), as well as more complex subjective feelings like CONSONANCE or DISSONANCE (how two tones seem to "go together" or "clash"). Our experience is composed of these and other qualitative feelings, and it is not simply the registration of the frequency and the intensity of the stimulus. We will discuss some of these subjective qualities in more detail in the sections that follow.

Loudness. Although we began our discussion of the subjective qualities of sound by stating that we cannot completely predict a subjective experience from a single physical dimension, we must acknowledge that the experienced loudness of a sound is greatly affected by stimulus intensity. As we increase the amplitude of the stimulus, we increase how loud it appears to be to an observer. However, the experience of loudness is *not* identical to stimulus intensity, and decibels are *not* measures of phenomenal loudness.

In order to study loudness, we must use psychophysical scaling procedures such as the magnitude estimation techniques we discussed in Chapter 3, or the matching of one stimulus to another on a different sensory continuum (cross-modality matching). Stevens (1956) did a classic study of this type. He gave an observer a standard stimulus tone and a set of tones that varied in intensity but

had the same frequency as the standard. The standard tone was assigned a value of 100 units. The observer's task was simply to assign numbers to the variable tone on the basis of its perceived loudness. Thus a tone that sounded twice as loud as the standard would be called 200 units, and a tone that sounded half as loud would be called 50 units. Stevens showed that the perception of loudness varies according to a simple equation: $L = aI^{2/3}$, where L is the apparent loudness, I is the physical intensity of the sound (in decibels of sound pressure), and a is a constant. This means that the loudness of the stimulus was increasing as approximately the $\frac{2}{3}$ power of the physical sound pressure. Other exponents have also been found depending upon the specific stimuli used and the test conditions employed (Marks, 1974).

On the basis of his and others' work, Stevens suggested a new unit by which to measure loudness. He called this unit the SONE. One sone is defined as the loudness of a 1000-Hz stimulus at an intensity level of 40 dB. For most of the stimulus range there is a linear relationship between the loudness measured in sones and the intensity measured in decibels. To double the loudness (for instance, from 1 to 2 sones) we have to increase the intensity of the sound by about 10 dB. For very weak sounds (below 20 dB), however, the change in apparent loudness is much more rapid with increases in intensity. This relationship is shown in Figure 9-8, which also indicates the loudness in sones of some typical sounds.

Sound intensity does not provide a full description of how loud a sound will be. For example, our perception of the loudness of a tone is also affected by its frequency. A typical procedure to measure the relationship between frequency and loudness involves presenting an observer with a standard tone of a given frequency and intensity. She is then asked to adjust the intensity of another tone

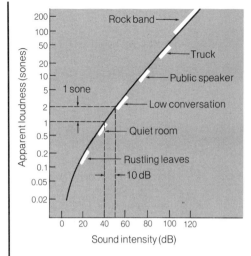

Figure 9-8.
The relationship between loudness (measured in sones) and stimulus intensity (measured in decibels).

(differing only in frequency) until it matches the loudness of the first. When this is done for a number of comparison tones, a curve may be plotted that describes the intensity at which tones of varying frequencies appear to be equally as loud as the standard tone. Such a curve is called an EQUAL LOUDNESS CONTOUR.

A series of such equal loudness contours based upon a study by Robinson and Dadson (1956) is shown in Figure 9-9. Each curve represents a different sound intensity for the standard tone in decibels. Notice that the lines are not flat. If sounds of various frequencies sounded equally loud when they were the same intensity, all of the curves would be straight lines. The fact that the contours rise and fall with frequency (much as the graph of absolute threshold varied with frequency) means that tones of equal intensity but of different frequencies appear to differ in loudness. Tones of less than 1000 Hz, or greater than around 6000 Hz, need to be considerably more intense to match the loudness of tones between 1000 and 6000 Hz. Thus tones in the middle range of frequencies sound considerably louder than equally intense tones outside this range.

There is a unit of measurement that is useful in determining the apparent loudness of a stimulus independent of the frequency. This measure is called a PHON. It uses the loudness of a 1000-Hz tone as the reference stimulus. If we set the 1000-Hz tone to 50 dB we will call the loudness 50 phons (the number of phons is just the decibel level of the 1000-Hz tone). Any tone of another frequency that matches this loudness will also be at 50 phons. For example, consider the curve labeled 30 on Figure 9-9. This curve defines the 30-phon level (since 1000 Hz is at 30 dB). Any sound with a frequency and intensity that lies on this curve will appear to be equal in loudness to any other sound on the curve. From that it is easy to see that an 8000-Hz tone at an intensity of 40 dB will appear to be equal in loudness to a 300-Hz tone at 30 dB. Both of these tones would be said to have a loudness equal to 30 phons. The advantage of the phon scale is that it provides a loudness measure that does not have to be further corrected for the frequency of the stimulus.

There are other factors that also influence the apparent loudness of a tone. One of these is the length of time the tone is sounded. For tones less than about 200 msec in duration, we must increase intensity to match the loudness of a longer tone. We could create an equal loudness contour, of a type similar to that for variations with frequency, by having a standard of fixed duration and requiring an observer to match its loudness with a comparison tone of different durations. When we do this we get a curve similar to that shown in Figure 9-10. Thus a 2-msec burst of sound must be 15 dB in order to sound as loud as a 90-msec burst at 5 dB. This sort of finding suggests that the auditory system may sum all

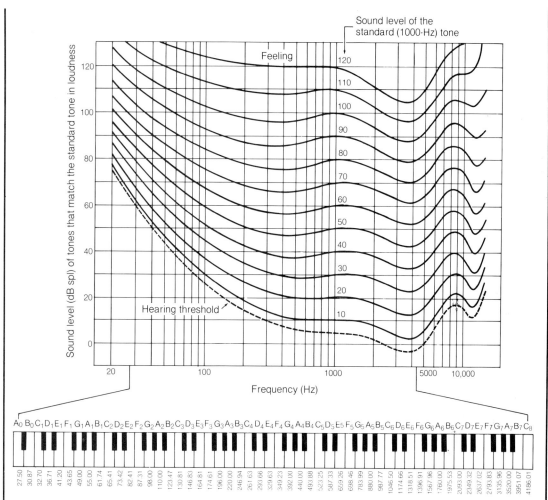

Figure 9-9.
Equal loudness contours (numbers on curve represent the
number of phons—see text) (from Lindsay & Norman, 1977;
data from Robinson & Dadson, 1956).

of the inputs coming in over a 200-msec window of time (Gulick, 1971).

The duration of the stimulus can have another effect upon our response to loudness. If a tone is presented for a very long time, the stimulus comes to appear less loud than it did when it first began. We can measure this ef-fect by having an observer match the loud-ness of the persistent or adapting tone to that of a comparison stimulus (usually of a differ-ent frequency). As the adapting stimulus re-mains on for longer and longer periods of time, the intensity of the matching stimulus must be decreased. This indicates that the

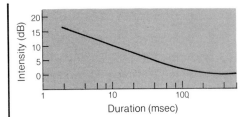

Figure 9-10.
Equal loudness contour showing the changes in intensity needed to maintain a constant loudness as the duration of the standard is varied (from *Hearing: Physiology and Psychophysics* by Lawrence W. Gulick. © 1971 by Oxford University Press, Inc. Reprinted by permission).

loudness of the adapting stimulus has itself decreased. This process is called AUDITORY ADAPTATION. A related phenomenon, called AUDITORY FATIGUE, is caused by exposing the ear to very intense sounds. The resultant *reduction* of loudness of other stimuli presented after the intense sound ceases may persist for a considerable period of time, depending on the intensity and duration of the stimulus. For instance, Postman and Egan (1949) exposed observers to an intense noise (115 dB) for 20 min. They then measured the sensitivity of their observers over a period of several days. The results are shown in Figure 9-11. The horizontal line represents their

preexposure sensitivity, while the other curves represent the hearing loss, which could be interpreted as a reduction in loudness, for varying periods of time following the exposure to the stimulus. As can be seen, the largest hearing loss immediately follows the exposure to the intense noise; however, it does persist to a measureable extent over a period of 24 hr. There is an interesting analog to this experiment that you can experience for yourself using Demonstration Box 9-4.

Another factor that influences our perception of the loudness of a sound is the complexity of the stimulus. Most laboratory experiments in audition have used tones of a single frequency, while most of the sounds we hear in our everyday environment are made up of mixtures of a large number of different frequencies. We can match the intensity of a pure tone to a complex sound in much the same way we matched different frequencies to 1000 Hz when we constructed the phon scale. Thus we have listeners adjusting the intensity of a pure tone of 1000 Hz until it matches the loudness of a complex tone, giving a new kind of equal loudness function.

Suppose we take a group of frequencies centered around a standard tone. We can systematically increase or decrease the range of frequencies included. One usually refers to

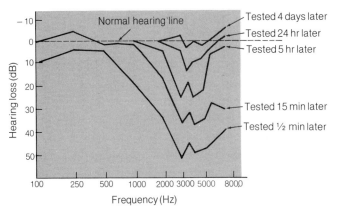

Figure 9-11.
Prolonged reduction of loudness following exposure to an intense (115 dB) stimulus for 20 min (based upon Postman & Egan, 1949).

During an average day you are exposed to many noises and sounds, from individuals who talk with you, from stereos, televisions, radios, and numerous other sources. Set a radio or a stereo to an intensity level where the sound seems comfortable for listening in the evening before you go to bed. At the day's end, your auditory system has adapted to the ongoing, persistent noise of the day. However, when you awaken in the morning you may find that the radio, set to be the same sound level, will appear to be too loud. During the night your ears have recovered from the auditory adaptation caused by exposure to the sounds you heard during the previous day. The quiet of the night has given you a chance to recover your sensitivity, hence all sounds now seem louder. This may explain why an alarm clock, whose bell seems low and pleasant when bought one evening in a department store, will seem so jarring and loud when used the following morning.

Demonstration Box 9-4:
Auditory Adaptation

the range of frequencies as the BANDWIDTH. Figure 9-12 displays an equal loudness contour for a complex tone with a center frequency of 1000 Hz as we gradually increase its bandwidth. Notice that when only a small band of frequencies make up the complex sound, increasing the bandwidth does not affect our perception of the loudness of the stimulus. This is reasonable, since the overall intensity of the sound is not changing but only the number of different frequencies included in it. However, notice what happens when the frequencies reach a critical bandwidth of about 160 Hz. From this bandwidth onward, loudness begins to increase as we include a greater number of frequencies, although the overall intensity of the sound is unchanged (Gulick, 1971).

Researchers have acknowledged that loudness depends upon all of the factors that we have been discussing, including the frequency, duration, and complexity of the tone. However, they have persisted in a search for one simple underlying physiological variable that might serve as the basis for our phenomenal experience of the loudness of a sound. The most frequent suggestion is that our sensation of loudness simply depends upon the total amount of neural activity per unit time taking place in some region of the brain. In Chapter 5 we discussed how the overall level of neural activity in the auditory nerve is mainly a function of the intensity of the sound reaching the ear. Since the primary physical determinant of loudness is sound intensity, it seems reasonable to suppose that the amount of neural activity in some higher brain center simply corresponds to our sensation of loudness. This is supported by evidence that the relationship between the amount of neural activity and the

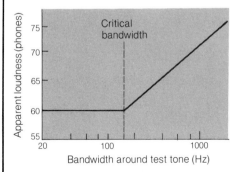

Figure 9-12.
The effects on loudness of increasing the range of frequencies in a complex tone (based upon Gulick, 1971).

sound intensity follows the same sort of power function that we observe when we look at the relationship between sound intensity and the loudness sensation (Stevens, 1970). In the auditory nerve, the exponent of this power function is similar to that derived from magnitude estimation experiments for loudness ($\frac{2}{3}$), although exponents obtained at higher levels are somewhat smaller. Stevens suggested that the power function obtained for loudness is determined by the operating characteristic of the ear (the way in which it transduces sound energy to neural activity), and that the remaining levels in the auditory system only relay the total intensity of the firing onto the next center, with the message ultimately "becoming" loudness at some more central site in the brain.

A recent study of neural responses in the auditory system of the cat indicates that the situation might not be so simple. Atkinson (1976) found evidence for a power function between stimulus intensity and the amplitude of the neural response in the medial geniculate body (an auditory center in the lower brain), which does suggest that there is a direct physiological basis for some aspects of loudness perception. However, Atkinson also reported evidence for another neural mechanism operating at this level. When he used very intense sounds (stimuli that sound like clicks to humans), he found an inhibitory response. It seems that for loud sounds this brain structure actually inhibits its own response. This process would set limits on the range of loudness that can be signaled. It also suggests that although there is a strong correlation between the overall amount of neural activity in the auditory system and perceived loudness, this relationship does not account for the entire range of our sensory experience of this quality of sound.

Pitch.   Every time you sing or play a musical scale, you are varying the subjective experience of PITCH. Your *do, re,* and *mi* differ in this tonal quality. The most important physical determinant of our perception of pitch is the frequency of the sound stimulus. The high notes on the piano have higher frequencies than the low notes. For instance, the dominant frequency of A-4 (for those of you who are not musically inclined that is the forty-ninth key on the piano counting from the left to the right) is 440 Hz. The dominant frequency of the A note one octave higher (A-5 or the sixty-first key from the left) is 880 Hz (see Figure 9-9).

Perhaps the first demonstration of the relationship between frequency and pitch was performed by Robert Hooke in 1681. In order to determine the relationship between pitch and frequency, Hooke placed a card against a wheel that had teeth notched in it. He then spun the wheel. The spinning teeth hit the card and the resultant vibrations sent out a sound wave—a sort of rough musical note. When the speed of rotation was increased the frequency of vibration of the card increased, and so did the pitch. Thus the relationship between frequency and pitch had been established. For centuries thereafter, the terms pitch and frequency were used interchangeably on the assumption that pitch rises and falls in exact step with frequency.

Perhaps the most commonly used measure of the pitch of a sound is the musical scale. It is basically logarithmic in nature. Any note one octave higher than another note of the same name has exactly twice the frequency of the lower note. Thus the note A-3 (the thirty-seventh key from the left) has a frequency of 220 Hz, while A-4 (the forty-ninth key from the left) is one octave higher and has a frequency of 440 Hz (see Figure 9-9). The musical scale has undergone very little change over the years, although some attempts have been made to adjust the spacing between the notes in an attempt to represent more accurately the pitches of different musical notes. For example, there is a version of the musical scale called the EQUAL TEMPER-AMENT SCALE (Ward, 1970). Here each octave is divided into 12 equal parts representing standard intervals between the musical notes. These intervals are called semitones and each semitone can be further divided into 100 cents. Thus an octave consists of 1200 cents, and the pitch of any tone can be precisely described in terms of what octave it is in and how many cents it lies above the lowest tone in that octave. This scale has proven quite useful for musicians, although there are still arguments about the spacing of the standard intervals within an octave. The reason for such arguments seems to lie in the fact that the musical scale is not a direct representation of the psychological scale for pitch.

The most useful psychological scale for pitch to date is the MEL scale proposed by Stevens, Volkman, and Newman (1937). Like the sone scale of loudness, the mel scale can be created by various psychophysical scaling techniques. For instance, in one experiment these researchers created a sort of electronic piano with 20 keys and 20 corresponding knobs set above the keyboard. Turning a knob varied the tone produced by the corresponding key through a wide range of frequencies. Subjects were asked to sit before the keyboard and to tune the "piano" to produce pitch intervals that appeared to be equally wide. The results were somewhat surprising. Subjects did not tune the piano to equal steps on the frequency scale, nor did they tune them to equal steps on a scale of musical intervals.

As in other psychophysical scaling techniques, one must designate a standard against which all other items will be scaled. By definition, a sound with a frequency of 1000 Hz and an intensity of 60 dB has been assigned a pitch of 1000 mels. This frequency lies between the notes B-5 and C-6 on the piano (the sixty-third and sixty-fourth keys

from the left). When we compare the mel scale with the musical scale we find several large discrepancies. For instance, the one octave difference between C-3 (Key 28) and C-4 (Key 46) is 167 mels, while the scaled distance between C-6 (Key 64) and C-7 (Key 76) is 508 mels. Such measurements confirm the feelings, often expressed by musicians, that the higher musical octaves sound "larger" than the lower ones. This helps to explain why melodies often have a somewhat different character when played in different keys. The relationships between mels, frequency, and the musical scale are shown in Figure 9-13.

Just as a variety of factors other than sound intensity affect the perceived loudness of a sound, we find that factors other than frequency affect its perceived pitch. The very existence of the mel scale demonstrates that pitch is not identical to frequency, since when someone is asked to find a sound that is half the pitch of a standard sound, she does not produce a sound that is half the frequency of the standard. Perhaps the major physical factor, other than frequency, that affects the perceived pitch of a pure tone is its intensity. There is a classic demonstration, first performed over a quarter of a century ago, in which an investigator struck a tuning fork tuned to middle C (C-4 or 262 Hz) a few feet from the ear of a trained singer. She was asked to sing the note she heard, and she reproduced the sound reasonably accurately. Next the investigator held the same tuning fork a few inches from her ear. This increases the intensity of the sound reaching her ear, but it leaves the frequency unchanged since a tuning fork (when properly struck) produces sounds of only a single frequency. Nonetheless the pitch that the singer heard did change. She now sang a note that was considerably lower in pitch than middle C. This clearly demonstrated that sound intensity affected perceived pitch.

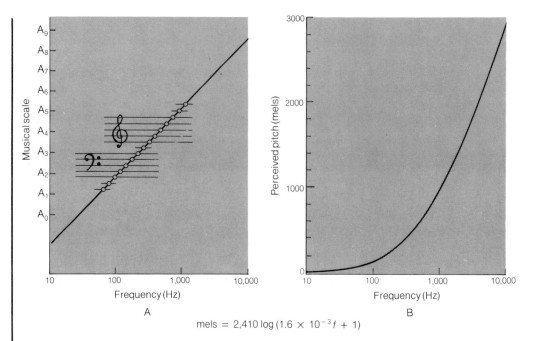

$$\text{mels} = 2,410 \log (1.6 \times 10^{-3} f + 1)$$

Figure 9-13.
(A) The relationship between frequency and the musical scale and (B) the relationship between mels and frequency (from Lindsay & Norman, 1977).

Using an experimental technique similar to that used in producing equal loudness contours, we can perform an experiment in order to trace out EQUAL PITCH CONTOURS. The observer can be asked either to match the apparent loudness of two tones that differ in frequency (Stevens, 1935) or to adjust the frequency of one of two tones that differ in intensity until it matches the other in pitch (Gulick, 1971). Figure 9-14 shows the results from one observer measured by Stevens (1935). The graph shows the percentage change in the frequency necessary to keep the pitch constant as intensity is changed. The ordinate was chosen so that lines moving upward mean that the pitch is increasing (sounds higher) while lines moving downward mean that the pitch decreases (sounds lower). As the figure shows, varying the intensity of the tone greatly alters its perceived pitch. For high-frequency tones the pitch tends to rise as we increase the intensity, whereas for lower frequency tones an increase in intensity tends to lower the pitch.

A second factor that affects our perception of pitch is the duration of the stimulus. A pure tone that lasts for only a few milliseconds is always heard as a click, regardless of the frequency. Before a tone is perceived to have the quality of pitch, one of two conditions must be met. For high-frequency tones (greater than 1000 Hz) the minimum length of time the stimulus must be sounded is around 10 msec. For low-frequency tones (less than 1000 Hz) at least 6–9 cycles of the frequency must reach the ear before it is per-

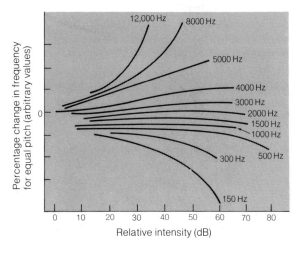

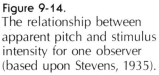

Figure 9-14.
The relationship between apparent pitch and stimulus intensity for one observer (based upon Stevens, 1935).

ceived to have pitch. This means that most lower frequency tones must be on for considerably longer than 10 msec before they have pitch (Gulick, 1971). Even for tones that exceed the minimum duration for number of cycles, the tonal quality continues to improve as the duration is increased up to about 250 msec. Listeners are better able to discriminate between tones of different frequencies when their duration is longer. You may recall that the loudness of a tone also increases as we increase stimulus duration up to around 200–250 msec. Perhaps $\frac{1}{4}$ of a second represents some sort of fundamental time period for sensory systems such as the ear. Our phenomenal impressions of the world seem to be based upon averages or sums of energy changes taken over this small window of time.

Theories of pitch perception. The realm of pitch perception has proven to be a testing ground for the major theories of auditory perception. Several tests have been based upon some interesting characteristics of our subjective impressions of sound. Suppose we have created a complex sound by adding together several different sinusoidal sound waves. The auditory system conducts its own waveform analysis of the complex sound,

and we are able to perceive the pitch of the various components separately. For instance, if two notes are played at the same time, you perceive a musical chord containing two distinct pitches. You do not hear a single, unitary sound (as you discovered in Demonstration Box 5-1). The visual system lacks this property of analyzing light stimuli into their component frequencies. In vision two stimulus frequencies are combined into a single percept and the individual components cannot be resolved in consciousness (this is discussed in Chapter 8).

When we are considering a complex stimulus composed of several sound wave frequencies, the lowest (usually most intense) frequency sound wave is called the FUNDAMENTAL. Musical instruments tend to produce complex sounds in which HARMONICS (frequencies higher than the fundamental) occur at whole number multiples of the fundamental frequency. For example, we have already noted that a sound wave of 220 Hz corresponds to a musical note that we call A (it would be A-3, or the thirty-seventh key from the left on the piano). When a musical instrument sounds this note, the complex waveform produced will also contain some sound energy at frequencies of 440 Hz, 880

Hz, 1320 Hz, and so on. These would be called *high even harmonics* (because they represent frequencies of 2, 4, and 6 times the fundamental frequency). Actually, the characteristic sound of an instrument depends upon the specific harmonics it produces. This quality, which gives the characteristic sound to a particular instrument, is called its TIMBRE. Different instruments emphasize different higher harmonics (sometimes called *overtones*). The number of higher harmonics or overtones and their strength determines the complex phenomenal perception that allows us to distinguish between a note played on a piano and the same note played by plucking a violin or a guitar string. Thus the pitch of a sound is greatly determined by the frequency of the fundamental, while the timbre is determined by the harmonics. Helmholtz (1863) summarized the various subjective feelings pertaining to the composition of a complex tone. This summary is shown in Table 9-1.

Since the fundamental frequency is the greatest common denominator of all of the harmonics present in a complex sound, we could correctly determine the fundamental from our knowledge of the way in which harmonics work. For example, if we had harmonics of 600, 900, and 1200 Hz, the fundamental frequency must be 300 Hz. As we noted in the preceding, a waveform normally contains both a fundamental frequency and several higher harmonics. It is possible (through the use of special electronic filters) to remove the fundamental frequency without changing the higher harmonic structure. Such an artificial sound complex, from which the fundamental frequency has been eliminated, would be called a stimulus with a MISSING FUNDAMENTAL.

An interesting and puzzling problem comes from a particular illusion associated with the missing fundamental. Suppose you are presented with two complex sounds. One contains the fundamental and higher harmonics and the other does not contain the fundamental frequency, but contains only the higher harmonics. The illusion lies in the fact that both of the sounds are subjectively the

Table 9-1 *Sound Composition and Timbre (Based upon Helmholtz, 1863)*

Makeup of Complex Tone	Subjective Impression
Fundamental alone	Soft
Fundamental plus first harmonic	Mellow
Fundamental plus several harmonics	Broad or full
Fundamental plus high harmonics	Sharp
Fundamental intense, harmonics less intense	Full
Harmonics intense, fundamental less intense	Hollow
Odd harmonics (for example, 1, 3, 5) dominating	Nasal
Frequency ratios of 16 : 15, 9 : 8, 15 : 8, 7 : 5, or 7 : 6	Rough or screeching

same. In both cases, the pitch will sound like that associated with the fundamental frequency, even though the fundamental frequency is not physically present in the waveform of the second sound. This unusual phenomenon of hearing plays an important role in a test of the two major theories of hearing. The first is based upon the PLACE PRINCIPLE and the second is based upon the FREQUENCY PRINCIPLE. Let us consider each in turn.

Over 100 years ago, Helmholtz became intrigued by the fact that the ear could separate a complex sound stimulus into its component simple frequencies. He observed that since the basilar membrane consists of many fibers stretched across its triangular shape, we could think of it as a harp with strings. He suggested that the longer strings resonate to (i.e., vibrate in sympathy with) lower frequency tones, while the shorter strings resonate to tones of higher frequency. Thus if we sounded a complex tone it would be automatically decomposed into its component frequencies on the basilar membrane. Each different tone would cause a different *place* on the membrane to vibrate. This is the place principle.

This basic idea was later supported by von Békésy in a precise series of experiments (see von Békésy, 1960). His basic procedure was to cut tiny holes in the cochleas of guinea pigs and to observe the basilar membrane with a microscope as the ear was being stimulated by tones of different frequencies. He discovered that high-frequency tones maximally displace the narrow end of the basilar membrane near the oval window, while tones of intermediate frequency cause displacement further toward the other (wider) end of the basilar membrane. Unfortunately, the action of the basilar membrane was not quite as simple as Helmholtz's resonance notion, since low-frequency tones activated the entire membrane with roughly an equal

amount of displacement (see Chapter 5). This fact, together with the result that tones of intermediate frequency also displace a fairly broad area of the membrane, would seem to make it unlikely that differential displacement or vibration of the basilar membrane is sufficient to fully explain our ability to discriminate pitch (at least for lower to intermediate frequencies).

The place theory also has difficulty in explaining the phenomenon of the missing fundamental. Helmholtz attempted to deal with this experience by suggesting that the transduction process in the middle ear introduces distortion before the waves enter the cochlea. This distortion could then create a new fundamental frequency, so that the fundamental is present inside the cochlea even though it is missing in the stimulus that actually reaches the outer ear. Von Békésy (1960) modified this notion somewhat so that the distortion became part of the response of the basilar membrane, which was said to respond "as if" the fundamental were also physically present.

Unfortunately, several experimental procedures seem to throw doubt upon this distortion hypothesis for the missing fundamental. The basic form of such experiments (Patterson, 1969) involves the presentation of pairs of tones, such as 2000 Hz and 2400 Hz, which would produce a missing fundamental of 400 Hz. If we now add a low-frequency band of noise to the complex wave, centered around 400 Hz, we would expect that when the noise is sufficiently intense it would be very effective in masking the fundamental tone, since it is stimulating approximately the place on the basilar membrane that is said to be vibrating by the place theory. Nevertheless, despite the presence of this noise, the pitch of the complex wave is still perceived as if the fundamental frequency is present. Since the missing fundamental phenomenon cannot be explained by distortions in the ear, or the local response of the basilar membrane, it presents a problem for a place theory.

The second major class of theory is based upon the frequency principle. It also has a long history. It was first championed by August Seebeck in the 1840s (Green, 1976) and has been carried forward to the present by Wever (1970). This theory argues that the basilar membrane vibrates as a whole, reproducing at least partially the vibrations of the incoming sounds. The frequency of the sound is transmitted by the pattern of neural excitation resulting from this vibration. This situation is analogous to the microphone end of a telephone transducing the pattern of vibrations into variations of electrical signals as it vibrates in unison with your voice. According to this theory, pitch is determined by the frequency of impulses traveling up the auditory nerve. The greater the frequency, the higher the pitch. Some studies have shown that for tones of up to about 4000 Hz, the electrical response of the auditory nerve tracks the frequency of the tone. A tone of 500 Hz produces a pattern of response that contains some 500 bursts of electrical responses per second in the nerve, while a tone of 1000 Hz produces twice as many responses.

Such a theoretical position could explain the missing fundamental. Since there are many harmonics but only one fundamental frequency, masking the region of the fundamental should not appreciably change the overall pattern of sound excitation. Thus the low frequency of the fundamental may actually be signaled by the neurons that respond to the higher harmonics, since it is these neurons that convey most of the information about the pattern of excitation. This may seem somewhat topsy-turvy in that we are saying that the fundamental is *not* fundamental, yet consider the example we used earlier in our discussion. Given a sound wave

with harmonics of 600, 900, and 1200 Hz, the fundamental is easily inferred to be 300 Hz. In much the same way that we *infer* the fundamental from knowledge of the harmonic structure, the higher auditory center could infer the fundamental from the pattern of excitation reported by neurons that respond to higher frequencies. This can be verified to a certain extent by the following experiment. If we present an individual with a pair of tones, such as 2000- and 2400-Hz tones, this produces a missing fundamental of 400 Hz. If we then introduce a high-frequency noise, centered at about 2200 Hz (which should mask the higher harmonics), the missing fundamental is no longer heard (Patterson, 1969).

There are still a number of problems with a frequency theory for pitch perception. One difficulty is that an individual neuron cannot fire at high enough rates to account for the perception of high-frequency signals. Actually, an individual neuron can conduct only about 1000 impulses per second. Thus the ability of the auditory nerve to track frequencies above this point (up to about 4000 Hz) has to be explained in terms of a VOLLEY PRINCIPLE (Wever, 1970). This argues that there is cooperation between neural fibers so that they fire in groups or squads. While one neuron is ''reloading'' its neighbor can discharge. The overall effect is that the neural pattern of firing is in direct correspondence to the frequency of the stimulus, since if one counts the total number of discharges, or volleys, per unit of time, they correspond to the frequency of the stimulus. An example of how this can work is shown in Figure 9-15.

The major problem with a volley or frequency principle of pitch perception is that we are requiring the frequency of neural firing to encode both the intensity and the frequency of the sound. Although at first this seems impossible, one way to resolve the problem is to differentiate a concept of over-

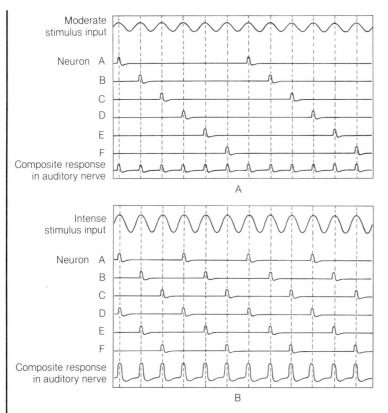

Figure 9-15.
The volley principal for encoding both frequency and pitch.
Note that the composite neural response follows the
frequency. However, for the weaker stimulus (A) fewer
neurons are firing in each volley than fire for the stronger
stimulus (B).

all *density* of neural activities from one of a *number* of volleys (or bursts of firing) per unit time. The density of neural firing could be defined as the total number of neural responses in each volley, or, if you will, the number of "shots" being fired in each volley down the auditory nerve. An increase in the intensity of the sound, while not changing the volley frequency, could increase the number of neurons joining in the firing, or cause the rate of each individual neuron to increase

somewhat. If all of the neurons were connected to some higher center that ascertained pitch by the frequency of volleys and loudness by the number of responses per volley, the problem would be solved. An example of how this could work is also shown in Figure 9-15.

Since both the place principle and the frequency principle seem to be supported by some data, it seems likely, as Wever (1970) has suggested, that the ultimate explanation of pitch perception will include some aspects of both theories. It is certainly the case that some primitive animals respond differently to different pitches, although they lack a basilar membrane (Fay, 1970). In the low-frequency region (less than 4000 Hz) they respond similarly to man. Wever has proposed that in humans pitch is coded by the frequency principle for frequencies lower than about 4000 Hz (the theoretical upper limit for volleying). For frequencies from 500 to 20,000 Hz, the place principle seems to be capable of explaining pitch perception. Below 500 Hz the vibration pattern on the basilar membrane seems too broad to explain an excellent pitch perception by this principle. Notice that for frequencies between 500 and 4000 Hz, both principles are operating. This could explain the superior performance of the ear for sounds in this range as compared to sounds of higher or lower frequencies. Frequencies outside of this range must rely upon only one mechanism, hence performance is poorer.

This place–frequency compromise is somewhat supported by research. For example, Simmons *et al.* (1965) placed electrodes in the auditory nerve corresponding to different parts of the basilar membrane of a subject's deaf ear. They found that electrical stimulation at different locations produced the perception of different pitches. This of course supports the place principle. However, varying the stimulus frequency from about 20 to 300 Hz produced the appropriate changes in pitch perception, regardless of the place in which the stimulating electrode was located. This supports the frequency principle. Clearly both mechanisms are needed to explain such data.

Volume, Density, and Subjective Impressions. Suppose you were asked to write music for a science fiction film in which the opening sequence is a panoramic view of outer space with glimpses of stars and distant planets. Your first inclination might be to use French horns and big booming drums, followed by the swelling sounds of a full orchestra playing in unison. You would write this type of sound track to evoke a feeling of the expansiveness of space in the listener. One would not be tempted to convey an impression of infinity by using the sound of a xylophone, a banjo, or a piccolo. Subjectively some sounds or tones seem "bigger" or more "expansive" than others. We can call this attribute VOLUME.

Although some psychologists deny that volume can be given a status as a separate attribute, it certainly seems to differ from pitch and loudness. In a phenomenological sense we can understand what is meant by volume, or the "space filling quality" of a sound, if we compare notes played on an organ with equivalent notes played on a flute. Although the notes may be musically equivalent in the characteristics of pitch and loudness, the sounds made by the organ appear to be *larger* or *broader* than those of the flute. Stevens (1934) investigated volume as a separate tonal attribute. He had observers adjust the intensity of each of a series of tones that differed in frequency until they seemed to match the volume of a standard tone of 500 Hz at 60 dB. In general, he found that volume grows as we decrease the frequency of the stimulus. Thus a tone of 450 Hz at 58 dB has the same volume as a tone of 500 Hz at 60 dB.

Another attribute of tonal quality is DENSITY, which is the impression that some tones are more *compressed,* more *concentrated, harder,* or *tighter* than others. Stevens (1934) measured density using a procedure similar to that used for volume. Observers generally regarded tones of higher pitch as being denser. Similarly, high-intensity tones are denser than low-intensity tones. Thus density seems to be a separate attribute, distinguishable from volume in that it operates in an inverse fashion. When two tones that differ in frequency are to be matched in density, one must increase the intensity of the lower frequency tones. Guirao and Stevens (1964) suggested that the dominant physical variable related to density is the sound pressure level. Direct magnitude estimations of density increase as a power function of sound pressure. However, although much guesswork still surrounds the question of the acoustical and psychological correlates of volume and density, an observer who is instructed to attend to density undeniably becomes more sensitive to variations in that attribute, as does an observer who is instructed to attend to volume. These observers will react in different ways than when they are asked to make judgments of pitch or loudness.

If we wanted to explore totally the subjective dimensions of sound, we would soon find ourselves dealing with very complex phenomenal impressions, even if aesthetic considerations were ignored. For instance, suppose you were a cartoonist who wished to provide voices for an ogre and the frail princess whom he is abducting. You would have the ogre speak in low tones. His voice would be loud and his speech would be slow. The frightened princess, on the other hand, would speak quickly and softly (when not screaming) with a high-pitched voice. Thus one finds that the frequency range, the intensity, and the duration of voice-produced sounds are related to our subjective impressions of the power and confidence of the individual who emits that sound.

Although the sound patterns emitted by animals are species specific, both in their nature and in the information they convey, the dimensions of frequency, intensity, and duration in specific combinations seem fairly typical of the power–confidence dimension in many mammalian species. For instance, the low-frequency, sustained angry growl of a wolf about to attack is quite different from the high-pitched squeaky yaps of pain of the same animal when hurt (Theberge, 1971). Many primates also use sound signals to exchange information. The most heavily studied subhuman group has been the Rhesus monkey. When we look at the characteristic pattern of monkey sounds, we find again that power and confidence are shown by low-frequency, loud, and long-duration sounds, whereas fear and defeat are associated with high-frequency, low-intensity, and short-duration sounds (Rowell, 1962). This can be seen in Table 9-2.

Since so many subjective impressions seem to be reliably produced by sound stimuli, including volume, density, perhaps power or confidence, and many more, it is but a short step to the conscious manipulation of sound stimuli to convey specific signals from one individual to another. Thus the complex subjective feelings evoked by sound stimuli, and the reliable ways in which they can be produced in many individuals, may have served as the basis upon which language and speech developed. For instance, consider the word "high" and the corresponding word "low." Notice that if asked to describe the subjective feelings associated with the pitch of those two complex stimuli, the word "high" has a higher pitch, and somehow feels higher than the word "low." In further support of such speculation, note that musical notes move up the page as the frequency rises, and down the page as the frequency falls. The interrelationship between the subjective impressions from simple sound stimuli and the evolution of language is an area that remains to be fully explored. Still, it is interesting to consider demonstrations such as Demonstration Box 9-5, which seem to show that some of the subjective feeling associated with sound input may have been encoded in our language use.

Table 9-2 *Patterns of Monkey Sounds (Based upon Rowell, 1962)*

Type	Frequency	Intensity	Duration	Meaning and Context
		Characteristics		
Roar	Low	Loud	Long	Used by confident animals threatening an inferior
Pant–threat	Low	Loud	Short bursts	Less confident animal, seeking support to make attack
Bark	Midrange	Loud	Short	Threat by animal too timid to attack
Growl	High midrange	Moderate	Extended, short bursts	Mildly alarmed animal
Geckering screech	High	Loud	Long volleys of short bursts	When threatened by another animal
Scream	High	Loud	Short	When losing a fight or being bitten
Squeak	Very high	Low	Short	From a defeated exhausted animal

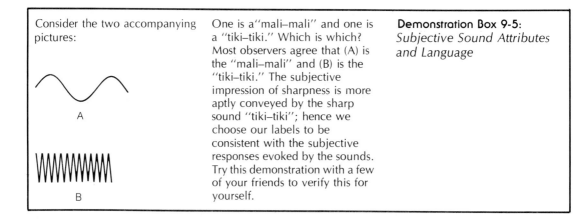

Consider the two accompanying pictures:

A

B

One is a "mali–mali" and one is a "tiki–tiki." Which is which? Most observers agree that (A) is the "mali–mali" and (B) is the "tiki–tiki." The subjective impression of sharpness is more aptly conveyed by the sharp sound "tiki–tiki"; hence we choose our labels to be consistent with the subjective responses evoked by the sounds. Try this demonstration with a few of your friends to verify this for yourself.

Demonstration Box 9-5:
Subjective Sound Attributes and Language

10
Taste, Smell, Touch, and Pain

TASTE
TASTE THRESHOLDS AND ADAPTATION
TASTE INTENSITY AND QUALITIES

SMELL
SMELL THRESHOLDS AND ADAPTATION
SMELL INTENSITY AND QUALITIES

TOUCH
TOUCH THRESHOLDS AND ADAPTATION
TOUCH INTENSITY AND QUALITIES

WARMTH AND COLD
THERMAL THRESHOLDS AND ADAPTATION
THERMAL INTENSITY AND QUALITIES

PAIN
PAIN THRESHOLDS, INTENSITY, AND ADAPTATION
ANALGESIA

The jungle man stopped and looked at the fresh gash in the tree. He touched his tongue to it. The lingering taste of metal verified that humans were near. He turned and sniffed the wind. There it was—the faint scent of two men. He could tell by the scent that they were city people, not from the jungle. He could also tell by the message in the wind that she was with them.

When you read a passage like this your mind probably flits back to memories of Tarzan or the wolf boy. Clearly, such sensory abilities lie only in the realm of fantasy. However, if we change the term "jungle man" to "large bloodhound," the element of fantasy dissipates. To the popular mind, animals seem to have incredible (almost supernatural) sensitivity, especially for taste, smell, and touch. Yet although we do not rely upon these senses as much as we do upon sight and hearing, much of our image of the world is dependent upon our chemical and mechanical senses.

TASTE

Taste Thresholds and Adaptation. Exactly what are the limits of a human's sensitivity to taste? It is difficult to study the thresholds for taste stimuli, since there are so many different stimuli to consider, and it is not easy to specify the relevent stimulus property for intensity (see Chapter 6). The study is further complicated by the fact that the various parts of the tongue and mouth are not equally sensitive to different stimuli. Let us begin by indicating how we can physically measure how much of a taste stimulus is present at any moment. Although there is still much debate on the appropriate measurement procedures for taste stimuli, one useful procedure may be to talk in terms of the MOLAR CONCENTRATION of a substance (Pfaffman, Bartoshuk, & McBurney, 1971). Molar concentration is based upon the weight of a substance dissolved in a given amount of a solution (usually water, when we deal with taste). A solution is said to have a concentration of one *mole* if the molecular weight of the substance (in grams) is added to enough water to make one liter of solution. This results in solutions that have the same number of stimulus molecules in a given volume of liquid.

Once we have specified the stimulus concentrations, we can begin to look at thresholds. However, we must be careful to note that the region of the mouth or tongue stimulated also determines our sensitivity. For many years it was thought that the back of the tongue was especially sensitive to bitter taste, while the front of the tongue was more sensitive to sweet and salty stimuli, and the sides of the rear part of the tongue were most sensitive to sour stimuli. However, recent work by Collings (1974) altered this picture. She used as a stimulus a tiny piece of filter paper that had been soaked in a stimulus solution. This gave more precise control over the location of the stimulus on the tongue. Figure 10-1 shows a summary of her results for four different parts of the tongue and the soft palate. For the bitter substance the lowest threshold on the tongue is at the front. However, an even lower threshold occurs on the palate for this substance. The tip and back of the tongue are most sensitive to sweet, while the front and sides are most sensitive to salt. An interesting explanation for the differences in taste thresholds across the tongue comes from von Békésy (1964), who found that each individual taste papilla seems to convey only one single taste quality (salty, sweet, sour, or bitter), although as we have seen in Chapter 6, all of the taste buds seem to respond to all stimuli. Perhaps more of the receptors that produce a particular class of sensation are concentrated on particular regions of the tongue, thus producing the threshold differences.

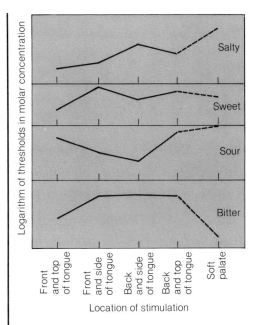

Figure 10-1.
Average absolute thresholds for four different taste stimuli at four locations on the tongue, and at a location on the soft palate (based upon Collings, 1974).

Individuals often differ in marked ways in their sensitivity to certain tastes. This is shown in a study by Blakeslee and Salmon (1935), who tested the taste thresholds for 47 people using 17 different substances. Figure 10-2 summarizes some of their results. Most substances, such as table salt or saccharine, have a moderate to very narrow range of thresholds across different people; others such as vanillin and phenyl thiocaramide, have very large ranges in these data. These latter two substances are interesting because they are substances about which it has been said that some people are "taste-blind." That is, at ordinary concentrations some people cannot taste these substances at all. For instance, phenyl thiocarbamide (PTC) produces a bitter taste for those who are sensitive

to it. Yet there is a large group of people who seem to be taste-blind for PTC. This is not the same as visual blindness, as Figure 10-2 shows, for if the stimulus is intense enough, even the taste-blind can taste PTC. One similarity between taste blindness for PTC and visual blindness for colors is that both often seem to have a genetic component and tend to run in families.

You might be surprised to learn that another substance often associated with taste blindness is caffeine, the stimulant found in

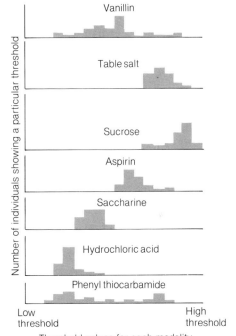

Figure 10-2.
Frequency distributions of absolute thresholds of 47 observers to various taste stimuli. Phenyl thiocarbomide (PTC) and vanillin have particularly wide ranges of thresholds, and PTC clearly shows two modes, tasters with low thresholds and nontasters with high thresholds (based upon Blakeslee & Salmon, 1935).

coffee (Hall, Bartoshuk, Cain, & Stevens, 1975). For caffeine the taster and nontaster groups are not as distinct as they are with PTC, but the range of thresholds is still quite large and two groups clearly appear. Furthermore, tasters of PTC tend to be tasters of caffeine and vice versa, indicating that there may be a common mechanism responsible for this threshold variation. This is not due simply to a general "bitter" taste mechanism, for in the same study Hall *et al.* (1975) found that thresholds to two other bitter-tasting substances were unrelated to thresholds for PTC and caffeine. In general, the attempt to explain such cases of taste blindness by attributing them to deficiencies in some general taste system (as is often possible for color blindness) has not succeeded very well.

Taste thresholds can also be affected by stimuli that have reached the tongue prior to the threshold test. The taste system adapts very readily to continued stimulation of the same type, and this adaptation temporarily raises the absolute threshold for the particular substance to which it has been adapted. Figure 10-3 shows an example of the effects of previous stimulation on absolute threshold. Here both the adapting stimulus and the test stimulus are table salt (NaCl). As you can see from the figure, the absolute threshold varies both with how long the tongue has been exposed to the adapting stimulus and the strength of the stimulus (Hahn, 1934). This sort of adaptation explains why at dinner some people resalt their food again and again. As they eat the salty food, they are adapting to the salty taste and come to need more salt to experience the taste at the same level. You can avoid having to resalt the food if you eat something else that is not salty between bites of salty food. As Figure 10-3 shows, recovery from adaptation is virtually complete in about 10 sec, no matter how much salt you were eating previously.

Adaptation to one substance can also

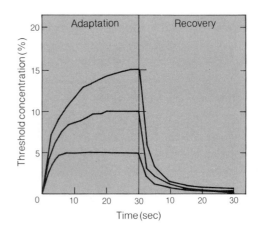

Figure 10-3.
Adaptation and recovery from adaptation to continued stimulation of the tongue with table salt (NaCl). The three curves represent three different adapting concentrations. The time axis represents amount of exposure to the adapting concentration, or recovery time, before determination of absolute threshold. Note the resemblance to dark adaptation curves (see Chapter 7) (based upon Hahn, 1934).

have an effect on the threshold of (and the subsequent taste of) different substances. This is called CROSS-ADAPTATION. In some cases exposure of the tongue to one stimulus may actually *lower* the threshold to another taste stimulus (or make its taste more intense). This is called POTENTIATION. More specifically, adaptation to one salt will raise the threshold to other salts. Similarly, exposure to a sour substance will raise the threshold to different sour stimuli. On the other hand, adaptation to an acid, while reducing the sourness of another acid, may increase the sweetness of a sugar. Adaptation to urea (the bitter substance contained in human urine) will increase the intensity of salty sensations (McBurney, 1969). Perhaps the most striking phenomenon associated with adaptation is the variability of the taste of ordinary tap water with adaptation to various substances. In fact, all four of the basic tastes can be induced in water by previous adaptation to a suitable taste stimulus (McBurney & Bartoshuk, 1972). You can experience this for yourself by trying Demonstration Box 10-1.

Taste Intensity and Qualities. Our ability to discriminate intensity differences in taste, regardless of the stimulus tested, is really quite poor. The Weber fraction (the difference threshold divided by the level at which it is measured) for different stimuli under different conditions ranges from a relatively poor 1/10 to an awful 1/1, making taste the least sensitive of the senses for this criterion (Pfaffman, et al., 1971).

To see how the sensation of taste grows as we increase the stimulus intensity, a number of investigators have used the magnitude estimation technique discussed in Chapter 3. In general, they find that the sensation increase is predicted by a typical power function of the form $S = aI^n$, where S is the sensation, I is the intensity of the stimulus, a is a constant, and n indicates the rate at which the sensation increases. The interesting fact that emerges is that the exponent n is usually above 1 (i.e., for table salt it is 1.4 and for refined cane sugar it is 1.3), which means that at greater concentrations a small addition to the stimulus produces a larger change in the sensation than if the same amount were added to a weaker solution (Moskowitz, 1970; Stevens, 1969). This is exactly the opposite of what happens in vision and hearing, where the corresponding exponents are less than one and changes in weaker stimuli are perceived as greater.

Several studies have compared the changes in the rate of neural response with changes in stimulus intensity to the psychophysical data. They have shown that the two types of response vary with stimulus

---

Water has a distinctive taste, especially when you have been eating or drinking some other substance before you taste the water. In this demonstration you will be able to make water taste sweet, bitter, sour, or salty. Although you may not be able to (or want to) try all of the demonstrations, be assured that all of them work under the carefully controlled conditions of the laboratory (Bartoshuk, 1974). The most pleasant of the demonstrations requires that you eat a few cooked artichokes of any variety (canned, fresh, or frozen) and then taste a sip of water. Be sure to thoroughly mash the artichoke onto your tongue and palate while eating it. Water tasted after eating the artichoke usually tastes sweet.

Another way to obtain the sweet taste is to swish a mouthful of strong (caffeinated) coffee on the tongue for 30 sec before tasting tap water. A foolproof way to make anything taste sweet is to eat miracle fruit first. However, this fruit is not readily available, so this is more difficult to demonstrate. To make water taste bitter/sour, take some very salty water and swish it around in your mouth for 30 sec and then spit it out. Afterwards, taste some tap water. Something that has been tried in the laboratory but which you may not want to try is to swish some urea (a major component of urine) on the tongue for 30 sec. Tap water tasted after this treatment tastes salty.

Demonstration Box 10-1:
The Taste of Water

intensity in a similar fashion (Borg, Diamant, Oakley, Strom, & Zotterman, 1967; Diamant & Zotterman, 1969). It seems likely that our sensation of the intensity of a taste is directly related to the overall amount of neural activity evoked by the stimulus, which in turn depends upon the intensity of the stimulus.

Modern psychophysical scaling techniques have also been used to look at the relationships among taste *qualities*. In 1916 Henning proposed that we could specify the qualities of all tastes using a figure in a three-dimensional geometrical space, in much the same way we specified colors in Chapter 8. He proposed that it would be in the form of a pyramid, with the primary tastes at the corners. Intermediate tastes would be represented by points on the surface of this space, which is shown in Figure 10-4A. Schiffman and Erikson (1971) used a sophisti-

cated mathematical technique to test this notion. The technique is based on the judged similarity between stimuli. Using a procedure called MULTIDIMENSIONAL SCALING, observers' similarity judgments can be converted into a set of distances between points in a geometric space with the smallest possible number of dimensions. Figure 10-4B shows their results. Notice that Henning's taste pyramid fits nicely into this space (perhaps with the exception of alkaline tastes). This has been verified in a more recent study using a larger set of stimuli (Schiffman & Dackis, 1975). One major challenge for any theory of taste would be to relate this three-dimensional "quality space" to the physiochemical properties of the substances that are the taste stimuli. Preliminary steps in this direction indicate that molecular weight and groupings of molecules accord-

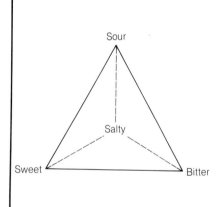

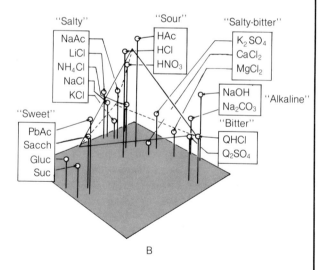

Figure 10-4.
(A) Henning's taste pyramid. (B) Multidimensional scaling results for similarity judgments of taste stimuli. Henning's taste pyramid is superimposed on the three-dimensional space so that you can see the correspondence. Since the "alkaline" stimuli are not on the pyramid, they may represent a fifth primary taste (from Schiffman & Erickson, 1971).

ing to common parts will be important properties to consider (Schiffman, 1974).

Taste qualities interact with each other in complex ways. For instance, von Békésy (1964) showed that when two different taste stimuli are presented to opposite sides of the tongue, they may add together to produce a sensation in the middle of the tongue or they may stay separate. Von Békésy found that only certain groups of taste stimuli will interact to produce a sensation in the center of the tongue. Other groups remain as two separate sensations. Generally, sweet and bitter substances interact, as do salty and sour substances. However, salty and sour do not interact with bitter, nor does sweet interact with salty or sour. In addition, the temperature qualities of warm and cold seem to interact with certain aspects of taste. Thus von Békésy found that a warm stimulus on one side of the tongue and a sweet stimulus on the other would interact to produce the sensation of a warm, sweet stimulus in the center of the tongue. Warm also interacted with bitter, while cold combined only with salty and sour. This total set of results is summarized in Figure 10-5, where it can be seen that there are two separate clusters of stimuli that interact. Von Békésy offers these data as support for a DUPLEXITY THEORY of taste, which postulates two separate, noninteracting systems for taste. Each of these (sweet–bitter and salty–sour) is thought to be an opponent-process system, in which the two processes act in opposition to each other, much as do opponent processes in color vision (see Chapter 8). This theory could possibly begin to make some sense of the bewildering variety of data we have just considered.

SMELL

Smell Thresholds and Adaptation. A dog's sense of smell can be amazingly acute. For

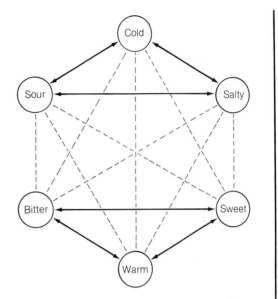

Figure 10-5.
Von Békésy's (1964) duplexity theory of taste. The solid arrows denote interaction, and the broken lines show no interaction. Warm, bitter, and sweet form one interacting group of qualities; cold, salty, and sour form another. The two groups do not interact with each other.

example, Dröscher (1971) tells the story of a dog trainer who had worked with dogs for years. He brought his dog to a university professor for testing. He felt that the dog's ability was "supernatural" since it could track people by scent, even if they were wearing rubber boots! Actually the dog was simply using his acute sense of smell to detect the millions of sweat molecules that leak through the rubber boots. Why can't we smell such things? The sensitivity of each smell receptor is about the same for dogs as for humans. The only difference is that the dog has many more smell receptors, with more hairlike cilia projecting from each (see Chapter 6).

Stuiver (de Vries & Stuiver, 1961) studied the absolute sensitivity of human smell receptors. He made a model of the nasal passages around the olfactory epithelium. He used this model to calculate just how much of an olfactory stimulus actually arrived at the surface of the epithelium (see Figure 10-6). When threshold stimuli were considered, he found that it takes eight molecules at most to stimulate a single receptor in the human. When one considers all aspects of the manner in which odor molecules are distributed in the nose, it can be argued that a single receptor cell needs to be contacted by one stimulus molecule in order to respond (de Vries & Stuiver, 1961). Since this is as sensitive as any single cell can get, a dog's (or any other animal's) receptors can be no more sensitive than a human's. However, since the dog has more receptor sites, the likelihood that a very weak stimulus will stimulate enough receptors to produce a noticeable sensation is larger for the dog.

More traditional attempts to determine the absolute threshold for various odors have

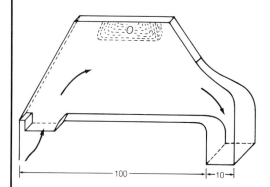

Figure 10-6.
Model of the nasal passage used by Stuiver to calculate the proportion of molecules in a smell stimulus that reach the olfactory epithelium (O). Air follows the path indicated by arrows. Stimulus molecules reach O via eddy currents (like the eddies in a stream) (from de Vries, H., & Stuiver, M. In W. A. Rosenblith (ed.), *Sensory Communication.* New York: Wiley, 1961. © 1961 by The MIT Press).

similar problems to those in taste. Thresholds vary across methods. They seem to depend upon the purity of the odorant, the way in which it is delivered to the olfactory epithelium, and how the stimulus intensity is measured. Different substances also have different thresholds. Some of these threshold differences seem to depend upon the ability of various molecules to stick to the receptive surfaces (to be adsorbed) rather than upon receptor sensitivities.

In much the same way that we found individual differences in taste sensitivity, there are also individual differences in smell sensitivity. Some individuals are relatively "odor-blind" to certain substances. Amoore (1969, 1975) has reported the results of an extensive search for instances of odor blindnesses as a part of his plan to identify the primary odors. By 1975 he was able to report 76 different ANOSMIAS (odor blindnesses), ranging from the smell of a skunk to the smell of vanilla. Some of these are quite common (32% of those tested could not smell a strong stimulus of isobutyraldehyde, which produces a sweaty smell), while others are rare (only 4 of 4030 individuals, or .1%, couldn't smell a strong stimulus of *n*-butyl mercaptan, which has a foul, putrid odor). Amoore was able to classify these 76 anosmias into about 31 classes. However, there is some question as to whether a group of 31 or so basic odors could in any useful sense be called primary.

As in most sensory systems, adaptation affects smell thresholds and the perceived intensity of an odor. It is one of the great disappointments of wine tasting that the aroma and the bouquet of the wine seem to last only for a few sniffs. The rich complexity of a great wine soon fades into a bland, featureless odor, even for the most experienced "smeller," unless frequent breaks of about 15 sec of nonsniffing are taken. Luckily, the odors of sweaty bodies, rotten eggs, or the sulfurous smell of air pollution also soon fade away, as long as you continue sniffing.

An important early study of adaptation of the smell sense was that of Moncrieff (1956). He studied the effects of previous exposure to an odorant on the threshold for that odorant (SELF-ADAPTATION). He also looked at the way in which exposure to one odorant affected the threshold for different odorants (CROSS-ADAPTATION). As you might expect, the largest loss of sensitivity was found for conditions of self-adaptation. Cross-adaptation effects varied with the similarity of the smells of the two stimuli. Stimuli with similar smells gave large cross-adaptation effects, while those that differed in smell gave smaller effects. Surprisingly, all of the adapting odors had some effects on observers' sensitivity for the others. This means that it was not possible to classify the various stimuli into a small number of primary classes. This is similar to Amoore's conclusions based on anosmias.

While Moncrieff (1956) looked at the effects of adaptation on smell thresholds, Cain and Engen (1969) looked at the effects of adapting stimuli on the perceived intensity of odorants. They used a magnitude estimation procedure and found that higher concentrations of the adapting stimulus produced greater reduction in the apparent intensity of the test stimuli. Surprisingly, *very* intense test stimuli all appeared to arouse about the same sensory response, regardless of the state of adaptation.

Smell Intensity and Qualities. When we consider how our sensation of the strength of an odor varies as we vary the stimulus intensity, we again find it useful to refer to the exponent of the psychophysical power function to describe this relationship. As is the case with the various taste substances, the exponents of power functions fitted to magnitude estimations of odor intensity differ across the various odors scaled. Cain (1969) found that exponents ranged from about .7 to a low of about .15. Remember that the higher the exponent the faster the sensation in-

creases as we increase stimulus intensity. Cain reports that the size of the exponent is directly related to the degree of water solubility of the odorant, with exponents for completely water-soluble odorants always about 2.5 times as large as those for non-water-soluble odorants.

In absolute terms the sense of smell is remarkably acute. However, previous investigations have found that the human ability to discriminate between odors of different intensities is rather poor. Typical values of the Weber fraction for various odorants have ranged from a low of about .20 to a high of 1.0, which is roughly the same range as for taste (Geldard, 1972). However, a recent study by Cain (1977) indicates that the differential sensitivity of olfaction is considerably greater than previously thought. Cain did a signal detection analysis (see Chapter 2) of the performance of human observers and of a gas chromatograph (an extremely sensitive physical instrument that measures amounts of gases in samples) under carefully controlled conditions. He found that they performed about equally well, indicating that much of the "noise" that limits discrimination performance in smell is stimulus noise. That is, there are large fluctuations in the number of molecules of odorant that reach the olfactory epithelium, or the relevant part of the chromatograph, even when the same measured concentration is used. These fluctuations are caused mainly by differential adsorption (from trial to trial) of the molecules onto the surface of the nasal passages, or onto the various valves and passages in the stimulus delivery device or the chromatograph. When Cain corrected for these stimulus factors, he obtained Weber fractions that were about ten times lower than those usually obtained. This would place maximum differential sensitivity in olfaction at about the same level as that in vision or audition with sequentially presented stimuli.

Another recent and somewhat surprising

set of results pertaining to the sense of smell deals with the ability of humans to identify human body odors. Since a variety of animals communicate via the sense of smell, it seems reasonable to ask whether humans are responsive to human scents. Two separate studies (McBurney, Levine, & Cavanaugh, 1977; Russell, 1976) have demonstrated that people can reliably detect their own body odor from among a set of similar stimuli contributed by other people. The actual stimuli were collected by having people wear T-shirts for several days. When asked to rate the pleasantness of the body odors and to describe the individual whose odor they were smelling, there was a remarkable degree of consistency across people. In general, the individuals having unpleasant odors were usually associated with socially undesirable traits. They were supposedly dumb, ugly, fat, and unhealthy. The more pleasant odors were described as coming from people with the more desirable traits (McBurney et al., 1977). Subjects seemed able to discriminate reliably the sex of an odor donor; the odors of males were characterized as "musk" while female odors were described as "sweet" (Russell, 1976). This sensitivity to human odors seems to be present from an early age, since Russell (1976) found that a small sample of 2-week-old babies reliably responded to the odor of their own mother's breast and not to that of a strange mother. Russell mentions a similar study that found a differential response of 6-day-old infants to their own and a strange mother's odor. It is possible that odors play a part in human social relationships similar to that played by odorous excretions in lower animals and insects. The most recent work even suggests that for some people, at least, body odors affect sexual activity (Hassett, 1978).

In the taste modality as in the visual perception of color it was possible to isolate a simple set of primary qualities. All sensations were then simply the result of a combination of the primary responses. Data from adaptation and amosmias do not suggest a small cluster of primaries for smell. The classical attempt to describe smell primaries was that of Henning (1915). Figure 10-7 shows his "smell prism," which had six primary qualities arranged at the corners of a prism. More recently, Amoore (1975) argued that there may be as many as 31 primary odors. Some of these primaries seem to be associated with receptor systems that respond to odors produced by the human body in various situations relevant to the survival of the species, such as danger and sexual contact. The data we discussed above on the identification of human body odors would suggest that this may be a possibility.

On the other hand, there is evidence that there may be no small set of primaries in odor perception at all. When we use multidimensional scaling techniques to provide us with a geometrical representation of odor judgments, in much the same way as we did for taste judgments earlier, neither Henning's

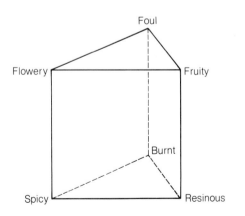

Figure 10-7.
Henning's (1915) smell prism. Six "primary" odors are at the corners; the surfaces represent stimuli that resemble more than one primary.

smell prism nor any other readily identifiable classification scheme emerges. Figure 10-8 displays some representative results from this kind of study. Erickson and Schiffman (1975) argue that such results indicate that only a complex set of physiochemical considerations could account for the interrelationships shown in the qualities of smell stimuli. At the present time, a successful explanation of our sensory experiences of smell seems unlikely to be as simple as comparable theories of sensory qualities in other modalities.

TOUCH

Given the fact that any point on our body's surface can evoke the sensation of touch, it is interesting to see how often this modality is ignored. For instance, one seldom considers that major components of most sexual experiences are touch sensations. The very act of

touching another person, in Western society, is considered to be an act of considerable intimacy, whether it is the gentle touch of a friend or lover or the violent punch of an aggressor.

Touch Thresholds and Adaptation. One of the most striking aspects of our sense of touch is the variability of sensitivity from one region of the body to another. Figure 10-9 shows the absolute touch thresholds for several different regions of the body (excluding most of the erogenous zones, which probably contain some of the lowest thresholds). Such thresholds are obtained by applying a small rod or hair (pig bristles were used in some of the earliest work) with differing amounts of force to the surface of the skin. When an investigator is always using the same hair, these thresholds can be expressed in terms of the amount of force applied to the hair, as they

Figure 10-8.
Composite replotting of selected odors from multidimensional scaling of similarity judgments of odor pairs (Schiffman, 1974). Dimension I is thought to be "pleasantness." This mapping bears little resemblance to Henning's smell prism (Figure 10-7).

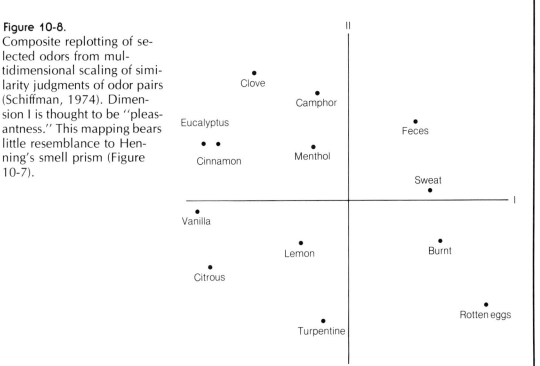

Figure 10-9.
Absolute pressure thresholds for different regions of the female skin. Relative values for males are similar but average thresholds are somewhat higher (from Weinstein, S. In D. R. Kenshalo (ed.), *The Skin Senses*, 1968. Courtesy of Charles C. Thomas, Publisher, Springfield, Illinois).

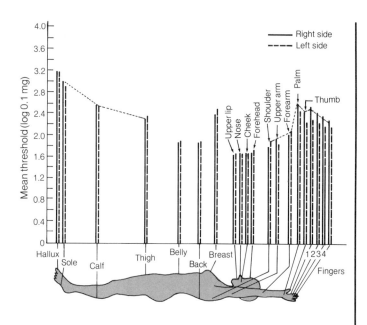

are in Figure 10-9. However, it is probably best to express absolute thresholds in units of force per unit area, since the actual stimulus is the change in the amount of tension in the skin and not the force itself (von Frey & Kiesow, 1899). At any rate, it is apparent in Figure 10-9 that absolute thresholds vary considerably over the body surface.

There are even more dramatic variations of threshold within a relatively small area of skin, say, the surface of the arm. If you explore a 2 × 2 cm area on your forearm with a toothpick or hairbrush bristle, pressing with the same light pressure every time you touch the skin (just enough to make the bristle bend slightly is good), you will discover a number of spots that respond to this stimulus with a distinct sensation of touch. However, there will also be a large number of places that will give only a faint sensation, or none at all.

The sensitivity of the skin is often tested using a *vibrating* stimulus, which alternately applies and releases a force to the same small surface region at frequencies similar to those common in auditory stimuli (20–20,000 Hz).

Generally, vibration of a touch stimulus results in a lower absolute threshold. That is, when the stimulation is intermittent (on again–off again) the skin seems to be more sensitive. This is reasonable since it is the change in the tension in the skin that is the stimulus for touch sensation, and the vibrations cause these changes continually. The frequency of vibration of a vibrotactile stimulator on the skin acts in a similar fashion to the frequency of a sound wave on the ear, resulting in a sense of vibrational pitch. Again, like the ear, the skin is sensitive only to a limited range of frequencies of vibration. The range most investigators agree upon is from about 40 to about 2500 Hz. However, some researchers have claimed, under special conditions, to have produced sensations at frequencies of up to 20,000 Hz (Verrillo, 1975).

One aspect of all tactual stimuli is that each touch sensation seems to be localized at a particular place on the skin. Our ability to localize the sensation accurately varies across different regions of the skin. Localization accuracy seems to be directly related to the amount of neural representation each area has in the touch cortex. In general, the greater the representation of a particular area, the smaller are the errors of localization for that area. A similar relationship may also hold between the amount of cortical representation and absolute and differential sensitivity, explaining the threshold differences seen in Figures 10-9 and 10-10. Another interesting aspect of localization is studied in Demonstration Box 10-2.

Touch sensations adapt, as do all other sensations. This can be shown by simply applying a stimulus to the skin and observing the gradual disappearance of the sensation. Zigler (1932) demonstrated this adaptation using several different areas of the body. He reported that the heavier the stimulus, the longer it took for the sensation to disappear. On the other hand, the larger the area covered by the stimulus, the less time it took for the sensation to disappear. You can demon-

strate this result using Demonstration Box 10-3.

Another technique for measuring adaptation is to present a stimulus for some period of time and then to introduce a second stimulus. The observer is asked to adjust the intensity of the second stimulus until it matches the sensation caused by the first. Since adaptation has reduced the apparent intensity of the first stimulus, the difference between the magnitude of the two stimuli is a measure of the amount of adaptation that has taken place. This technique assumes that the two stimuli would be matched in magnitude of sensation when they were equal in intensity. Using this technique, von Frey and Goldman (1915) determined that adaptation to touch stimuli is similar to that for other modalities. The adaptation is very rapid for the first second or so and then gradually slows down. After 3 sec the sensation level has decreased to about $\frac{1}{4}$ of the beginning value.

Von Békésy (1959) used this same tech-

Figure 10-10.
Average two-point thresholds for different regions of the male skin. Relative values for females are similar but absolutely somewhat lower (from Weinstein, S. In D. R. Kenshalo (ed.), *The Skin Senses,* 1968. Courtesy of Charles C. Thomas, Publisher, Springfield, Illinois).

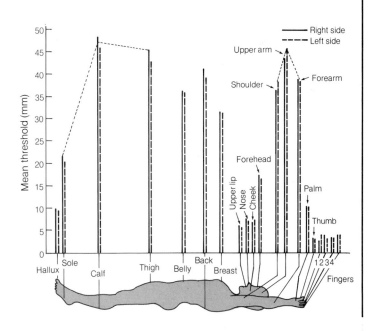

Von Békésy has studied localization in all of the major sensory modalities and has discovered similar phenomena in all of them. One of the most striking is the discovery that a touch can be localized as being outside of the body under the appropriate circumstances (von Békésy, 1967). We will demonstrate a somewhat simpler phenomenon that apparently depends upon the difference in arrival times of neural impulses from different parts of the skin surface to the primary sensory areas of the brain.

Touch your two index fingers together. Try to concentrate on experiencing *where* the sensations of touch are felt, that is, on which of the two fingers. Most people report sensations of about equal intensity from both fingertips. Now touch your fingertip (either one) repeatedly to your lower lip with light, quick touches. When asked to say where the sensation is, most people report that they feel it mostly on the lip and little or not at all on the fingertip, even though both are of about equal sensitivity and are being stimulated approximately equally. Now use the same finger to touch, with the same light, quick touches, your little toe or your ankle. Most people now report that the sensation seems to be located mostly in the finger, rather than in the toe or the ankle, even though both are being equally stimulated. As it turns out, it takes somewhat more than 1 msec longer for the nerve impulses to travel from the fingertip to the brain than for them to travel from the lip to the brain. Similarly, it takes more than 1 msec longer for impulses to travel from the foot to the brain than from the finger to the brain. The impulses that arrive at the brain first (providing the difference is more than 1 msec) seem to dictate where the sensation will be experienced, even though the two places on the skin are being stimulated equally. The various other parts of the body fall in between these extremes, but in all cases the localization depends upon the relative lengths of the pathways from the touching parts to the brain.

For this demonstration you will need a watch with a sweep second hand, two pieces of cardboard (cut into small circles with diameters of about 1 cm and about 4 cm), and a friend. Lay one piece of cardboard on the skin of your friend's back and record the amount of time before the sensation of touch disappears. Repeat this with the other piece of cardboard. Try the experiment again, only this time press gently on the cardboard. Notice that the lighter touches and the larger surface area stimulation disappear faster from consciousness. Thus they show faster adaptation.

nique to measure the time course of adaptation for vibratory stimuli. It is of quite a different character on the lip and on the forearm. On the lip the adaptation curve resembles that of von Frey and Goldman (1915), except that adaptation is complete only after about 20 sec. However, for the forearm, loss of sensation is much more gradual, and adaptation is not completed even after 60 sec. These longer adaptation times are consistent with the greater effectiveness of the vibratory stimulus.

Although stimulus intensity is important in touch, most studies of differential sensitivity of simple touches have focused on a kind of differential threshold unique to touch. It is called the TWO-POINT THRESHOLD. It was discovered by von Frey, who found that the two-touch stimuli (such as the points of a drawing compass) will be felt as a single touch if they are close enough together. The two-point threshold is a measure of how far apart the stimuli must be before they are felt as two separate touches. It was during investigations of this kind that von Békésy (1967) discovered inhibitory interaction in the skin (see Demonstration Box 6-1). A comprehensive determination of two-point thresholds was provided by Weinstein (1968). A summary of his results is shown in Figure 10-10. Notice the remarkable differential sensitivity of the lower face and the hands, and even the feet. Presumably this reflects the use of these areas in manipulation of objects; the high sensitivity of the feet may be a leftover from our primate ancestors, who could manipulate objects with their feet!

Touch Intensity and Qualities. Measurement of the intensity of tactile sensation has focused mostly on the vibrotactile stimulus. An early study by Stevens (1959) demonstrated that magnitude estimations of the in-

tensity of a 60-Hz vibratory stimulus on the fingertip followed the standard psychophysical power function, with an exponent of about 0.95. When the stimulus was applied to the forearm the results did not support the power law. The less sensitive areas of the skin may operate somewhat differently from those that are more sensitive.

It was mentioned in the preceding that the effect of the vibratory stimulus on the skin is quite similar to that of sound on the ear. Nowhere is this more apparent than when we look at variations of sensation intensity (given constant stimulus intensity) as we vary the frequency of the vibrating touch stimulus. Figure 10-11 shows a set of equal-sensation curves, for a vibrating stimulus on the skin, that are highly similar to the equal-loudness contours we presented in Figure 9-9. Here, maximum sensitivity seems to be in the re-

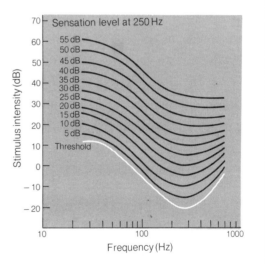

Figure 10-11.
Equal-sensation contours for a vibrating stimulus. These contours are very similar to equal-loudness contours over the same range of frequencies (see Figure 9-9) (from Verrillo, Fraioli, & Smith, 1969).

gion of about 200–400 Hz, with sensitivity decreasing dramatically as frequency declines. Notice that stimulus intensity is measured in decibels in Figure 10-11. This makes the vertical scale a logarithmic scale (see the Special Topic in Chapter 5). The standard to which these intensity measurements (dB) are relative is a displacement of the vibrator surface by one millionth of a meter. This small displacement would thus be a stimulus intensity of 0 dB.

The sense of touch has been employed as a means of communicating complex ideas. Most of you have probably heard about Louis Braille's tactile pattern alphabet, by which blind people can read any suitably translated book or paper. In this alphabet, patterns of raised dots on paper play the role of the patterns of ink on paper that sighted people use for letters. The speed with which an experienced blind person can read with this alphabet is a testimony to Louis Braille, long hours of practice, and the remarkable sensitivity of the touch system. But more is involved here than simply a sensitive touch system. Some complicated cognitive processes are also probably involved. These processes are just beginning to be studied in the area of touch.

One way of studying pattern processing in the touch modality was invented by a group of individuals who were trying to find a way to substitute patterns of touch for those of vision. White, Saunders, Scadden, Bach-y-Rita, and Collins (1970) developed a VISION SUBSTITUTION SYSTEM in which a television camera is used to scan a visual pattern. The information gathered by the television camera is then converted into a pattern of vibrating points on the skin of the back of an observer (see Figure 10-12). The subjects can move the camera to view different parts of the visual scene. When visual stimuli are presented tactually in this way, observers can recognize a wide variety of different stimulus patterns (up to 25). Remarkably, the relative distance of several visual objects in a scene can be perceived from the tactile pattern. Even visual illusions (such as the Mueller–Lyer illusion) can be experienced in a tactile pattern on the back. These types of findings raise questions about the role of the specialized feature detectors that seem to be available for recognition of visual and auditory patterns. (Are there also such feature detectors for touch?) They also point to the importance of higher level cognitive processes in even the simplest types of perceptual experiences.

Another vision-to-touch device was first aimed at making reading material more available for the blind. Reading in Braille requires that the paper or book be translated into Braille. This is especially difficult to do with newspapers, which pour from the presses in incredible numbers. The OPTACON (Bliss, Katcher, Rogers, & Shepard, 1970) works similarly to the system just described, except that the visual field scanned is about the size of a single printed letter, and the pattern of vibrations corresponding to each letter is formed on the fingertip instead of the back. After about 50 hours of training, blind users can read untreated material at about 20 words per minute. Experienced users attain rates as high as 60 words per minute. According to one source (Craig, 1977) nearly 2000 blind people now use the Optacon for reading. This device is beginning to be used for research into the mechanisms of tactile pattern perception. Recently, two sighted people were discovered who can read with the Optacon better than anybody previously studied, including blind people (Craig, 1977). Perhaps careful scrutiny of this extraordinary ability to process tactile patterns will lead to a new understanding of the functioning of this ancient sensory system.

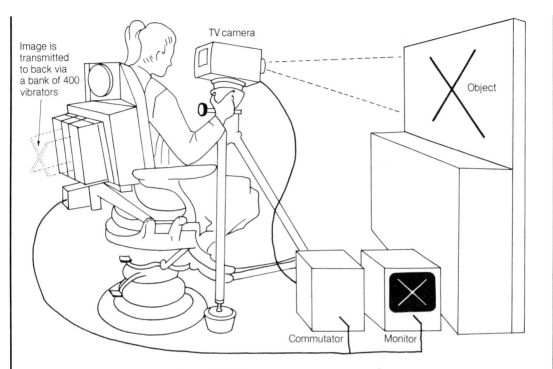

Image is transmitted to back via a bank of 400 vibrators

TV camera

Object

Commutator

Monitor

Figure 10-12.
The vision substitution system (from White *et al.*, 1970).

WARMTH AND COLD

Are you cold right now? Are you warm? Probably you are feeling rather neutral, that is, comfortably unaware of any temperature sensations. Our bodies contain a remarkable system of thermal sensors and reflexes to regulate the flow of blood in the blood vessels in our skin, as well as the activity of the sweat glands and the tiny muscles located around the roots of hairs in the skin. When our internal body temperature is too high (above 37°C), the blood vessels open up, allowing more blood to flow and thus radiating more heat into the air. We also begin to sweat, thus losing heat both by the carrying of the overheated sweat to the surface of the skin where it can radiate more efficiently, and also by the cooling of the skin surface through the process of evaporation. When we are too cold the blood vessels in the skin contract, thereby slowing heat loss, and we begin to shiver, which generates more heat from our muscles. The skin is a major part of a complex, mostly reflex-operated temperature-regulating system that keeps our internal body temperatures around 37°C. Usually this system functions so well that we do not notice any temperature sensations, at least in temperate environments. However, the ability of this system to regulate body temperature is limited, and when the limits are exceeded the body needs to take more dramatic steps, like changing clothing or starting a fire, to bring the temperature of the skin's environment within its safe limits again. Such necessities are signaled by sensations of warmth or cold.

Thermal Thresholds and Adaptation. Since the skin is trying to maintain a constant internal body temperature, sensations of warmth or cold are generally caused by *departures* from a particular skin temperature level. Thus when we talk about a cold stimulus, we mean one that has caused the *skin temperature* to depart from a kind of neutral point, called PHYSIOLOGICAL ZERO. The thermal receptors seem to adapt completely within a broad range of temperatures (perhaps from about 18 to about 40°C). Thus when the skin is at some temperature within this range, no thermal sensation will be felt. Also there is a NEUTRAL ZONE around physiological zero, within which no sensation will be felt if a stimulus of that temperature is applied to the skin. This zone is seldom more than a couple of degrees on either side of the zero, but it varies in width depending on what the zero point is, where on the body the change occurs, and what kind of stimulus is applied. A good average value for physiological zero in a temperate environment (room temperature) would be around 33°C, with a neutral zone of about 1°C on either side of this value. At room temperature this skin temperature suffices to maintain the internal body temperature at about 37°C.

Overall, the sensation of warmth or cold will be determined largely by the temperature to which the skin has been adapted before the stimulus is applied. (You can experience this in Demonstration Box 10-4.) Absolute thresholds for these sensations can be

defined as the amount of temperature change (from the adapting temperature) necessary to cause an experience or a report of warmth or cold. A determination of absolute thresholds by Kenshalo, Nafe, and Brooks (1961) found that the threshold for increases of temperature generally became lower as the adapting temperature increased (up to 44°C). The results were just the opposite for decreases in temperature, with thresholds becoming lower as the adapting temperature decreased (down to 27°C). Thus at relatively high or low temperatures we are more sensitive to fluctuations in temperature. This makes sense, since the low or high values can be dangerous for the body; the detection of thermally unsafe environments is more important when the stimuli are more extreme. The minimum thresholds for both sensations were about .1°C of temperature change from the adapting temperature. Kenshalo *et al.* (1961) also made determinations of differential thresholds over the same adapting temperatures. In general, differential thresholds were about the same size as absolute thresholds, except that for temperature increases at low temperatures, and decreases at high temperatures, differential thresholds stayed relatively low (about .5°C), while absolute thresholds grew quite large (well over 1.0°C). These changes in relative sensitivity to temperature change are shown in Figure 10-13.

As with other aspects of touch, the exact place on the body surface to which the stimulus is applied also determines sensitivity. If the stimulus is small in area (say, the size of the head of a pin) it is possible to find spots that only yield sensations of warmth and others that produce sensations of cold. There are also regions that produce no temperature sensations at all (although they may respond to touch). Figure 10-14 shows a set of maps of such warm and cold spots from an area of 1 cm² on the skin of the upper arm (Dallenbach, 1927). The spots were mapped

For this demonstration you will need to create three water baths of different temperatures. You can use a meat thermometer to measure the temperatures, or try the following formulas.

Assuming that your tap water has temperatures of 10°C (cold) and 60°C (hot), you can make a 30°C bath by adding $3\frac{2}{3}$ cups of cold tap water and $2\frac{1}{3}$ cups of hot tap water to a bowl. A 35°C bath requires 3 cups each of hot and cold tap water. For a 40°C bath, use $2\frac{1}{3}$ cups of cold water and $3\frac{2}{3}$ cups of hot water. It is best to have a friend help with preparing the water baths and with keeping them at a nearly constant temperature (by adding a little hot water every minute or so). Your friend can then try it while you make the baths.

The procedure is as follows. First prepare the 30 and the 40°C baths. Place one hand in the 30°C and one in the 40°C bath. Keep the hands in the baths for about 5 min. Under these conditions most people report that after 5 min there is no longer any sensation of warmth or cold, although the cooler bath initially felt cold (as it should have relative to your average skin temperature of about 33°C) and the warmer one felt warm. Now prepare the 35°C bath (quickly, if you are doing it by yourself), and plunge both hands into it at once. The hand that was in the 30°C bath should now feel as if it is in warm water, while the other hand (40°C) will feel as if it is in cool water. Since the water is actually the same for both hands, but their physiological zero has been changed by the previous 5-min adaptation period, the sensations of warmth and cold must be caused by the relationship of the stimulus temperature to the current temperature of the skin (physiological zero). You can experiment with this phenomenon further by trying out more extreme adapting temperatures and adapting to them for longer times. See if you can find points beyond which all stimuli feel either warm or cold. Changes in temperature near these points only result in changes in the intensity of that sensation, rather than resulting in a change in sensation quality (Kenshalo & Scott, 1966).

Demonstration Box 10-4:
The Dependence of Thermal Sensation on Physiological Zero

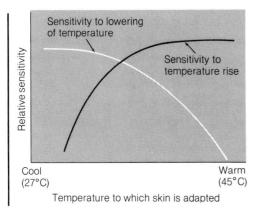

Figure 10-13.
Sensitivity to increases and decreases in temperature varies as a consequence of the temperature to which the skin is adapted.

Figure 10-14.
Maps of cold and warm spots on a 2-cm² area of the skin of the upper arm of a single observer on four successive days. Notice how the spots seem to be in the same places from day to day (from Dallenbach, K. M. *American Journal of Psychology,* 1927, **39.** © The University of Illinois Press).

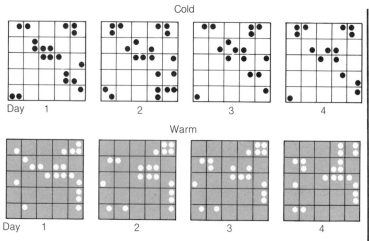

on four successive days so that the permanence of the spots could be determined. As you can see from the figure, the spots do tend to be in the same places from day to day. However, examination of the underlying skin generally shows no differences in the distribution of different types of nerve endings between the cold spots and the warm spots. It is still uncertain as to what the physiological basis is for such dramatic differences in sensitivity to thermal stimuli. There is no evidence at all that specialized receptors are stimulated by the different stimuli, and yet there do seem to be specialized warm and cold nerve fibers at higher levels of the nervous system (Zotterman, 1959; see also Chapter 6). Dallenbach (1927) found only free nerve endings beneath all of the spots for several observers, indicating at least that such endings can respond to thermal stimuli. However, they are probably not the only type of nerve endings that respond to thermal stimulation.

We have mentioned that the measurement of absolute thresholds for warm and cold sensations is complicated by the fact that complete adaptation to thermal stimuli takes place over some range of temperatures, and that thermal sensations seem to be relative to the temperature to which the skin has be-

come adapted. Because of this, thermal adaptation is an important area of study. Several techniques have been used to measure adaptation. Typically, an area of the skin is exposed to very high or low temperatures for some period of time (usually by dipping it in water at the required temperature) and then a threshold for warmth or cold is determined. In a different technique, observers are exposed to a particular thermal stimulus and asked to report when they no longer feel any thermal sensation at that temperature. These studies usually report that adaptation occurs over a wide range of temperatures, from about 15 to about 40°C (Kenshalo & Scott, 1966). Adaptation to temperatures close to that of the skin is rapid. When the temperature is far from that of the skin, complete adaptation takes longer.

A more recent determination of the time course of adaptation, and the range of complete adaptation, has considerably altered these earlier findings. Kenshalo and Scott (1966) had observers change the temperature of a sophisticated thermal stimulator by just enough to maintain a detectable sensation as adaptation proceeded. The stimulator started at the previously measured temperature of the observer's skin. Adjustments were made whenever the experimenter asked for them, every minute at first, and then every 5 min for up to 40 min. Figure 10-15 shows the results obtained for four observers. Using this technique, Kenshalo and Scott (1966) found that complete adaptation could occur only over a range of about 4–8°C centered around the average skin temperature. This is shown in the figure by the leveling off of the curves at between ±4°C, instead of continuing to increase or decrease. Kenshalo and Scott argue that it is only within this narrow band of complete adaptation that sensation is determined by the direction of change from the physiological zero point. Outside this range, or before complete adaptation has occurred within it, the direction of small temperature changes seems only to increase or decrease the intensity of the sensation that is established by the absolute temperature.

Thermal Intensity and Qualities. Owing to the complexity of the situations under which

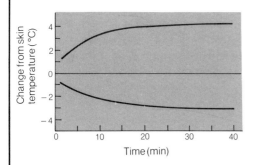

Figure 10-15.
Adaptation to thermal stimuli. Each curve represents the average amount by which four observers adjusted the temperature of a thermal stimulator in order to maintain a just noticeable warm or cool sensation.
Adaptation is shown by the adjustments becoming larger as time progresses from the beginning of thermal stimulation (based upon Kenshalo & Scott, 1966).

warm and cold sensations occur, you might be thinking that it would be difficult to measure the apparent intensity of thermal stimuli. However, we can measure these sensations using direct scaling techniques. For instance, Stevens and Stevens (1960) had observers make magnitude estimations of the thermal sensations caused by the application (to the skin of the forearm) of pieces of aluminum that had been warmed or cooled in water baths. They used stimuli above the average skin temperature (about 33°C) for warm sensations, and stimuli below this temperature for cold ones. They found that warm and cold sensations also follow the psychophysical power law when measured in this way, with exponents of the power functions for warmth around 1.6 and for cold about 1.0. The sensation of warmth thus grows somewhat more rapidly with stimulus intensity than does that of cold.

Because of the close relationship between the sensations of warmth and cold, it should not surprise you to learn that there are some very interesting and somewhat paradoxical phenomena associated with thermal stimuli. One of these, called PARADOXICAL COLD, was discovered by Max von Frey in 1895. He found that if cold spots like those we discussed in the preceding are touched with a very warm stimulus (above about 45°C) a sensation of cold will result. The opposite phenomenon, paradoxical warmth, has been much sought after, but never convincingly demonstrated. This asymmetry is consistent with the tendency of nerve fibers that respond to cooling (cold fibers) to respond both in the range of temperatures between about 12 and 35°C and between 45 and 50°C. Warm fibers respond only in the range between about 25 and 47°C (Zotterman, 1959; see also Chapter 6). When the skin temperature rises above 47°C, only the cold fibers are responding, and a sensation of cold results.

A variety of theories has been proposed to

account for the different phenomena of thermal sensation. Only two of these are given much consideration today, and there are serious problems with both of them (Geldard, 1972; Verillo, 1975). The first is the CHANNEL THEORY proposed by von Frey in 1895. He argued that each sensation (warmth and cold) has a specific receptor and a specific neural pathway. Von Frey made tentative proposals about which skin nerve endings were responsible for the two sensations, but these have not been supported. In fact, it has proven to be very difficult to identify the specific functions of any of the nerve endings in the skin. However, there seem to be nerve pathways, or at least nerve fibers, that respond specifically to one or the other of the stimuli (Hensel, 1966, 1968; Zotterman, 1959; see also Chapter 6). Some of these fibers fire at rates that depend on the *absolute* temperature of the skin. Thus there seems to be some support for von Frey's idea that warmth and cold sensations are mediated by separate sensory channels, although we cannot find distinct warm and cold receptors that trigger the activity in these fibers.

The second major theoretical approach to warmth and cold is the NEUROVASCULAR THEORY (Kenshalo & Nafe, 1962). This theory emphasizes the close relationship between cold and warmth sensations. The theory proposes that a single mechanism is responsible for both sensations. This mechanism is associated with nerve fibers located in the smooth muscle of the walls of the tiny blood vessels of the skin. These muscles respond to warmth by relaxing and to cold by contracting. Such relaxations and contractions could mechanically stimulate the nerve endings in the muscles and signal the presence of a warm or cold skin condition. This theory is capable of explaining the dependence of the warm and the cold sensations on the physiological zero. Such a theory would predict that sensations of cold and heat should have similar proper-

ties since they share a common mechanism. However, as we have seen in the preceding, sensations of warm and cold increase at different rates, depending upon stimulus intensity, and seem to be triggered by stimulation in different areas of skin. Although neither theory is completely satisfactory, both have some appealing aspects. Perhaps some combination of the two viewpoints will prove more useful than either alone.

PAIN

Throughout the history of man, pain has been recognized as an important experience, capable of motivating the basest and the most beautiful of human actions. Yet, although everybody acknowledges its importance in human experience, nobody is quite sure just what it is. Most individuals would agree that most pain is unpleasant, and indeed many authors simply classify pain as an emotional or affective experience that is the opposite of pleasure. This is consistent with the fact that pain seems to have no specialized sense organs. Furthermore, it does not convey information about any single class of stimulus energy in our environment. It comes from anywhere and everywhere and can be experienced in virtually every part of the body.

On the other hand, when we experience pain it has a distinct sensory quality. Also, much of the physiological evidence argues that the neural response identified with pain travels along specific pathways, and anesthetics that abolish pain can leave the other senses unaffected (see Chapter 6). Pain apparently has absolute and differential thresholds, it adapts, and it can be measured in a variety of ways. Thus pain acts much like a separate sensory system. Although the sensory versus the emotional viewpoints of pain have resulted in intense controversies in the history of psychology, there is no consensus as to exactly how we should define and deal with the concept of pain. In this section, we take the stand that pain must be considered to partake of both affective and sensory aspects. Thus we will first briefly review the available information on the sensory aspects, and then proceed to consider some of the interactions of affective and sensory qualities of pain.

Pain Thresholds, Intensity, and Adaptation. To treat pain as a sensation it is first necessary to define a pain threshold. Usually this is taken to be the intensity of a stimulus that will just barely produce a sensation of pain. Obviously thresholds will vary across the different conditions under which they are measured, since pain can be aroused in so many different ways. As in the case of touch and thermal sensitivity, there are specific tiny points on the skin that respond selectively to pain. These points will give the sensation of pain for stimuli that do not produce painful sensations when applied to places other than "pain points." The distribution of such pain points over the body also seems quite variable, as can be seen from Table 10-1.

One major advance in the standardization of conditions for measuring the pain threshold was made by Hardy, Wolff, and Goodell (1943). They used a device that focused an intense beam of light on the ink-blackened forehead in order to produce a painful heat stimulus. Since the device used radiant heat as a stimulus, it could be precisely controlled and measured. They called the device a DOLORIMETER (meaning a measurer of pain). This development permitted the investigation of the various conditions that affect the level of the pain threshold. The exact thresholds measured in this way are of little importance to us here, since the units of any pain threshold stimulus vary with the pain-producing device or stimulus modality. However, Hardy *et al.* (1943) were able to

Table 10-1 *Distribution of Pain Sensitivity (Based upon Geldard, 1972)*

Skin Region	Pain "Points"/cm²
Back of knee	232
Neck region	228
Bend of elbow	224
Shoulder blade	212
Inside of forearm	203
Back of hand	188
Forehead	184
Buttocks	180
Eyelid	172
Scalp	144
Ball of thumb	60
Sole of foot	48
Tip of nose	44

show that pain thresholds acted very much like the thresholds for other sensations. Pain thresholds were shown to be relatively stable as long as the conditions were stable, but they varied systematically with changes in the neurological, pharmacological (drugs), or psychological state of the individual. Since then, these results have been replicated many times. More recently, even social situations have been shown to affect pain thresholds (Craig & Weiss, 1971).

Pain has a differential threshold too. The first good measurement of the differential threshold was done by Hardy, Wolff, and Goodell (1947) using a modification of the dolorimeter. Since the stimuli all had to be above the pain threshold and since pain is a warning of potential damage, subjects for these experiments were understandably hard to come by. Since the authors felt the knowledge was important, they served as their own subjects and as a result experienced both a large amount of pain and considerable tissue damage. They even moved the site of the painful stimulation from the forehead to the forearm because the latter was more easily cared for when blistered by the pain stimuli. These rather extreme measures resulted in some very important results. It was found that the differential threshold could be measured for pain, and that it is reproducible under constant conditions. Moreover, Hardy *et al.* (1947) also found that the Weber fraction remains remarkably constant (as Weber's Law would assert) at about .04 over quite a large range of stimulus intensities. This indicates that we are quite sensitive to variations in pain intensity. Weber fractions begin to increase dramatically at only the highest stimulus intensities. However, these were not very reliable data because the skin damage sustained made it difficult for the observers (the authors themselves) to concentrate on the stimulus intensities.

Hardy *et al.* (1947) also created the first scale of pain intensity. Since they had established the validity of Weber's Law for pain, they merely added up *jnd*s, as Fechner had done, to create a scale of pain intensity based on the discriminability of painful stimuli. They appropriately called this scale the DOL SCALE (which means pain in Latin). Later scales of pain intensity were created by more direct methods. Stevens (1961) obtained magnitude estimations of the intensity of pain produced by electric shocks. He found that the magnitude estimations were a power function of the stimulus intensity with an exponent of about 3.5, making pain produced by electric shock the sensory modality with the highest power function exponent. This implies that the sensation of pain grows faster with increasing stimulus intensity than does any other sensory experience. The actual size of the exponent varies as a function of a variety of stimulus and even social factors (Craig, Best, & Ward, 1975; Sternbach & Tursky, 1964).

If one wants to argue for a sensory basis for the experience of pain, it is important to ask if pain sensations adapt as do all other sensations. Dallenbach (1939) demonstrated that pain caused by needles, heat, and cold does adapt. A more recent investigation of heat-induced pain was reported by Hardy, Stolwijk, and Hoffman (1968). Observers judged the degree of experienced pain as they sat with their hands in hot water over a period of time. As can be seen from Figure 10-16, adaptation is complete for the lower temperatures, which are only mildly painful, and less complete for the more painful stimuli. Adaptation may not take place at all for the extremely painful stimuli.

Analgesia. Since pain is unpleasant it is only natural to seek to minimize it. After it has served its function of warning us that damage to our body is likely, or has already been sustained, the pain signal is no longer necessary or desired. Yet strong pain signals seem to persist, and we do whatever we can to alleviate these sensations. Thus humans have assembled an impressive array of analgesics and anesthetics to rid themselves of pain. Perhaps the major modern effort in pain research is concerned with ways to induce analgesia. The most potent and reliable of these are chemicals that we eat (such as aspirin) or that are injected into certain nerves or muscles (such as the novocaine used by dentists). We can even buy a spray or a tube of salve that contains a substance that causes a temporary analgesia on cut or burned skin. When the pain promises to be too severe, we use narcotic drugs (such as morphine, an opium derivative) or opt for unconsciousness (as with ether or chloroform). More recent work attempts to alleviate chronic, severe pain by brain stimulation with electricity or chemicals (Marx, 1977). The mechanism of the action of these techniques is not always known, but it is

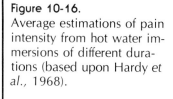

Figure 10-16.
Average estimations of pain intensity from hot water immersions of different durations (based upon Hardy et al., 1968).

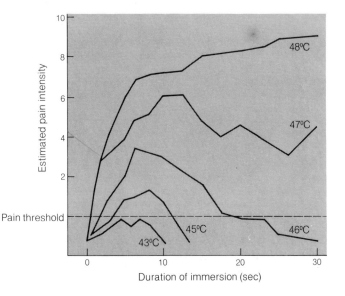

thought that most of them produce their effects by blocking neural responses at one or another of the sites on the pain pathways.

However, there is another class of analgesics that we do not understand. In this class are included such techniques as the masking of dental pain by intense sounds (Gardner, Licklider, & Weisz, 1960), acupuncture (Chapman, Wilson, & Gehrig, 1976; Clark & Yang, 1974), hypnosis (Hilgard, 1971), and more cognitive factors including suggestion, attitude, concentration of attention, or social factors (Craig & Weiss, 1971; Wolff & Goodell, 1943). An example of a cognitive approach to pain control is given in Demonstration Box 10-5. Several studies have suggested that the chemical analgesics affect the sensory aspects of pain, while the more cognitive techniques work on the affective response to the pain. In particular it is thought that these procedures affect the readiness to report the experience of pain (Clark & Yang, 1974). However, several studies using a signal-detection analysis sup-

port the view that the cognitive techniques may actually alter the pain sensation (Chapman et al., 1976; Craig & Coren, 1975).

An extension of the theory of pain proposed by Melzack and Wall (1965) is particularly relevant here, since it deals with the possible effects of various central nervous system processes on the experience of pain. You might remember from our discussion in Chapter 6 that Melzack and Wall proposed that there is a neural gate in the spinal cord composed of the substantia gelatinosa (a part of the spinal cord) and some T cells that transmit pain information up the spinal cord to the brain (see Figure 6-13). Activity in fast-conducting nerve fibers tends to close this gate, while activity in slow-conducting fibers tends to open it. Pain is experienced when the T cells are transmitting at a high enough rate. The theory also allows inputs from higher levels of the nervous system to open or close the gate. Thus motivational states, attentional factors, or other stimulation such as high-intensity hissing noises, electric-

A cognitive technique to alleviate the pain of childbirth is now being taught in many places in North America and Europe. The basic idea was that of a French medical doctor named Lamaze. One demonstration of how this technique works requires a friend to assist you.

Have your friend grasp your leg just above the knee with a hand. Have your friend squeeze gently at first, then with steadily increasing force until you can feel a fairly severe pain. This should convince you that the stimulus is actually painful. Now you have three things to practice simultaneously. First, you have to breathe in a particular way. To do this you must take five short panting breaths in a row, followed by a strong blow outward (pant-pant-pant-pant-pant-blow). Repeat this pattern during the entire period during which the painful stimulus might occur. Do not breathe too quickly for you might hyperventilate and get dizzy. If you do get dizzy, stop for a moment and then start up again at a slower pace. Second, you must count the

breaths (1-2-3-4-5-blow) or say a short poem or nonsense sentence over and over again to the rhythm of your breathing ("Am I a bird or a *plant?*"). Third, you must concentrate your visual attention on (e.g., look intently at) some clearly visible object during this entire period. Practice these behaviors for a few minutes until you feel fairly confident of your ability to maintain them for a couple of minutes. Then have your friend give you the gradually increasing pressure on the leg, while you do your breathing. Under these conditions, if your concentration is really intense, you might not feel the pain (or the pressure) at all, or at least it will be of much lesser intensity. According to the Melzack–Wall–Casey (Melzack & Casey, 1968; Melzack & Wall, 1965) approach; to pain, what is happening here is that your central control system is closing the pain gate. Thousands of mothers claim that this basic technique of concentrating on something removed from the source of the pain effectively alleviates the pain and distress of childbirth.

Demonstration Box 10-5:
Cognitive Effects on Pain: The Lamaze Technique

ity, music, or acupuncture needles could all be responsible for controlling the gate via the pathway *descending* from the brain to the spinal cord gate. Theoretically the gate could also be opened by such stimuli, so that pain sensitivity could be increased. Thus in this theory pain can have sensory aspects via the T cells, and affective aspects via the descending pathways that may control the gate. This theory, or some modification of it, seems to have the potential to explain the wide variety of pain phenomena, including the variety of analgesics, within a single coherent framework. Perhaps at some future time all of the effort put into the study of pain and analgesia will be rewarded when pain is relegated to the status of a transient signal of organic damage.

11
Space

One day a tourist stopped his car on a road and asked a country boy how far it was to Douglasville.

The boy looked up and said, "It's 24,999 miles the way you're going, but if you turn around it isn't more than four."

We live in a three-dimensional space composed of distances and directions. It is a commonplace task for us to estimate the distance between our hand and the pencil we wish to grasp. We also automatically calculate the direction of arm movement. We can even estimate whether our coffee cup is a few inches farther away than the pencil. These extractions of spatial information are made automatically and with remarkable accuracy.

The perception of depth, distance, and direction are vital to our survival. We must know how far we are from the edge of a cliff or we may stray too close to the edge and fall. We must further know the direction of the edge from our bodies, otherwise we might step toward it rather than away from it. We cannot get cut by a knife edge pictured in a flat photograph, but the real blade extending toward us in space can produce painful contact. Thus our lives and safety may depend upon the accuracy of our space perception.

Spatial perception involves a number of different facets. The first is called EGOCENTRIC LOCALIZATION. Most of us are familiar with the word egocentric in everyday use, where it pertains to a person who only thinks about his own activities and their effect on himself. In the context of space perception, the word egocentric means that we have a good sense of where our bodies are positioned relative to other objects in the external environment. The concept of space perception also includes the ability to make OBJECT-RELATIVE LOCALIZATIONS. Just as we can correctly estimate our own position relative to other objects, we can also perceive the distance between objects within the environment.

Yet another aspect of space perception involves the comprehension of whether an object is flat (as in a two-dimensional picture) or solid (three dimensional). The accomplishment involved in seeing objects in depth is quite amazing given that the basic information available to the nervous system is only two flat projections of the external world on the two retinas. You might not be surprised at this at all, since painters have been representing three-dimensional scenes on two-dimensional surfaces (such as paper or canvas) for centuries. As a starting place let's look at the techniques available to these artists, as they strive to "deceive" us into seeing a flat surface as an expanse containing solid objects at different distances.

DEPTH AND DISTANCE

Pictorial Cues to Depth and Distance. Our discussion will start with CUES that allow us to have the impression of depth or distance in pictures, drawings, or photographs, as well as in the real world. Notice that we use the word *cue* rather than clue. In the theater a *cue* is a signal that prompts an action from an actor who then automatically goes to the next line or motion in the script. A *clue* suggests conscious consideration that leads to the deduction of the correct answer. Since we derive depth from stimuli using mostly unconscious processing, the "triggers" that "prompt" the perception of depth will be called *cues*. The cues used by an artist, or those we interpret from photographs, are usually called PICTORIAL or MONOCULAR CUES, since they appear in pictures and only require one eye to register (remember a camera has only one eye). Some of these are commonly discussed in art classes as well as in courses in psychology. Basically they derive from geometrical considerations, and from the fact that objects are solid and light does not bend around them. These cues serve as the basis for our perception of monocular depth.

Interposition or overlay. Most objects in the world are not transparent. Thus, if one object is in front of another it will block part of the more distant one from view. This is called INTERPOSITION or OVERLAY. Thus in Figure 11-1A the square is seen as the most distant object, and the circle as the nearest, because of the partial covering of one object by another. Figure 11-1B shows an example of ambiguous interposition. Which rectangle is nearest to you? Here the inconsistent interposition cues give inconsistent depth impressions.

Size. As objects vary in distance the size of their retinal image changes. Consider Figure 11-2A; notice that the more distant person casts a smaller RETINAL IMAGE SIZE. We utilize this information in making judgments

of depth or distance. Thus in Figure 11-2B we see a row of faces that seems to recede in space because of their decreasing image size.

Our familiarity with the actual size of the targets plays a role in these judgments. We presume that all of the faces in Figure 11-2B are the same physical size, and hence that their retinal size differences are caused by differences in distance. Ittelson (1951) demonstrated the importance of familiarity with the size of the targets judged. He presented observers with a series of playing cards. One of the playing cards was normal in size, a second was twice that of normal size, and a third was one-half that of normal size. He found that observers tended to judge the double-sized playing cards as being much closer to them than the normal-sized ones. As you might expect, the half-sized cards were judged to be much more distant. Ittelson conducted his experiment under what have come to be called *reduction conditions*. This means that the observers were making their

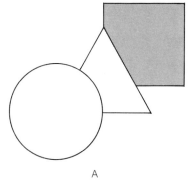

A

Figure 11-1.
Interposition. (A) The circle is perceived as the closest form since it is completely visible, while the triangle and square seem more distant since our view of them is partially blocked. (B) An example of ambiguous interposition.

B

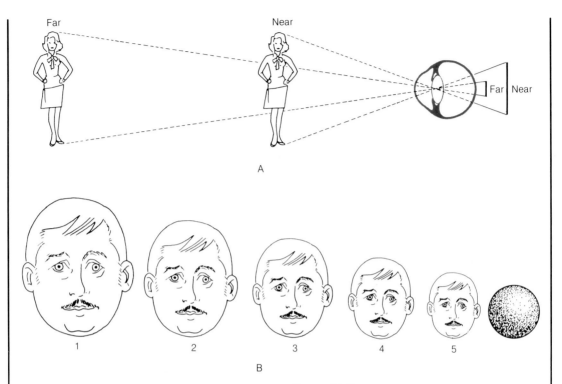

A

B

Figure 11-2.
The size cue to distance. (A) Objects of the same physical size produce smaller retinal angle sizes with increasing distance from the observer. Thus, relatively speaking, smaller images are perceived to be more distant. (B) The interaction between familiar and relative size (see Demonstration Box 11-1).

distance judgments under conditions that did not allow them to use any of the other distance cues.

Epstein and Baratz (1964) showed that FAMILIAR SIZE is a potent cue for the perception of distance. They found that differences in image size led to differences in distance estimates when the objects used in the experiment were ones that had a familiar size. Thus if we see a very tiny elephant, we can use our knowledge that elephants are relatively large creatures to deduce that the elephant has not shrunk in size but rather has moved away from us and is now more distant. You may demonstrate the effect of familiar size for yourself by following the instructions in Demonstration Box 11-1.

Perspective. PERSPECTIVE is simply an extension of the size cue to distance. Look at Figure 11-3A. Here you see a bundle of lines that seems to converge. If the lines represented physically parallel structures, the changing distance between the lines would result from increasing distance of the lines from the observer. Thus pole X appears to be

Look at Figure 11-2B. Notice that we have a row of faces that seems to recede into the distance. Off to the right is a ball. Imagine that it is a ping-pong ball or a golf ball. Study the figure for a moment and decide which face is at the same distance as the golf ball. Then return to this box. Now imagine that the ball is a volleyball or a basketball. Which face is at the same distance as the ball? Notice that the ball "moved backward" in depth when you assumed it was a larger object. This shows how retinal size and familiar size work together to give you an impression of depth or distance.

Demonstration Box 11-1:
Familiar Size and Distance

Figure 11-3.
Examples of linear perspective.

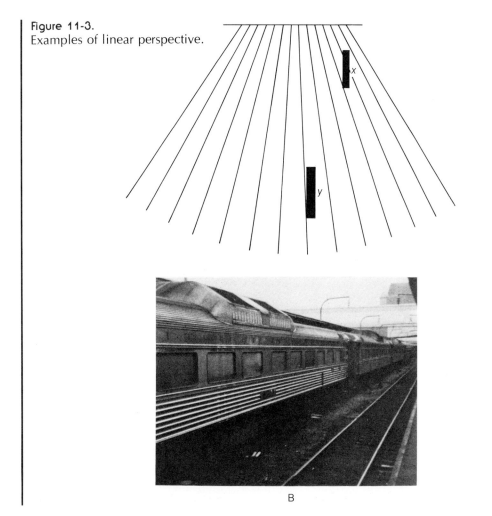

B

further away than pole Y, since it is associated with lines that are squeezed more tightly together due to the perspective cue. Figure 11-3B shows a real life scene in which linear (line) perspective is operating. We know that the sides of the train are parallel. In other words, the roof of the train is parallel to the underside. However, as these parallel planes recede into the distance (in this case, as they recede toward the entrance to the railway station) you will notice that they begin to converge. In general, we find that the world is arranged so that parallel lines converge toward a *vanishing point* as their distance from the eye increases. Probably the best real world example of this would be to stand in the middle of a railroad track and take note of how the tracks appear to converge as they become more and more distant from you.

Texture gradient. A cue that combines both linear perspective and relative size is the TEXTURE GRADIENT cue. A *texture* is any collection of objects, and the *gradient* (continuous change) is a change in the relative size and compactness of these object elements. The more distant points of the texture have smaller elements and are more densely packed together (Gibson, 1950). This cue is sometimes called DETAIL PERSPECTIVE. Figure 11-4A shows a texture of dots. It is usually seen as a plain receding in depth. On the other hand, Figure 11-4B is usually seen as a flat surface since the texture is uniform and unchanging. Figure 11-4C shows a texture of lines that again seems like a plain receding away toward the horizon. One important feature about texture gradients is that sudden changes in the texture usually signal a change in direction or distance of a surface. Thus Figure 11-5A shows how the gradient changes when we shift from floor to wall; Figure 11-5B shows how the gradient changes at a cliff or step down.

Height in the picture plane. Another cue to distance used by artists is HEIGHT IN THE PICTURE PLANE, which refers to where an object is relative to the horizon line. As can be seen in Figure 11-6, post B seems farther away than post A because its base is closer to the horizon line. Hence it is higher in the picture plane. The reverse holds for targets above the horizon. Bird C seems farther away than bird D because it is *lower* in the picture plane. The cue is, the closer to the horizon line, the farther away seems the object.

Light. There are three cues that are dependent upon the way light interacts with objects. The first and most obvious is SHADOWING. Light travels in straight lines and regions of an object that intercept the light are usually bright, while those shielded from the light are in shadow. Thus an object that has some protruding or indented portions will show a distribution of shadowing. Figure 11-7A shows a flat gray disk with no shadowing and no apparent depth. We add shadows and it is immediately seen as a three-dimensional sphere (Figure 11-7B). An interesting aspect of the shadowing cue is that it seems to involve the assumption that light generally comes from above. Notice that Figure 11-7C looks like a "bump" sticking out of the surface while 11-7D looks like a "dent." This is because the upper portion of 11-7C is light (as would be expected if a bump were illuminated from above) while 11-7D is shadowed in its upper portion (as would be a dent illuminated from above). Turning the figure upside down reverses this shadowing effect and also reverses the apparent depth, turning C into the dent and D into the bump.

The second lighting cue is RELATIVE BRIGHTNESS. Ittelson (1960) has shown that the brighter of two identical objects (viewed in a dark room that allows no other cues to be used) will be seen as closer. This cannot be predicted from any physical, geometric, or

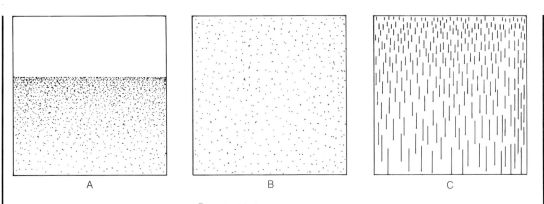

Figure 11-4.
Examples of texture gradients in (A) and (C), which appear as surfaces receding in depth. (B) shows no decreases in element size or spacing and thus is perceived as a flat surface.

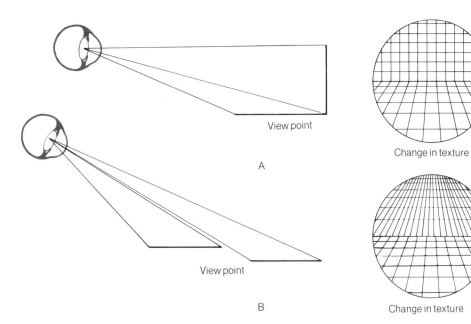

View point

Change in texture

A

View point

Change in texture

B

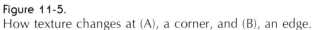

Figure 11-5.
How texture changes at (A), a corner, and (B), an edge.

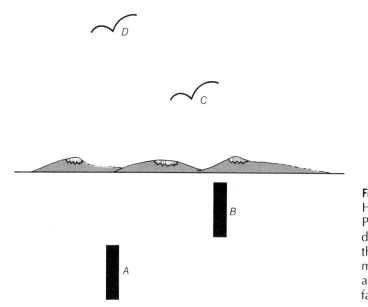

Figure 11-6.
Height in the picture plane. Proximity to the horizon will determine which elements in the diagram are perceived as more distant. In this case B and C are seen as being farther away.

photometric considerations. Perhaps it arises out of our experience with working in dim surroundings under a light source. Objects close to the light (and hence to us) will be bright, and more distant objects will be dimmer. However, such an explanation is extremely speculative.

The last cue pertaining to lighting is based upon the fact that light, as it travels through the air, tends to be absorbed and somewhat scattered by minute particles of dust and moisture in the atmosphere. This means that the image of a very distant object, such as a distant mountain, will be slightly bluer in hue and hazier in appearance. Such changes in appearance can provide information about distance. This cue is called AERIAL PERSPEC-TIVE. In some geographic regions (such as the Western United States) this can lead to considerable errors in distance judgments, since the clear dry air reduces aerial perspective. Thus a plateau that appears to be only 1 or 2 miles away may actually be 20 or 30 miles distant.

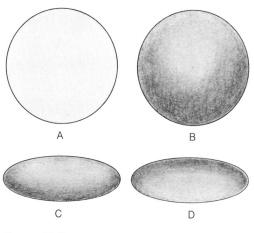

Figure 11-7.
Shadows. With the addition of shadowing a flat surface (A) can be made to appear as a solid object (B). Also, because we assume overhead lighting, shadowing can cause differences in the direction of perceived depth. (C) is seen as a "bump" while (D) is seen as a "dent." If you turn the book upside down, the direction of depth will change.

Motion. Some cues to depth and distance are not available to the artist or still photographer, although the cinematographer can make use of them. These involve the changes that come about in the pattern of retinal stimulation as we move, or are moved, through the world. One of these concerns the pattern of movement of objects as you travel past them. Suppose that you were traveling in a car or bus and looking at the scene in Figure 11-8. Let us also suppose that your direction of movement is from right to left and you are gazing at the spot marked "fixation point." Under these conditions all of the objects closer to you than the fixation point would appear to move in a direction opposite to your movement. On the other

hand objects that are farther away will appear to move in the same direction you are moving. Not only the direction, but also the speed of movement varies with the objects' proximity to you and to your point of fixation. This cue to distance is called MOTION PARALLAX.

There is an interesting variation of the linear perspective cue that involves motion. In linear perspective all objects and points in space seem to converge as they recede into the distance. When we directly approach a surface, objects and points in space seem to diverge outward from a point directly in front of our eyes and straight ahead of our movement. Walking down a corridor while looking at a distant point will give the flow pattern

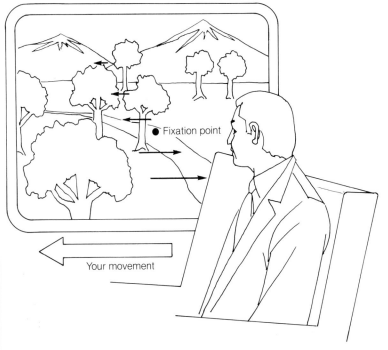

Figure 11-8.
Motion parallax. When an observer moves, objects at varying distances from the observer will move in different directions at differing speeds. Thus depth cues are also found in movement situations.

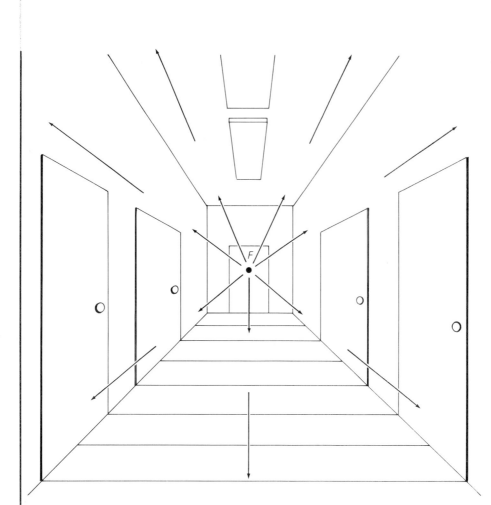

Figure 11-9.
Optical expansion. Movement toward and away from objects causes typical expansion and contraction patterns that can provide information about distance.

shown in Figure 11-9. The cue is often called motion perspective or optical expansion (Gibson, Kaplan, Reynold, & Wheeler, 1969).

Physiological Cues to Depth and Distance. We have considered cues for depth and distance that depend upon the geometry of the world and the way light interacts with objects. Certain other cues for distance arise simply because of the way the visual system is structured. These STRUCTURAL or PHYSIOLOGICAL CUES may also play a role in our perception of depth.

Accommodation. In Chapter 4 we discussed the action of the crystalline lens when the eye changes its distance of regard. As you may remember, when we shift our gaze from one object in the visual field to another that lies at a different distance from us, the lens changes shape (actually it changes its amount of curvature) so that the new object of regard is focused on the retinal surface. This process is called *accommodation*. Only a lens of one particular curvature will clearly focus the retinal image of any given object viewed at a specified distance from the eye. For instance, relaxed accommodation (or a relatively thin lens) is necessary if distant objects are to be clearly focused on the retina, while a curved lens is needed to clearly image closer objects on the retinal surface. Since we are continually changing the tension on the ciliary muscles, which control the lens shape, it seems reasonable to expect that the particular pattern of muscular tension needed to bring an object into focus could provide important information about the relative distance of objects from the eye. This process is analogous to the contraction and the expansion of the muscles of your arm giving you information about the relative degree of arm extension.

Unfortunately, accommodation by itself can only give information about distance and depth over a limited range of observer-to-object distances (Graham, 1965). The lens reaches its fullest point of relaxation when an object is about 3 m away from us. If the object moves beyond that distance, the lens will no longer change its degree of curvature. A similar restriction exists for close objects. Once a target has come within 20 cm of the face, the lens has reached its point of maximum curvature. Thus there is only a limited range over which accommodation of the lens alone can provide adequate information about distance and depth (Kaufman, 1974). Hochberg (1971a) has surveyed a body of literature spanning 70 years of research into the distance information available from accommodation in the absence of other cues. He concludes that accommodation is not a very good cue to distance even within the range where it could potentially work (20–300 cm from the observer).

Convergence and divergence. Other physiological cues for distance arise from our having two eyes. Since the best visual acuity is obtained when the image of a target is on the foveal region of the eye, eye movements are executed to bring the image to the fovea. When the object is close to the observer, the two eyes must rotate inward (toward the nose) as shown in Figure 11-10A. Such movements are called CONVERGENCE. When a target is farther away, the eyes must engage in an outward rotation (toward the temples) in order to BIFOVEALLY FIXATE (the technical term for the situation in which an image stimulates both foveas) the target (see Figure 11-10B). These are DIVERGENCE movements. Each target distance (up to about 6 m) is associated with a unique angle between the eyes (usually called the *convergence angle* as indicated in Figure 11-10A and B) and hence a unique pattern of muscular contractions. Thus information about the amount of ocular rotation needed to image the targets on both foveas could serve as a cue to target distance. Unfortunately, there is still much dispute about the usefulness and reliability of convergence as a distance cue (Gogel, Gregg, & Wainwright, 1961; Hochberg, 1971a).

Binocular Disparity. The last of the physiologically based cues for depth is probably the most important. In humans the two eyes are horizontally separated by the nose. This separation can result in a distance of up to 6.5 cm between the two pupils. Although seemingly not important, this results in different directions of view and, hence, different images in the two eyes. You can see this for yourself in Demonstration Box 11-2. The two eyes' images are said to be DISPARATE, and the process by which these disparate views come to be merged into one common percept is called FUSION.

The process of fusion is not perfect, and many parts of the total visual image remain disparate. This failure of the two eyes' views to merge completely gives rise to double vi-

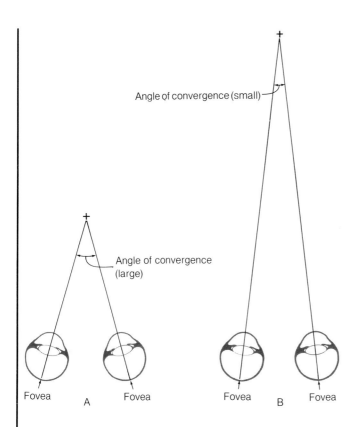

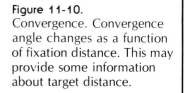

Figure 11-10.
Convergence. Convergence angle changes as a function of fixation distance. This may provide some information about target distance.

sion or DIPLOPIA. Although we are not consciously aware of this diplopia under normal viewing conditions, we can readily learn to see the double images. Demonstration Box 11-3 shows how this is done. Notice that in this demonstration the pattern of double images is different, depending upon whether the unfused image is in front of or in back of the target that you have fixated. These CROSSED and UNCROSSED IMAGES (see Demonstration Box 11-3 for definition of these terms) can serve as a cue to the relative distance of objects. Objects more distant than the point of fixation are seen in uncrossed disparity, while closer objects are seen with crossed disparity. Only objects at about the same distance as that at which you are converged will be fused and seen singly. If we map out all the points where targets are at about the same con-

vergence or fixation distance, we have traced out an imaginary plane called the HOROPTER. The region around this curved plane, which includes all points in space where the images are fused, is called PANUM'S AREA. A diagram of this is shown in Figure 11-11. The shape of the horopter will change with varying fixation distances; however, it is a convenient way to talk about the zone of fused images surrounded by areas of unfused or disparate images.

The physicist Wheatstone is credited with the discovery of STEREOPSIS. This term is used to describe the ability to see depth based solely on the disparity of the two retinal images. He maintained that when two objects are physically located at different depth planes, the two eyes cannot possibly get the same view of these two objects. This is dem-

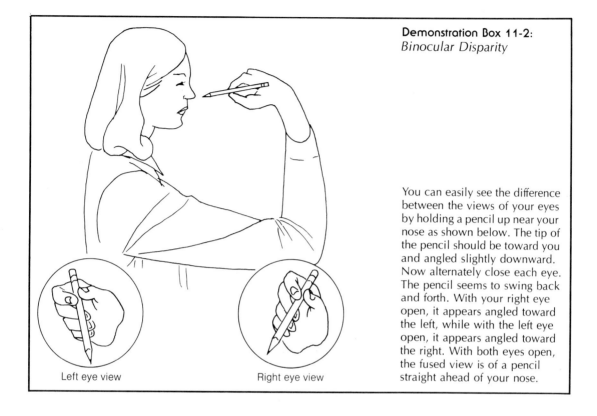

Demonstration Box 11-2:
Binocular Disparity

You can easily see the difference
between the views of your eyes
by holding a pencil up near your
nose as shown below. The tip of
the pencil should be toward you
and angled slightly downward.
Now alternately close each eye.
The pencil seems to swing back
and forth. With your right eye
open, it appears angled toward
the left, while with the left eye
open, it appears angled toward
the right. With both eyes open,
the fused view is of a pencil
straight ahead of your nose.

Left eye view   Right eye view

onstrated in Figure 11-12. As you can see,
the two rods are spatially separated in depth.
The image of these two rods differs for the
right and for the left eyes. The rods are more
widely separated in the right eye's image
than in the image in the left eye. Thus the
images in the two eyes are disparate; in other
words, they are not exactly alike.

Wheatstone wondered what would hap-
pen if he drew a flat picture of the right eye's
view of the two rods and another flat picture
of the left eye's view of the two rods. After
making these drawings, he positioned them
so that the right eye could only see its view
and the left eye could only see its view. He
was curious to see if he could simulate a real
world depth situation by artificially creating
the disparity of the two eyes' views. He accomplished this by devising an optical in-

strument known as a STEREOSCOPE (a stereoscope allows you to put different images into
the two eyes simultaneously). When he did
this he found that even though the pictures
were really flat, one of the rods was seen
behind the other. For a period of time every
Victorian living room had a stereoscope and
a set of travel pictures of famous places that
had been taken using a two-lensed camera.
This produced the "visual magic" of depth
from flat images. Unfortunately, the trend
toward more prurient photographic subjects
ended this craze, although it did not end the
interest in stereoscopic depth.

Depth and Distance: The Interaction of Cues.
In natural viewing situations we are exposed to a number of sources of distance and
depth information simultaneously. Normally

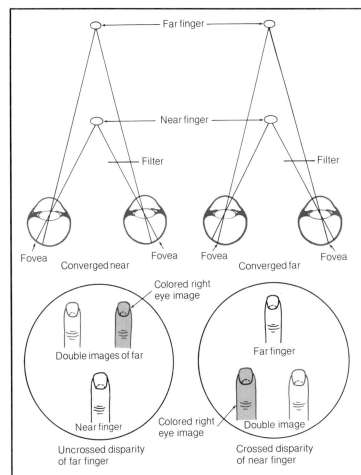

Far finger

Near finger

Filter · Filter

Fovea · Fovea · Fovea · Fovea

Converged near · Converged far

Colored right eye image

Double images of far

Near finger

Colored right eye image

Uncrossed disparity of far finger

Far finger

Double image

Crossed disparity of near finger

Demonstration Box 11-3:
Double Images and Disparity

appear as a double image. Targets that lie away from the area surrounding the point of fixation are not fused into a single image. They produce *disparate* retinal images. Disparate, unfused images are always present in the visual field; however, we are usually not aware of them unless forced to attend to them as in this demonstration.

Once you have become comfortable with this procedure, fixate the near target and then close the right eye. You should notice that the image of the far target (the uncolored image) appears to lie to the left of the nearer, fixated object. Now close the left eye and open the right and you will notice the opposite. The image of the far target (the colored image) now appears to lie to the right of the closer, fixated target. The fact that the right eye is seeing the right disparate image and the left eye is seeing the left disparate image means that when both eyes are opened the far target is seen in UNCROSSED DISPARITY. On the other hand, the opposite will happen if you change your fixation to the far target. Now the closer object appears as diplopic (double). If you once again alternately close each eye, you will notice that the right eye is now seeing the image that lies to the left of the fixated target (the colored image) while the left eye is viewing the image that lies to the right. In the case of double images that lie closer to us than the point of fixation, we have a situation of CROSSED DISPARITY. As the text explains, these differences in disparity may be a cue to distance.

Find a piece of transparent colored material like cellophane (any hue will work). Place it before your right eye. If you wear glasses you can affix it to the frame over the lens in front of your right eye; if not, use a piece of tape to hold it to your forehead. Now align two index fingers directly in front of your nose with the closer finger about 10–20 cm from your nose and the farther finger about 8 cm behind the closer one.

Now that you have arranged the appropriate situation, fixate your nearer finger. However, simultaneously try to pay attention to what the far finger looks like. This is a pretty difficult feat to accomplish at first, but with practice you should be able to fixate one target while simultaneously paying attention to what is going on beyond the fixated area. When you fixate the near target, you will notice that two images of the far target will be seen. The fact that one eye is viewing the image through a colored filter should help make the presence of double images beyond the fixation point more apparent. If you switch your fixation to the farther object, the closer of the two targets will

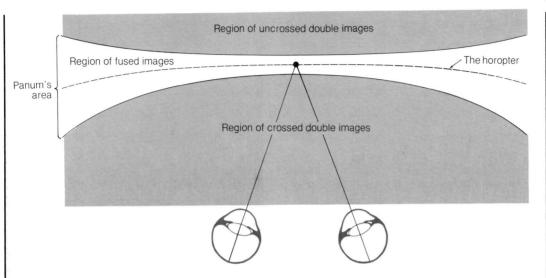

Figure 11-11.
The horopter and Panum's area for one fixation distance. The regions of fusion and disparate images are shown. Crossed disparity is present at distances closer to the observer than the fixation distance, while uncrossed disparity is present beyond the fixation distance. The presence of disparate images may provide a cue to distance.

they are in agreement. For example, if interposition tells you that object A is closer to you than object B, other cues such as relative size will be in agreement with this type of visual organization. However, investigators have been interested in the relative efficiency of each cue alone as well as how various cues interact with each other. In this context, Jameson and Hurvich (1959) have reported that an observer's sensitivity to a difference in distance when all cues are available is close to the arithmetic sum of the sensitivities obtained with each cue alone. In other words, your sensitivity to a depth difference between two objects when texture gradient and interposition are present in the field is equal to the sum of your sensitivity to this depth difference when interposition is the only available cue,

and when texture gradient is the only available cue.

However, much earlier work done by Schriever (1925) indicates that the interaction may not be that simple. He placed drawings and photographs of solid objects in a stereoscope. As you might expect, with only binocular disparity present Schriever found good perception of depth. He then added additional cues to this stereoscopic array. He wanted to know whether the appearance of depth could be changed or reversed if these additional cues were placed in conflict with the binocular disparity cue to depth. Thus, for example, the disparity information might indicate that object A was closer than object B, while the linear perspective information might indicate the reverse effect. In general,

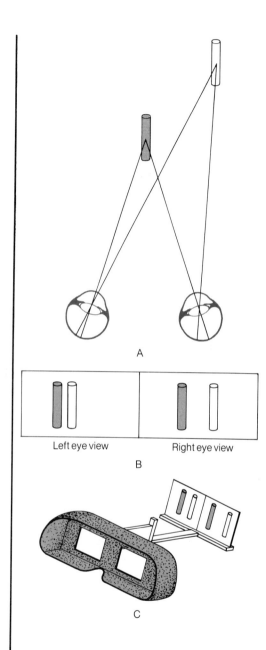

A

Left eye view   Right eye view

B

C

Figure 11-12.
Disparate retinal images. (A) The two retinal images of a scene can be different because the two eyes view the world from slightly different directions. (B) A stereogram is a flat representation that mimics the differences within the two retinal images. (C) A stereogram is viewed in a stereoscope that allows for the separate but simultaneous stimulation of the two eyes. When this is done, depth is seen. The phenomenon is called stereopsis.

Schriever found that the cue of disparity tended to dominate the organization of depth within the percept for all cues except interposition, which seemed to be the single most powerful depth cue he investigated.

Brunswik (1952, 1956) has argued that each separate distance and depth cue is ambiguous. Sometimes it may lead us to an incorrect interpretation of depth or distance within a scene. Thus the power of a particular cue will be determined by its reliability and our past experience with its accuracy. This approach implies that our use of depth cues, and our ability to decipher how they interact with each other to organize a visual space, is a learned ability that becomes more efficient with experience. Brunswick's approach is shared by some investigators, but historically the issue of the learned versus the innate nature of our spatial percepts has been a controversial one. It is often referred to as the *nativist* versus *empiricist* question (Hochberg, 1962). The nativists argue that these perceptual abilities and our capacity to use them are inborn, while the empiricists maintain that interaction with the world, through which we learn about its properties and organization, is crucial to our spatial awareness and abilities. One of the ways in which one can explore this issue is to observe the behavior of young organisms when they are placed in situations that call upon their abilities to perceive distance and depth. Since very young organisms have limited experience with the world, their abilities to deal with such situations should shed some light on the role of inborn versus learned components in the perception of visual space.

The Development of Depth and Distance Perception. The study of newborn and very young organisms is the principal technique used to study the origins of distance and depth perception. Investigators frequently use *controlled rearing* procedures that enable them to make a more exact statement about the experiential factors that contribute to these percepts (as you may remember, we discussed some controlled rearing experiments in Chapter 4). A common form of controlled rearing is *dark rearing*. In this procedure, young animals are raised from birth (or very close to birth) to adulthood in total darkness (Riesen, 1947). This eliminates all externally generated visual experience. If experience with various visual depth cues is necessary for the development of depth perception, these dark-reared animals should have measurable impairments. If depth perception simply matures within the animal, then this restriction of visual experience should not affect the animal. The only important thing should then be its chronological age.

The most popular method for measuring depth perception in young organisms is the VISUAL CLIFF. This apparatus was devised by Walk and Gibson (1961). A diagram of the typical visual cliff arrangement is shown in Figure 11-13. In the visual cliff a central start platform divides the floor of the apparatus into two sections. Each section provides a different kind of visual stimulation. The "shallow" side is a piece of glass that lies directly over a patterned surface. The "deep" side has the same type of patterned surface, but it is placed at some distance below the glass. In the usual experimental situation, a young organism is placed on the central starting platform that separates the shallow and the deep surfaces. It is assumed that from this position the organism can see that the shallow side is safe. However, the deep side, since it simulates a clifflike drop-off, would be perceived as being dangerous. The experimenters make the assumption that the organism would want to avoid a fall. The ability to perceive the drop-off in the visual cliff would lead it to prefer walking on the shallow side and to avoid any contact with the deep side.

Researchers have exposed a wide variety of animal species to the visual cliff. Walk and Gibson (1961) looked at visual cliff behavior in adult and infant rats, adult and infant chickens, turtles, goats, infant and adult sheep, pigs, kittens, puppies, infant monkeys, and infant humans. In all cases there was a preference for the shallow over the deep side of the cliff. It is interesting to note that aquatic turtles did not show the marked preference

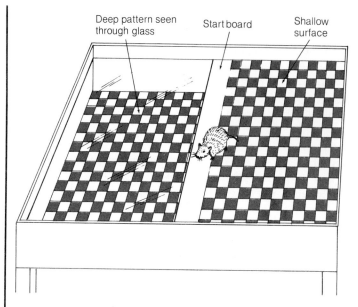

Deep pattern seen through glass   Start board   Shallow surface

Figure 11-13.
The visual cliff.

for the shallow side that the other, more landbound species displayed. In like fashion, Walk (1962, 1964) showed that rabbits chose the shallow side with perfect consistency, but ducklings walked on either side of the cliff with equal ease. Once again, ducklings are aquatic animals. The survival value of cliff avoidance may not be as pronounced in animals that spend much of their lives swimming, since changes in depth of water are not as perilous as sudden sharp drops on land.

Although these cross-species studies are of interest, the visual cliff apparatus has been primarily used to generate data concerning the development of depth perception. The combination of controlled rearing followed by observations of behavior on the visual cliff has been a widely used experimental technique. Several interesting interactions between experience and innate factors have emerged from these types of studies. For example, Walk and Gibson (1961) reared kittens in the dark for four weeks. Initially, they showed no depth discrimination on the visual cliff. However, as they received more and more experience in a lighted world their

depth discrimination rapidly improved. Thus the lack of early visual experience caused initial deficits that were remedied by later visual experience.

There seem to be crucial ages at which restricted or controlled rearing can have an effect on the behavior on the visual cliff. Adult cats and monkeys, even following dark rearing for three months, show no deficits in their abilities to discriminate depth on the visual cliff (Jones & Pasnak, 1970; Slomin & Pasnak, 1972). Tees (1974) demonstrated how physical maturation and experience can interact in a complex way in the development of depth perception. Dark-reared rats were compared to light-reared rats on their preference for the deep versus the shallow side of the visual cliff. The animals were tested at 20, 40, 60, or 80 days after birth. In addition, the depth of the drop in the visual cliff was varied from 10 to 25 cm. Tees reported that the age of the animal and the size of the drop interact. It was found that both the light-reared and dark-reared rats, regardless of the age at which they were tested, preferred the shallow side when the depth difference between the two sides was 20 or 25 cm. At the two shallowest depths (10 and 15 cm) the very young animals (20 days of age) showed no effect of either light or dark rearing. Neither group showed a significant preference for the shallow side at that age. Thus there was no significant effect of light versus dark rearing at the two deepest depths, nor was there an effect of rearing conditions for the very young animals at the shallowest depths. It was only among the older animals, those that were 60 and 90 days of age when tested, that the effects of rearing conditions revealed themselves. At these ages, at least 75% of the light-reared animals, regardless of the depth difference, showed a preference for the shallow side of the visual cliff. However, the dark-reared rats seemed to be insensitive to depth differences below 15 cm. These data indicate that there may be inborn components in the ability of rats to discriminate depth on the visual cliff. These are probably sharpened through experience with depth cues in the environment.

Similar data have emerged from studies with humans. Clearly, use of the visual cliff requires an organism who is old enough to be independently mobile. Therefore, to test human newborns who are still too young to crawl, other response measures have been employed. One such response involves a component of the *orienting reflex* (this will be discussed more fully in Chapter 15). When there is a change in stimulation in the external field, we find a series of physiological changes that coincides with the turning of attention toward novel or changed stimulation. One of these changes is the *deceleration* or slowing of the heartbeat when we orient toward a novel stimulus. There is evidence that this heart rate deceleration is part of a human observer's response of interest and attention to a novel and interesting stimulus (Graham & Clifton, 1966; Graham & Jackson, 1970). On the other hand, our

heartbeat *accelerates*, or speeds up, as a component of our reaction to intense, alarming stimuli. This may be part of a defensive reaction against potentially dangerous stimulation. This means that changes in heart rate can be used by experimenters to differentiate between situations an observer finds alarming and those that are found to be interesting or novel (Sokolov, 1960).

A number of investigators have used this technique to look at the patterns of response of young infants when placed upon the two sides of the visual cliff. For example, Campos, Langer, and Krowitz (1970) placed infants of two months of age face down alternately upon the shallow and upon the deep side of the visual cliff. Greater heart rate deceleration occurred when the infants were placed upon the deep side. This was interpreted as indicating that the infant could discriminate the difference between the two sides of the cliff but as yet was not sensitive to the dangerous implications of the depth drop-off. On the other hand, Schwartz, Campos, and Baisel (1972) found that infants of nine months of age showed a heart rate acceleration when placed upon the deep side of the visual cliff. These results seem to imply that between two and nine months of age the lack of visual stimulation indicating bodily support becomes a danger signal for infants.

Most contemporary psychologists would agree that capabilities to orient oneself in visual space are present at a very early age. However, they would also agree that experience in the world itself seems to play some useful role in the full development of distance and depth perception. Thus the contemporary emphasis is on understanding the interaction between these two factors. The earlier, very strict, dichotomy between the nativist and the empiricist has been replaced by an acknowledgment that there are both innate and learned components in depth perception.

DIRECTION

At the beginning of this chapter, we stated that space perception includes not only the ability to judge distances, but also the ability to assess direction. The simplest form of directional percept involves the location of objects relative to our body. For instance, is the target in front of you or to your left or right? Actually, such directional judgments are possible through both the visual and the auditory modalities.

Visual Direction. Most judgments involve the direction of objects relative to the body. If we imagine the body as the center point of a circle, we can refer to RADIAL DIRECTION as in the points of a compass (Rock, 1975). Unfortunately, several problems of definition immediately arise. For instance, when we perceive an object as being *straight ahead,* what do we mean? A first guess might be to suppose that objects whose images are stimulating the foveas of both eyes would be seen as straight ahead. Such a target would certainly be centered in the visual field. Hill (1972), however, has shown that observers whose eyes are viewing a target off to the side do not call this point straight ahead. Instead they localize the straight ahead direction as being around the *median plane* of the head (this is a line that vertically divides the head down the middle of the nose). This implies that the observers are "taking account" of their eye position in their judgments of direction.

Because straight ahead seems to be in front of the middle of the head, researchers often refer to direction in terms of a CYCLO-PEAN EYE. This is an imaginary point that lies midway between the two eyes. It derives its name from the Greek myth of the giant Cyclops who had a single eye in the middle of his forehead. Unfortunately, this is probably an oversimplification since it seems that the two eyes are not used equivalently. In tasks in which only one eye can be used, such as

in peering through a telescope, 65% of all observers consistently use their right eye, while the remainder consistently use their left. Thus it seems that one eye is preferred. We call this eye the SIGHTING DOMINANT EYE, and the direction "straight ahead" may be positioned in front of this eye (Porac & Coren, 1976). Demonstration Box 11-4 shows this more clearly.

Our sense of straight ahead also varies with the visual information available. Our judgments are much less stable in the dark. Also, specific visual configurations influence these judgments. If the observer is viewing a target, for example, a square or rectangle, that is not exactly centered in the visual field, there will be a tendency to judge the straight ahead direction in terms of the center of this displaced square or rectangle. It is as if the perceptual system confuses what is straight ahead of the observer with what is centered with respect to the other contents in the visual field (Roelofs, 1935). This is demonstrated in Figure 11-14.

What about the innate versus learned origins of the perception of direction? Here the evidence is somewhat clearer than that encountered in our discussion of depth and distance. Lower animals seem to have an inborn sense of direction. Hess (1950) has shown that immediately after birth chicks peck at small objects with reasonable accuracy. If one optically displaces the images of the targets to one side (using special lenses attached to hoods) the chicks now peck systematically to one side, and this pattern of inaccuracy shows little improvement over time. In salamanders it is possible to rotate the eye 180°, inverting the retina. When this is done, animals consistently swim and snap in the opposite direction when presented with a food lure (Sperry, 1943). Since the same results occur when similar operations are performed during the animals' embryonic stage, it is clear that visual direction is in-

It is easy to show that straight ahead may depend upon a single eye (Porac & Coren, 1976; Walls, 1951). Try the following demonstration to see how this works. Stand in front of a wall at a distance of about 3 m. Pick a point on the wall that is directly in front of you (a small crack or bump will do). Now, with both eyes opened, *quickly* stretch out your arm and align your fingertip with the point on the distant wall. When the alignment has been completed, alternately close each eye. You will find that the point on the distant wall will shift out of alignment for one of the eyes. However, the other eye will seem to be aligned with the point on the wall whether one or both eyes are opened. The eye that maintains the alignment is called the SIGHTING DOMINANT EYE. You will notice that regardless of which hand you use to perform the alignment, you will tend to line up a near (your fingertip) and a distant (the point on the wall) target in terms of the same eye. The presence of a sighting dominant eye, and our tendency to make a straight ahead alignment in terms of this eye, indicates that the locus of the egocentric straight ahead direction may be shifted toward the side of the sighting dominant eye and may not lie at a hypothetical point midway between the two eyes.

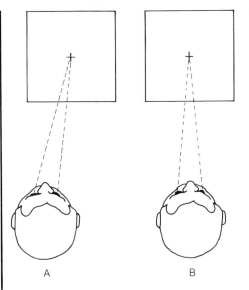

Figure 11-14.
Shifts in the position of objects in the field of view can produce shifts in the perceived straight ahead direction. (A) Actual situation (+ to right side). (B) Perceived situation (+ straight ahead).

nately related to the location of retinal stimulation in this species (Stone, 1960). In humans there appear to be learned components to the assessment of visual direction, since we readily learn to compensate for optical distortions in spatial direction, as we shall see in Chapter 16.

Auditory Direction. The auditory system can also construct percepts of distance and direction. Sounds are clearly localized as emanating from sources that are to the right or left, above or below our bodies. Some sounds appear close and others appear distant. Thus the analysis of auditory space perception follows much the same pattern as the analysis of visual space perception.

Direction cues: simple tones. When a sound is coming from some distance away and from a particular angle to the listener, there are a number of cues that can serve to indicate the direction, or AZIMUTH, of the sound source. Figure 11-15 shows a typical situation when a sound is coming from a source positioned at about 45° azimuth. Notice that one ear receives the sound directly from the source, while the other ear is in what could be called a SOUND SHADOW. The shadowed ear receives only those sounds from the source that are *bent* around the head, or *diffracted* by the edge of the head. The presence of a sound shadow means that the sound intensity at one ear is less than the intensity at the other ear.

Very careful measurements have been made of ear INTENSITY DIFFERENCES as we vary both the azimuth of the sound source and the frequency of the emitted sound. These measurements have shown that the intensity difference between the ears increases as a sound source is moved more toward the side. In addition, low-frequency sound waves (those less than 3000 Hz) bend around the head very readily while high-frequency sound waves do not. Thus high-frequency tones tend to rush right past the hidden ear unless deflected into it. This exaggerates the intensity differences caused by the presence of the sound shadow for higher frequency sounds. The intensity differences as we vary the angle of the sound source can serve as a cue to direction. A large intensity difference be-

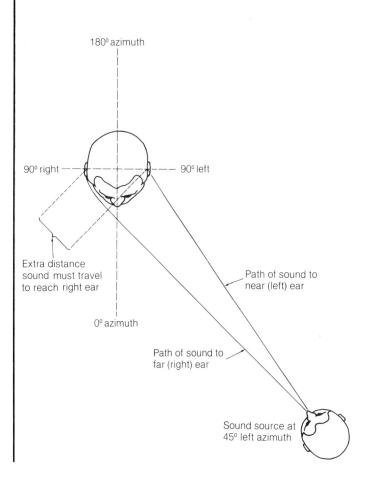

Figure 11-15.
The sound shadow for a sound source at 45° left azimuth (based upon Lindsay & Norman, 1977).

tween the two ears means that the source of the sound is positioned off to one side. The ear receiving the loudest input is closest to the source of the sound.

Another factor also serves as a cue to the direction of a sound. It is based upon the fact that when the sound source is off at an angle sound has to travel different distances to reach the two ears. This is always the case unless the sound source is positioned at either 0 or 180°, when the ears are at equal distances from the source of the sound. Since sound takes time to travel through space, this results in a TIME DIFFERENCE in the arrival of the sound to the two ears. For example, for a sound at 0° azimuth there is no time difference between the stimulation of the right and the left ears since they are at equal distances from the sound source. However, for a sound at 90° azimuth, in either direction, the ear closer to the sound is stimulated approximately 0.8 msec earlier than the hidden ear. Intermediate azimuths result in intermediate values for this time difference. Thus we have another source of information about the directional origin of the sound. You may demonstrate it for yourself using Demonstration Box 11-5.

Under certain circumstances the time difference between the stimulation of the two ears results in a PHASE DIFFERENCE. If a sound is arriving earlier at one ear it will be in a different portion of its cycle of compression and rarefaction of the air molecules than the sound arriving at the other ear (this aspect of sound is discussed fully in Chapter 5). This is especially true for low-frequency sounds where the time taken to complete one cycle is more than the maximum time difference of the arrival of sound at the two ears. For example, it takes a 1000-Hz tone exactly 1 msec to complete one cycle. If such a tone arrived .5 msec earlier at one ear (as it would if the sound source were positioned at about 62° azimuth), it would always be .5/1 msec

or $\frac{1}{2}$ cycle ahead of the sound arriving at the opposite ear. Although phase difference could be considered to be a cue to sound direction, it provides ambiguous information when we consider the full range of sound frequencies. For instance, with a tone of 10,000 Hz at 62° azimuth, the time difference between the arrival of the sound at the two ears would once again be .5 msec. However, a 10,000-Hz tone takes only .1 msec to complete one cycle. This implies a phase difference of .5/.1 msec or 5 cycles. Thus the sound at the ear closest to the source is 5 cycles ahead of the sound arriving at the more distant ear. However, every cycle is identical. Therefore, how can the observer tell just what the phase difference may be? It could be 5, 4, 3, 2, or 1 cycle since they are all alike. There seems to be some ambiguity attached to the use of phase difference information as a cue to sound localization. Even at the lower frequencies, where it could potentially be more useful, the same pattern of phase delay is characteristic of sounds positioned opposite to one another (in reference to a line drawn through the head in any direction).

What is the general effectiveness of various types of cues to sound localization? You should be familiar with this type of investigation from our previous discussion of distance and depth cues. Given that there are multiple sources of potential information that can be used to construct our spatial percepts, it is important to investigate not only how they interact but also the extent of their relative influences under differing conditions.

In 1907, Lord Raleigh proposed a dual, or two-process, theory of sound localization. He suggested that we localize low-frequency sounds by using time and/or phase differences at the two ears, while localization of high-frequency sounds makes use of intensity differences at the two ears caused by the sound shadow and differences in distance

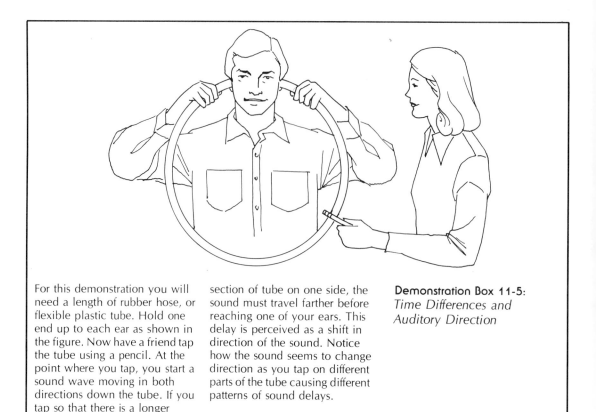

For this demonstration you will need a length of rubber hose, or flexible plastic tube. Hold one end up to each ear as shown in the figure. Now have a friend tap the tube using a pencil. At the point where you tap, you start a sound wave moving in both directions down the tube. If you tap so that there is a longer section of tube on one side, the sound must travel farther before reaching one of your ears. This delay is perceived as a shift in direction of the sound. Notice how the sound seems to change direction as you tap on different parts of the tube causing different patterns of sound delays.

Demonstration Box 11-5:
Time Differences and Auditory Direction

from the sound source. This notion has been confirmed by later research. For example, Stevens and Newman (1934) had observers make judgments as to the direction of a sound source with their eyes closed. They played sounds of different frequencies from a variety of azimuths and recorded the listener's errors of localization for each sound. Their data are shown in Figure 11-16. The solid line in this graph represents a summary of the data they collected, with errors averaged over all of the locations at a particular frequency. As you can see, most errors occur in the region of 1500–3000 Hz. There are fewer errors both above and below this frequency range. One can interpret this as indicating the efficient use of at least one cue in the low- and high-frequency ranges. However, performance is worst in the midrange where neither cue to localization is particularly useful. This interpretation has been confirmed by Mills's (1958) work on the MINIMUM AUDIBLE ANGLE, which is the smallest amount of movement of a sound source that can just be detected. Minimum audible angle also varies as a function of frequency and location of a sound source; the variations are consistent with those observed in experiments like those of Stevens and Newman (Mills, 1960).

It is clear from this discussion of sound localization that the auditory system makes use of physical differences in stimulation that arise between the two ears because of their

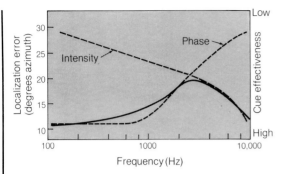

Figure 11-16.
Relative cue effectiveness in arbitrary units
for sound intensity and phase (dashed lines)
as a function of frequency. The solid line,
read against the left ordinate, shows mean
sound localization errors as a function of
frequency (from *Hearing: Physiology and
Psychophysics* by Lawrence W. Gulick. ©
1971 by Oxford University Press, Inc.
Reprinted by permission; data from Stevens
and Newman, 1934).

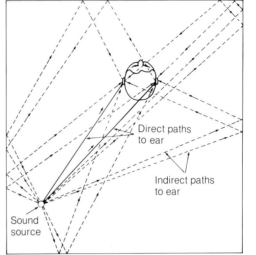

Figure 11-17.
Some of the echoes produced by sound
reflecting from the walls of a room. Unless
the walls are quite far away, the echoes are
not perceived (from Lindsay & Norman,
1977).

separation in space. In many respects, the
binaural use of phase, intensity, and time differences in the construction of auditory direction is analogous to the use of binocular
image disparity in the construction of three-
dimensional visual percepts. Thus it seems
that differences in sensory stimulation caused
by the physical separation of bilateral organs
(eyes and ears) are important to the construction of spatial percepts in both modalities.

**Direction and distance cues: complex
tones.** When we are in an ordinary room,
the sound from any source may go bouncing
around the room, reflecting from the walls,
ceiling, and floor many times before it
reaches our ears. Figure 11-17 illustrates this
phenomenon. Why do we not experience an
overwhelming auditory confusion as these
sounds richocet around us? Typically we respond only to the first of the many replicas of

a particular complex sound in echo-
producing surroundings. We do not respond
to the echoes that arrive several milliseconds
later. In fact, we do not even experience
echoes until the reflecting surface, which
hurls the sound back at us, is far enough
away so that the echoes take a substantial
time to reach us (about 34 msec or so).
Groups of sounds that arrive at interstimulus
intervals of less than 35 msec are fused together into one sound. The first arrival appears to be the major determinant of where in
space we perceive the sound source to be.
This phenomenon is called the PRECEDENCE
EFFECT and has been extensively studied by
Wallach, Newman, and Rosenzweig (1949).
Their experiments indicated that the earliest
of a pair of fused sounds (separated by 2
msec) was 6–20 times more important than
the later of the pair in determining the perceived direction of the sound source. Wal-

lach *et al.* (1949) also pointed out that the precedence effect is an important part of our ability to listen selectively to one source of sound out of a larger group of competing sounds (see the discussion of the cocktail party problem in Chapter 15).

Under appropriate conditions, echoes can be important to the judgment of the location of sounds. For example, blind individuals apparently use echoes to help them locate obstacles and thus avoid them. They seem to *feel* rather than hear these reflected sounds (Supra, Cotzin, & Dallenbach, 1944; Worchel & Dallenbach, 1947). Animals such as bats and whales have highly developed ECHOLATION SYSTEMS, similar to sonar, which they can use to locate objects with the same facility with which we use our eyes.

There are a number of other cues to the spatial location of complex sounds. Head movement has been shown to be important both in resolving ambiguities of location, such as whether the sound is in front of or in back of the observer, and in providing a feeling that the sound is *out there* as opposed to inside the head (Wallach, 1939). It has also been argued that the *pinnae* (the fleshy parts of the ears outside of the head) delay sounds of different frequencies by different amounts (Batteau, 1967). These differential delays apparently provide cues as to the location of complex sound sources.

Distance information is also carried by complex sounds. One major source of this information is the relative intensity of a sound, with nearer sources being louder. Changes in sound distance are thus reliably coded by changes in sound intensity (Mershon & King, 1975). Of course any intensity could be produced by a sound source that is nearby or by a louder sound source that is farther away. Thus this cue is unreliable for absolute distance unless the sound is a familiar one. Through experience we know what a bell on an ice cream truck or what a car en-

gine sounds like when the sound is made relatively close to us. At some other time, we can use this knowledge to judge how far away a similar sound source may be by the loudness of the sound. This type of auditory information is very similar to the distance cue of familiar size used by the visual system to assess distance. Thus previous experience with the unique qualities of a given piece of sensory input is an important distance cue in both modalities.

Another important source of distance information is the relative amount of REVERBERATION in the impinging sound. As we stated above, sound reaches our ears both directly from a source and after being reflected from (*reverberating* from) various surfaces such as walls (see Figure 11-17). In general, as a sound source gets further away from an observer, the amount of sound that directly reaches the ears decreases more rapidly than the amount reaching the ears after reverberation. Thus the relative amount of "reverberation sound" (which has a distinct quality, like an echo) is a cue to the distance of a sound source from an observer. Von Békésy was one of the first to investigate this cue systematically. In 1938 (von Békésy, 1960) he showed that altering the proportion of reverberant sound alters judgments of perceived distances of sounds. More recent work by Mershon and his colleagues (Mershon & Bowers, 1976; Mershon & King, 1975) has confirmed and extended this earlier work.

Throughout this chapter we have looked at the types of information observers use to place themselves and external objects into appropriate distance, depth, and directional relationships. We have also looked at the development of spatial percepts, and have learned that some of the information used by organisms to organize their world spatially appears to be part of our physiological heritage. Although we have made artificial separations and have discussed each of these processes separately, it should be clear that in normal everyday situations all of the visual and auditory cues are interacting to provide you with a unitary spatial experience. For example, we usually localize an object in space by both seeing its image and hearing any sound it makes as emanating from a common direction and distance. Although the evidence is still somewhat sketchy, there is reason to believe that this *cross-modal* integration of spatial information is also present from a very early age (Aronson & Rosenbloom, 1971; McGurk & Lewis, 1974; Yonas & Pick, 1975). Given the complexity of space perception, we are prompted to recall a line from a letter Charles Lamb wrote to a friend in 1802: "Nothing puzzles me more than time and space; and yet nothing troubles me less, as I never think about them." Perhaps now we have equipped you to think about them for yourself.

12
Time and Motion

The exasperated mother glared at her teen-aged son. "Have you no sense of time?" she growled. "This afternoon you said that you just wanted to talk on the phone to Judy for a few minutes and you were at it for two hours!"

"Mom, it only seemed like five minutes!"

"And tonight, you said that you were going to put in a full evening studying for your exams and you're back downstairs in ten minutes!"

"But Mom," came the puzzled reply, "it felt like I had been studying for three hours!"

The passage of time is a psychological experience. However, in some ways time can be treated as a stimulus continuum, just as any other perceptual event has its physical stimulus. Fraisse (1963) has pointed out that our notion of time seems to be tied to our experience of successive change. Changes occur continually, sometimes with the regularity of night following day, and sometimes with irregularity, as of moving to a new house. Our experience of the swift or slow passage of time appears to be linked to the experience of a continual flux of events. Change is also responsible for the perception of motion. Here the change refers to spatial position. If an object is perceived to have changed its position from one moment to the next, then, under the appropriate circumstances, we perceive it as moving. Time and motion thus represent dynamic qualities of perceptual experience.

TIME

There are two general theoretical approaches that characterize investigations into the perception of time. The first approach can be called the INTERNAL TIMER HYPOTHESIS. This approach assumes that there is a biological or physiological basis to our perception of time. Just as we have a sense organ that is sensitive

to light (the eye), we must also have a sense organ that accounts for our ability to keep track of the passage of time. The phrase "a sense of time" stems from this general orientation. An issue for the internal timer hypothesis is the search for the basic unit of time. There are several lines of evidence suggesting that time is an integral aspect of naturally occurring processes. For example, many physical phenomena have their own rhythm or timing. There are the day–night cycles, cycles of the moon, cycles of the seasons, and many others. Living organisms often display rhythmic activities. Many flowers open at particular periods of the day, and the cycle of opening and closing of a flower may follow a particular temporal sequence. Certain physiological processes in animals have a cycle of periodic change. One of the most obvious of these is the waking–sleeping cycle. For humans, periods of wakefulness and sleep follow regular rhythms throughout a 24-hr period.

There are other, more subtle physiological processes that have their own periodic changes. For example, the pulse, blood pressure, and temperature of the body demonstrate day–night variations in humans as well as in many animals. There is more than a 1°C difference in body temperature between the coolest point, which occurs during the night, and the warmest point, which occurs during the afternoon. There are also rhythmic aspects of other bodily functions. Heartbeats, breathing, walking steps, and finger tapping also seem to occur at regular intervals. All of these physiological processes, at one time or another, have been suggested as candidates for an internal biological timing mechanism (Ornstein, 1969; Treisman, 1963).

The second general approach to the investigation of the experience of time can be called the EVENT PROCESSING HYPOTHESIS. It dismisses the notion that our perception of time depends upon a continuous internal timer. Here time is viewed as a purely cognitive process that is not tied to any objective or "clock" time. Our experience of time is simply based upon how much sensory information is processed during a particular interval. According to this view time is not a real entity that we can perceive by means of a sensory system; rather, we experience time by attending to the number of psychological events occurring over a physically defined period. Within this second approach to the problem of time perception, the experience of time is not tied to any physiological process but it is a mental construct that comes about through our processing of differing amounts and types of incoming information.

Before we go any further, let us be clear as to what we mean by time. Imagine that there are three clocks that control our lives. The first is a *physical clock*. Each tick of this clock represents a regularly occurring physical event, such as the vibrations of the nitrogen atom in ammonia (the international standard of time) or the revolution of the earth around the sun (solar time). Physical time is marked off by the number of these regularly occurring events (conveniently grouped into larger and smaller units such as centuries or seconds). The second clock is a *physiological clock*. Each tick of this clock is represented by internally generated physiochemical events. Thus we have regular sleeping and wakefulness patterns based upon a CIRCADIAN RHYTHM (from the Latin *circa dia*, meaning "approximately a day"), which ticks off approximately 24-hr units. Females have a 28-day cycle marked off by the hormonal shifts of the menstrual cycle, while males manifest an approximate 9-week physiological cycle that is also based on hormonal fluctuations. Finally, our third clock is a *psychological clock*. This clock determines our conscious experience of time, and it is the clock with which we will be concerned here.

Perceived Duration. Both of the approaches we mentioned above have attempted to explain the estimation of duration. According to our psychological clock, how long does an event endure? How does psychologically clocked time compare to physically clocked time? Approaches to the problem have included the study of both brief (under 1 sec) and relatively long (minutes, hours, and days) durations. Evidence supporting both the internal timer and the event processing interpretations of temporal perception has been uncovered.

Let us consider the perception of brief intervals of time. Within this context, 5 sec is a "long" interval while 1 sec or less is short. In general, when asked to estimate the duration of time, observers tend to overestimate very brief intervals and underestimate longer intervals (Ward, 1975; Woodrow, 1951). There also seems to be a particular duration that does not give rise to either an overestimation or an underestimation of its length. This duration seems to be around .7 sec (700 msec). It has been termed the INDIFFERENCE INTERVAL (Ornstein, 1969; Treisman, 1963). Since this duration is measured as equally long by both the physical (real passage of clock time) and psychological (estimated passage of clock time) clocks, some investigators have hypothesized that it represents the basic time unit of the internal timer.

Stroud (1955) has proposed a slightly different concept. He maintains that time is not a continuous dimension; rather it is broken into discrete bits he calls *moments*. These PERCEPTUAL MOMENTS would be the psychological unit of time. By drawing upon information from various research findings (including patterns of electrical activity in the brain), he estimates that each moment is about 100 msec. According to this point of view, the shortest perceived duration a stimulus can have is one moment or 100 msec. Stimuli presented within the same moment would either be perceived as occurring simultaneously, or, depending upon the nature of the stimulus, would not be distinguishable from each other. White (1963) tested this notion by having observers estimate the number of clicks they heard. He presented the clicks at different rates up to 25 per second. Observers were fairly accurate at rates of up to 5 per second. At the highest click rates, however, observers still estimated a presentation rate of about 6–7 clicks per second. This corresponds to a perceived rate of one stimulus every 150 msec. Thus, information could not be processed in "bites" smaller than 150 msec, which would be the resolution limit of the internal timer.

Efron (1967) also tried to measure the perceptual moment. In one study he presented two brief pulses of light and asked observers to say which one was longer. One of the flashes was always 1 msec in duration. The other was of a variable duration. Both flashes were always seen as being of the same length until the exposure time of the variable flash exceeded a value of 60 or 70 msec. At this duration, it was seen as being longer than the 1-msec flash. From this Efron concluded that the minimum duration of a stimulus in consciousness (which should be one perceptual moment) was around 60 or 70 msec. Thus Stroud's assumption that the basic unit of perceived time was about 100 msec is supported by these data.

The existence of a fixed perceptual moment is what one would expect if we had an internal timer. Hence work on the perceptual moment supports this hypothesis. On the other hand, there is also support for the contention that our experience of duration is tied to the amount and type of stimulus information we process during a given time interval, and is not tied to an internal clock (Ornstein, 1969). For example, let us look at a phenomenon called the FILLED DURATION ILLUSION. A duration filled with stimulus events is perceived as being longer than an identical duration empty of any external events. In other words, if we fill a one second interval with brief tones, this interval will be perceived as being longer than an identical 1-sec period defined only by a beginning and an ending tone (Ornstein, 1969; Thomas & Brown, 1974). The presence of this illusion supports the position of those individuals who argue for an event processing approach to time perception. Since there are more stimuli to process within a filled duration, this period is perceived as being longer than one that is identical in physical time but devoid of information processing requirements.

Evidence from research on longer time intervals (those that extend over several minutes, hours, and even days) also provides evidence for both the internal timer and the event processing theories of time perception. For example, Hoagland (1933) suggested that if there were an internal timer, it would speed up or slow down along with other physiological processes in the body. When his wife became ill with a fever he took the opportunity to engage in some experimental observations. He asked her to estimate the duration of 1 minute by counting to 60 at a rate of what she perceived to be one number per second. He found that the duration of her count varied as a function of the degree of her fever. When her body temperature was approximately 39°C (103°F) her perceived minute was only 37.5 sec by objective clock time. Hoagland reasoned that at higher body temperatures, when physiological activities increase their speed, the internal timer should tick more rapidly. This means that when asked to reproduce a given physical time interval, a person with a high body temperature should produce an interval that is too short. An alternate way of looking at this is to note how our perception of physical time will seem to change when psychological time is running quickly. A given physical duration will appear to be too long since there are more ticks of the psychological clock during a fixed unit of physical time (see Figure 12-1).

Hoagland's observations would lead one to expect that lowering body temperature would have an opposite effect. Baddeley (1966) tested this notion with scuba divers diving in cold water off the coast of Wales. He also asked his subjects to count to 60 at a rate of about one number per second. After the dive, when their body temperature was approximately 1°C lower than it had been prior to entering the water, he found that his subjects required approximately 70 sec to count to 60. Their behavior indicates that their internal timer was ticking at a slower rate than the physical clock. They were counting time using the slower ticking rate of their internal timer. This should lead them to underestimate the passage of time. In other words, when your internal clock is too slow, physical time seems to whiz by (see Figure 12-1). You may demonstrate the effects of temperature upon your own time sense by using Demonstration Box 12-1.

The notion of a physiologically controlled internal timer is also supported by data concerning the effect of drugs on the experience of time. As a general rule, one can say that drugs that accelerate vital functions lead to an overestimation of physical time while those that have a sedative effect lead to its underestimation (Fraisse, 1963). For example, a number of investigators have found that drugs like amphetamines and caffeine (both of which are stimulants) lead to a lengthening of time experience (Frankenhauser, 1959; Goldstone, Boardman, & Lhamon, 1958). General anesthetics, on the other hand, have been shown to lead to a shortening of time experience (Adam, Rosner, Hosick, & Clark, 1971; Steinberg, 1955). Drugs such as marijuana, mescaline, psilocybin, and LSD seem to produce a lengthening of perceived time relative to a nondrug state (Fisher, 1967; Weil, Zinberg, & Nelson, 1968). Although it is argued that these changes in time perception are based upon physiological acceleration or deceleration of the internal timer, there are alternative explanations that we will consider shortly.

There is also a rather wide body of evidence to support the notion that our experience of longer periods of time involves the processing of stimulus events as well. Ornstein (1969) has provided evidence that durations filled with more elements are judged to be longer than durations filled with fewer elements (this is the filled-duration illusion

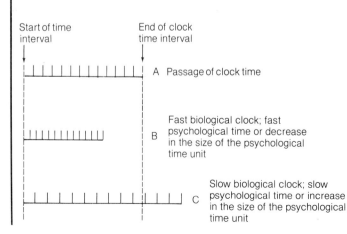

Figure 12-1.
Each unit on lines A, B, and C represents a unit of time. Those in B are one-half the size of those in A, while those in C are one and one-half the size of those in A. When the biological clock speeds up, leading to a decrease in the size of the psychological time unit, we tend to overestimate the passage of time and clock time seems to "drag" by. The opposite occurs when the biological clock slows down.

Start of time interval

End of clock time interval

A Passage of clock time

B Fast biological clock; fast psychological time or decrease in the size of the psychological time unit

C Slow biological clock; slow psychological time or increase in the size of the psychological time unit we talked about above). He presented his observers with tape recordings marking off the same physical time (approximately 10 minutes). The tapes differed from each other only in that sounds were recorded on the tapes at different rates per minute. These rates varied from 40 to 120 tones per minute. In confirmation of the event processing hypothesis, which says that time estimation is based upon the amount of information processed during a given interval, Ornstein found that the tape that had 40 tones per minute was judged to be shorter than the tape that had 120 tones per minute. Similar results have also been reported in the visual and tactual modalities (Buffardi, 1971; Mescavage, Heimer, Tatz, & Runyon, 1971). Thus durations filled with more elements are judged to be longer than durations filled with fewer elements. You may have had similar experiences contrasting periods of time when you are furiously busy, and those boring times when there is "just nothing to do."

There is other experimental evidence supporting the hypothesis that variations in time perception are caused by variations in information processing rates. For example, this hypothesis predicts that situations that increase one's awareness or heighten one's motivation to attend should lead to a lengthening of time perception relative to control situations where these factors do not operate. Under such aroused situations we attend to more stimuli and process information more rapidly. In a study by Filer and Meals (1949) subjects were given different motivational sets in the performance of simple tasks. Subjects who were told that a desirable goal would be obtained upon completion of their tasks tended to overestimate the passage of time relative to control conditions, where subjects were not given these expectancy sets. These findings are consistent with the folk saying that "a watched pot never boils," or the common experience of time dragging by as we await the fun of Christmas morning gift opening. Ornstein (1969) would interpret this as the result of the expectancy leading to a greater awareness of the input of information and thus a lengthening of subjective duration. A study by Falk and Bindra (1954) is consistent with this idea. They placed observers in a stress situation (they were receiving electrical shocks) and found that their observers also tended to overestimate the passage of physical time.

Other factors such as the complexity of stimuli being processed also affect time estimates. Complex stimuli, which would be expected to cause an increase in attention and awareness, cause increases in subjective time estimates over situations where less complex stimuli are being processed (Burnside, 1971; Ornstein, 1969). Given such data, we can now reinterpret the effects of various drugs on the perception of time using the event processing viewpoint. Drugs used to attain a heightened state of awareness (such as LSD, psilocybin, and others) also lead to a lengthening of perceived time. One could argue that the drug is not affecting an internal timer, but rather is increasing the amount of sensory input processed per unit of time. This in turn is what leads to the increase in perceived time.

It seems clear that there is support for both the internal timer and the event processing hypotheses of time perception. Neither of these viewpoints, however, provides a complete picture. Time is really an intangible aspect of our experience. We are aware of its effects but we do not experience it in ways that are similar to the experience of light or sound. The elusive nature of our experience of time makes it susceptible to variations due to individual styles, motivations, attitudes, and expectations. For example, estimates of a given duration may change as we vary the observer's perceptual task. If an observer is asked to reproduce a time interval, as opposed to giving a verbal estimate of its length, different types of data may result (Ornstein & Rotter, 1969). Similarly, duration judgments may also be affected by whether observers know in advance that they may be asked to make a time estimate (Hicks, Miller, & Kinsbourne, 1976).

There also seem to be age trends in the ability to make accurate time estimates. For instance, when elementary school-aged children are asked to make estimates of the duration of a 1-sec interval, their estimates are extremely variable. This variability in time estimation decreases with age. When one gives feedback as to the accuracy of the estimates, 6–7-year olds do not seem to benefit. It is not until around the age of 8 years that children are able to improve their performance as a result of information about the accuracy of their time estimates (Smythe & Goldstone, 1957).

Such data indicate that the strategy an observer uses when estimating time can affect measurements of subjective duration. Although such data do not directly address themselves to the event processing hypothesis of time perception, they do seem more compatible with such a view than with the internal timer hypothesis. They support the notion that the judgmental strategy and the distribution of attention in particular tasks can affect subjective estimates of duration. Thus we are led to conclude that it is unlikely that our time perception is based solely on a physiological or a biological clock.

There may be a resolution between the internal timer and the event processing hypotheses of time perception. Polzella, Dapolito, and Hinsman (1977) had observers estimate the duration of various patterns of dots, which differed in terms of the number of stimulus elements. They varied whether the dots appeared on the left or the right sides of the visual field. The simple procedure of varying the side of the visual field on which a target appears actually alters where the inputs are first processed in the brain. As we noted in Chapter 4, all stimuli imaged on the left side of the retina of either eye are first processed in the left cerebral hemisphere, while all those imaged on either right retina are first processed by the right hemisphere. The findings of Polzella et al. (1977) supported the suggestion that the left hemisphere of the brain relies on an internal timer to estimate duration, while the right hemisphere relies on event processing (Thomas & Weaver, 1975). Since both hemispheres are available for most tasks, this implies that both methods of estimating time may be used by observers in the majority of tasks involving time perception.

Perhaps the most intriguing aspect of time is the way it interacts with other sensory experiences. For instance, time and space affect each other. Suppose that we flash two spatially separated lights in a dark room, one after the other. Now we ask an observer to estimate the distance between the two lights. As we increase the time between the offset of one light and the onset of the other, the observer's estimates of the distance between the two lights will also increase. This is called the TAU EFFECT. Exactly the opposite manipulation distorts time. If we decrease the distance between the two lights, keeping the time interval between the flashes constant, the observer reports that the time between the offset of the first light and the onset of the second has shrunk. This is called the KAPPA EFFECT. Both the tau and kappa effects illustrate that time (and space) exist in the consciousness of the observer and that they are not dictated by physical events alone. You can experience the tau effect by following the instructions in Demonstration Box 12-2.

MOTION

The physicist Albert Einstein created a revolution in physics when he proposed that time and motion do not have absolute values but can only be measured relative to one another. In his *theory of relativity* he maintained that physical time actually slows down as we move more quickly. We have already seen an example of *psychological relativity* in the *kappa effect* where the distance that an object moves affects our

judgment of time. In fact, time and motion are psychologically inseparable phenomena. Max Wertheimer demonstrated this interdependence in 1912 with the following example. Once again we begin with two lights, separated in space, that can be flashed on and off one after the other. In addition, we can vary the time interval between the offset of the first light and the onset of the second (we can call this variable period the INTERSTIMULUS INTERVAL). If the interstimulus interval is very brief (under 30 msec), observers report seeing two lights that have flashed on simultaneously. When the interstimulus interval is increased to around 60 msec, observers report they see *movement*. In other words, observers report that a light comes on and *moves* from the first position in space to the second. If the interstimulus interval is longer than 200 msec the perception of movement is lost. Now observers report that they see a light come on and then go off, followed by a second light that comes on in a different position. The illusion of movement, which is perceived under certain interstimulus intervals, was called the PHI PHENOMENON by Wertheimer, although today the more usual term is STROBOSCOPIC MOVEMENT. Stroboscopic movement is interesting because it demonstrates that time relationships between stimuli can determine whether or not movement is perceived. You can demonstrate this effect for yourself using Demonstration Box 12-3.

The Nature of Motion Perception. Under more normal viewing conditions, how do we perceive movement? At first you might be tempted to say that we perceive motion when an image of an external object moves across the retinal receptors. However, we have just seen that this condition is not necessary since stroboscopic movement exists. Furthermore it is possible for us to perceive movement when our eyes are in motion with the image of an

The **TAU EFFECT** is an interaction between time and space. Suppose that we have two pairs of stimuli, pair A and pair B. The members of each of the pairs are separated by the same physical distance, and we can alter the time interval between the offset of one member of the pair and the onset of the other. Under these conditions, we find that as we increase the offset–onset interval between the members of one pair, we will increase the perceived distance between them relative to the other pair of stimuli. Thus increases in the time interval between successively stimulated points will lead to increases in the perceived distance between the two points.

Try the following demonstration. Cut an index card so that it has two points about 5 cm apart. Diagram A will help you visualize the stimulus. Make sure that the ends are rather narrow and come to a relatively sharp point. Simultaneously touch the ends of the notch to the underside of your forearm. Take note of the apparent distance between the two points of stimulation as they touch your skin. Next place one point on your skin. With a gentle twist of your wrist you can lift the point touching your skin and make contact with the other point. In other words, instead of stimulating your skin with both points simultaneously, you are applying the stimulation in a sequential order with one end of the notch following the other (see diagram B). Under these

Demonstration Box 12-2:
The Tau Effect

circumstances, you should experience the distance between the two points of stimulation as being longer than it was when the two stimuli were applied simultaneously. A sequential presentation means that the time interval between the offset of one stimulus and the onset of the second stimulus has increased. Thus the tau effect should operate to increase the perceived distance between the two points of stimulation on the skin during the sequential presentation.. Try this experiment several times not only on yourself but on someone else. See how varying the time between touches varies the apparent distances.

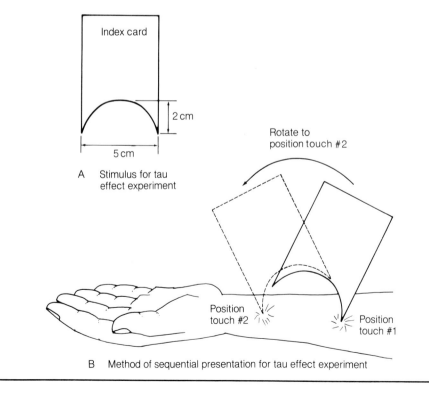

Index card

2 cm

5 cm

A   Stimulus for tau effect experiment

Rotate to position touch #2

Position touch #2

Position touch #1

B   Method of sequential presentation for tau effect experiment

You can experience stroboscopic movement for yourself by following this simple demonstration. Take a small piece of paper and draw a short line (about 1 cm in length) in the center of it. Hold it directly in front of you at a distance of about 15–20 cm from your nose. Alternately close each eye while looking at the line. You will notice that the line seems displaced in the two separate views (this is due to the separation of the two eyes in space—see Chapter 11). Now alternately wink each eye in turn (you may have to do this with moderately rapid alternations between the eyes). At an appropriate rate of alternate winking, you will see the line apparently *move* between the two positions. This is phi or stroboscopic movement.

Demonstration Box 12-3:
Stroboscopic Movement—The Phi Phenomenon

object remaining fixed on only one portion of the retinal surface, such as when we follow a moving car with our eyes. There are also times when we should see movement but do not. For instance, our eyes are in continual motion. This means that the images of objects that are stationary in the environment are sliding across our retinal receptors in stops and starts almost all of the time. Despite all of these image movements, we still perceive the world as remaining stationary. Thus movement of the retinal image does not fully account for the perception of motion. Actually, there are two movement perception systems that act in concert; they are the IMAGE–RETINA SYSTEM and the EYE–HEAD SYSTEM (Gregory, 1966). Both act together to deal with the many complexities involved in determining whether a given movement on the retina has been caused by an observer or an eye movement, or whether it has been caused by the real movement of an external object.

The image–retina movement system.
The image–retina system signals movement when there is motion in the retinal image but the eye is stationary. This situation is diagrammed in Figure 12-2A. The image–retina system seems to operate by means of physiological *movement detectors*, such as those found by Lettvin, Maturana, McCul-

loch, and Pitts (1959), Hubel and Wiesel (1968), Barlow, Hill, and Levick (1964), and others. You will probably recall from Chapter 4 that some of the complex cells in the cortex of mammals respond only to moving targets. Furthermore these cells seem to be directionally sensitive, discharging strongly when a properly oriented stimulus drifts in one direction across the visual field, and responding less strongly (or not at all) when the same stimulus moves through the field in the opposite direction (Hubel & Wiesel, 1962; Wurtz, 1969).

There is a psychophysical technique called SELECTIVE ADAPTATION that can tell us about the nature of these movement-sensitive cells in humans (Sekuler, 1975). First, the eye is continually exposed to a moving pattern such as a field full of stripes. After prolonged exposure, the motion-specific cells that have been responding to the direction of the pattern's movement begin to fatigue and become less sensitive. In other words, we have selectively adapted the visual system to movement in one direction by fatiguing the cells that are sensitive to that type of movement. When this is done, we find that an observer's sensitivity to movement of other patterns, which are moving in the same direction and at the same speed as the previously exposed *adapting pattern*, has been reduced.

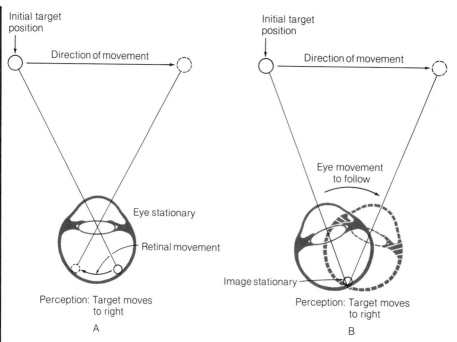

Initial target position

Direction of movement

Eye stationary

Retinal movement

Perception: Target moves to right

A

Initial target position

Direction of movement

Eye movement to follow

Image stationary

Perception: Target moves to right

B

Figure 12-2.
(A) The image–retina movement system. The image of the moving object stimulates the retina when the eyes are held stationary. This gives information about object motion possibly due to the involvement of movement detecting cells. (B) One of the functions of the eye–head movement system. When the eye pursues a moving target, the image remains stationary on the fovea of the eye but we still perceive the movement of the object.

However, this drop in sensitivity does not carry over to faster or slower movements, nor does it generalize to movements in the opposite direction (Sekuler, 1975; Sekuler & Ganz, 1963). Thus the selective adaptation procedure reveals that there are movement-sensitive cells having very specific ranges of responsiveness. To experience an interesting illusion, thought to be caused by the fatigue of motion sensitive cells, try the demonstration in Demonstration Box 12-4.

The eye–head movement system. The second system, the eye–head movement system, operates in a very different fashion. It seems to have two tasks to perform. First, this system enables us to detect the movement of external objects when they remain in a stationary position upon the retina. This happens when we move our eyes to follow the path of a physically moving object as shown in Figure 12-2B. These types of eye movements, called SMOOTH PURSUIT MOVEMENTS, function to keep the fovea (the most acute part of the retina) on the target. Since the image of the target remains on the fovea, the only way the observer can know

To experience the SPIRAL AFTEREFFECT, cut out (or trace) the accompanying stimulus and place it on the turntable of your stereo or record player as if it were a record. Let the stimulus rotate for about one minute while you stand over it and watch it closely. Stop the turntable and hold it so that it is completely stationary. You should notice that you now see a spiralling movement in a direction opposite to that in which the stimulus physically rotated. This is an illusory movement since the stimulus itself is no longer in motion. The spiral aftereffect is not well understood, but it may be due to the satiation or fatiguing of a particular group of movement detectors, which is caused by excessive stimulation in one direction of movement. It is one of several such movement aftereffects.

Demonstration Box 12-4:
The Spiral Aftereffect

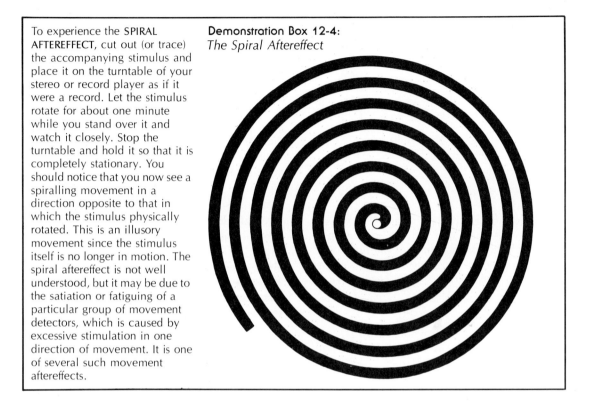

the path and the speed that an object has traveled is to monitor the path and speed of the eyes' movements. Given this fact, it is remarkable that we can accurately report the shape and the length of the path of a moving target (Epstein & Hanson, 1977; Rock & Halper, 1969).

Unfortunately, since most of our information about the course of a moving target comes from our record of the path that our eyes have traveled, discrepancies between the path of the stimulus and the path that the eye has followed can lead to perceptual errors. Actually, the eye does not pursue moving targets accurately. There is a tendency for the eye to follow some distance behind, with the degree of the lag dependent upon the speed of the target (Puckett & Steinman, 1969; Fender, 1971). Under some circum-

stances the eye never really catches up to the stimulus (Young, 1971). Festinger and Easton (1974) had observers track a spot of light that moved over a square path. The eye lagged behind (as usual) but also did not change direction as quickly as the spot; the spot had turned a corner of the square while the eye was still pursuing along a side. When asked to describe the path of the target, most observers did not describe squares but paths such as those in Figure 12-3. These are the kinds of shape distortions one would predict, given that the eye was tracking behind the target. The importance of eye movements in this illusion is confirmed by the disappearance of distortion, and the square appearance of the path, when the eye views the moving light without trying to follow it. Similarly, Coren, Bradley, Hoenig, and Girgus (1975)

Figure 12-3.
Festinger and Easton (1974) asked observers to follow the path of a moving spot of light. Although the physical path of the light was square, observers most often reported shapes like those shown (based upon Festinger & Easton, 1974).

have shown that the size of the circular path of a rotating spot of light can be distorted when the eye movements used to pursue the rotating light are erroneous.

The eye–head movement system also enables us to compensate for the effects of image motion on the retinal surface when it is caused not by an external movement but by the eye movements generated by the observer. Although we do not know exactly how this second movement system works, it must be based in part upon a system that monitors the changing position of the eye relative to the position of the head, either when we are tracking a moving target, or when we are making eye movements to scan a stationary scene.

Two major types of theories have been proposed to explain the eye–head movement system. Sir Charles Sherrington (1906) suggested that motion is detected via feedback information from the six extraocular muscles that control the movement of the eyes. This feedback information, called proprioceptive or position information (see Chapter 6), en-

ables the observer to monitor eye position. The proprioceptive information tells the brain that the eyes have moved. This information allows the brain to interpret movement across the retina as being observer generated rather than object generated. There is evidence that there are cells in the superior colliculus and in the cortex of the cat brain that monitor eye position. These cells fire at different rates depending upon the extent and direction to which the eye is turned (Kasamatsu, 1976; Noda, Freeman, & Creutzfeldt, 1972). These cells could provide the information required to monitor eye position. Sherrington's theory is often called an INFLOW THEORY because it is the information "flowing in" from the eye muscles to the brain that constitutes the crucial message for the interpretation of movement.

Hermann von Helmholtz (1909/1924) had a different view about how this eye–head system worked. He felt that it worked on an OUTFLOW PRINCIPLE. When the visual system in its entirety initiates an eye movement, signals are sent out from the brain commanding the eyes to move. In outflow theories it is this signal, emanating from central regions in the visual system, that cancels the movement information coming from the retina as the eyes move. Thus the interpretation of the origin of movement does not come from information from the extraocular muscles, but from the message sent out from the brain that initiates an eye movement. As in the case of inflow information, there seem to be some cells in the cerebellum and the cortex of monkeys that contain information about eye position. Since these cells respond before the actual movement takes place, they could represent the source of outflow information (Miles & Fuller, 1975; Wurtz & Goldberg, 1971).

There is also some experimental and observational evidence indicating that the initiation of VOLUNTARY EYE MOVEMENTS (eye movements under command of the brain, such as smooth pursuit movements) may contain the outflow information that is an important aspect of the eye–head movement system. For example, try this little experiment. Place your hand over one eye and try tapping or pushing the side of your other (uncovered) eye very gently with your fingertips. This rotates the eye in a movement similar to one that could be initiated by the brain. However, the brain has given no signal to move the eye. When the eye is rotated in this passive fashion, the visual field will be seen to swing around in the direction opposite to the movement of the eye. Thus the stability of the visual field holds only for eye movements initiated by signals from the brain. Passive eye movements result in an apparent movement of the visual field.

To maintain the stability of the visual world during eye movements, the eye–head movement system seems to operate in a complex fashion, whereby signals to the eye muscles are compared to signals arriving from the retina indicating changes in retinal image position. Figure 12-4 illustrates the difference between the inflow and the outflow theories of the eye–head movement system. As is the case with many phenomena we discuss, both inflow and outflow may be needed to provide a full explanation of this movement system. Table 12-1 presents a summary of the actions of the image–retina and eye–head movement systems. Demonstration Boxes 12-5 and 12-6 give other interesting examples that illustrate the relationships between eye movements, visual stability, and the perception of motion.

Movement Sensitivity. Now that we have discussed the conditions under which we can discern the movement of objects, we can ask "What is the minimum amount of motion that is necessary before we perceive an object as moving?" To answer this question, we must measure a movement threshold just as we established thresholds for the minimum amount of light or sound needed for perception (see Chapter 2). Our sensitivity to the movement of an external target depends upon several variables. In experimental settings, movement thresholds have usually been studied using a small point of light that moves against some sort of stationary background. For instance, Hermann Aubert (1886) found that observers could detect the movement of a luminous dot in the dark 50 cm from the eye, when it was moving at about 2.5 mm per sec (which is about two-tenths of a degree of visual angle per second).

However, our ability to detect motion increases when there is a stationary background, such as a square frame surrounding the dot, that is visible to the observer. Under these circumstances one finds that observers are 10 times more sensitive. The minimum movement that can be detected is about .25 mm per sec (or three-hundredths of a degree per second). This small displacement per unit of time represents an incredible degree of movement sensitivity. If a snail were to crawl across a desk $1\frac{1}{2}$ m wide at this rate, it would take it an hour and forty minutes to go from end to end. This finding demonstrates that our perception of movement is facilitated by the presence of other stimuli that are stationary or moving at different rates. When such stimuli are present, the observer can take advantage of the spatial change relative to the other background stimuli. Thus we can say that observers are more sensitive to *relative* movement than they are to *absolute* movement.

Movement sensitivity will also vary depending upon whether the eye is stationary or moving. This is shown by a phenomenon known as the AUBERT–FLEISCHL PARADOX (named for the two researchers who explored the effect). These investigators noted that when we track a target with our eyes while it

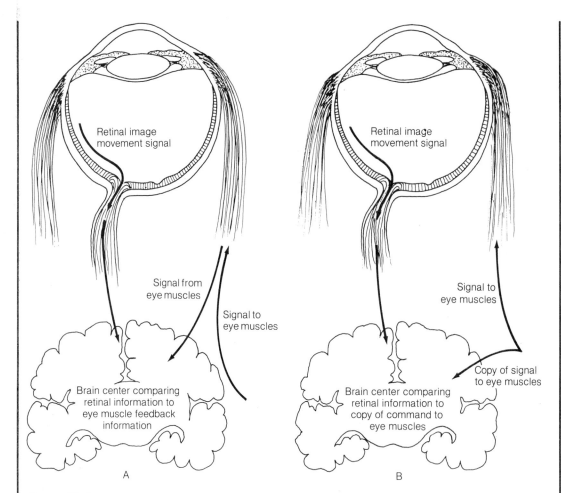

Figure 12-4.
The second function of the eye–head movement system is to maintain the stability of the visual world during eye movements. The inflow theory (A) states that this is accomplished by comparing movement signals from the retina with proprioceptive feedback from the eye muscles which indicates that the eye has moved. The outflow theory (B) maintains that commands from the brain to initiate voluntary eye movements cancel the movement information coming from the retina as the eyes move.

moves relative to a stationary background, it appears to move more slowly than it would if we were to fixate steadily upon the stationary background. This phenomenon was called a paradox because it seemed that pursuit of the moving target should provide a more salient impression of motion, since both the image movement of the background and the signals

Table 12-1 *The Effect of Retinal Image Change and Voluntary Eye Movements on the Perception of Motion*

Physical Target	Action of Eye	Retinal Image	Commands to Eye (Head)	Perception
Image–retina				
Moving	Stationary	Moves	None	Movement
Eye–head				
Moving	Tracks target	Stationary on fovea	Yes	Movement
Stationary	Moves	Moves	Yes	No movement
Stationary	Passively pushed	Moves	None	Movement in direction opposite eye motion
Image stabilized on retina	Moves	Stationary on retina	Yes	Movement in same direction as eye motion

One can readily experience one of the ways in which the eye–head movement system differentiates external from observer movement. The first thing that is needed is to generate a STABILIZED RETINAL IMAGE. Ordinarily, the retinal image is in constant motion and stimulates varying groups of receptors at a rapid rate. However, by quickly satiating or fatiguing a single group of retinal receptors, we can generate an image that maintains its position regardless of eye movements. Many of you are probably familiar with the technique used to give rise to such an image if you have ever had your picture taken with a flashbulb attached to the camera. If you looked at the light while it flashed, you may have noticed a purple dot that tended to linger in your field of view for some time after the picture was taken. This purple dot is called an AFTERIMAGE. It is one example of a stabilized retinal image. The afterimage does not shift position on the retina. It stays in a constant position regardless of how we move our eyes. We can use the afterimage to demonstrate the operation of the eye–head movement system.

Perhaps the easiest way to generate an afterimage is to look at a rather bright but small source of light for a brief period of time. Make a 1-cm hole in an index card and hold it up in front of a light bulb. Look at the hole for a few moments and this should provide a clearly visible afterimage when you look away from the light. Now notice that each time you move your eyes the afterimage seems to jump in the same direction. This apparent movement is due to the action of the eye–head system. Commands have been issued to the eye to move, yet the image remains on the same place on the retina. This could only occur if the image had moved as much as the eye (see Table 12-1). You may also notice that the image sometimes seems to drift smoothly from place to place. Again, the image never moves; the movement is signaled from the movements of your eyes. This is one example of how the action of the eye–head movement system can lead to illusions of motion.

Demonstration Box 12-5:
Afterimages and Apparent Movement

Demonstration Box 12-6:
The Autokinetic Effect

There is an interesting phenomenon in which movement is seen in the absence of any physical motion of the target. The word used to describe the occurrence is *autokinesis*, which means self moving. For this experiment, you will need a *very dark* room. No stray light of any sort should be visible. In addition you will need a small dim point of light (a lighted cigarette works fine). Place the point of light about 2 m away from you and look at it steadily. After a few minutes it should appear to move, perhaps slowly drifting in one direction or another. Of course the light is still stationary; hence the movement is an illusion, which is called the **AUTOKINETIC EFFECT**.

The autokinetic effect demonstrates the outflow principle that operates in the eye–head movement system. The visual system only monitors commands to initiate voluntary eye movements. However, these are not the only types of eye movements possible. Our eyes also exhibit involuntary eye movements. As you may have guessed, these are not monitored by the visual system. One type of involuntary eye movement is **EYE DRIFT**, and this is the mechanism that has been implicated in the autokinetic effect (Matin & MacKinnon, 1964). When we steadily fixate or stare at a target, it is difficult for the eyes to maintain steady and accurate fixation on that one point in space (Ditchburn, 1973). The eyes will tend to drift off of the fixation point; however, the visual system does not monitor this movement until it exceeds a critical point. In the autokinetic situation, retinal image movement has been signaled in the absence of commands to initiate voluntary eye movements. This is the situation under which the movement of the retinal image is attributed to an externally moving object (see Table 12-1). There is no information that the eyes have moved, so illusory movement of the dim spot of light is seen.

from the moving eye are present. This phenomenon can lead to several perceptual distortions. An observer will not only underestimate the velocity of a target that is tracked with the eye but will also tend to underestimate the distance that the target has moved (Mack & Herman, 1972). Overall, these data may simply indicate that the eye–head movement system is not as sensitive as the image–retina system.

Movement sensitivity also varies for different retinal locations. You will probably recall from Chapter 7 that visual acuity diminishes as we move away from the fovea. In a similar fashion our ability to detect slow target movements (up to about 1.5° per second) decreases with distance from the fovea (Lichtenstein, 1963; McColgin, 1960). For higher target velocities, however, this relationship reverses. At moderate to fast velocities, the peripheral retina seems better able to detect movement, even though the decrease in acuity is so great that the observer may not be able to recognize what is moving (Bhatia, 1975; B. Brown, 1972).

There are probably anatomical reasons for this difference. As we noted in Chapter 4 there are two major types of retinal ganglion cells, which differ in terms of the speed of information transmission, receptive field size, and in the nature of their neural response. These are usually called X and Y cells. The Y cells produce faster, more transient responses than X cells (Enroth-Cugell & Robson, 1966; Hoffman, 1973). Furthermore, X cells seem to be more frequently found in the central retina and Y cells in the periphery (Stone & Dreher, 1973). Some investigators have suggested that the X cells in central vision are specialized for maximum visual acuity, while the Y cells in the periphery are specialized for the detection of motion (Breitmeyer, Love, & Wepman, 1974; Tolhurst, 1973). It may be this retinal specialization that permits easier detection of a moving rather than a stationary target in the peripheral retina. You can experience this effect for yourself using Demonstration Box 12-7.

Context and Movement. In the preceding

Demonstration Box 12-7:
The Troxler Effect

The **TROXLER EFFECT** can be used to demonstrate the salience of movement stimulation in the peripheral retina. The Troxler effect deals with the fact that stationary targets, which stimulate the peripheral retina, will disappear under conditions of steady, unmoving stimulation. However, it can also be used to illustrate how movement in the periphery can revitalize the percept of a target that has faded.

Take a sheet of blank typing paper. Using the longer side (the 27.5-cm side), place a small fixation dot at one end of the paper and a straight line at the opposite end. The diagram given below can help you to visualize the stimulus conditions. Now hold the paper in front of you at a distance of about 25 cm. Make sure that the fixation dot is directly in front of you so that you can look directly at it. While fixating the dot, try to pay attention to the straight line in your peripheral visual field (but keep your eyes on the dot). After about 10–15 sec, you should notice that the line in the peripheral field has faded from view (i.e., the Troxler effect). Now, gently shake the paper, and the line will reappear. Thus the movement of an image can cause its reappearance in the peripheral retina.

● Fixation point

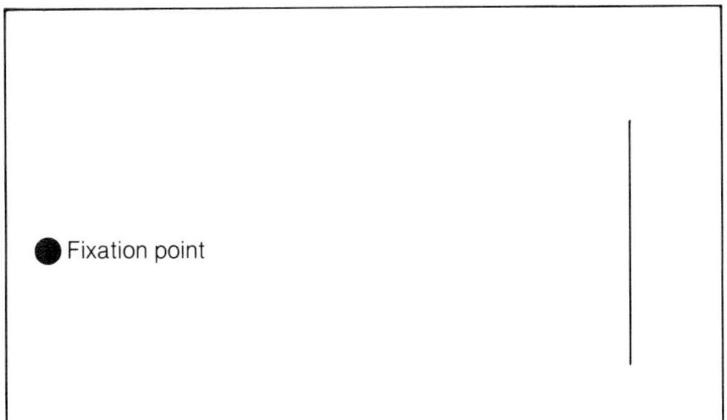

section we saw how the addition of a visual context or background can increase our sensitivity to motion. Actually, under certain conditions a visual context can also distort our perception of movement. For example, Duncker (1929) placed a bright dot in a dark visual field. When the dot was moved very slowly, observers were not certain whether or not it was moving. However, when a stationary dot was placed near the moving dot (in effect becoming the visual context), it became quite clear that one of the dots was in motion. Curiously, observers could not identify *which* of the two dots was moving. Duncker then altered the context somewhat. He replaced the stationary dot with a stationary luminous frame that was rectangular and surrounded the dot. Under these circumstances the former ambiguity was removed. Observers were now able to tell that the dot rather than the frame was in motion. Duncker now varied his experiment so that the dot was stationary and the surrounding rectangular frame was moving. Under these circumstances it was the dot rather than the frame that appeared to be moving. In other words, Duncker had produced an illusion of movement in the stationary dot by moving the surrounding context. Duncker called this INDUCED MOTION since the perceived movement of the dot was induced or brought about by the real movement of the surrounding context.

A common example of this same phenomenon occurs in everyday life. On a moonlit night we sometimes perceive the moon as rushing through clouds, when actually the clouds are moving while the moon maintains a stationary position in the sky. The clouds provide a surrounding context that is in motion and, consistent with the principle that Duncker discovered in the laboratory, they induce an apparent motion of the stationary moon. Duncker's PRINCIPLE OF SURROUNDEDNESS, in which an enclosed or sur-

rounded object is perceived to move relative to an enclosing or surrounding object, summarizes both the laboratory results and the everyday experience.

There is another interesting everyday example of this principle. Probably most of you have had the experience of sitting in a bus or a train parked next to another vehicle. All at once the adjacent vehicle starts to move. However, instead of correctly attributing the movement to the vehicle next to your own, you have a powerful sensation of yourself in motion. In this case the principle of surroundedness has produced an *induced motion of the self*. As the surrounded object, you feel yourself to be in motion. It is a very powerful sensation that can be difficult to overcome even when you become aware of the source of real movement.

Induced motion seems to depend upon certain relationships between the target and the frame. For instance, Wallach (1972a) used an arrangement in which a small target was surrounded by a rectangular frame, which in turn was surrounded by a larger circular frame as shown in Figure 12-5. An interesting thing happens when we move the rectangle in one direction and the circle in another. Suppose the rectangle was moved toward the left and the circular framework was moved downward. In both cases, the speed of movement was quite slow. One would expect that since the dot was enclosed by two frames, the rectangle and the circle, the motion induced in the dot would be affected by both the direction of the movement of the rectangle and by the direction of the movement of the circle. If the final induced motion is the average of that caused by each frame alone, we might expect it to move along a diagonal path upward and to the right. However, the induced movement of the dot is only affected by the closest frame. Thus the dot seems to move to the right along a horizontal path in a direction opposite to the real

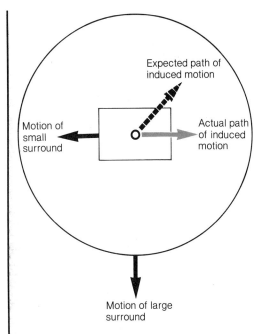

Expected path of
induced motion

Motion of
small
surround

Actual path
of induced
motion

Motion of large
surround

Figure 12-5.
The direction of induced motion seems to be affected only by the immediate context or surround. Here real movement is indicated by the heavy black arrows, induced motion by the gray arrow, and the expected motion by the dotted arrow.

movement of the rectangle. This is the same path that the dot would take (in terms of its induced motion) if only the rectangular frame was present and moving.

Gogel and Koslow (1972) have shown that in order to induce motion, the target and the background must be at the same distance from the observer. If the frame that supplies the context is too far in front of or behind the target, no motion will be induced. This *principle of spatial adjacency* makes it possible to put two different frames on separate sides of the visual field, and by moving them in opposite directions to induce motion in two opposite directions for enclosed targets (Gogel, 1977). These results show that our perception of movement does not depend simply upon physical motion, but it also involves complex processing of many variables. The background is as important as the moving target.

Biological Motion. Many of the experiments that we have been describing use rather simple stimuli. However, we could question the relevance of these experimental findings to real-world situations where we experience very complex motion patterns. Thus it is of interest to know if observers can detect and identify more complex movement patterns that can be related more directly to our everyday experience of movement. In a series of recent studies, Johansson (1976a) has investigated what he has called BIOLOGICAL MOTIONS. Although he and his co-workers have done a number of studies that have shown how various perspective transformations can predict the motion of differing objects, perhaps his most interesting work is with movement patterns.

Consider the intricate coordinations of the series of movement patterns accomplished by the skeletal structure when one walks across the room. Even in this simple act many precise movements are occurring in a coordinated pattern. Would an observer be able to identify these motions as the act of walking even in the absence of any other information? To answer this question Johansson and his co-workers used the following technique. They attached small flashlight bulbs to the shoulders, elbows, wrists, hips, knees, and ankles of an individual (see Figure 12-6A). They then made a motion picture film of the person as he moved around in a darkened room. Observers who watched the film saw only a pattern of lights moving about in total darkness. Observers were not only able to tell that it was a person walking, but they were also able to detect abnormalities, such as the simulation of a small limp. In another experiment two people with similar arrays of lights were filmed while performing a spirited folk

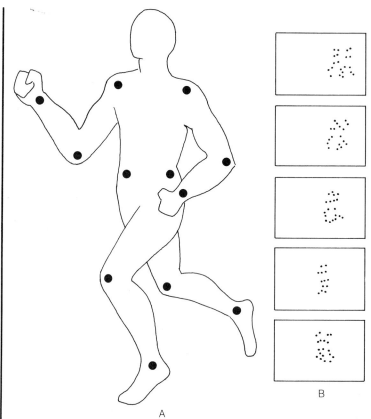

A

B

Figure 12-6.
An example of the type of displays used by investigators to study patterns of humans in motion. (A) Positions of lights affixed to individuals. (B) A sequence of movement positions made by a dancing couple.

dance. (Figure 12-6B shows a series of sequential positions from the folk dance in which the black dots mark the positions of the lights.) Once again, even with only a moving pattern of lights, observers had no difficulty recognizing that the motion was actually a dancing couple. Johansson (1976b) was also able to show that observers need very little time to make these identifications. In fact, 200 msec seems to be sufficient for the recognition of a pattern of lights as a human body in motion.

Other investigators (Barclay, Cutting, & Kozlowski, 1978; Cutting & Kozlowski, 1977; Kozlowski & Cutting, 1977) have extended and elaborated upon these findings. For example, in one study they photographed a group of people who were acquainted with

one another, in a manner similar to the technique used by Johansson. The individuals were photographed with only lighted portions of several joints visible. Several months later these same individuals were invited to watch the films and attempt to identify themselves and their friends in the motion picture. The observers were able to identify themselves and others correctly on a fair percentage of trials, although their performance was not perfect. These investigators also asked their observers how they went about making their identifications of various individuals in the film. Observers mentioned a variety of motion components such as the speed, bounciness, and rhythm of the walker, the amount of arm swing, or the length of steps as features that allowed them to make their identification. In other studies, these same investigators found that observers could tell, even under these conditions, whether a person was a male or a female, despite seeing only a moving pattern of dots. In fact, it was not necessary for all of the bodily joints to be represented in the light display for people to make correct identifications. Even when only the ankles alone were represented in the light display, observers could detect the sex of the walker. They could also make these gender identifications within about 5 sec of viewing. This indicates that not only are there biological motion patterns that can be readily identified, but also there are motion patterns that become part of one's sex identification as well as part of one's identity itself. It seems analogous to the uniqueness of a person's facial feature composition. This type of research lends support to the notion that motion perception is a primary ability that is integrated into our ability to recognize familiar objects. It is part of our perceptual world, and it is not derived from a simple series of successive transformations of static objects in the environment.

13
Form

The inventor sat musing at his workbench. Although he had a robot that could move incredibly fast, and that was remarkably strong, he still had problems. Despite the fact that the eye sockets had been equipped with extremely sensitive television cameras, he still could not decide how to instruct the robot to respond to the patterns that represent objects in the world. The first problem arose when he had directed the mechanical man to pick up the object in front of him, which was simply a cup on a table. Instead the robot lifted the entire table. Certainly any child can tell the difference between an object and its background. Why couldn't this marvelous machine do it? He had checked the circuits carefully, and they had picked up every contour and every change in brightness that passed in front of the camera lens. Perhaps there is more to the perception of forms and patterns than simply the perception of the contours defining them. The inventor mused, "I wonder how I know where the cup ends and the table begins?"

CONTOUR

The basic element needed for visual form perception is the presence of a CONTOUR. A contour can be defined as an area within the visual array where there is an abrupt change in luminance. For example, a simple contour, and probably one of the simplest visual forms, would be generated by drawing a black line on a white sheet of paper. The sharp change from black to white would define this line as a visible contour. The normal optic array is filled with contour information, and an area completely enclosed by a contour is usually seen as a distinct and separate form. The presence of a series of contour bounded "blobs" in the incoming visual stimulation is usually perceived as a group of objects in the external environment.

Visual Contour and Stimulus Change. In many respects all visual perception is dependent upon the presence of contours. This can be demonstrated by eliminating any abrupt brightness changes in the visual field. A field that contains no visible contours is called a GANZFELD (which is German for "blank field"). A series of studies have shown that perception in a Ganzfeld is quite unusual. Observers generally report that all they see is "a shapeless fog which goes on forever." If the field is filled with colored light, any hint of hue fades in a few moments, and all returns to the gray fog (Cohen, 1958). After prolonged exposure to the Ganzfeld, many observers experience a perceptual *blank out,* which is the phenomenal impression that all sense of vision has been lost. It is almost as if one had gone blind. Vision, however, can be quickly returned by simply casting a shadow or introducing a change in brightness in one local region of the field (Avant, 1965; Cohen, 1957). If the luminance difference is large enough, observers report that they see a contour bounding the luminance change. Blank out never occurs with an adequate number of contours in the field. The very existence of blank out, and its dissipation when contours are in the field, indicates that areas of abrupt intensity change (in other words, contours) are necessary for vision. Blank outs can also occur in natural environments. For instance, in the Arctic when the terrain is covered by snow and there is little luminance change within the retinal image, we have a naturally occurring Ganzfeld. *Snow blindness,* where observers report that they lose their sense of sight under these conditions, is nothing more than an instance of blank out. You may experience some of the sensations associated with the Ganzfeld for yourself by using Demonstration Box 13-1.

There are other conditions that can lead to a disruption of normal contour information and also tend to eliminate form perception. In

Although Ganzfeld situations have been produced with elaborate laboratory equipment, there are several simple ways to produce a Ganzfeld that will allow you to experience this contourless field for yourself. You can take a table tennis ball and cut it in half, placing one-half over each eye, or you can use two white plastic spoons (like those probably available in any campus cafeteria) to produce a Ganzfeld by placing the bowls of the two spoons over each eye as shown in the accompanying figure. Direct your gaze toward a light source (a flourescent lamp, say) prior to placing either of these objects before your eyes, so that your field of view will be flooded with diffuse, contourless light. Stay in this position for a few minutes and monitor any changes or alterations in your conscious perceptual experience. If the light originally had a tint, you will soon notice that the color will fade into a gray. After a while you will suddenly feel that you cannot see. This feeling of blindness is called "blank out." It seems that in the absence of contours in the field, vision ceases. If a friend now casts a shadow over part of the field (say, with a pencil across the spoons), vision will immediately return with the introduction of this contour.

Spoon

Chapter 12 we discussed an experimental technique that produces a STABILIZED RETINAL IMAGE. You may remember that a stabilized retinal image is one that stimulates the same group of retinal receptors regardless of how the eye moves. In other words, the image is stopped or immobile and does not move across the retinal surface as we shift our eyes from target to target. Research has demonstrated that when an image is stabilized upon the retinal surface, it does not stay visible for very long. In fact a general loss of color and contour information seems to occur within a few seconds after the image is presented to the eye (Heckenmueller, 1965; Pritchard, Heron & Hebb, 1960; Riggs, Ratliff, Cornsweet & Cornsweet, 1953; Yarbus, 1967). Since we normally have little difficulty in keeping nonstabilized targets in view for as long as we wish to look at them, we must ask what causes the stabilized retinal image to fade.

Our eyes are always scanning the visual field. Even when we fixate (stare steadily at) a particular place in the visual field, tiny involuntary eye movements, called microsaccades, continue to occur. These small eye movements occur many times per second; thus the retinal image is constantly slipping and sliding over different retinal receptors as the eye quivers. For any given retinal receptor there will be a period of time when it is being stimulated by one part of the visual array, followed by a period of time when that image has slipped off of this receptor due to a tiny eye movement, and another stimulus has taken its place. In other words, there are temporal variations ("on" times followed by "off" times) in the stimulation. When we artificially stabilize the retinal image, we remove these temporal variations. Since the stabilized image fades from view after a brief period, this means that a luminance difference in the visual field is not sufficient for contour perception. Continual change in the stimulation is needed for one percept to re-

main active. This is further supported by the fact that flickering the stabilized image on and off will tend to keep it from fading (Cornsweet, 1956).

We can interpret the information gained from research using the Ganzfeld and the stabilized retinal image technique as indicating that vision requires temporal or spatial change to function normally. When changes or local luminance differences are removed, such as when the visual field contains no contours at all, or when we stop temporal variation across the retinal receptors, consciousness of visual stimulation ceases, and no forms, patterns, or stimulus gradations are seen. The importance of change may explain the function of lateral inhibition (as discussed in Chapter 7), which tends to emphasize contours by accentuating the spatial change from a bright to a dark area. In any event, contours are one form of local stimulus change to which the visual system seems to be especially attuned (Arend, 1973).

Emergence of Visual Contours. An important characteristic of visual contours is that they do not appear immediately to our conscious experience. Some time must elapse between the presentation and the perceptual experience of a contour. If we interfere with the process before this time has passed, we may never see the contour. This was first demonstrated in an ingenious experiment by Werner (1935). He briefly flashed a stimulus that was simply a black disk on a white background (the target), and then followed this a short time later with a quick exposure of a black ring (the mask) in the same region of the visual field. The inner circumference of the ring just matched the outer circumference of the disk. He varied the time between when the disk disappeared from view and when the ring first appeared (as you recall, this is known as the interstimulus interval). When the interstimulus interval was between 100 and

200 msec, observers often reported that they could not see the disk at all, or that it had become less distinct, or dimmer, and that its boundary was hazy. This experiment and its results are diagrammed in Figure 13-1. Werner (1935) interpreted the apparent disappearance of the disk as indicating that the inner contour of the ring had interfered with the formation of the contour of the disk, thus preventing it from appearing in consciousness. When the interval between the stimuli was too great, the disk contour had already formed and its perception was impervious to interference. This general kind of phenomenon, in which one stimulus interferes with the perception of another, has come to be called BACKWARD MASKING (backward, because the second stimulus masks a target that has already come and gone). When contours on adjacent parts of the retina interfere with each other, we sometimes call this situation METACONTRAST to differentiate it from other forms of visual masking. We now know that contours can be masked by flashes of light, by random conglomerations of contours or dots, by fields of bars, stripes, and curves of all descriptions, and by a wide variety of more specific visual contours (Kahneman, 1968; Lefton, 1973). Metacontrast is of most interest to us here, since it deals with the interaction of adjacent contours. Since Werner's (1935) study, a number of investigators have produced the general finding that there is a particular interstimulus interval between a target and a mask that results in the most contour interference. This time is usually between 30 and 100 msec (Lefton, 1973). Because of this, the results of masking experiments may be shown as an inverted U-shaped function as indicated by the solid line in Figure 13-2. The actual relationship between the temporal separation of the stimuli and the amount of masking is still a matter of some controversy. Inverted-U rela-

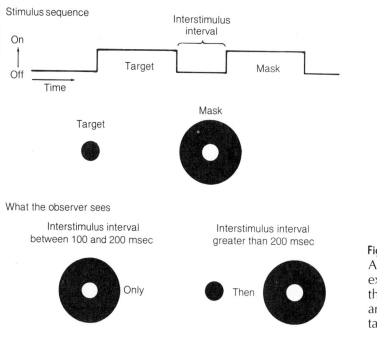

Figure 13-1.
A typical metacontrast experiment. Notice that when the interstimulus interval is of an appropriate length, the target is not seen at all.

tionships are reported by many people when the target and mask are about equally intense; otherwise, if the mask is very much brighter than the target, a different relationship is found. The most masking is found for the shortest target and mask separations, and the effect diminishes as the interval increases as shown by the dotted line in Figure 13-2.

Since visual masking tends to obliterate our perception of contours, it is probably involved with some of the same mechanisms that give rise to our perception of contours in the first place. On the basis of masking data, three ideas have been offered to explain how contours interact over time. The first suggests that the contour interactions result from lateral interactions between visual neurons (as we discussed in Chapter 7). One contour can mask another when the excitation aroused by the target contour is overcome by the inhibition aroused by the mask's contours (Weisstein, 1968; Weisstein, Ozog & Szoc, 1975). The second idea involves a notion similar to the psychological moment discussed in Chapter 12. It uses the concept of ICONIC MEMORY, which contends that each stimulus has an effect on the sensory system that lasts for a little while after the stimulus itself ceases (usually about 250 msec). If two stimuli enter the system within this brief time period, they add together (if they are sufficiently similar); or, the processing of the first set of contours may be canceled or blocked in order to process the most recent contour information (see Reed, 1973). The last idea maintains that contour perception requires more than the simple detection of a luminance difference between two regions of the visual field. There are even suggestions that the visual system decomposes brightness variations into their separate spatial components in much the same way that the ear can separate the various frequencies that make up a musical chord (see the Special Topic in Chapter 7). Simple contours are thus not so simple.

FIGURE

In our discussion of contour we said that the simplest perceptible form is a straight line. However, most of our visual experience is composed of integrated units that we call FIGURES. A group of straight lines of equal length joined together to form four equal angles of 90° is the figure we call a square. Thus, figures are integrated groups of contours. The perception of figure is basic to our other perceptual experiences. We must be able to differentiate figures as distinct from the backgrounds (or just GROUNDS) from which they emerge. Therefore, we must be able to distinguish that a pen or a coffee cup are separate entities which are different from the desk upon which they rest (remember the robot's problem). Unfortunately, the simple

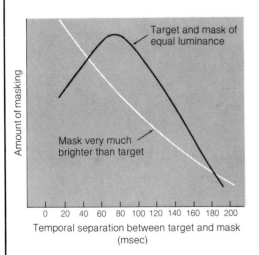

Figure 13-2.
The relationship between the amount of visual masking and the time interval between target and mask. Notice that different relationships are found depending upon the relative luminance of target and mask.

perceptual separation of figures, from each other and from the surrounding stimuli that make up their background, involves some complex processes.

Figure–Ground Separation. Figure 13-3 illustrates one of the complexities of the figure–ground problem. It is an example of an ambiguous or reversible pattern. By reversible we mean our perception of what is seen as ground (background) within this configuration can alternate or reverse. When you look at this picture you might see a bird bath or a vase which appears as a white figure clearly standing in front of the black background. Yet a few moments of viewing might cause the percept to change. Now you see two silhouette faces looking at each other. The black of the faces seems to be in front of the white of the background. Another in-

teresting aspect of this reversal is that the contour (defining the face or the vase) always "belongs" to the figure. It seems to "hold the figure together." Notice also that you cannot "see" both the faces and the vase simultaneously. They seem to alternate in consciousness. This demonstration points out that the perception of figures is a psychological act of interpretation, and not necessarily directly predictable from the stimulus array. Thus, to see a bear emerge from the bushes, one must first process the information to determine that bear and bush are separate entities.

We have already noted some of the perceived differences between figure and ground. Rubin (1915, 1921) also noted that figures usually appear closer than the ground, appear to be more "thinglike," and seem to have a shape, as opposed to the

Figure 13-3.
A reversible figure-ground stimulus in which a pair of black faces or a white bird bath are seen alternately.

background, which is relatively formless. Figures usually are seen as more meaningful and are more easily remembered. To these characteristics we can add Coren's (1969a) observation that the region perceived as figure shows more brightness contrast than the same area perceived as ground. Although we can list the perceptual attributes that distinguish figures from ground, we are still a long way from fully understanding the stimulus factors and psychological processing that distinguish the figure from the ground. Some factors have been isolated, however. For instance Figure 13-4A shows a reversible figure that alternately appears as a light X or a dark Maltese cross. In Figure 13-4B we have simply altered the size of the sectors, yet it is now much easier to see the dark X than it is to see the light cross. It becomes apparent that the smaller the stimulus the more likely it is to be seen as figure.

It may have occurred to you that there is another factor that aids in separation of figure from ground in normal viewing situations. Invariably there is a discriminable difference in depth between them. Remember that one of the properties mentioned by Rubin in his catalog of figure-ground differences was that the figure appears to be closer than ground. Perhaps it is this depth difference that *causes*

the separation of figure and ground, which would imply that reversible figure-ground percepts only arise in situations where we are dealing with flat stimulus arrays where the usual depth information (see Chapter 11) cannot be employed. There is an interesting phenomenon that illustrates how form can emerge through the use of depth cues in a two-dimensional array. Look at Figure 13-5. Here we have an array that seems to contain a white triangle, which is seen as figure, against a background of three black squares and an outlined triangle. Despite the fact that the perception of the white triangular figure is quite compelling, there are actually no real contours (abrupt changes from dark to light) that define the triangular figure. The contours we "see" are not physically present. Figures like this triangle are called SUBJECTIVE CONTOUR FIGURES since the observer perceptually "creates" the contours defining the form.

One of the explanations offered for subjective contours is relevant to our discussion of the emergence of figure from ground in two-dimensional arrays. Coren (1972) has suggested that subjective contours arise when we use depth cues within a configuration to help organize an otherwise meaningless array into a simpler, more meaningful figure. In the case of Figure 13-5, the depth cue that

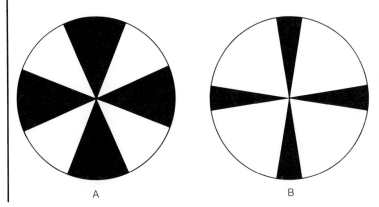

A   B

Figure 13-4.
Figure (A) is an ambiguous figure-ground stimulus in which a white X and a black Maltese cross are seen alternately. In (B), the smaller figure (the black cross) is now dominant.

Figure 13-5.
A subjective contour figure in which a white central triangle is seen although none actually exists (from Coren, S. *Psychological Review,* 1972, **79.** © 1972 by the American Psychological Association. Reprinted by permission).

is present within this array is interposition. As you may remember from our discussion of depth cues in Chapter 11, when one object blocks our vision of another object, the occluded object is perceived as being the more distant one. In the case of subjective contour figures, the presence of interposition cues helps to provide a meaningful figural organization for the gaps in the squares and in the outlined triangle. Figure emerges from ground as a consequence of this process. An imaginary contour arises to separate the figure from the ground, which heightens the perceived depth separation. The figure defined by such a subjective contour acts remarkably like a "real" contour, even to the extent that it can *mask* a real contour (Weisstein, Matthews & Berbaum, 1977). The emergence of subjective contours may indicate that the segregation of figure from ground is related to the separation of our visual world into various depth planes.

There is additional evidence that depth cues of some sort may be important in the emergence of visual forms. Julesz (1971) has shown this in an imaginative series of demonstrations and experiments. One of the very powerful physiological cues used to discriminate depth is BINOCULAR DISPARITY. Since the eyes view the world from slightly different directions, the images in the two eyes are not exactly the same. They are said to be binocularly disparate. As we noted in Chapter 11, we can simulate this natural disparity by drawing flat pictures that mimic the difference between the two eyes' views. These are called STEREOGRAMS. When placed in a stereoscope, the visual system responds to the simulated disparity and the observer perceives depth. Julesz made a set of stereograms out of computer-generated random dot patterns. In the center of one eye's view, he displaced (or made disparate relative to the other eye) a rectangular group of dots. This shift in the center group of dots in half of the stereogram introduced the depth cue of binocular disparity into the random dot array. The manner in which this was done is shown in Figure 13-6. When viewing the two halves of the stereogram with each eye separately, one only sees a group of random dots. However, when viewed stereoscopically so that the depth cue can operate, the rectangular form emerges, apparently floating in front of a random dot background. Thus the disparity that was introduced into this meaningless pattern is used by the visual system not only to organize the array into two separate depth planes, but also to create the rectangular form. Julesz has coined the term CYCLOPEAN PERCEPTION, referring to the mythical one-eyed cyclops, to describe such percepts. Not until the two views are fused into one is either the depth or the form seen. You may experience the emergence of form from a random dot array using Demonstration Box 13-2.

Implicit depth cues may carry over to

Left eye view · Right eye view

A

1	0	1	0	1	0	0	1	0	1
1	0	0	1	0	1	0	1	0	0
0	0	1	1	0	1	1	0	1	0
0	1	0	Y	A	A	B	B	0	1
1	1	1	X	B	A	B	A	0	1
0	0	1	X	A	A	B	A	1	0
1	1	1	Y	B	B	A	B	0	1
1	0	0	1	1	0	1	1	0	1
1	1	0	0	1	1	0	1	1	1
0	1	0	0	0	1	1	1	1	0

1	0	1	0	1	0	0	1	0	1
1	0	0	1	0	1	0	1	0	0
0	0	1	1	0	1	1	0	1	0
0	1	0	A	A	B	B	X	0	1
1	1	1	B	A	B	A	Y	0	1
0	0	1	A	A	B	A	Y	1	0
1	1	1	B	B	A	B	X	0	1
1	0	0	1	1	0	1	1	0	1
1	1	0	0	1	1	0	1	1	1
0	1	0	0	0	1	1	1	1	0

Displaced center square

B

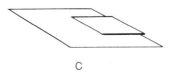

C

Figure 13-6.
Figure (A) is a random dot stereogram. Figure (B) shows how (A) is
constructed, while (C) illustrates that a central square is seen
floating above the background when the upper views are
perceptually combined in a stereoscope (from Julesz, B.
Foundations of Cyclopean Perception. © 1971 by The University
of Chicago Press).

You may demonstrate how depth cues can bring about the perception of form by using the accompanying figure, which incorporates the same principle used by Julesz (1971) in his demonstrations. You will need a pocket mirror, which should be placed on the dotted center line of Figure B while you hold your head as shown in Figure A. Adjust the images until the two views seem to overlap and the frames around the outside seem to be at the same distance. Viewing it in this way you will see a square form emerge, floating above the background, created completely by the depth cue of binocular disparity.

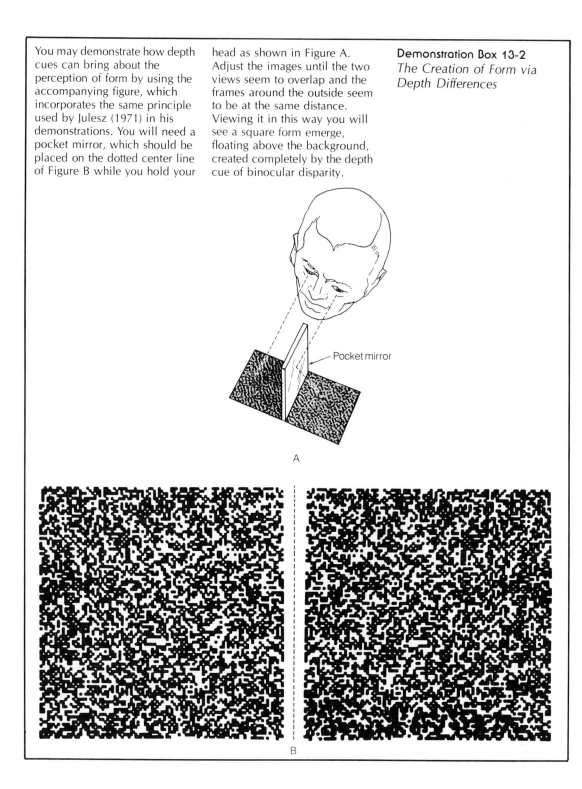

A

B

two-dimensional situations and assist us in achieving meaningful figural organizations. An outlined square on a piece of white paper may be seen as a figure because it blocks part of our perception of the white surface (via interposition), thus being perceptually pushed forward as a figure. Hochberg (1971b) has proposed an alternate view, maintaining that we make certain eye and head movements to take in information from real world scenes. These regular movement patterns lead us to expect certain kinds of figures and grounds to appear in certain ways. These expectations are called SCHEMAS or COGNITIVE MAPS, which are internal models of objects in the world based upon our experiences and habits. These may form the basis of figure-ground separation in perception. An example of such habits in operation can be seen when we consider how stimulus motion can give an array the quality of being an object, thus changing its perceived form. This is the so-called KINETIC DEPTH EFFECT discussed by Gibson (1966), Rock (1975), and Kaufman (1974). Demonstration Box 13-3 illustrates this effect.

In order to see how movement can create the impression of a three-dimensional form in a two-dimensional array, you will need a candle and a piece of stiff wire (a coat hanger or long pipe cleaner will do). Bend the wire into a random three-dimensional shape. Now light the candle and darken the room. Place the bent wire so that it casts a shadow on a blank wall as shown in the figure. Notice that, when the shape is absolutely motionless, the shadow is easily seen as a flat pattern of lines. Now, if you rotate it with your hand, the shadow suddenly changes form, becoming a three-dimensional object that cannot be seen as flat, despite the fact that you are viewing a two-dimensional shadow.

Demonstration Box 13-3
Kinetic Depth

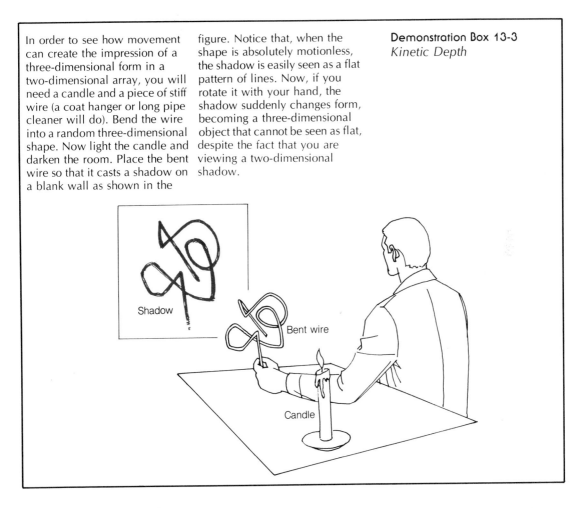

Shadow

Bent wire

Candle

Laws of Figural Organization. Most of the visual patterns we perceive are composed of a number of elements. Another way that a figure and a ground could be differentiated is by the grouping of elements to form a figure. This approach was emphasized by a group of psychologists (Max Wertheimer, Kurt Koffka, and Wolfgang Köhler were the most influential), who formed the GESTALT School of psychology. Gestalt is a German word that can be translated to mean "form," "whole," or even "whole form." The Gestaltists were interested in processes that cause certain elements to seem to be part of the same figure or grouping, while others seem to belong to other figures or groups. They formulated several laws of perceptual organization that govern the emergence of a visual figure (Wertheimer, 1923). They argued that elements within a pattern do not operate independently. Rather, there are attractive "forces" among the various elements that cause them to form a meaningful and coherent figure, much as gravity organizes the planets, sun, and moons of our solar system. They described how certain regular properties of elements within a pattern bring about the emergence of stable figures.

Figure 13-7A is usually seen as two clusters of dots. Although the array actually contains 12 individual elements (dots), our perception reduces this to the experience of two groups. This is an example of the LAW OF PROXIMITY, which states that elements close to one another tend to be seen as a perceptual unit or figure. Figure 13-7B is generally seen as a triangle composed of black dots on a background of (or surrounded by a swarm of) *X*'s. This is an example of the operation of the LAW OF SIMILARITY, which maintains that similar objects tend to be grouped together. Another example of this law is seen in Figure 13-7C where the two halves of the circular field appear quite separate because of grouping by similarity. Figure 13-7D is usually

viewed as a spiral of dots with one standing outside. This is an example of the principle of GOOD CONTINUATION, which holds that elements that appear to follow in the same direction (as in a straight line or simple curve) tend to be grouped together. Figure 13-7E is an example of the principle of CLOSURE, which maintains that when a space is enclosed by a contour it tends to be perceived as a figure. Most people see a diamond between two vertical lines here. Actually Figure 13-7E also could be seen as a letter *W* stacked on a letter *M*, were it not for the compelling nature of closure. Closure also allows us to complete broken contours as in Figure 13-7F, which is seen as a triangle rather than as three separated acute angles.

Figural Goodness. The Gestalt psychologists felt that the principles of figural organization worked in harmony to bring about perception of the most stable, consistent, and simple forms possible from the visual array. They described this process as the LAW OF PRAGNANZ, which maintains that the psychological organization of the percept will always be as "good" as the prevailing conditions allow. In this definition the term "good" is not fully specified; however, it includes properties such as regularity, symmetry, simplicity, and others we will encounter in the course of our discussion. The German word *Pragnanz* is not easy to translate into English; in general, it refers to "conveying the essence of something." In perception the essence is often better than the reality. In normal viewing, the differentiation of figure from ground and the organization of a coherent form are simultaneous and perhaps the same processes. Thus, although we discussed each component separately, you must keep in mind that all these basic processes in the perception of form operate to *reduce perceptual ambiguity.* They also seem to operate to *produce perceptual simplicity,* and this is the

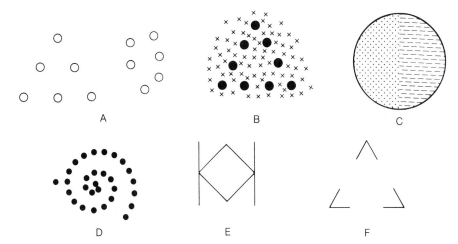

Figure 13-7.
Examples of the Gestalt principles of figural organization. (A) grouping by proximity; (B) and (C) grouping by similarity; (D) good continuation; (E) an extreme example of closure in which two common figures are hidden; and (F) closure.

issue to which the notion of figural goodness is related. Demonstration Box 13-4 gives you a method for exploring the operation of Pragnanz.

Earlier we showed how depth cues can assist in the separation of figure from ground. In some instances depth is the result of figural organization rather than an aid to it. For

---

Look at the accompanying figures for a moment and (without looking back again) draw them on a separate piece of paper. When you have finished, return to this box.

Now carefully compare the figures you drew to the actual figures. Did you pick up the fact that the "circle" is actually a

tilted ellipse? that the "square" contains no right angles? that the "triangle" has two rounded corners and an open one? that the X is actually made up of curved lines? Look back at your reproductions. If you drew (or remembered) just a good circle, square, triangle, and X, your percepts have been "cleaned up" by the action of Pragnanz.

Demonstration Box 13-4
Pragnanz

example, Kopfermann (1930) used figures similar to those shown in Figure 13-8 to study the circumstances under which people perceive drawings as either two- or three-dimensional. She demonstrated that a two-dimensional percept will dominate when such an organization is figurally good or simple. In other words, when the two-dimensional organization is compact and symmetrical with good continuation between the lines, this organization will dominate. When this is not the case, observers will tend to perceive the drawing as being three-dimensional. Therefore, in Figure 13-8 the figures are graded from *A* through *D*, with *D* being the least likely to be perceived as three-dimensional. Hochberg and Brooks

(1960) suggested that this results from the fact that when the two-dimensional array is complex, the three-dimensional organization may actually be simpler, and hence may show the operation of Pragnanz. Thus Figure 13-8A is seen as a three-dimensional "cube" because to imagine it as a two-dimensional pattern made up of triangles, trapazoids, and a parallelogram, interlocked like a puzzle, is more complex. Actually Hochberg and Brooks (1960) suggested a quantitative representation of figural complexity which was based on the stimulus itself. Their calculations used the following expression: figural complexity = (number of angles + number of different angles)/(2 × number of separate continuous line segments) + (total number of

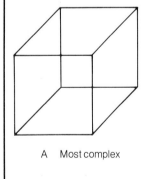

A   Most complex

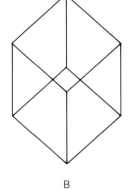

B

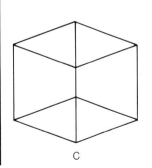

C

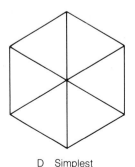

D   Simplest

Figure 13-8.
Various projections of a cube. The figures are gradually seen as more two-dimensional as one moves from the most complex (A) to the least complex (D).

angles). They found that the higher this value, the more likely a figure is to be seen as three-dimensional.

One of the interesting aspects of the work by Hochberg and Brooks (1960) is the notion that figural organization or "goodness" can be defined in terms of the amount of information needed to specify a particular coherent organization. Aspects of the form such as the number of line segments, the number of angles, and the size and differing varieties of lines and angles can be considered to be information needed to provoke the percept of a particular type of figure. Actually, information theory (which was discussed in Chapter 2) has been used to study the problem of figural goodness. To see how information theory applies to patterns, consider Figure 13-9. There we have broken up a square visual field into separate, smaller squares called "cells" (we call the whole figure a *matrix*). Notice that we can construct a variety of patterns by simply filling in cells as we have done in Figure 13-9A. If we did this randomly, in order to guess the complete pattern you would need 64 guesses (1 for each

cell) or 64 bits of information (1 for each guess needed). Suppose we told you that the left side was the mirror image of the right side. This is called a *vertically symmetrical pattern* since the mirror images are symmetrical around a vertical line. Under this condition, you would only need to guess either the 32 cells on the right or on the left in order to guess the pattern, thus reducing the amount of information to 32 bits. Therefore, a symmetrical figure such as 13-9B contains less information than an asymmetrical figure such as 13-9A. Figure 13-9C, which is symmetrical around both the vertical and horizontal axes, contains even less information (16 guesses or bits) than the other two patterns.

Attneave (1954) proposed that quantifying patterns in this manner could lead to an understanding of figural goodness. In general, he reasoned that "good" patterns are simpler in that they contain less information. Thus they are often more symmetrical or predictable. Attneave (1955) argued that observers should be better able to remember symmetrical patterns than irregular ones, simply because symmetrical patterns require the reten-

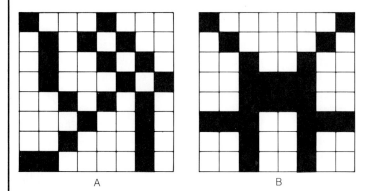
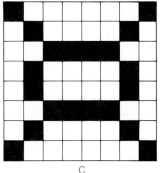

A   B   C

Figure 13-9.
Examples of symmetry in patterns: (A) no symmetry; (B) symmetrical around vertical axis; and (C) symmetrical around both horizontal and vertical axes.

tion of less information. Using matrices of dot patterns, some of which were symmetrical and some of which were not, Attneave (1955) verified this prediction, and he also showed that it was the amount of information in the pattern rather than symmetry per se that was the important aspect. Thus an 8×8 matrix (containing 64 cells) with horizontal and vertical symmetry is remembered as easily as a 4×4 matrix (16 cells) with no symmetry, since both contain 16 bits of information.

Garner (1962, 1974) has offered a different information theory approach to the problem of figural goodness. He notes that many figures alter their appearance when they are rotated or when they are presented in mirror image form. The total number of different patterns that can be produced may be classified as the set of stimuli from which a given example is drawn. Consider the 3×3 dot-matrix patterns shown in Figure 13-10. Notice that each is shown with all possible unique rotations and reflections. Figure 13-10A always produces four unique patterns, and 13-10C produces eight. Garner found that the smaller the set of possible figures the more likely an observer was to rate the pattern as "good" (Garner & Clement, 1963; Handel & Garner, 1965). Thus we are again drawn to the conclusion that the "good" figures are simple and contain less information.

In some respects Attneave and Garner represent two different approaches, both with the goal of quantifying the aspects of figures that satisfy the needs of Pragnanz. Attneave analyzed patterns into many separable components, each of which conveys information, while Garner considered the whole figure as a unit. The global and the analytic approaches will reappear in many guises during our discussion of form perception. Each is useful when we attempt to answer certain questions, although neither gives the complete answer by itself.

VISUAL PATTERN PERCEPTION

The inventor sat beside his robot. He continued to speculate on how he could construct the circuits to allow his mechanical marvel to recognize objects on the basis of the pattern of visual information available in the image. His first thought had been to design a circuit to match each possible stimulus element. Thus one could synthesize the perception of a face from knowing that the pattern contained a curved element like a mouth, two oval elements like eyes, and so on. Of course, he would need an extremely large collection of elements to recognize all of the typical patterns available in the world. He was worried that such an element-by-element analysis didn't seem to be the way that humans approached the problem. Their perception was much better than that. He remembered the masked ball he had once attended. Everybody had dressed in bizarre costumes and had worn wigs, masks, and make-up. Yet he was still able to identify almost all of his friends by sight—how could that be if each of the individual facial elements were changed? Worse yet, how could one go about designing a set of circuits to do the same thing? If a small child can recognize complex patterns, certainly the task cannot be that involved. He looked at the metallic hulk beside him and continued to muse.

When we consider all the processes that underly the recognition of complex, everyday patterns, we find that they can be conveniently classified into two types. One type, called DATA-DRIVEN PROCESSING, begins with the arrival of sensory information reaching the receptors (data). This input is said to *drive* a series of analyses, beginning with the registration of luminance differences in the image, colors, lines and angles, and other DISTINCTIVE FEATURES of the input pattern. This

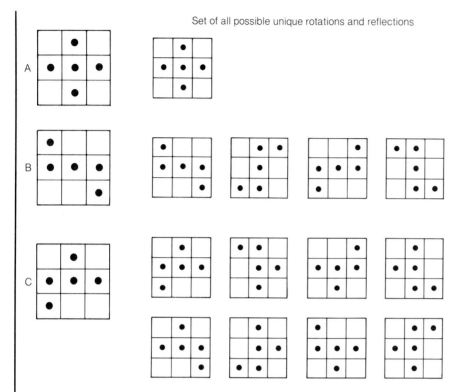

Set of all possible unique rotations and reflections

Figure 13-10.
Relationship between figural goodness and the set of possible
alternative stimuli that can be created by rotations and
reflections: (A) is the "best" figure and (C) is the "worst"
(based upon Handel & Garner, 1965).

analysis proceeds from the retina up through the various levels of the visual pathways, until it reaches the higher centers of the brain. The other type of processing is termed CONCEPTUALLY-DRIVEN PROCESSING: It operates in quite a different way using higher level *conceptual* processes including memories of past experiences, general organizational strategies, knowledge of the world, and expectations based upon the surrounding context or situation. Both types of analysis can be occurring simultaneously, or they may occur one after the other, as the data-driven processes inform the conceptually-driven processes about specific features in the pattern, while the conceptually-driven processes guide the data-driven processes in the search for specific details necessary to complete the percept. Let's look at the evidence for these two basic types of processing separately before we consider how they interact in the recognition of complex patterns.

Data-Driven Processing. At the physiological level it is relatively easy to find a number of data-driven mechanisms that seem to respond to local features of patterns. For instance, lateral inhibition accentuates local changes in brightness and perhaps color. In Chapter 4 we indicated that there are neural units that respond to specific features, such as the orientation of a line, its length, whether it forms an angle with another line, and so forth. An interesting source of evidence for processing patterns on the basis of features such as these comes from work on stabilized images (a technique that we discussed earlier in the chapter). As you recall, we mentioned that when we stop the image on the retina, keeping it from moving as the eye moves, it fades. This fading is not a gradual uniform disappearance of the whole figure, nor is it a disappearance of little random bits of the figure; rather, it is a chunk-by-chunk disappearance of whole lines and units (Evans & Wells, 1967; Heckenmueller, 1965; Pritchard et al., 1960). For instance, if we presented an observer with a stabilized outline square, we would expect the fade out to look something like the sequence shown in Figure 13-11A. It would not appear as shown in 13-11B. Since the disappearance is feature by feature, some researchers have taken this as evidence for an initial feature-by-feature

build-up of the percept in the first place. This may occur through data-driven cortical feature analyzers (Arend, 1973).

We have been using an intuitive definition of "features" in speaking of pattern analysis. However, there are more objective ways to approach features. One early study that is still suggestive is that of Attneave (1954), who asked observers to represent a figure by means of a series of ten dots. They tended to place the dots on points of the form that changed direction most sharply. We can represent common objects or pictures quite easily by indicating only points where the contours change direction. Thus in Figure 13-12A it is easy to recognize the alphabetic letters even though only dots, representing points where angles meet, lines end, or directions change, are indicated. In Figure 13-12B only the points of maximum curvature have been extracted and connected with a straight edge, yet the form of a sleeping cat is clearly seen. Local aspects of a stimulus, related to more intuitively defined features,

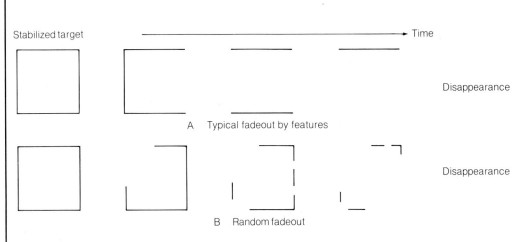

Stabilized target   ⟶ Time

Disappearance

A   Typical fadeout by features

Disappearance

B   Random fadeout

Figure 13-11.
Typical feature-by-feature fading of stabilized retinal image is shown in (A), as opposed to what would be expected if disappearance was random in its time course, as seen in (B).

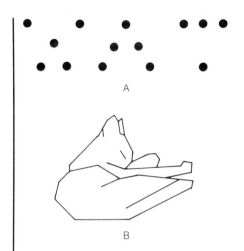

A

B

Figure 13-12.
The importance of points of change in contour direction for pattern recognition. In (A) the letters are recognizable even though points of change are merely indicated by dots. In (B) the cat is recognizable even though points of change are merely connected by straight lines (Figure (B) from Attneave, F. *Psychological Review,* 1954, **61.** © 1954 by the American Psychological Association. Reprinted by permission).

may provide adequate information about a pattern. In some cases local information can be so striking that it actually interferes with perception of the whole pattern, as can be seen in Demonstration Box 13-5.

There are several other ways that one can go about investigating the relative importance of local features in pattern recognition. For instance, Cheatham (1952) tried a visual masking situation. He used simple targets (such as triangles and squares) and followed them with a very bright masking stimulus. As we showed in Figure 13-2, under these circumstances the amount of masking decreases as the interval between the target and mask is increased. Cheatham noticed that, when the intervals were small,

the target was not seen; however, when the intervals became longer, his observers began to report seeing something. They did not simply see a dim image of the target but rather reported features in a specific order. He reasoned that the most important features would be processed first and would be visible after a short masking interval, while less important features would be processed more slowly and could be masked by a stimulus presented even after a substantially greater period of time. Observers reported that the first parts of the figures that were seen were the sides (often only one or two would appear). As the interstimulus interval increased, they could next report the presence of angles. The color of the figure only became apparent after the whole contour was visible. This finding indicates that specific features must be processed before the perception of form emerges.

Another approach to the problem of isolating features used in the recognition of patterns involves looking at the types of confusions that people make when performing a recognition task. For instance, if we use alphabet letters as our target patterns, we find that when an *R* is confused with another letter, it is most often confused with *P*, while *C* is most often confused with a *G* or an *O* (Kinney, Marsetta & Showman, 1966). Gibson, Osser, Schiff and Smith (1963) suggested a set of local features that could be used to recognize letters. They included the number of lines, their orientation, curvature, and symmetry, among others. Geyer and De Wald (1973) were able to show that letter confusions could be accounted for by a small set of such local features.

All the evidence we have presented suggests that the isolation and later combination of distinctive features plays a role in pattern perception. However, a conceptual difficulty remains. Any of the "features" we have discussed (i.e., a line or an angle) would be called a figure itself if it were not

Demonstration Box 13-5
The Role of Local Features in Pattern Recognition

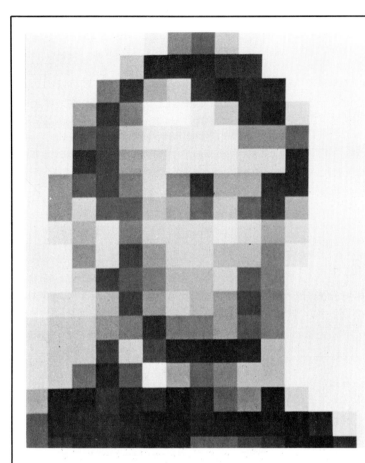

Harmon (1973) and Harmon and Julesz (1973) have presented an interesting set of demonstrations that illustrate how local features can interfere with a more global percept. One of their demonstrations is presented in the figure, a computer-processed block representation of a photographic portrait. It is made by taking a computer scan of a photograph. The brightness information from this scan is then locally averaged, so that the brightness value in each of the squares is an average of a number of brightness samples taken in that area of the picture. This technique can be used to see if such local brightness information can elicit the percept of the original photograph. To try this, look at the figure at normal reading distance. Do you recognize the person? Try again, viewing from 2 m this time. (It will also help if you squint your eyes.) If you follow these instructions, you should be able to identify this block portrait as a very famous historical person. If not, the name of the individual in the picture is printed upside down in the bottom right-hand corner of this page (From Harmon, L. D., & Julesz, B. *Science,* 1973, **180,** 1194–1197. © 1973 by the American Association for the Advancement of Science).

Abraham Lincoln

part of a larger form. How do we know what is the overall shape or pattern as opposed to what is merely a part? Somehow an extraction of the GLOBAL aspects of the figure must be made to distinguish it from the smaller, LOCAL details. It is interesting to consider whether we first process the global overview and then fill in the local details as the Gestalt principles of organization suggest, or whether we start with the details and build the global pattern feature by feature as some of the research above seems to imply.

Alternatively, the sequence of processing might depend upon the task that the observer is required to perform. Navon (1977) addressed himself to this problem by using stimuli like those in Figure 13-13. You will notice that Figure 13-13A contains two large *H* figures. One is composed of small *H*'s and one of small *S*'s. Navon named these figures either *globally-locally consistent* or *globally-locally inconsistent*. For example, the large *H* composed of small *H*'s is globally-locally consistent since the overall organization of the figure (a large *H*) agrees with the more local contour information (the small *H*'s). On the other hand, the large *H* composed of small *S*'s is globally-locally inconsistent since the overall organization disagrees with the local information. Figure 13-13B shows a similar pair of large *S*'s. Navon asked his observers to indicate whether the global character of the letter was an *H* or an *S* (he called this the globally directed condition). Other observers were to indicate whether the large letters were composed of smaller *H*'s or *S*'s (he called this the locally directed condition). He recorded how long it took observers to make these identifications, and he reasoned that if global processing has precedence over local processing, then observers in the globally directed condition would not be affected by inconsistent information at the local level. If local processing normally occurs first, then

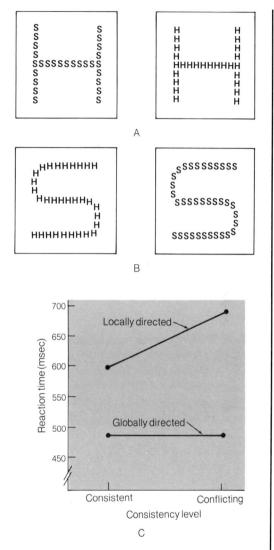

Figure 13-13.
Examples of figures that are globally and locally inconsistent or consistent are shown in (A) and (B); (C) shows the effect of task instructions on recognition time (based upon Navon, 1977).

the opposite would be the outcome.

The results of his experiment are shown in Figure 13-13C. It appears that global processing is the more powerful under these conditions. The recognition time for the locally directed observers was much longer when the information at the global level was inconsistent with their task at hand. However, the globally directed observers showed the same identification speed regardless of the consistency or inconsistency of local information.

Several other investigators have arrived at similar conclusions, although from different arguments. Pomerantz, Sager, and Stoever (1977) have shown that, in groupings of simple linear features, those that form closed, "good" figures are much easier to recognize than those composed of the same features in a different arrangement. These data seem to indicate some kind of direct (faster or earlier) perception of such "good" figures. A related concept is that of the INTEGRAL stimulus, which is seen in all of its aspects simultaneously, such as a lightbulb, which is seen to have shape and color all at once (Lockhead, 1966). A SEPARABLE stimulus is one that has single features that cannot be easily integrated, such as the letter Q, in which the circle and the "tail" appear to be distinct parts. Lockhead (1972) argued that integral stimuli (at least) are processed first as "blobs" at a global level, *before* they can be analyzed into their component parts. This seems to be the only way to explain how some stimuli are identified more quickly than other stimuli made of the same features but combined in a different way. More recent work has expanded upon and confirmed this notion (Lockhead & King, 1977; Monohan & Lockhead, 1977).

This evidence indicates that the first stage of data-driven analysis, at least for "good" figures, may be a global analysis rather than a local one. For other kinds of figures, more global aspects may not emerge until higher levels of processing piece them together from smaller features (Ward & Wexler, 1976). Clearly, both types of information must be

extracted if patterns or forms are to be accurately recognized.

Conceptually-Driven Processing. Data-driven processes do not operate in isolation. Many facts surrounding pattern recognition simply cannot be accounted for by the operation of this type of process alone. For example, the CONTEXT in which it appears can affect our ability to recognize a letter or word symbol. The context provides one type of conceptual information relevant to interpreting any stimulus. Look at Figure 13-14. Most people read these two lines as being *A, B, C, D, E, F* and 10, 11, 12, 13, 14, respectively. Notice, however, that the symbol you "saw" as *B* and the one you "saw" as 13 are identical. The context in which the two patterns occur alters our recognition of the figure. This is a conceptually-driven alteration since it depends upon knowledge and assumptions. Remember the "data" (the actual stimulus input) is identical for both the perceptual organizations of *B* and 13.

The use of a general organizing scheme in the recognition and remembrance of complex picture scenes has been demonstrated in a study by Mandler and Parker (1976). These investigators showed drawings, similar to the one shown as Figure 13-15A, to observers. They then asked them to reconstruct the pictures either immediately after viewing or after a period of one week. In addition a group of

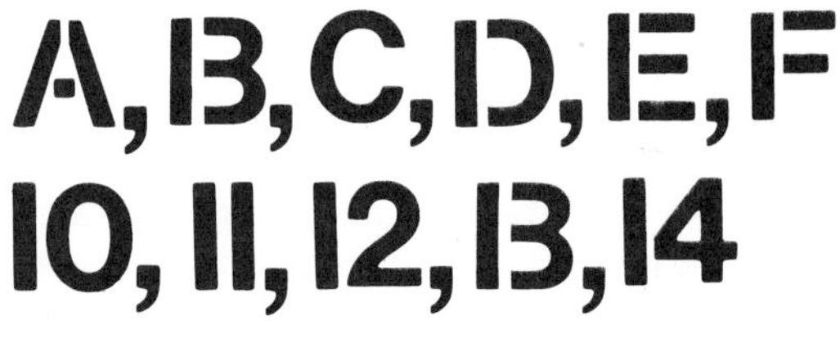

A,B,C,D,E,F
10,11,12,13,14

Figure 13-14.
The effect of context on pattern recognition. The *B* and the 13 are identical figures.

Figure 13-15.
Meaningful objects in (A) natural or (B) scrambled locations.

control observers, who had never seen the pictures, was given the array of objects within the pictures (as in Figure 13-15B). They were asked to reconstruct them as if they had seen a picture of them together. These researchers found that all the observers accurately reproduced the position of items on the vertical dimension. This was the case even for observers who had not previously seen the actual target pictures. Mandler and Parker (1976) argue that this reflects the use of a conceptual framework based upon our experience with real world scenes. There are characteristic up–down organizations; for example, some objects usually appear above the horizon line while other objects appear below the horizon line. This type of information, which is part of our expectations about the organization of the world, can also help us to recognize scenes and to place objects within them (Mandler & Johnson, 1976). When "naturally" organized pictures such as Figure 13-15A are viewed for only 10 sec, observers can correctly recognize whether the objects have been rearranged or are in the same position better than 80% of the time when tested four months later. On the other hand, spatial rearrangements in "unorganized" pictures such as Figure 13-15B are remembered less than 50% of the time (Mandler & Ritchey, 1977).

Palmer (1975a) has studied a related problem. He looked at the ability of observers to recognize specific items within a picture when they were placed within an appropriate as opposed to an inappropriate context. He argued that we have expectations about which objects should appear in particular scenes. Looking at Figure 13-16, which is a kitchen scene, one might state that the top figure on the right, a loaf of bread, is the one that could be most appropriately inserted into that scene. Palmer presented observers with a set of such scenes. The presentation of each scene was followed by a briefly ex-

posed target object that the observer was asked to identify. The contextual fit between the scene and the target object was either appropriate (such as in the case between a kitchen scene and a loaf of bread) or it was inappropriate (a kitchen scene followed by a drum). As you might expect, there was greater recognition of a target object when it was preceded by a scene that provided an appropriate context. This type of experiment also reflects the use of prior expectations in the recognition process.

Interaction of Data-Driven and Conceptually-Driven Processing. How does the data-driven analysis of local or global features interact with memories, expectations, context, and other concepts concerning the meaning of a pattern? Palmer (1975b) and Norman (1976) have argued that the two types of processing must proceed simultaneously and jointly. Our final interpretation of a particular pattern results from a melting together of the individual features and the context in which they occur. Palmer (1975b) demonstrated this notion in relation to facial perception. Look at Figure 13-17. Notice that when seen as part of a face, any bump or line will suffice to depict a feature. When we take these features out of context, they do not really portray the objects very well. We actually require more of a detailed presentation (such as those on the lower row in Figure 13-17) to recognize facial features unambiguously, when presented in isolation.

Meaning and expectation can direct which details within a pattern are chosen for analysis. This is shown in a study by Yarbus (1967). He recorded eye movement patterns while observers scanned pictures. He asked his observers to look at the pictures with different intentions in mind. He found that, when observers were asked to estimate the material wealth of the persons in the picture, they would scan and fixate different features

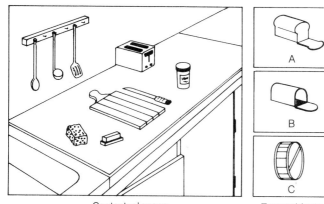

Contextual scene   Target objects

Figure 13-16.
Context and target stimuli
used by Palmer (1975a).

than when they were asked to determine the ages of the persons depicted. An example of these differences is shown in Figure 13-18. Thus, different features were used in the completion of different types of identification tasks. This is another example of the interaction between feature analysis and the expectation and context within which an observer approaches a pattern recognition task.

Theories of Visual Pattern Recognition. Since pattern recognition is such an important visual phenomenon, it isn't surprising that many investigators have offered theories and/or models that attempt to account for the major facts. In general, these fall

into two major groups. There are those that emphasize data-driven analysis of features and are more *passive,* and there are those that emphasize conceptually-driven processes and are more *active.* Neither type has had complete success in explaining pattern recognition, so it is important to examine a major example of each type to see what we can use to formulate a general view that is more successful.

As has been mentioned above, there is a large amount of evidence that seems to be most interpretable when we view pattern recognition as a data-driven process requiring feature analysis. Models based upon such an interpretation conceive of the pattern rec-

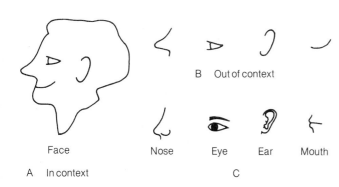

Face

Nose   Eye   Ear   Mouth

A   In context   C

B   Out of context

Figure 13-17.
Facial components are easily recognized in context (A) but out of context they are much less identifiable (B) unless they are made more detailed (C) (Palmer, 1975b) (From Donald A. Norman, David E. Rumelhart, and the LNR Research Group. W. H. Freeman and Company. Copyright © 1975).

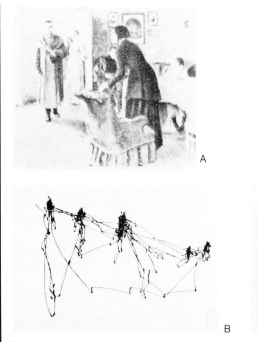

A

B

C

Figure 13-18.
Eye movement patterns viewing the picture shown as (A) vary
depending upon the questions asked of the observer. When
asked the age of the individuals the pattern shown as (B)
appeared, while when asked about the wealth of the
individuals the pattern shown as (C) was produced (from
Yarbus, 1967. Copyright © Plenum Publishing Co. Reprinted
by permission).

ognition process as one that involves a hierarchical system in which the sensory input is passed from lower to higher levels until it is finally combined at some central site. Let's look at one such model called PAN-DEMONIUM (Selfridge, 1959). Figure 13-19 pictures one kind of Pandemonium system. This system of pattern recognition, which actually began as a computer program, is based upon a series of successive stages of feature analysis and recombination. Each stage has been given the descriptive term *demon*; you can conceive of each stage as a series of little demons shouting out the results of their analyses.

Pandemonium works in the following way. The first stage, or the *image demon,* merely passes on an ''image'' or copy of the signal that has been registered in the visual system. This image is then analyzed by all of the *feature demons* simultaneously (in *parallel*). The feature demons look for particular features within the incoming pattern, such as lines, angles, and curves. The feature demons are monitored by *cognitive demons,* and each cognitive demon is responsible for searching for a particular pattern. So, for example, if we are talking about letters presented to an observer, each cognitive demon might be responsible for recognizing a particular letter. The cognitive demons monitor the feature demons in order to detect the presence of

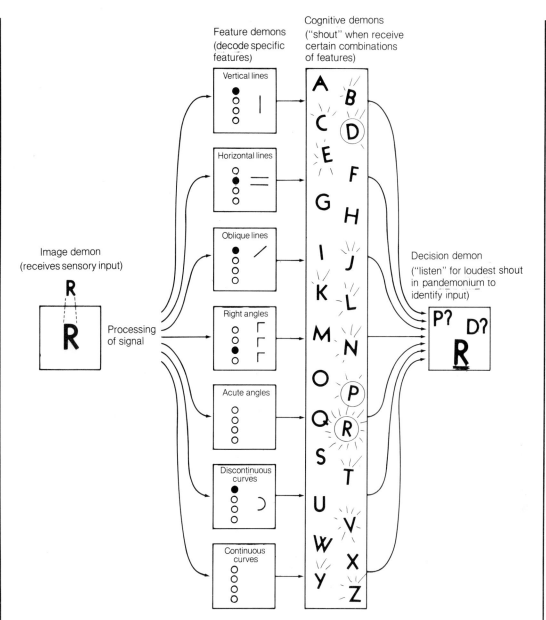

Figure 13-19.
A Pandemonium model in action. The *image demon* receives the input whose features are then decoded by specific *feature demons*. The number of each feature that is found is indicated by the blackened circle in each feature demon box. *Cognitive demons* are alert for the specific set of features that identify a particular letter. When these features are found they begin to shout, with the loudest pandemonium being made by the cognitive demon that corresponds to the original input. The *decision demon* listens to this pandemonium and makes a decision about the input based upon the loudest "shout."

features within the input that are included in the pattern for which they are responsible. Therefore an *A* cognitive demon would be looking for the presence of certain oblique straight lines, certain acute angles, and a horizontal line. As the information is analyzed by the feature demons, the cognitive demons start "yelling" when they find a feature appropriate to their own pattern, and the more features they find, the louder they yell. A *decision demon* listens to the Pandemonium caused by the yelling of the various cognitive demons. It chooses the cognitive demon (or pattern) that is making the most noise as the one that is most likely to be the pattern presented to the sensory system.

Programming a computer to act according to the rules that define the Pandemonium model and others like it (Selfridge & Neisser, 1963; Uhr & Vossler, 1963; Wallingford, 1972) has demonstrated that in certain cases, such models can perform about as well as humans in identifying handwritten letters. Such models also can account for confusions between letters (Geyer & De Wald, 1973). However, although these models do contain some primitive conceptual processes, they have considerable difficulty with problems such as figure-ground separation, context effects, and faster processing of "good" figures or "blobs." It is apparent that the greatest lack in these models is in the area of conceptually-driven processes.

The most important idea concerning conceptually-driven processes in pattern recognition is probably ANALYSIS-BY-SYNTHESIS. This concept appears to have been invented by Halle and Stevens (1962) to describe Stevens's (1960) computer program that attempted to recognize spoken speech. It has been popularized by Neisser (1967). Analysis-by-synthesis requires two steps. First, a hypothesis as to the identity of the stimulus is generated by the higher centers on the basis of context and expectations. A first guess might be that the stimulus is, for example, a square. The first guess is then used to guide the second stage, which is a search for the specific features that make up the "guessed" target. This is usually called matching to a *prototype* or testing a *schema* (Neisser, 1976; Reed, 1973). The prototype or schema here would be a square. If the features actually present do not match those expected, a new prototype is generated and the process is repeated. Thus higher level conceptual processes always guide lower level feature extraction processes. This could be used to explain context effects in which features are more easily detected when they are a part of a meaningful whole (Weisstein & Harris, 1974; Womersley, 1977). Analysis-by-synthesis requires an active central processor to continually monitor the outputs of feature detectors, give tips to the cognitive demons, remember what has gone on before, and predict what will come next. The second aspect of analysis-by-synthesis, the reanalysis of a pattern when recognition fails, resembles Bruner's (1957) suggestion about *perceptual readiness*. Bruner argued that under some conditions we have to search for cues as to what a visual pattern is and that we have a hierarchy of possible identities to work with. We go back and forth between the hierarchy and the features of the input, looking for a match. We identify the pattern as the highest category in our hierarchy (which represents our motivations and expectations) that sufficiently matches the input features. Reed (1973) suggests that we seldom use this aspect of analysis-by-synthesis, but it is available for use on ambiguous or novel patterns.

Some sort of combination of the above theoretical ideas seems necessary to deal with visual pattern recognition. Milner (1974) has made an ambitious start toward integrating a detailed set of physiological feature-analyzing mechanisms with other higher level processes to handle aspects of analysis-by-synthesis, especially the guiding of feature analysis by a higher level concept. However, there is still a long way to go and still many intriguing findings to be dealt with.

SPEECH PERCEPTION

The inventor stood looking at the ocean waves lapping over his short-circuited robot. His thoughts ran back over recent events—while setting up a set of stimuli for the mechanical man to practice its pattern perception, he had directed it to look at one stimulus by commanding, "Go see!" The machine had turned, crashed through the wall, and ran until it finally stopped chest deep in the ocean. "Maybe it thought that I said, 'Go sea,'" he mused. Yet that was so stupid a mistake. Although the machine had difficulty with visual patterns, certainly the sound patterns that make up speech are easy enough to encode. "Why even a child can understand a simple bit of language like 'Go see.'" Perhaps he should work first on the interpretation of speech sounds in the next model of the machine. He listened to the waves and mused on.

The meaningful interpretation of speech is usually taken for granted until we have to learn a foreign language. At that time we suddenly become aware that speech is just a collection of sound stimuli. The coherent understanding of speech requires us to look at the organization of these "noises" rather than at individual sounds. In other words, we are looking for an auditory pattern, and recognition of the pattern gives us the "meaning" of the utterance.

One might be tempted to think that listening to a spoken sentence is much like reading a printed sentence. In written sentences we have letters and words separated by spaces of various sizes, while in spoken sentences we might have a series of sounds alternating with silences along with longer silences between words and at the end of sentences. If this were the case it would be easy to identify the individual segments or features of the speech signal. However, there are problems with this model of decoding speech signals (Clark & Clark, 1977). For example, speech is usually continuous and it is not composed of clearly separated, individual segments of sounds. There may appear to be silences between words and sentences, but these are largely illusory. Speech is better described as a continuously varying auditory signal, which is much like a siren with very few breaks in sound.

Another problem with the comparison of the printed and spoken word has to do with the fact that each letter of the spoken word does not have very constant properties. For example, the letter *l* is printed very much the same way regardless of the word in which it appears. However, an *l* is pronounced quite differently depending upon the word in which it appears. The *l*'s in *lip* and *pill*, although printed alike, are pronounced differently. Furthermore, people speak with differing accents, differing voice qualities, and perhaps even through barriers (such as food in the mouth). The decoding of each speech segment is quite remarkable given the variability in how speech sounds are produced.

A third aspect that makes speech production difficult to compare to printed sequences of words is speed. Speech normally occurs at about 12 units per sec, but it can be understood at rates of up to about 50 units per sec (Foulke & Sticht, 1969). This rate of processing is much faster than would be expected from experiments involving nonspeech sounds. Such experiments indicate that individuals can only determine the correct order of nonspeech sounds when they are occurring more slowly than about 1 every 1.5 sec or $\frac{2}{3}$ unit per sec (Warren, Obusek, Farmer, & Warren, 1969). If we are processing speech by listening to each unit and then putting the units together in proper order, we could not possibly be accomplishing this task at the speeds at which human observers have been shown to comprehend speech. This means that recognition of speech poses some interesting perceptual challenges.

Stimulus Features in Speech.   In many ways speech perception is best understood as a form of auditory pattern perception. It is, therefore, important to isolate the stimulus features that allow us to recognize speech stimuli. Unfortunately, the specific features that distinguish one passage of speech from another are more difficult to isolate than those that differentiate various visual patterns. Quite often it is simpler to characterize a sound on the basis of the way it is produced by the speaker than to isolate all of the sound frequencies and temporal characteristics of the stimulus. Consider, for instance, the *p* sound in *pill* and in *spill*. At the pronounciation level, these two sounds are different. The *p* in *pill* is accompanied by a small puff of air (which would extinguish a lighted match held in front of your mouth), whereas the *p* in *spill* is not. The two *p* sounds are distinct PHONETIC, or sound, segments.

Let us look at how speech sounds are produced. In general, speech sounds are divided into *vowels* and *consonants*. Roughly speaking, vowels are formed when the vocal chords vibrate as air moves through the open mouth. Consonants are formed when the mouth constricts, temporarily interrupting the rush of air through the mouth and producing a distinctive sound. We can further subdivide the consonants. One group is called the *stop* consonants or the *plosive* sounds. These cannot be held for any duration and include *b, p, t, d, k,* and *g.* Other consonant sounds can be sustained, and these are called the *aspirate* or *fricative* sounds. They are produced by letting air escape through the constriction between the lips and teeth. These include *sh, ch, th, h, z, s, f,* and *v.* Sounds like *w, y, l, r, m,* and *n* are called *semivowels.* This is a class of sounds that falls between vowels and consonants.

Consonants are also characterized by the feature of VOICING. A *voiced* consonant is one whose pronounciation is accompanied by the vibration of the vocal chords, while *unvoiced* consonants are not. You can feel this for yourself by placing your hand on your throat and pronouncing the *s* in *sip* (which is unvoiced) versus the *z* in *zip* (which is voiced). Vowels can also be subdivided on the basis of how they are produced. These subdivisions are associated with the position of the tongue. Not only are the different parts of the tongue involved (front, center, or back) but the height of the tongue in the mouth also differs. Table 13-1 shows a classification of vowels on the basis of tongue positions.

An alternate way of characterizing speech features depends upon the features of the sounds themselves rather than upon the way the sounds are produced. In this feature-classification system, the basic unit is the PHONEME, which is defined as the smallest sound unit distinguishing one speech sound from another. The English language has about 40 phonemes (there is some dispute as to the exact number), and these are listed in Table 13-2 (these are the phonemes of general North American English and exclude regional dialect sounds). Some languages use as few as 20 phonemes while others use as many as 60 or more. The list of phonemes may be used as a first catalog of acoustical speech features.

Because of the diversity in the articulation of speech sounds, the speech signal that reaches the ear is a rather complex tone. As you learned in Chapter 5, sounds can be classified according to their frequency, which is usually expressed in terms of cycles per second, or Hz. Speech can be studied acoustically as one would study any complex

Table 13-1 *Classification of English Vowels Based upon Tongue Positions (based upon Clark & Clark, 1977)*

Height of Tongue	Part of the Tongue Involved		
	Front	*Central*	*Back*
High	The *ee* in beet	The *y* in marry	The *oo* in hoot
	The *i* in bit		The *u* in put
Middle	The *a* in ate	The *a* in sofa	The *oa* in boat
	The *e* in bet		The *ou* in bought
Low	The *a* in bat	The *u* in but	The *o* in pot

sound. In other words, we can analyze complex speech sounds into a list of the different frequencies that compose them. The most common way to display this information graphically is in the form of **SPEECH SPECTROGRAMS**. Some representative spectrograms are shown in Figure 13-20. The horizontal axis of the spectrogram shows time in milliseconds from the onset of the speech signal. The vertical axis gives the frequency of the speech sounds in Hz. The variations in the lightness and the darkness of the smudges shown on the spectrogram indicate how intense the sound is at each frequency and at each point in time. For example, in the spectrogram depicted in Figure 13-20A, there

Table 13-2 *The Major Phonemes of General North American English*

Consonants		Vowels
The *p* in pea	The *th* in thigh	The *ee* in beet
The *b* in beet	The *th* in thy	The *i* in bit
The *m* in meet	The *sh* in short	The *ai* in bait
The *t* in toy	The *s* in measure	The *e* in bet
The *d* in dog	The *ch* in chip	The *a* in bat
The *n* in neat	The *g* in gyp	The *oo* in boot
The *k* in kill	The *l* in lap	The *u* in put
The *g* in good	The *r* in rope	The *u* in but
The *f* in foot	The *y* in year	The *oa* in boat
The *s* in sit	The *w* in wet	The *ou* in bought
The *ng* in sing	The *wh* in whet	The *o* in dot
The *v* in vote	The *h* in hot	The *a* in sofa
The *z* in zip		The *y* in marry
		The *i* in bite
		The *ou* in out
		The *oy* in toy

are very loud sounds from about 300 to 700 Hz for about 200 msec in the pronounciation of the syllable *bab*.

The spectrogram provides some useful information that will become important in our later discussion of feature detection in speech perception. However, let us discuss for now the interpretation of the light and dark smudges on these spectrograms. The human voice starts in the throat with the vibration of the vocal chords. For men the vocal chords vibrate about 80–200 times per sec, while in women they can vibrate as often as 400 times per sec (Ladefoged, 1975).

These differences in the vibration frequency of the vocal chords result in a fundamental frequency for each voice. As you may remember from Chapter 9, any complex tone has a fundamental frequency; therefore, speech in this way is very much like other complex tones. Let us say that the vocal chords are vibrating at 128 times per sec. This will give us a fundamental frequency of 128 Hz. Simultaneously with the production of this fundamental frequency, the voice also produces harmonics of this frequency. In other words, frequencies that are whole-number multiples of the fundamental frequency are also produced. In our example, with a fundamental frequency of 128 Hz we would also find harmonics of 256, 384, and 512 Hz. As these vibrations pass through the pharynx and the oral cavity, some of these harmonics are enhanced while others are diminished. This strengthening and weakening leads to a particular pattern of sound.

If you look once again at Figure 13-20A and note the spectrogram for *bab*, you will notice that frequency enhancement has occurred in a band around 500 Hz and also in a

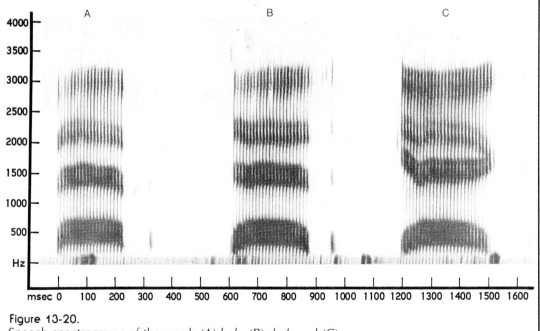

Figure 13-20.
Speech spectrograms of the words (A) *bab*, (B) *dad*, and (C) *gag*, spoken with a British accent (from *A Course in Phonetics* by Peter Ladefoged © 1975 by Harcourt Brace Jovanovich and reproduced with their permission).

band around 1450 Hz. This is where the darkest smudges on the spectrogram occur. These bands of enhanced sound have been named FORMANTS. The lowest (at 500 Hz) is the *first formant,* and the next lowest (at 1450 Hz) is the *second formant.* These two formants correspond to two major cavities in the vocal system, the pharynx and the oral cavity. The shape of these cavities is responsible for the first and second formants, and any changes in the shapes of these cavities will change the frequency placement of the first and second formant. It is this change in formants that distinguishes one vowel sound from another. For example, the pronounciation of the word *had* might produce average frequencies for the first two formants at 690 Hz and at 1660 Hz (Ladefoged, 1975). It seems that only vowels have this quality. Consonants are distinguished by abrupt changes in the formants. These are sometimes accompanied by wide bands of sound spread over the whole frequency range. For example, the pronounciation of *she* would give a broad smear of energy up and down the spectrogram.

The spectrogram reveals that speech is a very complex sound with frequency and energy differences produced across time. Each consonant and each vowel sound within the English language seems to consist of a different pattern (or distribution) of differing amounts of energy at the various sound frequencies. It is quite remarkable that this pattern can be recognized by a listener as quickly as it is, so that speech is intelligible and meaningful.

Data-Driven and Conceptually-Driven Processing. Having discussed the mechanics of speech production, we have set the stage for a discussion of how the various physical features of the speech sound contribute to the ultimate recognition of the speech signal. Just

as changes in brightness, contours, and color are physical features that seem to contribute to the perception of patterns in the visual modality, it is of interest to ask if the various physical differences in articulation, voicing, and other domains contribute to the perception of speech. Jacobson, Fant, and Halle (1952, 1961) and more recently Abbs and Sussman (1971) and many others have argued that speech perception is mediated in part by a system of "feature detectors." This discussion can be considered parallel to our discussion of visual pattern recognition.

Several acoustical features of the speech signal have been studied as potential feature units that are crucial to the perception of speech. In a study by Klein, Plomp, and Pols (1970), the role of *formants* in the perception of vowel sounds was studied. We have already said that vowels are characterized by the modulation (changing in a particular way) of sound as it passes through the oral cavity, giving rise to formants which are bands of high energy output positioned at characteristic frequencies in a speech spectrogram. These investigators had individuals pronounce 12 different vowels in a *b-vowel-t* context (such as *bat* or *bit*). They made test vowels by removing 100-msec segments of the steady vowel sound from this pronounced word. They then had observers attempt to identify the 100-msec segments of the vowels. These observers achieved about 74% correct identification of these segments. Klein *et al.* (1970) then looked at confusion errors between the vowels. You will notice that this is very similar to the technique used to study feature detection in letter perception. They reasoned that if observers tended to confuse vowels it may be because the vowels were physically similar to each other. They found that two vowels were confused with one another to the extent that the first two formant frequencies of the vowels were similar. Thus they found that acoustical properties (features) of the vowel sound could predict perceptual confusions.

In another approach, Eimas and Corbit (1973) (see also Chapter 9) wanted to investigate whether there might be physiological feature detectors tuned to the various physical properties of the speech sound, much as there seem to be cortical feature detectors tuned to some properties of a visual input (see Chapter 4). Eimas and Corbit (1973) reasoned that if such physiological feature detectors exist for specific speech properties then one should be able to fatigue these physiological systems by exposing them to stimulation to which they are particularly sensitive. They chose to study the characteristics of voiced versus unvoiced stop-consonants in English (*p, t,* and *k* are unvoiced; *b, d,* and *g* are voiced). In producing a stop-consonant sound followed by a vowel sound, there is a period of time after the column of air has been stopped by the lips and/or tongue before the vocal chords begin to vibrate to produce the voiced sound or the vowel sound. This latency is called the VOICE ONSET TIME. Small differences in voice onset time are usually sufficient to distinguish between voiced and unvoiced stop-consonants in English. For example, there is a 60-msec time difference between the onset of the vowel sound in *ba* and *pa* with the voiced *ba* being the faster.

It can be shown that by varying the voice onset time systematically, the point of transition, where observers recognize a target such as *ba* as opposed to *pa,* can be determined (Lisker & Abramson, 1970). Eimas and Corbit (1973) now adapted observers to one specific category (e.g., *ba*) by repeatedly presenting the stimulus sound. After this period of adaptation it was found that the boundary between *ba* and *pa* had shifted, and observers would now call certain stimuli *pa* even though they had originally classified them as *ba.* This suggests that adaptation to

the repeated sound characteristic had occurred.

These researchers argued that these results implied that the neural detectors for the feature of voiced versus unvoiced had been fatigued. Other investigators have shown that a variety of other characteristics of speech can also be adapted through repeated exposure (Cooper & Blumstein, 1974; Tartter & Eimas, 1975). Some of these include features associated with the place of articulation, while others deal with purely acoustic cues (Cooper, 1975). It may be that there are physiological mechanisms that monitor and respond to the physical characteristics of speech. These could operate similarly to those in vision. Unfortunately, little direct physiological evidence is as yet available.

Just as we found that pattern perception in vision cannot be explained solely on the basis of a data-driven analysis of separate components, we also find that there are more conceptual aspects to the processing and recognition of speech signals that aid us in our comprehension of speech sound patterns. When talking about conceptually driven processing involved in speech recognition, we must shift from the so-called *phonetic* level of analysis to the psychologically more important *phonological* level of analysis. Phonology is concerned with the meaning of speech stimuli. Meaning is often more important than the actual stimulus in determining what we hear. This point has been demonstrated by Day (1968, 1970), who presented observers with sequences of sounds, some to the right ear and some to the left ear. The left ear might hear *b-a-n-k-e-t* while the right ear would hear *l-a-n-k-e-t.* Some observers heard the individual sequences of sounds; however, other observers fused the two sequences of sounds and heard the word *blanket.* It is interesting that none of the observers ever heard *lbanket,* a sequence that would be excluded by the phonological rules of English. In English an *l* is never followed by a *b* at the beginning of a word. Individuals even fused the two sequences of sounds appropriately when *lanket* was presented a few milliseconds before *banket.* There seem to be some conceptually-driven constraints operating against our perceiving a sound sequence that is not appropriate for the language we are decoding. Our expectations thus form an interpretive context.

Thus far we have been discussing the perception of isolated words. However, normal speech is continuous and conveys information. This continuity of normal speech provides a detailed context that increases our ability to recognize words, which is demonstrated in an experiment by Pollack and Pickett (1964). They secretly recorded people engaged in spontaneous conversation. They then played back single words extracted from these tape recordings to other observers and asked them to identify the words. They found that single words were correctly identified 47% of the time. However, when you listen to an entire stream of continuous speech, you do not have the impression that words have to be guessed. The stream of speech seems intact and quite intelligible. In an interesting addition to their experiment, Pollack and Pickett (1964) continued to present longer and longer strings of words to surround the single words they had presented first. As the amount of speech surrounding the word increased, observers became increasingly accurate in identifying the word. Therefore, the more acoustic, syntactic, and meaningful information available, the better the recognition of words.

In a similar vein, Warren (1970) discovered that the context of a sentence can actually cause an observer to fill in a gap present in a continuous speech. He called this the PHONEMIC RESTORATION EFFECT, and it

works in the following way. Warren (1970) presented observers with a taped sentence: "The state governors met with their respective legislatures convening in the capital city." A segment corresponding to the *s* in "legislatures" was deleted and replaced with a cough. Only one observer out of twenty noticed that any speech sounds were missing. In other words, observers restored the deleted phoneme in the course of processing and recognizing the taped material.

Theories of Speech Perception.   Theories of speech perception—or rather, the recognition of individual spoken words as opposed to the understanding of language—fall into the same two broad categories as those of visual pattern recognition: passive theories emphasizing data-driven processing and more active ones emphasizing conceptually driven processing. One of the most interesting started as a computer program. Speech theorists have often resorted to computer models for their theoretical presentation. They reason that if a theory is specified well enough to allow us to program a computer to act in much the same way that the human observer does (not better, but even making the same sorts of mistakes), then the rules and processes used to create the program are probably similar to those going on within the human.

Hughes and Hemdal (1965) attempted to develop a program that could convert acoustic signals into phonemes. Their program examined a speech input for the presence of several critical features such as voicing, high frequency sounds, silence before the sound, and whether it was a vowel or a consonant. If it was a vowel, the formants were then examined to see which vowel it was. These few features served to allow the program to identify the phonemes contained in spoken nonsense words about as well as human listeners can (90% correct). This program demonstrates the potential power of a purely passive, data-driven analysis of speech input using a few critical features.

Unfortunately, data-driven theories of speech perception run into a number of immediate difficulties. There are too many speakers in the world. They differ in terms of the fundamental pitch of their voices, their speed of talking, articulation, dialect, and inflection. Their speech also differs depending upon whether they are excited or calm, have a mouthful of food, or are shouting to a distant listener. Each of these conditions drastically alters the pattern of the sound stimuli. Since the number of variations on a set of linguistic stimuli is almost infinite, a simple feature-detection system based upon the matching of stimulus features to stored copies seems doomed to failure. To solve some of these problems, a version of the *analysis-by-synthesis* theory has been offered (Stevens & Halle, 1964). It works on a sort of matching principle; however, it is not the physical stimulus itself that is matched. Observers are assumed to have an internal speech production system by which they can generate or "synthesize" speech sounds for themselves. The presumption is that when a string of speech sounds is encountered, an attempt is made by the listener to match these sounds in terms of the articulatory movements that she would have to make to produce similar sounds herself. In other words, the central concept in speech perception becomes speech production—the hearer is metaphorically repeating the sounds to herself. Since such a theory depends upon the movements used in the speech production sequence it is often called a MOTOR THEORY of speech perception. (Leiberman, Cooper, Shankweiler, & Studdart-Kennedy, 1967; Stevens & House, 1972).

Evidence for such a motor theory has been derived from the way in which sounds are classified. For instance the *d* in the composite sound *di* is given the same name as the *d* in the sound *du,* despite the fact that they are different acoustically. Their sound structures are certainly no more similar than the *d* in *di* is to the *b* in *bi.* Yet why are the *d*'s classified together? The motor theory argument states that both *d*'s are pronounced with the same articulatory movement of the tongue, accompanied by voicing. Listeners concluded that since the same motor sequence was used, the speaker intended to produce the same *d* sound both times. The fact that the sound is not the same is irrelevant, just as the pitch of voice, speed of speech, or speech defects are irrelevant. This conceptually-driven process ignores the local features of the sound and attempts to match speech input to how the listener would reproduce it.

A study by Lehiste and Peterson (1959) gives other evidence in favor of such a conceptually driven analysis of speech. They looked at the perception of the loudness of vowels. Vowel sounds may differ widely in the amount of sound energy they contain when spoken with the same effort. Thus the *ee* sound in *beet* contains much more sound energy than the *oa* sound in *boat,* when spoken with the same effort. Lehiste and Peterson were able to show that when observers are presented with the *ee* sound and the *oa* sound at exactly the same acoustical energy, the *oa* was judged to be louder. Thus the judgment of loudness followed the conceptually-driven inferences about the amount of effort needed to reproduce the sound, rather than the data-driven analysis of the actual stimulus features.

A motor theory, such as the one outlined, can only work in a weak sense. For instance, there are cases reported of individuals who, for neurological reasons, could not speak. If a motor theory were taken as the only mechanism involved in speech perception, these individuals should also not be able to understand speech; yet, many can (Lenneberg, 1962; Fourcin, 1975). We can also understand the speech of both sexes, people with extreme dialects, stutterers, and many other groups whose speech we could not possibly hope to reproduce. Thus a motor theory must be taken as an abstract, perceptual strategy used by a conceptually-driven process that tries to determine how the speaker would have to say what has been said. Since we have adopted the rules, grammar, and continuity of our language, as we attempt to match the inputs we will also tend to fill in gaps, and we will correct or guess at distorted word sounds. Often the perception is better than the stimulus. Thus the "sentence" *Pooh klus free eatwell size* should make more sense if we tell you that it is the answer to the request, "Add the numbers two and three." We hear the interpretation, not the sounds.

14
The Constancies

The range of stimuli that reaches our receptors is huge. Many of these different stimuli result in unique sensory experiences, but some of them are totally unnoticed. Let us consider what happens when you simply leave your chair to step outside for a brief stroll. You are probably quite conscious of the change in your auditory environment, as the sounds shift from the quiet of the interior to the roar of traffic on the street. Tactual sensations also change, from the softness of the carpet to the hard feeling of the concrete. The street smells are different too, with the exhaust fumes of cars now more salient, or perhaps the smell of newly mown grass. The visual input undergoes striking changes as one moves from a dim interior to a blazing, sunlit street, or from the warm glow of a living room to the darkness of the night.

This diversity and change contributes to the excitement and richness of our sensory world; yet, at the level of perceptual analysis, it is the unnoticed changes that are more mysterious and puzzling. To see this more clearly, imagine that you are looking at the actual image projected on the retina of your eye. What changes are actually taking place in the retinal image as you walk down the street? Human observers execute between two and four eye movements per second. Therefore, as you scan the environment, objects momentarily appear in the visual image and then disappear, as if they are blinking out of existence as you change your direction of gaze. Even if you fixated an object as you approached it, the retinal image would still not be constant; rather, it would grow larger as you come closer and smaller as you move away. Should you pass under a tree and look at your hand swinging by your side, its retinal image would become much dimmer than it was in the sunlight. However, you do not consciously experience these changes in the retinal image. You are merely walking down the street. Objects remain in a permanent po-

sition despite the fact that their images appear and disappear within your eye. You feel as though you draw closer to objects of a fixed size, and your hand seems to be the same color and brightness regardless of the intensity of the light falling upon it.

The discrepancies between retinal image properties and conscious experiences are examples that we "construct" the world from our visual input rather than "seeing" it directly. Since the physical world does not change as the light, our direction of gaze, or distance from a target changes, we construct a corresponding stable world in consciousness. The way in which this stability is created and maintained is an interesting story, which revolves around a set of visual phenomena known as the CONSTANCIES. There are three varieties of perceptual constancies, each of which defines a class of phenomena. There are constancies related to visual objects, such as their size and shape; constancies related to qualities of those visual objects, such as their brightness and hue; and constancies that deal with relationships between visual objects, such as their position or orientation. Let us begin our discussion with the first of these.

OBJECT CONSTANCIES

Size Constancy. To understand size constancy, you must be aware of the relationship between the size of the visual image on the retinal surface and the distance between the observer's eye and the object being observed. As the distance between the eye and the object increases, the size of the retinal image decreases. This relationship is shown in Figure 14-1. As you probably recall from Chapter 7 (see Figure 7-10), retinal image size is usually expressed and measured in terms of its visual angle. The visual angle for S_1 (stimulus 1) is α_1 and for S_2 is α_2. Like other angles, these are expressed in degrees, minutes, and seconds of

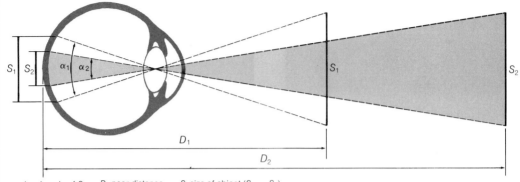

α_1 visual angle of S_1 D_1 near distance S, size of object ($S_1 = S_2$)
α_2 visual angle of S_2 D_2 far distance

Figure 14-1.
The visual angle. Although the physical size (S) of the object does not change, changes in distance (D) will result in changes in the size of the visual angle (α or alpha). Here α_1 (object S_1 close to the eye) is larger than α_2 (object S_2 far from the eye).

arc. Thus the image size of a quarter (25-cent piece) held at arm's length is about 2°, while at a distance of about 80 m the quarter would have a visual angle of 1 minute of arc. At a distance of 5 km it would have only the tiny retinal image size of 1 second of arc. Thus as its distance from an observer increases its retinal image size decreases.

Let us return to our earlier description of the physical changes in visual stimulation as one walks down the street. Now you may have begun to realize what would be happening if an observer perceived an object's size only in terms of its retinal image size. If such were the case, then a man who is 180 cm (about 6 ft) tall would look like a small child when he was at a reasonable distance from us, and he would appear to "grow" as we approached him. Of course this does not happen. Instead, we perceive him to be "man size" regardless of his relative distance from us. This stability of perceived size despite changes in objective distance and retinal image size is called SIZE CONSTANCY. In essence it involves assigning to an object a

constant size in consciousness, no matter what its distance or retinal size may be.

A good example of the operation of size constancy in human observers is found in a common experience that may have happened to you. While on vacation you discover a magnificent panoramic scene that overlooks a range of majestic mountains far in the distance. You are overawed. In great excitement, you quickly snap a photograph to share with your friends when you return home. However, after having gathered your friends together for a slide show of your trip, you are greatly disappointed to discover that the photograph does not convey the same impression of the scene as your personal view. In fact, those formerly majestic mountains appear to be puny. In disgust, you attempt to explain how "it was really quite awesome." Such occurrences can be explained in terms of the operation of size constancy. Although the eye can be compared to a camera in many ways, ultimately a camera does not act like a human observer. It does not compensate for the size changes that are related to distance changes. Since the camera registers only angular size, it does not make the perceptual correction needed to keep those distant objects "mountain size," and our own size constancy mechanism does not work as effectively when we view pictures as when we view the real objects (Coren & Girgus, 1977). Demonstration Box 14-1 can allow you to experience the relationship between retinal image size, distance, and the size constancy correction for yourself.

Shape Constancy. Epstein and Park (1963) have defined shape constancy as the "relative constancy of the perceived shape of an object despite variations in its orientation."

Hold out your hand in front of you at arm's length. Keep your eyes fixed on your hand as you move it toward your face and away again for several times. Although the retinal image size of your hand is smaller when it is seen at arm's length, you probably perceived no difference in size as you moved your hand.

Now hold up the index finger of your left-hand in front of your face, as shown in the figure, at a distance of about 20 cm. Fixate it carefully. Now position your right hand at arm's length behind your fixated finger. While maintaining fixation on your fingertip, bring your right hand toward and away from your face. Do not let your fixation waver from your finger, but also try to pay attention to the image of your hand as it moves closer to and farther away from your face. Under this second set of circumstances, you should suddenly see your hand change in size. You will perceive it as being smaller when it is held at arm's length, and you will see it enlarge as you move it toward your face. This simple demonstration allows you to experience the relationship between retinal image size and distance. Ordinarily, when we are paying attention to an object, the size constancy mechanism is immediately called into operation and the changes in retinal image size with distance are not perceived. When our attention is slightly diverted, we can experience the proximal (retinal) rather than the distal (objective or real) size.

Demonstration Box 14-1
Distance and Retinal Image Size

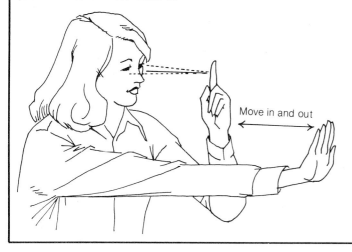

Move in and out

You might ask, "Why should an object look any different if its orientation changes?" Figure 14-2 attempts to answer this question. If you take a rectangular card or object and tilt or slant it so that the top is now farther from you than the bottom, you have changed the shape of the retinal image. As we increase the tilt, the retinal image becomes more like a trapezoid with the formerly vertical sides tapering outward. Yet the object still "looks"

rectangular. The same happens when we swing a door outward. The large changes in the shape of the retinal image are ignored, and the door still appears to be rectangular. In achieving shape constancy, the perceptual system appears to compensate for changes in slant in a way that is analogous to the compensation for distance changes in size constancy. Follow the instructions in Demonstration Box 14-2 to see this for yourself.

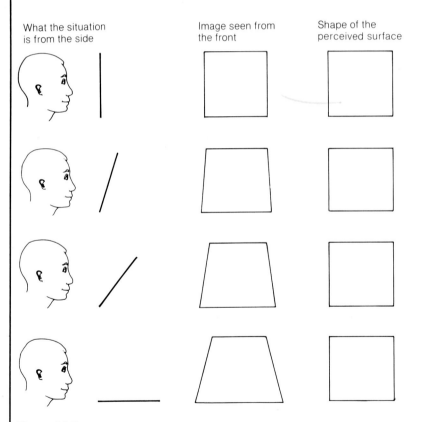

Figure 14-2.
Shape constancy. Changes in the tilt or slant of forms will cause changes in the shape of the retinal image. However, *perceived* shape remains constant (based upon Lindsay & Norman, 1977).

Demonstration Box 14-2
Shape Constancy

Look at the box in the accompanying figure. Most individuals believe that a dime will fit inside the top of this box. Try placing a dime (flat on one face) into the box. Does it fit?

The reason that the top surface of this box appeared to be large enough to accommodate the dime is because you made a shape (and size) constancy correction. The shape constancy correction changed the appearance of the top of the box into a square; the size constancy correction made the sides of the box top appear equal. Look back at the box and notice that its real physical shape is a parallelogram, not a square.

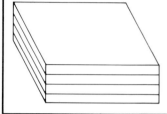

CONSTANCIES OF OBJECT PROPERTIES

After we have identified the presence of any object within the visual field, two of the most salient aspects of its visual existence are its qualities of brightness and color (hue). The identification of an object and the sensory processing of the qualities of that object are very closely tied. We perceive most visual stimuli as a totality and not as a bundle of distinct and discrete sensations. Since the qualities of an object are an integral part of the stability of its perceptual existence, it seems reasonable to expect such qualities to also remain stable despite variations in physical stimulation.

Brightness Constancy. In the case of perceived brightness there is a clear analogue to the operation of size constancy. Consider the retinal image first. Its brightness depends upon two things. The first is the amount of light from any source, such as the sun or a light bulb, that falls upon the object. This is called *illuminance* and is often symbolized by the letter E. Secondly, different object surfaces reflect differing amounts of light to the eye of the observer. For example, a white surface will reflect most (perhaps 80–90%) of the light that falls upon it back to the eye. On the other hand, a black surface will absorb a great deal of the light, and the amount reflected from the surface of the object will be quite small (often less than 4–5%). As you may remember from Chapter 8, the percentage of light reflected from a surface is called its *reflectance* and is often symbolized by the letter R. We can roughly express the physical parameters associated with the retinal image intensity L (for *luminance* at the eye) of an object by the following equation:

$$L = E \times R$$

Let us see how this works by putting some

numbers into the formula. If we have a light source that has a physical intensity of 100 units falling upon a surface that reflects 90% of the illuminating light, we would calculate a luminance value of 90 units ($L = 100 \times .90 = 90$). Now if we take that same surface and illuminate it with a physical intensity of 10 units, the luminance drops to 9 units ($L = 10 \times .90 = 9$). One might suppose that this simple example indicates that our perception of how light or dark an object appears should depend upon the solution to this equation. Certainly the intensity of the retinal image changes as the values within the equation change. However, just as perceived size does not appear to vary as the

retinal image size changes, perceived brightness remains relatively constant even as the physical intensity of the retinal image changes. A piece of white paper appears to be approximately the same brightness whether it is viewed in the dim light of an artificially lit room or in bright sunlight. This is in spite of the fact that the intensity of the retinal image differs for the two viewing conditions. One can observe the operation of BRIGHTNESS OR LIGHTNESS CONSTANCY very clearly in experimental situations like the one shown in Figure 14-3.

In Figure 14-3, an observer is sitting in a room with a piece of gray cardboard hanging from the ceiling a few feet in front of the

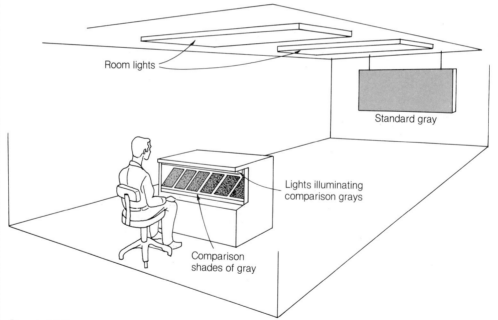

Figure 14-3.
An example of the classical experimental setup for the measurement of brightness constancy. The observer sees a standard gray target illuminated by room lights and is asked to choose the matching gray from a comparison series. The comparison series is seen through a box that provides independent illumination and prevents the intrusion of room light (from Cornsweet, 1970).

chair. Directly in front of the observer is a box with a window through which can be seen a series of papers graded in brightness from black through shades of gray to white. This graded or comparison series is independently illuminated, and it is not affected by the illumination in the room that falls upon the suspended gray cardboard. With identical illumination in the room and within the box, we ask our subject to choose a comparison gray that appears to be the same as the gray cardboard hanging in front of the chair. Based upon our knowledge of the luminance formula, we are not surprised when our observer chooses a comparison gray that is physically identical to the gray of the stimulus hanging in the room. Now we cut the room illumination by one-half but do not change the illumination on our comparison series. If our observer were making matches based upon the physical intensity of the retinal image, what would he do?

Table 14-1 shows that matches based upon the strict solution of the luminance equation would dictate that the observer should choose a comparison gray that has one-half of the surface reflectance of the standard. Typically, however, the observer will choose the comparison gray that is physically identical to (of the same reflectance as) the standard, and this pattern will continue regardless of the illumination changes we may impose upon the suspended gray cardboard. Perhaps it is just this type of behavior that prompted Thouless (1931) to talk of the constancies in terms of a "regression to the real object." It is quite clear that, in the experimental situation used to study brightness constancy, it is the relative reflectance of the stimulus hanging in the room and not the $L = ER$ solution that determines which comparison stimulus is chosen as its match. Thus we can define brightness constancy in terms of the dependence of perceived brightness on

the reflectance of a surface rather than on luminance values at the retina.

Color or Hue Constancy. Based upon the previous discussion of color vision in Chapter 8, you should be aware that our perception of

Table 14-1. $L = ER$ *Solutions for Observer's Behavior in a Brightness Constancy Experiment*

Test situation #1: Equal illuminance (100 units) in the room and on the comparison series.

Room	Comparison Series
$L = ER$	$L = ER$
$L = 100$ (.50)	$L = 100$ (.50)
$L = 50$	$L = 50$

The two grays match perceptually and physically.

Test situation #2: Room illuminance (50 units), one-half of that on the comparison series (100 units).

Perceptual Match

Room	Comparison Series
$L = ER$	$L = ER$
$L = 50$ (.50)*	$L = 100$ (.50)*
$L = 25$	$L = 50$

Physical Match

Room	Comparison Series
$L = ER$	$L = ER$
$L = 50$ (.50)**	$L = 100$ (.25)**
$L = 25$	$L = 25$

* Identical reflectances chosen although the value of L differs.
** The reflectance of the comparison gray is one-half that of the stimulus in the room. However, the value of L is equal in the two cases.

a color is a result of a complex interaction between the reflectance properties of a given pigment and the wavelength composition of the light that falls upon that pigment. Since properties of both lights and pigments are in a continual flux as we move about in our environment, one might expect that an object's color would appear to change as we changed the lighting conditions. However, we can identify red as red whether it is viewed under flourescent lights that have a dominant blue hue or incandescent lights that are basically yellow. Thus COLOR CONSTANCY refers to our ability to maintain the percept of a particular hue throughout variations in the quality of the illuminance and the reflectance properties of the surface pigment. Based upon our discussion of brightness constancy, we know that such variations will change the properties of the retinal image in terms of both luminance and wavelength; however, just as in brightness constancy, our percept of color is not based completely upon the properties of the image on the retina. Although we may be able to respond to variations within a given color, our ability to state, "Yes, it is a red of some type," remains intact. The nature of this perceptual ability is shown in Demonstration Box 14-3.

Color and brightness constancy share common aspects. First, they both relate to the surface qualities of objects in the visual environment. Brightness constancy is associated with ACHROMATIC (or noncolored) aspects of the objects. In other words it deals with the perception of things as dark or light. On the other hand, hue constancy lends stability to our perceptual experience of colored objects. Both hue and brightness constancy demonstrate how physical variations relate to, but do not fully account for, our final perceptual experience. Sensory psychologists often use the constancies of size, shape, brightness, and hue to demonstrate how the properties of the object in the visual environment (termed the DISTAL STIMULUS) tend to determine our emerging percepts in spite of variations in the retinal image (or PROXIMAL STIMULUS). We have introduced the terms distal and proximal because they are commonly used in discussions and research relating to the visual constancies. It may help you to remember which word describes each stimulus if you keep in mind that distal is derived from the Latin "dist," meaning "to stand apart" or "to be distant." It is easy to see how this term applies to the object standing apart from us in the visual environment. Proximal stems from the Latin "proxima," meaning "nearest." Of the two stimuli, the retinal image is the

---

Demonstration Box 14-3
Color Constancy

To carry out this demonstration you will need a reduction screen, which is simply a $\frac{1}{2}$-cm hole cut into the center of a dark piece of cardboard. In addition, you will need a fluorescent and a tungsten light source (such as your desk lamp and your room light, respectively) and a piece of colored paper (green works best). Hold the paper under the tungsten light. Notice its color. Next hold the colored sheet under a fluorescent lamp and notice that it still appears to be the same color under both light sources. Now look at the paper through the reduction screen, making sure that nothing else is visible through the hole except the patch of color. If you have used green paper, it should appear to be yellow-green under the tungsten light but blue-green when under the fluorescent lamp. In a full-cue situation with context information available, the operation of color constancy prevented you from seeing this hue change.

closest to us, yet our percept is a reconstruction of the object in the world.

CONSTANCIES OF OBJECT RELATIONS

The constancies of size, shape, brightness, and color deal with the perceptual stability of static objects within visual space. However, there are additional visual constancies that maintain perceptual regularity throughout movements of either the observer or the object of regard.

Position Constancy. When we freely walk about or move our heads, the image of the world stimulating the retinal surface moves in an orderly and systematic fashion. For example, when you move your head to the right, the retinal image of all stationary objects slides across the retinal surface to the left. Despite the fact that the retinal image moves, we do not experience the world as moving (see Chapter 12). Stationary objects seem to remain in a constant position regardless of our own movement. This is known as POSITION CONSTANCY. Retinal displacement can arise from two sources. First, the observer can move while the world remains stationary (although its retinal image has moved). On the other hand, the world may have moved while the observer has remained in a constant position. Either way, the relationship between the observer and the objects in the external field of view is monitored, and the visual system correctly discriminates between the two origins of retinal displacement or movement.

Direction Constancy. In Chapter 11, we discussed the notion of *egocentric localization,* the ability to localize external objects in relationship to our own bodies. When our eyes look straight ahead and the image of an object is stimulating both foveae, we perceive the object we are looking at as lying directly in front of our bodies. However, we can move our eyes and look off to the side, away from the object. Under these circumstances we are still able to localize the object as lying straight ahead of our bodies. Thus, in spite of eye movements, the egocentric direction of objects (where they lie relative to our bodies) remains constant. This is called DIRECTION CONSTANCY.

Position and direction constancy can be distinguished from each other in the following way. Eye movements do not change egocentric direction since, in spite of eye movements, objects are still perceived to lie in a particular and constant direction relative to our bodies. However, head and body movements can change egocentric direction. For example, look at an object that is straight ahead of your body. Now shift your head to one side. Since we tend to use the head as the reference point for egocentric direction (see Chapter 11), the object no longer seems to be directly straight ahead. Although the object is now perceived to lie in a different direction, its position in space is the same as it was before the head movement. Position and direction constancy are related but still separable phenomena (Shebilske, 1977).

The constancies exemplify how changes in proximal stimulation (the retinal image) are not exactly reproduced in our final perceptual experience. Our visual world remains stable, and the perceived qualities of the distant objects remain constant. Objects in the visual field are often more predictive of our experience than the retinal image, which supposedly provides our contact with the world. Hence the perceptual constancies also reveal the complex interaction that takes place between the structures of the visual system and the properties of incoming visual stimulation.

MECHANISMS IN THE CONSTANCIES

The constancies demonstrate that the physical realities are interwoven in a complex manner. One must ignore some aspects of the retinal situation if one is to represent the object more accurately in perception. In addition, each constancy seems to represent a coupling of several perceptual abilities. For example, size constancy couples our ability to perceive size with our ability to perceive distance. Epstein (1973, 1977) proposes that the visual system operates according to rules of processing whereby certain variables are combined to achieve constancy in perception. In the following discussion, we will attempt to see which variables are involved and what rules of combination are used.

Size Constancy. Leibowitz (1971, 1974) has likened size constancy to other biological processes that tend to involve a number of causal mechanisms. Some of these mechanisms are related to physiological structures within the visual system, while others are related to properties of the incoming visual stimulation and higher level processing of this information.

Size and distance information. The first approach to the problem of size constancy must be to ask why the perception of size does not change as retinal image size varies. Somehow the distance of the target is taken into account and the size percept is adjusted. In other words, we estimate distance and size together. This suggests that changes in apparent distance should alter our perception of apparent size. This is not a bad suggestion, as can be seen from Demonstration Box 14-4. Unfortunately, the suggestion that size constancy simply involves "taking distance into account" evades the question. How does one "take distance into account?" And, still unanswered, what is the actual underlying causal mechanism? Let us start by considering the interaction between size and distance information.

As you have discovered in Chapters 4 and 11, when we fixate objects at different distances, the lens of the eye changes shape to accommodate for changes in fixation distance. Simultaneously, the eyes either converge for near objects or diverge for distant objects to produce stable binocular foveal fixation. These two processes, working together, bring about a focused binocular retinal image over a wide range of fixation distances. We know that the retinal image size decreases as the observer–target distance increases; however, we also know that we do not perceive these changes in retinal image size. Why not? One explanation concerns the information available from the physiological changes brought about by convergence and accommodation changes.

In our discussion of position constancy, we mentioned that the visual system can differentiate between internally generated and externally generated movement, both of which cause image displacement across the retinal surface. If the visual system "knows" that the observer has made a head movement, it takes this into account and attributes the retinal displacement to internally generated sources. As a result, the external world remains stable. Such a phenomenon implies that the visual system has the physiological capability of monitoring changes in proximal stimulation. Suppose the same situation holds for accommodation and convergence changes. These changes could "inform" the visual system that distance is changing and, thus, retinal image size is varying. If this is monitored by the visual system, image changes can be anticipated and a perceptual compensation applied. The essence of this ar-

An easy way to demonstrate how apparent distance affects apparent size requires that you carefully fixate the point marked X in the accompanying white square while holding the book under a strong light. After a minute or so, you will form an afterimage (see Chapter 8) of the square. If you now transfer your gaze to a blank piece of paper on your desk, you will see a ghostly dark square floating there. This is the afterimage, which will appear to be several centimeters long on each side. Now shift your gaze so that you are looking at a more distant, light-colored wall. Again you will see the dark square projected against the wall, but now it will appear to be much larger in size. Because of the nature of an afterimage, its visual angle does not change. But as you project it against surfaces at varying distances from you, its apparent size changes. It appears to be larger when it is projected upon a distant surface. This is an example of how size and distance perception interact by means of the size constancy mechanism. The quantitative expression of this relationship is often called EMMERT'S LAW.

Demonstration Box 14-4
Size Constancy and Apparent Distance

gument is that information from convergence and accommodation changes, which signal distance variation, are taken into account so that alterations in retinal image size are not perceived.

How does one go about testing this theory? First of all, if this line of reasoning has any validity, we would expect that in the absence of any other information about the distance of the target (such as the pictorial cues to distance cataloged in Chapter 11), changes in accommodation and convergence would result in changes in perceived size. After all, if retinal image size is kept constant, but the visual system receives a signal that the object forming this image is close to the observer, the object should be perceived as being smaller. An identically sized target that is indicated to be more distant from the observer should be processed as being larger (remember that size constancy functions to "blow up" or enlarge the size of distant objects in consciousness).

In general, then, one has to set up a situation in which retinal image size remains constant, but physiological sources signal changes in distance. Such a situation should result in changes in perceived size. This experiment was conducted by Leibowitz and Moore (1966). Their experimental observers viewed a white triangle in an otherwise completely dark field. They matched the size of this stimulus by making size adjustments in a similar triangle. Accommodation and convergence were varied by inserting prisms and lenses before the eyes. This forced the subjects to adjust their convergence and accommodation to closer or farther distances when viewing the target, although the retinal size remained constant. If these depth cues help to stabilize the perception of size, this experimental manipulation should result in changes in perceived size.

The prediction of these investigators was confirmed. The size of the target, judged to be equal to that of the standard triangle, increased as accommodative and convergence changes were manipulated to indicate increasing target distance. Hence it seems that the state of the oculomotor (eye muscle) system, which varies with the distance of the distal stimulus, conveys information that helps to stabilize size perception. Since the perception of size seems to be linked to the perception of distance in some way, this is one way in which structures within the visual system "take distance into account" in computing the size constancy correction.

Information about the extent of accommodative and convergence movements is not the only mechanism at work in size constancy. Leibowitz (1971) has indicated that these sources of distance information appear to be useful in the preservation of size constancy only for fairly close distances (within

arm's length). This makes sense since most of these adjustments take place for targets within 1–2 m of the observer. In fact, current data indicate that the resting position of the eyes (where the fixation control mechanisms are relaxed) is between 0.5 and 1.0 m. Thus, when the distance information mechanism breaks down, it is not surprising to find that size constancy also fails. It is easy to demonstrate the disruption of size constancy at very large target–observer distances. One need only to climb to the top of a tall building and note that people appear to be tiny dolls and cars appear to be little toys.

Size and stimulus relationships. There is a geometric regularity in the visual array that provides us with much information. Thus the convergence of parallel lines as a function of distance (called linear perspective), or the increasing textural density of more distant fields of elements that we discussed in Chapter 11, are sufficiently regular in their occurrence to serve as reliable cues for distance. Such cues may assist in the maintainence of size constancy. Gibson (1950) and Rock (1975) have pointed out that constant relationships within the visual array may contribute to size constancy.

For example, we can imagine two objects of the same size sitting on a surface at different distances from the observer. As you know from Chapter 11, the fact that textured surfaces show gradations of coarseness as they recede into the distance is a very powerful distance cue. If two objects at different distances appear to cover the same number of textured elements (in other words, their relationship to the textured surface remains constant), they will remain perceptually the same size. This principle is exemplified in Figure 14-4. You will notice that here we have three cubes that appear to be about the same size, but that appear to vary in distance. Despite the fact that their image size differs, notice

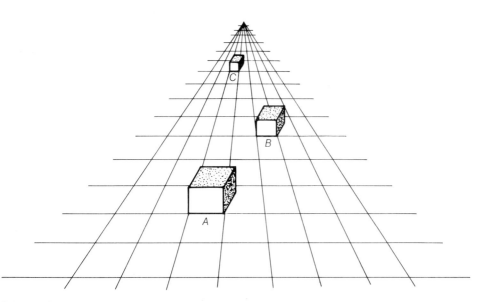

Figure 14-4.
Relational determinants of size constancy. Cubes *A, B,* and *C*
cover the same number of textured elements on the receding
ground. Hence they stand in a constant relationship to other
aspects of the visual environment. This helps to maintain size
constancy.

that each cube covers just slightly more than
one texture element. Thus the observer could
derive the fact that the cubes are physically
equal (which is simply the result of size constancy correction) by comparing the relative
size of the objects to the size of the surrounding texture elements.

To be convinced of this argument, however, we need to rely upon some experimental evidence that indicates that an observer's ability to make judgements consistent
with the preservation of size constancy differs
in the presence and absence of context.
Many experiments have demonstrated how
cues in the visual array contribute to the
maintenance of size constancy (for example,
the classic experiment was performed by
Holway and Boring, 1941). In one such experiment by Harvey and Leibowitz (1967),

observers were asked to choose a size match
for a standard target that was placed at various distances. There were two viewing conditions. One corresponded to natural situations
with many contextual cues, and the second
involved the removal of the surrounding context by having the subjects observe the standard target through a small opening that
blocked the view of everything but the target
to be observed. The visual angle of the standard target was kept constant at all viewing
distances. Hence, if size constancy were
maintained, each observer should continue
to choose a larger and larger variable target
to match the standard as the viewing distance
increased.

Under natural viewing conditions, size
matches conformed very well to the predictions based upon the efficient operation of the

size constancy mechanism. This was the case for all of the observer–target distances used in this experiment. However, when the context was removed, size matches conformed to constancy predictions only at viewing distances of up to about 120 cm. After that, size matches began to deviate from the predictions based upon size constancy. This experiment shows the role of context in the maintenance of size perception. In addition, it demonstrates the operation of several mechanisms in size constancy. Since there is no difference between the two viewing conditions at relatively small observer–target distances, one might argue that accommodation and convergence information about distance is primarily responsible for size perception when the observer is relatively close to the object. On the other hand, when the observer is not located in close proximity to the object, contextual cues appear to play a more prominent role in maintaining the stability of perceived size. Hence both physiological and stimulus variables appear to be involved in this perceptual process.

The ability to use information from the geometric relationships within the stimulus context seems to be affected by experience. This is demonstrated by the fact that children show patterns of size constancy that differ from those of adults. The size matching behavior of children and adults does not differ at close observation distances where information from convergence and accommodation seems to operate. However, when the target is farther away and contextual information is more important to the maintenance of size constancy, children have greater difficulty making the appropriate size constancy responses. This type of data, reported by Zeigler and Leibowitz (1957), suggests that the effective use of context information is based upon some learned components. Since children have a lesser amount of experience with the way in which the world is structured,

they exhibit deficits in size constancy at the observation distances that appear to be governed by those external cues. Contextual information appears to be more efficiently utilized by adult observers. This makes their size matching behavior stable across a wider range of observation distances. Thus the accuracy of size constancy seems to depend upon both the availability of depth information and the observer's ability to use it.

Size constancy and illusion. Size constancy allows our perception of the relative size of objects to differ from what is predicted on the basis of knowledge of the retinal image's size. This is quite important in that an accurate picture of the size of objects in the real world should not depend upon our distance from such objects. Thus, consider Figure 14-5A in which we see two logs lying in the middle of a road. Notice that the upper log appears to be the same size as the lower one, although it is quite clear that they have been drawn two different sizes on the paper. Since the contextual distance cues in the visual array (perspective, texture, and others) indicate that the upper log is more distant, we see it as being the same size as the closer log in spite of the fact that it is drawn slightly smaller. Hence this is another example of size constancy.

Now consider Figure 14-5B. Here we have two logs that appear to be different in size, with the more distant one seemingly longer than the closer one. A ruler will quickly reveal that they have been drawn exactly the same physical size. Once again this merely represents the operation of size constancy. To the extent that the picture mimics the conditions in the real world, the upper log appears to be more distant. Hence it can cause the same size retinal image as the lower log only under conditions where it is physically longer. Since in the picture the logs have been drawn the same size, the percept is appropriately corrected.

Figure 14-5.
(A) The two logs lying on the road appear to be at different distances. Therefore their apparent size is the same despite the fact that the apparently more distant log is physically smaller than the other one. (B) The logs are identical in size; however, the one that appears to be more distant looks larger. The application of size constancy can lead to illusions of size. (C) The Ponzo illusion. A similar effect to that in (B) in the absence of any context for distance and depth.

Now let us look at Figure 14-5C, where we see two converging lines and two horizontal lines. Notice that the upper line appears to be slightly longer. Like the logs in Figure 14-5B, the two lines are physically equal in length; hence, the percept of unequal size is an illusion. This configuration is usually called the *Ponzo illusion*. Let us note, however, that this is an illusion only in the sense that no context for depth or distance has been deliberately drawn into the figure. Yet the constancy corrective mechanism has been inappropriately evoked, resulting in this distorted, illusory percept of the relative length of the two horizontal lines. In some instances there is a very fine distinction between a picture and a simple array of lines that produces a visual illusion. Thus one might easily imagine a child with poor drawing ability producing 14-5C when asked to draw 14-5B.

In some instances the cues that inappropriately elicit size constancy are more difficult to see. Consider Figure 14-6. The vertical line marked *A* appears to be shorter than the vertical line marked *B* although they are equal in length. This distortion, which is called the *Mueller–Lyer illusion,* has also been explained in terms of size constancy. For example, the wings turned toward the vertical line might mimic the perspective cues of the outside of a building (shown in dark lines in C), while the wings turned away from the vertical line might mimic an interior corner of a room (shown in *D*). To the extent that the closest point in the array is the plane of the paper, it is easy to see that if the wings imply increases or decreases in distance away from that plane, the vertical shaft in *B* is more distant than that pictured in *A*. Hence the operation of size constancy would enlarge the apparent length of *B* relative to *A*. Notice again that this is an illusion of size only in the sense that no depth or distance was intended; therefore, the application of size constancy is inappropriate in this situation. Several other illusion distortions also act as though observers were responding to implied depth cues in the configuration (Ward, Porac, Coren, & Girgus, 1977).

Shape Constancy. There seems to be an intimate relationship between size and shape constancy. Both are related to distance per-

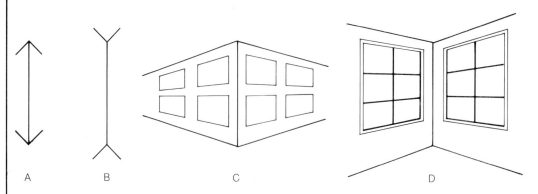

A   B   C   D

Figure 14-6.
(A) The underestimated segment of the Mueller–Lyer illusion.
(B) The overestimated segment. (C and D) The corresponding perspective configurations.

ception. However, for shape constancy, the distance information pertains to the relative distance of different *parts* of the object from the observer, in other words, its orientation in space or its slant. When we ask the question, "How does the observer take slant into account?" the resulting answers are similar to those for size constancy. To begin with, the amount of available information indicating the slant of the object seems to be critical. In unrestricted viewing, with many contextual cues available, observers tend to perceive the shape and slant of objects with remarkable accuracy (Lappin & Preble, 1975). As in the size constancy situation, when observers are prevented from using contextual information that would indicate the degree of slant, the operation of shape constancy becomes less accurate, and the percept comes to reflect the retinal situation rather than the actual object (Leibowitz & Bourne, 1956).

The degree of shape constancy one obtains can be further altered by the type of instructions that the observer is given in the experimental task. Carlson (1977) has analyzed the effects of instructions for both size and shape constancy and found that they affect judgment quite drastically. Essentially, observers can either be asked to report the size and shape of the objects that they are viewing (the OBJECTIVE INSTRUCTION) or asked to report the size and shape of their retinal image (the PROJECTIVE INSTRUCTION). The objective instruction is closest to normal viewing, where the perceptual task is to derive what is "out there." The objective instruction is similar to what an artist must do in trying to translate the scene being viewed onto a canvas consisting of sizes and shapes of colored regions that will represent objects in space when viewed by an observer. It has been shown many times (Gilinsky, 1955; Leibowitz & Harvey, 1969) that when observers are asked to adopt the projective viewing set, they show lesser degrees of con-

stancy. These data suggest that the constancies depend upon higher level cognitive corrections that may include some learned components.

One especially interesting aspect of the data is that observers, judging the projective shape of objects, cannot completely "turn off" the constancy correction. They continue to make constancy corrections although the judgments do become more like the retinal image than in the objective instruction condition (Lappin & Preble, 1975; Lichte & Borresen, 1967). These data, combined with the recent findings of Epstein, Hatfield, and Muise (1977) (which showed that, much like any cognitive task, the more processing time available, the more shape constancy is found), plus the failure to find physiological mechanisms for either size or shape constancy (Richards, 1977), suggest that shape constancy is an automatic, higher-level process. The shape constancy correction probably involves cognitive adjustments of the percept to bring it into closer correspondence with the external reality.

Brightness and Color Constancy. Of all the constancies, brightness and color have aroused the most heated theoretical debates. While some investigators have attempted to deal with these in terms of more cognitive, higher level information processing mechanisms, others have suggested that they can be completely explained in terms of relatively inflexible *structural* processes (structural processes refer to known physiological mechanisms). To be successful such theories must explain why the brightness and color of an object remain constant despite changes in the illumination falling upon it. Let us look at each in turn.

The structural mechanism that has been offered to explain brightness constancy (and by extension, color constancy) involves some of the same processes of neural interaction proposed to explain brightness contrast and Mach bands in Chapter 7. These involve lateral inhibitory interactions between adjacent regions of the retina. Thus Cornsweet (1970) suggests that when we uniformly increase the amount of light falling upon a region of the visual field containing a number of items of different reflectances, the actual response of the neural units that signal brightness does not change significantly. On the basis of animal experimentation, there is some evidence that the neural response of the earliest levels of processing in the retina changes logarithmically with luminance changes. (It is important to note that this does not mean that brightness grows logarithmically.) Because of this, if we increase the illumination over an area uniformly, all regions of the retina increase their response rate by the same relative amounts. For example, suppose that we have two stimuli in the visual field, one with 30% reflectance and the other with 80% reflectance. If the light falling upon each one is 10 units, we get 3 units of luminance from one and 8 units of luminance from the other, reflecting from the surface to reach the eye. If we double the amount of light falling upon the surface, we have increased the illumination intensity to 20 units, and the reflected light becomes 6 and 16 units, respectively. Although it looks as though we should get different amounts of brightness increase for both stimuli (since one has increased by 3 units and the other by 8 units), we have kept a constant ratio between the two stimuli. The ratio of 6/16 is equal to that of 3/8. When we take the logarithm of each value, we find that we have increased each by the same amount (we have added .3 log units of response as we doubled the input). Cornsweet now adds one additional assumption. He assumes that the amount of lateral inhibition increases as we increase the rate of response of any retinal region. Since the amount of stimulation and the amount of inhibition both increase

equally, the overall response of the eye to increased illumination remains relatively unchanged.

There are several predictions made by such a theory. For instance, brightness constancy should depend upon having several different levels of reflectance under the same illumination in close proximity in the visual field. This prediction is confirmed in the results of a classic experiment by Gelb (1929). He illuminated an object with a concealed light source. This illuminated object was placed in a dimly lit field as shown by the experimental situation in Figure 14-7. The illuminated object was a black disc; however, observers reported seeing a white disc in dim light rather than a black disc that was very brightly lit. This of course represents a complete failure of constancy. If constancy were operating, the observers would see the black disc as black even though it was very brightly lit. Gelb then tried a second manipulation. He placed a piece of white paper in front of the brightly lit black disc. As soon as this was done, observers reported that the disc looked black. In other words, with the addition of the reference white paper, constancy returned. However, as soon as the piece of white paper was removed, the black disc returned to its former white appearance. Thus, although the observers now had information that the target was a brightly lit black object, the additional information did not help them to maintain constancy in the absence of the additional brightness level in the field (the piece of white paper).

There is other evidence that supports the constant-ratio notion of brightness constancy. Wallach (1948, 1972b) found that the perceived brightness of a target is a constant ratio of its light intensity compared to that of its surroundings. Look at Figure 14-8. Here you see two central targets, each surrounded by an outer ring (which serves as a variable intensity background). Both the central cir-

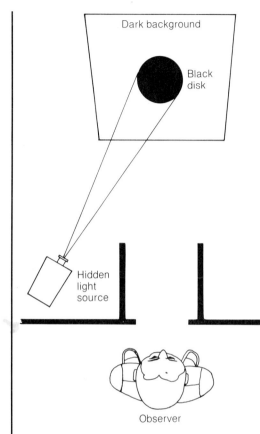

Dark background

Black disk

Hidden light source

Observer

Figure 14-7.
Experimental situation used by Gelb (1929) to disrupt brightness constancy.

cles and the outer rings are independently illuminated. The observers are asked to set the two inner circles until they appear to be equally bright. When this is done, we find the observers have set the intensity so that the ratios of the two sets of stimuli are the same. For example, suppose we set the central circle in Figure 14-8A to be 50 intensity units and the outer ring to be 100 intensity units. In order for the central circle in Figure 14-8B to appear to be equally bright, it must also be in a 2/1 ratio with its outer circle. Therefore, if

the outer circle's intensity in Figure 14-8B is 50 units, a central circle of 25 units (another 2/1 ratio) will appear to be as bright as the central circle of 50 intensity units in Figure 14-8A. It is not the absolute intensity levels that matter; rather, it is the brightness ratio between targets and their surroundings or between adjacent objects that seems to maintain brightness constancy.

The equal ratios reported in the preceding and the necessity of having more than one object in the field appear to support a structural basis for brightness constancy. Several recent investigators have elaborated on this mechanism (Richards, 1977; Marr, 1974). Unfortunately, other data show that this theory works both too well and too poorly. It works too well in terms of experiments that have attempted to directly measure the brightness interactions between adjacent areas. Such work suggests that the inhibitory effects do not reproduce the ratios exactly (Heineman, 1955; Diamond, 1960). Therefore, brightness constancy is better than the physiology would lead us to predict. The simple structural theory also cannot explain a number of observations. For instance, one does not reproduce Wallach's ratio results if the target is simply suspended on a thread a few centimeters in front of the background, as opposed to placing the target at the same level as the background (Mershon & Gogel, 1970). Certainly if the only important factor is adjacent areas of brightness on the retina, this simple manipulation would make no difference. Finally there is evidence that observers do "take into account" the amount of illumination falling on targets. This brings us to a second theoretical position.

Since the time of Helmholtz (mid-1800s) investigators have suggested that brightness and color constancy are maintained by mechanisms similar to those involved in shape and size constancy. In the present case, however, the observer adjusts the

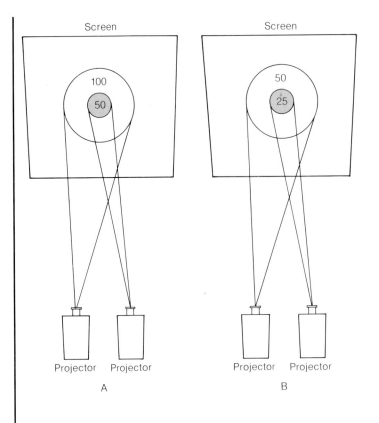

Screen

Screen

100

50

50

25

Projector   Projector

Projector   Projector

A

B

Figure 14-8.
Relational determinants of brightness constancy. Wallach (1948, 1972b) found that regardless of absolute physical intensity, equal brightness would be perceived when targets stood in an equal intensity ratio with their surroundings. In this example, which demonstrates the experimental technique used by Wallach, the central circles will appear to be equally bright because they both stand in a 1/2 intensity ratio with their respective surroundings.

percept not according to distance cues, but according to cues that suggest the amount of illumination and the direction from which it comes. Thus in the Gelb experiment they would argue that the introduction of the white piece of paper provides a cue indicating that there is an intense, hidden light source. This information evokes the formerly inoperative constancy correction.

Several such cues seem to be important in triggering brightness constancy. For instance, the presence of visible shadows seems to produce a brightness correction (MacLeod, 1947). Another factor is the perceived orientation of the target relative to the light. For example, one set of experiments arranged a situation so that an observer viewed a

trapezoidal object as in Figure 14-9. When viewed with one eye the target appeared as if it were a flat rectangle (Figure 14-9A). When viewed with both eyes it appeared to be standing upright (Figure 14-9B). Shadows cast by the surrounding objects gave observers information about the direction of the light source. The orientation of the object relative to the light source determines the amount of light falling on it and, therefore, it also determines the magnitude of brightness constancy needed to maintain an accurate percept. As would be expected, if the perceptual system were making its corrections on the basis of cues to illumination, the apparent brightness of the target would change according to its perceived orientation relative to the

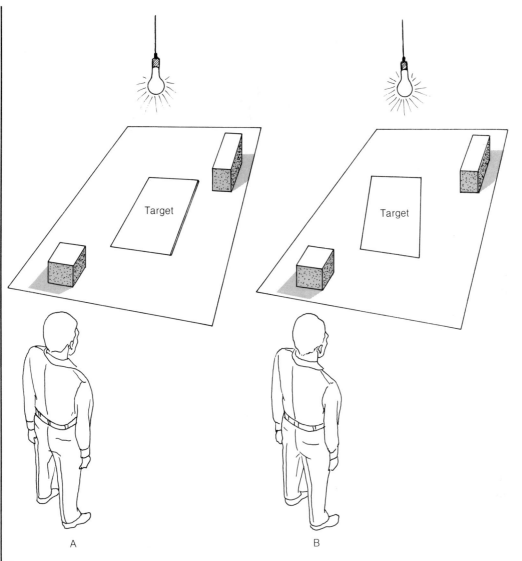

A

B

Figure 14-9.
Direction of illumination and brightness constancy
experiment. (A) Apparently flat configuration. (B) Apparently
upright configuration.

light source (Beck, 1965; Flock & Freedberg, 1970; Hochberg & Beck, 1954). Of course, the same amount of light is reaching the eye from the target, regardless of its perceived orientation. When the target appears flat the perceptual system "presumes" that much light is falling upon it from the light bulb directly above it. Because of this, the constancy correction operates to make the target appear darker when it is seen as flat (to correct for the extra light) than when it is seen as upright. It is probably useful now to turn back to Figure 7-9, which shows an example of brightness constancy correcting for the amount of illumination *presumed* to be present.

As with the structural theory, the cognitive-correction approach does not account for all of the data. For instance, the change in apparent brightness, as we change the apparent orientation of the object, is smaller than would be expected if the 90° difference in slant were taken completely into account. Thus brightness constancy involves both cognitive and structural mechanisms, as do most other perceptual phenomena.

The simplicity of our visual world is derived from a complex interaction of variables. Some of these processes are within the visual system itself, and some appear to be related to how the world is structured and how this structure presents itself to the human observer. At any rate, we must look beyond simple properties of the proximal stimulus to answer our questions concerning how and why things look as they do. Often the unnoticed changes, such as those associated with the size of the retinal image as we change distances from a target, or its brightness as we change illumination levels, are more important than those that are noticed.

15
Attention and Search

The policeman ran up to the dazed pedestrian, "Did you see the license number of the car that just hit you?"

"Well," came the shaky answer. "Actually I was looking at the dog next to the driver. It was a huge St. Bernard wearing a jewel-studded collar with a gold medallion hanging from it that said LOVE. It was wearing sunglasses, a red beret, and a green and yellow paisley scarf. Come to think of it, I guess I just didn't pay much attention to the license number of the car."

What is the relationship between attention and perception? The notion of attention involves selection. To "pay attention" to something means to process some portion of the incoming sensory information and to let other aspects of the external scene slip away. In our example, the pedestrian's attention was captured by the apparel worn by the dog and not by the license number of the car that struck her. Although the dog, the driver, and the car were all part of the scene the pedestrian observed, only one portion of it was selected for sensory processing. The dog became the only portion of the incident that could be related to the police. Paying attention means to be *perceptually selective*. Not everything that we are exposed to becomes part of our conscious perceptual experience.

The concept of attention, as well as investigations into the phenomena associated with it, have a stormy history. Its importance was recognized quite early by William James (1890), who noted that ". . . what is called our 'experience' is almost entirely determined by our habits of attention. A thing may be presented to a man a hundred times, but if he persistently fails to notice it, it cannot be said to enter into his experience." In the early part of the present century, many psychologists, such as William James and E. B. Titchner, felt that the study and examination of attention was of crucial concern. However, this view was not shared by other researchers, including behaviorists such as J. B. Watson; hence intensive investigation was dropped until about 1950. As a result of this gap in research time, contemporary notions of attention have a rather brief history by scientific standards, which may account for much of the lack of agreement and the controversy about the issue that is characteristic of the current literature. For example, we find that many researchers cannot even agree on the scope of the phenomenon to be covered by the word *attention*. Some individuals feel that there are as many as ten different types of behavioral events that can be classified under attention, while others choose to include only seven and still others mention only two types of attention (Boring, 1970; Moray, 1969; Posner & Boies, 1971; Swets & Kristofferson, 1970; Treisman, 1969).

Given this diversity, is there anything that is typical of an attentive state? Perhaps the phrases "to catch one's attention" or "to pay attention to" provide a good starting point. Usually when we are "paying attention" to something or someone, we have pointed our sense organs toward the source of the sound or light stimulation. To use the technical term psychologists prefer, we say that an observer has emitted an ORIENTING RESPONSE, in which the sense organs have been positioned so that we can optimally receive the stimuli (Mostofsky, 1970). In Chapter 4 you learned that the fovea is the very small region in the retina that provides the clearest and most detailed vision. When paying attention to a visual object, we generally orient our eyes so that the image of the object of interest falls within the foveal area. Unfortunately, attention as a psychological process is not nearly as simple as receptor orientation alone.

Simply noting which target is imaged on the fovea does not guarantee that the target is being attended to. It is possible to look without seeing, although it is more difficult to see without looking. Thus the study of attention will take us into realms of information processing beyond pure sensory experience. We must also deal with the role of memory and with the role of expectations that have been built up through continual exposure to sensory stimulation of a particular type. In other words, we must deal with attention as a COGNITIVE PROCESS, where cognitive is the word used to describe the aspects of our experience that involve thinking and memory. We might say that attention also·involves a sort of cognitive orienting response whereby one learns to expect various events and various sequences of events. As you will see, these expectations can affect how well we can extract information from the incoming sensory information. In our discussion of attention, we will generally follow a classification scheme proposed by Posner and Boies (1971), which seems to incorporate many features of the attentional process that are important for the perceptual process.

VIGILANCE

VIGILANCE refers to a form of attention that emphasizes the maintenance of alertness and accuracy of observation during long, often boring tasks where an observer tries to detect some type of signal (such as a blip on a radar screen). Research into vigilance began as a result of attentional problems found among radar operators during World War II (Jerison, 1970). After a certain time on duty, these operators tended to become tired, and this resulted in a decrease in their ability to detect signals caused by incoming planes. As a result of such observations, Mackworth (1950) conducted some experiments to investigate problems associated with sustaining attention over prolonged periods of time. In these original experiments, observers watched a hand moving in steps around a blank clock face. The hand moved in regular steps, but occasionally a double step took place. The ob-

server was asked to detect the occurrence of this double step by pressing a key each time one occurred. Mackworth found that after only one-half hour of watching, detection performance had dropped; the observers were actually missing more than one out of every four events. Physical fatigue seemed to be an unlikely explanation for this poor performance since the workload in this situation was really very light.

Later research attempted to examine this performance decrease over time. Was the sensory system (in this case, vision) becoming fatigued and thus losing its original sensitivity? Or was the performance decrease due to some factor that resulted in the observer just failing to respond, even though the sensory system was able to detect the critical stimulus event? Either factor, or both, would lead to the observed decrease in detection over time.

The questions being asked in the study of vigilance are very similar to those associated with Signal Detection Theory (which was discussed in Chapter 2). If you remember, when a detection problem is couched in signal detection terms, a researcher can calculate a d' score, which is a measure of the observer's sensitivity, and also a β score, which indicates changes in the way the observer is responding to the stimulus. Since either a decrease in sensitivity or a decrease in an observer's overall tendency to respond "yes" to a signal would account for the decrease in vigilance performance, such an analysis suits the present situation very well. When various investigators analyzed the vigilance problem from this viewpoint, they found that sensitivity (or d') did not change over time. However, observers became more cautious in saying "yes" as their time on watch progressed (Broadbent & Gregory, 1963, 1965). This seems to indicate that changes in performance during a vigilance task may not be due to a fatiguing of the sensory system so much as to a change in an observer's willingness to say that the signal has been detected.

The notions of vigilance and sustained attention demonstrate some interesting aspects of the phenomenon of attention. Vigilance tasks illustrate that paying close attention to an external stimulus is an intense activity that requires MENTAL EFFORT. Effort is not expended unless the observer is aroused in some way. Certain levels of physiological arousal, including maintenance of certain bodily positions, tensing of specific muscle groups, and continual active concentration, are necessary in order to pay attention. You can relate this to any situation in which you have "snapped back" to an alert posture after you have found yourself dozing off during a dull lecture. However, what happens during vigilance tasks illustrates that ever increasing levels of arousal may not bring about the best performance. As arousal levels increase, attention becomes more narrowly focused on the central target of interest while other information is ignored. In the case of the vigilance task, this may lead to the enforcement of an increasingly strict criterion for saying "yes" to the presence of a signal. Performance suffers when this happens. In 1908, Yerkes and Dodson formulated the relationship between arousal and performance in a way now known as the YERKES–DODSON LAW. This relationship is shown graphically in Figure 15-1. As you can see, it has the shape of an upside-down U, which indicates that there is a midrange of arousal that brings about optimum performance on a given task.

The relationship between arousal, or some level of alertness, and performance is not simple. This fact can be demonstrated in another way. When observers are given a warning signal that lets them prepare themselves to take in some sensory information, they seem to do better than if no warning were given prior to the presentation of a sensory stimulus. The best performance seems to

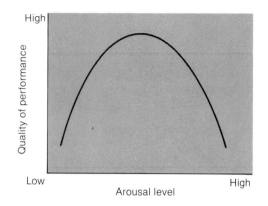

Figure 15-1.
The Yerkes–Dodson Law. The quality of performance seems to be best at middle levels of arousal.

occur when the warning signal is presented between 200 and 500 msec before the onset of the target. Once again these data indicate that a certain degree of alertness is optimal, and that it takes a certain period of time for an observer to achieve this level. However, if the forewarning period is too long, the critical arousal period for optimal performance passes and accuracy declines (Posner & Boies, 1971).

DIVIDED ATTENTION

Most of us have little difficulty in carrying on two or more activities simultaneously. We can read this book, scratch our heads, and chew on a snack—all at the same time. You might be tempted to say that you are conscious of the words in the book, while the rest of your activities remain unconscious. However, the evidence indicates that you are probably expending some mental effort on all these activities, although reading the book is taking the most effort. One can think of gaining mastery over a skill (such as driving a car) as a gradual withdrawal of mental effort until it can be performed almost automatically and with seemingly little attention. This leaves us free to expend mental effort on other things (such as talking to a friend or singing with the radio as we drive). Hence the old saying, "Practice makes perfect," can be rephrased to, "Practice makes automatic," or even, "Practice makes unconscious." Thus a practiced typist is totally unconscious of the individual key strokes involved in forming each word.

Norman (1976) describes this process as establishing schemes that allow us to organize large chunks of information which are then stored in memory for later, and very efficient, retrieval. Chess masters, for example, have engaged in extensive study of the possible combinations of pieces and squares on the board that characterize typical attacks or defenses. Thus the individual game becomes an expression of, or a deviation from, these well-learned patterns. This automatic control, gained through extensive practice, allows the chess master to seemingly expend less overt effort in the completion of a game than does a novice player. AUTOMATICITY of such cognitive processes allows us to divide our attention between various mental activities (LaBerge, 1973, 1975; Schneider & Shiffrin, 1977; Shiffrin & Schneider, 1977). Divided attention, in many instances, is highly dependent upon memory and the efficient systems that we have developed for the storage and retrieval of information.

It is also intriguing to look at other processes related to the issue of dividing attention. These processes have to do with the ease or difficulty one has in splitting attention within various sense modalities themselves. For example, we have two eyes and two ears. Do the individual channels carrying stimulus information merge so that it is impossible to distinguish between them? Or can we, given the right set of circumstances, divide our attention between these bilateral (two-sided) sense organs? If so, at what cost? These are interesting questions that we will investigate in the following sections. You can get a hint about the nature of the problem in Demonstration Box 15-1.

Divided Attention in Vision.   Moray (1969) has commented that one of the most striking differences between hearing and vision is the fact that, without the help of closing one eye, we are not able to tell which eye is receiving the visual stimulation. This is not true in audition where, when only one ear has received a signal, we can easily designate which one was involved. The two eyes appear to operate in a parallel or simultaneous fashion in which the binocular (two-eyed) information is perceived as a unit. Each eye's input seems to lose its particular identity (often lyrically called its *eye signature*). Researchers, interested in whether or not observers could tell if their right or their left eyes had received visual stimulation, tested this by placing observers in a dark room and secretly covering one eye. When a stimulus was presented monocularly (to one eye), observers were asked to guess which eye had seen it. They were unable to do this with any reliability, which seems to indicate that the separate channels from the two eyes are not usually distinguishable (Smith, 1945; Pickersgill, 1961).

There is, however, one condition in which the two eyes compete for conscious attention. This situation involves an experimental procedure known as BINOCULAR RIVALRY. As the name suggests, we can set up conditions in which the two eyes will act as rivals for attention. Using a stereoscope, which is an optical instrument that allows us to stimulate the right and the left eyes separately (discussed in Chapter 11), we can present an observer with a set of stimuli that will not combine into a normal, single unified image. Rather, each

You can perform a simple experiment to demonstrate the ease with which you can divide your attention and how this ability interacts with the amount of effort you are expending on a task. As you read these words, it is hoped that you are paying close attention to them, and you are probably not really attending to other things. Now shift your attention to the pressure of your buttocks against the chair on which you are sitting. The activity of sitting is well-practiced, and you need to expend very little effort on its performance. However, you can easily shift your attention to the activity if you are asked to do so. Now concentrate on the act of sitting and try to continue reading the book. Is it easier or more difficult to understand the words in the book while you are concentrating on another activity? Reading new material usually requires large amounts of mental effort. Therefore, it is difficult to divide one's attention when performing such a demanding task.

eye's view will alternate in consciousness. In other words, the right eye's view will be seen for a short time, but then the left eye's view will take over. The alternations will continue as long as the observer views the rivaling stimuli.

Binocular rivalry can be most effectively produced by presenting an observer with lined stimuli that are grossly different in orientation. For example, we might put a grid of horizontal lines in one eye and a grid of vertical lines in the other. Also, we might present different colors to the two eyes, such as red in one and green in the other. In both instances the stimuli will not combine, or *fuse,* and binocular rivalry will occur. Demonstration Box 15-2 allows you to experience binocular rivalry for yourself. Although binocular rivalry illustrates that the two eyes can operate somewhat independently, you should note that it can only be produced under certain laboratory conditions. In everyday viewing, we do not seem to be able to divide our attention between the two eyes.

Divided Attention in Audition. As was mentioned in the previous section, observers can more easily distinguish the origin of stimula-

tion (right ear versus left ear) in the auditory modality. In the early 1950s, Donald Broadbent took advantage of this fact to study divided attention with auditory stimulation. He called each ear a *channel* of information and asked a rather straightforward question. He wanted to know if it was easier to respond to input within one channel than to respond to input across different channels. In other words, would observers perform with greater efficiency when they were asked to respond to only one channel at a time, or when they were asked to divide their attention between two channels?

Broadbent (1954) had his observers wear a set of stereophonic headphones through which a different stimulus could be presented to each ear. This is sometimes called DICHOTIC presentation. On each trial three different numbers were presented to each ear; for example, the right ear might receive 6, 9, 2 while the left ear simultaneously receives 3, 4, 8. Broadbent had already ascertained that observers could recall a string of six numbers with about 96% accuracy when all the numbers were presented to both ears in a single sequence. He now wanted to know how they would perform given two types of recall in-

You may demonstrate binocular rivalry by using the accompanying figure and a pocket mirror. Place the mirror on the center line of Figure B and hold your head as shown in Figure A (this is the same technique that was used in Chapter 13 to demonstrate form in random-dot stereograms). Adjust it until the figure seen in the mirror appears to be at the same distance as the picture when seen directly. Now view the pictures for a few moments. At first you will see one set of lines; then they will be replaced by the other as they rival each other, alternating in and out of consciousness.

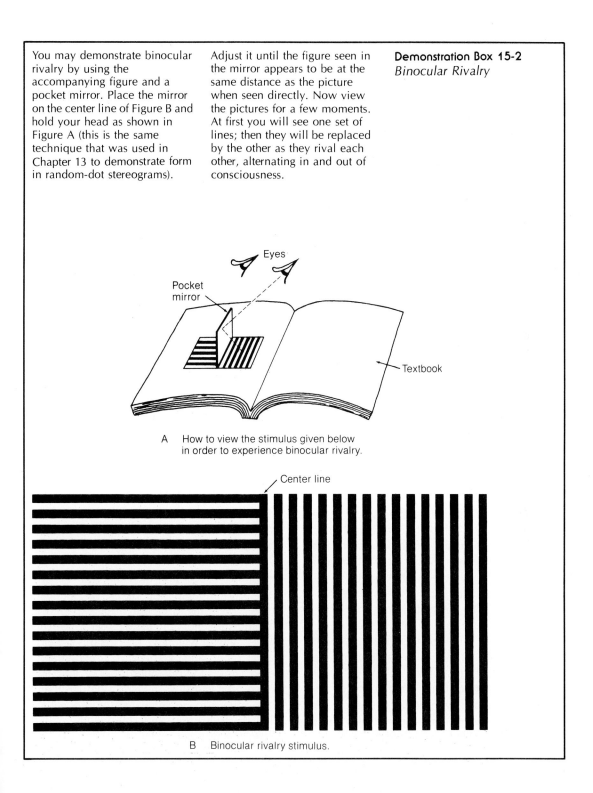

A   How to view the stimulus given below
in order to experience binocular rivalry.

B   Binocular rivalry stimulus.

structions. First, they were asked to recall the three numbers presented to one ear and then the three numbers presented to the other ear. Therefore, a correct response in our example would be 6, 9, 2, 3, 4, 8. In the second condition, observers were asked to repeat the numbers in their order of presentation. Since the numbers had been presented to both ears simultaneously, the correct order of report in this instance would be 6, 3, 9, 4, 2, 8 (or 3, 6, 4, 9, 8, 2). Broadbent found that observers could report the entire string of numbers about 65% of the time when they were responding ear by ear, but only 20% of the time when they were repeating the numbers by order of presentation across the two ears. He interpreted this as reflecting a loss of information processing capability when attention was switched between channels several times. In essence, Broadbent was suggesting that the order of auditory processing was determined by the channels of input and that switching between channels would bring about a division of attention and poorer performance.

It wasn't long before other researchers took exception to this line of reasoning. In 1960, Gray and Wedderburn published results that led them to question the assumption that the two ears function as separate channels. They used Broadbent's technique but they modified his six stimulus items. They used both numbers and words, three in each ear, with each ear receiving some words and some numbers. However, the words composed a meaningful phrase, so that the simultaneous stimulus presentation went something like "three, aunt, eight" in the left ear and "dear, two, Jane" in the right ear. You will notice that this stimulus series contains the organized and meaningful phrase, "Dear Aunt Jane." Under these conditions the observers performed with equal efficiency, regardless of whether they reported the items by ear or by order of presentation.

These results contradict the notion that

separation of physical channels will determine the order of information processing, and they also indicate the important role of memory in our ability to divide our attention. The expectations built up through our knowledge and experience with language are stored in memory. These can aid us in overcoming physical constraints on information processing. From the moment of input into a sensory system, various memorial expectations are alerted, and these interact in the final production of a perceptual experience. In other words, not only the physical aspects of the stimulus but our own interpretations and expectations can determine the order of processing and the allocation of attention.

Perhaps a good way to think of the above distinction is to use the framework suggested in Chapter 13 during our discussion of form perception. There we spoke of DATA-DRIVEN versus CONCEPTUALLY-DRIVEN processes (Lindsay & Norman, 1977; Norman, 1976). Data-driven processes are those based upon the limits and actions of physiological structures in direct response to incoming sensory information. For example, a stimulus enters the eye and proceeds through the various structures that process the image and respond to color, shape, and contrast. Such data-driven mechanisms have been discussed in Chapters 4, 7, 8, and 13. On the other hand, conceptually-driven processes are those that depend upon our prior knowledge or our expectations concerning the nature of the incoming stimulation. Suppose a facelike image enters the eye; our prior experience and knowledge of human faces can guide the efficiency with which we process this sensory input. Gray and Wederburn's experiment demonstrates the operation of conceptually-driven processes very nicely. Although there does appear to be some loss of processing efficiency when we shift our attention between the two ears (Massaro, 1975), let us point out again that physical characteristics alone do not seem to determine how well we can allocate our effort to produce optimum performance on a task.

SELECTIVE ATTENTION

In many ways a separation between selective and divided attention is artificial. This is because most research on selective attention has dealt not only with how well we can process the information on the channel to which we are attending, but also with the fate of the information on the unattended channel. In other words, if information is coming in to both ears and you are asked to pay close attention to the stimulation in the right ear, it would be of interest to know how well you can do this. Also, while you are attending to the right ear, what is happening to the information in the left ear? Can you respond to any of it or is it all lost? Our everyday experience tells us that what we pay attention to is seen or heard sharply and clearly while everything else is vague, ill-defined, and certainly not remembered. Let's see how research evidence bears out our casual observations.

The Cocktail Party Problem and Selective Attention in Audition. Although there are many intriguing diversions that occupy your time when you attend a cocktail party, it may be of scientific interest to observe your patterns of attention the next time you find yourself in such a situation. Even given a certain amount of surrounding noise and hubbub, it is not difficult to listen to a conversation that has engaged your interest. In effect you "tune out" the rest of the party in order to selectively attend to the portions of the incoming stimulation that are important to you.

You can demonstrate the restriction of attention under high levels of arousal, which was mentioned in the early part of the chapter, by reflecting on party conversations that you have had with attractive members of the opposite sex. When you have had the good fortune to encounter such a person at a party, how much of the rest of the party do you remember? However, you can also switch your attention rather rapidly if something happens across the room. If you are waiting for the arrival of more refreshments, for example, you can also monitor events at the doorway while still participating in a conversation. Hence, a cocktail party demonstrates not only selective listening, but also an ability to monitor a barrage of sensory input in order to pick up elements that are meaningful to your present situation.

Around the time that Broadbent was conducting his research in England, Colin Cherry, in the United States, became interested in the problems represented by cocktail party behavior. To study them he introduced a new experimental technique called SHADOWING. In a shadowing experiment, an observer is presented with two messages in different channels. For instance, one may be presented auditorially and the other visually, or one message may be sent to the right ear while a different one goes into the left ear. The observer is asked to repeat aloud (shadow) one of the messages as it occurs. This technique is used to force observers to pay attention to one of the messages, and it was thought that repeating it aloud would require close attention. Therefore, during a shadowing experiment, an experimenter can discover how well an observer can shadow a message and discover the amount of information picked up from a competing message that is not shadowed.

First let us consider a series of variables that appear to affect an observer's ability to shadow a message. Observers can easily shadow a message if it is organized prose, for example, a selection from a novel. They have more difficulty in shadowing randomly arranged words and the most difficulty with nonsense words (collections of letters that are assumed to have no meaning, such as *glak*). In addition, when shadowing a message, an observer tends to lag behind the words slightly, so that whole phrases are grouped together. This is called *phrase shadowing*. If an observer is asked to shadow syllable by syllable, or to repeat each sound as it is presented (called *phonemic shadowing*), the task is much more difficult. Thus grammatical structure and our familiarity with language help us to attend to a stimulus in the face of competing input. This is another example of conceptually-driven involvement in selective attention. On the other hand, data-driven aspects of the message can help you attend to one of the two competing messages. If the two auditory messages come from spatially separated places, are different in pitch (for instance, a male voice speaking one message and a female voice speaking the other), or are presented at different speeds, this can help direct and maintain attention on one of the inputs. For an example of such a data-driven process, see Demonstration Box 15-3.

Now let's look at what Cherry found out about the rejected, or unshadowed, message. Essentially he discovered that his observers could relate relatively little about the rejected message except that they assumed it was prose. Later, Moray (1959) tried to determine exactly how much information from the unshadowed message was processed. He found that although some words were repeatedly presented, and the observers were told that they would be asked about the information in the rejected message, his observers were unable to report the unshadowed words. There are several possible explanations for this result. Perhaps observers were not processing any information from the unattended channel, and thus they did not hear it. However, if

this were the case, we would not be able to perceive anything except that which was the object of our attention, and no one could ever be diverted from attending to a conversation by an extraneous stimulus. Of course this is not the case, since at one time or another you have probably heard your name mentioned by someone nearby, even though you were not attending to the conversation.

Another possibility stems from a lack of memory for the rejected message. Both Cherry and Moray had waited a few seconds after the end of the experimental messages before asking their observers about the unshadowed message. Perhaps when you are not paying attention to something, it is processed by your sensory system but is not committed to a long-lasting memory. To test this idea, an experimenter need only interrupt shadowing to ask the observer about what had just occurred in the competing message. When this is done, more of the rejected message can be recalled; the recalled material usually includes the last five to seven words, numbers, or whatever units are being shadowed (Glucksberg & Cowen, 1970; Norman, 1969). Once again we encounter the role of memory, with the data indicating that attending to a stimulus allows it to be more fully and more permanently entered into memory. Unattended input, on the other hand, is more fleeting and seems to be quickly lost from memory. Try the shadowing task in Demonstration Box 15-4 to experience the relationship between selective attention and memory.

Selective Attention in Vision. Unlike the ears, which are stationary organs whose movement is dependent upon head movement, the eyes are always moving, searching, and exploring the visual field. Since the small foveal area in the retina is most highly suited to a detailed analysis of visual information, we must move our eyes to allow targets of

You may remember our discussion of the precedence effect from Chapter 11, where we listed some variables that affect our ability to localize the position of sound sources in space. When sounds are emitted in enclosed spaces, they tend to cause echoes as they bounce from walls, ceilings, and floors. However, we can still make a correct localization of the sound source because the sound emanating directly from this source will reach our ears before its echo. The auditory system is sensitive to these time differences and can use this information in the localization of sound-producing sources. The direction of the sound, emanating directly from the sound source, takes precedence over other sounds in localization, hence the name *precedence effect*.

The precedence effect can also be helpful in selective attention, when we are attempting to process one of many simultaneously occurring stimulus events. A good example of this is found in cocktail party situations, where you may try to follow one of many competing conversations. This aspect of selective attention is helped by the spatial and temporal separation of the auditory inputs. You can demonstrate this for yourself with the aid of two friends (preferably of the same sex) and a door. First have your friends stand as shown in Figure (A), while each reads passages from a book or newspaper simultaneously. Notice that even with your eyes closed you can easily separate and locate the two messages. Now have your friends stand as shown in Figure (B). Notice that in this situation each is standing out of your line of sight, and the messages must travel out through the open door. This means that they will tend to reach you at the same time and come from the same direction. Now, again with your eyes closed, notice how difficult it is to locate the voices and to separate their messages.

Demonstration Box 15-3
Selective Attention and the Precedence Effect

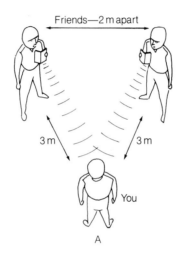

Friends—2 m apart

3 m   3 m

You

A

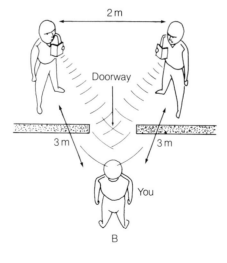

2 m

Doorway

3 m   3 m

You

B

Demonstration Box 15-4
Selective Attention and Memory

In the accompanying passage, the relevant message is shaded while the irrelevant message is printed in the normal fashion. You are to read the shaded passage aloud as rapidly as possible, ignoring the irrelevant (unshaded) message. Now without cheating and looking back, write down all of the words you remember from the irrelevant message. Go back and read the shaded passage again, but this time stop after each line to write down the words you recall from the irrelevant message (without looking back at it). You should find that the list of remembered words is longer when your reading is interrupted and you are not asked to recall all the irrelevant message at once (from Lindsay & Norman, 1977).

In performing an experiment like this one on man attention car it house is boy critically hat important shoe that candy the old material horse that tree is pen being phone read cow by book the hot subject tape for pin the stand relevant view task sky be read cohesive man and car grammatically house complete boy but hat without shoe either candy being horse so tree easy pen that phone full cow attention book is hot not tape required pin in stand order view to sky read red it not too difficult.

interest to stimulate the fovea. Therefore, attentive processes in vision relate both to situations in which the eye is moving and to situations in which the eye remains immobile.

A typical way to study selective attention in vision during eye movements is to engage the observer in a visual search task. For example, we could ask an observer to find a target letter that is embedded in a long list of other distracting letters. The observer must then move the eyes or *scan* the array until the target is found. This technique was used by Neisser and his associates (Neisser, 1967) in a series of experiments. They used 50-line lists of letters, and the observers were asked to look for a target letter that appeared in an unpredictable position. The observers scanned the list from top to bottom, and the experimenter recorded the amount of time it took them to find the target item. As you would expect, when the target was close to the end of the list, observers spent more time searching for it. But in general they performed the search task with great speed. Neisser estimated that after some practice his observers could scan at a speed of about ten lines of letters (each containing six letters) per second.

In much the same way that we analyzed the shadowing task, we can look at the search experiments and ask what factors affect the ability to find an embedded target with speed and efficiency. Practicing the task certainly increases one's speed; however, the nature of the lists can also have an effect. It is much more difficult to discriminate the target letter when it is embedded in a list of letters that are visually similar to it. Thus, like the shadowing task, physical similarities and differences can alter our ability to selectively attend to one aspect of the input. You can demonstrate this effect for yourself in Demonstration Box 15-5. Neisser also showed that search speed is not affected by increasing the number of targets for which one is simultaneously searching. Individuals seem to be

Demonstration Box 15-5
Stimulus Characteristics and Search Time

For this demonstration you will need a stop watch or a clock with a sweep second hand. Look at the time and then search List A for the letter Z. When you are finished note the time it took you to find it. Now do the same for List B and then return to this text.

You probably found List B much less difficult and your search to be faster (even though the Z's are both at the same line). This is because the letters in List B are quite dissimilar from the target (all of the letters except the Z have a round segment), while in List A they are all angular like the target. Thus the characteristics of the target and nontarget items interact in a search task.

VWMIEX	GODUCQ
VMWIEX	QCURDO
XVWMEI	DUCOQG
WXVEMI	CGRDQU
XMEWIV	UDRCOQ
MXIVEW	GQCORU
VEWMIX	GOQUCD
EMVXWI	GDQUOC
IVWMEX	URDCGO
IEVMWX	GODRQC
IVMXEW	CGUROQ
EWVMIX	UCGROD
EXWMVI	DQRCGU
IXEMWV	QDOCGU
VXWEMI	ODUGQR
MXVEWI	QCDUGO
XVWMEI	CQOGRD
MWXVIE	QUGCDR
VIMEXW	URDGQO
EXVWIM	GRUQDO
WVZMXE	DUZGRO
XEMIWV	OCDURQ
WXIMEV	UOCGQD
EMWIVX	RGQCOU
IVEMXW	GRUDQO
(A)	(B)

able to focus their attention during scanning with equal efficiency for several targets as for one.

What happens to the unattended channel in visual search tasks? In other words, what happens to the other letters in the list that are not targets? Neisser states that his observers reported that the other letters were just a blur and that they did not "see" individual letters. This implies that the observers are not searching letter by letter but that they are taking in the information in chunks. As these chunks are processed, only the distinctive features of the target stimulus appear to be noted and stand out. This type of reasoning would explain why physical similarities between targets and nontargets make the visual search somewhat harder.

As we have mentioned, selective processes in vision are closely tied with the movement of the eyes to fixate a target of interest. Neisser's work has indicated that information during visual search is processed in chunks. Therefore it seems reasonable to ask about the size of these chunks and to investigate just how much visual information can be taken in within one glance. Hernandez-Peon (1964) has described attention as a "beam of light in which the central brilliant part represents the focus." If this description is adequate, we are asking how wide this beam of light may be. In other words, how much visual information can we pick up at once during one fixation. This type of research has often been grouped under the general name of investigations into the SPAN OF APPREHENSION.

Perhaps the most well-known contemporary studies on this issue were conducted by Sperling (1960). He used a TACHISTOSCOPE, which is an experimental device that allows the presentation of visual material for very brief periods of time. In tachistoscopic terms 1 sec is very long; many studies using this piece of apparatus have studied information processing with exposure periods of less than $\frac{1}{10}$ of a sec (or 100 msec). Sperling used displays containing from 3 to 12 letters, and presented them to his observers for 50 msec each. An observer was given a score sheet that looked like the spatial arrangement of the display. She was asked to mark each letter in its correct position once the display was no longer visible. With displays of three to four letters, Sperling's observers were very accurate; however, when the displays contained more than four letters, observers were still averaging only about four correct items per display.

Before concluding that the span of apprehension was approximately four items,

Sperling felt he had to investigate another possibility. Perhaps his observers actually saw more than they could report, and since the presentation time was so brief, it was difficult to hold the entire display in memory. Even though the observers started writing down their answers as soon as the display had disappeared, perhaps their memory of the remaining items had faded by the time they reached the fourth item. Sperling wanted to separate the limitations of memory from the limitations of perception. To do this he devised an experiment in which he showed his observers three horizontal rows of four letters each as in Figure 15-2. After the display had been flashed for 50 msec, an auditory cue was presented to the observer. This was a short tone that varied in pitch. If the pitch was high, the observer was to repeat the top row, and if it was low or in a midrange, the bottom or middle row was to be repeated. The observer never knew which of these tones would be presented after the visual display. This experimental technique has been called PARTIAL REPORT since the observer is asked to repeat only part, not all, of the array.

By taking the number of letters correctly identified from each row and multiplying it by three (for the three rows in the display), an experimenter can make an estimate of how much information is being processed while

A R P I
X W H Q
Y Z E D

Figure 15-2.
Typical experimental stimuli used by Sperling in studying apprehension span.

the display is visible. Sperling found that with practice his observers could correctly recall about three letters out of each row. Multiplying this figure by three, we can see that the information available from this brief visual display is nine rather than four items.

When the effect of memory decay is taken into account, we find that the span of apprehension is much wider than that shown by the original experiment. Once again we find that memory interacts with attentional processes. When information is entering the visual system very rapidly (for example, during a series of eye movements) much more may be "seen" than can be effectively entered into memory and stored for later use.

A series of more recent studies demonstrates this point (Shiffrin & Grantham, 1974; Shiffrin, Pisoni & Castaneda-Mendez, 1974). These researchers compared the detection of a visual target under conditions of *simultaneous presentation,* where all targets to be detected are presented at the same time, and under conditions of *successive* presentation, where all targets are presented one after another so that the observer sees only one at a time. They felt that observers should be better at detecting targets during the successive presentation since they could allocate their attention fully to each target as it occurred. On the other hand, during the simultaneous presentation of all the targets, the observers had to divide their attention between them. This divided attention should have lowered the efficiency with which they could detect the presence of targets. The interesting aspect of these studies is that no differences were found between detection performance in the simultaneous and the successive presentation conditions. These researchers argue that all incoming information is processed automatically and quite extensively without selection. Any information selection that seems to occur is the result of selectivity in memory. This is very similar to the explanation that has

been given for the selective attention effects found in audition.

Both the Sperling study and the studies by Shiffrin and his co-workers tried to minimize the involvement of memory in the performance of the visual detection task. As a result, not only was the span of apprehension shown to be rather wide, but also divided attention did not bring about lowered performance.

In discussing divided attention in audition, we had mentioned the distinction between data-driven and conceptually-driven processing. The second term refers to the store of expectations and memories we have about the nature of the incoming information. In the case of divided attention, it was shown that such expectations can help an observer to switch attention between incoming channels of sensory input. However, there is an interesting phenomenon that occurs in the visual modality and demonstrates how conceptually-driven processes can actually interfere with our ability to focus our attention. This is called the STROOP EFFECT. In 1935, Stroop found that observers had difficulty screening out meaningful information even when it was irrelevant to the task at hand. He devised three situations. In the first he recorded how long it took individuals to read a list of color names, such as red, blue, and green printed in black ink. He then took an equal number of color patches and recorded how long it took observers to name each one of the series. Next he devised a clever trick. He took each color name and printed it in a colored ink that did not coincide with the linguistic information. In other words, he printed the name *red* in *blue* ink or the name *green* in *yellow* ink. When he had his observers name the color of the ink in this series of words, he found that they often erroneously read the color name rather than the color of the ink. As you might expect, it took them much longer to complete this third series correctly.

Meaningful linguistic information is difficult to ignore, and the automatic expectations that have come to be associated with the presence of words often take over, resulting in difficulties in focusing attention. The Stroop phenomenon is another example of how certain types of processing have become automatic, and, in the case of the Stroop situation, can cause interference when we are actively trying to process the incoming stimuli in a completely different way. You may experience this effect yourself with the aid of Demonstration Box 15-6.

MODELS OF ATTENTION

We have made repeated references to the relationship between processes of attention and stored memories and expectations. This interaction seems to hold in vision as well as in audition, and probably in other sensory systems as well (Shiffrin & Grantham, 1974). Psychologists are not content to just acknowledge the relationship without making some attempt to describe precisely and symbolically what may be going on when you pay attention to something. To do this, several investigators have devised MODELS of attention. A model of a process is like a hypothesis devised to explain a series of events and how

they relate to each other. The researchers who have devised these models feel that they describe the process of attention, including its association with memory. They have conducted experiments to test these models so that they can assess the fit between their idealized versions of the attention process (the model) and actual human behavior during a task that requires attention. We have already discussed some of this research, and we can now refer to it as we look at how various individuals have conceptualized the process of attention.

Bottleneck Models of Attention. The term used to describe this class of models has been borrowed from Kahneman (1973). BOTTLENECK MODELS assume a biological limitation on the amount of information that can be processed at one time. Incoming sensory information must be sequenced through a narrow processing channel like a droplet of water awaiting its turn to flow through the narrow neck of a bottle. Since the potential incoming information exceeds the limited processing capacity, the information must be filtered in some way. Only certain portions of the input pass through this filter for complete analysis and processing. The analyzed portion of the input can be compared to the attended material while the information blocked by the filter is the unattended material.

Color plate 7 is an example of the Stroop Color-Word Test. Have a friend time you with either the second hand of a watch or with a stop watch, if you have one, as you read each group. Start the timing with the word "go" and read across the lines in exactly the same fashion for each group. When the last response is made in each group, stop the timing and note your response time.

You should find that reading the color names will take the least amount of time, while naming the colors of the ink when the printed word names a different color will take you the most time. Naming the color patches will fall in between these two.

Demonstration Box 15-6
The Stroop Phenomenon

Where does the selection or filtering process take place? Some types of bottleneck models state that the selection process occurs right after sensory registration. We can call these the EARLY SELECTION MODELS (Broadbent, 1958). One of these is graphically shown in Figure 15-3A. Unlimited information can stimulate the sense receptors, but only a limited amount can be let through for contact with later processing stages such as memory. For example, visual stimulation reaches all of the retinal receptors. However, attention, and therefore processing priority, is usually given to the fovea. The limitations of the fovea determine the information processing limitations, and information from the peripheral retina is usually not processed further. Since all levels of information processing are needed for a perceptual experience to occur, we can say that we experience our foveal stimulation (which is fully analyzed) but do not experience our peripheral retinal stimulation (which is not processed beyond the retinal level). This is a very

simple way to conceptualize a limited capacity system. However, it does not seem to fit with our everyday experience. If nonfoveal stimulation is not processed, how can we shift our attention to other objects in the visual field? In addition, we appear to have some conscious awareness of the identity of objects around us, even if they are not in the direct line of sight. These are major problems for a model that sees selectivity as operating very early in sensory processing.

A second type of bottleneck model takes care of these objections. This model states that selectivity occurs in memory, and thus it is rather late in the stages of information processing (see Figure 15-3B). These are LATE SELECTION MODELS (Deutsch & Deutsch, 1963; Norman, 1968; Schneider & Shiffrin, 1977; Shiffrin & Schneider, 1977). We have already discussed some of the research that demonstrates the relationship between attention and memory. For example, when subjects are asked to recall information from an unattended channel in a shadowing task after

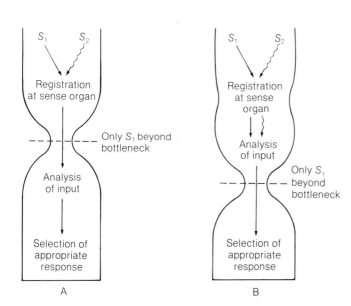

Figure 15-3.
Schematic diagrams of two types of bottleneck models of attention. Both models assume that perceptual selectivity stems from a structural limitation on our capacity to process all of the incoming stimulation (stimuli S_1 and S_2). (A) The early selection models see the limitation as occurring at the earliest stages; only limited amounts of stimulation are channeled along for further processing. (B) The late selection models conceptualize stimulus selection (attention) as occurring at later stages of information processing.

the session is completed, they have difficulty in doing so. However, if they are interrupted during the shadowing, they can retrieve some information from the unattended channel. In the second instance the role of memory in the performance of the task has been reduced. This suggests that the preference shown for attended material is intimately involved with its stability in memory. In late selection models, all channels of incoming information are monitored and processed at least to a limited extent, with the attentional selectivity occurring when it is time to make entrance into a more long lasting memory storage. At the very least, all input makes contact with the appropriate memories so that, unlike the early selection models, processing of unattended material does not stop at the sensory organ.

We can conceptualize the differences between these two types of bottleneck models in the following way. Both types assume a biological limitation on our capacity to process incoming information. However, the early selection models assume that attention is determined by the limitations of the sensory systems themselves and that physiological restraints determine attentional restraints. On the other hand, the late selection models assume that the selectivity of our memories and expectations greatly influence what we attend to and what we process further.

Capacity Models of Attention. CAPACITY MODELS do not assume biological limitations on our ability to process information. Rather, they assume that there are limits on our ability to exert mental effort in the performance of activities that may occur simultaneously (Kahneman, 1973; Moray, 1967). We have already mentioned that paying attention seems to require mental effort and a cer-

tain degree of arousal. Therefore, it seems to make sense to think that each of us has a limited capacity to perform mental work, and consequently, that each of us must allocate (or distribute) this capacity as effectively as possible. The important distinction between these models and those that are termed bottleneck is in the source of information processing limitations. Bottleneck models assume *structural* limitations within the observer, and these determine the filtering process that is called attention. On the other hand, capacity models assume that the distribution of mental effort is determined by the demands of competing tasks. This type of model is more concerned with limitations on the allocation of processing capacity. An important aspect of this type of model is the allocation *strategy*. If one task is very demanding, then it will claim all of our mental effort, leaving us with little to expend on a competing task. Figure 15-4 summarizes this type of model in a schematic diagram.

Let us see how this class of model might work. When we are first learning to drive a car, it requires a great deal of effort to attend to the integration of skills needed to perform this complex task. Novice drivers find it very difficult to do anything but drive the car. However, as the skill becomes more automatic it begins to require less of the total processing capacity. This reduction in effort leaves us free to pay attention to competing activities, such as carrying on a conversation. Thus the notion of allocating limited amounts of effort is highly compatible with everyday activities. Highly practiced skills require very little processing capacity once they are learned, allowing us to divide our attention rather effectively when a competing activity arises. This class of model is more fluid in the sense that it does not specify the types of

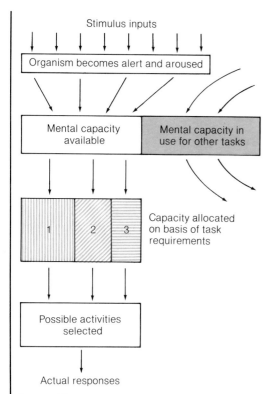

Stimulus inputs

Organism becomes alert and aroused

Mental capacity available

Mental capacity in use for other tasks

1　2　3

Capacity allocated on basis of task requirements

Possible activities selected

Actual responses

Figure 15-4.
Schematic diagram of a capacity model of attention. This type of model assumes that there are limitations on our processing strategies or capacities. We have a limited amount of processing capacity that we can allocate between different stimuli, or tasks, that occur simultaneously. The stimulus, or task, that takes the greater amount of processing capacity will be the one engaging most of our attention.

interference that may occur to disrupt attention. Interference depends solely on the types of tasks involved. On the other hand, bottleneck models predict that certain tasks will interfere with each other. For example, two highly similar prose passages fed into the two ears will tap into the same groups of perceptual analyzers, linguistic expectations, and memories. When this happens it will be very hard to attend to one of the passages and to ignore the other.

Where does this leave us with the notion of attention? We know from our experience that we can be alert, we can divide and switch our attention with relative ease, and we can selectively attend to only one of several events occurring simultaneously. Although the models presented here attempt to make some sense of this complex process, it is clear that some research supports each one of them. In the final "perfect" explanation of attention, it will most probably be shown that both structural limitations and limitations on processing capacities play a role in perceptual selectivity. Our discussion of attention has demonstrated how perception is dependent upon memories, prior expectations, and learning. This dependency has already emerged in Chapters 11 and 13, and we will see it again in Chapters 16 and 17. Clearly we must go beyond the mere registration of sensory input at the sense organ to understand how we construct our perceptual experiences.

16
Learning and Development

The camp counselor turned to the newest arrival and asked, "And how old are you, son?"

"Well," said the boy, "it all depends. According to my latest set of anatomical tests I'm 7. According to my physical dexterity test I'm 10. I've got a mental age of 11, a moral age of 9, and a social age of 10. If you are referring to my chronological age though, that's 8, but nobody pays any attention to that these days."

While one might not relish the thought of spending a summer with this child, his comments point out that there are significant changes in many of our physical and psychological characteristics as we age. Each of these changes has its own time course. Some changes simply represent physiological transformations occurring as the body matures (such as a person's anatomical age). Others represent patterns of behavior that are learned as the individual grows older (such as social or moral age). Still others may represent a combination of both learning and maturation (such as mental age). Although no one refers to a *perceptual age,* there are also changes in perceptual characteristics that occur as an individual develops and matures. These changes tend to represent improvements producing conscious experiences that more accurately represent the physical environment. However, there are also some perceptual capacities that seem to deteriorate with age.

In considering how an individual's perceptual functioning changes we can adopt two different perspectives. The first is long term, viewing people over their entire life span. This is the *developmental approach,* which assumes that knowledge of a person's chronological age will allow us to predict many aspects of perceptual behavior. The alternate approach is short term, viewing the changes that occur in perceptual responses as a result of a circumscribed set of experiences. This is the *perceptual learning approach.* It is based upon the presumption that our interactions with the world can shape our percepts. These two approaches are not mutually exclusive; understanding the nature of perception often requires us to use both viewpoints. Both lead to the conclusion that, despite our lack of awareness of it, perception is continually undergoing change. Your experience of the world differs from individuals who are 10 years older or 10 years younger than you.

PERCEPTION IN INFANTS

Before speaking about how perception changes as we age and develop, we must first know what perceptual capacities we had at the moment of birth. Unfortunately, newborn infants (*neonates*) are difficult to test. They tend to be asleep most of the time, and in addition they do not respond to instructions nor answer our questions in any direct verbal fashion. Finally, they produce only a limited range of observable behaviors. These problems require experimenters to be rather ingenious in devising measures of the perceptual abilities of the very young.

Basic Perceptual Functions. Let us begin by looking at the physiology of the infant's visual system. The infant's retina contains rods and cones as does the adult's. Electrical measures seem to indicate that these receptors are functioning from birth (Aantaa, 1970; Maurer, 1975). We can determine how well the visual cortex of the infant is functioning by measuring what is called the VISUALLY EVOKED RESPONSE (often abbreviated VER). This is a change in the electrical activity produced by the brain in response to a visual stimulus. One usually records a VER by fixing electrodes (generally flat pieces of silver) to the scalp and connecting them to very sensitive amplifiers. Almost all newborn infants (and even most premature infants) show some VER, although it differs somewhat from the adult response in its pattern, size, and speed (Ellingson, 1968; Umezaki & Morrell, 1970). Over a period of about three months, the infant's electrical responses to visual stimuli come to look more and more like those of adults (Harter & Suitt, 1970; Jensen & Engel, 1971). It is generally agreed that during the first year the actual neural functioning of the visual system may continue to mature, and it may not fully reach adult capabilities until the end of the second year (Ellingson, Lathrop, Nelson, & Donahy, 1972).

At a behavioral level we can find some responses in newborns to the direction, distance, or movement of stimuli. Perhaps the most impressive demonstration comes from Wertheimer (1961), who tested an infant girl's ability to localize stimuli 3 min after birth. With the infant lying on her back, a toy "cricket" was sounded next to her right or left ear. Two observers noted whether the eyes moved to the infant's right or to her left—or not at all. On 18 out of the 22 times when the child's eyes moved, they moved in the direction of the click. When the experiment was completed the child was still only 10 min old; hence, these data allow us to conclude that some directional aspects of auditory stimuli are accurately processed and are capable of guiding behavior from birth.

Further spatial abilities are shown by the fact that infants are capable of directing their eye movements toward targets. Neonates tend to move their eyes in a conjugate fashion (both eyes together) and seem to have the capacity to make convergent and divergent eye movements. When newborns are presented with a target, which appears and then moves to one side or another, they will track it (Dayton, Jones, Steele, & Rose, 1964; Schulman, 1973). If we present a young infant (about 2 weeks of age) with a target that suddenly appears 15° or 20° from the fovea, he will turn his eyes in the direction of the stimulus (Tronick, 1972). As the infant grows older, he will direct his eyes toward targets that appear even farther away in the periphery (Harris & MacFarlane, 1974).

The fact that an infant's eye movements respond to moving or displaced stimuli can be used to measure other capacities in the newborn. For instance, if we show an adult observer a field with a continuously moving pattern (such as a screen full of stripes all moving in one direction), we get a characteristic eye movement pattern. The eye will smoothly track in the direction of the movement for a distance, and then snap back in the opposite direction. After this return movement the observer's eyes lock on to another stripe and follow it, and this process repeats itself continually while the observer views the array. This repetitive eye movement sequence in the presence of a moving pattern is called OPTOKINETIC NYSTAGMUS. These same eye movements are found in infants younger than 5 days (Gorman, Cogan, & Gellis, 1957). In fact its appearance is so reliable that the absence of optokinetic nystagmus often indicates the presence of neurological problems (Brazelton, Scholl, & Robey, 1966).

We can use the optokinetic response to measure other aspects of visual function. If an infant cannot see the pattern of moving stripes (because visual acuity or brightness responses are insufficient to make them visible), she will not be able to track the moving pattern. This provides a good methodological tool for the study of infant vision. For instance, Doris, Casper, and Poresky (1967) varied the brightness difference between dark and light stripes. They found that when the stripes were very bright, even babies as young as 4 days of age showed the optokinetic response. As the infants became older they were more likely to respond to dimmer stripes, up to the age of 4 months, when their response level stabilized. This result suggests that the sensitivity to brightness differences improves over the first few months of life.

One can also use the optokinetic response to test the visual acuity of infants. The technique involves finding the most narrow stripes that will still produce the tracking response. This method has shown that the visual acuity of neonates is quite poor. It is around 6/120 in Snellen values. This is quite low when we consider that 6/12 is usually given as the legal definition of impaired vision. Such poor acuity is probably due to the fact that infants younger than 1 month have virtually no accommodative ability. They act as if their lenses were fixed for focusing on stimuli at about 19 cm from the eye (White, 1971). By 3 months, however, the accommodative response is functioning well and acuity improves steadily until about 6 months of age.

Pattern Perception and Discrimination. With the limited response repertoire available to a young baby, we can appreciate the methodological breakthrough accomplished by Fantz (1961). His procedure involves placing young babies in a special chamber (they either lie on their backs or sit in an infant chair). Visual stimuli are placed on the walls or the roof of the chamber, and there is a tiny hole through which the experimenter can watch the baby. When the baby views one of a pair of stimulus patterns placed in the chamber, the experimenter can detect this by noting the direction in which the eyes are turned. The experimenter triggers a timer that records how long each of the two stimuli are viewed, and if the baby looks at one target longer than the other, this is taken as an indication of a preference for it. The existence of a preference implies that the infant can tell the difference between the patterns. This simple

result does not tell us *why* the baby preferred to look at one stimulus rather than the other, nor can we be absolutely sure that the absence of any viewing preference necessarily means that the baby cannot discriminate between the two targets. However, the existence of differences in viewing times does suggest that the infants can discriminate between the patterns.

Using this procedure, Fantz was able to demonstrate that infants can discriminate among certain types of patterns. For instance, in one experiment 30 infants, ranging in age from 1 to 15 weeks, were shown pairs of targets. Infants showed a clear preference for viewing patterns (a checkerboard) over a plain square. They similarly showed a preference for a bull's-eye pattern rather than stripes, indicating that they could tell the difference between straight and curved lines. Simple shapes, such as a cross or a circle, produced no viewing preferences. Generally, infants prefer moderately complex stimuli over those that are very simple or very complex, although preferences do change with age (Karmel & Maisel, 1975). The apparatus used in these types of experiments is shown in Figure 16-1.

Some findings have indicated that certain meaningful patterns receive special attention, even from neonates. Fantz (1965a) studied the response of infants to targets that approximated the human face. Some targets were just head-shaped, others contained eyes, some contained scrambled facial features, and others actually looked like faces. Samples of such stimuli are shown in Figure 16-2. For infants younger than 1 month he reported a looking preference for stimuli containing facial features, but there was no preference for a normal versus a scrambled face (a fact that has been verified by Hershenson, Kessen, & Munsinger, 1967). This suggests that young infants are discriminating these patterns on the basis of simple elements rather than on the basis of total stimulus organization. In-

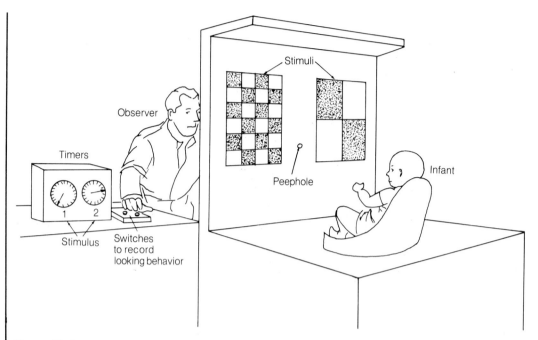

Figure 16-1.
An apparatus for monitoring how long infants view particular stimuli.

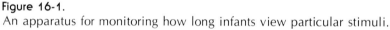

fants between 1 and 4 months of age, however, show a different pattern of response. For children of this age there is a definite preference for the unscrambled face, indicating that they can discriminate and identify the human face (Fantz, 1965a; Kagan, Henker, Hen-Tov, Levine, & Lewis, 1966).

A variation of the Fantz procedure is also useful in infant studies. This involves presenting the baby with only a single stimulus and monitoring the viewing behavior. At first the infant will spend some time looking at the stimulus, but as time passes she will become bored and cease to pay any attention to it. This process is called HABITUATION. If we now present a novel stimulus we will once again provoke looking behavior. This technique has been used to demonstrate that, from the very first days of life, infants can learn to recognize familiar

versus novel stimuli (Cohen & Salapatek, 1975). They can identify photos they have seen before (Fantz, 1964), familiar drawings, or patterns (Saayman, Ames, & Moffet, 1964), and even photographs of faces that they have seen previously (Fagen, 1973). This technique can be used to demonstrate basic perceptual processes as well. Bornstein (1976) has used habituation measures to demonstrate that infants show normal trichromatic color vision when tested at 3 months of age.

All the above data seem to indicate that the newborn child does have a reasonable set of perceptual capacities quite soon after birth. While these may not be as refined as those of the adult, we know that the world of the infant is not the ". . . great booming, confusion" suggested by the 19th century psychologist William James (1890). The in-

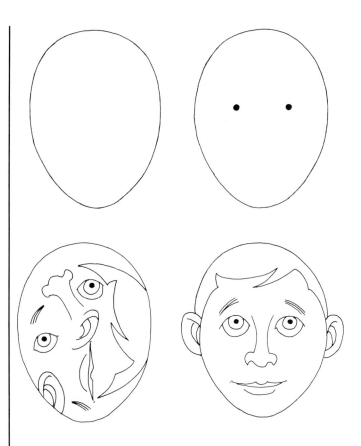

Figure 16-2.
Schematic and scrambled facial stimuli.

fant has a reasonable perceptual response range; however, as we shall see, these responses continue to change as the child matures.

PERCEPTUAL CHANGE THROUGHOUT THE LIFE SPAN

Sensory functioning and perceptual processing are not static; continual change occurs throughout the life span. As we age there seems to be a gradual decrease in the efficiency of our sensory structures. However,

this is accompanied by a gradual improvement in our abilities to perform complex perceptual integrations and discriminations.

Perceptual Change in Children. Throughout childhood we experience a general improvement in perceptual discrimination, recognition, and information processing. One of the most informative ways to monitor these changes is to observe the way in which a child selects information from external stimuli. In Chapter 4 we mentioned that visual acuity is best in the foveal region of the retina; it rapidly deteriorates with increasing distance from the foveal center. Eye movements are used to place the image of a target on the fovea where it can best be seen. There is no guarantee that an observer is paying attention to stimuli imaged upon the fovea, but it is the case that the eyes tend to fixate stimuli being studied by an observer. By monitoring eye movement patterns in children, we can determine the manner in which they are viewing, and hence constructing, their visual world. This line of reasoning is similar to that used by Fantz (1961) when he studied the perceptual world of infants.

Eye movements and information processing. When there is a distinct contour within the visual field of an infant, her eye is drawn toward it. Infants of 1 month tend to direct their eyes toward one distinctive feature of a visual stimulus, such as the corner of a triangle (Salapatek & Kessen, 1973). Their eyes seem to be captured by the feature since they dwell on it for prolonged periods. Since the gaze of a 1-month-old infant is caught by the first contour encountered, most of the viewing time is spent focused on the external contours of a form. If the stimulus has internal features, they seem to be ignored or missed. This picture changes by the age of 2 months. Now the infant scans the contours a little more and shorter periods are spent on each feature (Salapatek, 1975). In addition, the infant dwells almost exclusively on the internal features of the stimulus, seemingly ignoring the overall pattern. These differences are shown in Figure 16-3.

Changes in eye movement patterns continue beyond infancy. The patterns of 3- and 4-year-olds are similar to those of a 2-month-old infant. Children of this age spend most of their time dwelling upon the internal details of a figure with only an occasional eye movement beyond the contour boundary. This is shown in Figure 16-4A. The 4- or 5-year-old child has begun to make eye movement excursions toward the surrounding contour (Figure 16-4B). At 6 and 7 years of age, there is a systematic scan of the outer portions of the stimulus with occasional eye movements into the interior. This is shown in

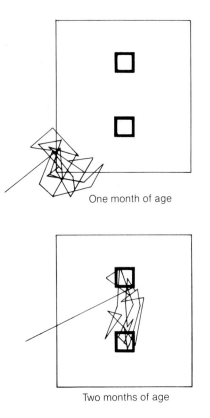

One month of age

Two months of age

Figure 16-3.
Eye movements typical of 1- and 2-month-old infants.

Figure 16-4C (Zaporozhets, 1965).

Eye movement patterns have important consequences for certain perceptual discrimination tasks. Vurpillot (1968) presented children, between the ages of 2 and 9 years, with pictures of houses. They were asked to indicate whether or not the houses appeared to be the same. As can be seen from Figure 16-5, the pairs of houses differ as a function of the contents of the windows; therefore, the most efficient strategy for determining the similarity (or lack of similarity) between the pairs is to compare the corresponding pairs of windows. In other words, the upper-left window of one house would be visually com-

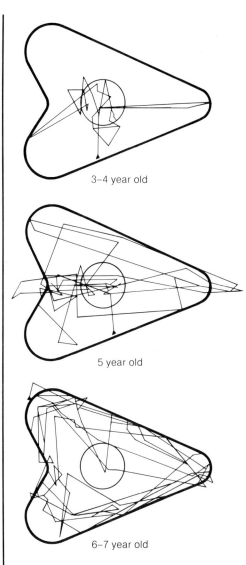

Figure 16-4.
Changes in eye movements from ages 3 to 6.
(A) 3–4 year old; (B) 5 year old; (C) 6–7 year
old (from Zaporozhets, 1965. © The Society
for Research in Child Development, Inc.).

pared with the upper-left window of the
other. This would continue until a difference
was found, thus allowing the observer to
make a same–different decision.

Vurpillot (1968) found that the youngest
children did not conduct a systematic search.
Rather, they often continued searching
through the houses even after looking at a
pair of windows that were quite different.
This lack of systematic viewing was accompanied by a low degree of accuracy in the
discrimination judgments of the younger
children. Older children, with more regular
and systematic viewing patterns, were much
more accurate.

**Pattern perception and discrimina-
tion.** As a child becomes older there is a
gradual movement toward a consideration
of the more global aspects of a pattern and its
elements (Elkind, Koegler, & Goh, 1964).
For instance, consider Figure 16-6. It consists
of a number of objects (fruits and vegetables)
that are organized into a larger figure (a bird);
children 4 and 5 years old report seeing only
the parts ("carrots and a pear and an orange"). By the age of 7, children report seeing both the parts and the global organization ("fruits and carrots and a bird"). By 8 or
9 years, the majority of children respond in
terms of both the parts and the global organization ("a bird made of fruits and
vegetables").

A number of other studies have shown
that the ability to discriminate between visual
patterns improves with age. For instance,
Gibson, Gibson, Pick, and Osser (1962) have
shown a steady improvement in a child's
ability to discriminate between nonsense patterns and their transformations between the
ages of 4 and 8 years. Von Mickwitz (1973)
has demonstrated that older children are
more efficient at extracting details that make
some targets differ from others. Since the discrimination ability of both older and younger
children improves with practice, it may be
that these age-related improvements are
themselves the result of learning.

There is one form of pattern discrimination error that seems to be characteristic of

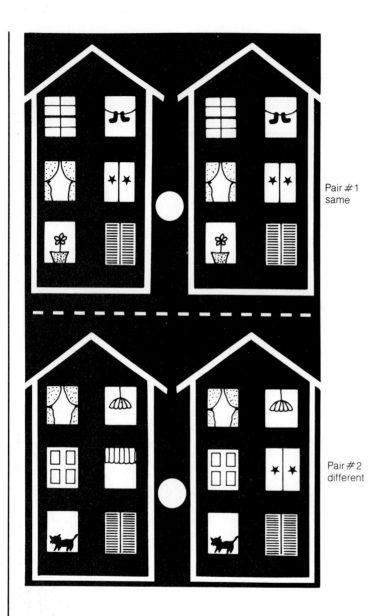

Pair #1
same

Pair #2
different

Figure 16-5.
Stimuli to measure developmental changes in discrimination (based upon Vurpillot, 1968).

young children. This involves mirror reversals. Davidson (1935) found that children confuse lateral mirror image pairs, such as *p* and *q*, or *b* and *d*, more frequently than up–down mirror image pairs, such as *p* and *b*, or *q* and *d*. These confusions seem to be quite common in young children (around 3 years old) and grad-

ually decrease until the child is about 10 or 11 (Rudel & Teuber, 1963; Serpell, 1971). Some of the improvement seems to be associated with educational processes, since between the ages of $5\frac{1}{2}$ and $6\frac{1}{2}$ there is a sudden increase in the ability to make these discriminations. It is likely that the improvement is caused by the

Figure 16-6.
A vegetable-fruit bird.

formal instruction in reading and writing that usually begins at about that age. With appropriate training, kindergarten-aged children can learn the left–right discrimination quite well, although it still seems to be more difficult than the up–down discrimination (Clark & Whitehurst, 1974).

When a child continues to have difficulties with left–right confusions, he can experience later problems with reading. The specific term used for such reading disabilities (when they are not associated with other disturbances such as mental retardation, sensory impairment, or emotional problems) is DYSLEXIA. While estimates of the incidence of dyslexia vary widely, it seems that the problem affects no less than 2% of all children in Western countries, with the incidence perhaps being as high as 10% (Bannatyne, 1971; Critchley, 1970). This is a problem that seems to have a perceptual rather than an intellectual basis. The dyslexic individual may be highly talented in all other respects, except for the reading problems. There are

many case histories of exceptional men who have been dyslexic. Among them one finds the inventor Thomas A. Edison, the surgeon Harvey Gushing, the sculptor Auguste Rodin, United States president Woodrow Wilson, and the author Hans Christian Andersen (Thompson, 1971). One characteristic of all children who have been diagnosed as dyslexic is that they show confusions between the left–right mirror images of targets, although they have no problem with the up–down mirror images (Newland, 1972; Sidman & Kirk, 1974).

Letter reversals in children suggest that a child is relatively insensitive to the orientation of a stimulus. There is an interesting quirk associated with this issue. Consider a stimulus, such as a human face, that has a familiar orientation. When a face is inverted it seems to lose much of its facelike quality, and even very familiar individuals are difficult to recognize when their photographs are turned upside down (Rock, 1974). Thus it is not surprising to find that adult observers show greater accuracy of identification when faces are upright than when they are inverted (Yin, 1970). However, the facial recognition performance of 6-year-olds is not affected by the orientation of the face. Their ability to recognize faces is the same regardless of whether the face is presented in a normal or in an inverted position. By the age of 10 years the child's facial recognition responses begin to look like those of adults; in other words, recognition ability is disrupted when the faces are inverted (Carey & Diamond, 1977). It seems that the adult's sensitivity to orientation differences gives rise to *poorer* discrimination performance than is found in a young child. You can explore the adult sensitivity to orientation in yourself by using Demonstration Box 16-1.

Perceptual Change in Adults. Perceptual and sensory functions continue to change

Adults are more rigid in their reliance upon normal orientations than are children. Look at Figures (A) through (D). They are quite difficult to identify, but turn the page upside down and watch them suddenly become recognizable. This effect is especially striking for faces and for handwritten script.

Demonstration Box 16-1
Orientation and Stimulus Recognition

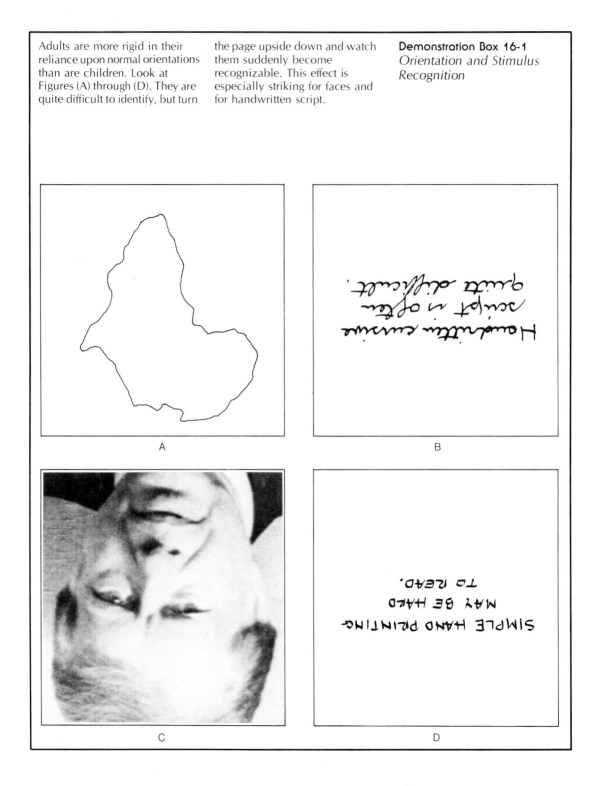

A

B

C

D

throughout the life span. The sensory receptors age, neural efficiency drops, and some sensitivity is lost (Weale, 1963). If we look at the period between 20 and 70 years of age, we find a consistent decrease in threshold sensitivities for the detection of spots of light. This is particularly evident in dark adaptation. Although the time to reach minimum threshold levels remains the same, the maximum sensitivity eventually achieved decreases with age. This is shown in Figure 16-7 (McFarland, Domey, Warren, & Ward, 1960). There is also a gradual deterioration in color vision. It seems that sensitivity to the shorter wavelengths of light (those in the blue range) continually diminishes from birth until death (Lakowski, 1962; Bornstein, 1977).

Although some basic sensory functions tend to diminish with age, responses to more complex visual problems become better, or more accurate, with age. One such set of phenomena concerns responses to visual-geometric illusions. These are simple line

drawings in which the *actual* size, shape, or direction of some elements differs from the *perceived* size, shape, or direction. We have already encountered some of these illusions in Chapters 1 and 14; two of them are shown in Figure 16-8. Figure 16-8A shows the Mueller–Lyer illusion, in which the line marked x appears to be longer than the line marked y. Figure 16-8B shows the Ponzo illusion, in which the line marked w appears to be longer than the line marked z. This is the case in spite of the fact that x and y are physically equal in length, and w and z are also physically equal to each other.

Susceptibility to the distortion in visual-geometric illusions varies with age. Coren, Porac, Green, and Dawson (1977) measured susceptibility to the Mueller–Lyer illusion (Figure 16-8A) in individuals ranging in age from 8 to 80 years. Illusion magnitude (the degree to which individuals are susceptible to the perceived differences in line length) was found to decrease until about the age of 25. After this point it remained relatively constant. In general, adults have been found to be less susceptible to the distortions in visual-geometric illusions (see Coren & Girgus, 1978; Pick & Pick, 1970). Since illusion figures cause complex perceptual errors, these data show that as we grow older our percepts become more related to the actual physical properties of the input.

LEARNING AND EXPERIENCE

Many of the developmental changes in perception we have observed so far are caused by changes in the physiology of the nervous system and in the sensory receptors themselves. Certainly, good visual acuity cannot be expected of infants until they have developed the apparatus needed to change

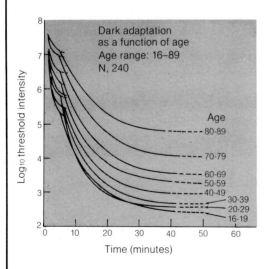

Figure 16-7.
Age changes in dark-adaptation (from McFarland, Domey, et al., 1960).

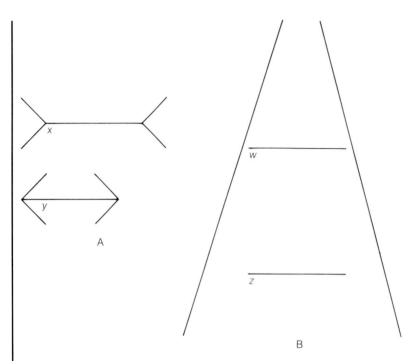

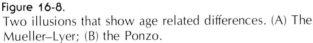

Figure 16-8.
Two illusions that show age related differences. (A) The
Mueller–Lyer; (B) the Ponzo.

the accommodation of the crystalline lens. The visual acuity of an older individual, on the other hand, might be expected to deteriorate as the lens becomes less plastic and less adjustable. Some developmental changes, however, are not directly attributable to changes in neural or receptor functioning. For instance, complex discriminations seem to be more easily done by the adult. It seems likely that this increase in accuracy is the result of a set of PERCEPTUAL STRATEGIES the adult has *learned*. A learning explanation for some developmental changes is suggested by the observation that one can often mimic age changes in perception through appropriate training. For example, the tendency of children to confuse patterns with their mirror

images, which we discussed in an earlier section, can be greatly reduced through appropriate training procedures (see Corballis & Beale, 1976). Another example may be found in the age trends in visual-geometric illusions that we have also discussed. These trends indicate that older (hence supposedly more experienced) individuals are not as susceptible to these perceptual errors as younger observers. However, we can produce a similar decrease in illusion magnitude with just a few minutes of exposure to the figure.

Suppose we present the Mueller–Lyer figure (Figure 16-8A) to an observer and measure susceptibility to the line length distortion. Then we instruct her to begin moving her eyes across the figure, scanning from one end of the line to the other on both portions of the figure. We ask her to be as accurate as possible with her eye movements. At one minute intervals we stop the scanning process and take measurements of illusion magnitude until a total of 5 min of viewing time has elapsed. This simple process of inspection will lead to a 40% reduction in the original illusion magnitude. This decrease is known as ILLUSION DECREMENT, and it has been demonstrated many times (see Coren & Girgus, 1972, 1978).

What is happening in this situation? How does the observer know that the percept is wrong? How does the process of correction occur? The answers seem to lie in the pattern of the observer's eye movements. If we measure the actual pattern of eye movements an observer makes over an illusion figure, we find that the eyes are directed to move as if the distorted percept were actually correct. In other words, if the eye were resting on the end of the line in the perceptually elongated portion of the Mueller–Lyer figure (Figure 16-9A), an attempt to look at the opposite end of the line would produce an eye movement that is too long. This eye movement error is in agreement with the percept, which tends to overestimate the length of the line. A corrective adjustment in the eye movement must be made if the fovea is to come to rest on the exact end of the line.

The opposite happens for the underestimated portion of the Mueller–Lyer figure (Figure 16-9B). Here the eye movements are too short (again in agreement with the perceptual underestimation of the line length), and a corrective adjustment must be made. These patterns of erroneous eye movements in the two segments of the Mueller–Lyer figure are shown in Figure 16-9.

In our discussion of infants and children, we have mentioned that patterns of eye movements can be used to tell us something about the information processing abilities of

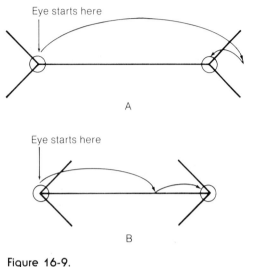

Figure 16-9.
Eye movement patterns over the Mueller–Lyer illusion.

an observer. The same type of reasoning can be applied to the study of eye movement patterns across illusion configurations. As the observer views the illusory array, eye movements and eye movement errors provide information about the existence (as well as the direction and the strength) of the illusory distortion. This error information can be used by the observer to correct the percept. This point of view is supported by the fact that an illusion decrement does not occur unless the observer is allowed to scan the figure (Coren & Hoenig, 1972; Festinger, White, & Allyn, 1968).

The phenomenon of illusion decrement implies that perceptual learning is taking place. The information obtained from the eye movements is being used to reduce a perceptual error, and the direction of this change (from greater to lesser illusion susceptibility) mimics that which is associated with age changes in illusion magnitude. The fact that learning and experience can produce changes similar to those observed as individuals become older chronologically has led some researchers to speculate that many age changes are the result of perceptual learning. This process may take place throughout a person's life, and it may form the basis for many developmental changes in perception. Let us look more directly at some ways in which learning affects perception.

Restricted Rearing. The most direct way of assessing the affects of learning on perception is to deprive an observer of the opportunity to use a sensory modality from the moment of birth. After the individual has fully matured, we could then test his perceptual capabilities in the deprived modality. If they are poorly developed (and if we have eliminated the possibility of physiological deterioration due to disuse), this would demonstrate the role of experience or learning in the development of perceptual capacities. This technique is called RESTRICTED REARING. In Chapter 11 we discussed its use in the study of the development of distance and depth perception.

Restricted rearing studies cannot be conducted with human observers because of the possibility of producing long-lasting perceptual difficulties. However, some clinical conditions reproduce the circumstances needed to study the effects of experience on perception. For example, Von Senden (1960) collected case reports of individuals who had suffered from lifelong blindness due to the presence of cataracts; these individuals later had vision restored through a surgical procedure. After the removal of the cataracts, these adults were unable to recognize familiar objects by sight, although they were capable of recognizing them if they were allowed to touch the objects. For instance, when asked to discriminate between a square and a triangle, these individuals had to undertake the painstaking procedure of seeking out and counting the corners of the figure before the

forms could be distinguished from each other. Their behavior was analogous to that of the infant whose eyes dwelt upon the corners of objects in view.

These newly sighted observers seemed able to detect the presence or absence of an object in the visual field, but this seemed to be the extent of their abilities. For example, one patient was shown a watch and was asked whether it was round or square. When he seemed unable to answer, he was asked whether or not he knew the shape of a square or a circle. He was able to position his hands to form both a square and a circular shape, but he could not visually identify the shape of the watch. When the watch was placed in his hands, he immediately recognized it as being round. Thus his sense of touch, which he had relied upon throughout his years of blindness, was able to compensate for his untrained sense of vision.

When restricted rearing studies are conducted with animals, a common procedure for the study of the visual sense is to raise the animal in total darkness from birth (dark rearing was also discussed in Chapter 11). However, problems can arise from this procedure. Prolonged light deprivation can lead to physiological deterioration within the visual system; therefore, animals are usually exposed for periods of time to diffuse, nonpatterned light by placing translucent contact lenses upon the eyes. The animals receive some light stimulation but are prevented from experiencing any patterned exposure (Riesen & Aarons, 1959). Dark-reared animals tend to show perceptual deficits. They have difficulty learning to make visual discriminations of patterns, and they show erratic or abnormal responses to the depth or distance of targets.

However, the relationship between perceptual development and visual experience is a complex one. Fantz (1965b) reared Rhesus monkeys in the dark from birth for varying lengths of time. Some were reared this way for only 3 days while others spent as long as 20 weeks in the dark. Afterward they were reared normally. The animals that were reared in the dark for less than 1 month quickly recovered their normal perceptual abilities after 3 or 4 days of exposure to light. Animals reared in the dark for longer than 2 months showed very little recovery of pattern and depth perception. Animals reared in the dark for between 1 and 2 months showed intermediate results, taking much longer to recover, and often never reaching normal levels. This seems to imply that there is some critical period during which the animal must have the opportunity to respond to visual stimuli if it is to see normally. If that critical period passes and the animal has not had a chance to interact with the visual environment, perceptual capacities will never achieve normal levels of functioning.

Sensory-Motor Learning. One variable that seems to be essential for the development of normal visual functioning does not involve only the eyes, but rather the entire body. It seems that normal perceptual development depends upon active bodily movement under visual guidance. Von Holst and Mittelsteadt (1950) offered a distinction between stimulus input that simply acts upon a passive observer, which they called EXAFFERENCE, and stimulation that changes as a result of an individual's own movements, called REAFFERENCE.

It has been suggested that reafference is necessary for the development of accurate visually guided spatial behavior. This is elegantly demonstrated in an experiment by Held and Hein (1963). They reared kittens in the dark until they were 8–12 weeks of age. From that time on, the kittens received 3 hours of patterned visual exposure in a "carousel" apparatus, which is shown in Figure 16-10. As you can see from the figure, one of the animals is *active* and can walk around freely.

The other animal is *passive* and is carried around in a gondola that moves in exactly the same direction and at exactly the same speed as the movements of the active animal. Thus the moving animal experiences changing visual stimuli as a result of his own movements (reafference); the passive animal experiences the same stimulation but it is not the result of self-generated movements (exafference).

The animals were later tested on a series of behaviors involving depth perception. These included dodging or blinking when presented with a rapidly approaching object and the avoidance of the deep side of the visual cliff (see Chapter 11). They were also tested for the *visual placing response,* which is a paw extension (as if to avoid collision) when the animal is moved quickly toward a surface. In all three measures the active animals performed like normal kittens while the passive animals showed little evidence of depth perception.

An interesting extension of this work, which shows the specificity of experiential effects, was done by Hein, Held, and Gower (1970). They repeated the carousel experiment; however, each animal received both active and passive exposure. One eye was used when the visual exposure was active while the other eye was used when the visual exposure was passive. They report that when tested on the actively exposed eye the kittens seemed to have normal depth perception, while when tested on the passively exposed eye they acted as if they did not.

How much of the development of our visually guided behavior requires practice and exposure? Consider the simple tasks of reaching out and picking up an object with one hand. This involves not only the accurate assessment of the distance and the size of the object, but the ability to guide your limb on the basis of the perceptual information. Held and Hein (1967) reared kittens in the dark

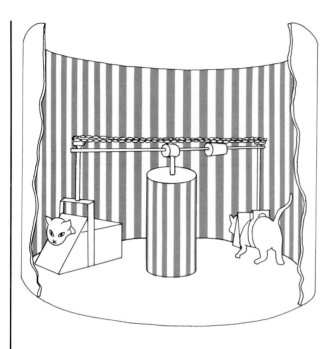

Figure 16-10.
Kitten carousel for active or passive exposure to visual stimulation (from Held, R., & Hein, A. *Journal of Comparative and Physiological Psychology*, 1963, **56.** © 1963 by the American Psychological Association. Reprinted by permission).

until they were 4 weeks old. After this period, they were allowed 6 hours of free movement each day in a lighted and patterned environment. However, during the time when the cats received their exposure to patterned stimuli, they wore lightweight opaque collars that prevented them from seeing their bodies or paws while they moved about (see Figure 16-11). The remainder of the time, the kittens were placed in a dark room. After 12 days of such exposure, these animals showed normal depth perception, but their ability to accurately place their paws by visually directing them toward targets was quite poor. Nonetheless, after 18 hours of free movement in a lighted environment, with their paws visible, all directional confusions seemed to have disappeared.

Hein and Diamond (1971) conducted a similar experiment in which each of the cats' front paws were placed in separate cones, rather than using collars. One cone was opaque, while the other one was transparent so that the animal could see its limb. When tested using the exposed limb, cats accurately placed their paws, but the unexposed limb could not be accurately directed toward the targets.

In another experiment, Held and Bauer (1967) reared a monkey for 34 days without sight of its limbs. When the animal was first exposed to a view of its arm, it acted startled and spent much time looking at its hand. The animal's reaching behavior was awkward and inaccurate but improved rapidly with practice. When the other hand (which had not been previously exposed) was tested, it also showed inaccurate reaching until some experience had been gained.

There are reports of behaviors in human infants that seem similar to the responses of the deprived monkey. White (1971) reports that after the first month of life (during which infants are alert about 5% of the time), infants

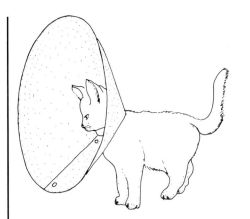

Figure 16-11.
Kitten in collar that prevents view of paws (from Hein, A., & Held, R. *Science,* 1967, **158,** 390–392. © 1967 by the American Association for the Advancement of Science).

spend many hours watching their hands. Their reaching is quite inaccurate at first but improves steadily. Actually, practice can speed up this process of perceptual development. If one arranges conditions so that there are many objects to reach for and to play with, infants develop accurate reaching behavior several weeks earlier than children who have not received this type of enriched experience. Experience with the sight of actively moving parts of the body seems to be a necessary condition for the successful development of visually guided behavior.

Perceptual Rearrangement. In 1896 George Stratton reasoned that if some aspects of the perception of space and direction were learned, then it ought to be possible to learn a new set of spatial percepts. To test this, Stratton used a technique that rearranged the visual world (Stratton, 1897a,b). His technique involved wearing a set of goggles that opti-

cally rotated the field of view by 180°, so that everything appeared to be upside down.

More recently, Kohler (1962, 1964) elaborated on this procedure. Kohler's observers often wore optically distorting devices for several weeks. Observers reported that at first the world seemed very unstable. The visual field appeared to swing as the observer turned his head. During this stage of the experiment observers often had difficulty walking and needed help to perform very simple tasks. However, after about 3 days one observer was able to ride a bicycle, and after only a few weeks he was able to ski. The observers reported that they sporadically experienced the world as being upright. If they observed common events that have definite directional components, such as smoke rising from a cigarette or water pouring from a pitcher, they reported that the world appeared to be upright. This seems to suggest that their ability to adapt to the optically rearranged visual input was facilitated by the notion of gravitational direction along with interaction with familiar events and objects. Kohler suggests that a real perceptual change has taken place because, when the inverting lenses were taken off, observers experienced a sense of discomfort. The world suddenly appeared to be inverted again, and they had difficulty moving about. However, the readaptation to the normal upright world was accomplished within a period of about 1 hour. Demonstration Box 16-2 shows how you can experience this inverted visual stimulation.

Most rearrangement studies involve a less dramatic change of optical input. A common technique is to use a *wedge prism,* which is a wedge-shaped piece of glass that bends, or refracts, light. The locations of objects viewed through the prism seem to be shifted in the direction of the apex (the pointed edge of the wedge). If an observer viewed the world through goggles containing such

You can experience some of the effects associated with inverted optical stimulation by holding a mirror as is shown in the accompanying figure. Walk around and view the world by looking up at the mirror. Notice that the world seems inverted, and also notice how the world swings as you turn. Now pour some water from a glass. Does the water pour up or down? Are you sure?

Demonstration Box 16-2
Optical Inversion

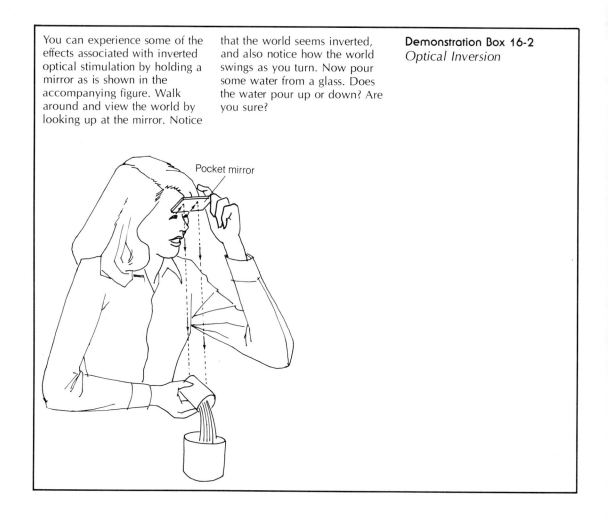

Pocket mirror

prisms and reached for an object, she would find herself missing it. After only a few minutes of practice, however, the observer's reaching would become quite accurate. We would say that she has *adapted* to the prismatic distortion; in other words, she has compensated for the optical distortion. If the observer is consciously correcting for the distortion (for instance, saying, "I must reach 10° to the right of where the object appears"), when removing the goggles she would recognize that the distortion is no longer present, and she should now reach with her usual accuracy. On the other hand, suppose that some perceptual change has occurred. Under these circumstances we would expect that the visual world now appears to be shifted several degrees to one side. When reaching for an object the observer should err in the direction opposite to that of the initial distortion. These errors, which occur after exposure to wedge-prism distortion, are called AFTEREFFECTS. The occurrence of aftereffects in prism adaptation seems to provide evidence that some perceptual rearrangement has occurred. This process is outlined in Figure 16-12.

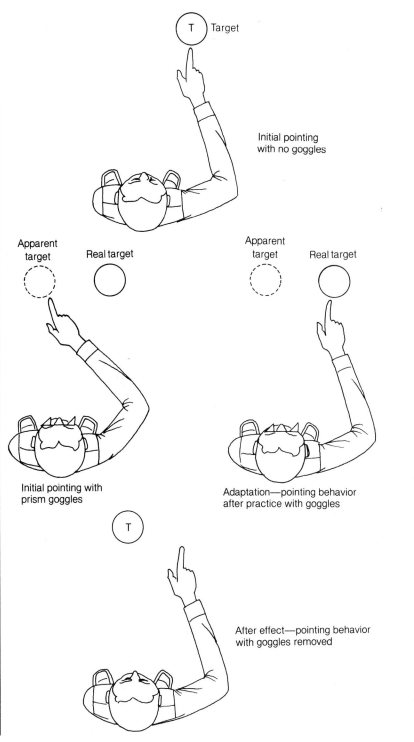

Figure 16-12.
Prism adaptation and
aftereffect.

A number of investigators have attempted to specify what conditions are necessary for adaptation to rearranged stimulation. Held and Hein (1958) have argued that adaptation depends upon active movements, as does the development of visually guided behavior. They tested this notion by having observers view their hand through a prism under one of three conditions. One was a no-movement condition in which the observers viewed their stationary hand. The second was a passive movement condition where the observer's arm was swung back and forth by the experimenter. The third was an active movement condition where the observers saw their hands through the prism while they actively moved it from side to side. There was considerable adaptation to the distortion produced by the prism under the active movement condition, while in the other conditions there was not. These results have been verified several times (Pick & Hay, 1965).

Another series of experiments used conditions similar to the kitten carousel (which we discussed earlier in the chapter). Observers wearing displacing prism goggles either walked around for about 1 hour (active exposure) or were wheeled around in a wheelchair over the same path for about 1 hour (passive exposure). They were then measured to see if any perceptual change had taken place. Adaptation to the prismatic distortion occurred in the active condition but not during the passive exposure condition (Held & Bossom, 1961; Mikaelian & Held, 1964).

One important aspect of active movement under the optically distorted conditions seems to be that it provides observers with some sort of error feedback, which informs them of the direction and the extent of the distortion. This information provides a basis for learning a new correlation between the incoming stimuli and the conscious percept. The more information we give observers about the nature of their errors, the greater is the adaptation to the distortion (Coren, 1966; Welch, 1969, 1971).

It has been suggested by some investigators that error information in the absence of active movement is sufficient to produce prism adaptation. Howard, Craske, and Templeton (1965) had observers watch a rotating rod through an optical system that displaced it to one side. For some observers the rod appeared to be displaced to the side, and they merely watched it rotate. For another group the rod appeared displaced to the same degree; however, as the rod swung about it brushed the observer across the lips, indicating that it was directly in front of the observer rather than off to the side as it appeared. Although both groups were passive, the groups receiving the information that their percept was erroneous (being touched by a stimulus that looked like it would pass them by) showed perceptual adaptation while the other group did not. Thus information indicating how our percepts are in error may be sufficient to produce adaptation (Howard, Anstis, & Lucia, 1974).

What actually changes during the adaptation process? This issue is still being debated. For a while it was believed that adaptation simply altered the *felt position* of various parts of the body. This was based upon the observation that after prism adaptation, when observers are asked to point to a straight ahead position (by feel alone), they tend to point off to the side. This indicated some proprioceptive component in the aftereffect (Harris, 1965). Other data indicate that this may be only part of the process. For example, animals can still adapt to the visual displacement when the nerves that provide information about the position of the arm are severed (Bossom & Ommaya, 1968; Taub & Berman, 1968). The consensus is that a perceptual shift is taking place, which is the result of recalibration of the higher centers used to interpret perceptual input.

Some evidence for this comes from an interesting experiment by Foley (1970, 1974). She placed wedge prisms in front of the eyes of observers so that the direction of displacement was different for each eye. Either one eye saw an upward displacement and the other a downward displacement, or one eye saw a displacement to the right and the other to the left. After several hours of exposure the two eyes were tested separately. The results indicated that each eye had adapted to its own particular distortion. This implies a perceptual recalibration. It seems likely that adaptation to optically rearranged stimuli involves some form of perceptual learning altering the appearance of visual space. However, whether the process of learning to deal with rearranged spatial stimuli involves the same mechanisms that may have gone into the original development of our perception of space is not clear.

Context and Meaning. Basically, all percepts are ambiguous. Consider a target that casts a square image upon the retinal surface. The object the image represents could actually be one of an infinite number of different shapes at any distance or inclination relative to the observer, as is shown in Figure 16-13. Since any retinal image can be caused by a variety of different physical targets in the world, it is surprising that our normal perceptual experiences are unambiguous. Actually, what we perceive is the result of a decision-

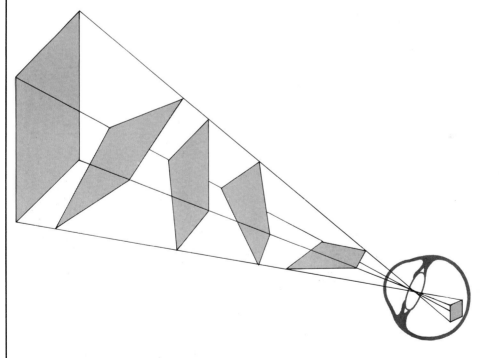

Figure 16-13.
Many different objects at different distances and slants, all of which cast the same square retinal image (from Coren & Girgus, 1978).

making process in which we deduce, on the basis of all available information, what the stimulus object is. This *transactional viewpoint* maintains that any current perceptual experience consists of a total complex of significances. Through our life experience we learn that certain objects or conditions have a high probability of being related to each other. On this basis we derive our best "bet" as to what we are viewing. In a sense, the world we are experiencing is a product of perception and not the cause of it (Ittelson, 1962). The transactional approach implies that if our expectations change, or our analysis of the situation changes, then our perceptual experience will also change (Ames, 1951; Brunswik, 1955). A simple example of the effect of context and expectations can be seen in Demonstration Box 16-3.

Most of our percepts are constructed from incomplete stimuli. Look at Figure 16-14A. It is clear that this represents a dog, yet it should also be clear that there is no dog present. The figure is completely constructed in

the *mind's eye* of the observer. The elephant in Figure 16-14B will probably be somewhat more difficult to recognize. The less familiar the object, the more difficult is the recognition. Once having seen (or "constructed") the figure, however, the meaningful organization will be immediately apparent when you look at it again. Our ability to perceive these stimuli as objects depends upon our prior experiences. This was shown by Steinfield (1967), who found that when observers were told a story about an ocean cruise they recognized Figure 16-14C as a steamship in less than 5 sec. Observers who were told an irrelevant story took six times longer to recognize the figure.

Some of the experiences that affect perception may take place at a preconscious level. For instance, Haber and Hershenson (1965) presented a word for so brief a time period that it could not be recognized. They found that if the word was presented several times, even though the length of time of each presentation was not increased, the word was eventually recognized. If the word was not

---

Read the accompanying handwritten message.

You probably read it as "My phone number is area code 604, 876-1569. Please call!" If you did, you were being affected by several contextual influences on perception. Go back to the message and look carefully at the script. You will see that the two pairs of characters you read as

the word *is* and the numbers *15* are identical. In addition, the *h* in the word phone and the *b* in the word number are identical, as are the *d* in the word code and the *l* in the word please. You saw each letter or number when you first read the message within a context, and this context determined how you interpreted the script character.

Demonstration Box 16-3
A Context Effect on Perception

My phone number 15 area
code 604, 876-1569. Please call!

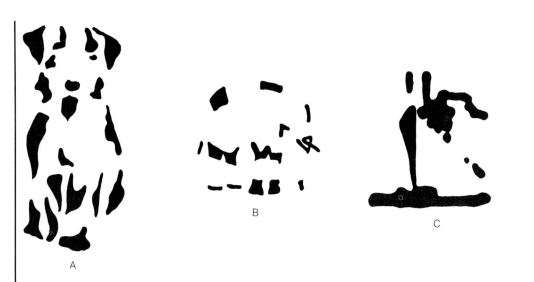

Figure 16-14.
Some degraded stimuli that may be seen as objects (based upon Street, 1931).

identified on the first presentation, why should an observer be able to recognize it after repeated exposures? Dodwell (1971) has suggested that very fast presentations of stimuli do not give the brain sufficient time to do the necessary computations required for recognition. The partially processed stimulus is held in memory, and as the information extraction continues, hypotheses are formed and checked until the stimulus appears to make sense. At this point, the conscious recognition response takes place (Doherty & Keeley, 1972).

The same perceptual hypotheses, allowing us to eventually formulate a percept from minimal or degraded input, can also be used to modify our perception so that it no longer accurately represents the stimulus. For example, Ross and Schilder (1934) presented observers with a series of briefly flashed line drawings. Some of the drawings were incomplete or distorted, such as three armed people, faces with a mouth missing, and others. A look at some of their observers'

comments is informative. When presented with the side view of a dog with the left hind leg missing, the subject reported, "It's a dog, a wolf, two ears stand upright, a round mouth, a long tail." The experimenter then instructed the observer, "Look at his legs."

Observer: "He has five toes on each leg."
Experimenter: "Look at the hind legs."
Observer: "I saw two; the tail goes up."

Despite continued pressure from the experimenter, the observer continued to correct the percept, filling in the missing leg on the hypothesis that dogs have four legs.

These researchers also used a drawing of a woman's head facing forward. She had two large eyes as well as a large third eye on her forehead. One observer described the picture as "a woman with long hair, black, two eyes, one nose, one mouth, two ears." The stimulus was briefly presented again, and the observer was asked if the forehead was in order, to which he replied, "Yes." After several other stimuli were presented again the observer now reported, "The same woman I saw before. She is funny: big eyes, a big nose, and a big mouth."

Experimenter: "Look at the forehead."

Observer: "She has a small curl in the middle."

Even with more brief presentations, this observer still insisted that all that appeared on the forehead was a curl of hair. Third eyes do not normally occur, so we apparently correct our percept on the basis of our expectations—we see extra hair, not extra eyes. You may see how expectations alter our perception in Demonstration Box 16-4.

Language as well as expectations may modify percepts. This view was advanced by Whorf (1956) and Sapir (1939), who suggested that specific language labels for certain types of stimuli increase the ease of perceptual recognition. They maintain, for example, that the Eskimo, whose language has a wide variety of different names for different kinds of snow, may be able to make better discrimination among types of snow than those of us who speak English and have only the single label "snow."

An example of how language can affect perception is seen in a classic experiment conducted by Gottschaldt (1926, 1929), who gave observers from 3 to 520 presentations of a simple target. He then asked them to find these targets in a more complex figure. Such a target is shown in Figure 16-15, where Figure 16-15A is embedded in Figure 16-15B. He reported that prolonged experience with the simple figure did not make it any easier to find it when it was hidden in the more complex stimulus. Djang (1937) repeated this experiment. However, her observers did not just look at the simple stimulus; they were required to draw it. She reports that when such active practice was combined with exposure, there was an improvement in later recognition of the simple component embedded in the more complex figure. Schwartz (1961) then added a language component. He had observers learn distinctive verbal labels to attach to each of the simple figures. This modification of the experiment resulted in an improved ability to find and recognize the named stimuli. However, verbal labeling can either help or hinder recognition. Ellis and Muller (1964) trained subjects using either a *narrow* labeling system (one label for each shape) or a *wide* labeling system (one label for four shapes). In later tests of recognition for these forms, the group using the narrow labeling approach performed better than the group simply observing the shapes without labeling; the group who used the wide labeling system had the fewest correct recognitions. Thus the wide labeling seems to emphasize the learning of similarities between the stimuli, which later results in poorer discrimination and recognition.

Language and expectation can also serve to modify the later reports of what we have seen. Carmichael, Hogan, and Walter (1932) presented observers with simple line drawings and associated each with a label. Observers were asked to reproduce these draw-

---

Turn to color plate 8 and *quickly* count the number of aces of spades that you see. Then return to this demonstration box. Although you probably only saw three aces of spades, there are actually five. Two of the aces of spades are printed in red ink, rather than in black. Since you "expect" spades to be black, your recognition process for incongruent or unexpected stimuli is impaired.

Demonstration Box 16-4
An Expectancy Effect on Perception

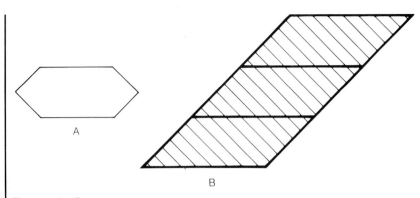

Figure 16-15.
Figure (A) may be found embedded in Figure (B).

ings. In general, their reproductions were biased in the direction of the verbal label. When presented with Figure 16-16A and told that it was a broom, observers tended to reproduce patterns similar to 16-16B. When told that it was a rifle, observers tended to reproduce patterns similar· to that in 16-16C. In this experiment the reproductions occurred only a few moments after the stimulus was taken away. Such distortions in our recollections of what we have seen may have important consequences for many behaviors, including such things as scientific observation and eye witness testimony. For example, eye witness reports of events that occurred during a crime tend to be remarkably unreliable, even when obtained immediately after the event. Observers have a tendency to include details that they could not have seen. Such details are often provided on the basis of the observer's expectations or biases (Buckhout, 1976).

Loftus (1974) demonstrated how words used to question observers about a filmed auto accident could cause them to distort their perceptual memory. When witnesses were asked about what happened when one car smashed into another (as opposed to using a more neutral term, such as made contact with the other car), they were more likely to report having seen broken glass flying about. One might argue that such distortion is a distortion in memory, rather than in perception. Unfortunately, when observers report what they have *seen*, they are always dealing with events that occurred in the past. This means that the report represents what is available in the observer's memory. Thus the same processes affecting memory will also affect perceptual reports. In many respects, it seems as if our perception of the world is more a product of our experiences, expectations, and mental processes than of the stimuli reaching our senses.

Stimulus

Reproduction when it was labeled a "broom"

Reproduction when it was labeled a "rifle"

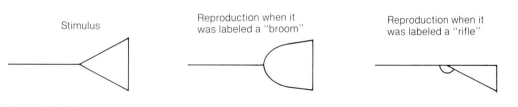

Figure 16-16.
The effects of labels on later perceptual recall.

17
Individual Differences

She waved the patch of cloth and raised her voice to say, "It's a dark blue, why do you insist on calling it a dark green?"

"It looks green to me."

"You mean you've chosen to call it green. My eyes are perfect and it looks blue to me; therefore it is blue."

"Listen, it looks green to me. I know what looks green and what looks blue. Maybe we just see the world in a different way. After all, you are always saying that I make coffee too strong and too bitter, while I think your coffee tastes too weak. Maybe your world is just different from mine."

Let us step back from this argument for a moment, to recall that perception is not simply a process by which the qualities of the world get transferred from "out there" to "in here." Remember that perception involves many levels of processing. Not only must the peripheral sensory receptors be stimulated, but stimuli must be interpreted and encoded. "The eyes are blind; only the mind sees." If this premise is accepted, it is possible that individuals can differ in the way that they perceive their worlds since their minds differ.

There are many factors that can cause individuals to have different perceptions even when encountering identical stimuli. For instance, in the last chapter we saw that individuals of different ages often perceived certain stimuli differently. We also discovered that an individual's past experience or expectations can alter perception. Actually, there are many mechanisms that operate to make each person's perceptual experiences somewhat unique. These include physiological factors, which can alter the sensory receptors themselves or the neural apparatus that decodes the sensory information. They can also include experiential variables, which have to do with the individual's life history. There is also a contribution from an individual's cognitive, or perceptual, style. This reflects personality differences and different approaches to gathering information from the environment, and all of these may lead to individual differences in perception. Let us now consider why the world you perceive may not necessarily be the same as the world of others.

PHYSIOLOGICAL DIFFERENCES

Basically, we are all complex physiological machines. We certainly know that any factors that alter the structure and function of our sensory apparatus will alter what we perceive. Thus, nonfunctional retinal cones will cause color vision deficits. Calcium deposits on the bones of the inner ear will lessen the intensity of sounds in the environment, while it will make your own voice seem very loud to you. In addition to such very specific factors, there are some physiological variables that affect the whole body and tend to also affect perception.

The Effects of Drugs. There are a number of drugs that can cause marked changes in sensory capacities. For instance, smokers are continually ingesting a number of active chemicals. The most important of these is the poison nicotine; next in importance is the gas carbon monoxide. Since these chemicals enter the body predominantly via the mouth, it is not surprising that the major sensory effects of smoking tobacco focus on the sense of taste. Evidence indicates that absolute taste thresholds are higher for smokers than for nonsmokers, with smokers being especially insensitive to bitter tastes such as quinine (Kaplan & Glanville, 1964; Sinnot & Rauth, 1937). On the other hand, you may be quite surprised to find that smoking also affects vision; most of these effects are probably due to the inhalation of carbon monoxide. Smoking tends to reduce one's ability to make brightness intensity discriminations, especially under scotopic illumination conditions (Rhee, Kim, & Kim, 1965). This might explain why smokers tend to have more nighttime driving accidents than non-smokers.

One general theme seems characteristic of the data describing the effects of drugs on perception. Commonly, drugs that depress neural activity, such as sedatives like barbiturates, tranquilizers, or alcohol, will decrease sensory acuity. For example, Hel-lekant (1965) measured the effect of alcohol on taste sensitivity by recording directly from the chorda tympani nerve of a cat. This nerve conveys taste sensations from most of the tongue. Alcohol reduced responsiveness to sweet (sucrose), acid (acetic acid), salt (sodium chloride), and bitter (quinine) stimuli. The strongest reduction of taste response was for the bitter stimuli.

The overall sensitivity of the visual and auditory systems is also affected by depressant drugs. A very popular technique for measuring visual responsiveness is the CRITICAL FLICKER FUSION FREQUENCY (usually abbreviated CFF). This task requires an observer to view a flickering light. As the rate at which the light flickers is increased, the observer will eventually see a steady, continuous light. The flicker speed that results in the perception of a steady light is the CFF. The *greater* the frequency needed to cause the perception of flicker to disappear, the better is the functioning of the receptor system. There is a similar task used in hearing. This is called the AUDITORY FLUTTER FUSION task (AFF). It is defined as the interval at which the listener first reports that a series of sequentially presented tones has merged into a continuous sound. Depressant drugs, such as alcohol and tranquilizers, tend to lower both the CFF and the AFF, thus indicating that the visual and auditory systems are acting sluggishly and with less sensitivity under the influence of such drugs (Besser, 1966; Holland, 1960).

While most of these drugs operate by making the observer generally less sensitive, alcohol seems to have a particularly potent effect in depressing visual functioning by direct action on the retina. This may account for some reports associating excessive alcohol intake with defects in red-green color vision (Granger & Ikeda, 1968).

Drugs that increase the arousal level of the observer, such as stimulants like caffeine or amphetamines (and even some of the B vitamins), may in some instances improve the sensitivity of the observer. These effects, however, do not seem to be as widespread or as reproducible as those obtained with depressant drugs. We do find that amphetamines and caffeine tend to increase the responsiveness of both the visual and auditory systems when sensitivity is measured using the CFF and the AFF. Such drugs seem also to increase the sensitivity of the olfactory system (Turner, 1968). Demonstration Box 17-1 provides a relatively simple perceptual task that can show you the effects of a stimulant on perception.

The hallucinogenic and psychoactive drugs, including LSD, mescaline, psilocybin, and marijuana, are often reported to have profound perceptual effects. For instance, Aldous Huxley (1963) described his visual experiences after taking mescaline saying: "First and most important is the experience of light. . . . All colors are intensified to a pitch far beyond anything seen in the normal state, and at the same time the mind's capacity for recognizing fine distinctions of tone and hue is notably heightened." The actual data seem to run contrary to Huxley's subjective impressions, however. Hartman and Hollister (1963) found that LSD, mescaline, and psilocybin all reduced the accuracy of color discriminations. Carlson (1958) showed that LSD reduced visual sensitivity in a threshold task. Furthermore, there are reports of blurred vision (Hoffer & Osmond, 1967) and slower

Look at the accompanying figure (which is called the *Necker Cube*) and notice that it tends to reverse its apparent orientation as you view it steadily. Sometimes the face with the corner labeled *A* seems closer than the face with the corner labeled *B*, and at other times *B* appears closer. Most people show a fairly constant rate of reversal for this figure. Have a friend monitor you for one minute as you look at the figure. Call out each time the figure reverses its apparent orientation, while your friend counts the number of reversals.

Now drink a cup of coffee. Don't use decaffeinated coffee since we want you to receive a dose of caffeine. Caffeine is a stimulant, and it should increase your visual responsiveness (as well as keeping you awake for the rest of

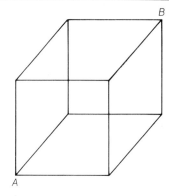

Demonstration Box 17-1
The Effects of Stimulants on Figure Reversals

the chapter). The effects of caffeine take about 10–15 minutes to appear. After this interval, repeat the viewing process. Look at the figure for 1 minute while a friend records the number of reversals. You should find that the stimulant has increased the number of perceptual shifts you experience.

---

than normal adaptation to darkness for observers under the influence of LSD (Ostfeld, 1961). Susceptibility to at least one visual geometric illusion (the Mueller–Lyer, shown in Figures 14-11 and 16-8) increases under the influence of LSD (Edwards & Cohen, 1961). On the other hand, LSD does seem to improve auditory acuity (Hoffer & Osmond, 1967).

Similarly, when observers are asked to describe their experiences, they often report that moderate doses of marijuana (*cannabis*) seem to improve visual clarity and acuity. Unfortunately the experimental results indicate that, as with LSD, the actual perceptual effects involve losses in sensitivity. For instance, in a vigilance task where observers were asked to fixate a target and report stimuli appearing in the periphery of vision, smoking marijuana produced fewer accurate reports. Such an effect could be due to a narrowing of attention induced by the drug. It also might occur because the observers could not be bothered to press the switch. This second explanation probably does not account for the results, since when the stimuli were reported the reaction times were as quick as when observers were not under the influence of the drug (Moskowitz, Sharma, & McGlothlin, 1972). Marijuana smokers also showed a loss of sensitivity when asked to report the offset of a brief light flash (Theodor & Miller, 1972).

Color discrimination has also been shown to be poorer after the use of marijuana. These effects are particularly marked in the blue region (Adams, Brown, Haegerstrom-Portnoy, & Flom, 1976). There are some more complex sensory effects that have been reported after the smoking of cannabis. Some observers experience changes in depth perception and distortions in the perception of size (Tart, 1971). In addition, there is a report that the autokinetic effect, which is the illusory movement of a stationary light viewed in total darkness (illustrated in Demonstration Box 12-6), may become exaggerated. This last observation has led one group of experimenters to caution against night driving while under the influence of marijuana (Sharma & Moskowitz, 1972).

Although contact with hallucinogenic drugs involves a departure from everyday behavior for most people, many of the stimulants (such as caffeine) and depressants (such as tobacco and alcohol) that alter perception are quite commonly used. Everyday drugs, including antihistamines and aspirin, can cause the perceptual responses of individuals to differ. For instance, aspirin may cause dimness of vision or ringing in the ears (Goodman & Gilman, 1965). Thus an individual who has just had a cup of coffee or a martini, or who has tried to tend to a headache, may differ from other individuals in perceptual responses due to the actions of the ingested drugs.

The Effects of Physical Pathology. There are many pathological conditions that affect perception. The most obvious of these are maladies damaging a particular receptor organ. Thus, glaucoma can produce blindness if left untreated, and otosclerosis, which causes the bones of the middle ear to become immobile, will impair hearing. There are, however, some pathological conditions that cause disturbances in very special and complex aspects of perception, rather than simply causing a loss of sensitivity to a given stimulus dimension. Such effects are often caused by severe toxic conditions, such as carbon monoxide poisoning, as well as diseases or injuries that damage or reduce the functioning in some parts of the brain (Critch-

ley, 1964; Davidoff, 1975; Luria, 1973). These can affect such complex functions as the ability to recognize objects or to place them in space, and they may also affect the ability to distribute attention. In general, these problems are called AGNOSIAS, from the Greek *a* meaning "not" and *gnosis* meaning "intuitive knowledge." People suffering from agnosias seem to perceive but do not seem to be capable of understanding the information presented to them.

Freud (1953) noticed a form of perceptual disturbance that he called VISUAL OBJECT AGNOSIA. Some of his patients were unable to recognize familiar objects, although there seemed to be no psychopathological disturbance or readily detectable elementary damage to the visual apparatus. More recent work (Luria, 1973) has suggested that agnosias might arise from lesions in the secondary visual areas of the cortex. These lesions do not cause blindness nor do they seem to diminish visual acuity. Rather, they make it difficult for a person to combine parts of an object and to recognize them. For example, Luria describes a patient who was given a picture of a pair of eyeglasses. The patient examined the picture carefully in a manner indicating that he was confused and did not know exactly what it represented. He then started to guess. "There is a circle . . . and another circle . . . and a stick . . . a cross bar . . . why it must be a bicycle?"

Such patients seem to have problems in separating the parts of the figure from the overall context. Thus, if the patient is shown a drawing of a clock, such as is shown in Figure 17-1A, the patient can usually identify it correctly. However, if one simply x's out the clock with a couple of lines, as in Figure 17-1B, the patient can no longer recognize what the picture represents. Such a patient may identify a telephone, with a dial, as a clock, or perceive a sofa, upholstered in brown fabric, as a trunk. Recognition difficul-

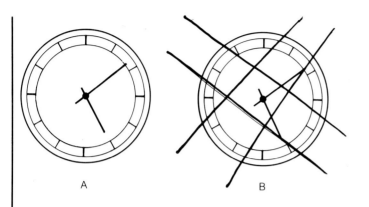

A   B

Figure 17-1.
(A) A figure recognized as a clock. (B) A figure no longer recognizable to a visual agnosic.

ties seem to be even more pronounced when the stimuli are presented for less than 500 msec.

What sort of underlying mechanisms are involved in these perceptual disturbances? As long ago as 1909, the Hungarian neurologist Balint made some observations that suggest an attentional mechanism. He found that his patients had a definite decrease in attention span, being able to see only one object at a time, regardless of its size. For instance, such a person could not place a dot in the center of a circle since this would require paying attention to both the circle and the dot simultaneously. This type of patient is said to be suffering from SIMULTAGNOSIA. Thus, if the patient were shown a series of overlapping objects, such as those in Figure 17-2, she might report a single object, for example, the hammer, and deny that she can see any of the others (Williams, 1970). If such individuals are asked to copy a simple drawing, such as the one shown as Figure 17-3A, they would depict only its individual parts. Essentially, they would give a visual list of most of the details, as opposed to an overall integration of the parts into a whole figure. A drawing typical of such a patient is shown in Figure 17-3B.

A number of physiological experiments tend to show that this defect is caused by disturbances in the temporal region of the cortex. It also seems to be specific to the way in which attention is distributed to the visual targets (Butters, Barton, & Brody, 1970; Gerbrandt, Spinelli, & Pribram, 1970). Luria (1973) claims that injections of caffeine (to stimulate the appropriate region of the cortex) can reduce some of the symptoms, thus allowing the patient to be able to attend to two or three objects in the visual field

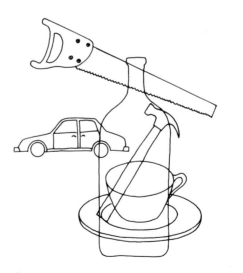

Figure 17-2.
A test figure for simultagnosia.

simultaneously. Unfortunately, this improvement lasts only as long as the drug is active.

Some of the agnosia effects are quite general and may involve more than one sensory modality. Patients with diseases of the parietal lobe of the brain may show a SPATIAL AGNOSIA. They have difficulty negotiating their way around the world. They make wrong turns even in familiar surroundings and do not easily recognize landmarks. They can become lost in their own homes. This problem does not appear to be caused by a defect in a single, specific sensory modality. These patients seem to be just as impaired using their tactile or kinesthetic senses as their visual (Heaton, 1968; Weinstein, Cole, Mitchell, & Lyerly, 1964). Such patients often show a unilateral neglect of space. For example, if asked to draw symmetrical objects, they will usually produce some sort of imperfection on one side. Thus an individual with left-sided spatial agnosia would reproduce Figure 17-3A as 17-3C.

While some of these perceptual effects are quite general, others are very specific. For instance, there is a rare disorder called PROSO-PAGNOSIA. In this type of agnosia the patient has difficulty recognizing human faces. In extreme cases the patient may not even recognize his or her own face in a mirror. Prosopagnosia is of interest because, as we saw in Chapter 16, the human face is a very important stimulus developmentally. Remember, your mother's face was probably one of the first visual forms to which you attended as an infant. When children draw, the face is usually the first part of the body to be depicted. Thus we find that facial perception is one of the aspects of form recognition that is lost only in cases of serious brain injury, and often returns much earlier than other cognitive functions when recovery from brain damage occurs (Heaton, 1968).

Although we have concentrated on the visual sense in this discussion, similar difficul-

ties are found in speech and sound recognition. These are usually grouped under the overall heading of APHASIA (from a meaning "not" and *phasis* meaning "utterance"). Such individuals suffer from an inability to name common objects or, often, to recognize the meanings of words designating common objects (Luria, 1972; Tsvetkova, 1972). Aphasia is the auditory analogue of agnosia. These problems indicate that, when the integrity of the nervous system is disrupted, severe perceptual consequences can result.

SEX DIFFERENCES

The sex of an individual can also influence perceptual capacities. Gender carries with it many physiological implications, not the least of which are massive chemical differences due to the presence of specific male or female hormones. Examples of the effects these hormones can have on perception are found in both taste and olfaction. For instance, women on the average have more acute senses of smell than do men (Money, 1965). This difference can be directly attributed to hormonal influences. The acuity of a female's sense of smell varies within the menstrual cycle, reaching its peak at midcycle when *estrogen* (one of the major female hormones) levels are at their highest. Women whose ovaries are less active than normal have impaired smell sensitivity, but this defect can be remedied by the administration of estrogen. On the other hand, doses of androgen (the male hormone) makes the sense of smell less sensitive (Schneider, Costiloe, Howard, & Wolf, 1958).

Some hormonal effects on perception are quite subtle. There is a sex difference in taste preference, with females showing a stronger preference for the sweet taste than males. This is true for rats as well as humans. When the ovaries of female rats are removed, their

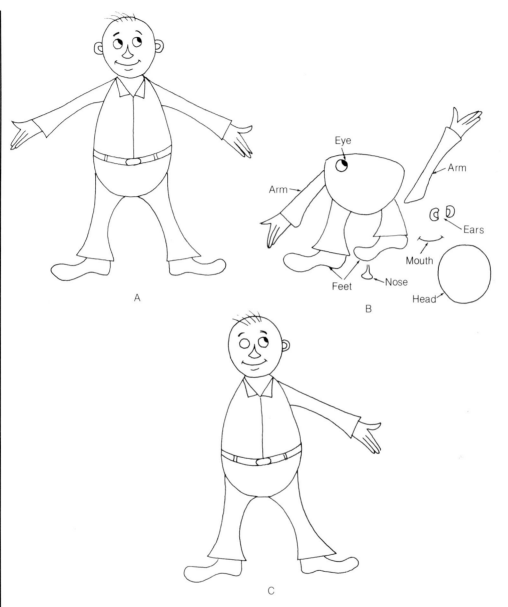

Figure 17-3.
(A) The target figure to be copied. (B) Reproduction typical of a
visual object agnosic. (C) Reproduction typical of a unilateral
spatial agnosic.

preference for the sweet taste diminishes, while therapeutic doses of estrogen can restore this taste preference again (Zucker, Wade, & Ziegler, 1972).

Male–female differences are found in other sensory modalities as well (McGuiness, 1976a). For example, women usually show greater touch sensitivity than do men (Weinstein & Sersen, 1961; Ippolitov, 1972—see also Chapter 10). Measurements of auditory thresholds have demonstrated that, on the average, females show superior sensitivity. This sex difference increases when higher frequencies are used to measure the threshold; it also increases with age (Corso, 1959; McGuiness, 1972). Responses to pain produced by electric shock show that women generally are more sensitive than men. These pain thresholds also seem to vary over the menstrual cycle (Tedford, Warren, & Flynn, 1977).

Sex differences in vision seem to be more complex. Males generally appear to have much better visual acuity under photopic conditions (Burg, 1966; Roberts, 1964). This sex difference does not appear until the middle to late teens (Skoff & Pollack, 1969). There is some evidence that the visual acuity of women varies with their menstrual cycle. It seems to be poorest just prior to and during menstruation. The hormone progesterone (another predominately female hormone) is often prescribed for women who suffer from severe anxiety or depression during menstruation. This hormone relieves these symptoms and also restores visual acuity to its normal level in most patients (Dalton, 1964). Under scotopic conditions, there is some suggestion that females tend to dark-adapt more rapidly than do males (McGuinness, 1976b).

One interesting and complex sex difference concerns visual-spatial abilities. There is a set of tasks requiring spatial abilities that seems to produce consistent sex differences favoring males. One of these involves *disem-*

bedding, which is the ability to disentangle a target object from a surrounding, and often confusing, context. For example, in Figure 17-4A, you see a figure marked "target" that is hidden, or embedded, in the more complex figure beside it. The observer's task is to find the simple shape as quickly as possible. Such tasks are usually called the EMBEDDED FIGURES TEST or the HIDDEN FIGURES TEST. A different spatial task involves the ability to recognize targets when they have been rotated. An example of this task is shown in Figure 17-4B. The observer has to recognize the shape marked "target" from among the three figures next to it. It is often difficult to recognize which shape is exactly the same as the target, since the correct shape has been rotated into a different spatial orientation.

Both these types of tasks produce sex differences favoring males (Maccoby & Jacklin, 1974; Wilson, DeFries, McClearn, Vandenberg, Johnson, & Rashad, 1975). Disembedding a figure, or recognizing it, when it has been rotated in space is a complex task that probably involves many learned skills. Therefore, it is surprising to find that there is a body of evidence suggesting that some of the same physiological factors distinguishing males from females could be responsible for some of these effects. Dawson (1967) used a series of these tests on a number of West African males who suffered from a disease that results in estrogen levels higher than those usually found in males. When tested on a series of spatial tasks, these males showed reduced spatial ability relative to a sample of nonaffected males. Males who are insensitive to androgen also show reduced spatial abilities, while females with high androgen levels show greater spatial ability (Masica, Money, Ehrhardt, & Lewis, 1969; Peterson, 1976).

Other factors also affect performance on these spatial tasks. There is a growing body of evidence suggesting that spatial abilities may be influenced by a sex-linked gene (Bock &

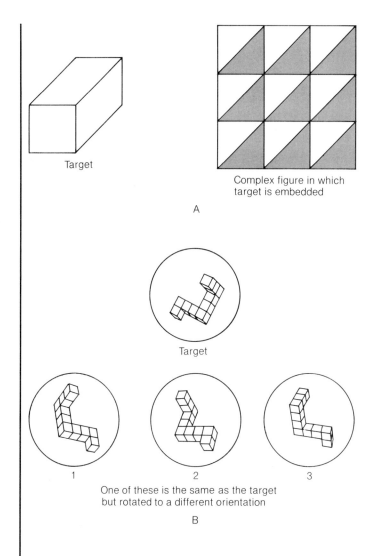

Target

Complex figure in which
target is embedded

A

Target

1   2   3

One of these is the same as the target
but rotated to a different orientation

B

Figure 17-4.
(A) An embedded figures test
in which the *target* is found in
the more complex array. (B) A
mental rotation test in which
the *target* is found as one of
the three test figures, but is in a
different orientation.

Kolakowski, 1973; Yen, 1975). In addition, the rate at which individuals mature seems to play a role. Typically, late maturing individuals (in this case maturing means showing their secondary sexual characteristics) are usually better on such spatial tasks than early maturing individuals (Waber, 1976, 1977).

We have been dealing only with some of the physical variables that seem to produce different patterns of perceptual abilities in males and females. Of course there will be many factors relating to experience, life history, and cultural influences, that will also affect perceptual behaviors. This is because many aspects of perception are subject to learning influences, as we discussed in Chapter 16. Males and females may differ in the types of tasks and activities in which they engage and in the tools, implements, or utensils used in their everyday activities. These factors can also influence some aspects of perception. Demonstration Box 17-2 provides a recognition task that usually produces different responses from males and females. The task in the demonstration shows differences that are most likely to have an experiential rather than a physiological basis.

ENVIRONMENTAL AND LIFE HISTORY DIFFERENCES

Up to now we have concentrated on physiological factors causing one individual to have perceptual experiences that differ from those of another. Each of us is also surrounded by a particular set of environmental stimuli that could teach us different patterns of perceptual response. If we live in the desert or on the pampas or the plains, we are exposed to broad vistas of open space that are never experienced by a forest dweller. If we live in a technologically advanced country, we are exposed to sets of visual stimuli (such as photographs and television) that are usually not available to someone dwelling in the African bush or the Australian outback. Frequent exposure to certain patterns of stimuli, along with isolation from others, may alter our perceptual experiences.

The Effects of Culture. Deregowski (1973) has collected some examples of perceptual responses that appear strange to those of us who live in a technologically advanced country. The following quote has been attributed to a Scottish missionary working in Malawi (a country in southwestern Africa between northern Rhodesia and Mozambique) nearly 75 years ago: "Take a picture in black and white, and the natives cannot see it. You may tell the natives: 'This is a picture of an ox and a dog'; and the people will look at it and look at you, and that look says that they consider you a liar. Perhaps you say again, 'Yes, this is a picture of an ox and a dog. Look at the horn of the ox, and there is his tail!' And the boy will say, 'Oh, yes and there is the dog's nose and eyes and ears!' Then the old people will look again and clap their hands and say, 'Oh yes, it is a dog. . . .' "

It may surprise you to learn that certain individuals have difficulty recognizing that a photograph is a representation of a real object. If you are surprised, then ask yourself how you recognize and interpret the contents of a picture you have taken with your camera or that has been drawn. Such an activity requires a certain amount of selection among the perceptual cues available; for instance, there may be cues in the photograph suggesting depth (such as those we spoke of in Chapter 11). These might include *linear perspective, interposition,* and *texture gradients,* among others. However, there are also cues indicating that the picture is flat. For instance, there is no *binocular disparity* between items in the picture, and all the elements in the photo require the same degree of *accommodation* and *convergence.* Thus to see a drawing or a photograph as representing an arrangement of objects in three dimensions, rather than as a flat surface with different shadings of dark and light, means that you are attending to some depth cues and ignoring others. The particular perceptual strategy an observer uses may well depend upon her life history and the relative frequency with which certain cues are encountered in the immediate environment.

Hudson (1960, 1962) has attempted to separate cultural factors associated with the use of pictorial depth information. His technique consisted of using a series of pictures that depicted certain combinations of picto-

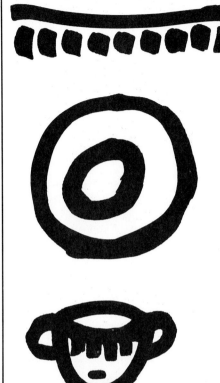

Demonstration Box 17-2
Sex Differences and Object Identification

Look at the three accompanying figures and decide what each looks like. Do this before reading any further.

Responses to patterns similar to these show differences depending on the sex of the observer. Most males view Figure (A) as a brush or a centipede, while females tend to view it as a comb or teeth. Most men view (B) as a target, while women tend to view it as a dinner plate (but both respond equally with ring and tire). Most men see Figure (C) as a head, while women tend to view it as a cup.

rial depth cues. Figure 17-5 shows one picture from Hudson's series, and as you can see, it depicts a hunting scene containing two pictorial depth cues. The first is *interposition,* in which objects closer to the observer block our view of portions of more distant objects. Since the hunter and the antelope are covering portions of the rocks, they appear closer to the observer than the rocks.

The second pictorial depth cue contained in this drawing is *familiar size.* We know the relative sizes of familiar objects; therefore, if an object is depicted as relatively small or large, we will judge its distance from us in a

way consistent with our expectations based upon its known size. For example, an elephant is a very large animal. However, in Figure 17-5 the elephant is one of the smallest items in the picture. If we are responding to the cue of familiar size, we would tend to see the elephant as being the most distant object in this hunting scene. This is consistent with the fact that the images of large objects decrease more slowly in size than images of small objects as the objects move away from us. When something as large as an elephant casts a smaller image than an antelope, the elephant must be

Figure 17-5.
A figure used to test the ability to respond to pictorial depth cues
(based upon Hudson, 1962).

farther away, since it is physically larger than the antelope.

Hudson used these particular stimuli because they are uniquely constructed to allow for both *two-dimensional* (no use of pictorial depth) and *three-dimensional* (full use of pictorial depth) types of responses. If we asked an observer to describe what she saw in this picture (after she had successfully identified all of the objects), a three-dimensional response would indicate that the hunter was attempting to spear the antelope (which is, of course, nearer to him than the elephant if you are perceiving pictorial depth). A two-dimensional response would state that the hunter is attempting to spear the elephant, which is actually physically closer to the tip of the spear in the picture. Such a response would indicate that the observer had not responded to either the interposition or the familiar size cues that place the elephant at a greater perceptual distance from the hunter than the antelope.

These stimuli have been used in a number of studies conducted throughout Africa, test-ing observers from a number of tribal and linguistic groups (Deregowski, 1973). The results indicate that relatively isolated and uneducated African observers have difficulty seeing pictorial depth within these pictures. This difficulty is still present in varying degrees at higher socioeconomic and educational levels within the African sample. This tendency to not respond to, or misperceive, depth in pictures seems to be a characteristic of some individuals that carries over into other tasks. You can explore your own tendencies to use certain depth cues but not others by trying Demonstration Box 17-3.

Several theories attempt to explain cross-cultural differences in the perception of pictures. One of the most popular is known as the CARPENTERED WORLD HYPOTHESIS (Davidoff, 1975; Gregory, 1966; Segall, Campbell, & Herskovits, 1966). This notion maintains that, in the Western world, rooms and buildings are usually rectangular. There are many objects in the environment that have right-angled corners, and those common objects give us frequent exposure to cer-

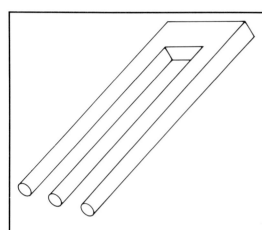

The figure accompanying this box is sometimes called the "Devil's tuning fork." Look at the figure for about 30 seconds or so; then close the book and try to draw it from memory. Return to this box when you have done this.

Most of you probably found this task to be quite difficult. The source of your difficulty comes from the fact that your cultural experience with graphic representations has caused you to interpret this two-dimensional stimulus as a three-dimensional object. Unfortunately, such an interpretation leads to problems since the depth cues implied in this figure are ambiguous. It is interesting to note that Africans who have not received formal education have no difficulty reproducing the figure. Since they do not interpret the figure as being three-dimensional they merely see a pattern of flat lines, which is easy to reproduce.

Demonstration Box 17-3
Cross-Cultural Differences in Perception

tain forms of linear perspective depth cues. Additional exposure to linear perspective comes from views of long expanses of highways and railroads. Surrounded by such an environment, we may learn to depend upon its cues when we construct our percepts. However, there are groups of people who live in environments that lack these abundant linear perspective cues. For example, the Zulus have been described as surrounded by a circular culture. They live in round huts with round doors. They do not plough their land in straight lines but tend to use curved furrows (Gregory, 1966). Individuals living in such a world would not be expected to rely on linear perspective as heavily as those of us living in a more linear environment.

In 1966, Segall, Campbell, and Herskovits reported a series of studies that compared the perceptual responses of individuals in carpentered versus noncarpentered environments. They did not use Hudson-like pictures as stimulus materials; rather they chose to explore the perceptual distortions associated with the Mueller–Lyer and other visual-geometric illusions. Some of these configurations have already been discussed in Chapter 14, where we pointed out how our susceptibility to size distortion in the Mueller–Lyer illusion may be dependent upon a three-dimensional interpretation of the figure (to refresh your memory refer back to Figure 14-11). For example, the apparently longer portion of the Mueller–Lyer figure may be interpreted as a corner of a room receding in depth because the wings of the illusion act as linear perspective cues. The inappropriate application of size constancy results in the distortion. Since pictorial depth information is thought to play a role in the formation of these illusory percepts, you can see how these types of configurations are well-suited to an exploration of the carpentered world hypothesis.

Segall *et al.* (1966) gathered data from throughout Africa and also from several groups of people living in Evanston, Illinois. Although there are variations within the noncarpentered samples, the average Mueller–Lyer illusion was greater for the more urban groups.

In another study, Killbride and Leibowitz (1975) studied the Ponzo illusion. This is another distortion that seems to result from the use of depth cues and the subsequent inappropriate size constancy correction (see Figure 14-10). They found that for a Ugandan sample, individuals who responded three dimensionally to the depth cues in pictures showed large illusions, while those who did not see depth showed little distortion. Some evidence suggests that schooling and the availability of graphic and pictorial materials in the environment may be important factors as well.

The observed differences in illusion susceptibility for different cultural groups may be partially caused by factors other than experience. Most of the Western observers from carpentered environments who were tested in these studies were Caucasian while most of the noncarpentered samples were Negroid. There is some evidence suggesting that racial characteristics (predominantly associated with the pigmentation of ocular structures, such as the iris and the lens) may also affect the perception of visual illusions (Berry, 1971; Pollack & Silver, 1967). Factors as seemingly inconsequential as the color of a person's eyes (whether the iris is light as in blue-eyed people or dark as in brown-eyed people) may make a difference in this class of percepts (Coren & Porac, 1978).

There are reported instances where isolation from experience with certain types of cues has led to changes in perception. One of the most striking examples of this was provided by the anthropologist Turnbull (1961) who was observing the behavior of the Bambuti Pygmies, who live in the Ituri Forest in the Congo. Since they are forest dwellers, their vision is primarily limited to vistas that only extend for, at most, 30 m. Thus, they would seem to lack the visual experience for greater distances that is necessary in order to learn the maintenance of size constancy at greater viewing distances. Turnbull noted an instance when he had first taken his Bambuti guide, Kenge, out of the forest. They were crossing over a broad plain and happened to spot a herd of buffalo:

"... Kenge looked over the plains and down to where a herd of about a hundred buffalo were grazing some miles away. He asked me what kind of insects they were, and I told him they were buffalo, twice as big as the forest buffalo known to him. He laughed loudly and told me not to tell such stupid stories. ... We got into the car and drove down to where the animals were grazing. He watched them getting larger and larger, and though he was as courageous as any Pigmy, he moved over and sat close to me and muttered that it was witchcraft. ... Finally, when he realized that they were real buffalo he was no longer afraid, but what puzzled him still was why they had been so small, and whether they really had been small and suddenly grown larger, or whether it had *been some kind of trickery.''* (From Turnbull, C. *American Journal of Phychology* **74.** © 1961 The University of Illinois Press)

Turnbull's description of Kenge's perceptual impressions suggests that our experience with particular environments can result in differences in perceptual experience and interpretation. It seems reasonable to assume that some of the other cross-cultural perceptual differences may also be a result of learning to utilize cues that are common to a particular environment while failing to learn to interpret cues that are rare.

The Effects of Occupation. Even within a given culture there are different sets of environmental stimuli to which some of us are selectively exposed. You are exposed to your occupational setting for about one-half of your adult working life, and specific sets of occupational experiences can affect your perceptual abilities both at the physiological and at the higher cognitive levels. One aspect of an occupation that may have physiological effects on a sensory system is the amount of noise present. While some job settings are relatively quiet (i.e., offices and small stores), others are associated with continuous, high intensity noise (i.e., factories and mills).

Figure 17-6 illustrates the effects of noise on hearing for different occupations. The horizontal axis represents the frequencies at which hearing was tested in a sample of male office, farm, and factory workers, and the 0 decibel point on the vertical axis represents the average minimum threshold for an auditory experience. The three curves on the graph plot the average threshold sound intensity at each of the frequencies used in the test. As you can see, the group of factory workers has a lower sensitivity (higher average thresholds). Fortunately, many factory workers have begun to wear earphones while working; these help protect them from the ill effects of continual noise exposure.

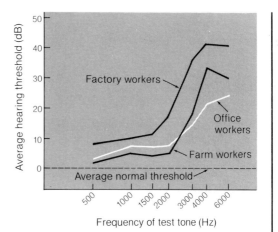

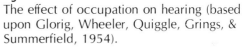

Figure 17-6.
The effect of occupation on hearing (based upon Glorig, Wheeler, Quiggle, Grings, & Summerfield, 1954).

According to Kryter (1970), factory workers are not the only group that should be concerned about continual exposure to very loud sounds. For instance, both soldiers exposed to gunfire and airline pilots have been shown to have hearing deficits. The loss tends to be greatest in the higher frequency ranges and seems to increase in severity as the length of the exposure increases. Thus, airline pilots who have from 1000–2000 hr flying time have an average audibility threshold of approximately 0 dB at a sound frequency of 4000 Hz. However, more experienced pilots, with 10,000–16,000 hr flying time, have an average audibility threshold of 10 dB at the same sound frequency.

Rice *et al.* (1968) have shown that performers of rock music may also suffer losses of hearing acuity. In Figure 17-7 we once again have average audibility thresholds plotted in decibels on the vertical axis and test frequencies plotted along the horizontal axis. The lowest curve represents the thresholds of the control group of nonperformers. Notice that relative to nonperformers of the

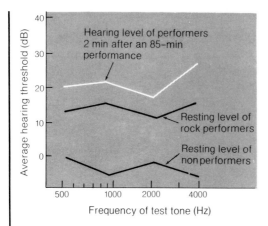

Figure 17-7.
A comparison of the hearing of rock musicians to that of nonperformers (based upon Rice, Hyley, Bartlett, Bedford, Gregory, & Hallum, 1968).

same age, the rock performers have elevated audibility thresholds (lower sensitivity). At 4000 Hz there is approximately a 20 dB difference between the thresholds of the performers and the controls. To give you a reference point, a 20 dB difference would be roughly equivalent to being able to hear a normal conversational tone as opposed to a shout. Figure 17-7 also shows the immediate effects of prolonged exposure to very loud sounds. The dotted curve on this graph plots the measured thresholds immediately after 85 min of exposure to very loud music, and as you can see, the threshold at 4000 Hz has risen to 25 dB.

There have also been reports of occupational effects of a more cognitive nature. Toch and Schulte (1961) wanted to know if specific past experiences would produce a sensitization or predisposition to "see" a situation in a certain way, especially when alternative perceptual experiences were possible (as when the stimulus is ambiguous or degraded). In other words, they were interested in problems of occupational influences in the development of PERCEPTUAL SET.

Perceptual set refers to the expectancies or predispositions an observer brings to the perceptual situation. In many respects, set can be thought of as another example of selective attention (as we discussed in Chapter 15), in which the observer is set to process some but not all portions of the incoming information.

Toch and Schulte (1961) studied police administration students and their abilities to perceive violence and crime in visual scenes requiring the resolution of some ambiguity. They simultaneously presented different pictures to each eye in a stereoscope. One eye was shown a violent scene and the other a nonviolent one, as in the pair of stimuli in Figure 17-8. If these two views were seen simultaneously by the two eyes, perceptual confusion would result. Observers tend to resolve this ambiguous situation in favor of one scene or the other; this scene then dominates the percept. Toch and Schulte were interested in exploring the notion that the police students would be predisposed to interpret this particular ambiguous situation in terms of the violent as opposed to the nonviolent scene. They compared the performance of their advanced police administration students with two control groups (beginning police students and university students). In general they found that the advanced police students interpreted the stereograms as depicting violence approximately twice as many times as the other two groups. Thus, their data provide

Figure 17-8.
A stereogram used to test for occupational influences on the perception of violence (from Toch, H. H., & Schulte, R. *British Journal of Psychology,* 1961, **52,** 389–393).

419
PERSONALITY
AND
COGNITIVE
STYLE
DIFFERENCES

some evidence that certain occupations, especially those requiring intensive training, may set an individual to interpret ambiguous stimulation in a particular way.

Another example of how occupational training can alter perception (especially in ambiguous situations) was recounted by Boring (1953). A biologist friend once showed him a set of drawings of the same microscopic specimen made before and after the discovery of chromosomes. While none of the "before" drawings showed or suggested any chromosomes at all, there were certainly plenty of chromosomes to be seen afterward!

PERSONALITY AND COGNITIVE STYLE DIFFERENCES

There are a myriad of nonperceptual ways in which individuals differ from one another. Some are outgoing and sociable; others are withdrawn and prefer to be alone. Some are careful and methodical in everything; others are haphazard and unsystematic. The total of all these behavior traits composes the individual's personality. People with different personalities tend to behave differently in many social situations and tend to respond differently to information of various sorts. Do they also perceive the world differently?

There have been many attempts to link individual differences in personality to individual differences in perception. Often the perceptual responses themselves are used to classify individuals as belonging to one personality type or another. One of the most popular of these attempts involves an *embedded figure task* (such as the one we have already discussed). Observers who have difficulty with this task (named FIELD-DEPENDENT people) have been classified by personality

tests as being socially dependent, eager to make a good impression, conforming, and sensitive to their social surroundings (Konstadt & Forman, 1965; Linton & Graham, 1959; Ruble & Nakamura, 1972). Individuals who have little difficulty with such perceptual disembedding tasks (FIELD-INDEPENDENT people) have been characterized by the same tests as being self-reliant, inner-directed, and individualistic (Alexander & Gudeman, 1965; Crutchfield, Woodworth, & Albrecht, 1958; Klein, 1970). Witkin has been one of the major proponents of this approach. He and his associates look upon both the personality and perceptual effects as examples of an individual's COGNITIVE STYLE (Witkin & Berry, 1975). They maintain that perceptual, cognitive, personality, and social interactions all are affected by the same set of processes that determine how a person approaches the world. In effect, cognitive style is part of what we call in everyday language "lifestyle."

While some investigators have begun with the perceptual behaviors and extended these into predictions about personality, others have attempted to predict individual differences in perception from prior considerations of personality theory. One theory that has produced a great deal of recent activity was proposed by Eysenck (1967). He divided individuals into two groups on the basis of whether they were outgoing and sociable (EXTROVERTS) or more withdrawn and self-contained (INTROVERTS). Eysenck found that he could classify individuals along this dimension on the basis of a simple questionnaire, and he next speculated on some physiological differences that might account for these personality traits. He suggested that extroverts have a neural system that is slower to respond and more weakly aroused by stimuli than that of introverts. In addition, they generate neural inhibition more quickly. If this physiological speculation is correct, then it is reasonable to expect introverts to be more perceptually sensitive than extroverts.

Several studies have investigated the effect of introversion–extroversion on perception. Introverts seem to have more sensitive perceptual systems as predicted by the theory. They show lower average thresholds for vision (Siddle, Morrish, White, & Mangen, 1969), hearing (Stelmack & Campbell, 1974), touch (Coles, Gale, & Kline, 1971), and pain (Halsam, 1967). In addition introverts have been shown to be better at tasks requiring sustained attention or vigilance (Harkins & Green, 1975).

When studying the effects of personality factors on perception, it is very important to be sure that we are actually measuring perceptual sensitivity rather than simply picking up differences in how observers respond. After all, it could be the case that introverts simply say, "Yes, I detected the stimulus," more often. One technique allowing us to separate these effects involves signal detection theory (discussed in Chapter 2). When Stelmack and Campbell (1974) analyzed their data from this point of view, they found that introverts have more sensitive hearing than extroverts, even though extroverts are more biased toward saying "yes." Another

way to ascertain sensitivity independent of the observer's response bias is to use direct physiological measurements. A popular technique of this type is called EVOKED RESPONSE recording. In this technique, an electrode is placed on an observer's head over the region of the cortex receiving the primary sensory information for the sense modality being tested. Another electrode, elsewhere on the body, serves as a reference electrode. Any changes in the electrical activity of this brain region can then be picked up by sensitive recording devices, and such activity presumably means that the sensory information has at least been registered in the brain. Using these evoked response measures, Stelmack, Achorn, and Michaud (1977) were able to verify the psychophysical findings. Introverts have greater auditory sensitivity than extroverts.

The startling aspect of all these results is that the answers to a few questions, giving us an insight into how persons interact with other individuals, can predict how the persons' perceptual responses may differ from those of other people. Demonstration Box 17-4 allows you to estimate for yourself whether you are more introverted or extroverted.

It is easy to determine your own standing on introversion versus extroversion by answering the following questions with a "yes" or a "no."

1) Do you often wish for more excitement in life?
2) Do you often say things without stopping to think?
3) Do you like going out a lot?
4) Do other people think of you as being lively?
5) Do you like interacting with people?

If you answered all the questions "yes," you are rather extroverted, while if you answered them all "no," you are rather introverted.

Have some friends and/or relatives answer these questions, but add one additional item to the list.

6) Do you like spicy foods?

What answer do you expect extroverts versus introverts to give? What *sensory data* would lead you to expect that answer?

Demonstration Box 17-4
Introversion–Extroversion and Taste Perception

18
New Approaches to Old Problems

ANALYSIS OF THE PERCEPTUAL EXPERIENCE
RETINAL BLUR
NEURAL INTERACTIONS
ATTENTION, COGNITION, AND LEARNING

SYNTHESIS OF THE PERCEPTUAL EXPERIENCE

PERCEPTUAL PUZZLES IN NEED OF SOLUTION
PUZZLE BOX #1: ARISTOTLE'S ILLUSION
PUZZLE BOX #2: THE PUZZLE OF RADIATING LINES
PUZZLE BOX #3: THE ONE-SPEAKER STEREO ILLUSION
PUZZLE BOX #4: THE HEAT GRILL
PUZZLE BOX #5: A SUBJECTIVE COLOR GRID
PUZZLE BOX #6: GEARS AND CIRCLES

FINAL NOTE

It is morning, and you are looking out of your window. What do you see? Perhaps it is a tree, a building, the sky, or a distant hill. Do you *see* the light rays that have been bent by the cornea and the crystalline lens of your eye? Do you *see* the pattern of neural firing carried from the retina up to the visual cortex of your brain? Do you *see* the three primary pigment colors, or the four primary neural colors, or the 350 different discriminable colors? Do you *see* continuous gradations of brightness, with sharp transitions that define contours?

Of course not. You see a tree, a building, and the sky. Despite the ponderous protestations of the perceptual psychologists, who maintain that all these features are characteristic of your perception, no amount of whimsical fantasy can cause you to see anything other than a tree, a building, and the sky. Your conscious percept has a specific coherence, with some things clearly separate from others and some features clearly nonseparable. There is no conscious reasoning necessary or possible to analyze the millions of separate neural responses, occurring in your retina, optic nerve, or brain, that result in the final percept of a tree. It simply happens. We are not aware of the individual stages of the process, only of the final product.

Much the same thing happens when we look at a painting. We are not conscious of the way in which the artist mixed the paints, prepared the surface, selected the brushes, composed the layout, and made thousands of brush strokes. Still, each stage was vital in producing the painting we see. Of course, completion of any one stage does not produce the final image either. A mixture of paints or a prepared surface or a thousand brush strokes are not a painting. All must be combined in a specific manner. To return to

our view from the window, light rays, visual pigments, retinal activity, brain responses, or cognitive organization does not provide us with a percept. All of these must be combined before we experience any perception as complex as the sight of a tree. Let us see how various levels of processing all interact in perception.

As an example we will consider one of the types of percepts we used to introduce this volume. You may recall from Chapter 1 that we considered our conscious response to a number of stimuli that produced percepts different from what would be expected on the basis of our knowledge of the physical reality. We called these *visual-geometric illusions.* We have occasionally alluded to such figures in Chapters 14, 16, and 17. The two configurations we will analyze are rather simple line drawings. The first, Figure 18-1A, is the *Mueller–Lyer illusion,* in which the upper horizontal line (with wings outward) appears to be longer than the lower horizontal line (with wings pointed inward), despite the fact that both lines are equal in length. The second is the *Poggendorff illusion,* in which the lower segment of the transversal (marked *X* in Figure 18-1B) looks as if it will pass under the upper segment (marked *Y*) if we extend its length. Actually *X* and *Y* are perfectly aligned as you can verify with a ruler or straight edge.

Why should we select these particular stimuli to demonstrate how various levels of processing combine to form the percept? First, these are physically quite simple stimuli, and they are created from a simple set of lines on paper. They are two-dimensional, hence should not be expected to involve different depth or distance processing for their elements. Only two levels of stimulus intensity are involved: light reflected from the lines and from the background. A second reason for selecting these stimuli for analysis is that the

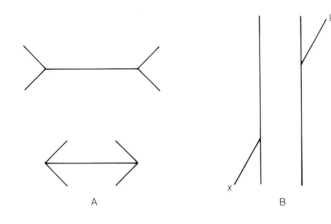

Figure 18-1.
(A) The Mueller–Lyer illusion in which the upper horizontal shaft appears larger than the lower. (B) The Poggendorff illusion in which line X looks as though it would pass under line Y, although both are portions of the same line.

percept differs from what would be expected on the basis of physical measurements. Percepts such as these may provide us with an opportunity to see how perception is shaped and formed within the individual rather than simply representing a snapshot of the environment, transmitted from the eye to the brain. A final reason for considering these figures is that there is a wealth of research knowledge about them; they have been studied for over a century.

While this analysis will concern a particular pair of visual percepts, a levels-of-processing analytic approach can be used to interpret any percept in any modality. We can do the same thing for hearing, touching, and tasting. Some aspects of perception will involve many stages, while others will involve only a few. Some percepts will be good, accurate reproductions of the external environment, whereas others will be shoddy, incomplete, erroneous, or systematically distorted. Any complete analysis must treat all stages, however. Ommission of any level of processing will, at best, result in an incomplete picture of the perceptual process. At worst it will be seriously in error.

ANALYSIS OF THE PERCEPTUAL EXPERIENCE

When we speak about vision we usually refer to "seeing" an object. Actually, the visual modality never makes contact with the object at all. There was an old theory of vision that maintained that the eye emitted rays serving the same function as our fingers. These rays reached out and *felt* the shape and size of objects that we viewed. While acceptance of such a theory may lead to erotic fantasies when viewing members of the opposite sex, the actual physics of the situation indicate that rays of electromagnetic radiation, which we call light, form an image on the surface of the retina. Our only direct interaction with the objects we view is through this image. In some respects, our percept can be no better than the image. Therefore, all considerations of a visual percept must consider the fidelity of the image after it has passed through the cornea and the crystalline lens of the eye, and has finally been projected onto the surface of the retina.

Retinal Blur. What can be said about this first stage of perceptual processing? As we noted in Chapter 7, when we discussed visual acuity, the eye is not a perfect image-forming system. Its optics are actually rather poor. The implications of this for the perception of the figures shown in Figure 18-1, or any other figures, is that the final retinal image is somewhat blurred or degraded. This blurring of the retinal image has important consequences. In addition to determining the minimum object size that can be seen, it also alters the actual pattern on the retina.

Since we rarely see our world as being blurred, it is quite clear that the visual system must be correcting for this blur in some fashion. Think about blurred lines such as the ones shown in Figure 18-2A. Obviously the blurred lines are brightest in the middle and get darker toward the edges. This is the same as saying that a blurred line on the retina stimulates fewer and fewer receptor cells as you move out from the center of the line to its edges. Suppose that the visual system searches for the region in the image where the stimulation is the most intense and then treats this region as if it were the actual location of the line. This would explain why the world usually looks sharp and clear despite the fact that the image itself is blurred.

While this is a useful procedure in cleaning up the blurred image, it can lead to a problem when two lines meet at an angle, as do the arrowheads of the Mueller–Lyer illusion (Chaing, 1968). In this case the edges of blurred contours can overlap on the retina because the blurred contours are coming close to one another. This could lead to a ridge of maximum stimulation where the blur from the two adjacent lines overlaps rather than where the centers of the two lines are located. When this happens for an angle, it

appears slightly more obtuse and the apparent location of the angle vertex is displaced into the body of the angle. This is shown schematically in Figure 18-2B. The solid lines represent the actual angles and the dotted lines represent the brightest portions of the image. Notice that if we simply use the brightest portions of the image as if they were the contours, the vertices will appear to have been shifted inward. It is this sort of distortion that could make the distance between two angles in the Mueller–Lyer look apparently longer or shorter than its physical length. The effect of blur on the illusion is demonstrated in Figure 18-2C. Notice that the illusion strength (the relative difference in size between the two horizontal segments) is greater when the figure is blurred.

The fact that blur of the retinal image plays a part in the creation of some perceptual distortions has been verified for a number of visual illusions containing converging lines (such as the Mueller–Lyer and the Poggendorff). In general, a given illusion increases its strength when it is optically blurred and decreases its strength when special optical procedures are used to reduce the image blur in a normal eye (Coren, 1969b; Coren, Ward, Porac, & Fraser, 1978; Ward & Coren, 1976). As you might expect, blurring does not act to distort percepts in figures that do not contain angles formed by intersecting lines. The importance of this analysis is that it indicates that, at the very first stage of processing, the stimulus relationships in the image differ from the physical relationships in the object being viewed. Since the final percept will be based upon this image, we have already found one mechanism that will produce a discrepancy between the world as it exists and as it is perceived.

Neural Interactions. Once the image is projected onto the retinal surface the photochemical response occurs and the neural

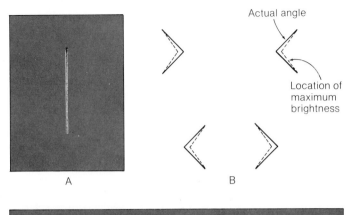

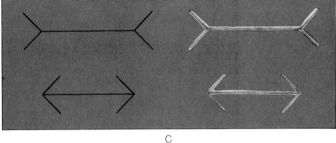

Figure 18-2.
(A) The effect of blur on a single line. (B) The effect of blur on the apparent location of the vertices of angles. (C) A demonstration of how blur alters the strength of the Mueller–Lyer illusion.

processing begins. However, the image is not simply transferred in an unmodified form from the retina to the higher centers. Changes that will affect the percept also occur at this level. As you probably recall from Chapters 4 and 7, interactions occur between retinal neurons, and these often involve inhibition. Thus the activity in one cell can decrease the activity in another nearby retinal cell. This process, which we called *lateral inhibition,* was shown to affect our perception of brightness. It can also affect our perception of where a contour is located.

Consider Figure 18-3A. Here we have a cross-sectional picture of the retinal response to a bright spot stimulus. Notice that in the central area the neural response is quite vigorous, well above the base line of neural firing, but on either side the surrounding cells are inhibited. Given this pattern of response, one would simply see the bright spot as shown (perhaps with a darker region imme-

diately around it). If we present two spots that are close enough together, as in Figure 18-3B, the two active and excited areas will tend to overlap, and we will see only one spot. If, however, the two spots are placed at an appropriate distance from each other, the inhibitory activity set up by one cell will overlap with the excited region set up by the other cell. This will distort the pattern of activity so that the two spots appear to be farther away than they actually are, as shown in Figure 18-3C (von Békésy, 1967; Ganz, 1966).

The combination of this pattern of fusion and repulsion, due to these lateral inhibitory effects, will cause figures made of converging lines to be somewhat distorted in terms of the neural response. For instance, a simple angle should appear to be slightly flared out at the wide portions and have its vertex pushed into the body of the angle near the point, as is shown in Figure 18-4. Notice that this should cause a distortion of length similar to that

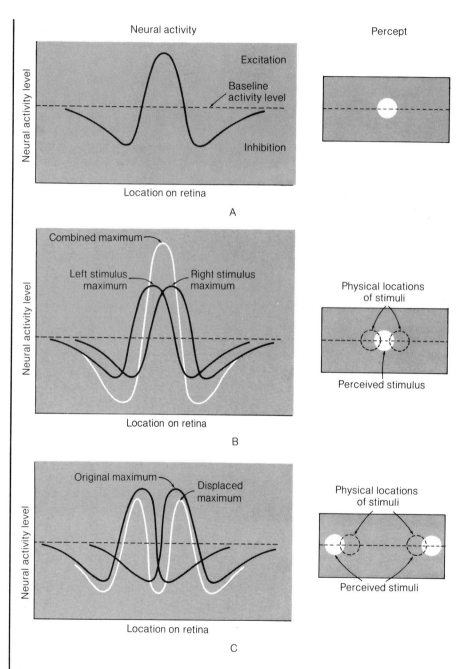

Figure 18-3.
(A) The spread of excitation and inhibition across the retina when stimulated by a single spot of light. (B) Two close spots result in a single distribution of neural activity that is seen as one spot. (C) At an appropriate distance the regions of maximum excitation are displaced away from each other, causing an apparent repulsion or spreading apart of the two spots of light.

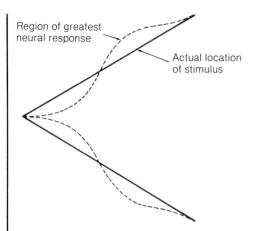

Region of greatest
neural response

Actual location
of stimulus

Figure 18-4.
The dotted line shows the expected ridge of
peak neural activity when the retinal image is
the angle shown as the solid line.

shown in Figure 18-2 in figures such as the
Mueller-Lyer. The fact that the angle seems to
open up slightly could cause the distortion
observed in the Poggendorff illusion by bending one transversal up and the other down. If
this effect is operating, we should also get
some apparent shape distortions. Thus the
Poggendorff illusion should no longer appear
as Figure 18-5A but should rather appear
bent slightly as in Figure 18-5B. Notice how
this bending seems to alter the lines so that
they no longer appear to be aligned. This picture is exaggerated since the actual bending
effects are relatively small.

Now suppose that we created a Poggendorff illusion that had bent lines, bent in such
a manner as to offset the distortion caused by
lateral inhibition. This is shown in an exaggerated form as Figure 18-5C. When we do
this, using the appropriate curvatures, the
magnitude of the illusion is greatly reduced
as is shown in Figure 18-5D (Kobayashi,
1956). This seems to demonstrate that the
contour distortions predicted from neural inhibitory interactions are actually taking
place.

There are other ways to show that these
effects are present. The neural interactions
require the presence of lines that converge or
intersect on the retina. Therefore, to eliminate
these effects we can simply remove all the
lines from the illusion, replacing the line ends
and vertices with dots. When this is done for
the Mueller–Lyer and Poggendorff illusions
(Figures 18-6A,B) the illusions are greatly
weakened but are still found (Coren, 1970).
An alternative procedure is to present one
part of the illusion to one eye and another
part of the illusion to the other eye. When
viewed in a stereoscope the two parts fuse
together to produce the illusion, and this is
shown in Figure 18-6C. Since the converging
lines are never present on the same retinal
surface simultaneously, we would not expect
neural interactions (at least at the retinal

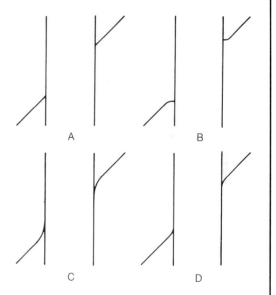

A

B

C

D

Figure 18-5.
(A) The usual form of the Poggendorff illusion.
(B) The expected shape distortions associated
with neural interactions (exaggerated). (C)
Offsetting shape distortions to compensate for
(B) (exaggerated). (D) The actual corrected
figure, which shows a greatly diminished
illusion.

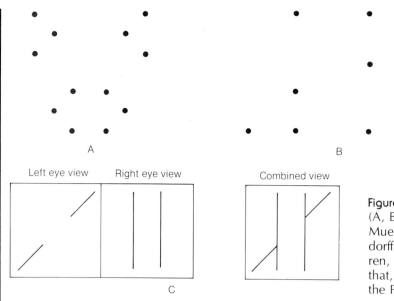

A

B

Left eye view   Right eye view   Combined view

C

Figure 18-6.
(A, B) Dot forms of the Mueller–Lyer and Poggendorff illusions (based upon Coren, 1970). (C) A stereogram that, when fused, produces the Poggendorff illusion.

level) to cause any further distortions. This has been done by a number of investigators, all of whom report that the illusion is still present, but is greatly reduced under these conditions (Day, 1961; Fisher & Lucas, 1969; Schiller & Weiner, 1962).

Such results appear to show that the interactions occurring during the first neural encoding process can, in fact, distort the final conscious percept. The fact that some distortion remains after these mechanisms are bypassed suggests that processes at higher levels in the visual system may be involved. There is some suggestion that interactions between adjacent neural units can occur at the level of the cortex and that these may serve to distort size or shape. Such interactions are complex and deal with the modification of the responses of adjacent orientation specific units or line detectors (Blakemore, Carpenter, & Georgeson, 1970; Burns & Pritchard, 1971). Such results suggest that both retinal and cortical neural processes may alter or modify any visual percept.

Attention, Cognition, and Learning. When physiological considerations can no longer provide us with any further insights, we must turn to psychological variables. Many of the factors we considered earlier in the text also play a role in the appearance of visual illusions. For instance, the manner in which observers distribute their attention over the figures can alter the size of the distortions. If an observer is instructed to carefully restrict her attention to only the horizontal lengths (and to attempt to ignore the wings) her judgments show considerably less illusory distortion. One can actually help the observer along by making the wings and the shaft of the Mueller–Lyer figure different colors. This assists the observer in her task of concentrating attention on the horizontal line and further reduces the size of the illusion (Coren & Girgus, 1972c).

In Chapter 14 we noted how depth cues, even if only suggested, can play a part in the formation of some illusions. Specifically, if certain aspects of these simple figures are seen as suggesting perspective, then the constancy mechanisms might be triggered. This could also lead to some perceptual distortions where constancy corrections are inappropriately applied. There is an interesting way to demonstrate the operation of such cognitive factors in illusions by using pictorial depth cues to correct for or to cancel out an already existing illusion.

Consider Figure 18-7A, which shows a Poggendorff figure containing two transversals. Both transversals on the lower left appear as if they will pass under their respective transversals on the upper right. Now, by including a few new lines and modifying the length of the vertical lines, we can transform this configuration so that it appears to be two sections of a fence, receding into the distance (Figure 18-7B). Under these conditions, the fence rails (the transversals) actually appear to be in alignment, showing that the magnitude of the illusion can be reduced by changing the cognitive interpretation of the stimulus (Gillam, 1971; Vurpillot, 1957).

Finally, let us remind you of some miscellaneous cognitive factors that seem to interact with illusion strength. In Chapter 16 we saw that a few minutes of free viewing of these illusion figures could reduce the strength of the distortion by a considerable amount. Thus the more practice an observer receives with the figure, the less the observed illusion effect. In addition, we saw that the age of the observer plays a role in the size of the illusion.

In Chapter 17, we discussed some cultural effects that cause observers to differ from one another. During that discussion, we saw that individuals who reside in cultures without much exposure to printed pictures or photographs tend to show less susceptibility to the illusory distortion in figures like the Mueller–Lyer. Thus perceptual strategies, involving how the observer attends to the stimulus, as well as to past experience with the stimulus or with other configurations that involve the same type of processing, can affect the final percept.

SYNTHESIS OF THE PERCEPTUAL EXPERIENCE

From where do these illusory percepts come? As you can see from the level-by-level analysis we have just outlined, we are dealing with at least six levels of visual processing. They include optical factors in the image, neural interactions in the retina, neural interactions in the cortex, attentional factors, learning factors, and cognitive factors associated with the meaning of the stimulus. Each of these levels plays a part in the formation of the final percept. Each contributes to, or subtracts from, the final distortion; there may also be complex interactions between various levels and mechanisms. Each level, however, plays a role in the stimulus relationships finally displayed in consciousness.

You might look at this multileveled process we call perception and ask, "Which levels are the most important?" They are all important. Coren and Girgus (1978) attempted to analyze the Poggendorff illusion to see how much of the distortion was caused at each level under the presumption that the various effects combined in a simple additive manner. They estimated that 22% of the distortion was caused by optical factors, 18% was caused by retinal neural interactions, 40% was caused by cognitive factors that could be affected by learning, and the remaining 20% was caused by some mixture of cognitive factors and cortical neural interac-

Figure 18-7.
(A) A two-transversal version of the Poggendorff illusion. (B) The illusion is greatly diminished when embedded in a meaningful context.

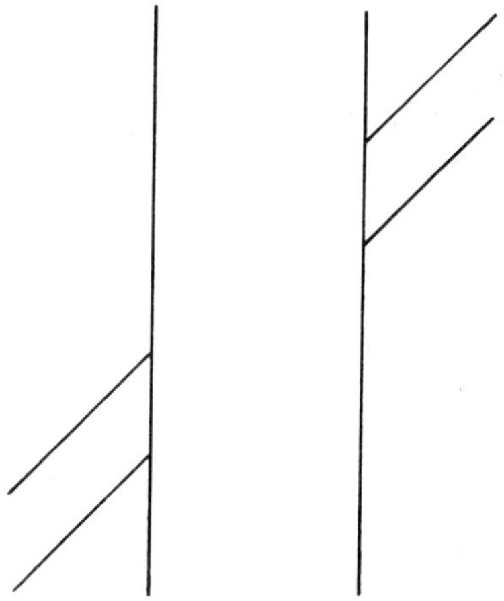

A

B

tions they could not identify. If they are correct, this means that approximately half the illusion results from *structural* factors associated with the physiological operation of the visual system, while the remaining half of the distortion is caused by information processing *strategies* associated with the history and personal style of the observer.

The current evidence suggests that most perceptual phenomena contain contributions from both the peripheral structural levels and the more central, cognitive levels of information processing. No level is dispensable. Should we remove the retina from the observer, the visual process stops. Should we strip off the primary visual cortex, the visual process becomes unresponsive to pattern information. Should we deprive an observer of all learned perceptual strategies and techniques of interacting with stimuli, the percept is no longer normal. All levels interact. It is hoped that this volume has shown you that perception is a multifaceted and multileveled phenomenon. To understand the perceptual experience in its entirety, we must deal with all levels and look at the way in which the levels interact with one another.

PERCEPTUAL PUZZLES IN NEED OF SOLUTION

The task of any textbook in science is not to provide all the answers in a given area. Unfortunately we never have all the answers. For every fact that science uncovers, ten new questions appear to be unearthed. The main purpose of a science textbook, then, is to provide you with a vocabulary of words and an arsenal of concepts to help you think about the problems you may encounter in the future. In this way you will be equipped to begin to analyze new problems as they are encountered. All the previous chapters have attempted to provide you with the concepts

and basic facts necessary to study perception, and you have seen many examples of methodologies that have been used to study perception.

We have also tried to demonstrate how a levels-of-processing approach can help in the understanding of perceptual functioning. The basic data upon which all our knowledge of the world depends are ultimately reduceable to our sensory experiences. Yet we have seen that the senses are not perfectly reliable. Sometimes our picture of the world is systematically in error because our perceptions do not agree with the actual physical relationships in the environment. However, these very instances in which the physical world and the perceptual world are discrepant can provide us with insights into human behavior. They can provide us with a fuller knowledge of how we perceive. Who knows the limitations of sensory abilities, and the capabilities and vagaries of perceptual analysis? The trained observer is the best and perhaps the only tool we can use to study the workings of the human mind.

In closing a textbook, authors often use the last chapter to summarize the current state of knowledge in an area. Sometimes this provides a useful backward look, and sometimes the synthesis provides insight as well as an overview. Yet, inevitably, the field has moved on; we learn more and the summary rapidly takes on the flavor of an antique. Perhaps a more useful device would be to look forward, to consider problems yet unsolved. Such an approach would provide two interesting benefits. First it would allow you, the newly trained student, fresh with ideas, and perhaps free of some of your mentors' biases, to wrestle with problems that do not as yet have clear answers. If you take a levels-of-processing approach, you will soon become aware of those areas about which we know the most and those about which we know the least. The second benefit lies in the future. Perhaps one of you reading this book will be stimulated enough to actually do the research that solves one of the problems.

The following few pages will present a series of demonstration boxes that should, perhaps, be called *puzzle boxes*. They will provide you with the information you need in order to demonstrate some puzzles or problems in the field of perception. You should have enough knowledge by now to at least make some preliminary guesses as to what is happening. Use a levels-of-processing analysis and see if you can account for all the stages of the percept's development. Some of the puzzles we will present to you have been the focus of much research. Some of the problems have been around for many years. While a few investigators would maintain that they have "the" answer to some of these problems, the majority of sensory and percep-

tual investigators would still classify these phenomena as unresolved.

Try the demonstrations for yourself. For each of them, ask yourself the following questions:

(1) What is my perceptual experience?
(2) What processes or mechanisms might be involved in producing this?
(3) Which levels of processing (structural or strategy) are most likely to be involved?
(4) What are the implications of this phenomenon for other perceptual processes?

At the end of some of the boxes we will ask you a few questions that may guide you in your explorations. Play with these puzzles. They are interesting, and they beg for solutions.

Perhaps one of the first illusory percepts to be discussed formally was an illusion of touch discussed by Aristotle. The illusion is quite easy to demonstrate. Hold your fingers as shown in Figure 18-8A and touch the point between them with a pencil as shown. Notice that you feel one item touching you and the sensation of one single touch. Now cross your fingers as is shown in Figure 18-8B, touching yourself again with a pencil in the place indicated between the fingers. Notice that you feel two distinct touches. Why? Is the illusion different if your eyes are open and viewing the touch as

Puzzle Box 1:
Aristotle's Illusion

opposed to their being closed? Does the illusion remain the same if you repeat the process many times?

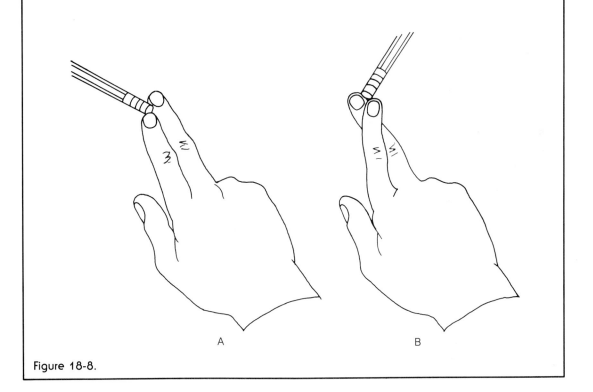

A   B

Figure 18-8.

This puzzle has two parts. Look at Figure 18-9. You will notice it is a series of regularly spaced black and white lines that radiate from a central point. If you look at the figure for a few moments, you will see that it takes on a rather unstable appearance. Curved lines and areas of different brightnesses seem to appear. Overall, the figure appears to be quite unstable, and this instability is the first puzzle. What is going on here? Does the size of the lines in the retinal image make a difference? You can test this by simply moving the pattern very close to you or very far away.

The second part of the puzzle takes a few moments more. Stare at the center spot in the figure for about 30–60 sec. Now transfer your gaze to a uniform wall or

Puzzle Box 2:
The Puzzle of Radiating Lines

surface. You will see a pattern resembling grains of light-and-dark rice streaming around in circles. What mechanism could cause this aftereffect? Does the level of illumination on the pattern affect the strength of the aftereffect or the time it takes to develop?

Figure 18-9.

For this demonstration you will need a radio, phonograph, or tape recorder that has stereo speakers located about 2 m apart. Turn on some music and stand about midway between the two speakers, facing a point between them. You will notice that the sound seems to envelop you. It comes from both sides, and you can clearly identify sounds coming from one speaker or the other. Take a few steps (you need not go very far) toward the side where one speaker is located. After only a step or two you will suddenly find that all the sound seems to be coming from the speaker nearest you. You no longer get any sensation of sound coming from the more distant speaker (although it still affects sound quality as you can demonstrate by turning it off). A few steps to the other side will reverse this effect, making it appear as though all the sound is coming from the other speaker. What mechanism is involved here? What does it have to do with the way in which we localize sounds? What does this say about the *cocktail party problem?*

Puzzle Box 3:
The One-Speaker Stereo Illusion

For this demonstration you will need two pipe cleaners, which should be bent as is shown in Figure 18-10A. Be careful to bend the pipe cleaners so that they can fit together fairly closely when both are laid upon a table, as shown in Figure 18-10B. Place one pipe cleaner in a glass of cool water and the other in a glass of very warm (not unpleasantly hot) water. Take the pipe cleaner out of the glass of cool water, and place it on a flat surface. Working quickly, take the pipe cleaner out of the glass of warm water and arrange it to form the configuration shown as Figure 18-10B. As soon as this is done, place your forearm over the set of pipe cleaners and press down as is shown in Figure 18-10C. The temperature sensation you receive will probably be quite surprising. Although the stimulus consists of alternately cool and warm surfaces, you will feel no coolness. Observers usually get a sensation of an intense stinging heat. Some individuals may find the heat sensation sufficiently intense to cause them to withdraw their arm. Of course, if your conscious experience with temperature were an accurate reproduction of the physical stimulus, you would feel alternating regions of warm and cool. There is no hot stimulus presented. Why is the sensation of cool lost? Where does the sensation of stinging heat come from? Why does this sensation appear to be slightly painful?

Puzzle Box 4:
The Heat Grill

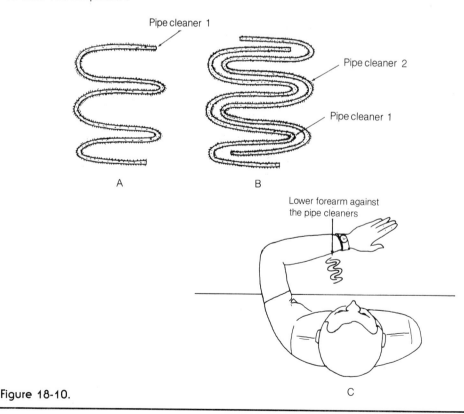

Figure 18-10.

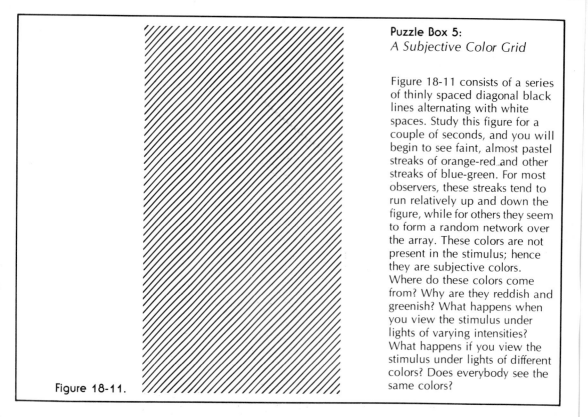

Figure 18-11.

Puzzle Box 5:
A Subjective Color Grid

Figure 18-11 consists of a series of thinly spaced diagonal black lines alternating with white spaces. Study this figure for a couple of seconds, and you will begin to see faint, almost pastel streaks of orange-red and other streaks of blue-green. For most observers, these streaks tend to run relatively up and down the figure, while for others they seem to form a random network over the array. These colors are not present in the stimulus; hence they are subjective colors. Where do these colors come from? Why are they reddish and greenish? What happens when you view the stimulus under lights of varying intensities? What happens if you view the stimulus under lights of different colors? Does everybody see the same colors?

Figure 18-12.

The pattern shown as Figure 18-12 should be viewed in motion. Move the book around so the motion resembles that which you would make if you were swirling or swishing coffee around in a cup without the use of a spoon. As you do so, notice that the six sets of concentric circles seem to show radial regions of light and dark that seem to move in the direction that you are swirling. They look as though they were covered by a liquid surface tending to swirl with the stimulus movement. Where does this effect come from? How is it tied to *motion perception?*

A second effect has to do with the center circle, which seems to have gearlike teeth. As you swirl the array, the center gear seems to rotate, but in a direction opposite to that of the movement of the outer circles. It may actually appear to some observers to move in a jerky rotating manner from one position to another; other observers may see a smooth rotation. What causes this effect? Why does it move in a direction opposite to the other effect? If you fixate your eyes on different parts of the stimulus, do these effects alter in strength?

Puzzle Box 6:
Gears and Circles

FINAL NOTE

We have taken you on a long intellectual journey in this book. If this journey has been successful, you have learned about the many steps involved in translating a physical stimulus in your environment into a conscious percept. One last warning though: Always remember that the percept and the object are two different things. We do not perceive what is "out there," rather, we perceive what is "in here." Our senses can only inform us of their own status. They can inform us of the status of their nerves, receptors, or the chemistry of their components. The outside world is never taken into our consciousness. It is created from the mass of sensations that surrounds us. In many respects, the ultimate question that perception must ask was stated by John Stuart Mill in 1865, when he asked, "What is it we mean, or what is it which leads us to say, that the objects we perceive are external to us, and not a part of our own thoughts?" This is the ultimate, unresolved puzzle.

Glossary

The following definitions are text specific. The reader should consult a dictionary for complete definitions.

Absolute threshold—The minimal amount of energy required for detection of a stimulus.

Acceleration—Change of rate of motion.

Accommodation—The process by which the lens of the eye varies its focus.

Across fiber pattern—A pattern of neural activity in which various neural units have different stimulus-specific response rates.

Action potential—A large rapid change in electrical potential of an axon.

Acuity—The ability of the eye to resolve or discriminate details.

Adaptation—A reversible change in sensitivity as a result of prolonged or ongoing stimulation.

Adaptation level—A subjective reference point against which stimuli are both quantitatively and qualitatively judged.

Additive color mixture—Color mixture resulting from the addition of one wavelength to another, e.g., projection of a blue light on top of a red light on a screen.

Aerial perspective—A distance cue in which objects appear hazy or less distinct due to the interaction of light with dust and moisture particles in the air.

Afterimages—A visual sensation that continues after an intense or prolonged exposure to a stimulus.

Agnosia—A pathological condition where an individual can no longer attach meaning to a sensory impression.

Amacrines—Large, laterally interconnecting neurones found in the retina.

Ampullae—Swellings at the base of the semicircular canals containing the crista.

Analysis-by-synthesis—In pattern recognition, a process in which some knowledge of the whole is used to help recognition of parts.

Anchor stimulus—In some types of psychophysical judgments, a stimulus that provides the background against which judgments of other stimuli are made.

Anomalous trichromatism—A defect in color vision in which color matches made by an individual are systematically different from normal, although the three primary color systems are still functioning.

Anosmia—Relative insensitivity to an odor.

Aphasia—Perceptual disorder usually resulting in difficulties involving speech and sound recognition.

Aqueous humor—The fluid occupying the small chamber between the cornea and the lens of the eye.

Area 17—According to Brodmann's numbering system, another name for the primary visual cortex which is part of the occipital lobe of the brain.

Aubert–Fleischl paradox—The phenomenon of perceived movement being slower when a moving target is fixated than when one fixates a stationary background behind a moving target.

Auditory adaptation—Transient reduction in auditory sensitivity due to prior exposure to sound stimuli.

Auditory canal—The channel conducting sound waves to the eardrum.

Auditory fatigue—Prolonged reduction in auditory sensitivity following exposure to very intense sounds.

Auditory flutter fusion—The rate of interruption of a continuous tone at which an observer first hears a continuous sound.

Auditory Masking—Presentation of one sound over another resulting in the initial sound being less audible.

Autokinetic effect—The illusion of movement of a stationary point of light viewed in an otherwise totally dark field.

Automaticity—When cognitive, perceptual, or motor processes can be accomplished with little conscious awareness and little allocation of mental effort.

Axon—The extended portion of a neuron that conducts the action potential to other cells.

Axon terminal—End of the axon through which action potentials trigger reactions in other cells.

Azimuth—The direction of a sound source indicated as degrees around a circle.

Background stimuli—Stimuli that form a context for a focal stimulus, but which are not themselves judged by an observer.

Backward masking—Masking of a previously presented visual target by a second stimulus. *See* Masking.

Bandwidth—The range of frequencies of a group of sound stimuli.

Basilar membrane—The membrane within the cochlea of the ear, upon which the Organ of Corti lies. Incoming sounds deform it.

Beat—When two tones similar in intensity but slightly different in frequency are presented, they are perceived as a single tone that varies in intensity, much like the vibrato of a singer.

Bel—Basic unit used to measure the intensity of a sound wave.

Benham's top—A black and white pattern that when rotated produces subjective colors.

Bezold–Brucke effect—The shift in the apparent hue of a color as the intensity is changed.

Bifoveally fixate—The situation in which an image stimulates both foveas.

Binaural—Sound presentations to both ears, from the roots *bi* and *aural*, for two and ear, respectively.

Binocular disparity—The difference between the images seen by the two eyes due to their separation in space.

Biological motions—The concept of the intricate movement patterns accomplished, for example, by the skeletal structure of a human crossing a room.

Bipolar cell—Neural cell in the retina between the photoreceptor and ganglion cells.

Bit—Measure of amount of information in a stimulus.

Blind spot—Portion of retina through which optic nerve passes and therefore an area without photoreceptors. This region shows no response to light.

Bloch's law—The relationship between stimulus duration and stimulus intensity.

Bony labyrinth—The structure inside the head that contains the cochlea and the vestibular organs. It is made of very hard bone.

Bottleneck models—Models of attention that assume a biological limitation on the amount of information that can be processed at one time.

Brightness—The phenomenological impression of the intensity of a light stimulus.

Brightness assimilation—The perceptual effect that is the reverse of brightness contrast. Here, added white lines lighten a stimulus and black lines darken it.

Brightness constancy—The process by which the apparent brightness of a stimulus remains unchanged, despite changes in physical illumination.

Brightness contrast—The apparent darkening of a target placed against a bright background.

Bril—A unit for measuring the apparent brightness of stimuli.

Brodmann's area 41—*See* Temporal cortex.

Bunson–Rosco law—The physical law defining the photochemical reaction of any light-sensitive substance as a function of the intensity and duration of light exposure.

Capacity models—Models of attention that do not assume biological limitations on the amount of information that can be processed at one time, but rather assume limits on an observer's ability to allocate mental effort to various stimuli.

Category scaling—A psychophysical scaling method in which stimuli are grouped into a predetermined number of categories on the basis of their perceived strength along a given dimension.

Catch trials—Trials in which no stimulus is presented. Used in threshold measuring experiments.

Cell body—Main part of cell (e.g., a neuron) containing the nucleus.

Channel theory—The theory of temperature perception suggesting that each sensation, warmth and cold, has a specific receptor and neural pathway.

Chlorolabe—Green-sensitive cone pigment.

Choice reaction time—A type of reaction time task in which different responses are made to different stimuli.

Chopper—A neuron that gives repeated bursts of impulses followed by short pauses, with the vigor of successive bursts decreasing in response to presentation of a pure tone.

Chromatic adaptation—Lowered response to color stimulus due to previous exposure to other chromatic stimuli.

CIE color space—A standard system used to describe colors based upon the mixture of three primary wavelengths.

Circadian rhythm—Rhythmic biological cycle occurring at approximately 24-hour intervals.

Closure—A principle of perceptual organization in which figures are recognized even though they may have missing contour segments.

Cochlea—A snail-shaped part of the labyrinth of the ear that contains the auditory receptors.

Cochlear duct—One of three canals in the cochlea.

Cognition—The process of knowing, incorporating both perception and learning.

Cognitive maps—*See* Schemas.

Cognitive processes—The aspects of experience involving thinking and memory.

Cognitive style—The overall personality and perceptual predispositions that are characteristics of a particular individual.

Cold fibers—Neurons that respond to cooling of the skin by firing at a more rapid rate and to warming of the skin by decreasing their firing rate.

Color atlas—A book in which each page represents a horizontal or a vertical slice through the color space.

Color blindness—A condition in which individuals lack the ability to make discriminations on the basis of wavelength of light.

Color constancy—The phenomenon whereby the color of an object does not appear to change despite changes of hue of the light falling on it.

Color circle—*See* Color wheel.

Color solid—*See* Color spindle.

Color spindle—A three-dimensional model in which the relationship between hue, brightness, and saturation are depicted.

Color wheel—A circular scheme in which colors are separated according to hue, with complementary colors placed directly across from each other.

Comparison stimuli—A graded set of stimuli differing in a specific dimension which are to be judged relative to a standard stimulus.

Complementary colors—Colors whose mixture produces an achromatic gray or white.

Complex cells—Cells in the visual cortex that respond to features such as line length and direction of movement.

Concentration test—Method for determining ability to discriminate objects following inferotemporal lobe loss.

Conceptually driven processing—Information processing that is guided by memories and expectations concerning the nature of the incoming stimulation.

Cone—Short, thick tapering cell in the photoreceptive layer of the retina, used in bright-light and color vision.

Consonance—The quality of two tones blending or "going together."

Consonants—One of two types of speech sounds, the other being vowels.

Constancies—The tendency for perceptual qualities (size, shape, hue, etc.) to remain stable despite variations in the properties of the retinal image.

Context—Stimuli present in the environment that alter the perception of other stimuli.

Convergence—The rotation of both eyes toward the nose as fixated objects become closer.

Cornea—The transparent, domelike part of the eye formed by the bulged sclera.

Correct negative—The trial when a stimulus signal is absent and the observer response is "no."

Crista—Movement-perceptive portion of the semicircular canal of the ear.

Criterion—In signal detection, a subjective value of sensation above

which a stimulus is judged to be present.

Critical flicker fusion frequency—The minimum rate of a flickering light that is perceived as continuous.

Cross adaptation—Exposure to one taste affecting the threshold stimulus taste of other substances.

Cross-modality matching—A scaling procedure in which the observer adjusts the intensity of a stimulus until it appears to be as intense as another stimulus from a different sensory continuum.

Crossed disparity—A cue for relative distance, where the unfused image of the right eye appears on the left and that of the left eye on the right.

Cupola—Jellylike material in which the hairs of the crista are embedded.

Cyanolabe—Blue sensitive cone pigment.

Cycle—In sound, the completion of a full sequence from air rarefaction to compression and back.

Cyclopean eye—An imaginary point midway between the eyes thought to be used as a reference point for the straight ahead direction.

Dark adaptation—Increase in the eyes' sensitivity following a change from a high to a lower level of illumination.

Data-driven processing—Information processing based upon the activation of structures within the sensory system that respond to individual properties of the incoming array.

Day blind—The condition of absence of or nonfunctioning of cones resulting in visual difficulty under bright-light conditions.

Decibel—Unit used for measuring sound intensity; one-tenth of a Bel.

Dendrite—Parts of neurons that receive stimulation from the axons of the neurons.

Density—The complex feeling of the compactness or hardness of a sound.

Depolarization—A change of the electrical potential of a neuron toward zero volts.

Dermis—The inner layer of skin, containing most of the nerve endings.

Detail perspective—See Texture gradient.

Detection—The perception that a stimulus is present.

Deuteranopia—A form of color blindness associated with the confusion of reds and greens due to insensitivity in the green system.

Dichotic—Presentation of different stimuli to each of the two ears.

Dichromats—Individuals whose color vision is defective allowing all hues to be matched with two rather than three primaries.

Difference threshold—The minimum amount of stimulus change needed for two stimuli to be perceived as different 50% of the time.

Diplopia—Double vision.

Direction constancy—The stability of an object's perceived direction despite changes in eye position.

Discrimination—The act of discerning stimulus differences.

Disparate—See Binocular disparity.

Dissonance—The quality of two tones being discordant or "clashing."

Distal stimulus—Stimuli from environmental objects.

Divergence—The outward rotation of both eyes away from the nose as fixated objects become more distant.

Dolorimeter—A device used to measure pain threshold.

Dominant wavelength—The wavelength of a monochromatic stimulus that best approximates the hue of a color mixture.

Dorsal cochlear nucleus—The point in the lower back part of the brain at which the majority of auditory nerve fibers end.

Double pain—The phenomenon of two distinct peaks of pain, differing in quality and separated in time, from one single pain stimulus.

Duplexity theory—The suggestion that two separate and noninteracting systems, sweet–bitter and salty–sour, are responsible for taste.

Duplicity theory—The concept of two separate visual systems, rod-dependent (low-light) vision, and cone-dependent (bright-light) vision.

Dynamic range—For a particular frequency, the difference between the absolute threshold and the pain threshold, measured in decibels.

Dyschromatopsias—Acquired color vision losses.

Dyslexia—Impaired reading ability.

Eardrum—Membrane at end of the auditory canal that vibrates in resonance with incoming sound waves.

Early selection models—Models of attention in which information selection occurs immediately following sensory registration.

Echolation system—System used by some animals, such as bats and whales, to locate objects by analysing sound waves reflected from them.

Efferent fibers—Neural fibers that carry outgoing information from the brain to muscles or other action systems.

Egocentric localization—The awareness of where our bodies are positioned relative to other objects in the external environment.

Embedded figures test—A task used to determine spatial abilities, in which a subject is asked to find a simple shape hidden in a more complex figure.

Emmetropic—An eye with normal accommodative ability.

Epidermis—The outer layer of skin.

Equal interval scaling—See Category scaling.

Equal loudness contour—A curve describing the intensities at which tones of varying frequencies appear to be equally loud.

Equal pitch contour—A curve describing the frequencies at which tones of varying intensities appear to have the same pitch.

Equal temperament scale—A version of the musical scale where each octave is divided into 12 equal parts, called semitones, that are further divided into 100 cents.

Error of anticipation—Change in response before the percept actually changes.

Error of perseveration—Continuing with the same response although the percept has changed.

Erythrolabe—Red-sensitive cone pigment.

Eustachian tubes—Channels from the back of the throat to the middle ear; when we swallow they open and allow the air pressure in the middle ear to equalize with that outside.

Event-processing hypothesis—The theory of time perception suggesting that perceived time is a purely cognitive process determined by the amount of sensory information processed during a particular interval.

Evoked response—Electrical response in the brain brought on by presentation of a stimulus.

Exafference—Stimulus input that acts upon a passive observer.

Extrovert—An outgoing and sociable person.

Eye-head system—A movement perception system that monitors and differentiates observer-generated from object-generated movement.

False alarm—A trial when a stimulus signal is absent and the observer reports he perceives it.

Familiar size—The known or remembered size of objects.

Fechner's law—The logarithmic relationship between the intensity of sensation and the intensity of physical stimulus proposed by Fechner.

Field-dependent—Individuals exhibiting difficulty with embedded figure tasks.

Field-independent—Individuals exhibiting little difficulty with embedded figure tasks.

Figures—Integrated visual experience that "stands out" in the center of attention.

Filled duration illusion—An interval filled with stimulus events perceived as being longer than an identical duration without stimulus events.

Focal stimuli—Stimuli at the center of observers' attention and those usually being judged.

Forced-choice procedure—The act of requiring an observer to respond "yes" or "no" even if the percept is uncertain.

Formants—The bands of enhanced sound, seen as dark smudges on a spectrogram.

Fourier components—Simple sine waves that add together to form a complex waveform.

Fourier analysis—The decomposition of a complex wave into simple sine waves.

Fovea centralis—A small depression in the retina which contains mostly cones and where acuity is best.

Frequency—The number of cycles a sound wave completes in one second.

Frequency principle—The principle of hearing theory that asserts that sound frequency is encoded in the *frequency* with which the auditory neurons fire.

Frequency sweep detector—A neuron that responds only to sounds that change frequency in a specific direction and range.

Fundamental—The lowest, usually most intense, frequency sound wave in a complex stimulus.

Fusion—The process by which disparate views are synthesized into one percept.

Ganglion cells—Third layer of the retina through which impulses travel after the photoreceptor and bipolar cells.

Ganzfeld—A visual field that contains no visible contours.

Glabrous skin—Type of skin that has no hairs (e.g., on lips, fingers, or toes); it is highly sensitive to stimulation.

Global—The overall aspects of a figure as opposed to the local details.

Golgi tendon organs—Nerve endings attached to tendons that respond to both stretching and contraction of muscle.

Good continuation—The principle that elements that appear to follow in the same direction tend to be grouped together.

Grating acuity—*See* Resolution acuity.

Ground—The background against which figures appear.

Habituation—The processes by which an observer ceases to respond to a repeated stimulus.

Hairy skin—Covering of the human body from which numerous hairs protrude; it is both a protective and stimulus-sensitive covering. *See also* Glabrous skin.

Harmonics—Frequencies higher than the fundamental in complex sounds.

Height in the picture plane—A cue for distance referring to where an object is relative to the horizon.

Helicotrema—An opening, between the vestibular and tympanic canals, at the apex of the cochlea.

Hertz—The unit (cycles per second) used to measure frequency of sound waves.

Hick's law—States that choice reaction time is a linear function of the amount of information in the stimulus.

Hidden figures test—*See* Embedded figures test.

Hit—The trial when a stimulus signal is present and the observer response is "yes."

Horizontal cells—Retinal cells with short dendrites and a long axonal process that extends horizontally.

Horopter—An imaginary plane in external space used to describe the region of fused images.

Hue—The term denoting the psychological dimension most clearly corresponding to wavelength of light and most often termed "color" in common language.

Hypercomplex cells—Cortical cells that respond to complex stimulus features regardless of where they occur in the receptive field.

Hypermetropia—Far sightedness.

Hyperpolarization—The change of the electrical potential of a cell toward increasing negativity.

Iconic memory—The short-lived persistance of a stimulus in consciousness after its physical disappearance.

Ideal observer—In Signal Detection Theory, a hypothetical observer who has complete knowledge of the detection situation and makes his responses in the optimum way.

Illuminance—The amount of light falling upon a surface.

Illusion decrement—The decrease in the strength of a visual illusion with prolonged free viewing.

Image–retina system—A movement perception system that detects movement within the retinal image.

Impedance matching—The process of amplification of sound energy received from the air so that equivalent vibrations are set up in the fluid medium of the inner ear.

Incus—One of the three middle ear bones involved in sound conduction to the cochlea. Also known as the anvil.

Indifference interval—A time duration, about .7 sec, that does not give rise to either an overestimation or underestimation of its length.

Induced motion—An illusion of movement of a stationary object by moving the background or surrounding context.

Inferior colliculus—Auditory processing centers in the midbrain which are the terminus for cells of the superior olives.

Inferotemporal cortex—Cortical region located in the temporal lobes of the brain which may be associated with recognition abilities and, pathologically, with aphasia.

Inflow theory—The suggestion that motion is detected via feedback information from the 6 extraocular muscles controlling eye movement.

Information processing—The process by which stimuli are registered in the receptors, identified, and stored in memory.

Information theory—The quantitative system for specifying the difficulty of a recognition task.

Information transmission—The degree to which the observer's response correctly represents the information in the stimulus.

In phase—Sound waves in which the peaks and valleys coincide over time.

Inner ear—The ear part responsible for transducing mechanical sound wave energy into electrochemical energy interpretable by the nervous system.

Integral—A stimulus that is experienced in all of its aspects at once and inseparably.

Internal timer hypothesis—The theory of time perception suggesting that there is a biological or physiological basis to time perception.

Interposition—The depth cue based upon the visual blocking of an object or part of an object from view by another closer object.

Interstimulus interval—The time span between end of one stimulus input and beginning of the next stimulus.

Interval of uncertainty—The range of stimulus differences between those which are detected 25% of the time and those detected 75% of the time.

Interval scale—A scale in which the spacing between adjacent numbers is meaningful, but which has no absolute zero point.

Introvert—A withdrawn and self-contained person.

Iodopsin—The cone pigment present in some birds. *See* Opsin.

Iris—The opaque, colored membrane controlling the amount of light entering the eye by changing the size of the pupil.

JND—*See* Just noticeable difference.

Just noticeable difference—The stimulus difference noticed 50% of the time, computed as the interval of uncertainty divided by 2.

Kappa effect—The phenomenon in which altering the distance between two successively presented stimuli alters the apparent interstimulus interval. *See* Tau effect.

Kinetic depth effect—Stimulus motion which imparts a perception of depth to a two-dimensional form.

Late selection models—Models of attention in which selection occurs rather late in the stages of information processing, e.g., in memory.

Lateral geniculate nucleus—The first major relay center for optic nerve fibers leaving the retina. It is in the thalamus in primates.

Lateral inhibition—The process of adjacent visual units inhibiting one another, e.g., the more a cell is stimulated, the more it responds and inhibits its neighbor cells.

Lateral olfactory tract—The main route, composed of axons, from the olfactory bulb to the smell cortex.

Lemniscal system—Composed of large, rapidly conducting nerve fibers; one route of information conduction from the skin to the brain.

Lens—A transparent body in the eye of primates. It can change shape, thus altering the focus of the retinal image.

Levels-of-processing analysis—Analysis of the contribution of each stage of processing to the final percept, beginning with the receptor, up through cognitive mechanisms.

Light adaptation—The change in visual sensitivity when an individual moves from a lighter environment into a dark one.

Lightness constancy—*See* Brightness constancy.

Line detectors—*See* Orientation detectors.

Local—The detailed aspects of a figure as opposed to the global aspects.

Lock and key theory—Suggests that variously shaped molecules fit into holes in the walls of cells in the olfactory epithelium like a key into a lock and that when this occurs, a chemical change occurs causing a neural response.

Lumen—The unit of luminous energy equal to the light emanating from a standard candle, which is slightly more than .001 watt at a wavelength of 555 nm.

Luminance—The amount of light reflected from a surface.

Luminosity curve—A plot of the relative brightness of different wavelengths.

mμ—*See* Millimicron.

Mach bands—The perception of dark and light lines at regions near an abrupt change in an intensity gradient.

Macula—The receptor organ of the utricle and saccule; it is responsive to linear acceleration.

Macula lutea—A yellow pigmented area centered over the fovea.

Magnitude estimation—A psychophysical scaling procedure requiring the observer to assign numbers to a stimulus on the basis of apparent intensity.

Malleus—The first of the inner ear bones. Also called the hammer.

Masking—General term used to describe the blocking of the perception of one target by the presentation of another one. *See also* Backward masking and Auditory masking.

Medial geniculate—Brain part through which the output of inferior colliculi cells are channeled to the cortex.

Medulla—Part of brain attached to spinal cord.

Mel—A scale used for apparent pitch.

Mental effort—Concept used to describe state of alertness in attentional tasks. Seems to be accompanied by changes in physiological arousal.

Metacontrast—A form of backward masking in which the second stimulus has contours that are adjacent to, but not overlapping, those of the first stimulus.

Metameric colors—Colors that appear to be the same but are composed of different wavelengths.

Metathetic continuum—A stimulus continuum involving quality of sensation, such as color or pitch.

Method of constant stimuli—A method for determining thresholds in which each of a limited number of stimuli are repeatedly presented and judged.

Method of limits—A method for determining thresholds in which stimulus intensity is systematically increased or decreased until a change in detectability occurs.

Microspectrophotometer—A device for measuring the amount and wavelengths of light emanating from microscopic target areas.

Middle ear—Part of the ear consisting of the ossicles, malleus, incus, and stapes, which transmit the eardrum vibrations to the inner ear.

Millimicron—The thousandth part of a micron, or the millionth part of a millimeter. Now usually called a nanometer.

Minimum audible angle—The smallest amount of movement of a sound source that can be detected.

Minimum audible field—The threshold value for a simulus presented and measured in a free field.

Minimum audible pressure—The threshold stimulus intensity for hearing for stimuli presented through earphones and measured at the eardrum.

Miss—The trial when a stimulus signal is present and the observer response is "no."

Modulus—In magnitude estimation, the standard numerical value assigned to one of the stimuli at the beginning of the judgment procedure; it determines the range of numbers to be used by the observer in the procedure.

Molar concentration—The weight of a substance dissolved in a given amount of solution, 1 mole equaling the molecular weight of a substance in grams added to enough water to make 1 liter of solution.

Monaural—Sound presentations to one ear, from the roots *mon* and *aural,* for one and ear, respectively.

Monochromatic stimulus—One that contains only one wavelength of light.

Monochromats—Individuals who see color as simply gradations of intensity, due to the absence of any functioning cones.

Monocular cues—Information requiring only one eye to be used.

Motion parallax—The relative apparent motion of objects in the visual field as the observer moves his head or body.

Motor theory—A theory of speech perception in which the hearer metaphorically repeats the sounds heard.

Myopia—Near sightedness.

Nanometer—Billionth of a meter (a millionth of millimeter).

Near point distance—The nearest point to which an object may be brought to an eye before it can no longer be in focus.

Negative time error—The circumstance that, in discrimination experiments, the first stimulus presented (generally the standard) is judged to be less intense than the following stimulus.

Neurovascular theory—The theory of heat perception suggesting that a single mechanism responds to both heat and cold.

Neutral zone—A temperature range surrounding physiological zero.

Stimuli within this range feel neither warm nor cold.

Night blindness—Due to an absence of functioning rods, individuals cannot see under low-light conditions.

Nominal scale—A scale consisting of naming of stimuli rather than ordering on the basis of intensity.

nm—See Nanometer.

Object-relative localizations—The estimation of the relative positions of objects within the environment which are external to the observer.

Occipital lobe—The rear portion of the brain which serves as the primary visual processing center.

Off response—A neural response commencing with the termination of a stimulus.

Ohm's Acoustical Law—The theory of separation of sound components in the ear.

Olfactory bulb—The termination point for the olfactory nerve in front of and below the main brain mass.

Olfactory cilia—Hairlike projections extending from the knoblike end of the olfactory rod, protruding through the surface of the olfactory epithelium.

Olfactory epithelium—The small area of oval-shaped cells in the upper nasal passages that receive smell stimuli.

Olfactory nerve—The bundle of axons of smell receptor cells that passes through the top of the nasal cavity.

Olfactory rod—A long extension from smell receptor cells toward the surface of the olfactory epithelium.

Ommatidium—An element, essentially a simple eye, consisting of one thin, translucent cylinder of a "compound eye."

On response—A neural response commencing with the onset of a stimulus.

On–off responses—Responses of neurons caused by both introduction and termination of a stimulus.

Opsin—Protein part of the rhodopsin pigment.

Optacon—A system, similar to the vision substitution system, that converts printed letters into vibration patterns on the fingertip.

Optic axis—An imaginary line through the center of the pupil.

Optic chiasm—The point at which the two optic nerves meet and the nasal fibers cross to the contralateral side.

Optic disk—Region of retina where the optic nerve leaves the eye. *See* Blind spot.

Optic nerve—Bundle of axons leading from the retinal ganglion cells.

Optic radiations—The large fans of fibers spreading out from the lateral geniculate nucleus to the occipital cortex.

Optic tract—The path of the optic nerve once it is past the optic chiasm.

Optokinetic nystagmus—Eye movement sequence in which there is a smooth movement and a quick return in the presence of a moving pattern.

Ordinal scale—A scale involving the ranking of items on the basis of more or less of some quantity.

Organ of Corti—The part of the cochlear duct that transduces mechanical sound wave energy into electrochemical energy interpretable by the nervous system.

Orientation detectors—Cortical cells that respond to visually presented lines at a particular orientation in a particular location.

Orienting response—The response where an observer turns toward and orients her receptors toward a novel stimulus.

Oscilloscope—A sensitive voltage measuring device used to display electrical activity of a cell.

Otocysts—In primitive vertebrates, fluid-filled cavities functioning as ears in maintaining balance and attitude to gravity. *See* Statocysts.

Otoliths—Bony bodies in otocysts.

Out of phase—Sound waves in

which the peaks and valleys of sound pressure do not coincide over time.

Outer ear—The pinna, the auditory canal, and the eardrum.

Outflow principle—The suggestion that brain commands initiating eye movements enable the eye–head movement system to differentiate object-generated from observer-generated movement in the retinal image.

Oval window—The membrane upon which the stapes footplate rests, which is the only part of the inner ear to receive sound vibrations directly.

Overlay—See Interposition.

Pandemonium—A computor model of pattern recognition based upon a series of successive stages of feature analysis and recombination.

Panum's area—The region around the horopter, where all images in space are fused.

Papillae—Small bumps on the tongue in which taste buds are located.

Paradoxical cold—The phenomenon of skin areas, cold spots, responding to warm stimuli with a sensation of cold.

Parietal region—Upper central region of the brain housing the part of the sensory cortex responsible for touch.

Partial report—An experimental technique used in span of apprehension experiments in which the observer is asked to repeat only part, not all, of the presented material.

Pauser neurons—Those, similar to on response neurons, that exhibit an initial response to stimuli, followed by a pause, and then a weaker, sustained response until the stimulus stops.

Payoff matrix—A set of rewards and penalties given an observer based upon his performance in a psychophysical experiment.

Perception—The conscious experience of objects and object relationships.

Perceptual moment—The hypothetical basic psychological unit of time, about 100 msec.

Perceptual set—The expectancies or predispositions that an observer brings to a perceptual situation.

Perceptual strategies—Complex cognitive sequences for extracting information from sensory inputs.

Perimeter—A device for measuring the extent of the visual field. Also used in locating the area of a scotoma.

Perspective, Linear—The convergence of parallel lines as they recede into the distance.

Phase—The particular point in the compression–rarefaction cycle of a sound wave at a given instant of time.

Phase angle—The degree to which one sound wave is out of phase with another, considering a complete cycle as 360°.

Phase difference—The difference in the phase of a sound wave reaching each ear since the distance the sound wave travels is slightly different.

Phi phenomenon—Apparent movement between two successive presentations of stimuli in different spatial locations.

Phon—A unit used to measure the apparent loudness of a stimulus, independent of frequency, using a 1000-Hz tone as a reference stimulus.

Phoneme—In analyzing speech, the basic unit of feature classification.

Phonemic restoration effect—The ability of an observer to fill in a blank in a sentence based on the context.

Phonetic—Sound segments.

Photometry—The process of light measurement based upon the eye as a reference.

Photon—The smallest unit of light energy.

Photopic—Vision under bright-light conditions.

Photopsin—The protein segment of the photochemical in cones.

Photoreceptors—Photo-sensitive cells in the retina (rods and cones).

Physiological cues—See Structural cues.

Physiological zero—A neutral point in the perception of heat and cold, usually taken to be the skin temperature.

Pictorial cues—Cues for distance that can be found in photographs and pictures.

Pigment epithelium—The light-absorbing dark layer backing the retina in diurnal animals.

Pinna—Fleshy visible parts of the outer ear.

Piper's law—The relationship between area and intensity in the detection of nonfoveal stimuli.

Pitch—The psychological attribute of sound associated with different sound frequencies (i.e., high or low tones).

Place principle—The theory of hearing suggesting that each different tone causes a different place on the basilar membrane to vibrate.

Point of subjective equality—The point at which the stimulus appears most like the standard.

Position constancy—Stable perceived position of objects despite body, eye, or head movements.

Potential—The difference between the electrical charge inside a cell and the electrical charge outside.

Power law—The relation that the magnitude of sensation varies as the intensity of the physical stimulus raised to some power. Also known as Stevens's Law.

Pragnanz—The principle that the psychological organization of the percept will always be as "good" as prevailing conditions allow.

Precedence effect—The first sound stimulus to arrive at the ear is a major determinant of where in space the sound source is perceived to be.

Presbyopia—Far sightedness found in older individuals.

Pressure amplitude—A measure of the degree of compression or rarefaction at the peaks or valleys of a sound wave.

Primaries—Three monochromatic light sources in appropriate amounts that, when combined, can match any other hue.

Primary auditory projection area—The temporal cortex.

Primarylike neuron—A neuron that gives an initial burst when fired in response to a stimulus and then continues firing at a lower level until the stimulus is stopped.

Probability distribution—A graphical representation of the likelihood that a given event will occur.

Prosopagnosia—A perceptual disorder in which an individual cannot recognize human faces.

Protanopia—A form of color blindness resulting in the confusion of reds and greens due to insensitivity in the red system.

Prothetic continuum—A psychological continuum that involves quantitative aspects (how much) of stimulation, such as loudness or brightness.

Proximal stimulus—The receptor responses to stimulation by an external object.

Proximity—The principle that elements close to one another tend to be seen as a perceptual figure or unit.

Psychic blindness—The ability of animals to locate objects without being able to identify them. *See* Aphasia.

Pupil—The opening in the iris of the eye through which light enters.

Purity—A spectrally pure stimulus is composed of only one wavelength.

Purkinje shift—The change in the apparent brightness of different wavelengths as one goes from a light to a dark-adapted state.

Quantum—A particle of any form of electromagnetic radiation. *See* Photon.

Radial direction—In judging visual direction, using the body as the center point of a circle, extensions outward can be referred to as points on a compass.

Radiance—The amount of energy coming from a light source.

Ratio scale—A measurement scale in which the rank order, spacing, and ratios of the numbers assigned to events have meaning; it also has an absolute zero point.

Reaction time—The interval between the onset of a stimulus and the beginning of an overt response.

Reafference—Stimulus input that results from an observer's own movements.

Receiver operating characteristic curve—The plot representing the probabilities of hits (ordinate) versus false alarms (abscissa).

Receptive fields—For any particular cell, the region of the visual field in which a stimulus can produce a response.

Recognition—The act of identification of a stimulus.

Reflectance—The proportion of light falling on a surface that is reflected off again.

Reflecting tapetum—The shiny surface backing the retina in some nocturnal animals.

Refractive error—Light-bending or focusing error due to inability to adequately accommodate for targets at given distances.

Reissner's membrane—One of two membranes comprising the cochlear duct.

Residual stimuli—Stimuli that are no longer present but that affect the current adaptation level.

Resolution acuity—The measure of an individual's ability to detect a gap between two bars or the orientation of a grid of lines.

Restricted rearing—An experimental technique in which an animal is reared without the opportunity to use a designated form of sensory input.

Reticular formation—Part of brain stem, associated with attentional processes.

Retina—The rear portion of the eye containing photoreceptors and neural elements.

Retinal illuminance—The amount of light reaching the retina.

Retinene—Part of the rhodopsin pigment, similar to vitamin A.

Reverberation—A cue in determining distance of a sound source; reverberant sound is sound that reaches the ears after having bounced off some surface.

Rhodopsin—The photosensitive pigment found in rods which is responsible for scotopic vision.

Ricco's law—The relationship between area and intensity in the detection of foveal stimuli.

ROC curve—*See* Receiver operating characteristic curve.

Rod—Long, thin cylindrical photoreceptor used in low-light vision.

Round window—The membrane at the base of the cochlea opening onto the middle ear.

S potentials—Graded electrical retinal cell responses which vary in direction and strength depending upon the wavelength of the stimulus.

Saturation—The psychological attribute of a color associated with "how much" of a hue is present.

Scaling—The measurement of how much of something is present; in this book we usually refer to scales of sensation.

Schemas—Patterns of expectations built up through continued exposure and experience with sets of stimuli.

Sclera—Strong, elastic outer covering, seen as the "white," of the eye.

Scoptic—Vision under low-light conditions.

Scotoma—A localized blind spot.

Scotopsin—The protein portion of rhodopsin.

Self-adaptation—The effects of previous exposure to an odorant on threshold for that same odorant on subsequent exposures.

Sensation—Simple conscious experience associated with a stimulus.

Set—See perceptual set.

Shadowing—Depth cue based upon characteristic light and dark areas on and between objects caused by directional lighting.

Sighting dominant eye—The eye whose use is preferred in monocular tasks such as looking through a telescope.

Signal detection theory—A mathematical, theoretical system that formally deals with both decisional and sensory components in threshold measurements.

Similarity—The principle that similar objects tend to be perceptually grouped together.

Simple cell—A cortical cell which responds to lines of particular orientation and location.

Simple reaction time—A task involving pressing or releasing a telegraph key or similar response upon stimulus detection.

Simultagnosia—An attentional disorder in which an individual cannot pay attention to more than one stimulus at a time.

Sine-wave grating—A pattern of light intensity that varies from light to dark following sinusoidal gradations.

Size constancy—The stability of perceived size despite changes in objective distance and retinal image size.

Smooth-pursuit movements—The continuous eye movement involved in following a smooth, steadily moving object.

Sone—A unit used to measure the apparent loudness of a sound.

Sound pressure level—The log-relative pressure amplitude.

Span of apprehension—The amount of visual information an observer can pick up at once during one fixation.

Spatial agnosia—A perceptual disorder in which individuals cannot accurately localize objects or themselves.

Spatial frequency—Rapidity of luminance changes in adjacent areas in the field of view.

Spatial modulation transfer function—A measure of the ability of a visual system to accurately register and interpret spatial frequencies.

Spectral Colors—Pure monochromatic stimuli as those produced in a prismatic spectrum.

Spindle organs—See Stretch receptors.

Spike potential—See Action potential.

Spino-thalamic system—A slow pathway of short fibers conducting information to the brain from the skin, muscles, tendons, and organs.

Spiral aftereffect—An illusion of continued motion after a rotating spiral has stopped moving.

Spiral ganglion—The component cells of the auditory nerve, which is the neural pathway to the brain.

Square-wave grating—Sharply alternating light and dark stripes.

Stabilized retinal image—An image whose retinal position remains constant regardless of eye movements.

Standard—A stimulus against which the comparison stimuli are judged.

Stapes—The final bone in the chain of middle ear ossicles. Sometimes called the stirrup.

Statocysts—In primitive invertebrates, motion-sensitive cavities lined with hair cells.

Statolith—A tiny stonelike body resting on the hairs in statocysts and responding to motion or position of the animal.

Stereograms—Pairs of pictures that mimic the binocular disparity of the eyes.

Stereopsis—The ability to see depth based solely on the disparity of the two retinal images.

Stereoscope—An optical instrument enabling two different images to stimulate the two eyes simultaneously.

Stereotaxic instrument—A device that permits accurate placement of electrodes in the head or brain.

Stevens' law—See Power law.

Stretch receptors—Nerve endings attached to muscle spindles that respond to stretching of the muscle.

Striate cortex—See Occipital lobe.

Stroboscopic movement—See Phi phenomenon.

Stroop effect—The difficulty of observers to eliminate meaningful but conflicting information from a task even when that information is irrelevant to the task.

Structural cues—Depth and distance cues based on the physiology of the visual system.

Subjective color—The experience of colors induced in black and white patterns.

Subjective contours—Contours which are consciously experienced, but not associated with physical stimulus change.

Substantia gelatinosa—Part of the spinal cord implicated in pain transmission through the gate-control theory.

Subtractive color mixture—Color mixture resulting from the subtraction or absorption of wavelengths.

Superior colliculus—The termination point of the optic fibers on the brain stem.

Superior olive—The brain terminus for axons leading from the dorsal or ventral cochlear nuclei.

Synapse—Point at which the axons of one cell come into proximity with the cell body or dendrites of another cell.

Tachistoscope—An experimental device allowing presentation of visual material for very brief periods of time.

Taste buds—The group of cells in which the major receptors for taste are located.

Taste pore—An opening in the surface of the tongue leading to the taste cells extending from the taste bud.

Tau effect—The interaction between perceived distance and temporal separation between two stimuli.

Tectorial membrane—Within the

cochlear duct, the membrane extending from Reissner's membrane laced with the hairs of the organ of Corti.

Temporal cortex—Cortex of brain on sides near temples.

Texture gradient—Distance cue based upon variations in surface texture as a function of distance from the observer.

Thalamus—Region of lower brain which relays impulses to the cortex.

Timbre—A sound attribute associated with the complexity of the sound wave.

Tonotopic—Whenever the place of response to a sound depends on the frequency of the sound.

Transmission cells—In the gate-control theory of pain, these transmit pain impulses to the brain.

Trichromatic theory—The theory that color vision is based on three primary responses.

Tristimulus values—The combination of the stimulus hue and brightness used in the CIE color system for determining any color stimulus.

Tritanopia—The color defect in which yellows and blues are confused due to reduced blue sensitivity.

Troxler effect—The effect that stationary targets that stimulate the peripheral retina will disappear under conditions of steady, unmoving stimulation.

Tuning curve—A plot showing the rate of firing of an auditory neuron for different frequencies of sound wave; it usually has a single peak.

Two-point threshold—The minimum distance necessary between two pointed touch stimuli (such as two toothpicks) so that they will be felt as two distinct sensations.

Tympanic canal—One of three canals running through the cochlea.

Tympanum—See Eardrum.

Uncrossed disparity—Cue to distance in which the unfused image of the right eye appears in the right field of view and that of the left eye appears on the left.

Ventral cochlear nucleus—The point of the lower back part of the brain at which the minority of auditory nerve fibers end.

Vernier acuity—The measure of an individual's ability to distinguish a broken line from an unbroken line.

Vestibular canal—One of three canals running through the cochlea.

Vestibular nuclei—In the brainstem, way stations along the route of nerve fibers from the crista and macula to the cerebellum and cortex.

Vibration theory—The suggestion that a stimulus molecule ruptures chemical bonds in the cell membrane of olfactory epithelium receptor cells, causing the release of stored energy, in turn generating an electrical current.

Vigilance—A form of attention that emphasizes maintenance of alertness and accuracy of observation during long tasks.

Vision substitution system—An instrument that converts a visual pattern from a television camera into a pattern of vibrating points on the skin of the back; used for the visually impaired.

Visual acuity—The ability of the eye to resolve visual details.

Visual agnosia—Syndrome in which all parts of a visual field are seen, but the objects seen are without meaning.

Visual angle—A measure of the size of the retinal image.

Visual cliff—A device used for measuring depth perception in young animals.

Visual cortex—See Occipital lobe.

Vitreous humor—The jellylike substance filling the large chamber of the eye.

Voice onset time—A latency in producing a vowel sound following a stop-consonant sound.

Volley principle—The theory that neural fibers fire in groups, one group of neurons firing while another group "recharges."

Volume—The sense in which a sound fills space and seems large or small.

Vowels—One of two classes of speech sounds, the other being consonants.

Warm fibers—Neurons that respond to warming by firing more rapidly and reduce the firing rate with cooling.

Wavelength—The distance in a sound wave from one peak to the next.

Weber fraction—The proportion by which the standard stimulus must be increased in order to detect change, $K = \Delta I/I$.

Yerkes–Dodson law—The principle that arousal and performance are related, a midrange of arousal yielding optimum performance levels.

References

Aantaa, E. Light-induced and spontaneous variations in the amplitude of the electro-oculogram. *Acta Oto-Laryngologica, Supplementum,* 1970, **267.**

Abbs, J. H., & Sussman, H. M. Neurophysiological feature detectors and speech perception: Discussion of theoretical implications. *Journal of Speech and Hearing Research,* 1971, **14,** 23–36.

Adam, N., Rosner, B. S., Hosick, E. C., & Clark, D. L. Effect of anesthetic drugs on time production and alpha rhythm. *Perception & Psychophysics,* 1971, **10,** 133–136.

Adams, A. S., Brown, B., Haegerstrom-Portnoy, G., & Flom, M.C. Evidence for acute effects of alcohol and marijuana on color discrimination. *Perception & Psychophysics,* 1976, **20,** 119–124.

Adams, J. A. Feedback theory of how joint receptors regulate the timing and positioning of a limb. *Psychological Review,* 1977, **84,** 503–523.

Alexander, J. B., & Gudeman, H. E. Personal and interpersonal measures of field dependence. *Perceptual and Motor Skills,* 1965, **20,** 79–86.

Allison, A. C. The structure of the olfactory bulb and its relation to the olfactory pathways in the rabbit and the rat. *Journal of Comparative Neurology,* 1953, **98,** 309–348.

Ames, A., Jr. Visual perception and the rotating trapezoid window. *Psychological Monographs,* 1951, **65** (14, Whole No. 324).

Amoore, J. E. A plan to identify most of the primary odors. In C. Pfaffman (Ed.), *Olfaction and taste III.* New York: The Rockefeller University Press, 1969. Pp. 158–171.

Amoore, J. E. Four primary odor modalities of man: Experimental evidence and possible significance. In D. A. Denton & J. P. Coghlan (Eds.), *Olfaction and taste V.* New York: Academic, 1975. Pp. 283–289.

Amoore, J. E., Johnston, J. W., Jr., & Rubin, M. The stereochemical theory of odor. *Scientific American,* 1964, **210,** 42–49.

Anderson, N. H. Averaging model applied to the size-weight illusion. *Perception & Psychophysics,* 1970, **77,** 153–170.

Anderson, N. H. On the role of context effects in psychophysical judgment. *Psychological Review,* 1975, **82,** 462–482.

Anderson, N. S., & Fitts, P. M. Amount of information gained during brief exposures of numerals and colors. *Journal of Experimental Psychology,* 1958, **56,** 362–369.

Andersson, S., & Gernandt, B. E. Cortical projection of

vestibular nerve in cats. *Acta Oto-Laryngologica, Suplementum,* 1954, **116,** 10–18.

Arend, L. E., Jr., Spatial differential and integral operations in human vision: Implications of stabilized retinal image fading. *Psychological Review,* 1973, **80,** 374–395.

Aronson, E., & Rosenbloom, S. Space perception in early infancy: Perception within a common auditory-visual space. *Science,* 1971, **172,** 1161–1163.

Atkinson, W. H. Electrophysiological evidence for Stevens' power law at the medial geniculate of the cat. *Brain Research,* 1976, **109,** 175–178.

Attneave, F. Some informational aspects of visual perception. *Psychological Review,* 1954, **61,** 183–193.

Attneave, F. Symmetry, information and memory for patterns. *American Journal of Psychology,* 1955, **68,** 209–222.

Aubert, H. Die Bewegungsempfindung. *Archiv füer die Gesamte Physiologie des Menschen and der Tiere,* 1886, **39,** 347–370.

Avant, L. L. Vision in the ganzfeld. *Psychological Bulletin,* 1965, **64,** 246–258.

Baddeley, A. D. Time estimation at reduced body temperature. *American Journal of Psychology,* 1966, **79,** 475–479.

Bannatyne, A. *Language, reading and learning disabilities.* Springfield, Illinois: Thomas, 1971.

Barclay, C. D., Cutting, J. E., & Kozlowski, L. T. Temporal and spatial factors in gait perception that influence gender recognition. *Perception & Psychophysics,* 1978, **23,** 145–152.

Barlow, H. B. Single units and sensation: A neuron doctrine for perceptual psychology? *Perception,* 1972, **1,** 371–394.

Barlow, H. B., Hill, R. M., & Levick, W. R. Retinal ganglion cells responding selectively to direction and speed of image motion in the rabbit. *Journal of Physiology,* 1964, **173,** 377–404.

Bartleson, C. J. Memory colors of familiar objects. *Journal of the Optical Society of America,* 1960, **50,** 73–77.

Bartoshuk, L. M. Taste illusions: Some demonstrations. *Annals of the New York Academy of Sciences,* 1974, **237,** 279–285.

Batteau, D. W. The role of the pinna in human localization. *Proceedings of the Royal Society of London, Series B,* 1967, **168,** 158–180.

Beck, J. Apparent spatial position and the perception of

lightness. *Journal of Experimental Psychology,* 1965, **69,** 170–179.

Beidler, L. M., & Smallman, R. L. Renewal of cells within taste buds. *Journal of Cell Biology,* 1965, **27,** 263–272.

Békésy, G. von. Synchronism of neural discharges and their demultiplication in pitch perception on the skin and in learning. *Journal of the Acoustical Society of America,* 1959, **31,** 338–349.

Békésy, G. von. *Experiments in hearing.* New York: McGraw-Hill, 1960.

Békésky, G. von. Duplexity theory of taste. *Science,* 1964, **145,** 834–835.

Békésy, G. von. *Sensory inhibition.* Princeton, New Jersey: Princeton University Press, 1967.

Berger, G. O. Uber den Einfluss der Reizstärke auf die Dauer einfacher psychischer Vorgänge mit besonderer Rücksicht auf Lichtreize. *Philosophische Studien, (Wundt),* 1896, **3,** 38–93.

Berlin, B., & Kay, P. *Basic color terms.* Berkeley: University of California Press, 1969.

Berry, J. W. Mueller-Lyer susceptibility: Culture, ecology, race? *International Journal of Psychology,* 1971, **6,** 193–197.

Besser, G. Centrally acting drugs and auditory flutter. In A. Herxheimer (Ed.), *Proceedings of the symposium on drugs and sensory functions.* London: S. A. Churchill, Ltd., 1966. Pp. 199–200.

Bevan, W., Maier, R A., & Helson, H. The influence of context upon the estimation of number. *American Journal of Psychology,* 1963, **76,** 464–469.

Bhatia, B. Minimum separable as a function of speed of a moving object. *Vision Research,* 1975, **15,** 23–33.

Blakemore, C. Central visual processing. In M. S. Gazzaniga & C. Blakemore (Eds.), *Handbook of psychobiology.* New York: Academic Press, 1975. Pp. 241–268.

Blakemore, C., Carpenter, R. H. S., & Georgeson, M. A. Lateral inhibition between orientation detectors in the human visual system. *Nature (London),* 1970, **228,** 37–39.

Blakemore, C., & Cooper, G. F. Development of the brain depends on visual environment. *Science,* 1970, **228,** 477–478.

Blakeslee, A. F., & Salmon, T. H. Genetics of sensory thresholds: Individual taste reactions for different substances. *Proceedings of the National Academy of Sciences of the U.S.A.,* 1935, **21,** 84–90.

Bliss, J. C., Katcher, M. H., Rogers, C. H., & Shepard, R. P. Optical-to-tactile image conversion for the blind. *IEEE Transactions on Man-Machine Systems,* 1970, **11,** 58–65.

Bock, R. D., & Kolakowski, D. Further evidence of sex-linked major gene influence on human spatial visualizing ability. *American Journal of Human Genetics,* 1973, **25,** 1–14.

Boles, J. Color and contour detection by cells representing the fovea in monkey striate cortex. Paper presented at the first annual meeting of the Society for Neuroscience, Washington, D.C., October 1971.

Borg, G., Diamant, H., Oakley, B., Strom, L., & Zotterman, Y. A comparative study of neural and psychophysical responses to gustatory stimuli. In T. Hayashi (Ed.), *Olfaction and taste II.* Oxford: Pergamon Press, 1967. Pp. 253–264.

Boring, E. G. The role of theory in experimental psychology. *American Journal of Psychology,* 1953, **66,** 169–184.

Boring, E. G. Attention: Research beliefs concerning the conception in scientific psychology before 1930. In D. I. Mostofsky (Ed.), *Attention: Contemporary theory and analysis.* New York: Appleton, 1970. Pp. 5–8.

Bornstein, M. H. Color vision and color naming: A psychopysiological hypothesis of cultural difference. *Psychological Bulletin,* 1973, **80,** 257–285.

Bornstein, M. H. The influence of visual perception on culture. *American Anthropologist,* 1975, **77,** 774–798.

Bornstein, M. H. Infants are trichromats. *Journal of Experimental Child Psychology,* 1976, **21,** 425–445.

Bornstein, M. H. Developmental pseudocyananopsia: Ontogenetic change in human color vision. *American Journal of Optometry & Physiological Optics,* 1977, **54,** 464–469.

Bornstein, M. H., Kessen, W., & Weiskopf, S. Color vision and hue categorization in young human infants. *Journal of Experimental Psychology: Human Perception and Performance,* 1976, **2,** 115–129.

Bossom, J., & Ommaya, A. K. Visuo-motor adaptation (to prismatic transformation of the retinal image) in monkeys with bilateral dorsal rhizotomy. *Brain,* 1968, **91,** 161–172.

Boyd, I. A., & Roberts, T. D. M. Proprioceptive discharges from the stretch receptors in the knee-joint of the cat. *Journal of Physiology (London),* 1953, **122,** 38–58.

Boynton, R. M. Color vision. In J. W. King & L. A. Riggs (Eds.), *Woodworth and Schlossberg's experimental psychology* (3rd ed.). New York: Holt, Rinehart & Winston, 1971. Pp. 315–368.

Boynton, R. M., & Gordon, J. Bezold-Brucke hue shift measured by color-naming technique. *Journal of the Optical Society of America,* 1965, **55,** 78–86.

Brazelton, T., Scholl, M., & Robey, J. Visual responses in the newborn. *Pediatrics,* 1966, **37,** 284–290.

Breitmeyer, B., Love, R., & Wepman, B. Contour suppression during stroboscopic motion and metacontrast. *Vision Research,* 1974, **14,** 1451–1456.

Broadbent, D. E. The role of auditory localization and attention in memory span. *Journal of Experimental Psychology,* 1954, **47,** 191–196.

Broadbent, D. E. *Perception and communication.* London: Pergamon, 1958.

Broadbent, D. E., & Gregory, M. Vigilance considered as a statistical decision. *British Journal of Psychology,* 1963, **54,** 309–323.

Broadbent, D. E., & Gregory, M. Effects of noise and of signal rate upon vigilance analyzed by means of decision theory. *Human Factors,* 1965, **7,** 155–162.

Brodmann, K. Physiologie des gehirng. In F. Krause (Ed.), *Allsemaine chirurgie der gehirnkrankheiten.* Stuttgart: F. Enke, 1914.

Brown, B. Resolution thresholds for moving targets at the fovea and in the peripheral retina. *Vision Research,* 1972, **12,** 293–304.

Brown, P. E. Use of acupuncture in major surgery. *Lancet,* 1972, **1,** 1328–1330.

Brown, P. K., & Wald, G. Visual pigments in single rods and cones of the human retina. *Science,* 1964, **144,** 45–52.

Brown, T. S. General biology of sensory systems. In B. Scharf (Ed.), *Experimental sensory psychology.* Glenview, Illinois: Scott-Foresman, 1975. Pp. 69–111.

Brown, W. The judgment of difference. *University of California, Berkeley, Publications in Psychology,* 1910, **1,** 1–71.

Bruner, J. S. Going beyond the information given. In J. S. Bruner et al., (Eds.), *Contemporary approaches to cognition: The Colorado symposium.* Cambridge, Massachusetts: Harvard University Press, 1957.

Bruner, J. S., Postman, L., & Rodrigues, J. Expectations and the perception of color. *American Journal of Psychology,* 1951, **64,** 216–227.

Brunswik, E. The conceptual framework of psychology. *International Encyclopedia of Unified Science,* 1952, **1,** No. 10.

Brunswick, E. Representative design and probabilistic theory in a functional psychology. *Psychological Review,* 1955, **62,** 193–217.

Brunswik, E. *Perception as a representative design of psychological experiments.* Berkeley: University of California Press, 1956.

Buckhout, R. Eyewitness testimony. In R. Held & W. Richards (Eds.), *Recent progress in perception.* San Francisco: Freeman, 1976. Pp. 205–213.

Buffardi, L. Factors affecting the filled-duration illusion in the auditory, tactual, and visual modalities. *Perception & Psychophysics,* 1971, **10,** 292–294.

Burg, A. Visual acuity as measured by dynamic and static tests: A comparative evaluation. *Journal of Applied Psychology,* 1966, **50,** 460–466.

Burns, B. D., & Pritchard, R. Geometrical illusions and the response of neurones in the cat's visual cortex to angle patterns. *Journal of Physiology (London),* 1971, **213,** 599–616.

Burnside, W. Judgment of short time-intervals while performing mathematical tasks. *Perception & Psychophysics,* 1971, **9,** 404–406.

Bush, R. R., Galanter, E., & Luce, R. D. Characterization and classification of choice experiments. In R. D. Luce, R. R. Bush, & E. Galanter (Eds.), *Handbook of mathematical psychology.* Vol. 1. New York: Wiley, 1963. Pp. 77–102.

Butters, N., Barton, M., & Brody, B. A. Right parietal lobe and cross-model associations. *Cortex,* 1970, **6,** 19–46.

Cain, D. P., & Bindra, D. Response of amygdala single units to odors in the rat. *Experimental Neurology,* 1972, **35,** 98–110.

Cain, W. S. Odor intensity: Differences in the exponent of the psychophysical function. *Perception & Psychophysics,* 1969, **6,** 349–354.

Cain, W. S. Differential sensitivity for smell: "Noise" at the nose. *Science,* 1977, **195,** 796–798.

Cain, W. S., & Engen, T. Olfactory adaptation and the scaling of odor intensity. In C. Pfaffman (Ed.), *Olfaction and taste III.* New York: Rockefeller University Press, 1969. 127–141.

Campbell, F. W., & Maffei, L. Contrast and spatial frequency. *Scientific American,* 1974, **231,** 106–114.

Campos, J. J. Langer, A., & Krowitz, A. Cardiac responses on the visual-cliff in pre-locomotor human infants. *Science,* 1970, **170,** 196–197.

Carey, S., & Diamond, R. From piecemeal to configurational representation of faces. *Science,* 1977, **195,** 312–314.

Carlson, V. Effect of lysergic acid diethylamide (LSD-25) on the absolute visual threshold. *Journal of Comparative and Physiological Psychology,* 1958, **51,** 528–531.

Carlson, V. R. Instructions and perceptual constancy judgments. In W. Epstein (Ed.) *Stability and constancy in visual perception: Mechanisms and processes.* New York: Wiley, 1977. Pp. 217–254.

Carmichael, L., Hogan, H. P., & Walter, A. A. An experimental study of the effect of language on the reproduction of visually perceived forms. *Journal of Experimental Psychology,* 1932, **15,** 73–86.

Carter, R. R., & Hirsch, J. An experimental comparison of several psychological scales of weight. *American Journal of Psychology,* 1955, **68,** 645–649.

Cattell, J. M. The influence of the intensity of the stimulus on the length of the reaction time. *Brain,* 1886, **9,** 512–515.

Chapman, C. R., Wilson, M. E., & Gehrig, J. D. Comparative effects of acupuncture and transcutaneous stimulation on the perception of painful dental stimuli. *Pain,* 1976, **2,** 265–283.

Cheatham, P. G. Visual latency as a function of stimulus brightness and contour shape. *Journal of Experimental Psychology,* 1952, **43,** 369–380.

Cheng, T. O. Acupuncture anesthesia. *Science,* 1973, **179,** 521.

Cherry, E. C. Some experiments on the recognition of speech, with one and with two ears. *Journal of the Acoustical Society of America,* 1953, **25,** 975–979.

Chiang, C. A new theory to explain geometrical illusions produced by crossing lines. *Perception & Psychophysics,* 1968, **3,** 174–176.

Chocolle, R. Relation de la latence d'une sensation auditive différentialle avec l'amplitude d'une variation brusque de fréquence. .d'intensité. *Bulletin de Biologie,* 1943, **137,** 643–644, 751–752.

Chocolle, R. Vairations des temps de réaction auditifs en fonction de l'intensité à diverses fréquences. *Annales de Psychologie,* 1945, **41–42,** 65–124.

Chocolle, R. Les effets des interactions interaurales dans l'audition. *Journale de Psychologie,* 1962, **3,** 255–282.

Clark, H. H., & Clark, E. V. *Psychology and language: An introduction to psycholinguistics.* New York: Harcourt, 1977.

Clark, J. C., & Whitehurst, G. S. Asymmetrical stimulus control and the mirror-image problem. *Journal of Experimental Child Psychology,* 1974, **17,** 147–166.

Clark, W. C., & Yang, J. C. Acupunctural analgesia? Evaluation by signal detection theory. *Science,* 1974, **184,** 1096–1098.

Cleland, B. C., Dubkin, M. W., & Levick, W. R. Sustained and transient neurones in the cat's retina and lateral geniculate nucleus. *Journal of Physiology (London),* 1972, **217,** 473–496.

Cohen, J., Hansel, C. E. M., & Sylvester, J. D. Interdependence of temporal and auditory judgments. *Nature (London),* 1954, **174,** 642.

Cohen, L. B., & Salapatek, P. *Infant perception: From sensation to cognition.* Vols. 1 & 2. New York: Academic Press, 1975.

Cohen, W. Spatial and textural characteristics of the Ganzfeld. *American Journal of Psychology,* 1957, **70,** 403–410.

Cohen, W. Color-perception in the chromatic Ganzfeld. *American Journal of Psychology,* 1958, **71,** 390–394.

Coles, M. G., Gale, A., & Kline, P. Personality and habituation of the orienting reaction: Tonic and response measures of electrodermal activity. *Psychophysiology,* 1971, **8,** 54–63.

Collings, V. B. Human taste response as a function of locus of stimulation on the tongue and soft palate. *Perception & Psychophysics,* 1974, **16,** 169–174.

Cooper, W. E. Selective adaptation to speech. In F. Restle, R. M. Shiffrin, N. S. Castellan, H. Lindeman, & D. B. Pisoni (Eds.), *Cognitive theory.* Vol. 1. Hillsdale, New Jersey: Lawrence Erlbaum Associates, 1975. Pp. 24–54.

Cooper, W. E., & Blumstein, S. E. A "labial" feature analyzer in speech perception. *Perception & Psychophysics,* 1974, **15,** 591–600.

Corballis, M. C., & Beale, J. *The psychology of left and right.* Hillsdale, New Jersey: Lawrence Erlbaum Associates, 1976.

Coren, S. Adaptation to prismatic displacement as a function of the amount of available information. *Psychonomic Science,* 1966, **4,** 407–408.

Coren, S. Brightness contrast as a function of figure-ground relations. *Journal of Experimental Psychology,* 1969, **80,** 517–524. (a)

Coren, S. The influence of optical aberrations on the magnitude of the Poggendorff illusion. *Perception & Psychophysics,* 1969, **6,** 185–186. (b)

Coren, S. Lateral inhibition and geometric illusions. *Quarterly Journal of Experimental Psychology,* 1970, **22,** 274–278.

Coren, S. Subjective contours and apparent depth. *Psychological Review,* 1972, **79,** 359–367.

Coren, S., Bradley, D. R., Hoenig, P., & Girgus, J. S. The effect of smooth tracking and saccadic eye movements on the perception of size: The shrinking circle illusion. *Vision Research,* 1975, **15,** 49–55.

Coren, S., & Girgus, J. S. Density of human lens pigmentation: In vivo measures over an extended age range. *Vision Research,* 1972, **12,** 343–346. (a)

Coren, S., & Girgus, J. S. Illusion decrement in interesecting line figures. *Psychonomic Science,* 1972, **26,** 108–110. (b)

Coren, S., & Girgus, J. S. Differentiation and decrement in the Mueller-Lyer illusion. *Perception & Psychophysics,* 1972, **12,** 466–470. (c)

Coren, S., & Girgus, J. Illusions and constancies. In W. Epstein (ed.), *Stability and constancy in visual perception: Mechanisms and processes.* New York: Wiley, 1977. Pp. 255–284.

Coren, S., & Girgus, J. S. *Seeing is deceiving: The psychology of visual illusions.* Hillsdale, New Jersey: Lawrence Erlbaum Associates, 1978.

Coren, S., & Hoenig, P. Eye movements and decrement in the Oppel-Kundt illusion. *Perception & Psychophysics,* 1972, **12,** 224–225.

Coren, S., & Keith, B. Bezold-Brucke effect: Pigment or neural locus? *Journal of the Optical Society of America,* 1970, **60,** 559–562.

Coren, S., & Komoda, M. K. Apparent lightness as a function of perceived direction of incident illumination. *American Journal of Psychology,* 1973, **86,** 345–349.

Coren, S., & Porac, C. Iris pigmentation and visual-geometric illusions. *Perception,* in press.

Coren, S., Porac, C., Green, S., & Dawson, I. The Mueller-Lyer illusion from age 8 to 80. Paper delivered at the meeting of The Psychonomic Society, Washington, D.C., November 1977.

Coren, S., Ward, L. M., Porac, C., & Fraser, R. The effect of optical blur on visual-geometric illusions. *Bulletin of the Psychonomic Society,* 1978, **11,** 390–392.

Cornsweet, T. N. Determination of the stimuli for involuntary drifts and saccadic eye movements. *Journal of the Optical Society of America,* 1956, **46,** 987–993.

Cornsweet, T. N. *Visual perception.* New York: Academic Press, 1970.

Corso, J. F. Age and sex differences in thresholds. *Journal of the Acoustical Society of America,* 1959, **31,** 498–507.

Craig, J. C. Vibrotactile pattern perception: Extraordinary observers. *Science,* 1977, **196,** 450–452.

Craig, K. D., Best, H., & Ward, L. M. Social modelling influences on psychophysical judgements of electrical stimulation. *Journal of Abnormal Psychology,* 1975, **84,** 366–373.

Craig, K. D., & Coren, S. Signal detection analysis of social modelling influences on pain expressions. *Journal of Psychosomatic Research,* 1975, **19,** 105–112.

Craig, K. D., & Weiss, S. M. Vicarious influences on pain-threshold determinations. *Journal of Personality and Social Psychology,* 1971, **19,** 53–59.

Creed, R. S., Denny-Brown, D., Eccles, J. C., Liddell, E. G. T., & Sherrington, C. S. *Reflex activity of the spinal cord.* London & New York: Oxford University Press (Clarendon), 1932 (Reprinted: 1972).

Critchley, M. The problem of visual agnosia. *Journal of Neurological Science,* 1964, **1,** 274.

Critchley, M. *The dyslexic child.* London: Heinemann, 1970.

Crossman, E. R. F. W. Entropy and choice time: The effect of frequency unbalance on choice response. *Quarterly Journal of Experimental Psychology,* 1953, **5,** 41–51.

Crutchfield, R. S., Woodworth, D. G., & Albrecht, R. E. *Perceptual performance and the effective person.* WADC-TN-58-60. Lackland Air Force Base, Texas: Wright Air Development Center, 1958. NTIS No. AD-151-039.

Cutting, J. E., & Kozlowski, L. T. Recognizing friends by their walk: Gait perception without familiarity cues. *Bulletin of the Psychonomic Society,* 1977, **9,** 353–356.

Dallenbach, K. M. The temperature spots and end-organs. *American Journal of Psychology,* 1927, **39,** 402–427.

Dallenbach, K. M. Pain: History and present status. *American Journal of Psychology,* 1939, **52,** 331–347.

Dalton, K. *The premenstrual syndrome.* Springfield, Illinois: Thomas, 1964.

Dartnall, H. J. A. *The visual pigments.* London: Methuen, 1957.

Davidoff, J.B. *Differences in visual perception: The individual eye.* New York: Academic Press, 1975.

Davidson, H. P. A study of the confusing letters b, d, p, q. *Journal of Genetic Psychology,* 1935, **47,** 458–468.

Davies, A. E. An analysis of elementary psychic process. *Psychological Review,* 1905, **12,** 166–206.

Dawson, J. L. Cultural and physiological influences upon spatial processes in West Africa. I. *International Journal of Psychology,* 1967, **2,** 115–128.

Day, R. H. On the stereoscopic observation of geometric illusion. *Perceptual and Motor Skills,* 1961, **13,** 247–258.

Day, R. S. Fusion in dichotic listening. Unpublished doctoral dissertation, Stanford University, 1968.

Day, R. S. Temporal order judgments in speech: Are individuals language-bound or stimulus-bound? *Haskins Laboratories Status Report,* 1970, **SR-21/22,** 71–87.

Dayton, G., Jones, M., Steele, B., & Rose, M. Development study of coordinated eye movements in the human infant. II. An electro-oculographic study of the fixation reflex in the newborn. *Archives of Ophthalmology,* 1964, **71,** 871–875.

Delk, J. L., & Fillenbaum, S. Differences in perceived color as a function of characteristic color. *American Journal of Psychology,* 1965, **78,** 290–293.

Deregowski, J. B. Illusion and culture. In R. L. Gregory & G. H. Gombrich (Eds.), *Illusion in nature and art.* New York: Scribner's, 1973. Pp. 161–192.

Deutsch, J. A., & Deutsch, D. Attention: Some theoretical considerations. *Psychological Review,* 1963, **70,** 80–90.

De Valois, R. L. Contributions of different lateral geniculate cell types to visual behavior. *Vision Research,* 1971, **11,** 383–396.

De Valois, R. L., & De Valois, K. K. Neural coding of color. In E. C. Carterette & M. P. Friedman (Eds.), *Handbook of perception.* Vol. 5. New York: Academic Press, 1975. Pp. 117–168.

de Vries, H., & Stuiver, M. The absolute sensitivity of the human sense of smell. In W. A. Rosenblith (Ed.), *Communication processes.* New York: Wiley, 1961. Pp. 159–167.

Diamant, H., Funakoshi, M., Strom, L., & Zotterman, Y. Electrophysiological studies on human taste nerves. In Y. Zotterman (Ed.), *Olfaction and taste.* Oxford: Pergamon, 1963. Pp. 191–203.

Diamant, H., & Zotterman, Y. A comparative study on the neural and psychophysical response to taste stimuli. In C. Pfaffman (Ed.), *Olfaction and taste III.* New York: The Rockefeller University Press, 1969. Pp. 428–435.

Diamond, A. L. A theory of depression and enhancement in the brightness response. *Psychological Review,* 1960, **67,** 168–199.

DiLollo, V. Contrast effects in the judgment of lifted weights. *Journal of Experimental Psychology,* 1964, **68,** 383–387.

Ditchburn, R. W. *Eye movements and perception.* Oxford: Clarendon Press, 1973.

Djang, S. The role of past experience in the visual apprehension of masked forms. *Journal of Experimental Psychology,* 1937, **20,** 29–59.

Dodwell, P. C. On perceptual clarity. *Psychological Review,* 1971, **78,** 275–279.

Doetsch, G. S., Ganchrow, J. J., Nelson, L. M., & Erickson, R. P. Information processing in the taste system of the rat. In C. Pfaffman (Ed.), *Olfaction and taste III.* New York: Rockefeller University Press, 1969. Pp. 492–511.

Doherty, M. E., & Keeley, S. M. On the identification of repeatedly presented visual stimuli. *Psychological Bulletin,* 1972, **78,** 142–154.

Doris, J., Casper, M., & Poresky, R. Differential brightness thresholds in infancy. *Journal of Experimental Child Psychology,* 1967, **5,** 522–535.

Dow, B. M. & Gouras, P. Color and spatial specificity of single units in the rhesus monkey foveal striate cortex. *Journal of Neurophysiology,* 1973, **36,** 79–100.

Dowling, J. E. Organization of vertebrate retinas. *Investigative Ophthalmology,* 1970, **9,** 655–680.

Dröscher, V. B. *The magic of the senses: New discoveries in animal perception.* New York: Harper, 1971.

Duke-Elder, S. *System of opthalmology.* London: Kimpton, 1963.

Duncker, K. Uber induzierte Bewegung (ein Beitrag zur Theorie optisch warigenommener Bewegung). *Psychologishe Forschung,* 1929, **12,** 180–259.

Duncker, K. The influence of past experience upon perceptual properties. *American Journal of Psychology,* 1939, **52,** 255–265.

Edwards, A., & Cohen, S. Visual illusion, tactile sensibility and reaction time under LSD-25. *Psychopharmacolosia,* 1961, **2,** 297–303.

Efron, R. The duration of the present. *Annals of the New York Academy of Sciences,* 1967, **138,** 713–729.

Egan, J. P. *Signal detection theory and ROC-analysis.* New York: Academic Press, 1975.

Eimas, P. D., & Corbit, J. D. Selective adaptation of linguistic feature detectors. *Cognitive Psychology,* 1973, **4,** 99–109.

Elkind, D., Koegler, R., & Go, E. Studies in perceptual development. II. Part-whole perception. *Child Development,* 1964, **35,** 81–90.

Ellingson, R. Clinical applications of evoked potential techniques in infants and children. *Electroencephalography and Clinical Neurophysiology,* 1968, **24,** 293.

Ellingson, R., Lathrop, G., Nelson, G., & Donahy, T. Visual evoked potentials of infants. *Revue d'Electroencephalographie et de Neurophysiologie Clinique,* 1972, **2,** 395–400.

Ellis, H. C., & Muller, D. G. Transfer in perceptual learning following stimulus predifferentiation. *Journal of Experimental Psychology,* 1964, **68,** 388–395.

Engen, T., & Tulunary, U. Some sources of error in half-heaviness judgments. *Journal of Experimental Psychology,* 1956, **54,** 208–212.

Enroth-Cugell, C., & Robson, J. G. The contrast sensitivity of retinal cells of the cat. *Journal of Physiology (London),* 1966, **187,** 517–522.

Epstein, W. The process of taking into account in visual perception. *Perception,* 1973, **2,** 267–285.

Epstein, W. Observations concerning the contemporary analysis of constancies. In W. Epstein (Ed.), *Stability and constancy in visual perception: Mechanisms and processes.* New York: Wiley, 1977. Pp. 437–448.

Epstein, W., & Baratz, S. S. Relative size in isolation as a stimulus for relative perceived distance. *Journal of Experimental Psychology,* 1964, **67,** 507–513.

Epstein, W., & Hanson, S. Discrimination of unique motion-path length. *Perception & Psychophysics,* 1977, **22,** 152–158.

Epstein, W., Hatfield, G., & Muise, G. Perceived shape at a slant as a function of processing time and processing load. *Journal of Experimental Psychology: Human Perception and Performance,* 1977, **3,** 473–483.

Epstein, W., & Park, J. N. Shape constancy: Functional relationships and theoretical formulations. *Psychological Bulletin,* 1964, **62,** 180–196.

Erickson, R. P. Sensory neural patterns and gustation. In Y. Zotterman (Ed.), *Olfaction and taste.* Oxford: Pergamon Press, 1963. Pp. 205–213.

Erickson, R. P., & Schiffman, S. S. The chemical senses: A systematic approach. In M. S. Gazzaniga & C. Blakemore (Eds.), *Handbook of psychobiology.* New York: Academic Press, 1975. Pp. 393–425.

Eriksen, C. W., & Hake, H. W. Absolute judgments as a function of stimulus range and number of stimulus and response categories. *Journal of Experimental Psychology,* 1955, **49,** 323–332.

Evans, C. R., & Wells, A. M. Fragmentation phenomena associated with binocular stabilization. *British Journal of Physiological Optics,* 1967, **24,** 45–50.

Evans, E. F. Cochlear nerve and cochlear nucleus. In W. D. Keidel and W. D. Neff (Eds.), *Handbook of Sensory Physiology. Auditory System (Vol. V/2).* Berlin: Springer Verlag, 1975.

Eysenck, H. J. *The biological basis of personality.* Springfield, Illinois: Thomas, 1967.

Fagen, J. F. Infants delayed recognition memory and forgetting. *Journal of Experimental Child Psychology,* 1973, **16,** 424–450.

Falk, J., & Bindra, D. Judgment of time as a function of serial position and stress. *Journal of Experimental Psychology,* 1954, **47,** 279–282.

Falmagne, J. C. Foundations of Fechnerian psychophysics. In D. Krantz, R. C. Atkinson, R. D. Luce, & P. Suppes (Eds.), *Contemporary developments in mathematical psychology.* Vol. II. San Francisco: Freeman, 1974. Pp. 121–159.

Fantz, R. L. The origin of form perception. *Scientific American,* 1961, **204,** 66–72.

Fantz, R. L. Visual experience in infants: Decreased attention to familiar patterns relative to novel ones. *Science,* 1964, **146,** 668–670.

Fantz, R. L. Visual perception from birth as shown by pattern selectivity. *Annals of the New York Academy of Sciences,* 1965, **118,** 793–814. (a)

Fantz, R. L. Ontogeny of perception. In A. M. Schrier, H. F. Harlow, & F. Stollnitz (Eds.), *Behavior of nonhuman primates.* Vol. 2. New York: Academic Press, 1965. Pp. 365–403. (b)

Fay, R. R. Auditory frequency discrimination in the goldfish (Earassius Auratus). *Journal of Comparative and Physiological Psychology,* 1970, **73,** 175–180.

Fechner, G. T. *Elemente der psychophysik,* 1860. Translated by H. E. Alder, *Elements of psychophysics.* New York: Holt, 1966.

Fender, D. H. Time delays in the human eye-tracking system. In P. Bach-y-Rita, C. C. Collins, & J. E. Hyde (Eds.), *The control of eye movements.* New York: Academic Press, 1971. Pp. 539–543.

Festinger, L., Allyn, M. R., & White, C. W. The perception of color with achromatic stimulation. *Vision Research,* 1971, **11,** 591–612.

Festinger, L., Coren, S., & Rivers, G. The effect of attention on brightness contrast and assimilation. *American Journal of Psychology,* 1970, **83,** 189–207.

Festinger, L., & Easton, M. Inference about the efferent system based on a perceptual illusion produced by eye movements. *Psychological Review,* 1974, **81,** 44–58.

Festinger, L., White C. W., & Allyn, M. R. Eye movements and decrement in the Mueller-Lyer illusion. *Perception & Psychophysics,* 1968, **3,** 376–382.

Filer, R., & Meals, D. The effect of motivating conditions on the estimation of time. *Journal of Experimental Psychology,* 1949, **39,** 327–331.

Fisher, R. The biological fabric of time. In Interdisciplinary perspectives of time, *Annals of the New York Academy of Sciences,* 1967, **138,** 451–465.

Fisher, G. H., & Lucas, A. Illusions in concrete situations. I. Introduction and demonstrations. *Ergonomics,* 1969, **12,** 11–24.

Flock, H., & Freedberg, E. Perceived angle of incidence and achromatic surface color. *Perception & Psychophysics,* 1970, **8,** 251–256.

Foley, J. E. Prism adaptation with opposed base orientation: The weighting of direction information from the two eyes. *Perception & Psychophysics,* 1970, **8,** 23–25.

Foley, J. E. Factors governing interocular transfer of prism adaptation. *Psychological Review,* 1974, **81,** 183–186.

Foulke, E., & Sticht, T. Review of research on the intelligibility and comprehension of accelerated speech. *Psychological Bulletin,* 1969, **72,** 50–62.

Fourcin. A. J. Speech perception in the absence of speech productive ability. In N. O'Connor (Ed.), *Language, cognitive deficits, and retardation.* London: Butterworth, 1975, Pp. 33–43.

Fraisse, P. *The psychology of time.* New York: Harper, 1963.

Frankenhauser, M. *Estimation of time.* Stockholm: Almqvist & Wiksell, 1959.

Freud, S. *An aphasia.* London: Imago, 1953.

Frey, M., von & Goldman, A. Der zeitliche Verlauf der Einstellung bei den Druckempfindungen. *Zeitschrift fuer Biologie,* 1915, **65,** 183–202.

Frey, M., von & Kiesow, F. Über die Function der Tastkörperchen. *Zeitschrift fuer Psychologie,* 1899, **20,** 126–163.

Fukada, Y., & Saito, H. A. The relationship between response characteristics to flicker stimulation and receptive field organization in the cats optic nerve fibers. *Vision Research,* 1971, **11,** 227–240.

Funakoshi, M., Kasahara, Y., Yamamoto, T., & Kawamura, Y. Taste coding and central perception. In D. Schneider (Ed.), *Olfaction and taste IV.* Stuttgart: Wissenshaftliche Verlagsgesellschaft MBH, 1972. Pp. 336–342.

Funkenstein, H. H., Nelson, P. G., Winter, P., Wolberg, Z., & Newman, J. D. Unit responses in auditory cortex of awake squirrel monkeys to vocal stimulation. In M.B. Sachs (Ed.), *Physiology of the auditory system.* Baltimore: National Educational Consultants, Inc., 1971. Pp. 307–326.

Galanter, E. Contemporary psychophysics. In R. Brown, E. Galanter, E. Hess, & G. Mandler (Eds.), *New directions in psychology.* New York: Holt, 1962. Pp. 87–157.

Galanter, E. *Textbook of elementary psychology.* San Francisco: Holden-Day, 1966.

Ganz, L. Mechanism of the figural after-effects. *Psychological Review,* 1966, **73,** 128–150.

Gardner, W. J., Licklider, J. C. R., & Weisz, A. Z. Suppression of pain by sound. *Science,* 1960, **132,** 32–33.

Garner, W. R. An informational analysis of absolute judgments of loudness. *Journal of Experimental Psychology,* 1953, **46,** 373–380.

Garner, W. R. *Uncertainty and structure as psychological concepts.* New York: Wiley, 1962.

Garner, W. R. *The processing of information and structure.* Potomac, Maryland: Lawrence Erlbaum Associates, 1974.

Garner, W. R., & Clement, D. E. Goodness of pattern and pattern uncertainty. *Journal of Verbal Learning and Verbal Behavior,* 1963, **2**, 446–452.

Garner, W. R., & Hake H. W. The amount of information in absolute judgments. *Psychological Review,* 1951, **58**, 446–459.

Gelb, A. Die ''Farbenkonstanz'' der Sehdinge. *Handbuch der normalen und pathologischen Physiologie,* 1929, **12**, 594–678.

Geldard, F. A. *The human senses.* (2nd ed.) New York: Wiley, 1972.

Gerbrandt, L. K., Spinelli, D. N., & Pribram, K. H. Interaction of visual attention and temporal cortex stimulation on electrical activity evoked in striate cortex. *Electroencephalography and Clinical Neurology,* 1970, **29**, 146.

Gesteland, R. C., Lettvin, J. Y., Pitts, W. H., & Rojas, A. Odor specificities of the frogs olfactory receptors. In Y. Zotterman (Ed.), *Olfaction and taste.* Oxford: Pergamon Press, 1963. Pp. 19–34.

Geyer, L. H., & DeWald, C. G. Feature lists and confusion matrices. *Perception & Psychophysics,* 1973, **14**, 471–482.

Giachetti, I., & MacLeod, P. Cortical neuron responses to odours in the rat. In D. A. Denton & J. P. Coghlan (Eds.), *Olfaction and taste V.* New York: Academic Press, 1975. Pp. 303–307.

Gibson, E. J. *Principles of perceptual learning and development.* New York: Appleton, 1969.

Gibson, E. J., Gibson, J. J., Pick, A. D., & Osser, H. A developmental study of the discrimination of letterlike forms. *Journal of Comparative and Physiological Psychology,* 1962, **55**, 897–906.

Gibson, E. J., Osser, H., Schiff, W., & Smith, J. An analysis of critical features of letters, tested by a confusion matrix. In *A basic research program on reading.* Cooperative Research Project No. 639. Washington, D.C.: U.S. Office of Education, 1963.

Gibson, J. J. *Perception of the visual world.* Boston: Houghton, 1950.

Gibson, J. J. *The senses considered as perceptual systems.* Boston: Houghton, 1966.

Gibson, J. J., Kaplan, G. A., Reynolds, H. V., & Wheeler, K. The change from visible to invisible: A study of optical transitions. *Perception & Psychophysics,* 1969, **5**, 113–116.

Gibson, R. H., & Tomko, D. L. The relation between category and magnitude estimates of tactile intensity. *Perception & Psychophysics,* 1972, **12**, 135–138.

Gilinsky, A. S. The effect of attitude upon the perception of size. *American Journal of Psychology,* 1955, **68**, 173–192.

Gillam, B. A depth processing theory of the Poggendorff illusion. *Perception & Psychophysics,* 1971, **10**, 211–216.

Glorig, A., Wheeler, D., Quiggle, R., Grings, W., & Summerfield, A. 1954 Wisconsin State Fair hearing survey: Statistical treatment of clinical and audiometric data. Cited in K. D. Kryter, *The effects of noise on man.* New York: Academic Press, 1970. P. 116.

Glucksberg, S., & Cowen, G. N., Jr. Memory for nonattended auditory material. *Cognitive Psychology,* 1970, **1**, 149–156.

Gogel, W. C. Independent motion induction in separated portions of the visual field. *Bulletin of the Psychonomic Society,* 1977, **10**, 408–410.

Gogel, W. C., Gregg, J. M., & Wainwright, A. *Convergence as a cue to absolute distance.* Report No. 467. Fort Knox, Kentucky: U.S. Army Medical Research Laboratory, 1961. Pp. 1–16.

Gogel, W. C., & Koslow, M. The adjacency principle and induced movement. *Perception & Psychophysics,* 1972, **11**, 309–324.

Goldstone, S., Boardman, W. K., & Lhamon, W. T. Effect of quinal barbitone dextro-amphetamine, and placebo on apparent time. *British Journal of Psychology,* 1958, **49**, 324–328.

Goodman, L., & Gilman, A. (Eds.) *The pharmacological basis of therapeutics.* New York: Macmillan, 1965.

Gordon, B. The superior colliculus of the brain. In R. Held & W. Richards (Eds.), *Recent progress in perception.* San Francisco: Freeman, 1976. Pp. 85–95.

Gorman, J., Cogan, D., & Gellis, S. An apparatus for grading the visual acuity of infants on the basis of opticokinetic nystagmus. *Pediatrics,* 1957, **19**, 1088–1092.

Gottschaldt, K. Über den Einfluss der Erfahrung auf die Wahrnehmung von Figuren. I. *Psychologische Forschung,* 1926, **8**, 261–317.

Gottschaldt, K. Über den Einfluss der Erfahrung auf die Wahrnehmung von Figuren. II. *Psychologische Forschung,* 1929, **12**, 1–87.

Graham, C. H. Visual space perception. In C. H. Graham (Ed.), *Vision and visual perception.* New York: Wiley, 1965. Pp. 504–547.

Graham, C. H., & Hsia, Y. Color defect and color theory. *Science,* 1958, **127**, 675–682.

Graham, F. K., & Clifton, R. K. Heart-rate change as a component of the orienting response. *Psychological Bulletin,* 1966, **65**, 305–320.

Graham, F. K., & Jackson, J. C. Arousal systems and infant heart-rate responses. In H. W. Reese & L. P. Lipsitt (Eds.), *Advances in child development and behavior.* Vol. 5. New York: Academic Press, 1970. Pp. 60–117.

Granger, G. W., & Ikeda, H. Drugs and visual thresholds.

In A. Herxheimer (Ed.), *Drugs and sensory functions.* London: Churchill, 1968. Pp. 299–344.

Gray, J., & Wedderburn, A. Grouping strategies with simultaneous stimuli. *Quarterly Journal of Experimental Psychology,* 1960, **12,** 180–194.

Green, D. M. *An introduction to hearing.* New York: Academic Press, 1976.

Green, D. M., & Swets, J. A. *Signal detection theory and psychophysics.* New York: Wiley, 1966. (Reprinted, New York: Krieger, 1974.)

Gregory, R. L. *Eye and brain.* New York: World University Library, 1966.

Gross, C. G., Rocha-Miranda, C. E., & Bender, D. B. Visual properties of neurons in inferotemporal cortex of the macaque. *Journal of Neurophysiology,* 1972, **35,** 96–111.

Guilford, J. P. *Psychometric methods.* (2nd ed.) New York: McGraw-Hill, 1954.

Guirao, M., & Stevens, S. S. The measurement of auditory density. *Journal of the Accoustical Society of America,* 1964, **36,** 1176–1182.

Gulick, W. L. *Hearing: Physiology and psychophysics.* London & New York: Oxford University Press, 1971.

Haber, R. N., & Hershenson, M. The effects of repeated brief exposures on the growth of a percept. *Journal of Experimental Psychology,* 1965, **69,** 40–46.

Hahn, H. Die Adaptation des Geschmackssinnes. *Zeitschrift fuer Sinnesphysiologie,* 1934, **65,** 105–145.

Hall, M. J., Bartoshuk, L. M., Cain, W. S., & Stevens, J. C. PTC taste blindness and the taste of caffeine. *Nature (London),* 1975, **253,** 442–443.

Halsam, D. Individual differences in pain threshold and level of arousal. *British Journal of Psychology,* 1967, **58,** 139–142.

Handel, S., & Garner, W. R. The structure of visual pattern associates and pattern goodness. *Perception & Psychophysics,* 1965, **1,** 33–38.

Hardy, J. D., Stolwijk, J. A. J., & Hoffman, D. Pain following step increase in skin temperature. In D. R. Kenshalo (Ed.), *The skin senses.* Springfield, Ill.: Thomas, 1968. Pp. 444–457.

Hardy, J. D., Wolf, H. G., & Goodell, B. S. The pain threshold in man. *Research Publications Association for Research in Nervous and Mental Disease,* 1943, **23,** 1–15.

Hardy, J. D., Wolff, H. G., & Goodell, H. Studies on pain: Discrimination of differences in intensity of a pain stimulus as a basis of a scale of pain intensity. *Journal of Clinical Investigation,* 1947, **26,** 1152–1158.

Harkins, S., & Geen, R. G. Discriminability and criterion differences between extraverts and introverts during vigilance. *Journal of Research in Personality,* 1975, **9,** 335–340.

Harmon, L. D. The recognition of faces. *Scientific American,* 1973, **229,** 70–82.

Harmon, L. D., & Julesz, B. Masking in visual recognition: Effects of two dimensional filtered noise. *Science,* 1973, **180,** 1194–1197.

Harper, R. S. The perceptual modification of coloured figures. *American Journal of Psychology,* 1953, **66,** 86–89.

Harris, C. S. Perceptual adaptation to inverted, reversed and displaced vision. *Psychological Review,* 1965, **72,** 419–444.

Harris, P., & MacFarlane, A. The growth of the effective visual field from birth to seven weeks. *Journal of Experimental Child Psychology,* 1974, **18,** 340–348.

Harter, M., & Suitt, C. Visually-evoked cortical responses and pattern vision in the infant: A longitudinal study. *Psychonomic Science,* 1970, **18,** 235–237.

Hartline, H. K. The receptive fields of optic nerve fibers. *American Journal of Physiology,* 1940, **130,** 690–699.

Hartline, H. K., & Ratliff, F. Inhibitory interaction of receptor units in the eye of Limulus. *Journal of General Physiology,* 1957, **40,** 357–376.

Hartman, A., & Hollister, L. Effect of mescaline, Lysergic acid diethylamide and psilocybin on color perception. *Psychopharmacologia,* 1963, **4,** 441–451.

Harvey, L. O. Jr., & Leibowitz, H. Effects of exposure duration, cue reduction, and temporary monocularity on size matching at short distances. *Journal of the Optical Society of America,* 1967, **57,** 249–253.

Hassett, J. Sex and smell. *Psychology Today,* 1978, **11,** 40–45.

Head, H. *Studies in neurology.* London & New York: Oxford University Press, 1920.

Heaton, J. M. *The eye: Phenomenology and psychology of function and disorder.* London: Tavistock, 1968.

Hecht, S., & Mandelbaum, J. Rod-cone dark adaptation and vitamin A. *Science,* 1938, **88,** 219–221.

Hecht, S., Shlaer, S., & Pirenne, M. H. Energy quanta and vision. *Journal of General Physiology,* 1942, **25,** 819–840.

Heckenmueller, E. G. Stabilization of the retinal image: A review of method, effects, and theory. *Psychological Bulletin,* 1965, **63,** 157–169.

Hein, A., & Diamond, R. M. Contrasting development of visually triggered and guided movements in kittens with respect to interocular and interline equivalence. *Journal of Comparative and Physiological Psychology,* 1971, **76,** 219–224.

Hein, A., & Held, R. Dissociation of the visual placing response into elicited and guided components. *Science,* 1967, **158,** 390–392.

Hein, A., Held, R., & Gower, E. C. Development and segmentation of visually controlled movement by selective exposure during rearing. *Journal of Comparative and Physiological Psychology*, 1970, **73**, 181–187.

Held, R., & Bauer, J. A. Visually guided reaching in infant monkeys after restricted rearing. *Science*, 1967, **155**, 718–720.

Held, R., & Bossom, J. Neonatal deprivation and adult rearrangement: Complementary techniques for analyzing plastic sensory-motor coordinations. *Journal of Comparative and Physiological Psychology*, 1961, **54**, 33–37.

Held, R., & Hein, A. Adaptation of disarranged hand-eye coordination contingent upon re-afferent stimulation. *Perceptual and Motor Skills*, 1958, **8**, 87–90.

Held, R., & Hein, A. Movement-produced stimulation in the development of visually guided behavior. *Journal of Comparative and Physiological Psychology*, 1963, **56**, 872–876.

Held, R., & Hein, A. On the modifiability of form perception. In W. Wathen-Dunn (Ed.), *Models for the perception of speech and visual form*. Cambridge, Massachusetts: MIT Press, 1967. Pp. 296–304.

Hellekant, G. Electrophysiological investigation of the gustatory effect of ethyl alcohol: The summated response of the chorda tympani in the cat, dog and rat. *Acta Physiologica Scandinavica*, 1965, **64**, 392–397.

Helmholtz, H. E. F. von. *De Lehre von den Tonempfindungen als physiologische Grundlage fur die Theorie der Musik*. Braunschweig: Viewig und Sohn, 1863. English translation by A. J. Ellis, The sensations of tone. New York: Longmans, Green, 1930.

Helmholtz, H. E. F. von. *Handbuch der Physiologischen Optik. Dritte Auflage*. Hamburg: Leopold Voss, 1909, 1910, 1911. English translation, J. P. C. Southall (Ed.). The Optical Society of America, 1924. Reissued by Dover, 1962.

Helson, H. Adaptation-level as a frame of reference for the prediction of psychophysical data. *American Journal of Psychology*, 1947, **60**, 1–29.

Helson, H. Adaptation level theory. In S. Koch (Ed.), *Psychology: A study of a science*. Vol. 1, New York: McGraw-Hill, 1959. Pp. 565–621.

Helson, H. *Adaptation level theory: An experimental and systematic approach to behavior*. New York: Harper, 1964.

Helson, H., & Bevan, W. An investigation of variables in judgments of relative area. *Journal of Experimental Psychology*, 1964, **67**, 335–341.

Helson, H., & Nash, M. Anchor, contrast, and paradoxical distance effects. *Journal of Experimental Psychology*, 1960, **59**, 113–121.

Heinemann, E. G. Simultaneous brightness induction as a function of inducing and test field luminance. *Journal of Experimental Psychology*, 1955, **50**, 89–96.

Henmon, V. A. C. The time of perception as a measure of differences in sensations. *Archives of Philosophy, Psychology and Scientific Methods*, 1906, No. 8.

Henning, H. Der Geruch. I. *Zietschrift fuer Psychologie*, 1915, **73**, 161–257.

Henning, H. Die Qualitatenreihe des Geschmaks. *Zeitschrift fuer Psychologie*, 1916, **74**, 203–219.

Hensel, H. Classes of receptor units predominantly related to thermal stimuli. In A. V. S. de Ruech & J. Knight (Eds.), *Touch, heat and pain*. Boston: Little, Brown, 1966. Pp. 275–288.

Hensel, H. Electrophysiology of cutaneous thermoreceptors. In D. R. Kenshalo (Ed.), *The skin senses*. Springfield, Illinois: Thomas, 1968. Pp. 384–399.

Hering, E. *Outlines of a theory of the light sense*, 1878. English translation by L. M. Hurvich & D. Jameson. Cambridge, Massachusetts: Harvard University Press, 1964.

Hernandez-Peon, R. Psychiatric implications of neurophysiological research. *Bulletin of the Menninger Clinic*, 1964, **28**, 165–185.

Hershenson, M. Perception of letter arrays as a function of absolute retinal locus. *Journal of Experimental Psychology*, 1969, **80**, 201–202.

Hershenson, M., Kessen, W., & Munsinger, H. Ocular orientation in the human newborn infant: A close look at some positive and negative results. In W. Wather-Dunn (Ed.), *Models for the perception of speech and visual form*. Cambridge, Massachusetts: MIT Press. 1967. Pp. 282–290.

Hess, E. H. Development of the chick's response to light and shade cues of depth. *Journal of Comparative and Physiological Psychology*, 1950, **43**, 112–122.

Hess, E. H. Attitude and pupil size. *Scientific American*, 1965, **212**, 46–54.

Hick, W. E. On the rate of gain of information. *Quarterly Journal of Experimental Psychology*, 1952, **4**, 11–26.

Hicks, R. E., Miller, G. W., & Kinsbourne, M. Prospective and retrospective judgments of time as a function of amount of information processed. *American Journal of Psychology*, 1976, **89**, 719–730.

Hilgard, E. R. Pain: Its reduction and production under hypnosis. *Proceedings of the American Philosophical Society*, 1971, **115**, 470–476.

Hill, A. L. Direction constancy. *Perception & Psychophysics*, 1972, **11**, 175–178.

Hirsch, H. V. B., & Jacobson, N. The perfectable brain: Principles of neuronal development. In M. S. Gazzaniga & C. Blakemore (Eds.), *Handbook of psychobiology*. New York: Academic Press, 1975. Pp. 107–137.

Hirsch, H. V. B., & Spinelli, D. N. Visual experience modifies distribution of horizontally and vertically oriented receptive fields in cats. *Science*, 1970, **168**, 869–871.

Hirsh, I. J. The influence of interaural phase on interaural summation and inhibition. *Journal of the Acoustical Society of America,* 1948, **20,** 536–544.

Hoagland, H. The physiological control of judgment of duration: Evidence for a chemical clock. *Journal of General Psychology,* 1933, **9,** 267–287.

Hochberg, J. Nativism and empiricism in perception. In L. Postman (Ed.), *Psychology in the making.* New York: Knopf, 1962. Pp. 255–330.

Hochberg, J. Perception. II. Space and movement. In J. W. Kling & L. A. Riggs (Eds.), *Woodworth and Schlossberg's experimental psychology.* (3rd ed.) New York: Holt, 1971. Pp. 475–550. (a)

Hochberg, J. Perception. I. Color and shape. In J. W. Kling & L. A. Riggs (Eds.). *Woodworth and Schlossberg's experimental psychology.* (3rd ed) New York: Holt, 1971. Pp. 395–474. (b)

Hochberg, J., & Beck, J. Apparent spatial arrangement and perceived brightness. *Journal of Experimental Psychology,* 1954, **47,** 263–266.

Hochberg, J., & Brooks, V. The psychophysics of form: Reversible-perspective drawings of spatial objects. *American Journal of Psychology,* 1960, **73,** 337–354.

Hoffer, A., & Osmond, H. *The hallucinogens.* New York: Academic Press, 1967.

Hoffman, K. P. Conduction velocity in pathways from retina to superior colliculus in the cat: A correlation with receptive-field properties. *Journal of Neurophysiology,* 1973, **36,** 409–424.

Holland, H. Drugs and personality. XII. A comparison of several drugs by the flicker-fusion method. *Journal of Mental Science,* 1960, **106,** 858–861.

Holst, E. von, & Mittelstaedt, H. Das Reaffenzprinzip (wechselwirkungen zeischenzentral Nervensystem und Peripherie). *Naturwissenschaften,* 1950, **37,** 464–476.

Holway, A. F., & Boring, E. G. Determinants of apparent visual size with distance variant. *American Journal of Psychology,* 1941, **54,** 21–37.

Howard, I. P., Anstis, T., & Lucia, H. C. The relative lability of mobile and stationary components in a visual-motor adaptation task. *Quarterly Journal of Experimental Psychology,* 1974, **26,** 293–300.

Howard, I. P., Craske, B., & Templeton, W. B. Visuomotor adaptation to discordant exafferent stimulation. *Journal of Experimental Psychology,* 1965, **70,** 189–191.

Hubel, D. H., & Wiesel, T. N. Receptive fields, binocular interaction and functional architecture in the cat's visual cortex. *Journal of Physiology (London),* 1962, **160,** 106–154.

Hubel, D. H., & Wiesel, T. N. Receptive fields and functional architecture of monkey striate cortex. *Journal of Physiology (London),* 1968, **195,** 215–243.

Hudson, W. Pictorial depth perception in subcultural

groups in Africa. *Journal of Social Psychology,* 1960, **52,** 183–208.

Hudson, W. Pictorial perception and educational adaptation in Africa. *Psychologia Africana,* 1962, **9,** 226–239.

Hughes, G. W., & Hemdal, J. F. *Speech analysis.* Lafayette, Indiana: Purdue Research Foundation, 1965.

Hurvich, L. M., & Jameson, D. Opponent processes as a model of neural organization. *American Psychologist,* 1974, **29,** 88–102.

Huxley, A. *The doors of perception and heaven and hell.* New York: Harper, 1963.

Ippolitov, F. W. Interanalyser differences in the sensitivity-strength parameter for vision, hearing and cutaneous modalities. In V. D. Nebylitsyn & J. A. Gray (Eds.), *Biological bases of individual behavior.* New York: Academic Press, 1972. Pp. 43–61.

Ittelson, W. H. Size as a cue to distance: Static localization. *American Journal of Psychology,* 1951, **64,** 54–67.

Ittelson, W. H. *Visual space perception.* Berlin & New York: Springer-Verlag, 1960.

Ittelson, W. H. Perception and transactional psychology. In S. Koch (Ed.), *Psychology: A study of a science.* Vol. 4. New York: McGraw-Hill, 1962. Pp. 660–704.

Jacobson, R., Fant, G. G. M., & Halle, M. Preliminaries to speech analysis. Acoustical Lab Technical Lab Report No. 13, 1952, Massachusetts Institute of Technology.

Jacobson, R., Fant, G. G. M., & Halle, M. *Preliminaries to speech analysis: The distinctive features and their correlates.* Cambridge, Massachusetts: MIT Press, 1961.

James, W. *The principles of psychology.* New York: Holt, 1890.

Jameson, D., & Hurvich, L. M. Note on factors influencing the relation between stereoscopic acuity and observation distance. *Journal of the Optical Society of America,* 1959, **49,** 639.

Jameson, D., & Hurvich, L. M. Theory of brightness and color contrast in human vision. *Vision Research,* 1964, **4,** 135–154.

Jensen, D., & Engel, R. Statistical procedures for relating dichotomous responses to maturation and EEG measurements. *Electroencephalography and Clinical Neurophysiology,* 1971, **30,** 437–443.

Jerison, H. J. Vigilance, discrimination and attention. In D. I. Mostofsky (Ed.), *Attention: Contemporary theory and analysis.* New York: Appleton, 1970. Pp. 127–148.

Johansson, G. Visual motion perception. *Scientific American,* 1975. Reprinted in R. Held & W. Richards (Eds.), *Recent progress in perception: Readings from Scientific American.* San Francisco: Freeman, 1976. Pp. 67–75. (a)

Johansson, G. Spatio-temperal differentiation and integration in visual motion perception. *Psychological Research,* 1976, **38,** 379–393. (b)

Jones, G., & Pasnak, R. Light deprivation and visual-cliff performance in the adult cat. *Psychonomic Science,* 1970, **21,** 278–279.

Julesz, B. *Foundations of cyclopean perception.* Chicago: University of Chicago Press, 1971.

Kagan, J., Henker, B. A., Hen-Tov, A., Levine, J., & Lewis, M. Infants' differential reactions to familiar and distorted faces. *Child Development,* 1966, **37,** 519–532.

Kahneman, D. Method, findings, and theory in studies of visual masking. *Psychological Bulletin,* 1968, **70,** 404–425.

Kahneman, D. *Attention and effort.* Englewood Cliffs, New Jersey: Prentice-Hall, 1973.

Kaplan, A., & Glanville, E. Taste thresholds for bitterness and cigarette smoking. *Nature (London),* 1964, **202,** 1366.

Karmel, B. Z., & Maisel, E. B. A neuronal activity model for infant visual attention. In L. B. Cohen & P. Salapatek (Eds.), *Infant perception: From sensation to cognition. Vol. I. Basic visual processes.* New York: Academic Press, 1975. Pp. 78–133.

Kasamatsu, T. Visual cortical neurons influenced by the oculomotor input: Characterization of their receptive field properties. *Brain Research,* 1976, **113,** 271–292.

Kaufman, L. *Sight and mind: An introduction to visual perception.* London & New York: Oxford University Press, 1974.

Keller, H. *The story of my life.* New York: Doubleday, 1931.

Kenshalo, D. R., & Nafe, J. P. A quantitative theory of feeling: 1960. *Psychological Review,* 1962, **69,** 17–33.

Kenshalo, D. R., Nafe, J. P., & Brooks, B. Variations in thermal sensitivity. *Science,* 1961, **134,** 104–105.

Kenshalo, D. R., & Scott, H. A., Jr. Temporal course of thermal adaptation. *Science,* 1966, **151,** 1095–1096.

Kilbride, P. L., & Leibowitz, H. W. Factors affecting the magnitude of the Ponzo illusion among the Baganda. *Perception & Psychophysics,* 1975, **17,** 543–548.

Kimura, D. Right temporal-lobe damage. *Archives of Neurology,* 1963, **8,** 264–271.

Kimura, K., & Beidler, L. M. Microelectrode study of taste receptors of rat and hamster. *Journal of Cellular and Comparative Physiology,* 1961, **58,** 131–140.

Kinney, G. C., Marsetta, M., & Showman, D. J. Studies in display symbol legibility. Part XII. The legibility of alphanumeric symbols for digitalized television. Bedford, Massachusetts: The Mitre Corporation, November, 1966, ESD-TR-66-117. Cited in P. H. Lindsay & D. A. Norman. *Human information processing: An introduction to psychology.* (2nd ed) New York: Academic Press, 1977. Pp. 267–268.

Klein, G. S. *Perception, motives and personality.* New York: Knopf, 1970.

Klein, W., Plomp, R., & Pols, L. C. W. Vowel spectra, vowel spaces and vowel identification. *Journal of the Acoustical Society of America,* 1970, **48,** 999.

Klüver, H., & Bucy, P. C. "Psychic blindness" and other symptoms following bilateral temporal lobectomy in Rhesus monkeys. *American Journal of Physiology,* 1937, **119,** 352–353.

Kobayashi, T. Analytical study of displacement in visual perception. I. *Japanese Psychological Research,* 1956, **3,** 37–47.

Kohler, I. Experiments with goggles. *Scientific American,* 1962, **206,** 62–86.

Kohler, I. The formation and transformation of the perceptual world. *Psychological Issues,* 1964, **3** (Whole No. 4).

Köhler, W. Zur Theories des Sukzessivvergleichs und der Zeitfehler. *Psychologische Forschung,* 1923, **4,** 115–175.

Konstadt, N., & Forman, E. Field dependence and external directedness *Journal of Personality and Social Psychology,* 1965, **1,** 490–493.

Kopfermann, H. Psychologische Untersuchungen über die Wirkung Zweickmen sconälar Darstellungen Korperlicher Gebilde. *Psychologische Forschung,* 1930, **13,** 293–364. Cited in K. Koffka, *Principles of Gestalt psychology.* New York: Harcourt, 1935. Pp. 159–160.

Kozlowski, L. T., & Cutting, J. E. Recognizing the sex of a walker from a dynamic point-light display. *Perception & Psychophysics,* 1977, **21,** 575–580.

Kryter, K. D. *The effects of noise on man.* New York: Academic Press, 1970.

Kuffler, S. W. Discharge patterns and functional organization of mammalian retina. *Journal of Neurophysiology,* 1953, **16,** 37–68.

Kupchella, C. *Sights and sounds.* Indianapolis: Bobbs-Merrill, 1976.

LaBerge, D. Attention and the measurement of perceptual learning. *Memory and Cognition,* 1973, **1,** 268–276.

LaBerge, D. Acquisition of automatic processing in perceptual and associative learning. In P. M. A. Rabbit & S. Dornic (Eds.), *Attention and performance.* Vol. 5. New York: Academic Press, 1974. Pp. 50–64.

Ladefoged, P. *A course in phonetics.* New York: Harcourt, 1975.

Lakowski, R. Is the deterioration of colour discrimination with age due to lens or retinal changes? *Farbe,* 1962, **11,** 69–86.

Lakowski, R. The Pickford-Nicolson anomaloscope as a test for acquired dyschromatopsias. *Modern Problems in Ophthalmology,* 1972, **11,** 25–33.

Lakowski, R., Aspinall, P. A., & Kinnear, P. R. Association between colour vision losses and diabetes mellitus. *Ophthalmic Research,* 1972, **4,** 145–159.

Lakowski, R., & Morton, B. A. The effect of oral contraceptives on colour vision in diabetic women. *Canadian Journal of Ophthalmology,* 1977, **12,** 89–97.

Landolt, E. Tableua d'optotypes pour la determination de l'acuité visuelle. *Societe Francais d'Opthalmologie,* 1889.

Lappin, J. S., & Preble, L. D. A demonstration of shape constancy. *Perception & Psychophysics,* 1975, **17,** 439–444.

Lashley, K. S. The mechanism. IV. The cerebral areas necessary for pattern vision in the rat. *Journal of Comparative Neurology,* 1931, **53,** 419–478.

Lefton, L. A. Metacontrast: A review. *Perception & Psychophysics,* 1973, **13,** 161–171.

Lehiste, I., & Peterson, G. Vowel amplitude and phonemic stress in American english. *Journal of the Acoustical Society of America,* 1959, **31,** 428–435.

Leiberman, A. M., Cooper, F. S., Shankweiler, D. P., & Studdert-Kennedy, M. Perception of the speech code. *Psychological Review,* 1967, **74,** 431–461.

Leibowitz, H. W. Sensory, learned, and cognitive mechanisms of size perception. *Annals of the New York Academy of Sciences,* 1971, **188,** 47–62.

Leibowitz, H. W. Multiple mechanisms of size perception and size constancy. *Hiroshima Forum for Psychology,* 1974, **1,** 47–53.

Leibowitz, H. W., & Bourne, L. E. Time and intensity as determiners of perceived shape. *Journal of Experimental Psychology,* 1956, **51,** 277–281.

Leibowitz, H. W., & Harvey, L. O., Jr. Effect of instructions, environment, and type of test object on matched size. *Journal of Experimental Psychology,* 1969, **81,** 36–43.

Leibowitz, H. W., & Moore, D. Role of changes in accommodation and convergence in the perception of size. *Journal of the Optical Society of America,* 1966, **56,** 1120–1123.

Lenneberg, E. H. Understanding language without ability to speak: A case report. *Journal of Abnormal and Social Psychology,* 1962, **65,** 419–425.

Lettvin, J. W., Maturana, H. R., McCulloch, W. S., & Pitts, W. H. What the frog's eye tells the frog's brain. *Proceedings of the IRE,* 1959, **47,** 1940–1951.

Lichte, W. H., & Borresen, C. R. Influence of instructions on degree of shape constancy. *Journal of Experimental Psychology,* 1967, **74,** 538–542.

Lichtenstein, M. Spatio-temporal factors in cessation of smooth apparent motion. *Journal of the Optical Society of America,* 1963, **53,** 302–306.

Lindsay, P. H., & Norman, D. A. *Human information processing.* (2nd ed.) New York: Academic Press, 1977.

Linton, H., & Graham, E. Personality correlates of persuasibility. In I. Janis (Ed.), *Personality and persuasibility.* New Haven, Connecticut: Yale University Press, 1959.

Lipetz, L. E. The transfer functions of sensory intensity in the nervous system. *Vision Research,* 1969, **9,** 1205–1234.

Lisker, L., & Abramson, A. The voicing dimension: Some experiments in comparative phonetics. *Proceedings of the 6th International Congress of Phonetic Sciences, 1967,* 1970, 563–567.

Lockhead, G. R. Effects of dimensional redundancy on visual discrimination. *Journal of Experimental Psychology,* 1966, **72,** 95–104.

Lockhead, G. R. Processing dimensional stimuli: A note. *Psychological Review,* 1972, **79,** 410–419.

Lockhead, G. R., & King, M. C. Classifying integral stimuli. *Journal of Experimental Psychology: Human Perception and Performance,* 1977, **3,** 436–443.

Loewenstein, W. R. Biological transducers. *Scientific American,* 1960, **203,** 98–108.

Loftus, E. Reconstructing memory: The incredible eye witness. *Psychology Today,* 1974, **8,** 116–119.

Lord Rayleigh. On our perception of sound direction. *Philosophical Magazine* [6], 1907, **13,** 214–232.

Löwenstein, O., & Sand, A. The mechanism of the semicircular canal: A study of the responses of single-fibre preparations to angular accelerations and to rotation at constant speed. *Proceedings of the Royal Society of London, Series B,* 1940, **129,** 256–275.

Luria, A. R. Memory disturbances in local brain lesions. *Neuropsychologia,* 1972, **9,** 367–375.

Luria, A. R. *The working brain.* London: Penguin, 1973.

Maccoby, E. E., & Jacklin, C. N. *The psychology of sex differences.* Stanford, California: Stanford University Press, 1974.

Mack, A., & Herman, E. A new illusion: The underestimation of distance during pursuit eye movements. *Perception & Psychophysics,* 1972, **12,** 471–473.

Mackworth, N. H. Researches on the measurement of human performance. *Medical Research Council (Great Britain), Special Report, Series,* 1950, **SRS-268.**

MacLeod, P. An experimental approach to the peripheral mechanisms of olfactory discrimination. In G. Ohloff & A. F. Thomas (Eds.), *Gustation and olfaction.* New York: Academic Press, 1971. Pp. 28–44.

MacLeod, R. The effects of "artificial penumbra" on the brightness of included areas. In A. Michotte (Ed.), *Miscellanea psychologica.* Paris: Librairie Philosophique, 1947. Pp. 1–22.

Mandler, J. M., & Johnson, N. S. Some of the thousand

words a picture is worth. *Journal of Experimental Psychology: Human Learning and Memory,* 1976, **2,** 529–540.

Mandler, J. M., & Parker, R. E. Memory for descriptive and spatial information in complex figures. *Journal of Experimental Psychology: Human Learning and Memory,* 1976, **2,** 38–48.

Mandler, J. M., & Ritchey, G. H. Long-term memory for pictures. *Journal of Experimental Psychology: Human Learning and Memory,* 1977, **3,** 386–396.

Marks, L. E. Stimulus range, number of categories, and form of the category scale. *American Journal of Psychology,* 1968, **81,** 467–479.

Marks, L. E. On scales of sensation: Prolegomena to any future psychophysics that will be able to come forth as science. *Perception and Psychophysics,* 1974, **16,** 358–376.

Marks, W. B., Dobelle, W. H., & MacNichol, E. F. Visual pigments of single primate cones. *Science,* 1964, **143,** 1181–1183.

Marr, D. The computation of lightness by the primate retina. *Vision Research,* 1974, **14,** 1377–1388.

Marx, J. L. Analgesia: How the body inhibits pain perception. *Science,* 1977, **195,** 471–473.

Masica, D. N., Money, J., Ehrhardt, A. A., & Lewis, V. G. IQ, fetal sex hormones and cognitive patterns—studies in testicular feminizing syndrome of androgen insensitivity. *Johns Hopkins Medical Journal,* 1969, **124,** 34.

Massaro, D. W. *Experimental psychology and information processing.* Chicago: Rand-McNally, 1975.

Matin, L., & MacKinnon, G. E. Autokinetic movement: selective manipulation of directional components by image stabilization. *Science,* 1964, **143,** 147–148.

Matthews, B. H. C. Nerve endings in mammalian muscle. *Journal of Physiology (London),* 1933, **78,** 1–53.

Maurer, D. Infant visual perception: Methods of study. In L. B. Cohen & P. Salapatek (Eds.), *Infant perception: From sensation to cognition, basic visual processes.* Vol. 1. New York: Academic Press, 1975. Pp. 1–77.

Maxwell, J. C. Treatise on electricity and magnetism. Oxford: Clarendon Press, 1873.

McBurney, D. H. Effects of adaptation on human taste function. In C. Pfaffman (Ed), *Olfaction and taste III.* New York: The Rockefeller University Press, 1969. Pp. 407–419.

McBurney, D. H., & Bartoshuk, L. M. Water taste in mammals. In D. Schneider (Ed), *Olfaction and taste IV.* Wissenshafliche Verlagsgesellschaft MBH, 1972. Pp. 329–335.

McBurney, D. H., Levine, J. M., & Cavanaugh, P. H. Psychophysical and social ratings of human body odor. *Personality and Social Psychology Bulletin,* 1977, **3,** 135–138.

McColgin, F. H. Movement threshold in peripheral vision. *Journal of the Optical Society of America,* 1960, **50,** 774–779.

McFarland, R. A., Domey, R. G., Warren, A. B., & Ward, D. C. Dark-adaptation as a function of age. I. A statistical analysis. *Journal of Gerontology,* 1960, **15,** 149–154.

McGuinness, D. Hearing: Individual differences in perceiving. *Perception,* 1972, **1,** 465–473.

McGuinness, D. Away from a unisex psychology: Individual differences in visual sensory and perceptual processes. *Perception,* 1976, **5,** 279–294. (a)

McGuinness, D. Sex differences in the organization of perception and cognition. In B. Lloyd & U. Archer (Eds.), *Exploring sex differences.* New York: Academic Press, 1976. Pp. 123–156. (b)

McGurk, H., & Lewis, M. Space perception in early infancy: Perception within a common auditory-visual space? *Science,* 1974, **186,** 649.

Melzack, R. *The puzzle of pain.* London: Penguin, 1973. (a)

Melzack, R. How acupuncture can block pain. *Impact of Science on Society,* 1973, **23,** 65–75. (b)

Melzack, R., & Casey, K. L. Sensory, motivational, and central control determinants of pain. In D. R. Kenshalo (Ed.), *The skin senses.* Springfield, Illinois: Thomas, 1968. Pp. 423–443.

Melzack, R., & Wall, P. D. Pain mechanisms: A new theory. *Science,* 1965, **150,** 971–979.

Merkel, J. Die zeitlichen Verhältnisse der Willensthätigkeit. *Philosophische Studien (Wundt),* 1885, **2,** 73–127.

Mershon, D. H., & Bowers, J. N. Reverberation and the specific distance tendency as factors in the auditory perception of egocentric distance. Paper presented at the meeting of the Psychonomic Society, November 1976.

Mershon, D. H., & Gogel, W. C. Effect of stereoscopic cues on perceived whiteness. *American Journal of Psychology,* 1970, **83,** 55–67.

Mershon, D. H., & King, L. E. Intensity and reverberation as factors in the auditory perception of egocentric distance. *Perception & Psychophysics,* 1975, **18,** 409–415.

Mescavage, A. A., Heimer, W. I., Tatz, S. J., & Runyon, R. P. Time estimation as a function of rate of stimulus change. Paper presented at the annual meeting of the Eastern Psychological Association, New York, April 1971.

Mickwitz, M. von. The effect of type and amount of familiarization training on pattern recognition. Doctoral dissertation, University of Pittsburgh, 1973.

Mikalelian, H., & Held, R. Two types of adaptation to an optically-rotated visual field. *American Journal of Psychology,* 1964, **77,** 257–263.

Miles, F. A., & Fuller, J. E. Visual tracking and the primate flocculus. *Science,* 1975, **189,** 1000–1002.

Miller, G. A. Sensitivity to changes in the intensity of white noise and its relation to masking and loudness.

Journal of the Acoustical Society of America, 1947, **19,** 609–619.

Miller, G. A. The magical number seven, plus or minus two: Some limits on our capacity for processing information. *Psychological Review,* 1956, **63,** 81–97.

Miller, N. D. Visual recovery from brief exposures to high luminance. *Journal of the Optical Society of America,* 1965, **55,** 1661–1669.

Mills, A. W. On the minimum audible angle. *Journal of the Acoustical Society of America,* 1958, **30,** 237–246.

Mills, A. W. Lateralization of high-frequency tones. *Journal of the Acoustical Society of America,* 1960, **32,** 132–134.

Milne, J., & Milne, M. *The senses of animals and men.* New York: Atheneum, 1967.

Milner, B. Intellectual function of the temporal lobes. *Psychological Bulletin,* 1954, **51,** 42–62.

Milner, B. Psychological defects produced by temporal lobe excision. *Research Publications, Association for Research in Nervous and Mental Disease,* 1958, **36,** 244–257.

Milner, P. M. *Physiological psychology.* New York: Holt, 1970.

Milner, P. M. A model for visual shape recognition. *Psychological Review,* 1974, **81,** 521–535.

Monahan, J. S., & Lockhead, G. R. Identification of integral stimuli. *Journal of Experimental Psychology: General,* 1977, **106,** 94–110.

Moncrieff, R. W. Olfactory adaptation and odour likeness. *Journal of Physiology* (London), 1956, **133,** 301–316.

Money, J. Psychosexual differentiation. In J. Money (Ed.), *Sex research: New developments.* New York: Holt, 1965. Pp. 3–23.

Moray, N. Attention in dichotic listening: Affective cues and the influence of instructions. *Quarterly Journal of Experimental Psychology,* 1959, **11,** 56–60.

Moray, N. Where is capacity limited? A survey and a model. *Acta Psychologica,* 1967, **27,** 84–92.

Moray, N. *Attention: Selective processes in vision and hearing.* London: Hutchinson Educational Ltd., 1969.

Moskowitz, H., Sharma, S., & McGlothlin, W. Effect of marijuana upon peripheral vision as a function of the information processing demands in central vision. *Perceptual and Motor Skills,* 1972, **35,** 875.

Moskowitz, H. R. Ratio scales of sugar sweetness. *Perception & Psychophysics,* 1970, **7,** 315–320.

Mostofsky, D. I. The semantics of attention. In D. I. Mostofsky (Ed.). *Attention: Contemporary theory and analysis.* New York: Appleton, 1970. Pp. 9–24.

Mountcastle, V. B., Poggio, G. F., & Werner, G. The relation of thalamic cell response to peripheral stimuli varied over an intensive continuum. *Journal of Neurophysiology,* 1963, **26,** 807–834.

Mountcastle, V. B., & Powell, T. P. S. Central nervous mechanisms subserving position sense and kinesthesis. *Bulletin of the John Hopkins Hospital,* 1959, **105,** 173–200.

Munsell, A. H. *Atlas of the Munsell color system.* Maldin, Massachusetts: Wadsworth, Howland, 1915.

Nafe, J. P., & Wagoner, K. S. The insensitivity of the cornea to heat and pain derived from high temperatures. *American Journal of Psychology,* 1937, **49,** 631–635.

Navon, D. Forest before trees: The precedence of global features in visual perception. *Cognitive Psychology,* 1977, **9,** 353–383.

Needham, J. G. The time-error in comparison-judgments. *Psychological Bulletin,* 1934, **31,** 229–243.

Neisser, U. *Cognitive psychology.* New York: Appleton, 1967.

Neisser, U. *Cognition and reality: Principles and implications of cognitive psychology.* San Francisco: Freeman, 1976.

Newhall, S. M., Burnham, R. W., & Clark, J. R. Comparison of successive with simultaneous color matching. *Journal of the Optical Society of America,* 1957, **47,** 43–56.

Newhall, S. M., Nickerson, D., & Judd, D. B. Final report of the O. S. A. subcommittee on spacing of the Munsell colors. *Journal of the Optical Society of America,* 1943, **33,** 385–418.

Newland, J. Children's knowledge of left and right. Unpublished master's thesis, University of Auckland, 1972. Cited in M. C. Corballis & J. L. Beale, *The psychology of left and right.* Hillsdale, New Jersey: Lawrence Erlbaum Associates, 1976. P. 167.

Noda, H., Freeman, R. B., & Creutzfeldt, O. D. Neuronal correlates of eye movements in the cat visual cortex. *Science,* 1972, **175,** 661–664.

Norman, D. A. Toward a theory of memory and attention. *Psychological Review,* 1968, **75,** 522–536.

Norman, D. A. Memory while shadowing. *Quarterly Journal of Experimental Psychology,* 1969, **21,** 85–93.

Norman, D. A. *Memory and attention.* (2nd ed.) New York: Wiley, 1976.

O'Connell, R. J., & Mozell, M. M. Quantitative stimulation of frog olfactory receptors. *Journal of Neurophysiology,* 1969, **32,** 51–63.

Ono, H. Difference threshold for stimulus length under simultaneous and non-simultaneous viewing conditions. *Perception & Psychophysics,* 1967, **2,** 201–207.

Ornstein, A., & Rotter, G. Research, methodology in temporal perception. *Journal of Experimental Psychology,* 1969, **79,** 561–564.

Ornstein, R. E. *On the experience of time.* London: Penguin, 1969.

Osterberg, G. Topography of the layer of rods and cones in the human retina. *Acta Ophthalmologica,* Supplementum, 1935, **6.**

Ostfeld, A. Effects of LSD-25 and JB318 on tests of visual and perceptual functions in man. *Federation Proceedings, Federation of American Societies for Experimental Biology*, 1961, **20**, 876–883.

Ottoson, D. Analysis of the electrical activity of the olfactory epithelium. *Acta Physiologica Scandinavica*, 1956, **35** (Suppl. 122), 1–83.

Oyama, T. A behavioristic analysis of Steven's magnitude estimation method. *Perception & Psychophysics*, 1968, **3**, 317–320.

Palmer, S. E. The effects of contextual scenes on the identification of objects. *Memory and Cognition*, 1975, **3**, 519–526. (a)

Palmer, S. E. Visual perception and world knowledge: Notes on a model of sensory-cognitive interaction. In D. A. Norman & D. E. Rumelhart (Eds.), *Explorations in cognition*. San Francisco: Freeman, 1975. Pp. 279–307. (b)

Parducci, A. Category judgment: A range-frequency model. *Psychological Review*, 1965, **72**, 407–418.

Patterson, R. D. Noise masking of a change in residue pitch. *Journal of the Accoustical Society of America*, 1969, **45**, 1520–1524.

Pedley, P. E., & Harper, R. S. Pitch and the vertical localization of sound. *American Journal of Psychology*, 1959, **72**, 447–449.

Penfield, W., & Rasmussen, T. *The cerebral cortex of man*. New York: Macmillan, 1950.

Peterson, A. C. Physical androgyny and cognitive functioning in adolescence. *Developmental Psychology*, 1976, **12**, 524–533.

Pfaff, D. Effects of temperature and time of day on time judgment. *Journal of Experimental Psychology*, 1968, **76**, 419–422.

Pfaffman, C., Bartoshuk, L., & McBurney, D. H. Taste psychophysics. *Handbook of Sensory Physiology*, 1971, **1**, 75–101.

Pfeiffer, R. R. Classification of response patterns of spike discharges for units in the cochlear nucleus: Tone-burst stimulation. *Experimental Brain Research*, 1966, **1**, 220–235.

Pick, H. L. Jr., & Hay, J. C. A passive test of the Held reafference hypothesis. *Perceptual and Motor Skills*, 1965, **20**, 1070–1072.

Pick, H. L., Jr., & Pick, A. D. Sensory and perceptual development. In P. H. Mussen (Ed.), *Carmichael's manual of child development*. New York: Wiley, 1970. Pp. 773–848.

Pickersgill, M. J. On knowing with which eye one is seeing. *Quarterly Journal of Experimental Psychology*, 1961, **13**, 168–172.

Plateau, M. H. Sur la mesure des sensations physiques, et sur la loi qui lié l'intensité de ces sensations à l'intensité de la cause excitante. *Bulletin de l'Academie Royale de Belgique*, 1872, **33**, 376–388.

Poggio, G. F. Spatial properties of neurons in striate cortex of unanesthetized macaque monkey. *Investigative Ophthalmology*, 1972, **11**, 368–376.

Poggio, G. F., & Mountcastle, V. B. A study of the functional contributions of the lemniscal and spinothalamic systems to somatic sensibility: Central nervous mechanisms in pain. *Bulletin of the Johns Hopkins Hospital*, 1960, **106**, 266–316.

Pollack, I. The information of elementary auditory displays. *Journal of the Acoustical Society of America*, 1952, **24**, 745–749.

Pollack, I. The information of elementary auditory displays. II. *Journal of the Acoustical Society of America*, 1953, **25**, 765–769.

Pollack, I. Iterative techniques for unbiased rating scales. *Quarterly Journal of Experimental Psychology*, 1965, **17**, 139–148.

Pollack, I., & Pickett, J. M. Intelligibility of excerpts from fluent speech: Auditory vs. structural context. *Journal of Verbal Learning and Verbal Behavior*, 1964, **3**, 79–84.

Pollack, R. H., & Silver S. D. Magnitude of the Mueller-Lyer illusion in children as a function of pigmentation of fundus oculi. *Psychonomic Science*, 1967, **8**, 83–84.

Polzella, D. J., Dapolito, F., & Hinsman, M. C. Cerebral asymmetry in time perception. *Perception & Psychophysics*, 1977, **21**, 187–192.

Pomerantz, J. R., Sager, L. C., & Stoever, R. J. Perception of wholes of their component parts: Some configural superiority effects. *Journal of Experimental Psychology: Human Perception and Performance*, 1977, **3**, 422–435.

Porac, C., & Coren, S. The dominant eye. *Psychological Bulletin*, 1976, **83**, 880–897.

Posner, M. I., & Boies, S. J. Components of attention. *Psychological Review*, 1971, **78**, 391–408.

Postman, L., & Egan, J. P. *Experimental psychology*. New York: Harper, 1949.

Poulton, E. C. The new psychophysics: Six models for magnitude estimation. *Psychological Bulletin*, 1968, **69**, 1–19.

Pritchard, R. M., Heron, W., & Hebb, D. O. Visual perception approached by the method of stabilized images. *Canadian Journal of Psychology*, 1960, **14**, 67–77.

Puckett, J. deW., & Steinman, R. M. Tracking eye movements with and without saccadic correction. *Vision Research*, 1969, **9**, 295–303.

Ratliff, F. *Mach bands: Quantitative studies on neural networks in the retina*. San Francisco: Holden-Day, 1965.

Reed, S. K. *Psychological processes in pattern recognition*. New York: Academic Press, 1973.

Restle, F. Visual illusions. In M. H. Appley (Ed.),

Schiffman, S. S. Physicochemical correlates of olfactory quality. *Science*, 1974, **185,** 112–117.

Schiffman, S. S., & Dackis, C. Taste of nutrients: Amino acids, vitamins, and fatty acids. *Perception & Psychophysics*, 1975, **17,** 140–146.

Schiffman, S. S., & Erikson, R. P. A theoretical review: A psychophysical model for gustatory quality. *Physiology and Behavior*, 1971, **1,** 617–633.

Schiller, P., & Weiner, M. Binocular and stereoscopic viewing of geometric illusions. *Perceptual and Motor Skills*, 1962, **13,** 739–747.

Schmitt, F. O., & Worden, F. G. (Eds) *The neurosciences: Third study program.* Cambridge, Massachusetts: MIT Press, 1974.

Schneider, G. E. Two visual systems. *Science*, 1969, **163,** 895–902.

Schneider, R., Costiloe, J., Howard, R., & Wolf, S. Olfactory perception thresholds in hypogonadal women: Changes accompanying administration of androgen and estrogen. *Journal of Clinical Endocrinology*, 1958, **18,** 379–390.

Schneider, W., & Shiffrin, R. M. Controlled and automatic human information processing. I. Detection, search and attention. *Psychological Review*, 1977, **84,** 1–66.

Schriever, W. Experimentelle Studien uber stereokopische Sehen. *Zeitschrift fuer Psychologie*, 1925, **96,** 113–170.

Schulman, C. Eye movements in infants using dc recording. *Neuropaediatrie*, 1973, **4,** 76–87.

Schwartz, A. N., Campos, J. J., & Baisel, E. J. The visual cliff: Cardiac and behavioral responses on the deep and shallow sides at five and nine months of age. Paper presented at the meetings of the Eastern Psychological Association, Boston, April 1972.

Schwartz, C. B. Visual discrimination of camouflaged figures. Unpublished doctoral dissertation, University of California at Berkeley, 1961.

Scott, T. R., & Erickson, R. P. Synaptic processing of taste-quality information in the thalamus of the rat. *Journal of Neurophysiology*, 1971, **34,** 868–884.

Segall, M. H., Campbell, D. T., & Herskovits, M. J. *The influence of culture on visual perception.* Indianapolis: Bobbs-Merrill, 1966.

Sekuler, R. Visual motion perception. In E. C. Carterette & M. P. Friedman (Eds.), *Handbook of perception.* Vol. 5. New York: Academic Press, 1975. Pp. 387–433.

Sekuler, R., & Ganz, L. A new aftereffect of seen movement with a stabilized retinal image. *Science*, 1963, **139,** 419–420.

Selfridge, O. G. Pandemonium: A paradigm for learning. In D. V. Blake & A. M. Uttley (Eds.), *Proceedings of the symposium on the mechanisation of thought processes.* London: HM Stationery Office, 1959. Pp. 511–529.

Selfridge, O. G., & Neisser, U. Pattern recognition by machine. In E. A. Feigenbaum & J. Feldman (Eds.), *Computers and thought.* New York: McGraw-Hill, 1963. Pp. 237–250.

Senden, M. von. *Space and sight: The perception of space and shape in congenitally blind patients before and after operation.* London: Methuen, 1960.

Serpell, R. Discrimination of orientation by Zambian children. *Journal of Comparative Physiology*, 1971, **75,** 312.

Shallice, T., & Vickers, D. Theories and experiments on discrimination times. *Ergonomics*, 1964, **7,** 37–49.

Shannon, C. E., & Weaver, W. *The mathematical theory of communication.* Urbana: University of Illinois Press, 1949.

Sharma, S., & Moskowitz, H. Effect of marijuana on the visual autokinetic phenomenon. *Perceptual and Motor Skills*, 1972, **35,** 891.

Shebilske, W. Visuomotor coordination in visual direction and position constancies. In W. Epstein (Ed.), *Stability and constancy in visual perception: Mechanisms and processes.* New York: Wiley, 1977. Pp. 23–70.

Sherrington, C. S. *Integrative action of the nervous system.* New Haven, Connecticut: Yale University Press, 1906.

Shiffrin, R. M., & Grantham, D. W. Can attention be allocated to sensory modalities? *Perception & Psychophysics*, 1974, **15,** 460–474.

Shiffrin, R. M., Pisoni, D. B., & Castaneda-Mendez, K. Is attention shared between the ears? *Cognitive Psychology*, 1974, **6,** 190–215.

Shiffrin, R. M., & Schneider, W. Controlled and automatic human information processing. II. Perceptual learning, automatic attending and a general theory. *Psychological Review*, 1977, **84,** 127–190.

Shipley, E. F. Detection and recognition with uncertainty. Unpublished doctoral dissertation, University of Pennsylvania, 1961.

Shower, E. G., & Biddulph, R. Differential pitch sensitivity of the ear. *Journal of Acoustical Society of America*, 1931, **3,** 275–287.

Siddle, D. A., Morish, R. B., White, K. D., & Mangen, G. L. Relation of visual sensitivity to extraversion. *Journal of Experimental Research in Personality*, 1969, **3,** 264–267.

Sidman, M., & Kirk, B. Letter reversals in naming, writing, and matching to sample. *Child Development*, 1974, **45,** 616–625.

Simmons, F. B., Epley, J. M., Lummis, R. C., Guttman, N., Frishkopf, L. S., Harmon, L. D., & Zwicker, E. Auditory nerve: Electrical stimulation in man. *Science.* 1965, **148,** 104–106.

Sinclair, D. C., & Stokes, B. A. R. The production and characteristics of "second pain." *Brain*, 1964, **87,** 609–618.

Sinnot, J., & Rauth, J. Effect of smoking on taste

Adaptation-level theory. New York: Academic Press, 1971. Pp. 55–69.

Restle, F. Assimilation produced by contrast. In N. S. Castellan & F. Restle (Eds.), *Cognitive theory* (Vol. 3). Hillsdale, New Jersey: Erlbaum, 1975.

Rhee, K., Kim, D., & Kim, Y. The effects of smoking on night vision. *14th Pacific Medical Conference (Professional papers),* 1965.

Rice, C. G., Ayley, J. B., Bartlett, B., Bedford, W., Gregory, W., & Hallum, G. A pilot study on the effects of pop group music on hearing, 1968. Cited in K. D. Kryter, *The effects of noise on man.* New York: Academic Press, 1970. P. 203.

Richards, W. Lessons in constancy from neurophysiology. In W. W. Epstein (Ed.), *Stability and constancy in visual perception: Mechanisms and processes.* New York: Wiley, 1977. Pp. 421–436.

Riesen, A. H. The development of visual perception in man and chimpanzee. *Science,* 1947, **106,** 107–108.

Riesen, A. H., & Aarons, L. Visual movement and intensity discrimination in cats after early deprivation of pattern-vision. *Journal of Comparative and Physiological Psychology,* 1959, **52,** 142–149.

Riesz, R. R. Differential intensity sensitivity of the ear for pure tones. *Physical Review,* 1928, **31,** 867–875.

Riggs, L. A., Ratliff, F., Cornsweet, J. C., & Cornsweet, T. N. The disappearance of steadily fixated visual test objects. *Journal of the Optical Society of America,* 1953, **43,** 495–501.

Roberts, J. *Binocular visual acuity of adults.* Washington, D.C.: U.S. Department of Health, Education and Welfare, 1964.

Robertson, P. W. Colour words and colour vision. *Biology and Human Affairs,* 1967, **33,** 28–33.

Robinson, D. W., & Dadson, R. S. A redetermination of the equal-loudness relations for pure tones. *British Journal of Applied Physics,* 1956, **7,** 166–181.

Robson, J. G. Receptive fields: Neural representation of the spatial and intensive attributes of the visual image. In E. C. Carterette & M. P. Friedman (Eds.), *Handbook of perception. Vol. 50 Seeing.* New York: Academic Press, 1975. Pp. 82–116.

Rock, I. *Orientation and form.* New York: Academic Press, 1974.

Rock, I. *An introduction to perception.* New York: Macmillan, 1975.

Rock, I., & Halper, F. Form perception without a retinal image. *American Journal of Psychology,* 1969, **82,** 425–440.

Rodieck, R. W. Receptive fields in the cat retina: A new type. *Science,* 1967, **157,** 90–92.

Rodieck, R. W. *The vertebrate retina: Principles of structure and function.* San Francisco: Freeman, 1973.

Rodieck, R. W., & Stone, J. Analysis of receptive fields of cat retinal ganglion cells. *Journal of Neurophysiology,* 1965, **28,** 833–849.

Roelofs, C. O. Optische Lokalisation, *Archiv fuer Augenheilkunde,* 1935, **109,** 395–415.

Rose, J. E., Galambos, R., & Hughes, J. Organization of frequency sensitive neurons in the cochlear nuclear complex of the cat. In G. L. Rasmussen & W. F. Windle (Eds.), *Neural mechanisms of the auditory and vestibular systems.* Springfield, Ill.: Thomas, 1960. Pp. 116–136.

Ross, N., & Schilder, P. Tachistoscopic experiments on the perception of the human figure. *Journal of General Psychology,* 1934, **10,** 152–172.

Rowell, T. E. Agonistic noises of the rhesus monkeys (macaca mulatta). *Symposium of the Zoological Society of London,* 1962, **8,** 91–96.

Rubin, E. *Synoplevede Figuren.* Copenhagen: Gyldendalske, 1915.

Rubin, E. *Visuell wahrgenommene Figuren.* Copenhagen: Glydendalske, 1921.

Ruble, D. N., & Nakamura, C. Y. Task orientation versus social orientation in young children and their attention to relevant social cues. *Child Development,* 1972, **43,** 471–480.

Rudel, R. G., & Teuber, H. C. Discrimination of direction of line in children. *Journal of Comparative and Physiological Psychology,* 1963, **56,** 892–898.

Rushton, W. A. H. Visual pigments in man. *Scientific American,* 1962, **205,** 120–132.

Rushton, W. A. H. Cone pigment dynamics in the deuteranope. *Journal of Physiology (London),* 1965, **176,** 38–45.

Russell, M. J. Human olfactory communication. *Nature (London),* 1976, **260,** 520–522.

Saayman, G., Ames, E. W., & Moffet, A. Response to novelty as an indicator of visual discrimination in the human infant. *Journal of Experimental Child Psychology,* 1964, **1,** 189–198.

Salapatek, P. Pattern perception in early infancy. In L. B. Cohen & P. Salapatek (Eds.), *Infant perception: From sensation to cognition, Vol. 1.* New York: Academic Press, 1975. Pp. 133–248.

Salapatek, P., & Kessen, W. Prolonged investigation of a plane geometric triangle by the human newborn. *Journal of Experimental Child Psychology,* 1973, **15,** 22–29.

Sapir, E. *Language.* New York: Harcourt, Brace & World, 1939.

Scharf, B. Audition. In B. Scharf (Ed.), *Experimental sensory psychology.* Glenview, Illinois: Scott, Foresman, 1975. Pp. 112–149.

Scharf, B. Partial masking. *Acustica,* 1964, **14,** 16–23.

Schenkel, K. D. Die beidohrigen Mithorschoellen von Impulsen. *Acustica,* 1967, **18,** 38–46.

thresholds. *Journal of General Psychology*, 1937, **17**, 155–161.

Sivian, L. S., & White, S. D. On minimum audible sound fields. *Journal of the Acoustical Society of America*, 1933, **4**, 288–321.

Skoff, E., & Pollack, R. H. Visual acuity in children as a function of hue. *Perception & Psychophysics*, 1969, **6**, 244–246.

Slomin, V., & Pasnak, R. The effects of visual deprivation on the depth perception of adult and infant rats and adult squirrel monkeys (Saimiri Scurea). *Vision Research*, 1972, **12**, 63–66.

Smith, S. Utrocular, or "which eye" discrimination. *Journal of Experimental Psychology*, 1945, **35**, 1–14.

Smythe, E., & Goldstone, S. The time sense: A normative, genetic study of the development of time perception. *Perceptual and Motor Skills*, 1957, **7**, 49–59.

Snellen, H. *Probebuchstaben zur Bestimmung der Sehschärfe*. Utrecht: Weijer, 1862.

Snodgrass, J. G. Psychophysics. In B. Scharf (Ed.), *Experimental sensory psychology*. Glenview, Ill.: Scott-Foresman, 1975. Pp. 16–67.

Sokolov, E. N. *Perception and the conditioned reflex*. New York: Macmillan, 1960.

Sperling, G. The information available in brief visual presentation. *Psychological Monographs*, 1960, **74**, (11, Whole No. 498).

Sperry, R. W. Effect of 180 degree rotation of the retinal field on visuomotor coordination. *Journal of Experimental Zoology*, 1943, **92**, 263–277.

Spoendlin, H. Ultrastructure and peripheral innervation pattern of the receptor in relation to the first coding of the acoustic message. In A. V. S. de Rueck & J. Knight (Eds.), *Hearing mechanisms in vertebrates*. Boston: Little-Brown, 1968. Pp. 89–125.

Sprague, J. M., & Meikle, T. H., Jr., The role of the superior colliculus in visually guided behavior. *Experimental Neurology*, 1965, **11**, 115–146.

Steinberg, A. Changes in time perception induced by an anaesthetic drug. *British Journal of Psychology*, 1955, **46**, 273–279.

Steinfield, G. J. Concepts of set and availability and their relation to the reorganization of ambiguous pictorial stimuli. *Psychological Review*. 1967, **74**, 505–522.

Steinman, A. Reaction time to change, compared with other psychophysical methods. *Archives of Psychology, New York*, 1944, No. 292.

Stelmack, R. M., Achorn, E., & Michaud, A. Extraversion and individual differences in auditory evoked response. *Psychophysiology*, 1977, **14**, 368–374.

Stelmack, R. M., & Campbell, K. B. Extraversion and auditory sensitivity to high and low frequency. *Perceptual and Motor Skills*, 1974, **38**, 875–879.

Sternbach, R. A. Congenital insensitivity to pain: A critique. *Psychological Bulletin*, 1963, **60**, 252–264.

Sternbach, R. A., & Tursky, B. On the psychophysical power function in electric shock. *Psychonomic Science*, 1964, **1**, 247–248.

Stevens, J. C., & Stevens, S. S. Warmth and cold: Dynamics of sensory intensity. *Journal of Experimental Psychology*, 1960, **60**, 183–192.

Stevens, K. N. Towards a model for speech recognition. *Journal of the Acoustical Society of America*, 1960, **32**, 47–55.

Stevens, K. N., & Halle, M. Remarks on analysis by synthesis and distinctive features. In W. Wathen-Dunn (Ed.), *Models for the perception of speech and visual form*. Cambridge, Massachusetts: MIT Press, 1964.

Stevens, K. N., & House, A. S. Speech perception. In J. V. Tobias (Ed.), *Foundations of modern auditory theory*. Vol. 2. New York: Academic Press, 1972. Pp. 3–62.

Stevens, S. S. The attributes of tones. *Proceedings of the National Academy of Sciences of the U.S.A.*, 1934, **20**, 457–459.

Stevens, S. S. The relation of pitch to intensity. *Journal of the Acoustical Society of America*, 1935, **6**, 150–154.

Stevens, S. S. On the theory of scales of measurement. *Science*, 1946, 103, 677–680.

Stevens, S. S. The direct estimation of sensory magnitudes—loudness. *American Journal of Psychology*, 1956, **69**, 1–25.

Stevens, S. S. Tactile vibration: Dynamics of sensory intensity. *Journal of Experimental Psychology*, 1959, **57**, 210–218.

Stevens, S. S. The psychophysics of sensory function. In W. A. Rosenblith (Ed.), *Sensory communication*. Cambridge, Massachusetts: MIT Press, 1961. Pp. 1–33.

Stevens, S. S. A metric for the social consensus. *Science*, 1966, **151**, 530–541.

Stevens, S. S. Sensory scales of taste intensity. *Perception & Psychophysics*, 1969, **6**, 302–308.

Stevens, S. S. Neural events and the psychophysical law. *Science*, 1970, **170**, 1043–1050.

Stevens, S S. *Psychophysics: Introduction to its perceptual, neural, and social prospects*. New York: Wiley, 1975.

Stevens, S. S., & Galanter, E. Ratio scales and category scales for a dozen perceptual continua. *Journal of Experimental Psychology*, 1957, **54**, 377–411.

Stevens, S. S., & Newman, E. B. The localization of pure tones. *Proceedings of the National Academy of Sciences of the U.S.A.* 1934, **20**, 593–596.

Stevens, S. S., Volkman, J., & Newman, E. B. A scale for the measurement of the psychological magnitude of pitch. *Journal of the Acoustical Society of America*, 1937, **8**, 185–190.

Stevens, S. S., & Warshovsky, F. *Sound and hearing.* New York: Time-Life Books, 1965.

Stone, J., & Dreher, B. Projection of X- and Y-cells of the cat's lateral geniculate nucleus to areas 17 and 18 of the visual cortex. *Journal of Neurophysiology,* 1973, **36,** 551–567.

Stone, J., & Hoffman, K. P. Very slow conduction ganglion cells in the cat's retina: A major new functional type? *Brain Research,* 1972, **43,** 610–616.

Stone, L. S. Polarization of the retina and development of vision. *Journal of Experimental Zoology,* 1960, **145,** 85–93.

Stratton, G. M. Some preliminary experiments on vision without inversion of the retinal image. *Psychological Review,* 1896, **3,** 611–617.

Stratton, G. M. Upright vision and the retinal image. *Psychological Review,* 1897, **4,** 182–187. (a)

Stratton, G. M. Vision without inversion of the retinal image. *Psychological Review,* 1897, **4,** 341–360. (b)

Street, R. F. *A gestalt completion test: A study of a cross-section of intellect.* New York: Bureau of Publication, Teachers College, Columbia University, 1931.

Stroop, J. R. Studies of interference in serial verbal reactions. *Journal of Experimental Psychology,* 1935, **18,** 642–643.

Stroud, J. M. The fine structure of psychological time. In H. Quastler (Ed.), *Information theory in psychology: Problems and methods.* Glencoe, Illinois: Free Press, 1955. Pp. 174–207.

Supra, M., Cotzin, M. E., & Dallenbach, K. M. "Facial vision:" The perception of obstacles by the blind. *American Journal of Psychology,* 1944, **57,** 133–183.

Svaetichin, G. Spectral response curves of single cones. *Acta Physiologica Scandinavica,* 1956, **1,** 93–101.

Svaetichin, G., & MacNichol, E. F., Jr. Retinal mechanisms for achromatic vision. *Annals of the New York Academy of Sciences,* 1958, **74,** 385–404.

Swarbrick, L., & Whitfield, I. C. Auditory cortical units selectively responsive to stimulus "shape." *Journal of Physiology (London),* 1972, **224,** 68–69.

Swartz, P. A new method for scaling pain. *Journal of Experimental Psychology,* 1953, **45,** 288–293.

Swets, J. A., & Kristofferson, A. B. Attention. *Annual Review of Psychology,* 1970, **21,** 339–366.

Swets, J. A., Tanner, W. P., Jr., & Birdsall, T. G. Decision processes in perception. *Psychological Review,* 1961, **68,** 301–340.

Szentagothai, J. The elementary vestibulo-ocular reflex arc. *Journal of Neurophysiology,* 1950, **13,** 395–407.

Tanner, W. P., Jr., Swets, J. A., & Green, D. M. *Some general properties of the hearing mechanism.* T. R. 30. Electronic Defense Group. Ann Arbor: University of Michigan, 1956.

Tart, C. *On being stoned.* Palo Alto: Science and Behavior Books, 1971.

Tartter, V. C., & Eimas, P. D. The role of auditory feature detectors in the perception of speech. *Perception & Psychophysics,* 1975, **18,** 293–298.

Taub, A. Acupuncture. *Science,* 1972, **178,** 9.

Taub, E., & Berman, A. J. Movement and learning in the absence of sensory feedback. In S. J. Freedman (Ed.), *The neuropsychology of spatially oriented behavior.* Homewood, Illinois: Dorsey, 1968.

Tedford, W. H., Warren, D. E., & Flynn, W. E. Alternation of shock aversion thresholds during menstrual cycle. *Perception & Psychophysics,* 1977, **21,** 2, 193–196.

Tees, R. C. Effect of visual deprivation on development of depth perception in the rat. *Journal of Comparative and Physiological Psychology,* 1974, **86,** 300–308.

Teghtsoonian, R. On the exponents in Stevens' Law and the constant in Ekman's Law. *Psychological Review,* 1971, **78,** 71–80.

Teghtsoonian. R. Review of *Psychophysics* by S. S. Stevens. *American Journal of Psychology,* 1975, **88,** 677–684.

Theberge, J. B. Wolf music. *Natural History,* 1971, **80,** 37–42.

Theodor, L., & Miller, R. D. The effect of marijuana on visual signal detection and the recovery of visual acuity after exposure to glare. In *Cannabis: A report of the Commission of Inquiry into the non-medical use of drugs.* Ottawa: Information Canada, 1972.

Thomas, E., & Brown, I. Time perception and the filled duration illusion. *Perception & Psychophysics,* 1974, **16,** 449–458.

Thomas, F. A. C., & Weaver, W. B. Cognitive processing and time perception. *Perception & Psychophysics,* 1975, **17,** 363–367.

Thompson, L. J. Language disabilities in men of eminence. *Journal of Learning Disabilities,* 1971, **4,** 39–50.

Thouless, R. H. Phenomenal regression to the real object. *British Journal of Psychology,* 1931, **21,** 339–359.

Thurstone, L. L. A law of comparative judgment. *Psychological Review,* 1927, **34,** 273–286.

Titchner, E. B. *Experimental psychology. Vol. II. Quantitative.* New York: Macmillan, 1905.

Toch, H. H., & Schulte, R. Readiness to perceive violence as a result of police training. *British Journal of Psychology,* 1961, **52,** 389–393.

Tolhurst, D. J. Separate channels for the analysis of the shape and the movement of a moving visual stimulus. *Journal of Physiology (London),* 1973, **231,** 385–402.

Torgerson, W. S. Distances and ratios in psychophysical scaling. *Acta Psychologica,* 1961, **19,** 201–205.

Tower, S. S. Pain: Definition and properties of the unit for sensory reception. *Research Publications, Association for Research in Nervous and Mental Disease,* 1943, **23,** 16–43.

Treisman, A. Strategies and models of selective attention. *Psychological Review,* 1969, **76,** 282–299.

Treisman, M. Temporal discrimination and the indifference interval: Implications for the model of an internal clock. *Psychological Monographs,* 1963, **77,** 1–31 (Whole No. 576).

Treisman, M. On the use and misuse of psychophysical terms. *Psychological Review,* 1976, **83,** 246–256.

Treisman, M., & Watts, T. R. Relation between signal detectability theory and the traditional procedures for measuring sensory thresholds: Estimating d' from results given by the method of constant stimuli. *Psychological Bulletin,* 1966, **66,** 438–454.

Troland, L. T. The enigma of color vision. *American Journal of Physiological Optics,* 1921, **2,** 23–48.

Tronick, E. Stimulus control and the growth of the infant's effective visual field. *Perception & Psychophysics,* 1972, **11,** 373–376.

Tsvetkova, L. S. *Rehabilitative training in local brain lesions.* Moscow: Pedagogika Publishing House, 1972.

Turnbull, C. Some observations regarding the experiences and behavior of the Bambuti pygmies. *American Journal of Psychology,* 1961, **74,** 304–308.

Turner, P. Amphetamines and smell threshold in man. In A. Herxheimer (Ed.), *Drugs and sensory functions.* Boston: Little, Brown, 1968. Pp. 91–100.

Uhr, L., & Vossler, C. A pattern-recognition program that generates, evaluates and adjusts its own operators. In E. A. Feigenbaum & J. Feldman (Eds.), *Computers and thought.* New York: McGraw-Hill, 1963. Pp. 251–268.

Umezaki, H., & Morrell, F. Developmental study of photic evoked responses in premature infants. *Electroencephalography and Clinical Neurophysiology,* 1970, **28,** 55–63.

Verriest, G. Recent advances in the study of the acquired deficiencies of color vision. *Fondazione "Gorgio Ronchi,"* 1974, **24,** 1–80.

Verrillo, R. T. Cutaneous sensation. In B. Scharf (Ed.), *Experimental sensory psychology.* Glenview, Illinois: Scott, Foresman, 1975. Pp. 150–184.

Verrillo, R. T., Fraioli, A. J., & Smith, R. L. Sensation magnitude of vibrotactile stimuli. *Perception & Psychophysics,* 1969, **6,** 366–372.

Vurpillot, E. L'influence de la signification du matériel sur l'illusion de Poggendorff. *Annee Psychologie,* 1957, **57,** 339–357.

Vurpillot, E. The development of scanning strategies and their relation to visual differentiation. *Journal of Experimental Child Psychology,* 1968, **6,** 632–650.

Waber, D. P. Sex differences in cognition: A function of maturation rate? *Science,* 1976, **192,** 572–574.

Waber, D. P. Sex differences in mental abilities, hemispheric lateralization and rate of physical growth at adolescence. *Developmental Psychology,* 1977, **13,** 29–38.

Wald, G. The molecular basis of visual excitation. *Nature (London),* 1968, **219,** 800–807.

Wald, G. Brown, P. K., & Gibbons, I. R. The problem of visual excitation. *Journal of the Optical Society of America,* 1963, **53,** 20–35.

Walk, R. D. Can the duckling respond adequately to depth? Paper presented at the 33rd meeting of the Eastern Psychological Association, Atlantic City, April 1962.

Walk, R. D. Class demonstration of visual depth perception with the albino rabbit. *Perceptual and Motor Skills,* 1964, **18,** 219–224.

Walk, R. D., & Gibson, E. J. A comparative and analytic study of visual depth perception. *Psychological Monographs,* 1961, **75,** 1–44.

Wallach, H. On sound localization. *Journal of the Acoustical Society of America,* 1939, **10,** 270–274.

Wallach, H. Brightness constancy and the nature of achromatic colors. *Journal of Experimental Psychology,* 1948, **38,** 310–324.

Wallach, H. The perception of motion. In R. Held & W. Richards (Eds.), *Perception: mechanisms and models: Readings from Scientific American.* San Francisco: Freeman, 1972. Pp. 310–315. (Originally published in *Scientific American,* 1959.) (a)

Wallach, H. The perception of neutral colors. In R. Held & W. Richards (Eds.), *Perception: mechanisms and models: readings from Scientific American.* San Francisco: Freeman, 1972. Pp. 278–285. (Originally published in *Scientific American,* 1963.) (b)

Wallach, H., Newman, E. B., & Rosenzweig, M. R. The precedence effect in sound localization. *American Journal of Psychology,* 1949, **62,** 315–336.

Wallingford, E. G., Jr. A visual pattern recognizing computer program based on neurophysiological data. *Behavioural Science,* 1972, **17,** 241–248.

Walls, G. L. A theory of ocular dominance. *AMA Archives of Ophthalmology,* 1951, **45,** 387–412.

Walls, G. L. *The vertebrate eye and its adaptive radiation.* New York: Hafner, 1963.

Ward, L. M. Some psychophysical properties of category judgments and magnitude estimations. Doctoral dissertation, Duke University, 1971.

Ward, L. M. Category judgments of loudness in the absence of an experimenter-induced identification function: Sequential effects and power function fit. *Journal of Experimental Psychology,* 1972, **94,** 179–184.

Ward, L. M. Repeated magnitude estimations with a variable standard: Sequential effects and other properties. *Perception & Psychophysics,* 1973, **13,** 193–200.

Ward, L. M. Power functions for category judgments of duration and line length. *Perceptual and Motor Skills,* 1974, **38,** 1182.

Ward, L. M. Sequential dependencies and response range in cross-modality matches of duration to loudness. *Perception & Psychophysics,* 1975, **18,** 217–223.

Ward, L. M., & Coren, S. The effect of optically-induced blur on the magnitude of the Mueller-Lyer illusion. *Bulletin of the Psychonomic Society,* 1976, **7,** 483–484.

Ward, L. M., and Lockhead, G. R. Sequential effects and memory in category judgments. *Journal of Experimental Psychology,* 1970, **84,** 27–34.

Ward, L. M., Porac, C., Coren, S., & Girgus, J. S. The case for misapplied constancy scaling: Depth associations elicited by illusion configurations. *American Journal of Psychology,* 1977, **90,** 609–620.

Ward, L. M., & Wexler, D. A. Levels of feature analysis in processing visual patterns. *Perception,* 1976, **5,** 407–418.

Ward, W. D. Musical perception. In J. V. Tobias (Ed.), *Foundations of modern auditory theory.* Vol. 1. New York: Academic Press, 1970. Pp. 407–447.

Warren, R. M. Perceptual restoration of missing speech sounds. *Science,* 1970, **167,** 392–393.

Warren, R. M., Obusek, C. J., Farmer, R. M., & Warren, R. P. Auditory sequence: Confusion of patterns other than speech or music. *Science,* 1969, **164,** 586–587.

Weale, R. A. *The aging eye.* London: Lewis, 1963.

Weber, E. H. *De pulen, resorptione, auditu et tactu: Annotationes anatomicae et physiologicae.* Leipzig, 1834.

Webster, W. R., & Aitkin, L. M. Central auditory processing. In M. S. Gazzaniga & C. Blakemore (Eds.), *Handbook of sensory psychobiology.* New York: Academic Press, 1975. Pp. 325–364.

Weil, A. T., Zinberg, E., & Nelson, J. N. Clinical and psychological effects of marijuana in man. *Science,* 1968, **162,** 1234–1242.

Weinstein, A. D., Goldstone, S., & Boardman, W. K. The effects of recent and remote frames of reference on temporal judgments of schizophrenic patients. *Journal of Abnormal Psychology,* 1958, **57,** 241–244.

Weinstein, E. A., Cole, M., Mitchell, M., S., & Lyerly, O. G. Anosognosia and aphasia. *Archives of Neurology,* 1964, **10,** 376–386.

Weinstein, S. Intensive and extensive aspects of tactile sensitivity as a function of body part, sex, and laterality. In D. R. Kenshalo (Ed.), *The skin senses.* Springfield, Ill.: Thomas, 1968 Pp. 195–218.

Weinstein, S., & Sersen, E. A. Tactual sensitivity as a function of handedness and laterality. *Journal of Comparative & Physiological Psychology,* 1961, **54,** 665–669.

Weisstein, N. A Rashevsky-Landahl neural net: Simulation of metacontrast. *Psychological Review,* 1968, **75,** 494–521.

Weisstein, N., & Harris, C. Visual detection of line segments: An object superiority effect. *Science,* 1974, **186,** 752–755.

Weisstein, N., Matthews, M., & Berbaum, K. Illusory contours can mask real contours. Paper presented at the meetings of the Psychonomic Society, Boston, November 1974.

Weisstein, N., Ozog, G., & Szoc, R. A comparison and elaboration of two models of metacontrast. *Psychological Review,* 1975, **82,** 325–343.

Welch, R. B. Adaptation to prism-displaced vision: The importance of target pointing. *Perception & Psychophysics,* 1969, **5,** 305–309.

Welch, R. B. Prism adaptation: The "target pointing effect" as a function of exposure trials. *Perception & Psychophysics,* 1971, **9,** 102–104.

Werner, H. Studies on contour. *American Journal of Psychology,* 1935, **47,** 40–64.

Wertheimer, M. Experimentelle Studien über das Sehen von Bewegung. *Zeitschrift fur Psychologie,* 1912, **61,** 161–265.

Wertheimer, M. Untersuchungen zur Lehre von der Gestalt. II. *Psychologische Forschung,* 1923, **41,** 301–350. Abridged translation by M. Wertheimer. In D. S. Beardslee & M. Wertheimer (Eds.), *Readings in perception.* Princeton, New Jersey: Van Nostrand-Reinhold, 1958. Pp. 115–137.

Wertheimer, M. Psychomotor coordination of auditory and visual space at birth. *Science,* 1961, **134,** 1692.

Wever, E. G. *Theory of hearing.* New York: Wiley, 1970.

White, B. L. *Human infants.* Englewood Cliffs, New Jersey: Prentice-Hall, 1971.

White, B. W., Saunders, F. A., Scadden, L., Bach-y-Rita, P., & Collins, C. C. Seeing with the skin. *Perception & Psychophysics,* 1970, **7,** 23–27.

White, C. Temporal numerosity and the psychological unit of duration. *Psychological Monographs,* 1963, **77,** 1–37 (Whole No. 575).

Whitfield, I. C. *The auditory pathway.* London: Arnold, 1967.

Whorf, B. L. Science and linguistics. In J. B. Carroll (Ed.), *Language, thought and reality: Selected writings of Benjamin Lee Whorf.* Cambridge, Massachusetts: MIT Press, 1956.

Whytt, R. *An essay on the vital and other involuntary motions of animals.* Edinburgh: Balfour & Neill, 1751.

Wiener, N. *Cybernetics.* New York: Wiley, 1948 (2nd ed.: Cambridge, Massachusetts, MIT Press, 1961).

Wiesel, T. N., & Hubel, D. H. Spatial and chromatic interactions in the lateral geniculate body of the rhesus monkey. *Journal of Neurophysiology,* 1966, **29,** 1115–1156.

Williams, M. *Brain damage and the mind.* London: Penguin, 1970.

Wilson, J. R., DeFries, J. C., McClearn, G. E., Vandenberg, S. G., Johnson, R. C., & Rashad, M. N. Cognitive abilities: Use of family data as a control to assess sex and age differences in two ethnic groups. *International Journal of Aging and Human Development,* 1975, **6,** 261–275.

Wilson, M. Effects of circumscribed cortical lesions upon somesthetic and visual discrimination in the monkey. *Journal of Comparative and Physiological Psychology,* 1957, **50,** 630–635.

Witkin, H. A., & Berry, J. W. Psychological differentiation in cross-cultural perspective. *Journal of Cross-Cultural Psychology,* 1975, **6,** 4–87.

Wolff, H. G., & Goodell, B. S. The relation of attitude and suggestion to the perception of and reaction to pain. *Research Publications, Association for Research in Nervous and Mental Disease,* 1943, **23,** 434–448.

Womersley, M. A context effect in feature detection with application of signal detection methodology. *Perception & Psychophysics,* 1977, **21,** 88–92.

Woodrow, H. Time perception. In S. S. Stevens (Ed.), *Handbook of experimental psychology.* New York: Wiley, 1951, Pp. 1224–1236.

Woolard, H. H., Weddell, G., & Harpman, J. A. Observations of the neuro-histological basis of cutaneous pain. *Journal of Anatomy,* 1940, **74,** 413–440.

Worchel, P., & Dallenbach, K. M. "Facial vision:" Perception of obstacles by the deaf-blind. *American Journal of Psychology,* 1947, **60,** 502–553.

Wright, R. H. Odor and molecular vibration: Neural coding of olfactory information. *Journal of Theoretical Biology,* 1977, **64,** 473–502.

Wright, R. H., & Burgess, R. E. Molecular coding of olfactory specificity. *Canadian Journal of Zoology,* 1975, **53,** 1247–1253.

Wright, W. D. A re-determination of the trichromatic mixture data. *Medical Research Council (Great Britain), Special Report Series,* 1929, **SRS-139,** 1–38.

Wurtz, R. H. Comparison of eye movements and stimulus movements on striate cortex neurones of the monkey. *Journal of Neurophysiology,* 1969, **32,** 987–994.

Wurtz, R. H. Extra retinal influences on the primate visual system. In R. A. Monty & J. W. Senders (eds.), *Eye movements and psychological processes.* Hillsdale, New Jersey: Lawrence Erlbaum Associates, 1976. Pp. 231–244.

Wurtz, R. H., & Goldberg, M. E. Superior colliculus cell responses related to eye movements in awake monkeys. *Science,* 1971, **171,** 82–84.

Wyburn, G. M., Pickford, R. W., & Hurst, R. J. *Human senses and perception.* Toronto: University of Toronto Press, 1964.

Wyszecki, G., & Stiles, W. S. *Color science: Concepts and methods, quantitative data and formulas.* New York: Wiley, 1967.

Yarbus, A. L. *Eye movements and vision.* New York: Plenum, 1967.

Yen, W. Sex-linked major gene influence on selected types of spatial performance. *Behavior Genetics,* 1975, **5,** 281–298.

Yerkes, R. M., & Dodson, J. D. The relation of strength of stimulus to rapidity of habit formation. *Journal of Comparative Neurology and Psychology,* 1908, **18,** 459–482.

Yin, R. K. Face recognition by brain injured patients—a dissociable ability. *Neuropsychologia,* 1970, **8,** 395.

Yonas, A., & Pick, H. L. An approach to the study of infant perception. In L. B. Cohen & P. Salapatek (Eds.), *Infant perception: From sensation to cognition. Vol. 2. Perception of space and sound.* New York: Academic Press, 1975. Pp. 3–31.

Young, L. R. Pursuit eye tracking movements. In Bach-y-Rita, P., Collins, C. C., & Hyde, J. E. (Eds.), *The control of eye movements.* New York: Academic Press, 1971. Pp. 429–443.

Zaporozhets, A. V. The development of perception in the preschool child. *Monographs of the Society for Research in Child Development,* 1965, **30,** 82–101.

Zeigler, H. P., & Leibowitz, H. Apparent visual size as a function of distance for children and adults. *American Journal of Psychology,* 1957, **70,** 106–109.

Zigler, M. J. Pressure adaptation time: A function of intensity and extensity. *American Journal of Psychology,* 1932, **44,** 709–720.

Zotterman, Y. Thermal sensations. *Handbook of Physiology: Section 1: Neurophysiology,* 1959, **1,** 431–458.

Zucker, I., Wade, G., & Ziegler, R. Sexual and hormonal influences on eating, taste preferences, and body weight of hamsters. *Physiology and Behavior,* 1972, **8,** 101–111.

Zwicker, E. Uber psychologische und methodosche Grundlagen der Lautheit. *Acustica,* 1958, **8,** 237–258.

Zwislocki, J. J., Damianopoulos, E. N., Buining, E., & Glantz, J. Central masking: Some steady-state and transient effects. *Perception & Psychophysics,* 1967, **2,** 59–64.

Author Index

Subject Index

B   9
C   0
D   1
E   2
F   3
G   4
H   5
I   6
J